Criminal Law

Palgrave Law Masters

Series Editor: **Marise Cremona**

Criminal Law

Third edition

Jonathan Herring
Fellow in Law
Exeter College, Oxford

(formerly Cremona and Herring)

Series editor: Marise Cremona
Professor of European Commercial Law
Queen Mary Centre for Commercial Law Studies
University of London

First published 2002 by
PALGRAVE MACMILLAN
Houndmills, Basingstoke, Hampshire RG21 6XS and
175 Fifth Avenue, New York, N.Y. 10010
Companies and representatives throughout the world

PALGRAVE MACMILLAN is the global academic imprint of the Palgrave
Macmillan division of St. Martin's Press, LLC and of Palgrave Macmillan Ltd.
Macmillan® is a registered trademark in the United States, United Kingdom
and other countries. Palgrave is a registered trademark in the European
Union and other countries.

ISBN 0–333–98770–5

This book is printed on paper suitable for recycling and
made from fully managed and sustained forest sources.

A catalogue record for this book is available
from the British Library.

10   9   8   7   6   5   4   3
11   10   09   08   07   06   05   04

Printed and bound in Great Britain by J. W. Arrowsmith, Bristol

Contents

vi   *Contents*

Preface to the First Edition

This book is intended as an introduction to the basic principles of criminal liability and some of the most important criminal offences. The offences have been chosen (from among the vast range of criminal offences) to illustrate clearly the principles underlying the criminal law; they also feature in most courses on substantive criminal law. There is a fundamental need for the law (and especially the criminal law) to be clear, and its content easily understood by the lay person, but first-time students of the subject often find its key concepts difficult to grasp and the major textbooks somewhat formidable. The Mastering Law series should provide a comprehensible account of major areas of the law and an introduction to the controversy and debate that is inseparable from any serious study of the law. This book was commissioned by the late Lady Oliver, who gave me much encouragement, and who was a firm believer in the need for accessible student texts as an adjunct to large-scale scholarly and reference works. Certain features of the book have therefore been designed to help those who are studying criminal law for the first time. There is a Case Notes section at the end of each chapter which gives, in respect of the key cases mentioned in the text, a short account of the facts and decision. Cases that are noted in this way are marked with an asterisk when they are first mentioned in the text, and the page on which the Case Notes appears is printed in bold type in the Table of Cases. In addition there is a selective bibliography (giving references to works mentioned in the text) and list of further reading for each chapter. Of the books listed, two are worth special mention; all students of English criminal law will come to know well Glanville Williams's *Textbook of Criminal Law* and Smith and Hogan's *Criminal Law*. The section of Exercises at the end of each chapter is designed both to test the reader's understanding and to stimulate further thought on the topics covered. The Workshop section gives an opportunity to practise the practical application of the rules and principles discussed. The book endeavours to state the law as at the end of March 1988.

MARISE CREMONA

Preface to the Third Edition

The third edition of this book sees the introduction of several new features. At the end of each chapter there is a section entitled *Hot Topic*. This provides an opportunity for a more in-depth analysis of a subject that is particularly topical or has received attention from academics in recent years. As the prospects for a criminal code now seem dim there is no longer a chapter devoted to it, although it is covered in Chapter 2. The book includes a chapter specifically on the potential effects of the Human Rights Act 1998, although references are made throughout the book to that legislation's potential impact. The new edition has also been thoroughly updated and many sections have been completely rewritten. The fact that the House of Lords has produced several important and highly controversial decisions in the past few years demonstrates that criminal law continues to be a vibrant, if contentious, subject of legal study.

Although this edition does not bear Marise Cremona's name her influence can be seen throughout the book. I have also enjoyed her advice and support during the preparation for this new edition. I have greatly appreciated the support of the team at Palgrave Macmillan, especially Helen Buglar and Esther Thackeray. Much of the writing of this book was witnessed by my daughter Laurel, who patiently played as I typed. I hope the experience has not harmed her too much. My wife, Kirsten Johnson, has been, and is, a constant source of love and support.

JONATHAN HERRING

As in the previous editions, cases marked with an asterisk* when they are first mentioned in the text are discussed in greater detail in the Case Notes at the end of the relevant chapter.

Table of Cases

A page number in **bold** type indicates a Case Note giving a short account of the facts and decision in respect of the case concerned

Table of Statutes

List of Latin Terms

Actus non facit reum, nisi mens si rea: An act does not make a person guilty of a crime unless the mind is also guilty.

Actus reus: The part of the definition of a criminal offence which does not relate to the defendant's state of mind.

Bona fide: Good faith.

Causa sine qua non: An event without which a result would not have occurred.

De minimis: Minimal.

Doli incapax: Being unaware of the difference between right and wrong and so not being liable to a criminal conviction.

Intercourse *per anum*: Anal intercourse.

Intercourse *per vaginum*: Vaginal intercourse.

Mala in se: A 'true' crime (in contrast to a regulatory offence).

Mala prohibita: A regulatory offence (in contrast to a 'true' crime).

Mens rea: The part of the definition of a criminal offence that relates to the defendant's state of mind.

Nolens volens: Not caring.

Novus actus interveniens: An act which breaks the chain of causation.

Obiter: A comment made by a judge in a case which is not binding on other courts.

Per se: In and of itself.

Prima facie: At first glance.

Regina: The Queen.

Rex: The King.

PART I

BASIC PRINCIPLES OF CRIMINAL LIABILITY

1 Introduction to Criminal Law

> ### Key words
>
> * **Culpability** – the blameworthiness of the defendant.
> * **Harm** – the wrong done to the victim of a crime.
> * **Objectivism** – a view that states the defendant should be judged by his conduct.
> * **Subjectivism** – a view that the defendant should be judged on the basis of his beliefs, intents and knowledge.

1.1 The Scope of this Book

This book is about the basic principles of criminal liability. These principles are the tools for understanding and applying the criminal law, and so can be used when you are faced by an unfamiliar or new offence. However, the common law, which is the foundation of criminal law, does not develop principles in the abstract, but in the context of concrete cases and specific crimes. Central offences against persons and property provide the basis upon which the judges have built the criminal law, and all students of criminal law need to understand them. Murder, for example, although a comparatively rare crime has played this role, because it is one of the most serious offences and so provides a testing ground for fundamental notions of culpability. The offences that are discussed in this book are chosen as examples of offences against persons and property. They have either (like murder) performed a key role in developing important legal principles, or (like theft) are common offences arising every day in the courts.

Although criminal law used to be thought a straightforward subject, it can be extremely complex and is often controversial. The aim of this book is to ensure that the basic principles are centrally presented, so that the wood does not disappear among the trees. Some of the underlying theoretical themes and conflicts are also introduced, as these are an inescapable part of current criminal law, which is undoubtedly alive and provocative. Tension between competing principles is inherent in the law: for example, in criminal law the interests of the accused can compete with the interests of the victim (see Chapter 8).

1.2 What is Criminal Law?

This is a question that is surprisingly difficult to answer. Most people would imagine the criminal law to be about murders, assaults and thefts, which, of course, it is; but the scope of criminal law is wider than this. It also includes pollution offences, crimes against public morals and traffic offences. It is the values and culture of a particular society which determine what conduct is regarded as being criminal. It should be noted that conduct that is contrary to criminal law at one point in time may not be seen as criminal at another time or in another country. For example, before 1956 sexual acts between two men were contrary to the criminal law, but following the Sexual Offences Act 1956 the legal prohibition on private sexual acts between two men over 21 was removed (the age limit has since been reduced to 18 and in 2001 it was reduced to 16). This was in part a result of a change in the general public's attitudes towards homosexual relationships. However, there are some crimes, such as murder, which have always been crimes and always will be. But even in the case of murder there are disagreements over whether euthanasia, abortion or capital punishment should be lawful.

But how can criminal law be distinguished from other parts of the law? Probably the best answer is given by Professor Glanville Williams, one of the great criminal law scholars, who argued that criminal law is best defined by the procedures it uses (see Chapter 2). He suggested that a crime is 'an act that is capable of being followed by criminal proceedings having one of the types of outcome (punishment etc.) known to follow these proceedings'. Although this may be the best definition, it is not especially useful, as it tends to be a circular one: – What is criminal law? It is that part of the law that uses criminal procedures. What are criminal procedures? Those that apply to criminal law.

1.3 The Role of Criminal Law

The criminal law plays a distinctive role in society, including the following functions: to deter people from doing acts that harm others or society; to set out the conditions under which people who have performed such acts will be punished; and to provide some guidance on the kinds of behaviour that are seen by society as acceptable. Of course, it is not only the criminal law that has a role in these areas. For example, deterrence from crime may occur as a result of pressure from families, friends and communities. But the criminal law is different from these other pressures. It is the established state response to crime. This is reflected in the fact that prosecutions under the criminal law are brought on behalf of the state in the name of the Crown (see Chapter 2.1). Further, the breaking of the criminal law is seen as different from the breaking of other kinds of law, in that a breach of the criminal law involves a degree of official moral censure. To be ordered by a court to pay damages following a breach of contract (which is not a criminal offence) does not carry with it the same kind of moral message of stigma that it would if you had been found guilty of a criminal act and then ordered to pay a fine. As Professor Ashworth has written, 'criminal liability is the strongest formal condemnation that society can inflict'.

1.4 What Conduct is Criminal?

There are two aspects to the definition of most serious crimes. The first, and most important, is that the defendant has done an act which has caused a prohibited kind of harm. The second is that the defendant is culpable, worthy of censure, for having caused that harm. We will now consider these aspects separately.

1.4.1 Causing Harm

The criminal law is not only concerned with the causing of direct harm to other people: it also outlaws harm to the state, public morals and the environment, for example. The criminal law goes further and punishes conduct that might not cause harm on a given occasion but endangers others (for example, dangerous driving); attempted crimes; and acts which help other people commit crimes. There are also a few criminal laws that are mainly designed to protect people from their own folly. An obvious example is the law requiring the wearing of seat belts in cars.

It is often argued that the criminal law should seek to punish only conduct that causes harm to others. Such an argument is in line with the well-known 'harm principle', articulated by J. S. Mill, who stated: 'the only purpose for which power can be rightfully exercised over any member of a civilized community, against his will, is to prevent harm to others'. Some conduct may be immoral but if it does not harm others or only harms the actor it is seen as unsuitable for punishment under the criminal law. Its prohibition is seen as too great an infringement on individuals' liberty. Although this principle has been widely accepted, there has been much dispute over what the term 'harm' means. For example, does it cover feelings of outrage some may feel at the conduct of their fellow citizens or damage to 'the moral fabric of society'?

The 'harm principle' has received support not just from academics, but also the judiciary. For example, Lord Hobhouse in the recent House of Lords case of *Hinks** stated:

'An essential function of the criminal law is to define the boundary between what conduct is criminal and what merely immoral. Both are the subject of the disapprobation of ordinary right-thinking citizens and the distinction is liable to be arbitrary or at least strongly influenced by considerations subjective to the individual members of the tribunal. To treat otherwise lawful conduct as criminal merely because it is open to such disapprobation would be contrary to principle and open to the objection that it fails to achieve the objective and transparent certainty required of the criminal law by the principles basic to human rights.'

It may be necessary to calculate the severity of the harm an act has caused. This can be important for two reasons. First, it is used to determine whether certain conduct is sufficiently harmful for it to be criminalized, and secondly to decide the hierarchy of offences. Generally the more harmful the conduct, the more serious the crime, and the higher the sentence is expected to be. But how to grade harm is controversial and difficult. From one perspective it is an impossible task as the victim's circumstances and perceptions vary from crime to crime. For example, some victims seem able to shrug off a burglary with little difficulty, while others find it a deeply traumatic and invasive experience. One could try to ignore the effect on a particular victim and instead look at the effect on an average victim, but then the victim may feel that he or she is being pigeonholed and his or her individual responses are not being taken seriously. The harm to society caused by any particular act is similarly difficult to gauge.

1.4.2   Culpability

Criminal law should be distinguished from civil law, which includes breaches of contract or claims for damages for negligent conduct. Civil law is more concerned with who should pay for a loss than determining blame. Given that the defendant has damaged the victim's property, the question in civil law is who should pay for that damage. If the victim is wholly innocent and the defendant even only a little to blame, then the defendant should shoulder the liability. However, in criminal law, as explained above, the censuring function plays a crucial role. Defendants should only be found guilty of a crime when they truly deserve the stigma of a criminal conviction, and so normally a higher level of blame needs to be shown in criminal law than in civil law, at least for serious offences. For less serious offences it is common for there to be a requirement of only a low level of culpability, partly because there is a correspondingly low level of censure attached to such crimes (see, for example, Chapter 6).

In deciding whether a defendant is to be blamed for his conduct, the criminal law generally presumes that a defendant is responsible for both his actions and the consequences of his actions. The criminal law does not accept that a person's conduct is simply a result of his environment and/or socio-economic background. Cases would become far too complex if each time it had to be carefully determined to what extent the defendant was responsible for his personality and the causing of the harm. Instead the law assumes that every person is a free autonomous agent who is responsible for his or her actions. Although generally the defendant's deprived background itself does not provide the defendant with a defence to a crime, the law does not ignore it entirely. For example, a defendant's social and financial circumstances may be taken into account at the sentencing stage of the criminal process.

Although the defendant is usually responsible for her actions and their consequences, there are four main ways that the law has of recognizing that a defendant may not be to blame, or not fully to blame, for the harmful results of her actions and so is not guilty of an offence:

1. Exemption from liability

The law recognizes that there are some people who are properly exempt from criminal prosecution, that is those who have not had the opportunity to develop fully moral characters and so are insufficiently responsible for their actions to justify the censure attached to a criminal conviction. Children below the age of criminal responsibility and persons classified as insane by the law are good examples. Such people may be subject to forms of restraint under the civil law, for example detention in a hospital under the Mental Health Act 1983.

2. Lack of capacity

The law may accept that the defendant (although not insane) was at the relevant time not responsible for her 'actions'. For example, if the defendant was pushed over and fell into a window breaking it, then the 'act' of falling into the window is not properly seen as the defendant's act. She was not acting in a 'human' way, as the result of conduct that was (or could have been) planned and thought about, but fell in the same way that a chair would have done had it been knocked over. It may well be, however, that the person who pushed the defendant would be criminally responsible for the broken window (see Chapter 17.2). Another example of this may be where the act was that of the defendant but was done under such circumstances that he was unable to exercise control over his actions, as when acting under hypnosis, for example. Here again it was not an act that he *could* have controlled. If the defendant could have controlled his actions but it was difficult for him to do so then this is not properly described as 'lack of capacity', but the defendant may be able to rely on a special defence (see point 4 below).

3. Lack of required mental state
Here the defendant was capable of exercising rational thought and of having considered her actions but lacked the necessary intention or foresight required for the particular offence. Often in such a case the defendant will still be guilty of a less serious crime. For example, as we will see later, in order to convict a defendant of murder it is necessary to show that she intended to kill or cause grievous bodily harm. If she lacks that intention, she may still be guilty of manslaughter.

4. Special defence
Although the defendant had the required mental state, she may claim that nevertheless she is not to be blamed because she had a particular defence. These defences arise when the circumstances of the offence lessen or remove any blame that the defendant would otherwise face. For example, she was acting in self-defence, or had been threatened with death or serious injury if she did not commit the crime.

Although we have discussed harm and culpability separately, they are in fact closely linked. A victim is likely to feel only slightly aggrieved if someone accidentally knocks into him causing him to fall over, but much more aggrieved if someone deliberately pushes him over. In other words intentionally inflicted injury is seen by victims as a different kind of harm to accidentally caused injury. Similarly the degree of culpability is perceived by most people, however illogically, to be different according to whether the harm caused is great or not. A person who drives dangerously and kills a pedestrian is seen as more blameworthy than someone who drives in an equally dangerous manner but injures no one.

1.4.3   Theories of Culpability

As you can imagine, there are many different theories on how to assess culpability and some of them have been developed to a high degree of sophistication. They have been expressed in many different ways and can only be discussed here in very bare outline. It is not possible to say that one of them is the 'right' theory or that the law clearly follows only one of these approaches. Indeed each has been influential in the law's developments and in the writings on criminal law. The three most popular will now be briefly discussed.

1. The choice theory

The argument here is that the defendant should only be responsible for the consequences of his actions that he has chosen to bring about, be that by deliberately acting in order to bring the consequence about or acting while aware that he might bring that consequence about. In *Lynch* Lord Simon stated 'the general basis of criminal responsibility is the power of choice included in the freedom of the human will'. The theory accepts that a defendant is not liable where he chose to act but that choice was not one for which he should be morally responsible. For example where the defendant acts under duress (for example where a person is kidnapped and told he must commit a crime or he will be killed) his choice was not one for which he should be responsible.

The choice theory has been highly influential in the development of the criminal law, but there are two particular problems with it. The first is that there are some offences which do not require proof that the defendant intended, foresaw or knew anything (for example, negligence and strict liability offences, see Chapter 6). These offences play an important part in our criminal law, but cannot be explained by the choice theory. A variant of the choice theory can deal with negligence-based offences by asking whether the defendant had a 'fair opportunity' to choose to act otherwise. Thus H. Hart has suggested, 'a moral licence to punish is needed by society and unless a man has the capacity and fair opportunity or chance to adjust his behaviour to the law, its penalties ought not to be applied to him'. This variant asks not whether the defendant *did* choose to bring about the consequence, but whether he *could have* avoided causing the harm. A second objection to the choice theory is that in making a moral judgement on the defendant's actions, choice is arguably only one criteria to consider; the defendant's attitudes and motives might also be thought to be relevant. These are excluded by this theory which focuses only on choice alone.

2. The character theory

This approach suggests that if the defendant's actions indicate a character trait that is unacceptable according to the standards expected by the criminal law, then the defendant deserves punishment. Whereas if the defendant's actions do not reveal bad character then there is no point in punishing him. This argument needs to be treated with care. The criminal law is not interested in discovering whether the defendant is generally 'a bad person' and so will only consider inferences of bad character from conduct prohibited by the criminal law. So the criminal law can infer bad character from the fact that the defendant assaulted someone, but not from evidence that he is a gossip. Assaulting is prohibited by the criminal law, gossiping is not. The strength of the theory is its ability to explain the defences that the criminal law provides. For example, the defence of duress can be explained because if the defendant commits a theft after he has been threatened with death, the theft does not lead us to conclude that he has a bad character. One difficulty with the theory is in explaining why, when considering the defendant's bad character, consideration is limited to criminal conduct alone. Another is that the law does not generally accept a defence of 'I was acting out of character'.

3. The objective theory.
This theory in its pure form focuses on what the defendant did, rather than what was going on in the defendant's head. It argues that it is necessary to have minimum standards of conduct that have to be met by every citizen. These standards should not be varied because of the defendant's individual characteristics because this would produce an unequal standard for different groups of people. The theory is capable of explaining those offences where the defendant is guilty if his conduct falls below the required standard, regardless of his state of mind (see, for example, Chapter 6). The objective theory is proposed by some for practical reasons. This may be because they feel the courts lack the evidence and capacity to make full moral judgements on the defendant. The court can declare certain conduct as harmful, but only an omnipotent God could decide the extent to which a defendant is morally blameworthy. Others argue a court is capable of deciding the moral blameworthiness of a defendant but that it would take too long and be too cumbersome to carry out an individual moral investigation in each case. This argument is particularly strong in minor offences. Opponents of the objective theory argue that it can produce unfair results, especially with those who lack the ability to meet the required standard (for example, because of a disability), although supporters argue that these difficulties can be dealt with at the sentencing stage. Opponents also point out that, as mentioned above, a criminal conviction carries with it a degree of censure and this is only appropriate if the defendant is in some sense to blame for what has happened. We can only know that, they argue, by looking at the defendant's state of mind.

1.4.4   The Objective/Subjective Dispute

The disputes between these different theories of culpability and how to achieve a balance between them in practical terms comes down to a debate over whether the law should take an objective or subjective approach to criminal liability. A pure subjectivist argues that a defendant should only be responsible for the foreseen or intended consequences of her actions. The actual consequences of a defendant's acts are to a large degree a matter of chance and beyond her control. She should be judged by those consequences with which she clearly associated herself, that is those she intended or foresaw. An example can be given of a defendant who throws a punch at a victim intending to give him a black eye. A pure subjectivist would argue that such a defendant should be punished in the same way for that act regardless of whether she does indeed cause a black eye; or the victim jumps out of the way at the last minute and so the punch misses completely; or the victim is knocked over by the punch, bangs his head and dies. The argument is that having thrown the punch, which of the different consequences occur is beyond the control of the defendant, and so the level of blame attached to the defendant should be the same whichever consequence occurs.

A pure objectivist focuses not on what the defendant believed would happen but on what actually happened; not on what the defendant foresaw but what a reasonable person would have foreseen. In other words while blame is the key concept for subjectivists, it is conduct which causes harm that objectivists see as fundamental. Objectivists argue that to say consequences are a matter of luck is unreal. For example, if a defendant dropped a pottery mug from the top of a high-rise building, it is surely not 'luck' that it breaks when it hits the ground, or at least not luck in the sense that it should affect our moral judgement of the defendant. Objectivists also often argue that it is better to have a clear conduct-based standard so that people know what conduct is or is not contrary to the law and that there should be the same standards for everyone. It is also claimed that generally we *do* see people as responsible for the consequences of their actions – be they good or bad consequences. What otherwise is the point of rewarding someone for doing well in an examination?

In an important recent decision of the House of Lords, *B* v. *DPP**, Lord Nicholls suggested that there is an important common law presumption that criminal offences require proof of a subjective state of mind. He explained:

'By definition the mental element in a crime is concerned with a subjective state of mind, such as intent or belief. To the extent that an overriding objective limit ("on reasonable grounds") is introduced, the subjective element is displaced. To that extent a person who lacks the necessary intent or belief may nevertheless commit the offence. When that occurs the defendant's "fault" lies exclusively in falling short of an objective standard. His crime lies in his negligence. A statute may so provide expressly or by necessary implication. But this can have no place in a common law principle, of general application, which is concerned with the need for a mental element as an essential ingredient of a criminal offence.'

Here then, Lord Nicholls argues that the common law supports the subjectivist school of thought, although Parliament can pass a statute that creates an offence which is objectivist.

In fact, overall the law, and indeed most commentators, rejects either of the extreme forms of objectivism and subjectivism, as outlined above. What is needed is a middle course to be taken between the two views. However, there is little agreement where exactly the course should be. Two areas where the dispute has been particularly fierce will now be mentioned briefly by way of example, but we will discuss the law's approach to these topics in more detail later.

1. Liability for indifference

The question here is how to deal with a defendant who fails to foresee that his action will cause harm. Take the example of a person who lights a match next to a haystack, which catches fire. The pure objectivist would argue that as a reasonable person would realize that such an act might lead to the burning of the haystack, the defendant should be liable for arson. However this pure objectivist position would be clearly unfair where the defendant is, for example, suffering from a mental illness which means that he is not able to foresee such a risk (see *Stephenson*). To say to such a person, 'you *should* have foreseen that', is only fair if the defendant *could* have foreseen that. The pure subjectivist would say the person who lights the match should only be liable if he foresaw that it might set the haystack ablaze. This might produce a fair result if the defendant is suffering from a mental illness, but it would not produce a satisfactory result if the defendant did not foresee the harm because he was indifferent to the welfare of others and simply did not care about other people's property. As this example shows, neither the pure subjective nor pure objective theory deals satisfactorily with indifference and a middle approach; maybe focusing on the defendant's attitudes and reasons for failure to foresee a risk needs to be adopted. Indeed it is interesting to note that in the *DPP* v. *B* case where Lord Nicholls stressed the allegiance of the common law to subjectivism, the House of Lords would in fact have convicted a defendant who was indifferent to the age of the victim.

2. Use of the term 'reasonable person' in defences

If a defendant is taunted, loses his self-control and kills someone, he may be able to use the defence of provocation. The law states that he can only do so if a 'reasonable person' would have reacted as he did. This looks like an objectivist test, as a subjectivist test would probably only be interested in whether the defendant actually lost his self-control. However, the strict objectivist test may be harsh when dealing with, say, a young defendant. Indeed the House of Lords has held it is not right 'to require old heads upon young shoulders', and so the defendant only has to react as a reasonable person of his age would have done. Here we see an attempt to forge a middle path between the objectivist and subjectivist positions. The defendant must behave in accordance with an objective standard, but one that is tailored to his own capabilities.

The Law Commission (the body which makes suggestions to the government of reforms of the law) when drafting the proposals for a Criminal Code (see Chapter 2.8) took pure subjectivism as its guiding principle and argued 'principles of personal autonomy and freedom require that the state should only . . . inflict punishment on those who know what they are doing and they could, but do not, choose to desist' (Law Commission 219). Thus Law Commission Report 218 defined the *mens rea* terms (the states of mind required of a defendant) in a purely subjective way. For example, a defendant is reckless with respect to a result 'when he is aware of a risk that it will occur, and it is unreasonable, having regard to the circumstances known to him, to take that risk'. This adherence to subjectivism has been criticized, especially as the Law Commission had not really discussed the relative advantages and disadvantages of objectivism, subjectivism, or a middle path between them. In fact, despite the earlier avowedly subjectivist approach, the Law Commission in some of its later papers departed from a purely subjective approach (for example in relation to manslaughter, rape and intoxication).

In practice there may be less difference between the subjectivist and objectivist positions than there appears to be at first sight. Subjectivists have to accept that it is impossible for the jury to discover what was going on inside the defendant's head while she was committing the crime. The jury must inevitably ask what would a 'reasonable person' have foreseen, and then assume that the defendant would have foreseen what any reasonable person would have foreseen. The difference in approach is only really apparent where the jury are persuaded that the defendant is in some way different from the reasonable person.

1.5   Other Influences on Criminal Law

Other factors apart from simply the harm caused by the act and the culpability of the defendant are relevant in the formulation of criminal law and we will consider these now.

1.5.1   Certainty

You could, in theory, have a very short criminal law. It might read something like this: 'It is an offence wrongfully to harm someone in a blameworthy way'. However, there would be two main objections to such a law. The first is that a citizen should be able, if she wishes, to arrange her life so that she does not breach the criminal law. This is particularly true of the criminal law, given the gravity of the consequence of breaching it. Therefore the law needs to be predictable, fairly certain and capable of being obeyed. These requirements are often called 'the rule of law'. In our imaginary very short criminal law mentioned above it would be very hard to predict how the phrase 'wrongfully to harm someone in a blameworthy way' would be interpreted. It would be difficult therefore to live your life making sure that it was not breached. It might also have the disadvantage in giving the police wide powers to decide whether or not to arrest or prosecute someone. Lord Bingham in *R* v. *K**** recognized this when he stated:

> 'The rule of law is not well served if a crime is defined in terms wide enough to cover conduct which is not regarded as criminal and it is then left to the prosecuting authorities to exercise a blanket discretion not to prosecute to avoid injustice.'

The second objection to the very short criminal law is that if the criminal law is to impose censure on those who do wrong, then that censure needs to be fairly apportioned. It would be inappropriate to censure someone who parks his car illegally with the same level of blame as a deliberate killer. Thus the law has a 'fair labelling function', as some commentators have put it (Williams, 1983). That is to say the offences should be so defined that one can know what level of blame is attached to which offence. On the other hand, if offences are too tightly defined, the way is left open for a defendant to attempt to use technical arguments that he was not charged with exactly the right offence and so escape a conviction.

1.5.2　Autonomy

Imagine a woman ends a relationship with her boyfriend. The boyfriend may feel deeply upset and pained, indeed much more so than if she had hit him. Although the physical assault would fall within the ambit of the criminal law, the breaking off of the relationship would not. The reason seems to be that the law gives protection to people's individual liberty or autonomy. Broadly speaking, freedom or autonomy means that we should be able to live our lives as we wish, in as far as that permits others to do with their lives as they wish. In the above example, although the harm caused to the boyfriend through breaking off the relationship is great, forcing the woman to remain in a relationship with him against her will by threat of a criminal sanction would be an even greater and an unacceptable infringement on her freedom of autonomy. Hence her conduct is not criminalized. Forbidding her to hit her boyfriend is much less of a restraint on her liberty than forbidding her to end the relationship, as she is still left with many other ways of expressing her anger towards him.

1.5.3　Political Expediency

The law is, of course, not just influenced by the high-sounding principles of autonomy and the rule of law but also by political expediency. Even if it could be shown that the taking of soft drugs caused little harm to the user or to society, it would be unlikely that a government would delegalize the drug, at least in the present political climate, given the outcry that would follow such a change in the law. Similarly, even though the consumption of alcohol is connected with a large number of crimes and other harms to society, it is unlikely that a government would make the consumption of alcohol illegal, at least if it wished ever to win an election!

1.5.4　Power Relationships

Ideally the criminal law should be of equal impact in that every member of society should have an equal opportunity to obey the law. However, some argue that the definitions of crimes reflect power structures within society: that the criminal law is designed to protect the interests of the rich and powerful, not the poor and weak. It is certainly true that among convicted criminals there is an over-representation of those in lower socio-economic groupings and those in ethnic minorities (Hood, 1992). It has also been suggested that crimes in which politically weaker sections of society are likely to engage and which are seen as dangerous by the 'middle classes' (for example, drug possession) are defined in such a way as to be easy for the police to prosecute (see Chapter 14.5). By contrast, 'middle-class' crimes, for instance white-collar fraud, are notoriously difficult to prosecute successfully.

1.5.5   Practicality

The law is also governed by practicality. There is no point in making an activity illegal if it would be almost impossible for the police to catch people doing it, or if the only way to do so would be to give police unacceptably wide powers. This may be one reason why adultery is not illegal. Linked to this is administrative efficiency. This is particularly important in the present political climate of seeking to cut public expenditure. An important recent Government White Paper, *Criminal Justice: The Way Ahead*, emphasizes the importance of streamlining the criminal justice system and cutting costs. The definition of criminal offences should aim to be as clear and readily comprehensible as possible to ensure the swift, but fair, conviction of those deserving of punishment. The more complex the legal definition of a crime, the longer the trial is likely to take and the higher the costs. Further, if criminal procedure become too complex and so ineffective it might well be that private vengeance would start to take its place.

1.6   The Reality of Criminal Behaviour

It would be easy to believe from reading some books that a picture of crime and criminal law is to be gleaned from the cases recorded in the law reports. However, considering only reported cases would be most misleading if you wanted to learn about day-to-day criminal activity. Many crimes are not disclosed to the police, even quite serious ones, because victims distrust the police, fear reprisals, or cannot be bothered. Further, the police are not able to catch every criminal, especially given the volume of crime with which they have to deal. Thus the perpetrators of less serious crimes are often not caught. If a criminal is apprehended the police have the discretion whether to charge, caution (give a formal police warning), or take no action. Even if the police do charge, the Crown Prosecution Service still have the discretion to decide not to prosecute, for example on grounds that there is insufficient evidence or that it is not in the public interest to do so. So, even if the perpetrator of a crime is found by the police there may well not be a court hearing. Indeed the Home Office has estimated that only 2 per cent of crimes end with the criminal being convicted. Of those that are prosecuted only a small number of cases reach the higher courts and even fewer are reported. Notably it is exceptional for cases where the defendant has been found not guilty, or had pleaded guilty, to reach the law reports, as there are very limited grounds of appeal in such cases. Thus the cases which appear in the law reports give a distorted picture of the criminal law. What they do provide is a picture of those topics where the law is in doubt and where important principles clash, and that is one of the things in which academic lawyers (and examiners!) are particularly interested.

Hot Topic: Should Fox Hunting be made Illegal?

The dispute over whether the hunting of foxes with dogs should be made illegal reveals many of the issues that need to be addressed when considering what conduct should be made illegal. The aim of this discussion is not to reach a conclusion on this controversial issue, but to demonstrate how the discussion on criminalization above applies to a particular topic.

The issues which are raised by those on either side of the issue include the following:

1 Are animals deserving of protection of the criminal law? Although there is widespread agreement that harming people or injuring people should be prevented by criminal law, there is much dispute over what else deserves protection. In relation to animals, some people would claim that animals deserve the same protection as humans; more popular would be a view that animals deserve some protection, but not at the same level as people. Others would argue that animals do not deserve any protection under the criminal law. Similar kinds of dispute surround the legal status of the foetus.

2 Are moral values to be protected by the criminal law? Even if it was felt that animals were not deserving of protection under the criminal law, it could be argued that the criminal law must protect the moral values that underpin society in order to prevent society sliding into barbarism. Preventing people harming foxes in the course of hunting could be said to uphold moral principles of part of a civilized society. This view would support a ban on fox hunting not on the basis of protecting the fox's interests, but rather protecting the interests of society. Others will not accept this argument for a range of reasons. This may be on the basis that there are no agreed moral values which can be said to underpin our society, because people have a wide range of religious, moral and cultural beliefs. Alternatively it may be accepted that there are values which underpin our society, but that the hunting of foxes does not infringe those moral values. Finally, it may be argued that even if the protection of foxes from being hunted is a fundamental moral principle in our society, nevertheless the criminal law is not an effective tool in protecting society's moral values. Instead education might be thought to be a more effective way of protecting core moral values.

3 Can the disgust of a majority of people be grounds to justify rendering the practice illegal? Is the fact that a majority (or maybe a sizeable minority) find fox hunting objectionable a good ground for rendering the practice illegal? We mentioned above that the 'harm' principle, advocated by Mill, would not permit the criminalization of an act unless it harms other people. The issue here is whether people's disgust will be sufficient to amount to a 'harm' under this analysis.

4 Even if one of the harms listed in points 1 to 3 above is regarded as sufficient to justify criminalization of fox hunting, it might be argued that the harm is outweighed by the good done to society by ridding the countryside of animals

whom some see as pests. There are many lawful activities which cause great harm, but are permitted because they also produce great good. The driving of cars would be on example.

5 Even if it is accepted that a *prima facie* case could be made for rending the practice illegal, can fox hunting be justified on the basis that to some people it is an important aspect of their cultural life? This argument is not quite the same as point 4 because it is not argued that an identifiable good can be demonstrated by the conduct, but rather that people have rights to pursue goals close to their hearts, unless there are very strong reasons against this. For example, our society encourages diversity in religious practice and a law which sought to outlaw a particular religious practice would require very strong justification. Of course fox hunting is not a religious practice, but some people argue that it is an important cultural practice; a crucial aspect of their 'way of life'. Those who adopt such an approach could justify a law generally preventing cruelty to animals, while permitting fox hunting. This is because no one could legitimately claim that being cruel to their pet was an important part of their cultural life; while some claim that fox hunting is an established cultural institution.

6 Even if there is a *prima facie* case that fox hunting causes harm to the animal or to society's values, is the harm a strong enough one to justify the intervention of the criminal law? Ashworth has advocated the principle of minimalism in the criminal law: that the criminal law should be restricted to offences where there are serious harms. This approach maximizes personal liberty (or autonomy) so each person has the greatest choice as to how to live their way of life.

7 Some might oppose a ban on fox-hunting on far more pragmatic grounds than the previous three points. It might be said that banning fox hunting would lead to such wide-scale protests and disruption that it would not be worth doing it. In other words, preventing the harm of fox-hunting would not be worth all the disruption to public order that would result. An alternative argument would be that any law would be unenforceable. It would be impossible for the police to know whether illegal fox hunting was taking place and so any attempted ban would be utterly ineffective.

What these arguments show is that decisions about criminalization are not straightforward. As can be seen from the above points, the factors to be taken into account can range from the practical to the philosophical. Certainly the widely respected 'harm principle' does not provide a ready answer. Indeed it poses almost as many questions as it answers.

Summary

1.1 This book is designed to provide the tools necessary to analyse the criminal law. It also seeks to discuss the tensions between the principles that underlie the law.

1.2 It is difficult to define what constitutes criminal law. Probably the best definition is to consider whether the alleged crime involves using the procedures that attend criminal law. Which conduct is classified criminal can change from society to society and generation to generation.

1.3 The criminal law seeks to deter people from conduct that causes sufficient harm to society and sets out the circumstances in which people may face punishment. A breach of criminal law is different from a breach of other kinds of law, for example contract law, as it contains an element of formal moral censure from society.

1.4 Most criminal offences involve two aspects: harmful conduct and culpability. The harm need not be the injury of another person but includes harm to the environment or society in general. The fact that conduct is simply immoral or harms only the accused is usually insufficient to justify a criminal conviction. The defendant may escape culpability by claiming to be exempt from the criminal law (for example because of age or insanity); or lacking the capacity to commit a crime; or lacking the mental state required for the defence; or having a special defence to the crime. There are several theories that seek to provide a theory of culpability that underpins criminal law, including the choice theory, the character theory and the objective theory. The different theories of culpability link into a dispute over whether the law should take an objective or subjective approach to the law. A subjectivist holds a defendant liable for the consequences of his actions that he has chosen to bring about. An objectivist will hold the defendant responsible for all of the reasonably foreseeable consequences that the defendant's act has caused.

1.5 The criminal law is also influenced by other factors, such as the need for certainty in the law in order that people can arrange their lives so as to ensure that they do not breach the criminal law. It also needs to be efficient in its operation. However, the law inevitably reflects society's attitudes and inequalities.

1.6 The vast majority of crimes do not reach the courts. Many are not reported or if they are the police are unable to find who committed the crime or decide not to prosecute the perpetrator. Thus the picture of crime as it appears in the law reports does not necessarily reflect that which occurs on the streets.

Case Notes

B v. *DPP* [2000] Crim LR 403. House of Lords
See Chapter 6 case notes.

Hinks [2000] 3 WLR 1590. House of Lords
See Chapter 11 case notes.

R v. *K* 25 JULY 2001; [2001] UKHL 41. House of Lords
See Chapter 6 case notes.

Further Reading

Williams discusses the definition of a criminal offence and von Hirsch explains the censuring function played by the criminal law. For the leading works on what conduct should be criminalized read Devlin, Fineberg, Hart and Mill,. For a discussion of the benefits of the character and choice theories of responsibility see Bayles, Duff and Horder. The arguments for and against a subjective or objective approach to criminal liability are to be found in Ashworth, Gobert and Tur. Duff and Garland provide an excellent set of writings on the justifications for punishment. Eaton and Hood discuss how the criminal justice system arguably discriminates against women and ethnic minorities. Norrie reveals the different political pressures that influence criminal law.

Ashworth, 'Taking the Consequences', in Shute, Gardner and Horder (eds), *Action*

20 Criminal Law

and Value in Criminal Law (1993, Oxford University Press).

Bayles, 'Character, Purpose and Criminal Responsibility' (1982) 1 Law and Philosophy 5.

Devlin, The Enforcement of Morals (1968, Oxford University Press).

Duff, 'Choice, Character and Criminal Responsibility' (1993) Law and Philosophy 345.

Duff and Garland (eds), A Reader on Punishment (1994, Oxford University Press).

Eaton, Justice for Women? (1987, Open University Press).

Fineberg, Harm to Self, Harm to Others; Harmless Wrongdoing; Offense to Others (1984, 1986, 1988, Oxford University Press).

Gobert, 'The Fortuity of Consequences', (1993) 4 Criminal Law Forum 1.

Hart, Law, Liberty and Morality (1963, Oxford University Press).

von Hirsch, Censure and Sanctions (1993, Oxford University Press).

Hood, Race and Sentencing (1992, Oxford University Press).

Horder, 'Criminal Culpability: The Possibility of a General Theory', (1993) Law and Philosophy 193.

Mill, On Liberty (1859).

Norrie, Crime, Reason and History (1993, Weidenfeld & Nicolson).

Tur, 'Subjectivism and Objectivism: Towards Synthesis', in Shute, Gardner and Horder (eds), Action and Value in Criminal Law (1993, Oxford University Press).

Williams, 'The Definition of Crime' (1955) Current Legal Problems 107.

Williams, 'Convictions and Fair Labelling' [1983] Cambridge Law Journal 85.

2 Procedures and Structures of Criminal Law

Key words

- **Burden of proof** – who must prove a particular fact.
- **The Crown** – the Crown refers to the Queen who represents the state.

2.1 The Role of the State in Criminal Proceedings

Civil and criminal law are both concerned with liability for wrongful conduct. The same act (such as an assault) may amount both to a civil wrong, called a tort, and a crime. So, if Sam hit Millie there would be consequences in both civil law and criminal law. Millie could sue Sam for damages for her injuries under the law of tort. The police may also decide to charge Sam with a criminal offence, as a result of which Sam may receive a punishment. These civil and criminal law consequences are quite different. In the case of a tort, liability is owed to the injured party and damages may be paid to the injured party to compensate for any losses. In the case of a crime, liability is owed to the state and the state supervises any punishment. Liability is owed to the state even where the crime has a human victim, because a crime is regarded as a breach of public order. One of the ways in which England was united under the Crown in the thirteenth and fourteenth centuries was by the enforcement of order (the King's peace) by the King's officials and judges. Serious infringements of order (called felonies) were offences against the Crown, and prosecutions were brought in the name of the King. This is still the case: serious offences are tried on indictment in the Crown Court, and the prosecution is in the name of the Crown. The prosecuting authority is called the Crown Prosecution Service, and the official title of the case will be for example, *The Queen* versus *Smith*, abbreviated to *R. v. Smith*, or even *Smith*.

The criminal law is about the control of behaviour by the state, backed up by the sanction of punishment. Judges have on occasion expressly recognized this: in describing the culpability necessary for the crime of manslaughter, Lord Chief Justice Hewart referred to 'such disregard for the life and safety of others as to amount to a crime against the State and conduct deserving punishment' (*Bateman*). However, it would be wrong to think that the criminal law is unconcerned about the victim. Indeed at the sentencing stage it is now possible for the judge to require the defendant to pay compensation to the victim for the harm done. This to some extent blurs the distinction between civil and criminal law.

2.2   The Role of the Judge in Criminal Proceedings

The criminal law is still largely common law, that is judge-made law. Of course, there are important statutes, mainly dating from the last 150 years, but these have tended to adjust the underlying common law, rather than radically change it. For example, the Homicide Act 1957 alters the law of murder without defining 'murder' and the definition of murder is still a matter of caselaw. Exceptions are the Theft Acts of 1968 and 1978, which completely reworked the law of theft; but even these have since been over-laid with a body of caselaw, interpreting the various statutory provisions. Now it would not be possible to understand the law of theft by simply looking at the Acts, the cases applying the Acts must be read as well.

A clear view of the importance of the judicial role is found in the judge-ment of Viscount Simonds in *Shaw* v. *DPP*, in which he denied that the courts have the power to create new crimes but asserted that in exercising their duty as 'servants and guardians of the common law . . . there remains in the courts of law a residual power to enforce the supreme and funda-mental purpose of the law, to conserve not only the safety and order but also the moral welfare of the State, and that it is their duty to guard it against attacks which may be the more insidious because they are novel and unprepared for'. In this case, the protection of public order justified the extension of the offence of conspiracy to cover conduct which was not itself criminal but which, in the view of the House of Lords, was a threat to public morals (see Chapter 18.3). Lord Millet, in an important recent case, *R* v. *K*, was willing to reform the law because he felt that Parliament had failed to ensure the law accorded with current standards of morality. The case concerned (in effect) the age at which teenagers could consent to sexual activities:

'But the age of consent has long since ceased to reflect ordinary life, and in this respect Parliament has signally failed to discharge its responsibil-ity for keeping the criminal law in touch with the needs of society. I am persuaded that the piecemeal introduction of the various elements of Section 14 [Sexual Offences Act 1956], coupled with the persistent failure of Parliament to rationalise this branch of the law even to the extent of removing absurdities which the Courts have identified, means that we ought not to strain after internal coherence even in a single offence. Injustice is too high a price to pay for consistency.'

In spite of the pre-eminence of judge-made law, it is only recently that the higher courts, the Court of Appeal and the House of Lords, have paid much attention to the development of the criminal law. Criminal practice used to be regarded as hackwork, with little intellectual interest, and this coloured the ideas of judges. In the last fifty years this has changed completely – the criminal law has attracted academic attention, the Court of Appeal has developed a strong tradition, and the number of criminal cases going to the House of Lords has increased.

Perhaps for this reason, considerable criticism has in recent years been directed at the courts, particularly the House of Lords, by writers and commentators who feel that the judges fail to achieve either clarity or consistency. Eminent academic writers such as J. C. Smith have speculated about the House of Lords' 'dismal record in criminal cases', and questioned whether we can really afford the House of Lords as an appellate criminal court. In several different areas of the criminal law there has been a striking divergence between the views of academic lawyers on what the law should be, and the decisions of the courts establishing what the law is. One of the drawbacks to the common law method of developing rules of law piecemeal in the context of individual cases is that concern for 'the right answer' in a particular case can obscure the wider logical implications of a decision. This tension between justice in individual cases and the coherence of a just legal system is a particular difficulty in the criminal law. Judges sometimes feel that academic writing is too theoretical and abstract, not grounded firmly enough in the need to explain the law clearly to juries. Lord Diplock (in the decision which prompted the reflections quoted above about the quality of the House of Lords' decisions) rejected a definition formulated by a legal writer and adopted by the Court of Appeal, because it created 'fine and impracticable distinctions' which were not appropriate for a jury (see *Caldwell**). Lord Reid, in *Haughton* v. *Smith**, said 'the life blood of the law is not logic but common sense', and very similar words were used by Lord Salmon in *Majewski**, both cases which attracted enormous academic criticism. This criticism is sometimes effective. Lord Bridge, in a case which reversed an earlier House of Lords' decision, referred to an article written by Professor Glanville Williams: 'The language in which he criticises the decision . . . is not conspicuous for its moderation, but it would be foolish, on that account, not to recognise the force of the criticism and churlish not to acknowledge the assistance I have derived from it' (*Shivpuri**). In the last few years however it has become increasingly common for judges, particularly in the House of Lords, to carefully analyse the academic writings in criminal cases, leading sometimes to longer and more carefully reasoned judgements. This has not, of course, meant that academics have stopped criticizing some of the decisions of the House of Lords.

2.3   Judge and Jury

Some criminal trials are carried out in front of a judge and jury (this is called trial on indictment, and takes place in the Crown Court), but most are tried summarily by magistrates. The difference between summary and indictable offences is explained below in Chapter 2.5. Magistrates, when they hear a case, combine the functions of both judge and jury: they decide any questions of law that arise (with the help of their clerk, who is a lawyer); they decide the facts; and they apply the law to the facts to reach a verdict. It is easier to explain these different functions in the context of a trial on indictment, but the same principles apply to a summary trial.

If the defendant pleads guilty to the offence with which he is charged then the jury have no role to play and a conviction will be entered. A defendant who pleads guilty may be influenced by the fact that a guilty plea may well lead to a lesser sentence. It may also be that if a defendant pleads guilty to a lesser crime then the prosecution will not pursue a more serious charge; this is commonly known as 'plea bargaining'. If the defendant pleads not guilty then there is a clear division of roles between the judge and the jury.

The judge has a duty to ensure that the trial is conducted according to the rules of procedure and evidence, a large subject in itself. The judge's function is to explain the *law* to the jury: this is a very important part of the judge's summing-up, in which she addresses the jury before they retire to consider their verdict. If any questions of law are raised during the trial, by either the prosecution, the defence or by the judge herself, it is the judge who must give a ruling on the point. The jury is bound to take the law from the judge. It may be possible for the defendant to challenge the judge's ruling on the law by appealing to a higher court after the verdict. Decisions on the law by magistrates can always be challenged in a higher court, either the Crown Court or the High Court.

It is the function of the jury to decide questions of *fact* and to apply the law to the facts so as to arrive at a verdict on the charge facing the defendant. The charge will be stated on a formal document, known as an indictment, which will specify, in brief, the nature of the allegation facing the defendant, including particularly the offence with which he is charged. It may well be that there are some aspects of the case on which the prosecution and defence agree. For example, the defendant may admit that he was at the scene of the crime, but deny that he hit the victim. In such a case, obviously the jury will focus on those factual issues that are in dispute.

The jury is only to consider whether the defendant committed the offence with which he is charged. For example if the defendant is charged with stabbing the victim and during his evidence the defendant admits stealing from the victim, but denies stabbing him, the jury cannot return a verdict of guilty of theft as it is only allowed to consider the offence with which the defendant was charged. That said, sometimes the jury can return a verdict of guilty to a lesser crime if the defendant is charged with a serious offence, the elements of which include the lesser offence. For example if the defendant is charged with murder, the jury could convict the defendant of manslaughter if the jury decided that it had not been shown that he intended to kill or cause serious injury. The judge will inform a jury if this may be possible. It is not true to say that the jury is not concerned with the law at all: if that were so, then the 'verdict' would merely be a series of statements of fact about what the jury think happened. A verdict is the law applied to the facts, which results in a conclusion of guilt or innocence.

An important aspect of the jury's function is to decide what happened: whether a particular witness is telling the truth, for example; or whether an identification that has been denied is reliable. 'What happened' does not only include actions (what the accused did) but also the state of mind of those who were involved, including particularly the accused. For example in a rape case, the jury have to decide whether sexual intercourse took place; whether the victim was consenting at the time (her state of mind); as well as, if she was not consenting, whether the accused knew that she was not consenting (his state of mind). Questions about states of mind are often called subjective questions (see Chapter 1.4). Of course, the jury cannot read minds, and even if it could, it is concerned with the state of mind at the time of the alleged offence, not at the time of the trial. So it has to rely on external evidence, which includes what was done and what was said as well as the surrounding circumstances. Sometimes the inference from the facts is overwhelming: if the accused has pointed a gun point-blank at the victim and fired, the jury will readily infer that the accused intended at least some injury. But this inference may be displaced by other evidence (see *Lamb** for an example), and it is important to remember that the jury is ultimately concerned with the actual state of mind of the accused, not what jury members themselves would have thought.

The jury not only deals with the facts of what happened: it is also asked to decide questions such as 'what would a reasonable person have done in this situation?' or 'would a reasonable person call this book obscene?'

When the criminal law poses questions such as these, it is setting an objective standard, and the jury acts as representatives of reasonable persons in assessing and applying that standard. The jury measures the conduct of the accused person against its view of what a reasonable person would have done or thought.

Yet another aspect to the jury's function is to determine the meaning of words used by statutes. Sometimes these words are defined, either in the statute itself, or by the judges. In such cases the definition is a matter of law, and the jury is bound to apply it: the jury cannot say that it disagrees with the definition given and apply a different one (if it was to do this, and convict the accused, the verdict may be overturned on appeal). An example is the definition of the word 'property' found in the Theft Act 1968, which is given a particular technical definition in the statute (see Chapter 11). Sometimes, however, words are not defined either by statute or by the courts, and the jury must apply the words as it understands them. There has been a tendency in modern statutes to use supposedly simple, non-technical language, and judges increasingly avoid giving exhaustive definitions of words used in this way. They say that these are ordinary, everyday words which the jury can be expected to understand and apply without definition. An example, also from the Theft Act 1968, is the word 'dishonesty'. This use of simple words is not confined to words used in statutes: the meaning of 'intention' in a common law crime such as murder is another example. The judges are willing to explain how the jury may infer intention from the evidence, but not to define it. The benefits and disadvantages of doing this will be discussed in the *Hot Topic* for this chapter.

2.4   The Burden of Proof

It is fundamental to a criminal trial that the prosecution must prove its case: a person, however clear the evidence seems to be, is innocent until proved guilty (*Woolmington**). The prosecution has to prove its case beyond reasonable doubt, and the judge must direct the jury that it is not to convict unless it is convinced that all the elements of the offence were present. The phrase 'beyond reasonable doubt' is the conventional way of expressing the idea that the jury must feel sure of the accused's guilt. It is stronger than the standard of proof in a civil case, such as an action for negligence, which only requires 'proof on the balance of probabilities': a conclusion that the plaintiff's version of events is more probable than not. It is therefore quite possible for the jury in a criminal case to believe that a defendant probably committed the crime but still to acquit her if it has some doubts over her guilt. In such a case the accused might be not guilty of a criminal offence, but be liable to pay damages in a civil case.

The judge cannot direct a conviction, because only the jury can find the facts and apply the law to those facts. However, it may be appropriate for the judge to say 'if you find the facts to be this then you should acquit but if you find the facts to be that you should convict'. The judge can direct an acquittal: it is sometimes the judge's duty to tell the jury that there is not, as a matter of law, enough evidence to justify a conviction, even if the jury were to believe every word of the prosecution evidence. The judge also ensures that the rules of evidence are complied with and can exclude evidence that is inadmissible. The judge may direct an acquittal on part of the indictment (one of the 'counts', alleging one offence) but leave the rest to the jury. This is sometimes explained by saying that the prosecution has both an *evidential* burden – to produce enough evidence to justify leaving the case to the jury – and a burden of proof – to prove the case beyond reasonable doubt. The evidential burden is to satisfy the judge, the burden of proof is to satisfy the jury.

Do these two burdens always rest on the prosecution, or may they sometimes rest on the defence? It is very important to remember the principle already stated: at the end of the trial, the prosecution must prove all the elements of the offence in order to obtain a conviction. However, this does not mean that the prosecution has to disprove every single defence on which an accused may possibly rely, such as lack of intention or knowledge, self-defence, provocation, drunkenness, duress and so on. If such a defence is raised on the facts as presented by the prosecution, the judge will direct the jury on the law relating to the defence in question. If the defence is not revealed by the prosecution's evidence, the accused has a burden of producing sufficient evidence of the defence to justify leaving it to the jury, and if he does not the judge will refuse to let the jury consider it. This is an evidential burden only: the accused does not have to prove the defence. What amounts to sufficient evidence will depend on the nature of the defence. If the accused denies the knowledge or intention required for the offence, his own evidence will be enough to put to the jury. But in the case of automatism, for example, where the accused claims that he was not in control of his actions, the courts have looked for medical evidence to back up the accused's own testimony (see Chapter 3.6). If he fails to produce any evidence in his defence, he puts himself at risk of conviction by making the prosecution's burden of proof easier to discharge. If the judge puts the defence to the jury, the prosecution then has the burden of disproving that defence in order to obtain a conviction.

There are exceptions to this rule (although we will discuss in Chapter 19 an argument that these exceptions are contrary to the Human Rights Act

1998). A person is presumed sane until proved otherwise, so there is a burden of proof on the accused if he seeks to rely on the common law defence of insanity or the statutory defence of diminished responsibility, both of which deny the accused's legal capacity (see Chapters 10 and 15 for a discussion of these defences). There are also occasions where a statute creating an offence expressly puts a burden of proof on the accused (see Healy, 1987). In all cases where there is a burden of proof on the accused, the standard of proof required is lower than that required for the prosecution: it is proof on the balance of probabilities, rather than beyond reasonable doubt.

Let us apply these principles to an example. Jack is charged with the murder of Jill and pleads not guilty. The prosecution has to prove the elements of murder: that Jack caused the death of Jill, and that he either intended to kill her or at least intended to cause her serious injury. The prosecution produces evidence that Jack shot Jill with a revolver at a range of four yards. This may include evidence of witnesses who saw the incident, and forensic evidence, such as that the bullet found in Jill's body carries markings consistent with being fired from the revolver owned by Jack. The prosecution also needs evidence that the shot caused the death of Jill, and this will be medical evidence from the autopsy. Then the prosecution needs evidence of Jack's state of mind: that Jack intended to kill or seriously injure Jill. The prosecution may rely on Jack's conduct (it is alleged that he shot Jill at close range and so the jury may be invited to infer that the only believable explanation for his conduct was that he intended to kill her) or his words at the time. There may be other circumstantial evidence, such as evidence of motive (for example Jack was due to receive a large inheritance from Jill).

At the close of the prosecution case, the accused can submit that there is 'no case to answer', which is a claim that the prosecution has not satisfied the evidential burden. The judge must decide whether all this evidence amounts to a case against Jack, in other words if there are sufficient grounds for a conviction if the evidence is believed and not denied. If the case is tenable, then the judge will let it continue: she will not direct an acquittal, as the prosecution will have satisfied the evidential burden. Faced with a 'case to answer', Jack has a choice. He can refuse to defend himself at all, and not produce any alternative explanation of the prosecution's evidence. This is possible, but it is scarcely consistent with a plea of not guilty, and it is likely to mean a conviction because the jury has no reason to doubt the prosecution evidence. A conviction is not inevitable, because the jury is not under an obligation to believe an unchallenged prosecution case and may think that there is still a reasonable doubt over Jack's guilt.

Jack can challenge the prosecution evidence, that he shot Jill or that the shot caused the death, or that he intended Jill any harm (or all of these). Or

Jack may accept all these facts, and rely on a defence: a claim that his act was justified because he was acting in self-defence; or that it was excusable because Jill had provoked him so that he lost his self-control. He will have to produce evidence, including his own testimony, to support his assertions. This is his evidential burden, and if he does not produce any evidence (and no such evidence is raised on the agreed facts) the judge will not put that defence to the jury. If the defence goes to the jury, the prosecution, in addition to proving the elements of murder already stated, must disprove the defence (for example that Jack was acting in self-defence). If Jack pleads either insanity or diminished responsibility, he will have to prove it, according to the legal definition of the defence.

At the end of the defence case, the judge will sum up to the jury, telling them the elements of the offence which the prosecution must prove, and summarizing the evidence. The judge will point the jury towards the issues in the case, the areas of dispute between the prosecution and the accused, and explain the burden of proof. The jury will then determine the facts (what happened?), apply the law to them (is this murder?) and reach a verdict.

2.5   Classification of Offences

The basic distinction when classifying criminal offences is between those that are tried on indictment, those that are tried summarily, and those that can be tried either way. In the first group are the more serious offences, such as murder, manslaughter and rape. They are tried before a judge and jury in a Crown Court. Relatively minor offences, such as many motoring offences, are in the second group and these are tried before magistrates, who have limited sentencing powers. In the third group are those offences such as theft, which may vary considerably in their seriousness according to circumstances. They may be tried either way, and the choice is made in the Magistrates' Court. Either the magistrates *or* the accused may insist on trial on indictment; only if both agree will the case be tried summarily. For the magistrates, the choice will depend on the seriousness of the charge, as indicated by the prosecution statements, and whether the case seems likely to raise a difficult question of law, which a judge would be better able to decide than lay magistrates. For the accused, the choice will depend on many factors: summary trial is faster and cheaper (this may be important if the accused is ordered to make a contribution to legal aid); the Crown Court can impose heavier sentences, although the magistrates can, if they convict, decide to commit the offender for sentence to the Crown Court; and magistrates have a reputation of being more likely to convict, especially if the defence relies on challenging police evidence. The rules of procedure applicable to the two forms of trial are different, the sentencing powers differ, as do the rights of appeal, but the definition of the offence (with which this book is concerned) do not change according to whether the accused is tried in the Crown Court or the magistrates' court.

A much earlier classification distinguished between felonies and misdemeanours. This distinction was abolished by the Criminal Law Act 1967 and is only mentioned here because references are still sometimes made in judgements to felonies or misdemeanours and may otherwise be puzzling. The Criminal Law Act 1967 also created the concept of an arrestable offence. This is now defined in s.24 of the Police and Criminal Evidence Act 1984, and includes all offences carrying a maximum sentence of five years' imprisonment or more (certain other specific offences are also included). Both police officers and members of the public are able to arrest without a warrant where a person has committed an arrestable offence. The powers of police officers are more extensive in relation to both arrestable and non-arrestable offences (s.24 and s.25 of the Police and Criminal Evidence Act 1984).

2.6   Punishment

Theories of punishment are more relevant in discussing sentencing than discussing the definition of criminal offences, and we are not going to discuss sentencing in any detail in this book. However, the definition of an offence and its punishment are linked. There would be little point in finding defendants guilty who were thought unsuitable for punishment. The main theories of why the state should punish criminals are well known and discussed in detail in many books on criminology and sentencing, but they can be summarized briefly. One theory is *reformation* – that the goal of punishment should be to reform the criminal so that he will not commit a crime again. Another is *deterrence* – that the criminal himself and other potential criminals will be discouraged from committing a crime through fear of punishment. A further theory is *incapacitation* – that the criminal should be prevented from committing a crime, typically by imprisonment. The dominant theory at present appears to be '*just deserts*' or *retribution*. This theory is that defendants should be punished in proportion to their blameworthiness, and is the main philosophy behind the Criminal Justice Act 1991, which is one of the main statutes governing sentencing. At different times in penal history, one or other of these theories have held sway and no doubt all four are factors weighing on a sentencer's mind, even though they are to some extent conflicting.

2.7   Reform of the Law

Reform of the criminal law, like any branch of the law, is dependent on Acts of Parliament. Over the last thirty years, Parliament has relied heavily on the work done and Reports produced by two committees: the Criminal Law Revision Committee, established in 1959; and the Law Commission, established in 1965. Reports prepared by these bodies often have a draft Bill attached, which may form the basis of legislation. The success of these Reports, judged purely in terms of whether they have been implemented, has been mixed; some, such as the Criminal Law Revision Committee Report on theft (Eighth report, Cmnd 2977, 1966) or the Law Commission Report on attempt (No. 102, 1980), have been implemented; others, such as the Law Commission Report on the mental element in crime (No. 89, 1978) and the recent Law Commission Reports on the Criminal Code (see Chapter 2.8), are yet to be implemented.

When a major revision of the law is envisaged, a Royal Commission may be set up. An example is the Royal Commission on Criminal Procedure, which reported in 1981 and eventually led to the Police and Criminal Evidence Act 1984. One of the major law reform issues is the desirability of codifying the criminal law.

2.8   The Proposals for a Criminal Code

2.8.1   The Definition of a Code

Some countries have a Code of criminal law; that is, a single statute which sets out the definitions of each offence and defence. Increasingly there have been calls for England and Wales to have such a Code. The Law Commission has been working on a Criminal Code for over two decades. It produced its first draft Code in 1985 and recently started to produce short draft bills to deal with specific topics. As yet none of these Law Commission draft bills have been enacted. This may be because what might be seen as 'tidying up' the criminal law is low on a government's list of priorities given governments' frantic legislative programmes. It is interesting that in more recent reports the Law Commission has highlighted the financial savings that a Code could produce for the criminal justice system, perhaps in an attempt to make the reforms politically more attractive. This may have had its desired effect because in a paper entitled *Criminal Justice: The Way Ahead* (2001) the government indicated that it wishes to improve the efficiency and effectiveness of the criminal justice system, including codifying the criminal law.

If the Law Commission's proposals for a Code are ever enacted they will signify a radical change in the nature of our criminal law. It would lead to a movement away from the primarily caselaw-based system to a statutory-based system. The Code would be a single statute that would aim to set out the entire criminal law. What is less clear is the extent to which the substance of the law would change. There has been much dispute over whether the Criminal Code should seek to reform the present law or to declare it. In fact the Law Commission has stated that in general the draft Code is seeking to state the present law. However, the Code seeks to reform the law if reform is necessary to deal with inconsistencies, arbitrary rules or lack of clarity; or if reform of a particular law has been proposed by an official body. However, it is clear that some significant reform will take place. For example one proposal is to abandon the *Caldwell* recklessness test, and another is to reformulate the basic principles underlining accessorial liability.

2.8.2   The Benefits of a Code

Many benefits have been claimed for the Criminal Code. One aim of the Code is to summarize the law in a single document written in simple language. The law would therefore be easier to ascertain, not only for citizens but also for lawyers and the judiciary. This helps fulfil the ideal of the rule of law (see Chapter 1.7) and ensures that the criminal law satisfies the requirements of the European Convention on Human Rights (see Chapter 19).

The Code is also seen as a means of improving the efficiency of the criminal justice system. Complex and uncertain laws take more time for judges and lawyers to ascertain, are more complex to explain to juries and are more likely to lead to appeals. All of this slows down and increases the cost of the legal process. By creating a Code the law can be put into a format that is easier and cheaper to use.

It is said that the present case-by-case and statute-by-statute system of law reform has meant that the criminal law is not internally consistent. There are cases and rules that are anomalous and seem not to be based on the moral principles that underlie the rest of the law. The Criminal Code could establish some cardinal principles and ensure that they are consistently applied throughout the law. Another argument is that at present many changes in the criminal law are judge-made (see, for example, *R* (see Chapter 8.2.1)), rather than authorized by Parliament, and are therefore undemocratic. One Law Commission report stated, 'a Criminal Code makes a symbolic statement about the constitutional relationship of Parliament and the courts', the argument being that the development of the criminal law should not depend upon how a judge chooses to interpret conflicting caselaw, but should be decided by Parliament in the form of a Code.

The Law Commission has summarized the benefits of the Code as accessibility, comprehensibility, consistency and certainty. However, this leaves the question of what is the ultimate aim of the Code. In one Law Commission report the efficiency and practical benefits were stressed, while in another report the 'rule of law' benefits were emphasized.

2.8.3   The Disadvantages of a Code

In the face of such arguments it is hard to argue against a Criminal Code, but there are some concerns. One is that a Code may become obsessed with guiding principles and internal consistency and overlook the fact that apparent contradictions within the criminal law may reflect the complexity of the many political, ethical and practical issues involved. Sometimes seemingly 'logically contradictory' rules may in fact reflect the best compromise between these competing values in particular circumstances. This may be true of the rules on intoxication (see Chapter 15.3.1) and mistakes in defences (Chapter 15.3.2).

Another argument is that it is easy to over-stress the benefits of a Code and that any advantages will be minimal. Inevitably the Code will need to be interpreted by the judiciary and it is suggested by some that a whole new body of caselaw would soon build up around the Criminal Code and so defeat the code's aims of accessibility and comprehensiveness. The Law Commission has stated that 'the creative role of the judge will therefore continue to play a part where the legislation does not provide an answer', and so it is clear that judicial inventiveness will not be completely curbed. Also, one might think that members of the public will not be quick to purchase and read copies of any new Code and so perhaps making the Code comprehensible to a lay person should not be high on the priorities for a Code. That said, there is still a strong argument that if a citizen does decide to try and find out what the criminal law is, the task should not be made unduly difficult.

Hot Topic: The Increasing Role of the Jury

The exact balance of power between the judge and jury is always controversial. One dominant theme in some of the important decisions of the House of Lords in recent years has been that complex questions that have troubled criminal lawyers have been classified as questions for the jury, about which the judge need give no detailed directions. To give a few examples:

1   Some legal terms should not be defined by the judge, but left to the jury to be given their 'normal meaning'. For example, the word 'intention' is to be given its 'ordinary meaning' by the jury and the judge does not normally need to give the jury a detailed explanation of the term (see Chapter 4.3.2).

2   Sometimes the definition of an offence will require the jury to apply the standards of the reasonable or ordinary person. For example, the word 'dishonesty' largely depends on what the jury assesses the standards of behaviour expected by ordinary people. The judge should not tell the jury whether a particular kind of conduct is dishonest or not; it is up to the jury to decide this on the basis of the current standards of morality. Another example is where the jury is asked to decide whether the defendant acted as the reasonable or ordinary person would have done (for example in the case of duress).

3   Most extraordinarily, in the offence of gross negligence the jury is quite openly required to assess whether the defendant's conduct was so bad as to justify a criminal conviction.

In all of these examples (and many others can be given) a move is made away from the judge (or the law) giving the jury detailed guidance as to what the legal requirements are for a particular offence to be made out. Instead the issue is left to the jury, by applying its common sense and the standards of ordinary people. Of course, there are still many issues where the judge does have to set out clearly what legal requirements have to be shown, but the trend appears towards giving the jury a greater role in establishing the legal standards.

Arguments can be made for or against such a move. Looking first at some of the arguments in favour of this trend:

1   Some argue that giving juries complex guidance on, for example, the precise meaning of intention will be of little use. In fact it may be that juries place greater weight on their own common sense and the standards of the common person than what the judge tells them are the technical rules of the law. If this is correct it can be argued that requiring juries to give words their normal meaning and to use the standards of the ordinary person is just being realistic. It should be added that relatively little is known about the reasoning process that juries in England and Wales use in reaching their conclusions, and the validity of these claims therefore remains unknown.

2   A significant argument in favour of the present approach is that it decreases the chances of a defendant successfully appealing against a conviction on the basis that the judge did not use precisely the correct wording towards the jury. For example if the courts developed a complete definition of dishonesty, without reference to the standards of ordinary people, it would almost inevitably consist of a lengthy number of points that would need to be mentioned by a judge. A failure to mention just one could lead to a successful appeal against conviction. By using the standards of the ordinary person the direction can be kept short and there is far less chance of judicial error in providing the direction.

3   By using the standard of the ordinary person or the normal meaning of the word, the law is able to keep abreast of changing attitudes within society. Any fixed complex legal definition of a term such as dishonesty may soon find itself out of tune with the times. The current trend should mean that it will be rarer for the courts or Parliament to have to change the law in response to shifts in public attitudes.

There are however many who oppose these trends and they raise a number of arguments, including the following:

1 Some argue that if the law claims to be based on principles and values of justice then the law cannot be based on the jury's understanding of justice. The values of the jury may not be those that the law wishes to uphold. For example, if the jury were to be permitted to give rape 'its ordinary meaning', an unenlightened jury may decide that if the victim was walking home alone at night she was 'asking for it' and therefore acquit the accused. The law would quite properly wish to reject any such analysis, but if it is to do so this may require the judge to clearly direct the jury that such a line of reasoning is forbidden.

2 It is also argued that allowing each jury to rely on its own understanding of fairness or the meaning of legal terms can lead to injustice. There may be two cases with identical facts, but where the juries reach opposite conclusions because they have different views on what are the standards of the ordinary person. A jury from Tunbridge Wells and a jury from inner-city Liverpool may well disagree on the ordinary standards of honesty.

3 There is a concern that if a jury is asked to apply its common sense, in reality this will mean its members applying their prejudices. Judges are often careful to ensure that juries decide a case based on the evidence and not on the appearance of the defendant. Juries may, however, regard a direction to apply common sense or the standards of ordinary people as permitting them to rely on prejudicial attitudes.

It should not be thought that it is juries alone who seek to rely on their common sense. A senior judge described very well how in a number of homicide cases, appeal judges who 'felt' that the accused was guilty of murder, rather than the less serious manslaughter, adjusted the legal meaning of words in order to achieve what appeared to their gut instincts to be the right result (Lord Goff, 1988). If judges in the House of Lords and Court of Appeal do this, why not juries?

As you read through this book, keep the issue discussed in this *Hot Topic* in mind. For each offence ask why the law does or does not leave the question to the jury as one of common sense.

Summary

2.1 Crimes, besides often having human victims, are wrongs against the state – infringements rendering the offender liable to be punished. Proceedings against the accused are brought in the name of the Crown, on behalf of the state.

2.2 Much criminal law is still common law although there are also important statutes. Some academic writers have been very critical of the way that the courts have developed aspects of the criminal law, including their interpretation of statutes.

2.3 In a criminal trial the judge decides questions of law and directs the jury on the law. The jury decides questions of fact, and applies the law to the facts. In a Magistrates' Court, the magistrates perform both functions. Some questions of fact are subjective and some are objective. Judges frequently leave words and concepts that have not already been defined in a statute or caselaw to the jury to interpret as to their ordinary meaning.

2.4 The burden of proof is on the prosecution, which has to satisfy the jury beyond reasonable doubt of all the elements of an offence. The prosecution has to produce sufficient evidence for the judge to leave the case to the jury; if the prosecution does not do this, the judge will direct an acquittal. The accused does not have to prove his innocence, but does have to produce evidence of a defence on which he wishes to rely.

2.5 Offences may be tried on indictment before a judge and jury, tried summarily before magistrates, or tried either way. There is also a distinction between arrestable and non-arrestable offences, which affects the powers of arrest given to police officers and ordinary citizens.

2.6 There are various theories of punishment including deterrence, reformation, incapacitation and 'just deserts'. 'Just deserts' is the dominant theory at present but the others often influence a sentencer.

2.7 The principal law reform body is the Law Commission. It produces reports and draft legislation, some of which gets onto the statute book. The Law Commission is working on a Criminal Code and has several reports in preparation.

2.8 A Criminal Code has been drafted and is being considered by the government. It seeks to describe in one document all the criminal offences.

Case Notes

***Caldwell* [1982] AC 341. House of Lords**
See Chapter 4 case notes.

***Haughton* v. *Smith* [1975] AC 476. House of Lords**
See Chapter 18 case notes.

***Lamb* [1967] 2 All QB 981. Court of Appeal**
See Chapter 10 case notes.

***Majewski* [1977] AC 443. House of Lords**
See Chapter 15 case notes.

***Shivpuri* [1987] AC 1. House of Lords**
See Chapter 16 case notes.

***Woolmington* [1935] AC 462. House of Lords**
The appellant was convicted of murder, having shot his wife. His wife had left him a short time after their marriage, and he went to see her, taking a shotgun with him. He claimed that he had intended to tell her that he would shoot himself if she would not return, and the gun went off accidentally, killing her. At the trial, the judge directed the jury that once it was proved by the prosecution that the accused had killed his wife, the shooting was presumed to be murder, unless the accused could satisfy the jury that the killing was accidental, or justified, or should be manslaughter rather than murder. His appeal was dismissed by the Court of Appeal, but allowed by the House of Lords. Viscount Sankey, the Lord Chancellor, said that the trial judge's direction had been based on a book by Foster, written in 1762, and not on any earlier caselaw authority. If the judge were able to rule that the burden of proof in a case had shifted to the accused, to prove that he was not guilty, that would be making the judge decide the case and not the jury. The accused is entitled to the benefit of any doubt: 'while the prosecution must prove the guilt of the prisoner, there is no such burden laid on the prisoner to prove his innocence, and it is sufficient for him to raise a doubt as to his guilt; he is not bound to satisfy the jury of his innocence. Throughout the web of the English criminal law one golden thread is always to be seen – that it is the duty of the prosecution to prove the prisoner's guilt subject to what I have already said as to the defence of insanity and subject also to any statutory exception.'

Further Reading

Ashworth (1999) provides an excellent discussion of the law on criminal procedure. The role played by a judge is described by Ashworth (1991), Goff and Devlin. Ashworth and Blake, Healy, Roberts and Smith discuss burdens of proof and the presumption of innocence. The criminal code is examined in da Burca and Gardner, and Glazebrook.

Ashworth, 'Interpreting Criminal Statutes: a Case of Legality' (1991) 107 *Law Quarterly Review* 419.

Ashworth, *The Criminal Process* (1999, Oxford University Press).

Ashworth and Blake, 'The Presumption of Innocence in English Criminal Law' [1997] *Criminal Law Review* 306.

da Burca and Gardner, 'The Codification of the Criminal Law' (1990) 10 *Oxford Journal of Legal Studies* 559.

Devlin, *The Judge* (1979, Oxford University Press).

Glazebrook, 'Structuring the Criminal Code', in Simester and Smith (eds), *Harm and Culpability* (1996, Oxford University Press).

Goff, 'The Mental Element in the Crime of Murder' (1988) *Law Quarterly Review* 30.

Healy, 'Proof and Policy: No Golden Threads' [1987] *Criminal Law Review* 355.

Roberts, 'Taking the Burden of Proof Seriously' [1995] *Criminal Law Review* 783.

Smith, 'The Presumption of Innocence' (1987) 38 *Northern Ireland Law Review* 223.

3   The External Elements

3.1   The Elements of a Criminal Offence

We must now examine some of the basic building blocks that make up the hundreds of different criminal offences. A criminal lawyer often approaches the analysis of an offence by separating its component parts into the 'external elements' (for example, the acts of the accused), called the *actus reus*, and the 'mental elements' (for example, the defendant's intention), called the *mens rea*. These Latin phrases, taken from a sentence in Coke's *Institutes* (written in the eighteenth century), can be misleading, as we shall see, and have been criticized by academic writers and judges. Lord Diplock recently stated that he preferred to speak of 'the conduct of the accused and his state of mind at the time of that conduct', rather than use the Latin terminology (*Miller**). However, these phrases are still so widely used by the courts and in writing on the criminal law that they make a sensible starting point.

Coke in his *Institutes* said that '*actus non facit reum, nisi mens sit rea*' (an act does not make a person guilty of a crime unless the mind is also guilty). The principle embodied in this phrase can be traced back to the laws of Henry I in the twelfth century. As a general rule in English law, for a person to be liable for a criminal offence he must have brought about a certain prohibited state of affairs by his conduct and this must be accompanied by a certain state of mind. This general rule has to be qualified: some crimes do not require any particular state of mind. These are crimes of strict liability and we will consider them further in Chapter 6. In other crimes, a particular state of mind (or *mens rea*) is required in respect of some elements of the *actus reus*, but not for others. In other cases, the conduct of the accused may extend over a considerable period of time, and it may not be necessary to prove that the accused had the specified *mens rea* throughout that period (see Chapter 4.7).

These are all qualifications to the general rule that the external elements (the *actus reus*) of the offence must be accompanied by a particular state of mind. What about the need for the external elements themselves, are they essential? The position taken by English law is that an evil state of mind is not by itself criminal: it must have manifested itself in some conduct in order to attract liability. However wicked the defendant's thoughts, unless she acts to put them into effect she will not have committed a crime. Professor Glanville Williams has said that 'the law governs conduct, not purity of intention'. Even in crimes where no direct harm is caused, for example an attempted crime, some conduct is required. Lord Hailsham said in *Haughton* v. *Smith** that there is a 'distinction between the intention to commit a crime and an attempt to commit it. In addition to the intention, or *mens rea*, there must be an overt act'. There are a few exceptional cases where this principle appears to be absent (for example, *Larsonneur**), but it remains a general rule of English criminal law.

3.2   Different Aspects of the *Actus Reus*

The *actus reus* or external elements will very often involve activity on the part of the accused, such as an assault, an act of appropriation of property (in theft), or entry into a building (in burglary). However, the *actus reus* of an offence is not solely a question of conduct by the accused. It can include a state of affairs, consequences caused by the act of the defendant, or circumstances in which the defendant acts. This requires further explanation.

The term *actus reus* can include a state of affairs for which the accused is responsible, such as *having* an offensive weapon in a public place (s.1 of the Prevention of Crime Act 1953) or *being in possession* of a controlled drug (s.5 of the Misuse of Drugs Act 1971), *permitting* the smoking of cannabis on premises of which the accused is the occupier (s.8 of the same statute), or even being in the neighbourhood of a prohibited place in certain circumstances (s.1 of the Official Secrets Act 1911). In some cases the *actus reus* can also include a failure to act or an omission by the accused (see Chapter 3.3).

In some crimes something more than conduct or a state of affairs is required: the accused must have produced a particular prohibited result or consequence. In murder, the death of the victim must result from the defendant's acts; in the case of criminal damage, property must be destroyed or damaged; in s.18 of the Offences Against the Person Act 1861, the accused must either wound or cause grievous bodily harm to the victim. The result is just as much part of the *actus reus* as the conduct of the accused, and in its absence the *actus reus* will be incomplete (though the defendant may well be guilty of an attempt to commit the crime).

Yet another aspect of the *actus reus* is found in relevant circumstances attached to the prohibited conduct or result. Sexual intercourse is only rape if performed without the consent of the victim. The appropriation of property is only theft if the property belongs to another. Going through a ceremony of marriage is only bigamy if the accused is already married to another person. Every offence includes some necessary circumstance, if only the requirement that the accused is acting 'unlawfully' or 'without lawful excuse', phrases that refer to certain defences (such as self-defence and the prevention of crime: see Chapter 15.3.1).

Although for simplicity we have been referring to the *actus reus* or *mens rea* (or 'external elements' and the 'mental elements' within an offence), it is often difficult to separate them in this simple way. The *actus reus* itself may contain a mental element: that of the victim. In rape, for example, the victim's lack of consent is part of the *actus reus* as a required circumstance. We can take this further: in some cases it is impossible to distinguish the purely physical or external from the state of mind of the accused himself. For example, a person commits aggravated burglary if he commits a burglary having with him any weapon of offence (s.10 of the Theft Act 1968); the term 'weapon of offence' is then defined to include any article *intended* by the person having it with him to cause injury to another person. Here, the definition of a term within the *actus reus* ('a weapon') depends on the state of mind of the accused (what the defendant intended to do with the item). Indeed, as we have already seen, the *actus reus* may consist of being in possession of something, such as a controlled drug. In such cases, the very notion of being in possession has been held to involve a mental element: the accused must know of the existence of a thing in order for it to be in his possession, although he need not know of its qualities (*Warner v. Metropolitan Police Commissioner**). Thus the defendant's mental state can turn what would otherwise be an innocent act into the *actus reus* of a crime. These examples reveal that a sharp distinction between the *actus reus* and *mens rea* of each offence cannot always be made. Despite this, the distinction is still a popular way of analysing offences.

3.3   Liability for Omissions

As a general rule criminal liability does not attach to omissions. So if you see a blind man about to walk over the edge of a cliff but do not shout a warning you will not have committed a crime if he were to fall over the cliff, unless you had a legal duty to take care of him. This is so even if it would have been easy for you to shout out and even if you deliberately refrained from issuing a warning in the hope that he might fall over the edge. The circumstances in which you have a legal duty to intervene will now be considered.

3.3.1   When there is a Duty to Act

There are four particular circumstances in which the duty will arise, although it appears open to the courts to find novel situations in which to impose a duty to act.

1. Statutory duties
Some of these are express: the statute explicitly imposes liability for a failure to act. For example, under s.7(4) of the Road Traffic Act 1972, it is a criminal offence to fail to supply a specimen of breath when required to do so in certain specified circumstances by a constable in uniform. In other cases, the courts have interpreted particular words in the definition of an offence in such a way that they may be applied to a failure to act: for example, 'assisting in the retention' of stolen goods in s.22(1) of the Theft Act 1968 (*Pitchley**).

2. Contractual duties
A duty to act may arise as the result of a contractual obligation. One example is *Pittwood*, where a railway-crossing keeper's failure to close the crossing gate in breach of his contract of employment led to a conviction for manslaughter after a person was killed when a train hit a hay cart. So in the hypothetical situation posed at the start of this section if you were employed as the nurse of the blind man to look after him, you would be under a contractual duty to care for him and so could be convicted of an offence for failing to warn him of the danger.

3. Assumption of responsibility
A duty to act arises in cases where the defendant has assumed responsibility for the wellbeing of the victim. This may be inferred from a blood relationship (parent and child, for example), but may also be inferred where the accused has undertaken to care for another person. In *Instan,* the accused lived with her infirm and elderly aunt; it was found that her neglect of her aunt had accelerated the latter's death, and she was liable for manslaughter. In *Stone and Dobinson**, the victim came to live with her brother (Stone) and Dobinson (Stone's cohabitee). According to the Court of Appeal, the jury were entitled to conclude that both defendants had assumed a duty to care for the victim on the grounds that she was living in their house, and

that they had made inadequate efforts to care for her. The fact that the victim was 'helplessly infirm' was also relevant: the jury 'were entitled to conclude that once [the victim] became helplessly infirm, as she had by 19 July, the appellants were, in the circumstances, obliged either to summon help or else to care for [her] themselves'. The two were convicted of manslaughter and the Court of Appeal dismissed their appeals against the verdict. The decision in *Stone and Dobinson* has been heavily criticized and was described by the House of Lords in *Airedale National Health* v. *Bland* as 'troubling'. This was because defendants were themselves suffering from learning difficulties and indeed had enough difficulties looking after themselves, let alone anyone else.

4. Creation of danger

A fourth circumstance in which the Court has found a duty to act is where the defendant has created a dangerous situation and then failed to prevent a harm occurring as a result. The case of *Miller** illustrates this. The accused was sleeping as a vagrant in an unoccupied house. He fell asleep on a mattress while smoking a cigarette, and the cigarette set light to the mattress. He woke up to find the mattress alight, but did nothing to put out the fire, merely moving into another room of the house. As a consequence, the house itself caught fire and considerable damage was caused. Miller was charged with arson, contrary to ss.1(1) and (3) of the Criminal Damage Act 1971. The trial judge ruled that, even though he started the fire unintentionally, Miller became under a duty to take some action to put it out once he became aware of its existence. Lord Diplock, in the House of Lords, agreed that in these circumstances a duty to act could be implied. The duty arises out of the creation (albeit unintentional) of a dangerous situation: that is, a situation likely to cause damage. Lord Diplock stated that the *actus reus* of criminal damage might legitimately include 'conduct which consists of failing to take measures that lie within one's power to counteract a danger that one has oneself created'.

5. Other cases

Miller indicates that the courts may be willing to find novel situations in which there is a duty to act. Another example is *Speck*, where a girl put her hand on a man's trousers. He allowed her to leave her hand there and was convicted of indecent assault. In effect the law found that he was under a duty to remove her hand and his failure to do so could be classified as an assault.

3.3.2 The Consequences of Being under a Duty to Act

Once it is found that the defendant is under a duty to act then he must act in a reasonable way. This may involve rescuing the victim or summoning help (*Khan*). If the defendant owes a duty to act because of his contract of employment he must act in accordance with that contractual duty. That may involve performing acts that would not be expected of a reasonable person. For example if Bob decides to swim across the English Channel and hires Ken to be his lifeguard in a boat following his adventure and Bob gets into trouble, Ken would be required to rescue Bob, even if the dangerous seas meant that an ordinary passer-by would not be expected to do so.

3.3.3 Distinguishing Omissions and Acts

In other cases the law has not relied on the concept of duty but interprets a situation that appears to concern an omission to in fact involve an act. Indeed Lord Diplock, in *Miller*, took the view that much of the apparent difficulty of fitting liability for omissions into the traditional analysis of the *actus reus* would disappear if a less rigid phrase, such as 'course of conduct', were used instead:

'it is the use of the expression "*actus reus*" that is liable to mislead, since it suggests that some positive act on the part of the accused is needed to make him guilty of a crime and that a failure or omission to act is insufficient to give rise to criminal liability . . . the habit of lawyers to talk of "*actus reus*", suggestive as it is of action rather than inaction, is responsible for any erroneous notion that failure to act cannot give rise to criminal liability in English law.'

In *Fagan**, the accused, having accidentally driven a wheel of his car onto a policeman's foot, for some time refused to move the car when asked to do so. He was convicted of assaulting a police constable in the execution of his duty, and his conviction was upheld by the Divisional Court on the ground that there was a continuing act of assault being committed throughout the time the car was on the victim's foot. In fact Lord Justice May in the Court of Appeal in *Miller** thought that *Miller* itself could be explained on this ground. He held that the whole of the accused's conduct, from the moment he lay on the mattress with the lighted cigarette until the time he left it smouldering, should be regarded as *one* act, forming part of the *actus reus* of criminal damage. As he had the *mens rea* at one point during the *actus reus* (when he woke up) he could be convicted. The House of Lords, while not rejecting the reasoning of the Court of Appeal, preferred the duty approach. Lord Diplock did not say why, except to say that he thought it easier to explain to juries.

3.4   Should the Law Punish Omissions?

The law thus places great weight on the distinction between acts and omissions. Apart from the exceptions outlined above a defendant is not liable for an omission, but can be for an act. This distinction has been criticized by Lord Mustill in *Airdale NHST* v. *Bland* who said that the distinction between acts and omissions in this kind of case is a 'morally and intellectually dubious distinction'. An oft-quoted example is where a doctor has a patient on a life-support machine – is there a distinction of any moral importance between a doctor who switches off a life-support machine and a doctor who fails to switch on a life-support machine which automatically turns itself off every twenty-four hours? Surely in such cases doctors should not be able to escape the real legal moral difficulties involved in the care of the seriously ill, by claiming they were omitting to switch the machines back on.

The House of Lords have recently authorized doctors to withhold essential supplies of food and drink to a patient in a persistent vegetative state (*Airdale NHST* v. *Bland*). This was classified as an omission, the 'withholding of treatment', and so the doctors were not liable to be charged with murder. Lord Mustill argued that a doctor should only provide treatment where this was in the patient's best interests and it was not in the interests of a patient in a persistent vegetative state to carry on receiving the nourishment. It may not be against his interests either, but it was not positively in his interests. It is important to stress that the doctors were not liable as they had no legal duty to feed the patient and they acted in accordance with a body of medical opinion, but it may well be that a relative caring for a patient could not decide that in his or her view the patient did not require food or liquid. Another argument was that by withdrawing the food and drink, the doctors were in effect returning Tony Bland to the position he had been in when he first arrived at the hospital and so the overall effect of the doctors' actions was nothing.

This demonstrates the real difficulty in distinguishing acts and omissions. So, what is the reason for the traditional insistence that omissions should not be punished?

3.4.1   Policy Arguments over Liability for Omissions

From a policy perspective, the law's approach to omissions is a compromise between various important competing values. On the one hand there is the need to preserve freedom of autonomy (see Chapter 1.5.2). A law that punishes an omission is a greater infringement on liberty than a law that punishes an act. This is because punishing an omission means that in the given circumstances the only way a defendant can avoid criminal liability is by performing the required act, whereas punishing an act means that a defendant can avoid liability by performing any act except the prohibited one. On the other hand the law also seeks to protect people's life and well-being. Does not the value we place on a person's life easily justify a minor infringement on other's liberty for as long as it takes to perform a rescue or summon help? Professor Ashworth has argued 'a level of social co-operation and social responsibility is both good and necessary for the realisation of individual autonomy. . . . Each member of society is valued intrinsically, and the value of one citizen's life is generally greater than the value of another citizen's temporary freedom'.

The present law balances these competing principles. Where an individual has assumed responsibility for another then the restriction on his liberty by punishing omissions is less problematic than if the duty to act is imposed on a passer-by. This balance is essentially a policy choice; other countries have 'easy rescue' statutes that punish those who fail to rescue a victim when it would be easy for them to do so.

3.4.2   Technical Legal Arguments over Liability

The second group of arguments explaining the law's reluctance towards the punishment of omissions is more technical. There are three particular problems here.

1. Causation
There are difficulties in explaining how an omission can cause a particular result. Applying the 'but for' rule of causation (see Chapter 5) seems to imply that omissions cannot in law cause a result. 'But for' an omission it is by definition true that the result would still have happened in exactly the same way. One response is to redefine the question and suggest that 'but for' the failure of the defendant to act, the harm would not have occurred.

2. The number of defendants
A second difficulty is the number of potential defendants. If the blind man

walked over the cliff on a popular day at the seaside then anyone walking by could be liable and this may involve a large number of people being said to have caused his death. It may be that the simple answer is that it is justifiable to hold many people responsible, because if any one of them had acted the blind man would have lived.

3. Mens rea *problems*
The jury normally has to decide whether the accused had the *mens rea* when he committed the *actus reus*. The problem with omissions is that there is no precise moment in time when the *actus reus* takes place and at which to consider whether the defendant had the relevant *mens rea*.

None of these are insuperable problems but they indicate that the traditional approach of the law is not easily suited to liability for omissions. It is interesting that the Draft Criminal Code recommends retaining the balance struck by the present law with the following provision which details the circumstances in which a defendant may be liable for failing to act:

'a person causes a result which is an element of an offence when . . . (b) he omits to do an act which might prevent its occurrence and which he is under a duty to do according to the law relating to the offence' (Clause 17(1)(b) Draft Criminal Code).

3.5   The Voluntary Nature of the *Actus Reus*

We have already seen that occasionally the *actus reus* does not require proof of an act, for example a state of affairs may be sufficient. However, if the *actus reus* does require action or conduct it is seen as a fundamental principle that such action must be willed or voluntary. This does not mean that the prosecution must show that the defendant has deliberately chosen to act in a particular way. Indeed a defendant rarely decides 'I will now move my right finger'; rather she thinks in terms of the consequences of her acts, for example, 'I will now fire a gun'. So what the voluntariness requirement means is that the defendant must have been able to prevent herself from acting in the way she did. In other words that the defendant was capable of controlling her behaviour when she acted. It is for this reason that there is no criminal liability for 'accidental' behaviour, such as breaking property after tripping over or injuring someone after jumping when startled. Clearly in such cases there is no *mens rea*, but the law goes further and says in such cases there is no *actus reus* either. The defendant is not just saying, 'I did not mean to do that' (a claim of having no *mens rea)* but

'I did not do that'. That is because such accidental or instinctive acts are not properly described as the defendant's acts – they are not done *by* the defendant but happen *to* her. In some cases it is important for a defendant to show that she did not commit the *actus reus* rather than simply showing when she did not have *mens rea*. For example, if she is charged with an offence of strict liability she has a defence if she can show she has not committed the *actus reus*, but not if she could only show that she had no *mens rea* (see Chapter 6).

The essence of the voluntariness requirement is that the act must have been under the control of the accused: she must have been able to choose not to act as she did in the particular circumstances; and to put that choice into effect. It should be stressed here that we are talking about the defendant having no physical choice. A claim of involuntariness is not available where the defendant could have chosen to act otherwise but was put into an awful dilemma (for example facing a threat: 'kill that person or be killed'). An act would be involuntary if it were the result of physical compulsion from some outside source – being pushed by someone else, for example, or having one's arm seized and used as a 'weapon' of aggression by another person. It is for these reasons that the case of *Larsonneur** is often criticized, on the ground that Ms Larsonneur was not acting voluntarily, and should not have been held to have been 'acting' at all.

More difficult cases of involuntary behaviour occur when the compulsion comes not from outside the accused, but from some internal physical or mental disturbance. For example, concussion can cause involuntary behaviour, as can an imbalance in insulin and blood-sugar levels in diabetics. Such involuntary behaviour has been labelled 'automatism' and will be discussed next.

3.6 Automatism

3.6.1 The Definition of Automatism

Automatism was defined by Lord Denning in *Bratty* v. *AG for Northern Ireland** as 'an act which is done by the muscles without any control by the mind such as a spasm, a reflex action, or a convulsion; or an act done by a person who is not conscious of what he is doing such as an act done whilst suffering from concussion or whilst sleepwalking'. The defence can be said to involve three elements:

• Total destruction of voluntary control
• Caused by an external factor

• The defendant was not responsible for his condition.

These elements will now be considered separately:

1. Total destruction of voluntary control
It is necessary to demonstrate 'a total destruction of voluntary control'. It is not sufficient to show that the accused had only impaired control over his acts (*Attorney-General's Reference (No. 2 of 1992)**). Nor is it enough simply to show that the accused did not control his actions or did not know what he was doing if he *could* have controlled his actions. What must be shown is that the defendant lost the ability to control his actions.

2. The condition must be caused by an external factor
There is a great difficulty in drawing the boundary between automatism and insanity. The essential distinction between automatism and insanity depends on whether the state of mind is caused by an external or an internal factor. If it is caused by the external factor (for example, a brick falling onto the defendant's head) then the defendant is an automaton; if an internal factor (for example, an epileptic fit) then the defence will be insanity. The difficulty is due to the very outdated and inadequate concept of insanity still found in English criminal law (see Chapter 15.2.2).

So how can we distinguish between external and internal factors? It has been accepted that a diabetic who harms someone involuntarily as a result of hypoglycaemia caused by an excess of insulin injected as part of medical treatment for diabetes is not insane, but may be entitled to an acquittal on the grounds of automatism. In *Quick** this was said to be because the excess of insulin was an 'external factor', comparable to concussion, rather than an internal factor. If, however, the diabetic failed to take insulin and suffers excess blood-sugar (hyperglycaemia) this will be due to an internal factor and only insanity will be available (*Bingham*). This demonstrates that the distinction requires some very fine lines to be drawn. Indeed although Lord Denning in *Bratty* mentioned sleepwalking as a form of automatism it has since been held that this was wrong, and that sleepwalking is in fact a form of insanity (*Burgess**).

The distinction can produce some bizarre results. The distinction between external and internal factors was relied upon by the House of Lords in *Sullivan** (1984), a case involving epilepsy. Epilepsy was held to fall on the insanity side of the boundary because it was not a 'temporary impairment' resulting from 'some external physical factor', such as a blow on the head or the administration of a drug, but an internal malfunctioning. Of course no doctor would ever describe an epileptic as insane.

This distinction between external and internal factors can be very difficult to draw in some cases. In a Canadian case (*Rabey*) a man killed his former girlfriend after she had left him. He tried to claim he was an automaton, arguing that he killed her in an unconscious state caused by an external factor, namely the break-up of the relationship. However, the court argued that 'the ordinary stresses and disappointments of life which are the common lot of mankind do not constitute an external cause'. The case could be explained on the ground that many people suffer the ending of a close relationship without acting in the way Rabey did and so the cause of his involuntariness must be peculiar to him (an internal factor) rather than the break-up. *Rabey* has been said to reflect the law in England in *Hennessy* where it was stated 'stress anxiety and depression can no doubt be the result of the operation of external factors, but they are not . . . in themselves separately or together external factors of the kind capable in law of causing or contributing to a state of automatism. They constitute a state of mind, which is prone to reoccur'.

3. The defendant is not responsible for his state of mind
If the automatism is self-induced it will not excuse a person from criminal liability. This was the view of the Court of Appeal in *Quick* and again confirmed by the House of Lords in *Sullivan*. This is in line with the courts' attitude towards drink and drugs (see Chapter 15.3.2). So a diabetic who could be shown to have known the effect of taking too much insulin may be liable for any harmful consequences (see, for example, *Bailey**, where such knowledge was said to be capable of amounting to recklessness, and thus supplying the *mens rea* of an assault). It is not clear whether the test to be used here is subjective or objective. For example, if a diabetic takes too much insulin and so has a fit and causes harm, is the question whether the defendant foresaw the consequences of taking the insulin or whether he *should* have foreseen the consequences. In one case the test was said to be subjective (*Bailey*) and in another objective (*Quick*). Until we have a further case we will not know the answer. The general tendency in the criminal law in recent years has been to prefer subjective tests and so it may be *Bailey* that is followed. However, it is clear that an automaton state produced by illegal drugs or alcohol provides no defence, even if the accused was unaware of the effects that the drugs or alcohol would have (see Chapter 15.3.2).

3.6.2 The Consequences of a Finding of Automatism

What then are the possible consequences for an accused that argues in her defence that her conduct was involuntary as the result of automatism? If there is evidence that the automatism was self-induced, then it will provide no defence, and the accused may well be convicted if she possesses the necessary *mens rea*. If the automatism is proved to be the result of legal insanity, then it will lead to the 'special verdict' of 'not guilty by reason of insanity', and detention in a mental hospital or whatever order the judge thinks appropriate (Criminal Procedure (Insanity and Unfitness to Plead) Act 1991). If the automatism is the result of external factors then it will lead to a complete acquittal. With the uncertainty surrounding the boundary between insanity and automatism it is not surprising that automatism is not a common defence, and an accused may well prefer to change her plea to guilty and risk a prison sentence, rather than risk the stigma of insanity and a possible detention in a mental hospital. This is what happened in the case of *Sullivan,* after a ruling by the trial judge that Sullivan's defence based on epilepsy amounted to a plea of insanity.

3.6.3   Reform of Insanity

The Draft Criminal Code has proposed a definition of the state of automatism as when a defendant's act:

'(i) is a reflex, spasm or convulsion; or (ii) occurs while he is in a condition (whether of sleep, unconsciousness, impaired consciousness or otherwise) depriving him of effective control of the act; and (b) the act or condition is the result neither of anything done or omitted with the fault required for the offence nor of voluntary intoxication.'

It should be noticed that this definition seems to require a loss of effective control, not the total loss of control that is required by the present law. Further, the clause seems to attempt to reverse *Burgess*, as it lists sleepwalking as automatism.

Hot Topic: Drug Dealers and Omissions

This *Hot Topic* will discuss one particular case. The case involves some interesting questions over liability for omissions, but also involves some issues relating to causation (Chapter 5) and manslaughter (Chapter 10). It is an interesting example of how the courts deal with a novel case involving omissions. The case is *Khan and Khan* and was heard in the Court of Appeal. Swinton Thomas LJ summarized the facts:

'The deceased was a young girl, Lucy Burchell, aged 15, who was working in Birmingham as a prostitute. In the evening of 15 August, 1996, she went to a flat at 27, Clark Street, Saltley, Birmingham, where the Appellants sold and supplied a quantity of heroin to her. She was inexperienced as a heroin user and this was probably the first occasion on which she had taken it. She snorted the heroin through her nose and swallowed it. The amount that she took was 10 times the recommended therapeutic dosage, and twice the amount likely to be taken by an experienced heroin user. The deceased began to cough and splutter and went into a coma. She was obviously very ill, and in need of medical attention. The Appellants, who were drug dealers and at risk for being found out as such, left the flat either later in the evening or next morning, leaving this unfortunate girl alone and without the medical assistance that she so clearly required. On the next day, 16 August, the Appellants returned and found that Lucy Burchell was dead. They dumped her body on some waste ground. The mattress on which she had been lying and some of her clothing was burnt. They disposed of the bed . . . It was . . . conceded that it was clearly proved on the medical evidence that Lucy Burchell died as a result of taking an overdose of heroin, and that if medical assistance had been summoned at any time prior to her death the probability is that she would have been saved.'

The appellants were charged with manslaughter. Before looking at what the Court of Appeal decided, it is worth considering how we might have expected the arguments to proceed.

The prosecution could argue that the appellants were guilty of manslaughter in two ways. First, it could be argued that the act of giving the drugs to the victim had caused her to enter the coma and die. Second, it could be argued that by running away when she needed medical attention they had caused her death. Let us consider these arguments in further detail.

First, the argument that the supplying of the drugs caused the victim's death. There is no problem here in seeing that as an act. The difficulty is that the appellants did not inject the heroin into Lucy Burchell; she took the drug herself. The appellants would argue that applying the rules of causation her free voluntary and informed act of injecting herself (*Pagett*, see Chapter 5.2) broke the chain of causation, meaning that they did not cause her death. The prosecution could respond to this argument in three ways:

1 It could be argued that because the victim was only 15 she cannot be said to have acted freely. At first this appears a convincing argument, but there is a difficulty. The law states that a person can be convicted of a crime from the age of 10 (see Chapter 15.2.1) and therefore clearly does deem young people criminally responsible for their actions.

2 The prosecution could argue that the victim did not act in a free, voluntary and informed way because she was not an experienced heroin user; indeed this may have been the first time she used the substance. Could it therefore be said that this was not an 'informed' act? Certainly, it appears she had no idea that she was taking a lethal dose. The defence are likely to refer to the law's approach to intoxication which suggests that a defendant who thinks he is taking a low alcohol drink, but which is in fact highly alcoholic will be regarded as voluntarily intoxicated (see Chapter 15.3.2). However that rule built up in relation to defendants who were seeking acquittals based upon their intoxicated state; the rule may be less strictly applied when discussing whether a victim's act broke the chain of causation.

3 The prosecution could rely on the argument advance by the Court of Appeal in *Kennedy* (see Chapter 5.4.2) that the victim's act of taking the heroin was a joint act on behalf of the victim and the defendant because the defendant had encouraged the victim to take the drug. In Chapter 5.4.2 it is explained that this line of argument is highly controversial and few commentators believe it to be correct. In any event, the strong encouragement from the defendant to take the drug that was reported in *Kennedy* was not noted in the *Khan and Khan* case.

So there is an arguable case that the defendant's supplying of the drug was an act that caused the death of the victim, but it is certainly not a watertight one. Even if it succeeds it is unlikely that it could be shown at this point that the appellants intended death or grievous bodily harm and so the most serious offence available would be manslaughter.

What about the argument that sought to attach liability to the time when the defendant left the victim alone? The running-away of course was an omission. Can we attach liability for the omission? Was there a duty to act? The prosecution could rely on two arguments to establish the duty:

1 It could be argued that the case is analogous with *Miller*. It will be recalled that the defendant in *Miller* had accidentally set off a chain of events which caused the fire and he was therefore under a duty to stop the fire when he woke up and became aware of it. When he moved off, leaving the fire burning, he committed an offence. It can be argued that this case is similar. In setting off the chain of events by supplying the drugs, the defendants created the danger to the victim and so were under a duty to assist her once it became apparent that she was seriously ill. By running off they were in breach of that duty and so can be criminally responsible for her death.

   Unfortunately there is not an exact analogy with *Miller* and the defendant could respond in two ways. First in *Miller* there was a direct causal link between the actions of the defendant and the dangerous situation, while as discussed above it is not clear whether there was a causal link (in the legal sense) between the supplying of the heroin and her coma. That said, it is notable that in *Miller* the House of Lords talked about 'setting off a chain of events' leading to the fire rather than using the legal terminology of causation. This might suggest that in deciding whether there is a duty to act under the *Miller* rule it is not necessary to show the defendant caused the danger in the legal sense, but rather that he is morally responsible for it.

   The second possible distinction with *Miller* is that it was clearly true in that case that the reasonable person in the defendant's shoes would have raised the alarm or put out the fire. This he could have done without any danger to himself. As noted above when discussing liability for omissions, the defendant is only required to act in a reasonable way and is not expected to put his own wellbeing at serious risk. In *Khan and Khan*, as the Court of Appeal noted, if the appellants had summoned help this would have alerted the police to their drug-dealing activities. Indeed it was arguable that the Khans did exactly what an ordinary drug dealer would have done in their shoes. It is unlikely that a court would be sympathetic to such an argument. It is more likely that the court would find that a reasonable person would never commit an offence and so the appellants behaved unreasonably.

2 It could be argued that a drug dealer owes a duty of care to a client, by virtue of his or her contractual relationship (or quasi-contractual relationship, because a contract for illegal items is a void one). If someone fell ill while eating at a restaurant is it not reasonable that the restaurant owner would be under a duty to summon help? The court may, however, be reluctant to impose this in the context of two people who are committing a crime (the dealing and possession of illegal drugs).

So that may be how we would expect the arguments to go. Unfortunately the judgment in the Court of Appeal is rather disappointing. It does not discuss in detail the above arguments. On the omissions issue and whether there was a duty to act, Swinton Thomas LJ stated:

'the Judge must first make a ruling as to whether the facts as proved are capable of giving rise to such a duty and, if he answers that question in the affirmative, then to give the jury an appropriate direction which would enable them to answer the question whether on the facts as found by them there was such a duty in the case being tried by them.'

As the issue of the duty was not left to the jury, the appeals had to be allowed and there was no need to discuss other issues raised.

This brings us back to the Hot Topic in chapter 1: whether or not there is a duty to act is to be left to the jury. One of the concerns expressed in that discussion is relevant: it is unlikely that a jury will be particularly sympathetic to a drug dealer and whatever the legal principles involved it is hard to believe that if it were left to their discretion most juries would not convict the appellants.

Summary

3.1 As a general rule, a criminal offence consists of both the *actus reus* (external elements) and a *mens rea* (state of mind). Not every offence requires *mens rea* for every element of the *actus reus*, but the presence of an *actus reus* is essential in every offence. There is no criminal liability merely for possessing a particular state of mind.

3.2 The *actus reus* is not just action or conduct on the part of the accused. It may involve bringing about a state of affairs, or causing a certain prohibited consequence. It will also include certain relevant circumstances surrounding the conduct, state of affairs or result. One of these circumstances may be the state of mind of another person, such as the victim. It is not always easy to separate the external elements of an offence from the state of mind of the accused.

3.3 The *actus reus* may involve a failure to act by the accused. As a general rule the criminal law does not impose liability for omissions. However, it may do so if a statute so provides, either expressly or implicitly. Liability for omissions may also be imposed by the courts in cases where there is found to be a duty to act on the part of the accused. Such duties may be the result of a statutory provision, of a contract, of a special relationship of dependence between the victim and the accused, or where the accused has by his own unintentional act brought about a dangerous situation. Sometimes the combination of unintentional act plus intentional omission can also be regarded as one course of conduct forming part of the *actus reus* of the offence, without expressly relying on the existence of a duty.

3.4 The law's approach to omissions reflects a tension between protecting the defendant's individual liberty and recognizing the value that the law places on the victim's life and well being. There are some technical difficulties in analysing a crime involving an omission, although these are not insuperable.

3.5 The *actus reus* must be voluntary. This means that it must be willed: the accused must have been able to choose not to act in those circumstances. If the accused acts involuntarily there is no *actus reus* and therefore no offence.

3.6 Some cases of involuntary action are the result of automatism, meaning that the muscles act without conscious control by the mind. Where this is the result of an external factor, such as a falling brick, it will provide a complete defence to criminal liability unless it was self-induced. Where the automatism is the result of an internal factor that falls within the legal definition of insanity, then the result will be a special verdict of 'not guilty by reason of insanity'.

Case Notes

Attorney-General's Reference (No. 2 of 1992) [1994] QB 91. Court of Appeal
The respondent was acquitted of causing death by recklessness after claiming he was 'driving without awareness'. The Court of Appeal held that the defence of automatism is only available if the defendant suffers a 'total destruction of voluntary control', and 'impaired, reduced, or partial control' is insufficient. The evidence showed that the defendant was aware of bright flashing lights and able to steer in a straight line, and so the Court of Appeal stated that the defence of automatism should not have been left to the jury.

Bailey [1983] 1 WLR 760. Court of Appeal
The accused was convicted of causing grievous bodily harm, contrary to s.18 Offences Against the Person Act 1861. He was a diabetic, and had taken insulin with insufficient food, giving rise to hypoglycaemia. He appealed against conviction on the ground of automatism. The appeal was dismissed, as there was insufficient evidence of automatism, but it was held that if the accused had known of the risk of hypoglycaemia, and resultant uncontrollable behaviour, then such self-induced automatism would have afforded no defence.

Bratty v. AG for Northern Ireland [1963] AC 386. House of Lords
The accused was convicted of murder. There was evidence that he was suffering from psychomotor epilepsy and he pleaded insanity and automatism at the trial, but the trial judge refused to let automatism go to the jury. The jury rejected the insanity defence. Appeals to the Court of Appeal and then to the House of Lords were both dismissed. Lord Denning defined automatism as an involuntary act, and held that if it was the result of a disease of the mind, then it gave rise to the defence of insanity and not automatism.

Burgess [1991] 2 QB 92. Court of Appeal
Burgess was found not guilty by reason of insanity of wounding with intent, after he attacked a neighbour while sleepwalking. The court upheld the verdict and stated that sleepwalking was caused by an internal factor, namely his sleep disorder which was a malfunctioning in the mind.

Fagan [1969] 1 QB 439. Divisional Court
Fagan was convicted of assaulting a police officer in the execution of his duty, contrary to s.51 (1) of the Police Act 1964. When asked to park his car by the side of the road, he inadvertently drove his car onto the constable's foot, and then when asked to remove it switched off the ignition and waited some time before reversing off the constable's foot. He appealed on the ground that at the time when he had the necessary *mens rea* for assault he did no act which could be said to amount to the *actus reus* of assault, as merely refraining from driving his car off the constable's foot was an omission and not an act. The court dismissed the appeal, holding that 'assault' in this offence included a battery, and that a battery could be inflicted through a weapon or instrument controlled by the accused. In this case, the battery was inflicted by means of the car that was deliberately left on the policeman's foot. Although assault could not be committed by omission, in this case the *actus reus* was an act which continued during the whole time when the car was on the constable's foot. The act was not complete at the time when the *mens rea was* formed and it was not necessary for *mens rea to* be present throughout the continuing act.

Haughton v. Smith [1975] AC 476. House of Lords
See Chapter 18 case notes.

Larsonneur (1933) 97 JP 206. Court of Criminal Appeal
Larsonneur, a French national, had been ordered to leave the United Kingdom, and she went to Ireland. She was then deported from Ireland, and, in the custody of the Irish police, brought back to the United Kingdom and handed over to the police at Holyhead. She was charged and convicted of being found in the United Kingdom, having been refused permission to land, contrary to the Aliens Order 1920. The court dismissed her appeal, and held that the circumstances in which she had returned to the United Kingdom (in police custody and against her will) were irrelevant.

Miller [1983] 2 AC 161. House of Lords
Miller was convicted of arson, contrary to ss.1 (1) and (3) of the Criminal Damage Act 1971. He was sleeping as a vagrant in an unoccupied house and fell asleep on a mattress with a lighted cigarette. When he awoke to find the mattress alight he did not attempt to put out the fire, but moved into another room. The house caught fire and substantial damage was caused. Miller appealed against conviction, and the Court of Appeal, dismissing his appeal, certified as a question of law for the House of Lords whether, having accidentally started a fire, the accused would be liable for arson if he thereafter (with the necessary *mens rea*) failed to take any steps to extinguish the fire or prevent damage being caused to property by the fire. The House of Lords dismissed the appeal and held that the *actus reus* of arson could include, as well as a positive act of setting fire to property, a failure to take measures that lie within one's power to counteract a danger that one has oneself created. The House adopted the view of the trial judge that once Miller became aware of the existence of the fire, he was under a duty to take some action to put it out, although not disapproving of the alternative view of the Court of Appeal that the whole course of conduct of the accused, both actions and omissions, should be seen as part of one uninterrupted *actus reus,* during the latter part of which he had the necessary *mens rea.*

Pitchley (1972) 57 Cr App Rep 30. Court of Appeal
The accused was convicted of assisting in the retention of stolen goods for the benefit of another, contrary to s.22 of the Theft Act 1968. He had been handed some money by his son to keep for him and had paid it into his post-office savings account. He subsequently discovered that the money was stolen and left it in the savings bank. His appeal against conviction was dismissed, and the court held that 'retain' meant 'not lose, continue to have'. Permitting the money to remain in the bank after finding out that it was stolen was sufficient to amount to assisting in the retention of the money.

Quick [1973] 1 QB 910. Court of Appeal
The accused was convicted of assault occasioning actual bodily harm. He was a nurse in a mental hospital and had assaulted a patient. He was diabetic and had been suffering a hypoglycaemic episode at the time; he pleaded automatism. On a ruling by the trial judge that this amounted to a plea of insanity, Quick changed his plea to guilty and then appealed against his conviction. The Court of Appeal allowed his appeal on the ground that automatism should have been left to the jury: hypoglycaemia arising from an excess of insulin was not insanity, it was the result of an external factor, comparable to the effect of other drugs or violence. Nevertheless, if the automatism were self-induced, or one which could reasonably have been foreseen, as where there was a failure to take medical advice, then it could not excuse from liability.

***Stone and Dobinson* [1977] 1 QB 354. Court of Appeal**
See Chapter 10 case notes.

***Sullivan* [1984] 1 AC 156. House of Lords**
Sullivan was charged with causing grievous bodily harm, contrary to s.18 of the Offences Against the Person Act 1861. He had attacked the victim during an epileptic fit, and pleaded automatism. However, the trial judge ruled that this amounted to a plea of insanity and refused to let automatism go to the jury, whereupon the accused changed his plea to guilty of the less serious assault occasioning actual bodily harm and then appealed against conviction on the ground that the ruling of the trial judge was wrong. The court dismissed his appeal and held that epilepsy amounted to insanity in law; it did not matter that its effects were merely transitory. Epilepsy affected the mind, in the sense of the mental faculties of reason, memory and understanding, and was not the result of some external cause such as drugs, alcohol or violence.

***Warner* v. *Metropolitan Police Commissioner* [1969] 2 AC 256. House of Lords**
See Chapter 6 case notes.

Further Reading

The *actus reus*/*mens rea* distinction is discussed in Robinson and A. Smith. The debates over when omissions should be punished are revealed in Ashworth, Meade, Simester, J. Smith and Williams. The 'voluntary act requirement' is discussed in Budd and Lynch, Glazebrook, Horder, Husak, Lanham and Simester. A detailed and complex discussion on what an act is can be found in Moore.

Ashworth, 'The Scope of Criminal Liability for Omissions' (1989) 105 *Law Quarterly Review* 424.

Budd and Lynch, 'Voluntariness, Causation and Strict Liability' [1978] *Criminal Law Review* 74.

Glazebrook, 'Situational Liability' in Glazebrook (ed.), *Reshaping the Criminal Law* (1978, Stevens).

Horder, 'Pleading Involuntary Lack of Capacity' (1993) *Cambridge Law Journal* 298.

Husak, 'Does Criminal Liability Require an Act?' in Duff (ed.), *Philosophy and the Criminal Law* (1999, Cambridge University Press).

Lanham, '*Larsonneur* Revisited' [1976] *Criminal Law Review* 276.

Meade, 'Contracting into Crime' (1991) *Oxford Journal of Legal Studies* 147.

Moore, *Act and Crime* (1993, Oxford University Press).

Robinson, 'Should the Criminal Law Abandon the Actus Reus/Mens Rea Distinction?', in Shute, Gardner and Horder (eds), *Action and Value in Criminal Law* (1993, Oxford University Press).

Simester, 'Why Omissions are Special' (1995) 1 *Legal Studies* 311.

Simester, 'On the So-called Requirement for Voluntary Action' (1998) 1 *Buffalo Criminal Law Review* 403.

A. Smith, 'On *Actus Reus* and *Mens Rea*', in Glazebrook (ed.), *Reshaping the Criminal Law* (1978, Stevens).

J. Smith, 'Liability for Omissions in the Criminal Law' [1984] *Legal Studies* 88.

Williams, 'Criminal Omissions: The Conventional View' (1991) 107 *Law Quarterly Review* 432.

4   The Mental Element

> ### Key words
> * **Intention** – the aim or purpose of the defendant.
> * **Recklessness** – the taking of a risk by the defendant.
> * **Negligence** – the defendant's failure to act according to the standard of the reasonable person.

4.1   Mental Element in a Criminal Offence

The majority of serious criminal offences require, in addition to the *actus reus*, a specific state of mind on the part of the accused, usually referred to as the *mens rea*. Many less serious crimes require no *mens rea*, but simply proof that the defendant caused the prohibited harm. These are known as strict liability crimes and will be discussed separately in Chapter 6. They tend to be crimes that carry lower sentences and focus on discouraging a particular harm rather than imposing moral blame. Most serious crimes require proof of some blameworthy state of mind, for example that the defendant intended or foresaw a particular result. The requirement of *mens rea* can be justified on several grounds. If the criminal law is to act as a deterrent it is only sensible to punish people who deliberately break the law. Likewise if a criminal conviction is to carry an element of censure (see Chapter 1.3) then the law should require a guilty state of mind. Of course, just because the defendant has the *mens rea* it does not follow that he is necessarily guilty because he may have a defence. For example a defendant may kill another intentionally but still be not guilty of murder if the killing was carried out in self-defence. So the *mens rea* requirement is part of, but not the whole of, the law's assessment of whether the defendant deserves criminal blame.

The definition of an offence, in a statute or in the common law, may contain a fairly precise description of the *mens rea* required (such as 'knowing or believing that the goods are stolen' in the case of handling stolen goods, in s.22 of the Theft Act 1968). In some cases, however, the definition either uses a general word such as 'maliciously' or does not contain any indication of the mental element required at all. This means that the courts must decide what if any mental element is required.

This area of the criminal law is one in which there is much disagreement between academic lawyers and many of the judges. The judges themselves are not unanimous or entirely consistent in their approach, which makes the task of reformulation and codification of the criminal law both more necessary and more difficult. For example, one recurring debate concerns the extent to which the criminal law should define the precise meaning of '*mens rea* words' such as 'intention' or 'belief.' Many judges feel that these words are best left undefined by the courts so that the jury (or magistrates) can give them their ordinary, 'common sense' meaning. (See the discussion in Chapter 2, *Hot Topic*.) The other main dispute in this area, mentioned in Chapter 1.4, is whether the law should require proof of a subjective state of mind, or whether an objective test should be used.

As the *actus reus* of an offence may contain a number of different elements, there may be a different *mens rea* required for each of these elements; so that the *mens rea* of an offence may consist of several components. The offence of handling stolen goods requires that the act of handling be dishonest, as well as the knowledge or belief that the goods were stolen. The offence of burglary, under s.9(1)(a) of the Theft Act 1968, requires entry of a building as a trespasser (the *actus reus*) with an intent to commit one of a range of offences such as an intent to steal, and in addition that the accused knows that he is entering a building as a trespasser, or realizes that he might be. The example of burglary is interesting, because although the intention (for example, to steal) is specifically mentioned in the statute, the *mens rea* attached to being a trespasser is not: it has been implied into the definition of the offence by the courts. Where the mental element is left unstated in the definition, a form of *mens rea* will often be implied by the courts. In *Tolson*, Stephen J said:

> 'the mental elements of different crimes differ widely . . . The full definition of every crime contains expressly or by implication a proposition as to a state of mind . . . Crimes are in the present day much more accurately defined by statute or otherwise than they formerly were . . . but it is the general – I might I think say the invariable – practice of the legislature to leave unexpressed some of the mental elements of crime.'

The general principle, then, is that an offence may contain several different *mens rea* elements, and that one or more of these may be left unexpressed in the definition and implied by the courts.

It should be noted that although the phrase *mens rea* literally means 'guilty mind' a defendant may have a *mens rea* even though he is blameless. For example in *Yip Chiu-Cheung**, the Privy Council stated that the defendant, who was an under-cover anti-drug officer, joined with a drug smuggler in arranging the importation of drugs in an effort to uncover a drug-smuggling gang. The court decided that he could be said to intend to conspire to arrange the importation of drugs. The fact that he was acting from the best of motives did not affect the question of whether the *mens rea* existed.

4.2   Different Types of Mens Rea

Although, as we have stressed, each offence has its own *mens rea*, there are a number of *mens rea* words which occur frequently in the definitions of offences and which need to be examined. It might appear logical and desirable for the criminal law to possess a 'library' of concepts, with clear definitions, which can then be used for a variety of offences: it would make the drafting, interpretation and application of the criminal law easier and more consistent. This aim was in part behind the Law Commission Report of 1978 on the Mental Element in Crime, and the accompanying draft bill; and it also influenced the draft Criminal Code published by the Law Commission in 1985 and the subsequent reports. In practice, there are problems with seeking to develop a set of strict definitions of the *mens rea* terms. Not only is there the debate referred to above (see Chapter 4.1) as to whether *mens rea* words can be defined too rigidly; there is also the difficulty of drafting a definition of a word such as 'intention' which is suitable for such widely different offences as, for example, theft, murder, attempts and criminal damage. In the English legal system this latter problem is exacerbated by the fact that the courts always approach the meaning of a word from the point of view of a particular case and therefore a specific offence. As a result it has not been unknown for the same word, such as 'intention', to bear a different meaning in two different offences. Such a position cannot be seen as logical or desirable and it certainly does not make the interpretation or application of the criminal law any easier. It is perhaps in reaction to this problem that judges have recently taken to avoiding the definition of *mens rea* words, preferring to trust the common sense of juries acting with the minimum of guidance.

We will examine three key *mens rea* concepts: intention, recklessness and negligence. They can be seen as on a scale, with intention being the most serious form of *mens rea*, recklessness the next most serious, and negligence the least serious.

4.3   Intention

4.3.1   The Different Roles Played by Intention

It has already been noted that *mens rea* terms can play a variety of functions in the criminal law. This is particularly true of intention. For example Jeremy Horder (Horder, 1995) has suggested four different roles for the term 'intention'.

1.   'Constituting a harm'.
Intention can be used as 'constituting a harm', meaning that an act which would otherwise be blameless is made criminal by the intention with which it is carried out. For example, causing a computer to function with an intent to secure access to unauthorized data is an offence that we will be looking at in Chapter 14. Clearly, causing a computer to perform a function is not itself harmful, it is the intention that makes the act deserving of criminal sanction.

2.   Protecting autonomy
The intention requirement can also be used to protect autonomy. It serves the useful function of restricting the potential width of an offence. This is particularly relevant when considering the causing of psychological injuries. Although the law may wish to punish a stalker who intends to cause his victim psychological injuries, the law not wish to punish an examiner who fails a candidate and who is aware that the candidate will suffer psychological harm as a result. The requirement of intention helps to distinguish these cases and convict the stalker, but not the examiner.

3.   Nature of the harm
Intention can be an important aspect of the harm. An intended push will be regarded by the victim as more serious than an accidental one. An intentional injury causes not just the victim physical injury, but demonstrates a lack of respect to her as an individual.

4.   Element of culpability
Finally, intention can be used as an element in determining how blameworthy the defendant is. Thus an intentional killing is seen as murder, whereas a reckless killing is a lesser offence, that is manslaughter.

4.3.2   The Meaning of Intention

In light of the different roles that intention can play, it is not surprising that the word 'intention' has proved difficult for the courts to define and has been given different meanings in different contexts. In fact it is rare for the courts to have to consider the precise meaning of 'intention'. This is partly because there are not many offences for which intention alone will suffice for the *mens rea*; it is much more common for the *mens rea* to include recklessness as well. For such offences there is no need to distinguish recklessness and intention. This means that the crucial theoretical question of the boundary between intention and recklessness is not often of practical importance. However, intention should be examined for two reasons. The first is conceptual: intention has been described as the 'paradigm of self-determined action'; that is, to intend a consequence is to associate oneself to that consequence to a greater extent than to be reckless or negligent towards it. So in a sense it is the most serious form of *mens rea*. The second is more practical. Most cases on intention have arisen in the context of homicide, where the difference between intention and recklessness marks the difference between murder and manslaughter.

What, then, does it mean to say that a person intends a particular result? A consistent theme in all the cases on intention is that the term should be given its normal meaning. Therefore the core meaning of intention is that a person intends a result when he wants or desires it to happen. In *Mohan*, a case dealing with the meaning of intention in the context of the offence of attempt, Lord Justice James explained that intention meant 'aim' or 'a decision to bring about a certain consequence'. He considered it is irrelevant whether the result was likely or unlikely to occur. You can intend to kill a victim by shooting at him hoping to kill him, even though he is a long way away and you are unlikely to succeed.

It has also been made clear that 'intention is something quite distinct from motive or desire' (Lord Bridge in *Moloney*). This means that the law is not concerned with why the defendant acted. So, in a case of a 'mercy killing', for example, there is an intent to kill, even though there may be a good motive (to put an end to the victim's pain and suffering). In *Hyam* v. *DPP**, the accused's motive may have been jealousy, or more immediately to frighten the intended victim into leaving the district, but the court was only interested in whether or not she had an intent to kill or cause grievous bodily harm to any person. In circumstances such as these, motive will only be relevant as a means of proving the existence of intention, making it more (or less) likely that the accused possessed the necessary intention.

The core definition of intention, then, is that it was the defendant's purpose in committing an action. This is thought to coincide with the normal understanding of the word and so Lord Bridge in *Moloney** suggested a 'golden rule' – that judges do not need to give juries detailed guidance on the meaning of intention. Juries simply use the normal meaning of the word.

However in difficult cases (which are 'rare and exceptional' (*Gregory and Mott*)) it may be necessary to give further direction. These cases arise when the defendant does an act in order to bring about one particular consequence but it is highly likely another result will occur. An oft quoted example (taken from a Law Commission report) is of a person who puts a bomb on an aircraft, with the purpose of collecting insurance money from the goods on board which will be blown up. Although his purpose is only to blow up the goods (indeed he will be delighted if the pilot is able to escape unhurt) he is aware that the pilot's death is effectively inevitable. Is this foresight sufficient to amount to intention to kill the pilot?

The courts have struggled with this question. To fully understand the law it is necessary to look at three cases where the House of Lords have discussed this issue:

1. Moloney

In *Moloney*, Lord Bridge firmly distinguished intention from the foresight that a consequence was likely or probable. In his view, unanimously accepted by the other judges in the case, foresight that a consequence was highly likely was merely evidence of intention, and was not intention itself. Proof of foresight was a step on the way towards proof of intention, but the two should not be confused. So in the example of the Law Commission's bomber, the fact the bomber foresaw that the pilot would die was evidence that the bomber intended to kill the pilot, but did not itself amount to intention.

Lord Bridge felt that in most cases the jury would not need to be given a definition of intention, and references to foresight would be confusing and unnecessary. However, in cases where the facts require some discussion of foresight by the trial judge, Lord Bridge laid down the following 'guidelines':

'I do not believe it is necessary for the judge to do more than invite the jury to consider two questions. First, was death or really serious injury in a murder case (or whatever relevant consequence must be proved to have been intended in any other case) a natural consequence of the defendant's voluntary act? Secondly, did the defendant foresee that consequence as being a natural consequence of his act? The jury should then be told that if they answer yes to both questions it is a proper inference for them to draw that he intended that consequence.'

Lord Bridge was not more specific than this in defining intention. What is a 'natural consequence'? Its meaning is not spelt out by Lord Bridge, but his judgement as a whole makes clear that it means a consequence which is virtually certain to occur unless something unexpected intervenes. However, the doubt as to the meaning of the phrase 'natural consequences' led (soon after *Moloney*) to another appeal to the House of Lords.

2. *Hancock and Shankland*

In *Hancock and Shankland**, the House of Lords approved Lord Bridge's approach to intention. Lord Scarman, giving the judgement of the House, confirmed that 'foresight does not necessarily imply the existence of intention, though it may be a fact from which when considered with all the other evidence a jury may think it right to infer the necessary intent'. However, Lord Scarman felt that the *Moloney* guidelines quoted above were defective, because the phrase 'natural consequence' might well be misunderstood. It might be thought that 'natural' meant that nothing unnatural occurred and the phrase did not convey the sense of near certainty that Lord Bridge intended. Lord Scarman suggested that it should be made clear to a jury that the greater the probability of a consequence, the more likely it is that the consequence was foreseen and the greater the probability that the consequence was intended. However, he also felt that specific guidelines were unlikely to be much help to a trial judge, who should encourage the jury to exercise its common sense in reaching its decision on the facts of a particular case.

3. *Woollin*

Despite the fact that in *Hancock and Shankland* the House of Lords had clearly indicated that they thought it inappropriate to set down general guidelines, the issue of intention still troubled trial judges. The Court of Appeal in *Nedrick* thought it appropriate to provide a model direction for judges to give the jury in 'difficult cases'. In due course the House of Lords in *Woollin* was asked to consider whether the direction was appropriate. This time the House of Lords were happy to approve the guidelines, with a slight modification. They suggested:

'Where the charge is murder and in the rare cases where the simple direction is not enough, the jury should be directed that they are not entitled to [find] the necessary intention, unless they feel sure that death or serious injury was a virtual certainty (barring some unforeseen intervention) as a result of the defendant's actions and that the defendant appreciated that such was the case.'

Woollin represents the current law. The law will now be summarized taking the example of murder where it must be shown that the defendant intended to kill or cause serious injury:

> In most cases the judge needs simply to tell the jury to give intention its ordinary meaning; that is, the defendant intended to kill or cause serious injury if that was his aim or purpose. If the case is one where the defendant had some other aim, but death or serious injury was very likely to occur as a result of the defendant's actions then the judge should invite the jury to consider two questions:
>
> 1. Was death or serious injury virtually certain to result from the defendant's acts?
> 2. Did the defendant appreciate that death or serious injury was virtually certain to result from his or her acts?
>
> Only if the answers to both these questions are 'yes' is the jury entitled to find intention.

A number of points should be stressed about the present law:

1 If it is not the defendant's purpose to kill or cause serious injury *and* death or serious injury was not virtually certain or appreciated to be so by the defendant, the jury is *not* permitted to find intention, even if it feels the evidence indicates this is so. Consider this example. A terrorist plants a bomb in a city centre and telephones a warning in plenty of time to evacuate the town, but the bomb goes off when it is touched by a passer-by, killing her. The jury may decide that the terrorist's purpose was to gain publicity and cause disruption, but not to kill or cause serious injury. If so, it cannot convict of murder because it cannot be said that it was virtually certain that the bomb would kill or injure anyone.

2 It must be shown that both death or serious injury was virtually certain *and* that the defendant realized that this was so. This means that if the defendant believed death or serious injury to be certain, but in fact they were not, the jury is not entitled to find intention. This seems surprising given that intent is seen as a subjective concept, looking at the defendant's state of mind. Smith and Hogan give the example of a defendant firing a gun at a person who, unknown to the defendant, has a bulletproof vest on, but whom the defendant still kills. Although it would not be virtually certain that the victim would die, is it sensible that the existence of the vest affects the defendant's intention?

3 The courts have stressed that foresight of virtual certainty is not intent, but it is evidence from which the jury may find intent. Intent is a subjective concept. The fact that a reasonable person in the defendant's shoes

might have foreseen or intended the consequence is only evidence of the defendant's state of mind. This is stressed by s.8 of the Criminal Justice Act 1967 which states:

'A court or jury, in deciding whether a person has committed an offence,
(a) should not be bound in law to infer that he intended or foresaw a result of his actions by reason only of it being a natural and probable consequence of those actions; but
(b) shall decide whether he did intend or foresee that result by reference to all the evidence, drawing such inferences from the evidence as appears proper in the circumstances.'

4 The direction approved in *Woollin* states that the jury is *entitled* to find intention. The word 'entitled' suggests that the jury may find intention, but it does not have to. In other words if death or serious injury was not the defendant's aim or purpose, the jury is permitted to decide that even though death or serious injury was virtually certain and the defendant realized this, the defendant did not intend death or serious injury. An example of where it may be appropriate not to find intention is given by Wilson (1999). A father is holding his baby at the top of a burning building. As the flames get very close he throws the baby to the ground, aware that this is virtually certain to kill or seriously injure the baby, but believing that it is the only way of saving the baby from burning. Even though he realized it was virtually certain that the baby would die, to say that the father intended to kill or seriously injure the baby seems wrong. In fact he was acting with the intention of saving the baby from death. By saying that the jury is entitled to find intention, this leaves the jury with 'moral elbow room' (to use Horder's phrase) to decide in cases such as the father's that there is no intention. It may be that, although not wanting to say so openly, the courts are saying that for these cases that are at the borderline of intention, motive can be taken into account by the jury.

Although the above explanation of the law is the natural meaning of the word 'entitled' used in *Woollin*, the issue is not beyond doubt. Some commentators argue that the jury *must* find intention if the result is virtually certain and the defendant realises this. Those who make this argument point to two arguments:

(i) The speech of Lord Steyn in *Woollin*. At one point Lord Steyn in his speech stated that: 'The effect of the critical direction [in *Nedrick*] is that a result foreseen as virtually certain is an intended result.' This has been picked upon by Smith (2000) to argue that this indicates that if the jury decides that the result was foreseen as virtually certain this state of mind amounts to intent. Those who reject Smith's analysis point out that Lord Steyn concluded his speech with the proposed direction from above which used the word 'entitled'. Lord Steyn also quoted with approval the House's previous decisions in *Moloney* and *Hancock*, both of which had stressed that foresight is evidence from which a jury may, not must, infer intent. Therefore looking at his speech as a whole although it is not entirely consistent there is much more in it to support the view that juries have an option to find intent from foresight of virtual certainty than there is for Professor Smith's view.

(ii) In *Re A(Children)*, the Court of Appeal recently addressed the issue. The case will be examined in detail at Chapter 16. The majority of the Court of Appeal assumed that if the virtually certain test was satisfied, that amounted to intention and there was no discretion to escape from this conclusion. It should be pointed out that the case (involving the separation of conjoined twins) raises a huge number of complex issues, the discussion of intention was necessarily fairly brief and there was a limited discussion of the relevant authorities on the meaning of intention. The case may, therefore, be regarded as a weak authority on the meaning of intention.

5   Lord Steyn in *Woollin* modified the direction in *Nedrick* to replace the word 'infer' with 'find'. Unfortunately he did not explain why he thought this was a better word to use and commentators have discussed the question at some length. Here are some of the possible explanations:

(i) There is no significance in the change. Lord Steyn simply thought that 'finding' would be an easier word for juries to understand than 'inferring'.

(ii) Lord Steyn was indicating that sometimes foresight of virtual certainty is not just intention from which evidence can be found, but rather foresight of virtual certainty can actually be intention (the jury can find that the foresight is intent).

(iii) It may be that 'finding' intention was seen as setting a lower hurdle than 'inferring' intent and therefore the change was designed to encourage juries to find intent.

4.3.3   Reform of the Definition of Intention

The Law Commission has proposed new definition of intention:

'a person acts –

(a) 'intentionally' with respect to a result when
  (i) it is his purpose to cause it, or
  (ii) although it is not his purpose to cause it, he knows that it would occur in the ordinary course of events if he were to succeed in his purpose of causing some other result.'

The thinking behind this clause is that intention should only be a little wider in meaning than purpose. If it is not the accused's purpose to produce the consequence then the only *mens rea* that will constitute intention is where the accused is aiming to do *A* which necessarily involves *B* occurring. For example if an accused fires a gun at a victim who is standing behind a window, she will necessarily break the window if she is to achieve her purpose of shooting the victim. So she could be said to intend to break the window under the Law Commission's proposed definition of intention.

4.4   The Meaning of Recklessness

The cases we have just been considering in relation to intention have focused on the distinction between intent and foresight of consequences. This is, in fact, the distinction between intention and recklessness. The cases on recklessness that we will now examine tend to focus on the distinction between recklessness and negligence.

Rather unsatisfactorily, the law has no settled meaning of recklessness. Indeed the House of Lords has formulated two different kinds of recklessness. These are usually known by the names of the House of Lords cases that defined them – *Cunningham* recklessness and *Caldwell* recklessness. The law has however developed in such a way that *Cunningham* recklessness is used for nearly all crimes where recklessness is an issue. Criminal damage is the most important crime for which *Caldwell* recklessness is used. The most significant difference between the two is the extent to which recklessness includes inadvertence to a risk, that is failure to consider a risk. As we have already seen this is one of the major grounds of dispute between objectivists and subjectivists (see Chapter 1.6). The position has very recently been made even more complex by the creation of what can be seen as a third form of recklessness, 'presumed *mens rea* recklessness', which applies to statutory offences where there is no indication as to the correct *mens rea* (see Chapter 6)

4.4.1   *Cunningham* Recklessness

There are two key elements in *Cunningham* recklessness:

1 *Cunningham* recklessness requires that the defendant 'has foreseen that the particular kind of harm might be done and yet has gone on to take the risk of it' (*Cunningham**). It does not need to be shown that the risk was a large one, just that the defendant was aware that there was a risk.
2 The risk must be one that it was unreasonable for the accused to take. In considering whether the risk is one that was unreasonable to take, the law will take into account the risk of the harm and the nature of the act. So, if a defendant was driving his car when a child ran into the road and in order to avoid the child he swerves, realizing that he is likely to crash into and damage a parked car, the jury may well decide that the taking of this risk of damage to property was reasonable and so was not *Cunningham* reckless.

In order to prove *Cunningham* recklessness it is necessary to show that the defendant was subjectively aware of the risk, albeit a small one, that her act would cause harm. If the defendant is found not to have foreseen the risk of harm that her conduct created then she is not *Cunningham* reckless, even if it was a blindingly obvious risk. For the purposes of *Cunningham* recklessness it does not matter whether a reasonable person would have foreseen the harm but only what the defendant herself actually foresaw. Of course, the jury is still permitted to infer that because a reasonable person would have foreseen the risk the defendant must have foreseen it, and so in effect the burden may be on the defendant to explain to a jury why she failed to foresee an obvious risk.

In *Parker*, a man in a rage slammed down a public telephone and broke its receiver. He was charged with criminal damage, which at the time used *Cunningham* recklessness as its *mens rea* requirement. He claimed he was so angry that he did not foresee he might damage the telephone. No doubt this was true because at the time he slammed down the telephone he was not consciously thinking of the risk of damage to it but rather thinking angry thoughts. The Court of Appeal held that if a defendant was aware of a risk but put it to the back of his mind he would still be found to be *Cunningham* reckless, and decided that this must have been true of Mr Parker. This decision seems to have stretched *Cunningham* recklessness to its limit in accepting that having a risk 'in the back of one's mind' is being aware of the risk. It is notable that *Parker* concerned criminal damage which is now governed by *Caldwell* recklessness and so it may be argued it is not a strong authority on *Cunningham* recklessness.

There is one very important addition to the definition of *Cunningham* recklessness. If a defendant is voluntarily intoxicated, for example through taking alcoholic drink or drugs, she is not allowed to rely on her intoxication as evidence that she did not foresee a risk. In effect she will be deemed to be *Cunningham* reckless if the risk was one which she would have seen had she been sober, even if, in fact, in her intoxicated state she was not aware of the risk (see Chapter 15 for further discussion of intoxication).

The *Parker* case mentioned above demonstrates a potential weakness in *Cunningham* recklessness, namely it is too narrow. Sometimes a defendant fails to be aware of an obvious risk, but is blameworthy. A defendant who fails to see a risk to others owing to anger, lack of consideration for others or a self-absorbed attitude should be regarded as blameworthy, but would not be found to be *Cunningham* reckless.

4.4.2 *Caldwell* Recklessness

This second kind of recklessness was set out in the cases of *Caldwell** and *Lawrence**, but it had been significantly modified by the later decision of the House of Lords in *Reid**. It is useful first of all to look at what *Caldwell* and *Lawrence* decided and then to see how *Reid** has changed the position. The House of Lords in *Caldwell* defined reckless as:

'(a) The defendant performed an act that created a serious risk of harm
 (b) either
   (i) he recognised that there was some risk of that harm occurring, but nevertheless went on to take it; or
   (ii) he did not even address his mind to the possibility of there being any such risk and the risk was in fact obvious.'

'Serious risk' in (a) means a risk that a reasonable person would not dismiss as negligible and that the harm would amount to the *actus reus* of a criminal offence. The requirement in (b)(i) is the same as *Cunningham* recklessness. If you foresee a risk of harm (it does not need to be a serious risk) then you will be *Caldwell* reckless. This means that anyone who is *Cunningham* reckless will also be *Caldwell* reckless. However, (b)(ii) states that if the defendant failed to consider the obvious risk she will be *Caldwell* reckless (although she would not be *Cunningham* reckless).

This means that if the risk is an obvious one then the only state of mind that will not constitute *Caldwell* recklessness is if a person considers whether or not there is a risk and decides that there is no risk. This state of mind is often referred to as 'the *Caldwell* lacuna'. It is important because without it the test for *Caldwell* recklessness would simply be 'is the risk obvious?', which is in effect the test for negligence (see Chapter 4.5). However, the courts have defined the lacuna strictly. In fact no defendant in a reported case has successfully shown that he fell within the lacuna. One case where it might have arisen but was not relevant is *Lamb**, in which a boy was playing with a gun. He pointed the gun at a friend and checked that there was no bullet opposite the hammer of the gun and fired it. What he did not realize was that the cartridge of the revolver turned and the hammer struck not the empty cartridge but the one next to it that had a bullet in it. He killed his friend. Here the defendant had considered whether or not there was a risk and decided there was none, and had it been relevant he would have fallen within the *Caldwell* lacuna. In *Shimmen** it was stressed that in order to fall into the lacuna it is necessary to show that the defendant believed that there was no risk at all. It is not enough to show that he thought there was a minimal risk. Further, if you create a risk you cannot claim to be in the lacuna by taking subsequent steps to cancel the risk (*Merrick*). So the lacuna is only available to a defendant who before acting considers whether or not there is a risk and decides there is none at all.

Caldwell recklessness has been strongly criticized by commentators and partly in response to them the House of Lords in *Reid* has modified the definition of *Caldwell* recklessness. Before considering the effect of *Reid* it is useful to outline the objections to *Caldwell* recklessness. There were three main objections.

The first was a claim that *Caldwell* recklessness is in effect an objective test as it does not need proof of a state of mind. Failing to avert a risk is not a state of mind but the absence of a state of mind, it was argued.

Secondly, it was said that the test fails to take into account the peculiarities of the defendant. In deciding whether the risk was obvious the jury must consider whether it is obvious to a reasonable person and not whether it should have been obvious to the defendant. The unfairness of this was shown in the case of *Elliot* v. *C** in which a fourteen-year-old with learning difficulties was out late at night and lit a fire in a shed, burning it down. It was said that the lighting of the fire created an obvious risk of damage to the shed and she was convicted, even though the risk may not have been obvious to a person of her age and in her circumstances. It is one thing to punish a defendant for failing to foresee a risk that he should have foreseen, but to do so is only fair in cases where a defendant could have foreseen the risk. This case was followed by others (for example *R* (1984)) and so has become an established part of the *Caldwell* test (*Coles**).

Thirdly, the lacuna was seen as unsatisfactory. The lacuna plays a crucial role in theory (as explained earlier, it separates *Caldwell* recklessness from negligence), yet it was nearly impossible to prove. Further, it was by no means clear why being in the lacuna meant that you deserved to be innocent. An arrogant javelin thrower who believes that he is such a good athlete that he could not possibly hurt someone as he throws a javelin into the middle of a crowd of people seems as blameworthy and dangerous as an incompetent javelin thrower who has never thrown a javelin before and does not consider that he might injure someone by doing so. It is particularly hard to see why someone who decides that there is no risk is less blameworthy than someone who thinks his conduct has created a risk and takes inadequate steps to remove the risk.

These criticisms have to some extent been answered by the reconsideration and explanation of *Caldwell* recklessness given by *Reid**. Although *Reid* was a case about reckless driving (an offence which is now abolished and has been replaced with dangerous driving) it is clear from the judgements that the case was regarded by their Lordships as of general application to *Caldwell* recklessness and this seems to have been accepted in a later Court of Appeal case (*Coles**).

In response to the first argument above, that *Caldwell* recklessness does not require proof of a state of mind, Lord Keith in *Reid* argued that failing to appreciate a risk, for example not caring whether you might injure people, is an attitude or state of mind, as much so as deliberately taking a risk.

In response to the concern raised by cases like *Elliot v. C*, the House of Lords in *Reid* stated that you may not be *Caldwell* reckless if you have a good reason why you failed to see the risk. Their Lordships gave several examples of good reasons: a sudden illness; or shock; or sudden disability; or 'some condition not involving fault on his part'; or an understandable mistake; or a sudden emergency; or a sudden distraction. (Lord Goff's example of overtaking a pretty girl and being distracted by her is not a good example of such a distraction! Maybe driving along and being distracted by your child who suddenly screams out in the back seat is a better example.) The House of Lords appears to be trying to move away from simply considering whether the defendant failed to foresee a reasonable risk, to considering why she failed to foresee that risk. This sophistication recognizes that not all forms of inadvertence are necessarily blameworthy, but that some are, particularly if they suggest an attitude of indifference to the welfare of others. It will be noted that this reasoning does not deal directly with the *Elliot* v. *C* case, which the House of Lords left open, as the excuses given in *Reid* are limited to sudden illness etc. and not pre-existing conditions, such as the learning difficulties of *C*. However, as was stressed by Lord Ackner, *Reid* was a driving case and people with illness or disabilities either should not drive or if they do they should take extra care to compensate for their disabilities. So it is not surprising that *Reid* did not take into account pre-existing conditions. However, a strong argument can be made that where the defendant has not undertaken a particularly dangerous activity then the pre-existing conditions should provide an excuse. Indeed Lord Ackner left open the possibility of *Elliot* v. *C* being overruled in relation to criminal damage. However, this option was not taken up by the Court of Appeal in *Coles*, which followed *Elliot* v. *C*, although it did not consider the judgements in *Reid* in detail. So it seems, at least at present, *Elliot* v. *C* still represents the law in respect of pre-existing conditions and that the exceptions in *Reid* only apply to sudden illnesses or disabilities.

In relation to the lacuna, the House of Lords narrowed it by saying that one could show that the defendant was in the lacuna only if the defendant's decision that there was no risk of harm was an 'understandable or excusable one' (Lord Keith) or a 'reasonable one' (Lord Brown Wilkinson), although Lord Goff only required a '*bona fide*' belief.

4.4.3   Presumed *Mens Rea* 'Recklessness'

Following *B* v. *DPP** and *R* v. *K** (discussed in greater detail in Chapter 6), if a statute is silent or unclear as to the *mens rea* requirement then the common law 'presumption of *mens rea*' applies. The presumption is that the defendant will be guilty unless she believes that an element of the *actus reus* is not present. The belief does not need to be reasonable in order to provide a defence. Presumably (although the House of Lords in *B* v. *DPP** and *R* v. *K* do not address this directly) if the belief is caused by intoxication this will not provide a defence. This means the defendant will be guilty if she either was aware of the circumstances of the *actus reus* or gave no thought to the existence of an element of the *actus reus*.

4.4.4   Contrasting the Forms of Recklessness

We can now contrast the three forms of recklessness. Six situations may be considered where a defendant (*D*) engages in conduct that creates an obvious risk of harm:

1 *D* foresees the risk and takes it.
2 *D* fails to see the risk because he is voluntarily intoxicated.
3 *D* fails to foresee the risk because of some blameworthy reason, apart from voluntary intoxication.
4 *D* fails to foresee the risk for some non-blameworthy reason (for example because of a sudden illness or distraction).
5 *D* considers whether or not there is a risk and understandably decides there is none.
6 *D* considers whether or not there is a risk and decides unreasonably that there is none.

1 and 2 are both *Caldwell*, *Cunningham* and 'presumed *mens rea*' reckless;
3 would be *Caldwell* reckless but not *Cunningham* or 'presumed *mens rea*'

reckless; **4** and **5** are neither *Cunningham* nor *Caldwell* nor 'presumed *mens rea'* reckless. **6** would be *Caldwell* and *Cunningham* reckless, but not 'presumed *mens rea'* reckless.

As can be seen, the difference between *Caldwell* and *Cunningham* recklessness is not very substantial (Gardner, 1993). Both agree that advertent recklessness and inadvertent recklessness due to drunkenness constitute recklessness. The only difference is where the defendant fails to foresee the risk for some blameworthy reason other than drunkenness.

4.4.3 Reform of Recklessness

The Law Commission has suggested the following definition of recklessness:

> 'a person acts . . . (b) "recklessly" with respect to (i) a circumstance, when he is aware of a risk that it exists or will exist, and (ii) a result, when he is aware of a risk that it will occur, and it is unreasonable, having regard to the circumstances known to him, to take that risk.'

Thus the proposal is that *Caldwell* be abolished. The Code also indicates that recklessness is to be the normal basic *mens rea*, and negligence will only be available where the Code specifically so states. It was said 'every offence requires a fault element of recklessness with respect to each of its elements other than fault elements, unless otherwise provided'.

4.5   The Meaning of Negligence

A considerable amount of the criticism directed at the decision in *Caldwell* centres on the proposition that by applying an objective test to recklessness, recklessness is confused with negligence. Negligence compares the actions of the accused with those of a hypothetical 'reasonable person'. A negligent act is one that falls below the standards expected of a reasonable ordinary prudent person. The state of mind of the defendant, what she intended or foresaw, is irrelevant. In fact, although negligence is of very great importance in the civil law of tort, it does not feature in many serious criminal offences. However, there are many statutory crimes that are negligence based, particularly in areas of professional regulation. Many believe that negligence should not play a role in criminal law; that criminal liability should require that the accused actually possess a specific state of mind, and does not merely fall short of some required standard of conduct. Lord Diplock himself expressed a similar view in *Caldwell* when he said that '*mens rea* is by definition a state of mind of the accused himself at the time he did the physical act that constitutes the *actus reus* of the offence; it cannot be the mental state of some non-existent, hypothetical person'. In *Sheppard**, Lord Diplock also expressed doubts as to the place of negligence in the criminal law:

> 'The concept of the reasonable man as providing the standard by which the liability of real persons for their conduct is to be determined is a concept of civil law, particularly in relation to the tort of negligence; the obtrusion into criminal law of conformity with the notional conduct of the reasonable man as relevant to criminal liability, though not unknown (e.g. in relation to provocation sufficient to reduce murder to manslaughter), is exceptional, and should not lightly be extended.'

The most serious offence in which negligence has formed part of the *mens rea* or fault element is common law manslaughter. In this case the negligence required has to be very great, or 'gross' (see Chapter 10.3).

Some argue that negligence should not be regarded as a form of *mens rea*, as that concept is concerned with states of mind and negligence is essentially a description of conduct. To include negligence within *mens rea* broadens the concept to include wider ideas of fault, blameworthiness or culpability. The leading exponent of such liability is Hart, who suggests that two questions should be asked: 'Did the accused fail to take those precautions which any reasonable man with normal capacity would in the circumstances have taken? Could the accused, given his mental and physical capacities have taken those precautions?' If both of these questions are answered 'yes' then the accused deserves punishment. It should be noted that Hart's approach is not a pure negligence standard as it requires the conduct of the accused to be compared with that expected of a reasonable person with the accused's mental and physical capacities, rather than a simple reasonable person.

There are several other words commonly found in criminal offences that import an element of *mens rea*, but these are best considered in the context of the specific offences in which they appear. For example, 'knowledge or belief' is found in the offence of handling stolen goods, and 'dishonesty' is commonly found in the offences against property discussed in Part III.

4.6   Transferred *Mens Rea*

A general principle, well established in the case law, though sometimes criticized by academics, is the doctrine of transferred *mens rea* (sometimes called transferred malice). This is a rule which is connected to the rules of causation in the criminal law (see Chapter 5). If Jennifer shoots at Mark intending to kill him, but in fact kills Jim, she will be held liable for the murder of Jim. It may be said that Jennifer's *mens rea* (intention to kill Mark) is transferred to the actual victim and so Jennifer can be convicted of Jim's murder. By contrast in *Pembiliton*, the defendant threw a brick at a person but missed and damaged a window. He was not guilty of maliciously damaging a window as he had no *mens rea*. Transferring the intention to injure a person did not enable the conviction because the *mens rea* transferred has to be the correct *mens rea* for the offence. Intention to injure a person plus damage to property does not create an offence. Had the defendant thrown the brick at a door and missed and hit the window then he would have been guilty as that *mens rea* (maliciously damaging property (the door)) was the *mens rea* needed for the offence with which he was charged.

In *Attorney-General's Reference (No. 3 of 1994)** the defendant stabbed his pregnant girlfriend. The stab wound injured the unborn child, who was born prematurely and died from the stab wound 121 days after birth. It was argued by the prosecution that it was possible to convict the man of murder on the basis of transferred malice: he intended to kill or cause grievous bodily harm to the mother and this could be transferred to the child. The House of Lords rejected this on the basis that at the time of the stabbing the unborn child was not a person in the eyes of the law. This meant that to convict the defendant there had to be a double transfer of malice: from the mother to the unborn child; from the unborn child to the person she would become. This they felt was to stretch the doctrine of transferred malice too far. Especially as the prosecution was relying on an intention to cause serious injury as the *mens rea* for murder, which Lord Steyn said was anomolous, even though it was well established in the caselaw. As we shall see in Chapter 10.2, the defendant could have been properly convicted of manslaughter. The House of Lords' decision has been criticized. The defendant caused the death of the child and intended to cause grievous bodily harm to someone. Is his argument 'I did not intend to injure the child I intended to injure the mother' any more attractive in this case than the standard case of transferred malice in a murder case?

It had been thought that the doctrine of 'transferred *mens rea*' was best seen as no more that the operation of the rules of *mens rea* at their most simple level. In other words Jennifer, in the example above, was guilty of murder because the *mens rea* for murder was simply an intention to kill someone and she had that intention. *Pembliton* was not guilty as it was not shown he had the malice to damage any property. Therefore in these cases there was no need to talk of transferring intention; at issue was simply the question of whether or not the defendant had the necessary *mens rea*. However, the House of Lords has recently rejected this interpretation of the rule. In *Attorney-General's Reference (No. 3 of 1994)** Lord Mustill stated that the *mens rea* for murder was an intention to kill or cause grievous bodily harm *to the victim*, not simply an intention to kill or cause grievous bodily harm to someone, as had previously been thought. However, their Lordships confirmed that if the death of someone other than the intended victim was caused then the doctrine of transferred *mens rea* could be used to convict a defendant of murder. The decision is strange as their Lordships were critical of the doctrine of transferred *mens rea* and thought that it lacked 'sound intellectual basis'. But their narrow interpretation of the *mens rea* of murder means that the doctrine will have to be relied upon more often than it would have been had they accepted the wider interpretation of the *mens rea* for murder. The doctrine of transferred *mens rea* is therefore still very much part of the law. Despite its artificiality it is useful as it stresses the point that for many crimes it is not necessary to show an intention or recklessness in respect of a specific person or piece of property.

It should be emphasized that whenever the doctrine of transferred *mens rea* operates there is also the alternative charge for attempting to commit the intended crime. So Jennifer could be convicted of the murder of Jim and the attempted murder of Mark.

Some commentators argue that the doctrine of transferred *mens rea* is too wide: one should not be liable for unintended and unforeseeable consequences. The correct charge, they argue, is of attempt against the intended victim. However, it is understandable that the law is unsympathetic to a defendant who seeks by way of excuse to say 'I did not intend to kill her, I meant to kill him'.

4.7   Coincidence of *Actus Reus* and *Mens Rea*

In order for a criminal offence to be complete, the *actus reus* and *mens rea* must coincide in time. As James J said in *Fagan**, 'the subsequent inception of *mens rea* cannot convert an act which has been completed into an assault'. The rule is of relevance in two different situations:

1 If the *mens rea* occurs after the *actus reus*. For example, if Brian was driving carefully and within the speed limits when Josh jumped out in front of his car and despite his best attempts Brian ran him over, there would be no offence. If Brian jumped out his car and saw it was Josh he had injured and jumped with joy because Josh was his enemy whom he wanted to kill, this later intent to kill could not turn the original accident

into a criminal offence. Of course, there would have been an offence if Brian saw Josh and deliberately drove into him.

2 If the *mens rea* occurs before the *actus reus*. If the *mens rea* exists before the *actus reus* but is not present at the time the *actus reus* is performed there is no offence. If Glen, in a fit of rage, says to his enemy Vladimir, 'I want to kill you', and several days later is involved in a car accident where quite without fault on his part, he happens to run over Vladimir, he would not be guilty of murder. That is because although at one point in time he had an intention to kill Vladimir (the *mens rea* for murder) and at another point in time he killed him (the *actus reus* of murder), the two did not coincide. He did not intend to kill when performing the act that killed the victim.

The requirement of coincidence of *actus reus* and *mens rea* seems a sensible limitation on the width of criminal law or else we would get dangerously close to punishing people just for their bad thoughts. However, there are situations in which there is an apparent separation in time between the *mens rea* and *actus reus*, but the law still convicts the defendant.

Considering the two kinds of situations discussed above:

1 There could be an *actus reus* with no *mens rea*, followed later in time by the *mens rea*. Imagine a different example from the Brian example above. Fred takes Penelope's umbrella from a stand, thinking it is his own, and later he realizes his error but decides to keep it. The law may enable a conviction in this situation. First, the law may see the first act as a continuing act. It could be held that Fred is continuing to appropriate Penelope's umbrella and therefore is continuing to commit the *actus reus* of theft at the time when the *mens rea* arises. An example of this is *Fagan*, where the defendant's act of parking a car on a policeman's foot was seen as an ongoing *actus reus* and once the *mens rea* arrived (he realized that the car was on the foot) the offence was complete. A second way that the law can deal with this is by looking at the later occasion when there is a *mens rea* and considering whether there may be liability for an omission. *Miller** can be analysed in this way (see Chapter 3.3). When falling asleep there was an *actus reus* but no *mens rea*. However, on awaking and seeing the fire then there was a *mens rea*. By stating that his failure to deal with the fire was an *actus reus*, the House of Lords was able to circumvent the problem of the apparent separation of the *actus reus* and the *mens rea*. In Fred's case it could be said that the moment he was aware the umbrella was not his, he was under a duty to return the umbrella. His failure to do was an omission but because he was under a duty to act this constituted the *actus reus*.

2 Sometimes it is possible to convict a defendant even though there is *mens*

rea but no *actus reus*, later followed by the *actus reus*. An example is *Church**, in which the defendant attacked a woman, with the *mens rea* for murder. He thought that he had killed her but in fact he had only injured her. He put the 'corpse' into a river and the victim died while in the river. Again, the law has used two devices to deal with this problem. The first is by developing a special doctrine. The Court of Appeal in *Church* held that the defendant was guilty if 'the jury regarded the appellant's behaviour from the moment he first struck her to the moment when he threw her into a river as a series of acts designed to cause death or grievous bodily harm'. The difficulty in applying this test has been in deciding exactly what constitutes a 'series of acts'. It is clear that if there is a plan and the defendants are mistaken as to when during their plan they have killed the victim, they are still guilty (*Thabo Meli*). However, the doctrine also applies where there is no preconceived plan, as *Church* itself shows.

In *Le Brun** the defendant and his wife had an argument in a street. He wanted her to come home with him and she did not want to go. He hit her and she fell over. He then tried to pick up her body in order to carry her inside the house. It appears that the defendant dropped his wife and she banged her head on the side of a pavement. This killed her. Although it was an accident when he dropped his wife, he had *mens rea* when he hit her. The Court of Appeal argued that, although they were not part of a preconceived plan, these acts formed a 'single transaction' and he was therefore guilty of manslaughter. It seems that their reasoning was that his act of picking his wife up was done in order to take her into the house, perhaps to cover up his crime. It is generally thought that the result would have been different had he picked her up to take her to hospital, as then he would have been seen to be trying to undo the earlier harm rather than exacerbate it. If this had been the case the *actus reus* and the act with *mens rea* could not have been linked and he would not have been guilty of manslaughter.

An alternative argument used by the Court of Appeal in *Le Brun* was to try to apply the rules of causation to this situation. It can be said that the defendant's initial act of hitting his wife caused him to pick her up, which caused her death. His act of picking her up would not then be seen as a break in the chain of causation (see Chapter 5).

4.8   'The Correspondence Principle'

It might be thought that there should be a correspondence between the *actus reus* and the *mens rea*, that is the *mens rea* should be a state of mind relating to the *actus reus*. For example the *mens rea* for murder would be an intent to kill; for an offence of causing grievous bodily harm that the defendant intended or foresaw grievous bodily harm. However, such a principle is not part of the law and the *mens rea* can relate to a lower level of harm than that which forms part of the *actus reus*. For example, the *mens rea* for murder includes an intent to cause grievous bodily harm. Also, there are some other offences which require an 'ulterior intent', that is performing an act with an intention to cause some harm in the future with different acts. For example, as we have seen, burglary involves entering as a trespasser with intent to do one of various crimes.

The *mens rea* therefore does not necessarily correspond to the *actus reus*, although it often will do so. Intention or foresight of a lesser harm than that involved in the *actus reus* may be sufficient in some cases; intention or foresight of a greater harm than the *actus reus* is required in others.

Some commentators argue that 'the correspondence principle' (that the *mens rea* should correspond to the *actus reus*) is one to which the law should aspire as an ideal. Others disagree and argue that if a defendant does an act foreseeing that it will cause some harm, then she should be responsible for any harm resulting from her acts; the consequence is not 'bad luck' as she has 'made her own bad luck'. She should be responsible for the consequences of her actions. She has lost any sympathy for 'bad luck' by acting in a way that she knows might harm another. Horder has proposed a 'proportionality' principle. This is that a defendant can be responsible for more harm than she intended or foresaw as long as it was proportionate to the harm she foresaw.

Hot Topic: Euthanasia and Mercy Killing

If a person is suffering from a terminal illness and asks a doctor to help her die, what can the doctor lawfully do? If the doctor hastens the death of the patient, could she be convicted of murder? Two key questions are involved. First, did the doctor cause the death of the victim? Second, did the doctor intend to kill or seriously injure the victim?

1 The law draws a sharp distinction in this context between acts and omissions. These will be dealt with separately:
   (a) If the doctor does an act (for example gives a lethal injection) the *actus reus* of murder will be established if the act was a substantial and operating cause of death (*Cheshire, Moor*). This must, of course, be demonstrated beyond reasonable doubt. In one trial of a doctor for murder, the trial judge withdrew the murder charge from the jury on the ground that there was insufficient evidence that the accused had caused the death (rather than the death resulting from the patient's illness). A charge of attempted murder went to the jury and the doctor was acquitted (*Arthur*).
   Devlin J in *Adams* stressed that if an act of a doctor shortened the life

expectancy of a terminally ill patient, the doctor would still be held to have caused the death of the patient even though the patient would have died a few weeks afterwards anyway. However he went on:

'But that does not mean that a doctor aiding the sick or dying has to calculate in minutes or hours, or perhaps in days or weeks, the effect on a patient's life of the medicines which he administers. If the first purpose of medicine – the restoration of health – can no longer be achieved, there is still much for the doctor to do, and he is entitled to do all that is proper and necessary to relieve pain and suffering even if measures he takes may incidentally shorten life.'

This suggests that a doctor who is seeking to relieve pain may not be found to have caused the death of a patient if he only shortens life expectancy by a few minutes or hours. It must be said that these *dicta* (at first instance) are not consistent with cases on causation in other contexts (such as *Dyson*). This may be seen as an example of the law on causation being influenced by policy considerations (see Chapter 5.1). This might be implied from Devlin J's direction to the jury in *Adams* to apply common sense to the case. In a more recent case on euthanasia, Hooper J preferred to simply ask the jury whether it believed that the doctor's acts were an operating and substantial cause of the death (Moor).

(b) Now we will consider the situation where the defendant does not act, for example, she does not provide the medical treatment necessary for the victim's life. Here, perhaps strangely, a distinction is drawn between doctors and members of the deceased's family.

(i) Doctors are required to act in the patient's best interests. This will never permit the doctor to act in a way that causes the death of the victim (*Bland, Cox*). However, the law has accepted that sometimes it is not in the patient's best interests to receive treatment, even if without it the patient will die. This will be true where either the patient's projected life will be intolerable (for example a baby is born with terrible disabilities and a short pain-filled life is predicted, *Re J*) or the patient is suffering from Persistent Vegetative State and so is unaware of what is happening to him or her (*Bland*).

(ii) Carers are expected to act as reasonable people. This means that they must follow medical advice. Therefore a carer who does not give the patient the drugs prescribed by the doctor will infringe his duty. If the patient falls seriously ill and the carer does not summon a doctor this would also infringe her duty. In both cases the defendant could be liable for murder or manslaughter. The law takes the view that it is for doctors, not carers, to decide whether or not it is in the patient's interests to receive further medical treatment.

2 If it is established that the doctor did cause the patient's death, the next question is whether there was an intention to kill the patient. It would be possible to distinguish three states of mind:

(a) If the doctor acts with the purpose of killing the patient this appears to be an example of direct intention and the *mens rea* of the murder would be established. The fact that the doctor or patient may be acting with the best of motives (for example, believing that the patient has suffered enough) is irrelevant if the doctor's purpose was to kill.

(b) A little more complex may be an argument that the defendant killed in order to prevent the patient suffering any more. It could be argued that the primary purpose was to end the suffering, not to kill. However, it is submitted that although this issue has not been directly addressed by the courts, this is a case where the end (ending the pain) necessarily involves the killing. The purpose is to be achieved through the killing. This should therefore be regarded as a case of directly intended death. Therefore the *mens rea* of murder could be established.

(c) The most controversial case is where the doctor or carer administers a substance which is a pain reliever, while being aware that this substance will also lead to a shortening of the patient's life. This is different from (b) where it is the death that will relieve the pain; here it is the drug that will ease the pain, and the death can be regarded as an incidental consequence. This therefore is a case of 'oblique intent' and the *Woollin* direction applies. The doctor or carer would have to admit that he was aware that death or serious bodily harm was a virtually certain consequence of his action and therefore the jury is entitled to find there is intent. Some people take the view that faced with such a case, the jury would in fact be sympathetic to a doctor or carer and decline to find intention. Indeed Lord Goff in *Bland* stated as a fact that if a doctor administers pain-relieving drugs and death is caused as a side-effect of this treatment, he would not be guilty of murder. Ognall J in *Cox* and Hooper J in *Moor* directed the jury that if the doctor's primary intent was to relieve pain there was no *mens rea* for murder. However, as discussed above, this loophole may no longer be available after *Re A (Conjoined Twins)*. As mentioned above, it may be that following this case, the jury *must* find intention once it is found that death or grievous bodily harm was a virtually certain consequence of his or her actions and the defendant realized this. So where does this leave Lord Goff's statement? If what he was saying was that a jury should not (or would not) find or infer intent in such a case, then after *Re A (Conjoined Twins)* it is arguable that the jury has no choice but to decide that the doctor intended to kill. It may, however, be that Lord Goff was explaining that in cases involving the treatment of terminally ill patients the normal law on intention does not apply.

To complete the picture, defences need to be briefly mentioned. It is, of course, no defence simply to rely on the fact that the patient had consented to the killing. A carer may be able to rely on diminished responsibility if the pressure of the caring had caused an abnormality of mind (see Chapter 10.9). Provocation may be available, but *Cocker* indicates that there will be difficulties in proving that the defendant lost his or her self-control (see Chapter 10.10). There is no special defence of mercy killing. There are those who argue that a special defence of mercy killing should be developed for carers who kill their terminally ill relatives. There is also a case for developing a special defence available to doctors who act in accordance with established medical practice. Indeed there are a few *dicta* which could suggest that such a defence already exists. In *Gillick*, Lord Scarman stated that 'the *bona fide* exercise by a doctor of his clinical judgement must be a complete negation of the guilty mind . . .'. Hooper J's direction in *Moor* also suggests that a special defence is available.

The issue of euthanasia is of course a moral minefield. Strong views are taken on either side of the issue. The present state of the law is unlikely to satisfy either those who are keen to legalize euthanasia or those who believe it is never justifiable to take another's life. As the above discussion reveals, the present law draws some very fine distinctions between acts and omissions and different forms of intention. It is therefore easy to criticize the law because it draws artificial distinctions. However, it must be accepted that in order to set the line between lawful and unlawful killings in this context, some very fine distinctions must be made.

Before leaving this issue there is a question of whether the law will need to be re-examined in the light of the Human Rights Act (see *ex p Pretty*). It can be argued that the right to life means that the present law is too lax and needs to be tightened. On the other hand it can also be argued that the right to protection from torture and inhuman or degrading treatment means that people have a right to authorize others to kill them. These arguments will be considered in Chapter 19.

Summary

4.1 *Mens rea* is the term used to describe the mental element in an offence, the state of mind that the offender must possess at the same time as committing the *actus reus*. It may consist of several different components, and may be implied by the courts as well as expressed in a statutory definition of the offence.

4.2 Some *mens rea* words, such as 'intention' and 'recklessness', are used in many different offences. Although it would be logical for these words to bear the same meaning wherever they occur, this does not in fact happen. As a result, words are given different interpretations by the courts and there is considerable variation in the context of the offences in which they appear.

4.3 The meaning of 'intention', according to the House of Lords, should be left to juries to define for themselves in the vast majority of cases, giving the words their normal meaning. Where further help is needed the judge can tell the jury the following: intention must be distinguished from motive; if the defendant foresaw a consequence as virtually certain and the result was virtually certain then the jury is entitled to find that the defendant intended the consequence.

4.4 There are two forms of recklessness: a more subjective definition (*Cunningham* recklessness); and a more objective one (*Caldwell* recklessness). The two are not, in fact, very different once the rules relating to intoxication are taken into account. Both cases hold a defendant who deliberately takes a risk or fails to foresee it because of intoxication. *Caldwell* is willing also to see as reckless certain other forms of blameworthy inadvertence.

4.5 Negligence is concerned with an objective standard of behaviour and often involves a failure to think rather than a state of mind. Negligence is rarely found as a component of serious criminal offences; manslaughter is an exception and here the negligence required is 'gross'.

4.6 If the accused intends to injure one person, but succeeds in injuring a different person, the *mens rea* is sometimes said to be 'transferred' from the intended victim to the actual victim. In many cases this rule will not be needed because of the definition of the offence, or because it will be possible and sufficient to prove recklessness with respect to the actual victim.

4.7 *Actus reus* and *mens rea* must coincide in time for the offence to be complete. However, if the *actus reus* takes place over a period of time, or consists of a series of acts, the *mens rea* need not be present throughout – it may be superimposed on a continuing *actus reus*.

4.8 Some commentators argue that the law should uphold the correspondence principle. This requires the *mens rea* of a crime to refer to the *actus reus*. Others support a proportionality principle, that there need only be a proportion between the *actus reus* and the harm referred to in the *mens rea*.

Case Notes

Attorney-General's Reference (No. 3 of 1994) [1997] 3 WLR 421. House of Lords
See Chapter 9 case notes.

Caldwell [1982] AC 341. House of Lords
The appellant was convicted of arson, contrary to s.1(2) and (3) of the Criminal Damage Act 1971. He had pleaded guilty to arson contrary to s.1(1) and (3). The appellant had set light to a hotel, in which there were guests staying, because he had a grudge against the proprietor. He pleaded intoxication as a defence, but the trial judge ruled that intoxication was no defence to s.1(2), which requires intention to endanger the life of another or recklessness as to whether life would be endangered. The Court of Appeal allowed his appeal on the ground that this was a misdirection. The House of Lords dismissed the appeal by the prosecutor, but held that intoxication was only a defence to s.1 (2) in cases where the charge was based on an intention to endanger life. In cases where recklessness was alleged, intoxication was no defence. The majority agreed with the judgement of Lord Diplock, who redefined recklessness for the purposes of the Criminal Damage Act 1971, overruling earlier Court of Appeal decisions such as *Stephenson*. He held that recklessness was not confined to persons who were aware of the risk that the harmful consequence would result. It included those who, in circumstances in which the risk was obvious, had not given any thought to the possibility of such a risk.

Church [1966] 1 QB 59. Court of Criminal Appeal
See Chapter 10 case notes.

Coles [1995] 1 Cr App Rep 157. Court of Appeal
The accused was fifteen when he set fire to a hay rick thereby endangering the lives of his friends. He sought to introduce evidence that he was of below normal intelligence for his age. The Court of Appeal followed *Elliot* v. *C* and stated that the test for recklessness was whether the risk was obvious to an ordinary person and not a person of the accused's age or intellectual abilities.

Cunningham [1957] 2 QB 396. Court of Criminal Appeal
See Chapter 7 case notes.

B v. ***DPP*** [2000] Crim LR 403. House of Lords
See Chapter 6 case notes

Edwards v. ***Ddin*** [1976] 1 WLR 942. Divisional Court
See Chapter 11 case notes.

Elliot v. ***C*** [1983] 2 All ER 1005. Divisional Court
The accused was acquitted of arson, contrary to s.1 (1) and 3 of the Criminal Damage Act 1971. She was a girl of fourteen who, after staying out all night, had set light to a garden shed by pouring white spirit over the floor and throwing two lighted matches onto the spirit. The magistrates accepted the defence argument that, in applying Lord Diplock's ruling in *Caldwell* as to the meaning of recklessness in this offence, they should take into account whether the risk of damage to property would have been obvious to the particular defendant if he or she had given any thought to the matter. The Divisional Court allowed the appeal by the prosecutor. The court rejected the magistrates' interpretation of Lord Diplock's judgement and held that an 'obvious risk' was one that would be obvious to a reasonably prudent person, not necessarily to the particular defendant.

Fagan [1969] 1 QB 439. Divisional Court
See Chapter 3 case notes.

Hancock and Shankland [1986] AC 455. House of Lords
See Chapter 9 case notes.

Hyam v. *DPP* [1975] AC 55. House of Lords
See Chapter 9 case notes.

R v. *K* 25 JULY 2001; [2001] UKHL 41. House of Lords
See Chapter 6 case notes.

Lamb [1967] 2 QB 98. Court of Appeal
See Chapter 10 case notes.

Lawrence [1982] AC 510. House of Lords
The accused was convicted of causing death by reckless driving. He had knocked down and killed a pedestrian while riding his motorcycle along a busy urban street. He appealed to the Court of Appeal on the ground that the trial judge had misdirected the jury on the meaning of 'recklessly', and the Court of Appeal allowed the appeal. The prosecutor appealed to the House of Lords and the House of Lords dismissed the appeal, holding that there had been a misdirection. The Court applied Lord Diplock's definition of recklessness, as stated in *Caldwell*, to reckless driving. Reckless driving involves (i) driving in such a manner as to create an obvious and serious risk of causing physical injury to some other person or of doing substantial damage to property, and (ii) in so doing, either not thinking about the possibility of such a risk, or recognizing the risk and nevertheless going on to take it.

Le Brun [1992] QB 61. Court of Appeal
The defendant hit his wife and she fell to the ground. He picked her up to carry her into their house but dropped her, causing her to bang her head, which caused her death. The Court of Appeal argued that the apparent separation in time between *mens rea* and *actus reus* could be dealt with by seeing the events as 'one transaction'; or on the basis of causation in that there had been no intervening causes between his hit and her death.

Miller [1983] 2 AC 161. House of Lords
See Chapter 3 case notes.

Moloney [1985] AC 905. House of Lords
See Chapter 9 case notes.

Nedrick [1986] 3 All ER 1. Court of Appeal
See Chapter 9 case notes.

Reid [1992] 3 All ER 673. House of Lords
Reid was convicted of causing death by reckless driving (an offence now abolished). He killed his passenger after trying to drive through a narrow gap. The offence involved *Caldwell* recklessness. The accused tried to argue that *Caldwell* recklessness should be abolished and *Cunningham* recklessness should be recognized as the appropriate form of recklessness. The House rejected this argument but reconsidered the test for *Caldwell* recklessness. It was suggested that a defendant would not be reckless if she had a reasonable excuse for why she did not foresee a risk, such as a sudden illness or distraction.

Sheppard [1981] AC 394. House of Lords
See Chapter 6 case notes.

Shimmen [1986] 84 Cr App Rep 7. Divisional Court

The accused was charged with criminal damage. He had broken a shop window in the course of displaying his martial-arts skills to some friends. He claimed that he had not intended to break the window, and had thought that he had minimized the risk of doing so. He argued that he was not reckless, applying the *Caldwell* definition, since he had satisfied himself that he would probably not damage the window. The magistrates accepted this argument and dismissed the charge. The prosecutor appealed and the court allowed the appeal, holding that this was not a case where the accused considered the possibilities and concluded that there was absolutely no risk (the court left open whether this state of mind was reckless). In this case, however, the accused did recognize that there was some risk, but thought that he had minimized it. This state of mind was reckless within the *Caldwell* definition.

Woollin [1999] AC 82. House of Lords

The appellant was charged with the murder of his baby son who had died of head injuries. He was convicted of murder after admitting that he had caused the injuries. The House of Lords allowed his appeal. A modified form of the *Nedrick* test was approved. The jury would be entitled to find intention if death or serious injury was virtually certain and the defendant realized that this was so.

Yip Chiu-Cheung [1995] 1 AC 111. Privy Council

See Chapter 18 case notes.

Further Reading

Theoretical discussions of the nature of intention and recklessness are found in Duff, Hart, Horder, Lacey and Norrie. The present law on intention is analysed in Norrie, Simester, Simester and Chan, Simester and Shute, and Williams. Recklessness and negligence are discussed in Gardner, Horder (1997) and Leigh. Issues surrounding the legal treatment of euthanasia and similar problems are examined in Arlidge, Ashworth, Goss and Smith. Sullivan reviews the link between *mens rea* and *actus reus*. The correspondence principle is discussed in Horder (1995 and 1999) and Mitchell.

Arlidge, 'The Trial of Dr David Moor' [2000] *Criminal Law Review* 31.

Ashworth, 'Criminal Liability in a Medical Context', in Simester and Smith (eds) *Harm and Culpability* (1996, Oxford University Press).

Duff, *Intention, Agency and Criminal Liability* (1990, Blackwell).

Gardner, 'Recklessness Redefined' (1993) 109 *Law Quarterly Review* 21.

Gardner, 'The Importance of *Majewski*' (1994) 14 *Oxford Journal of Legal Studies* 26.

Goss, 'A Postscript to the Trial of Dr David Moor' [2000] *Criminal Law Review* 568.

Hart, *Punishment and Responsibility* (1968, Oxford University Press).

Horder, 'Intention in the Criminal Law – a Rejoinder' (1995) 58 *Modern Law Review* 678.

Horder, 'A Critique of the Correspondence Principle' [1995] *Criminal Law Review* 759.

Horder, 'Gross Negligence and Criminal Culpability' (1997) 47 *University of Toronto Law Journal* 495.

Horder, 'Questioning the Correspondence Principle – A Reply' [1999] *Criminal Law Review* 206.

Lacey, 'A Clear Concept of Intention: Elusive or Illusory?' (1993) 56 *Modern Law Review* 621.

Lacey, 'In(de)terminable Intentions', (1995) 58 *Modern Law Review* 592.

Leigh, 'Recklessness after Reid' (1993) 56 *Modern Law Review* 208.

Mitchell, 'In Defence of the Correspondence Principle' [1999] *Criminal Law Review* 195.

Norrie, 'After *Woollin*', [1999] *Criminal Law Review* 532.

Simester, 'Moral Certainty and the Boundaries of Intention' (1996) *Oxford Journal of Legal Studies* 445.

Simester, 'Murder, *Mens Rea* and the House of Lords – Again' (1999) 115 *Law Quarterly Review* 17.

Simester and Chan, 'Intention Thus Far' [1997] *Criminal Law Review* 704.

Simester and Shute, Letter [2000] *Criminal Law Review* 204.

Smith, 'A Comment on Moor's Case' [2000] *Criminal Law Review* 41.

Sullivan, 'Cause and Contemporaneity of *Actus Reus* and *Mens Rea*' (1993) *Cambridge Law Journal* 487.

Williams, 'Oblique Intent' [1988] *Cambridge Law Journal* 417.

Wilson, 'Doctrinal Rationality after *Woollin*' (1999) 62 *Modern Law Review* 448.

5 Causation

Key words

- **Causation** – the rules which decide whether a defendant is responsible for a harm.
- **'But for' cause** – a finding that 'but for' the defendant's actions the harm would not have occurred.
- ***Novus actus interveniens*** – the intervention of the victim, third party or natural event which means that the defendant is no longer responsible for subsequent consequences of his or her actions.

5.1 The Nature of Causation

Some commentators have argued that you should be responsible for your actions, but not their consequences (see Chapter 1.4.3). The argument is that having acted (for example pulling the trigger of the gun), what happens next is to some extent a matter of chance (for example whether the victim jumps out of the way or whether the gun will work). However, this view has not been accepted by the law. The consequences of actions do play an important role in determining criminal liability. The difficulty lies in deciding for which consequences of our actions we are responsible. This is where the rules of causation come into play.

Imagine a situation in which Bob has been abused by his father in childhood and has been brought up under socially deprived circumstances. He is in a depressed state because his girlfriend has left him. He stabs a policeman with a knife given to him by a friend. An ambulance is called but arrives late on the scene because there is an ambulance strike, and by the time the policeman arrives in hospital his condition is serious. The doctor who sees him is terribly overworked and mistakenly concludes that the policeman does not need urgent treatment. The policeman dies shortly afterwards. In this situation who caused the policeman's death? Bob? His friend? His father? His girlfriend? The ambulance unions? The doctor? The hospital? The government? Society? A doctor, a sociologist, a theologian, a politician and the victim's relatives might all give different answers to this question.

It is often stressed that legal causation is different from factual causation. This is true because legal causation is not strictly a logical, factual or medical question, but more a moral one – 'is the defendant morally to blame for a consequence of her actions?' In *McKechnie* the defendant attacked the victim with a television set, causing him head injuries. On being taken to hospital it was discovered that the victim had a duodenal ulcer. It was not possible to operate on the ulcer because of the head injuries caused by the defendant and the victim died from the ulcer shortly after- wards. The defendant was held to have caused the victim's death in law. As a matter of pure factual causation this might be hard to justify, as the medical cause of death was the ulcer and not the injuries inflicted by the defendant. But as a matter of ascribing moral responsibility the decision appears correct. (It should be added that the case seems to be based on the assumption that, had he not been attacked, the victim would have sought medical help and he would have had a successful operation to deal with the ulcer.)

The problem is that moral responsibility is a controversial topic. As we have seen, ascribing responsibility for a criminal injury could involve consideration of contentious political or sociological factors. The criminal law tries to avoid these by focusing on one person, the defendant, and asking whether he or she can be said to have caused the consequences, regardless of the extent to which his or her background or social circum- stances may also have been responsible for the commission of the crime. So where a person carelessly driving a car at high speed kills a pedestrian, the law focuses on the driver. Whether car manufacturers who make cars that can travel at high speeds and advertise cars in a way that encourage high-speed driving are responsible is not considered in a criminal trial. That said, sometimes the law permits the rules of causation to be affected by policy considerations and this will become evident as we consider the legal rules of causation in further detail.

The question of causation is not simply left to the jury to be decided by its common sense. There are legal principles that the judge can use to guide it. As one judge explained:

'generally speaking causation is a question of fact for the jury . . . But that does not mean that there are no principles of law relating to causa- tion, so that no directions on law are ever to be given to a jury on the question of causation . . . It is for the judge to direct the jury with refer- ence to the relevant principles of law relating to causation, and then to leave it to the jury to decide, in the light of those principles, whether or not the relevant causal link has been established' (Goff ʟᴊ in *Pagett**).

5.2　The Guiding Rule of Causation

The cornerstone of the law on causation is that the prosecution must show that the defendant's act was 'a substantial and operating cause' (*Cheshire**) of the harm. The term substantial makes it clear that the defendant's act need not be the sole cause, but the act must be more than a *de minimis* (minimal) cause (*Cato*), or 'a slight or trifling' contribution to the result (*Kimsey*). As Goff LJ put it in *Pagett*, 'in law the accused's act need not be the sole cause, òr even the main cause, of the victim's death, it being enough that his act contributed significantly to that result'. It is therefore quite possible for a harm to be caused by two or even more people, each of whom contributed significantly to the creation of the harm. In such a case the jury is asked simply to consider whether the actions of the particular defendant before it contributed significantly to the death. The fact that someone else might also have contributed to the death is irrelevant to the jury's enquiry. For example, in one case (*Benge*) there was a railway accident after a foreman negligently arranged for tracks to be removed and the driver of the train failed to keep a proper lookout. The court held that the foreman could be criminally responsible for the accident even though the driver was also to blame. This has recently been confirmed by the Court of Appeal:

> 'The onus on the Crown is to make the jury sure that the injuries inflicted by the defendant were a significant cause of death. However, the Crown has no onus of establishing that any supervening event was not a significant cause of death . . .'(*Mellor*).

In order to explain further what the phrase 'operating and substantial cause' means, the law has developed a number of further rules.

5.3　'But for' Causation

A starting point for the law's approach to causation is to ask whether 'but for' the defendant's act the result would have happened. This test is sometimes known by its Latin tag *causa sine qua non*. The jury must ask itself what would have happened had the defendant not acted in the wrongful way that the defendant did. If the harm would still have occurred in the same way and at the same time then the act cannot be said to have caused the harm in law. For example, if Albert poisons Victoria's tea, but before she has drunk it she suffers an unrelated heart attack and dies, then Albert cannot be said to have caused Victoria's death (although he may be guilty of attempted murder). 'But for' his act Victoria would still have died in exactly the same way (see *White*, which has similar facts to this example). The converse of this is that if the defendant kills someone who was in fact due to die from other causes shortly afterwards she would still be said to have caused the victim's death. It is true that 'but for' her act the victim would still have died, but at a different time and in a different way. The jury will decide what would have happened 'but for' the defendant's act using their common sense and general experience of the world and the predictability of the way things or people behave.

It is important to remember that the defendant is only liable under the criminal law if a *wrongful* act of his own causes the injury. For example, in *Dalloway*, a man, who was driving a horse cart without properly controlling the reins or looking where he was going, ran over a young child. The court found that even if he had been exercising all due care and control he would not have been able to avoid injuring the girl as she jumped out in front of the cart without any warning. Although 'but for' the driving of the cart the child would not have been injured it was not true that 'but for' his negligence the child would not have been killed, and it was this that was the crucial question for the jury to decide.

Just because 'but for' causation is established does not mean that the accused will be said to have caused the result in law. Otherwise every criminal's parents could be said to have caused the crime, because 'but for' their act of procreation their child's crime would not have occurred! Hence the law has further requirements. A defendant is taken to be responsible for and to have caused the consequences of his actions unless there has been a break in the chain of causation, a *novus actus interveniens* as it is known. That is, an event by which someone or something else has taken over responsibility for the chain of events that follow.

5.4   *Novus Actus Interveniens*

The *novus actus interveniens* doctrine has been developed in a highly influential book by Professors Hart and Honoré. They argue that to understand the doctrine it is necessary to distinguish conditions from causes. To demonstrate this distinction they give the example of a fire. In order for the fire to start it is necessary to have a dropped match, oxygen in the air and combustible material. Only the dropped match would be seen as a cause and the others as conditions. The distinction is that conditions are those things that are normal, such as oxygen in the air. However, the dropping of the match is abnormal, it 'made the difference' and so can be said to have caused the fire. Only abnormal causes can be *novus actus interveniens* and break the chain of causation. Conditions cannot break the chain of events. The main difficulty with this approach is how to distinguish between normal and abnormal events. Three kinds of *novus actus interveniens* will now be considered to explore this distinction.

5.4.1 Acts by Third Parties

To consider the circumstances in which the acts of a third party may constitute a *novus actus interveniens* it is necessary to distinguish the following:

1.   Free and voluntary acts of third parties
Normally if a third party is of criminal capacity (that is, over ten and sane) then she assumes responsibility for the consequences that follow from her acts if the acts are 'free, deliberate and informed' (Goff LJ in *Pagett*). Hart and Honoré explain that this is because a third party's acts are 'abnormal' (they are unpredictable) and so break the chain of causation. It can also be explained as a matter of principle – that a person is not to be blamed in law for someone else's actions as otherwise that would be to make someone responsible for things outside his or her control. Thus if Anne puts poison into Charlotte's food, but before the poison takes effect Emily shoots and kills Charlotte, then Anne is no longer liable for her death, and Emily, by her act of shooting, assumes responsibility for the death. Anne would not have caused the death because Emily's act was a *novus actus interveniens*, breaking the chain of causation. Indeed this analysis reflects the general principle of causation because Anne's act is no longer an operating cause of Charlotte's death.

Although what has been said in the previous paragraph is generally regarded as the correct way to analyse causation and the acts of third parties, there are some cases which are not consistent with it. In a case on pollution, vandals had opened a tap on a company's oil tank, thereby releasing oil into a stream (*National Rivers Authority* v. *Wright Engineering*). It was held that the company could be said to have caused the pollution despite it occurring as a result of the acts of a third party. It may be that this is an example of public policy affecting the rules of causation – the law of pollution seeks to encourage companies to take all possible steps to prevent pollution and in this context that would include ensuring that third parties are not able to enter, and interfere with, the company's factories and so cause pollution. Alternatively the case has been dismissed as one where the courts simply got the law wrong.

As mentioned above, it is possible for two or more people to be responsible for a consequence. So, if *A* and *B* both poured poison into a victim's glass and the combination of the poisons killed *C*, then both *A* and *B* could be said to have killed *C*. They were both operating and substantial causes of *C*'s death. In *Dyos and others*, for example, the victim died of injuries received in a fight between groups of youths. It was found at the trial that the victim had suffered two main injuries to the head, one of which was caused by Dyos. There was no evidence as to the cause of the other injury. Both wounds were potentially fatal, and there was no way of telling which injury came first. As a result, at the end of the prosecution case the trial judge upheld a submission from the defence of 'no case to answer' on the murder charge, on the ground that there was another injury which may have been the sole cause of death. It would in these circumstances be impossible for the prosecution to prove beyond reasonable doubt that the injury caused by the accused was the cause of death. If, as was possible, the accused's act had occurred first, then the chain of causation between the act and the death could have been broken by the second injury.

If there is ever a case where it is unclear which act of a series of acts caused the harm, but all of the acts were committed by the accused, the above problem does not arise. There is no need for the prosecution to show which of the accused's acts caused the harm as long as it is clear that one of his acts did (*Attorney-General's Reference (No. 4 of 1980)**).

2.   *Lawful acts of third parties*
There are some circumstances when the act of a third party will not assume responsibility and it is necessary to look earlier in time to find the cause. This will occur where an act is not 'free, deliberate and informed'. The following are examples of where the acts of a third party will not break the chain of causation:

(a) **Lack of capacity.** If the third party lacks criminal capacity (for example he is insane or is below the age of criminal responsibility) his or her act will not break the chain of causation. In *Michael*, for example, the accused intended to kill her baby son. She gave his nurse a bottle of laudanum, telling her that it was medicine for the baby. The nurse put the bottle on one side, but her child, aged five, took the bottle and gave a large quantity of the laudanum to the baby, who died as a result. The mother's conviction for murder was upheld on appeal. Although two other people had acted in-between her, giving the bottle and the feed of the bottle to the baby, they were both 'innocent agents' (see Chapter 17) – the young child because she was below the age of criminal responsibility, and the nurse because she was completely unaware that the bottle was poisoned. Therefore their acts did not break the chain of causation and the mother could be said to have caused the death of the child.

(b) **Lack of *mens rea*.** If the third party has no *mens rea* and is unaware of the harm he or she is causing this will not break the chain of causation. For example, if Susan sends Anthony a poisoned chocolate cake through the post, the cake will be delivered by a post office worker. However, the postal deliverer will not be guilty of poisoning Anthony as he had no *mens rea*. If he was working in cahoots with Susan and was aware that the parcel was a poisoned cake then the result would be different, as he would be seen to have the *mens rea* and so can be said to have caused the death. Susan would then be his accomplice (see Chapter 18). In *Haystead v. Chief Constable of Derbyshire* the defendant deliberately pushed a woman. She dropped the baby she was carrying who hit his head on the floor. It was held that the defendant could be said to have caused the injuries to the child because the mother's act in dropping the baby was entirely accidental and was caused by the defendant. It could not be described as a free voluntary informed act.

(c) Defences. If the third party acts but is justified in so acting, this will not break the chain of causation. An example is the Court of Appeal decision in *Pagett*, where a defendant kidnapped his former girlfriend and was pursued by police officers. He fired a gun at the police officers while using the woman as a 'human shield'. The police fired back and unfortunately killed the women. The Court of Appeal decided that the defendant could be said to have caused the death of his former girlfriend. The police officer acted in self-defence, in pursuance of his legal duty, and so did not break the chain of causation. The court also argued that the police had acted 'involuntarily'; the accused caused them to fire and so could be held responsible for the consequences.

3. Medical treatment

There have been a number of cases where the defendant has tried to argue that the victim was killed not by the injury inflicted by the defendant, but by the bad medical treatment that he or she later receives. For example, in *Malcherek and Steel** the victim was so badly injured by the defendant that he had to be put onto a life-support system. Some time later, following normal medical practice, the doctors decided that the life-support machine should be switched off. The defendant tried to claim that he had not caused the death of the victim but that this had happened because of the doctor's act in switching off the life-support machine. Not surprisingly the court rejected this argument, saying that had the doctors not used the life-support machine the victim would have died quickly, and then the defendant would clearly have been guilty. A defendant cannot complain where the doctors try to save a patient but fail. The court applied the normal 'substantial and operating cause' test – the cause of the death was the wound inflicted by the defendant not just the lack of a life-support machine. Notably, had the machine been switched off by an intruder then the intruder could be said to have caused the victim's death and broken the chain of causation. There are two ways of explaining this. It may be that the doctors, in switching off the life-support machine, were acting in accordance with their legal duty and so did not break the chain of causation – in the same way that the police officers in *Pagett* in shooting were said to be carrying out their legal duty. Clearly an intruder would have no legal duty to switch off the machine and so his acts would be said to cause the death. A second possible explanation is that looking at the doctors' conduct as a whole they had first intervened to try and save the victim's life but had later taken away the assistance by switching off the life-support machine. This returned the victim to the same situation he would have been in had the doctors not intervened and the total effect of the doctors' actions was nothing. However, the same could not be said of the intruder who was not withdrawing help previously offered.

More difficult are cases where medical treatment provided by the hospital was inappropriate and caused death. In such cases the test is still whether the original wound was a 'substantial and operating cause (not necessarily the only or even main cause of death)' or whether the treatment 'was so independent of [the act of the accused], and in itself so potent in causing death, that [the jury] regard the contribution made by [the accused's] acts as insignificant' (*Cheshire*). So, for example, in *Jordan* the patient was recovering well from a stabbing and the wound had 'mainly healed' in hospital when he was given a drug to which he was allergic, despite the hospital having known of his intolerance. The patient's reaction to the drug was such that he died. The court called his medical treatment 'palpably wrong' and said that it broke the chain of causation. So the defendant did not cause the victim's death, although he would still be guilty of wounding him. However, *Jordan* seems to be an exceptional case and was referred to in *Smith*** as a 'very particular case depending on its exact facts'. The court in *Smith* went on to state 'only if it can be said that the original wound is merely the setting in which another cause operates can it be said that death does not result from the wound. Putting it another way, only if the second cause is so overwhelming as to make the original wound merely part of the history can it be said that it does not flow from the wound'. *Jordan* can be contrasted with the more recent case of *Cheshire* where the wound was so serious that the patient needed a tracheotomy. This was done negligently and it led to the victim's death. However, on this occasion the court decided that the defendant could still be said to have caused the death of the victim. The court argued that negligently wrong treatment is not completely abnormal (referring to Hart and Honoré's test mentioned above), and does necessarily break the chain of causation.

To summarize, it seems in cases where it is alleged that medical treatment has broken the chain of causation that the court will look at two issues:

1 How negligent or wrongful was the treatment?
2 Was the original wound still an operating and substantial cause?

Only if the treatment is manifestly wrong and the original wound no longer an operating and substantial cause of the injury will the medical treatment break the chain of causation. If the defendant's acts are a significant cause of death then the culpability of the doctors is irrelevant and should not be considered by the jury (*Mellor*).

As we have seen, the courts seem very reluctant to find that medical help can break the chain of causation. There may be two reasons behind this. Firstly, there is a feeling that it is no thanks to the defendant that the victim receives any medical help at all, and the defendant cannot really complain if it is not of the highest standard. Secondly, the courts are wary of turning a criminal trial into a trial of the doctors involved. The question of whether the doctors were negligent may be a suitable question in civil proceedings against the doctors, but their blameworthiness or otherwise is irrelevant when considering the criminal liability of the defendant.

5.4.2 Acts and Omissions of the Victim

It is important to distinguish between cases where it is argued that the victim does an act which is said to break the chain of causation and those which claim that the victim fails to do something and the omission is said to break the chain of causation.

1. Acts of the victim
Where the action of a victim contributes to his own death the law may accept that the victim's act breaks the chain of causation, but the law is often reluctant to do so. This is especially so in cases where the victim runs away from his attacker and in so doing injures himself (*DPP* v. *Dally and McGhie**). In *Roberts**, the defendant gave the victim a lift in his car, but started to molest her and she jumped out of the car, injuring herself. Stephenson LJ in upholding the defendant's conviction explained that if the action of the victim in trying to escape was reasonably foreseeable, then the accused may be held to have caused the resulting injuries. Here her response was reasonably foreseeable and so the defendant could be said to have caused the victim's injuries. On the other hand:

'if of course the victim does something so 'daft', . . . , or so unexpected, not that this particular assailant did not actually foresee it but that no reasonable man could be expected to foresee it, then it is only in a very remote and unreal sense a consequence of his assault, it is really occasioned by a voluntary action on the part of the victim which could not reasonably be foreseen and which breaks the chain of causation between the assault and harm or injury.'

The Court of Appeal in *Williams and Davis* slightly modified the *Roberts* test suggesting that the jury should consider:

'whether [the victim's act] . . . was within the range of responses which might be expected from a victim placed in the situation which he was. The jury should bear in mind any particular characteristic of the victim and the fact that in the agony of the moment, he may act without thought and deliberation . . .'

It should be stressed that the question is whether a reasonable person would have foreseen the way that the victim reacted, not whether the defendant foresaw the way that the victim reacted.

Even if the victim's reaction was unforeseeable it might still be held that the defendant's actions were a substantial and operating cause of the injury. So in *Dear*, where the victim made the wounds caused by the defendant worse by reopening them, the defendant was held to have caused the resulting death on the basis that the wounds inflicted by the accused were still operating and substantial. Less readily explained is *Kennedy** where the defendant was asked by the victim for some drugs. The defendant gave the victim a heroin-filled syringe and the victim injected himself. The victim died shortly after. Surprisingly the Court of Appeal held that the defendant could be said to have caused the death of the victim. Because the defendant had encouraged the victim to take the drugs their administration could be seen as a 'joint act'. The defendant could therefore be seen as a cause of the victim's death. Most commentators see this reasoning as misconceived. As the victim acted voluntarily in injecting himself, this free voluntary informed act broke the chain of causation.

2. Omissions of the victim

As we noted earlier, the criminal law is reluctant to ascribe responsibility for any act of omission. It follows that if a victim fails to seek treatment for a wound, the law would not find a break in the chain of causation. In *Holland*, the defendant failed to seek medical treatment for a wound which became infected and led to his death. The failure did not break the chain of causation. This is also the best explanation of *Blaue** in which the victim was stabbed and required a blood transfusion. She was a Jehovah's Witness and for religious reasons refused the blood transfusion. She in due course died. This refusal of treatment was an omission (that is a failure to consent to the treatment) and so did not break the chain of causation. The death was due to the stabbing of the victim by the defendant, not the refusal to consent to the transfusion. The decision is clearly correct. In *Blaue*, the victim died from the stab wounds inflicted by the defendant so it could hardly be said he was not an 'operating and substantial cause' of the victim's death.

3. *Condition of the victim*

In some cases the accused's actions may have unexpectedly serious consequences because of some pre-existing condition of the victim. The accused will be liable (provided she has *mens rea*) even though the condition was unknown to her and could not reasonably have been foreseen. This is sometimes known as the 'thin-skull rule'. You take your victim as you find him, whether he suffers from an unusually thin skull or from haemophilia, for example. In *Hayward*, the victim died after being chased into the street by her husband. She was found to have been suffering from an abnormality of the thyrus gland, and her husband was found guilty of manslaughter. Ridley J directed the jury that 'the abnormal state of the deceased's health did not affect the question, whether the prisoner knew or did not know of it, if it were proved . . . that the death was accelerated by the prisoner's illegal act'. In *Blaue*, the case with the Jehovah's Witness mentioned above, Lawton J argued, 'it has long been the policy of the law that those who use violence on other people must take their victims as they find them. This in our judgement means the whole man and not just the physical man'. So in *Blaue* the defendant had to take the victim as a Jehovah's Witness who would refuse a blood transfusion. The 'take your victim as you find her' argument is a little odd here as it should not really matter whether the victim became a Jehovah's Witness before or after the stabbing. Lawton J considered the argument that the appropriate test should be whether the victim acted in a reasonable way. However, he rejected this, pointing out:

> 'At once the question arises reasonable by whose standards? Those of Jehovah's Witnesses? Humanists? Roman Catholics/Protestants of Anglo-Saxon descent? The man on the Clapham omnibus?'

The case is best supported on the basis suggested above that the omission of the victim cannot break the chain of causation.

5.4.3 Acts of God

It may be that the defendant tries to claim that a freak occurrence of nature, or 'Act of God', broke the chain of causation. In *Pegrum*, it was said that an Act of God was 'an operation of natural forces so unpredictable as to excuse a defendant all liability for its consequences'. Of course, a defendant cannot claim that if he dropped a vase out of a second-floor window and the vase broke that he did not cause the damage to the vase but the law of nature (that is, gravity) did. However, if the Act of God was 'an abnormal and extraordinary' act (*Express Car Co* v. *NRA*) then the defendant might be able to claim that there was a break in the chain of causation. Thus, for example, if the defendant put a vase on a windowsill and it was struck by lightning, the argument would be more likely to succeed.

This is an area where the Hart and Honoré test of normality seems to work particularly well. However, policy factors can again be relevant. For example, a company was charged with a pollution offence (of allowing pig effluent to enter a river) and argued that they had not caused the pollution but that it had been caused by unusually high rainfall that had led to their lagoon of waste overflowing. This argument was rejected by the Divisional Court (*Pegrum*). The basis of the decision seems to be that the defendant company were engaging in an activity for profit which had the potential to pollute and therefore it should take all possible steps to ensure pollution did not occur, including taking precautions against highly unlikely occurrences. If the same rainfall had caused an individual's rotten manure heap to be transported over to a neighbour's garden, thereby killing his beloved plants, it may well be that the unusually high rainfall would be a break in the chain of causation. This is another example of policy factors affecting the rules of causation.

5.5 The Relevance of *Mens Rea* in Questions of Causation

It is, of course, quite possible that the person who causes a result is not to blame, for example because he was insane at the time. However, it is sometimes said that 'intended results are never too remote', subject to the 'but for' test. That is, if the defendant intentionally acts to produce a result, he cannot claim not to have caused that result unless the result would have occurred however he had acted. The idea here is that if a defendant acts hoping that the act will lead to a result then she will be said to cause that result, however peculiar the way in which the harm resulted from the defendant's act. To use an example above, if the accused put the vase on the windowsill hoping that it might be struck by lightning and amazingly it was, then he might be said to have caused that result. *Michael* is a good example from the caselaw of this principle at work. The mother intended that the baby be given the laudanum – the fact that it was given by the child rather than the nurse does not matter, given that her intended result occurred. It might be that here we see moral and policy considerations can become entangled in the questions of causation. If the defendant intended to cause an injury it would be understandable if the court was unsympathetic to an argument that he was not responsible for the consequence.

5.6   Reform of Causation

The draft criminal code suggests that:

'A person causes a result which is an element of an offence when
(a) he does an act which makes a more than negligible contribution to its occurrence; or
(b) he omits to do an act which might prevent its occurrence and which he is under a duty to do according to the law relating to the offence.

A person does not cause a result where, after he does such an act or makes such an omission, an act or event occurs
(a) which is the immediate and sufficient cause of the result;
(b) which he did not foresee, and
(c) which could not in the circumstances reasonably have been foreseen.'

These clauses are designed to largely replicate the present law. However, there are difficulties in that the 'reasonable foreseeability' test is not identical to the present law on third parties, where a third party's acts can break the chain of causation if it is 'free, voluntary and informed', even if unforeseeable (G. Williams, 1989).

Hot Topic: The Suicidal Rape Victim

A hypothetical case that has been much discussed in the academic literature is that of a victim raped by the defendant, who is so traumatized by the incident that she kills herself. Could the rapist be said to have caused the victim's death and be convicted of homicide? Three views could be taken:

1 One view is that the rapist must take his victim as he finds her. It is well established that a defendant who injures a victim cannot argue that the resulting death was caused by the victim's medical condition or physical frailty. If the defendant pushes over a person with a thin skull and she bangs her head,

breaks her skull and dies, then the defendant will be found to have caused the death. The Court of Appeal in *Blaue* held that this applies equally to psychological conditions and religious beliefs. The defendant there could not argue that it was the victim's religious beliefs that caused her death. He had to take the victim (the whole person) as her found her. In this hypothetical case it could be argued that the defendant had to take the victim with her propensity to commit suicide having been raped. He therefore can be said to have caused her death.

2 An alternative view is that the *Roberts* 'reasonable foreseeability test' should be applied. An analogy could be drawn between the woman jumping out of the car in *Roberts,* with the suicide in the hypothetical case. The question for the jury would therefore be whether the victim's suicide was a reasonably foreseeable consequence of the defendant's actions. It may be thought that the inevitable answer to this question would be 'no'. Only a tiny number of rape victims respond to the trauma of rape by committing suicide. However, this will not necessarily follow. First, remember the *Williams and Davis* modification to the *Roberts* test. Asking whether it was reasonably foreseeable that the victim (given her psychological condition) would respond to rape in this way may produce the answer 'yes'. Secondly, in *Roberts* it was asked whether the response was reasonably foreseeable *or* completely daft. Surely the suicide here could not be classified as 'daft' in which case maybe it should be regarded as reasonably foreseeable.

3 A third view is that the issue should be the extent to which the victim's acts are 'free, voluntary and informed'. There is 'but for' causation between the defendant's act and the death of the victim. So the question is whether there was a *novus actus interveniens*. In *Paggett*, it was confirmed that only the 'free voluntary and informed' act of a third party could break the chain of causation. It could be said that the act of suicide was not free or voluntary as it was committed while in a state of trauma (an analogy could be drawn with *Haystead*). In which case there was no *novus actus interveniens* and so the defendant caused the death.

It is difficult to predict which line of reasoning would be adopted by the court. Indeed there is caselaw which would support all three. This demonstrates the flexibility in the rules of causation which enables the courts to ensure that the rules of causation are able to achieve what is perceived to be 'the right result'. Whether or not that is desirable is, of course, a matter of much debate.

Summary

5.1 The question of causation raises complex moral and political questions about the extent to which we are responsible for our actions and the consequences of our actions. Although some cases have suggested that causation is a matter of common sense, the law has still formulated some rules to guide the jury.

5.2 The guiding rule for causation is to ask whether the defendant's act was an 'operating and substantial cause' of the consequence. If it was, then the defendant can be said to have caused the consequence. Simply because one act may also have been a 'substantial and operating cause' does not prevent any other act also being a cause.

5.3 If it can be said that had the defendant not acted in the way that he did the consequence would have occurred in exactly the same way that it did, then it cannot be said that the defendant caused that consequence.

5.4 An accused is assumed to be responsible for the consequences that flow from his acts unless another cause assumes responsibility and becomes a *novus actus interveniens*. A third party, an act of the victim or an act of God can be a *novus actus interveniens*.

5.5 If the defendant intends to produce a consequence then the law is likely to find that he caused the result, even if it occurred as a result of an unlikely set of events.

5.6 The Law Commission has proposed a straightforward formulation of the causation rules, but these proposals do not really resolve the difficult issues.

Case Notes

Attorney-General's Reference (No. 4 of 1980) [1981] 2 All ER 617. Court of Appeal

The Attorney-General asked the Court of Appeal for its opinion (under s.36 of the Criminal Justice Act 1972) on the following point of law: 'whether a person who has committed a series of acts against another, culminating in the death of that other person, each act in the series being either unlawful and dangerous or an act of gross criminal negligence, is entitled to be acquitted of manslaughter on the ground that it cannot be shown which of such acts caused the death of the deceased'. The accused was charged with manslaughter following the death of his fiancée. He gave evidence of a series of actions, any one of which might have been the direct cause of her death, but there was insufficient forensic evidence to prove which act had in fact caused the death. In the opinion of the court it was unnecessary to prove which act caused the death; the jury should have been directed to convict if they were satisfied that, whichever act killed the victim, each act was committed with the necessary fault element for manslaughter.

Blaue [1975] 3 All ER 466. Court of Appeal

The appellant was convicted of manslaughter on grounds of diminished responsibility. He had stabbed the victim, and in hospital she was told that a blood transfusion would be necessary to save her life. She refused a transfusion as being contrary to her beliefs as a Jehovah's Witness. She died; medical evidence at the trial indicated that if she had consented to a transfusion she would not have died. The appellant argued that causation was not established. The Court of Appeal dismissed the appeal, holding that the refusal of medical treatment on religious grounds did not break the chain of causation, as the rule that 'you take your victim as you find him' applies to the whole person and not just the physical person.

Cheshire [1991] 3 All ER 670. Court of Appeal

The defendant shot the victim who was taken to hospital. He required a tracheotomy that the doctors performed negligently and the patient died. The Trial Judge had suggested that the doctors' acts had broken the chain of causation if the jury decided that they had acted recklessly. The Court of Appeal suggested that the sole question for the jury was whether the defendant's acts were a substantial cause of death. If they were, he could be said to have caused the victim's death even though the doctors' mistreatment may also have contributed to the death.

DPP v. *Dally and McGhie* [1986] AC 237. Privy Council on appeal from the Court of Appeal of Jamaica
The accused were convicted of manslaughter and their convictions had been quashed by the Court of Appeal. The victim had been running away from the accused, who were attacking him by throwing stones at him. Lord Keith of Kinkel summed up what the prosecution needed to prove in a case of this kind:

> 'the essential ingredients . . . are (1) that the victim immediately before he sustained the injuries was in fear of being hurt physically; (2) that his fear was such that it caused him to try to escape; (3) that whilst he was trying to escape and because he was trying to escape he met his death; (4) that his fear of being hurt there and then was reasonable and was caused by the conduct of the defendant; (5) that the defendant's conduct which caused the fear was unlawful; (6) that his conduct was such as any sober and reasonable person would recognise as likely to subject the victim to at least the risk of some harm resulting from it, albeit not serious harm.'

The Privy Council reversed the decision of the Court of Appeal and restored the convictions and sentences.

Kennedy [1999] Crim LR 63. Court of Appeal
The appellant gave a syringe full of heroin to the victim. The victim injected himself with it. The victim died as a result. The appellant was convicted of manslaughter. He appealed on the ground that the victim has broken the chain of causation by injecting himself. The Court of Appeal dismissed his appeal, holding that because the defendant had 'wilfully encouraged' the victim to inject himself, the defendant's acts could be regarded as an operating and substantial cause of the victim's death.

Malcherek and Steel [1981] 2 All ER 422. Court of Appeal
The appellants were convicted of murder. In each case, the appellant had seriously injured a victim. The victims were both put on life-support machines, which were switched off when the victims were found to be dead, according to the medically accepted tests of brain death. The appellants argued that the juries in their respective cases had been misdirected on the issues of causation. The court held that switching off the life-support machines had not broken the chain of causation between the injuries and the death of the victims. The court approved the *dictum* of Lord Chief Justice Parker in *Smith* (see below), and was satisfied that the injuries were the operating cause of death. The court did not decide whether death occurred before or after the life-support machines were switched off, or which tests should be applied to determine death. Whichever tests were applied, the victims had died, and the medical treatment was 'normal and conventional', given *bona fide* by competent and careful medical practitioners. Evidence that other doctors might have acted differently did not affect the issue of causation. The appeals were dismissed.

Pagett (1983) 76 Cr App Rep 279. Court of Appeal
The appellant was convicted of manslaughter. He shot at police officers, using the victim as a shield against her will. The victim was hit by bullets shot in return by the police officers, and died. The court held that it was usually unnecessary to direct the jury on causation, it being enough to tell it that the act of the accused must have contributed significantly to the result. In this case, the intervention by the police officers did not break the chain of causation because it was not voluntary: it was a reasonable act of self-preservation. The appeal was dismissed.

Roberts (1971) 56 Cr App Rep 95. Court of Appeal
The appellant was convicted of an assault occasioning actual bodily harm, contrary to s.47 of the Offences Against the Person Act 1861. He had given the victim a lift in

his car and as a result of his advances she jumped out of the car while it was moving, and was injured. The court dismissed his appeal, holding that it is not a requirement under s.47 for the accused to have foreseen the actions of the victim that resulted in the actual bodily harm. The test was whether it was something that could reasonably have been foreseen, the 'natural consequence' of what the accused said and did. If the victim does something so unexpected that no reasonable person could be expected to foresee it, then the injury is caused by a voluntary act on the part of the victim, which breaks the chain of causation between the assault and the injury. The appeal was dismissed.

Smith [1959] 2 All ER 193. Courts-Martial Appeal Court

The appellant was convicted of murder. He had injured the victim in a fight in a barracks. The victim was dropped twice by a third man on the way to the medical station. On arrival, the seriousness of one of his wounds was not diagnosed and inappropriate treatment was given. He died. There was evidence that if the victim had received immediate and different treatment he might not have died. The court dismissed the appeal, distinguishing *Jordan*.

Further Reading

Hart and Honoré provide the leading analysis on causation. Bruder, Klimchuck and Norrie discuss some alternatives to their approach. Padfield and Shute discuss ambiguities within the present law.

Bruder, 'Owning Outcomes: On Intervening Causes, Thin Skulls, and Fault-undifferentiated Crimes' (1998) 11 *Canadian Journal of Law and Jurisprudence* 90.
Hart and Honoré, *Causation in the Law* (2nd edn, 1985, Oxford University Press).
Klimchuch, 'Causation, Thin Skulls and Equality' (1998) 11 *Canadian Journal of Law and Jurisprudence* 115.
Norrie, 'A Critique of Criminal Causation' (1991) 54 *Modern Law Review* 685.
Padfield, 'Clean Water and Muddy Causation' [1995] *Criminal Law Review* 683.
Shute, 'Causation: Forseeability v Natural Consequences' 55 *Modern Law Review* 584.
Williams, "*Finis* for *Novus Actus*" [1989] *Cambridge Law Journal* 391.

6 Strict and Vicarious Liability

Key words

- **Strict liability** – a crime in which a defendant can be convicted without proof of the defendant's state of mind.
- **Vicarious liability** – a crime in which the defendant can be convicted because of the acts of someone else.
- **Corporate liability** – the circumstances in which a company can be convicted of a criminal offence.

6.1   The Meaning of Strict Liability

'Strict liability' is the phrase used to refer to criminal offences that do not require *mens rea* in respect of one or more elements of the *actus reus*. They are nearly all offences created by statute. Although strict liability is sometimes said to be exceptional, in fact it has been estimated that over half of the criminal offences triable in the Crown Court require no proof of *mens rea* (Ashworth and Blake). The phrase 'absolute liability' is sometimes used, but this is misleading because it implies both that an offence of strict liability possesses no fault element at all and that it is not possible to plead a defence to such crimes, but neither of these suggestions is true. Often the statute itself will provide for a defence, such as a defence of 'due diligence' (the accused will be acquitted if he can show that he was not negligent) or the 'act of third party defence' (the accused attempts to show that the prohibited conduct or result was due to the act or default of a third party (see Chapter 5). It is also possible for the accused to plead a general defence if that defence is not a mere denial of *mens rea* (see Chapter 15.1). Examples would be self-defence or automatism, which deny either the unlawfulness of the *actus reus* or its voluntary nature, and so are not affected by the absence of *mens rea* in an offence of strict liability. That said, it was recently held that insanity is not a defence to a strict liability drink-driving offence, the argument being that insanity is a denial of *mens rea* (*Harper*). This is hard to accept as insanity is best seen as exemption of liability (see Chapter 15.1). The case may be explained by special policy reasons relating to road safety.

6.2   The Justifications for Strict Liability Offences

At first sight it seems unjust that people can be convicted of a criminal offence, even though they had no knowledge of the circumstances rendering their conduct unlawful. Indeed in some strict liability offences a person could be guilty even though he or she had behaved entirely reasonably. Can such offences be justified? Here are some of the possible explanations:

1. Protection of the public. The main justification of strict liability offences is that they protect the general public. It is significant that the nineteenth century saw a wider acceptance of strict liability by the courts alongside a considerable increase in legislation designed to protect people from dangers in the workplace and public places (see *Strict and Vicarious Liability* by Professor Leigh). In a decision of the House of Lords (*Lemon**), Lord Diplock explained:

> 'The usual justification for creating by statute a criminal offence of strict liability, in which the prosecution need not prove *mens rea* as to one of the elements of the *actus reus*, is the threat that the *actus reus* of the offence poses to public health, public safety, public morals or public order.'

Strict liability offences are most commonly found in statutes dealing with, for example, the sale of alcohol, food and drugs; the prevention of pollution; safety at work; and public health. The argument in favour of strict liability in these areas is that it ensures a company does everything it can to prevent there being, for example, any pollution or dangerous substances in food. The fear of a criminal conviction may encourage a company to take every step possible to ensure that it does not infringe the law. Just requiring a company to take 'reasonable steps' to prevent pollution may not be sufficient protection to the public as that might be interpreted to mean companies only need to do the minimum that is reasonable to prevent the harm. However, this argument can be countered: how will the punishment of a person who has taken all reasonable care, and so has not been negligent, encourage others to avoid liability by taking more care? Do we want people to take unreasonable steps to try and prevent harm?

2. Ease of proof. Strict liability offences are easier for the prosecution to prove. There is no need to produce evidence of the defendant's state of mind. All the prosecution need do to establish a case is prove that the defendant acted in a certain way. Requiring a court to find that the defendant knew certain fact makes cases more complex for the police to prepare and for courts to hear. Imagine that it was only possible to convict a motorist of a speeding offence if it was shown that he knew that he was driving over the speed limit. Making speeding a strict liability offence and only requiring proof that the car was being driven at excess speed makes the courts' and police's job so much easier. It is also notable that in the case of many strict liability offences, the defendant will be a corporation. As we shall see later, there can be great difficulty in finding that a company has *mens rea* and strict liability offences overcome this problem.

3. Strict liability offences not really criminal. Strict liability may also be justified in such cases by suggesting that strict liability offences are regulatory offences and not truly criminal. The argument is that there is no grave injustice if a person is convicted of a strict liability offence despite acting entirely reasonably because a conviction for a strict liability offence is not 'a real crime'. In *Sherras* v. *De Rutzen*, Wright J referred to strict liability offences as involving acts which 'are not criminal in any real sense, but acts which in the public interest are prohibited under a penalty'. However, there seems to be no objective criteria by which to differentiate between so-called true crimes (*mala in se*) and regulatory offences (*mala prohibita*). It is largely a matter of retrospective rationalization once the decision has been taken to impose strict liability: strict liability offences tend to be perceived as regulatory rather than truly criminal because they are sometimes committed without fault (see Richardson, 1987).

This alleged distinction between regulatory and truly criminal offences has no practical consequence relating to the procedures of trial or punishment. However, prosecution for some regulatory offences is carried out by a government agency rather than the police or Crown Prosecution Service. This can be significant as some regulatory agencies rarely prosecute and prefer to rely on negotiation and encouragement to enforce compliance with the law.

6.3   Construing Statutes which Appear to Impose Strict Liability

When courts are construing a statute which creates a criminal offence but does not state what the *mens rea* requirement is, the court must decide whether to imply a *mens rea* requirement or to treat the offence as one of strict liability. The law is governed by the presumption of *mens rea*, although this presumption can be rebutted.

6.3.1 The Presumption of *Mens Rea*

Two important recent decisions of the House of Lords (*B* v. *DPP* and *R* v. *K*) have emphasized the 'presumption of *mens rea*'. The presumption means that if there is any doubt over whether an offence requires *mens rea*, it should be presumed that it does. In other words there is a presumption against an offence being one of strict liability. This presumption is of relatively recent origin. The doctrine of *mens rea* evolved only gradually during the development of the common law, and the concept of subjective *mens rea*, which concentrates on the actual state of mind of the accused person, only developed once the accused was able to give evidence on his own behalf (the Criminal Evidence Act 1898; see Chapter 2).

The general presumption of *mens rea* was explained by Lord Nicholls in *B* v. *DPP*. In discussing cases where a statute did not explicitly state what the *mens rea* for an offence was, he stated:

'In these circumstances the starting point for a court is the established common law presumption that a mental element, traditionally labelled *mens rea*, is an essential ingredient unless Parliament has indicated a contrary intention either expressly or by necessary implication. The common law presumes that, unless Parliament indicated otherwise, the appropriate mental element is an unexpressed ingredient of every statutory offence.'

In *R* v. *K*, Lord Steyn appeared to go even further. He explained that the presumption does not only arise if the statute is silent or ambiguous as to any *mens rea* requirement. He stated:

'The applicability of this presumption is not dependent on finding an ambiguity in the text. It operates to supplement the text. It can only be displaced by specific language, i.e. an express provision or a necessary implication. In the present case there is no express provision displacing the presumption. The question is whether it is ruled out by a necessary implication.'

As a result of these decisions, an offence will be one of strict liability only if Parliament makes it quite clear in a statute that it is to be so.

But, if a *mens rea* is presumed, exactly what *mens rea* will that be? It appears from *B* v. *DPP* and *R* v. *K* that the defendant will have a defence if he believed that an aspect of the *actus reus* did not exist. So in *B* v. *DPP* the defendant was charged under section 1(1) of the Indecency with Children Act 1960 of inciting a girl under the age of 14 to commit an act of gross indecency with him. As the statute did not require any *mens rea* the House of Lords implied that the defendant would have a defence if he believed that the circumstances of the case were such that he was not committing an offence. Crucially here, the defendant would have a defence if he thought the girl in question was over 14. A fine distinction must be made. It does not have to be shown that the defendant was aware of the circumstances of the offence. What must be shown is that he did not believe that the circumstances were such that there was no offence. The distinction becomes important when considering a defendant who does not think about the age of the victim. In such a case he would be guilty under this rule.

Most controversially, their Lordships went on to hold that the defendant had a defence if he believed she was over 14, even if this was an unreasonable belief. Lord Nicholls rejected an argument that a belief had to be honest if it was to provide a defence, explaining:

'Considered as a matter of principle, the honest belief approach must be preferable. By definition the mental element in a crime is concerned with a subjective state of mind, such as intent or belief. To the extent that an overriding objective limit ("on reasonable grounds") is introduced, the subjective element is displaced. To that extent a person who lacks the necessary intent or belief may nevertheless commit the offence. When that occurs the defendant's "fault" lies exclusively in falling short of an objective standard. His crime lies in his negligence. A statute may so provide expressly or by necessary implication. But this can have no place in a common law principle, of general application, which is concerned with the need for a mental element as an essential ingredient of a criminal offence.'

6.3.2   Rebutting the Presumption of *Mens Rea*

The circumstances in which the presumption of *mens rea* will be rebutted is far from clear. The traditional approach of the courts has been summarized by Lord Scarman in *Wings Ltd* v. *Ellis*:

'at the end of the day the question whether an offence created by statute requires "*mens rea*", guilty knowledge or intention, in whole, or part, or not at all, turns on the subject matter, the language and structure of the Act studied as a whole, on the particular statutory provision under consideration construed in the light of the legislative purpose embodied in the Act, and on "whether strict liability in respect of all or any of the essential ingredients of the offence would promote the object of the provision".'

However recently the House of Lords has suggested that the presumption may be even stronger than this quote suggests. In *B* v. *DPP* the House of Lords indicated that the presumption of *mens rea* should only be rebutted if it is a *necessary* implication that Parliament intended the offence to be one of strict liability. The phrases used by their Lordships to indicate how strong the evidence had to be to rebut the presumption included: 'compellingly clear' (Lord Nicholls), 'sufficiently clear' (Lord Steyn) and 'necessary' (Lord Hutton and Lord Mackay).

The strength of the presumption is revealed by the decision in *R* v. *K*. The case involved the Sexual Offences Act, s.14:

'(1) It is an offence . . . for a person to make an indecent assault on a woman.

(2) A girl under the age of sixteen cannot in law give any consent which would prevent an act being an assault for the purposes of this section. . . .

(4) A woman who is a defective cannot in law give any consent which would prevent an act being an assault for the purposes of this section, but a person is only to be treated as guilty of an indecent assault on a defective by reason of that incapacity to consent, if that person knew or had reason to suspect her to be a defective.'

The case involved a man who had made an indecent assault on a 14-year-old. The defendant believed that the woman was over 16 and that she consented to the assault. The prosecution relied upon s.14(2) to show that as the victim was under fourteen she could not in law consent. Further it was no defence for the defendant to show he believed that the victim was over sixteen. The defence replied by relying on the presumption of *mens rea*, arguing that it should therefore be a defence if the defendant was unaware that the victim was under sixteen. The prosecution argued that the presumption could be rebutted because in s.14(4) (quoted above) the statute specifically provides that it is a defence if the defendant was not aware that the victim was a defective. The fact that s.14(2) does not include a similar provision indicates that Parliament did not intend a belief that the victim was over 16 to be a defence. Lord Steyn rejected that argument:

'Thus it is noteworthy that subsection (4) of section 14 but not subsection (2), makes specific provision, in the context of consent, for a defence of absence of *mens rea*. Nevertheless, I would hold that in the present case a compellingly clear implication can only be established if the supplementation of the text by reading in words appropriate to require *mens rea* results in an internal inconsistency of the text.'

This might suggest that only if there are words in the statute which specifically state that the defendant's mistaken belief will not provide a defence will the presumption be rebutted. However their other Lordships appear not to take such a straightforward approach. Lord Bingham undertook a detailed examination of the history of the Sexual Offences Act 1956. He pointed out that the Act was a consolidation statute. A consolidation statute is used where Parliament notes that there are a large number of statutes on the same theme (here sexual offences) and that it would be convenient to bring them all together in one Act. Lord Bingham noted that s.14 (2) had originated in one statute and s.14 (4) from another. It therefore did not necessarily follow that s.14(2) was intended by Parliament to be read in the light of s.14(4), which would be a natural implication had the statute not been a consolidation statute. Lord Mustill referred to public policy in deciding that the presumption applied. This might suggest that a court will take a more wide-ranging analysis when deciding whether the presumption is rebutted than just looking at the words.

In deciding whether the presumption of *mens rea* is rebutted, the courts will consider the following:

1. The wording of the statute
As is clear from *R* v. *K* and *B* v. *DPP*, the wording of the statute will be important. If the presumption is to be rebutted it now appears that there must be words in the statute indicating that the offence is to be strict. If the statute makes no mention of the defendant having a defence of mistake, it is very unlikely that the presumption will be rebutted. If there is some evidence in the statute that the offence is to be strict, the courts will consider the other factors.

2. The nature of the offence
The subject matter of the statute and the nature of the particular offence will be considered (*Sweet* v. *Parsley**). In *Alphacell Ltd* v. *Woodward*, the purpose of the statute (to prevent the pollution of rivers) was also stressed by the House of Lords. Lord Salmon said:

'If this appeal succeeded and it were held to be the law that no conviction could be obtained under the 1951 Act [the Rivers (Prevention of Pollution) Act 1951] unless the prosecution could discharge the often impossible onus of proving that the pollution was caused intentionally or negligently, a great deal of pollution would go unpunished and undeterred to the relief of many riparian factory owners. As a result many rivers which are now filthy would become filthier still and many rivers which are now clean would lose their cleanliness. The legislature no doubt recognised that as a matter of public policy this would be most unfortunate.'

The interpretation of drug offences also illustrates the importance of the subject matter of the offence. The House of Lords considered the issue of strict liability for the first time in a case involving the possession of controlled drugs (*Warner* v. *Metropolitan Police Commissioner**). The appellant had been convicted of possessing a controlled drug found in a box in his possession; he claimed that he did not know that the box contained the drug and that he had thought it contained perfume. Lord Reid, who was in a minority in the House of Lords, took the view that this was a 'truly criminal and disgraceful offence, so that a stigma would attach to a person convicted of it', and for this reason held that the offence should require knowledge on the part of the accused that he had prohibited drugs in his possession (not necessarily knowledge as to the precise drug). However, the majority held that this degree of *mens rea* was not required; as long as the accused knew that he possessed something there was no need to prove that he knew he had a prohibited drug. Lord Pearce thought that the 'efficacy of the Act' would be seriously impaired if it were to be held that the accused must know the nature of the drug concerned.

The case of *Sweet* v. *Parsley** also concerned drug offences, but in this instance the House of Lords was prepared to interpret the definition of the offence so as to include an element of *mens rea*. Lord Reid relied on the general presumption of *mens rea* as stated in *Tolson*; he held that in order to displace this presumption, the court should consider, in addition to the subject matter of the statute, the stigma attaching to conviction for this 'truly criminal offence': 'whether, in a case of this gravity, the public interest really requires that an innocent person should be prevented from proving his innocence in order that fewer guilty men may escape' (note that it is begging the question to refer here to 'an innocent person'). Lord Reid added that the court should also take into account that such a conviction may be perceived as unjust, 'and every manifestly unjust conviction made known to the public tends to injure the body politic by undermining public confidence in the justice of the law and of its administration'.

3. Profits-making activities

The imposition of strict liability may be more justifiable where the defendant is engaging in a profit-making activity which creates hazards for the public, than for 'the conduct of ordinary citizens in the running of their everyday life' (Lord Diplock in *Sweet* v. *Parsley*).

4.   Seriousness of the offence

There is some dispute over the relevance of the seriousness of the crime in deciding whether the offence is one of strict liability. Some cases suggest that the less serious the offence, the more likely the crime was intended by Parliament to be one of strict liability (*Alphacell Ltd* v. *Woodward*). However, in other cases the seriousness of the crime is seen as a reason in favour of imposing strict liability. In *Howells*, a case concerning possession of a firearm, the court stated:

> 'the danger to the community resulting from the possession of lethal firearms is so obviously great that an absolute prohibition against their possession without proper authority must have been the intention of Parliament when considered in conjunction with the words of the section.'

Lord Nicholls in *B* v. *DPP* appeared to prefer the earlier view, stating:

> 'The more serious the offence, the greater is the weight to be attached to the presumption, because the more severe is the punishment and the graver the stigma which accompany a conviction.'

The fact that imprisonment is available as a sentence does not necessarily indicate that the offence is not regulatory (*Blake* (1997)).

5.   Ensuring compliance

The Privy Council has held that courts should consider whether the imposition of strict liability will be effective in encouraging 'greater vigilance to protect the commission of the prohibited act' (*Gammon* v. *Attorney-General for Hong Kong*). However, it might be thought that imposing liability only if the defendant has failed to take reasonable steps (that is negligence-based liability) would fulfil this function.

6.   Justice and public interest

In *R* v. *K* Lord Steyn argued that the courts could take into account the public interest in deciding whether offence should be strict. He said it was not in the public interest that sexual acts involving anyone under 16 would automatically be a criminal offence. He did not say what the public interest was though. Lord Millet preferred to talk in terms of justice. He thought it would be unjust to convict a defendant of a sexual offence who honestly believed that the victim was over sixteen and was consenting.

6.4   The Future of Strict Liability

What is the future of strict liability? It is clear following *R* v. *K* and *B* v. *DPP* that in the courts the balance is tilted against the imposition of strict liability. Following those cases, if Parliament wants to create a strict liability offence the statute has to make it quite clear that this is what Parliament intended.

6.5   Alternatives to Strict Liability

Over the years, various alternatives to the rigours of strict liability have been suggested. Two in particular were mentioned by Lord Reid in *Sweet* v. *Parsley* and have attracted adherents. The first is to require *mens rea* for the offence, but to transfer the burden of proof to the accused, so that once the *actus reus* of the offence is proved, the burden of disproving *mens rea* lies on the defence. In *Sweet* v. *Parsley*, Lord Pearce favoured this approach, referring to it as a 'sensible half-way house', although he conceded that there may be difficulty in reconciling it with the opinion of Viscount Sankey in *Woolmington** (which puts the burden of proving every element of an offence on the prosecution; see Chapter 2.4).

The second possibility mentioned by Lord Reid would be to substitute negligence for '*mens rea* in the full sense'. Instead of having to prove intention, or knowledge or recklessness, the prosecution would merely have to prove that the accused was negligent. A variation of this comes from *Tolson*, and is sometimes referred to as the 'defence' of a reasonable mistake of fact. Lord Diplock in *Sweet* v. *Parsley* preferred this option, and explained that it involved:

'the implication that a necessary element in the offence is the absence of a belief, held honestly and upon reasonable grounds, in the existence of facts which, if true, would make the act innocent . . . This implication stems from the principle that it is contrary to a rational and civilised criminal code, such as Parliament must be presumed to have intended, to penalise one who has performed his duty as a citizen to ascertain what acts are prohibited by law (*ignorantia iuris non excusat* [ignorance of the law is no excuse]) and has taken all proper care to inform himself of any facts which would make his conduct unlawful.'

Professor Hogan has used more direct language: 'a provision which labels criminal a man who has taken all reasonable care to stay on the right side of the law is, on the face of it, just plain daft' (Hogan, 1978).

In the Draft Criminal Code (clause 24) there is a presumption that liability depends on fault (intention, knowledge or recklessness) unless a contrary intention appears from the terms of the enactment, which may specify a different fault element or that no fault element is required. If this proposal were implemented, the present high level of uncertainty over the interpretation of the fault element in criminal offences would be reduced by restricting the courts to considering the words of the statute itself: they would no longer be able to refer to the public interest, the nature of the offence or the type of penalty imposed in order to decide whether the offence is one of strict liability. Some flexibility would be sacrificed for a considerable increase in consistency and certainty.

6.6   Vicarious Liability

Normally a person is not liable in criminal law for the acts of another. Vicarious liability is an exception to this rule and can be regarded as a form of constructive liability, as the act, and in some cases even the *mens rea*, of another person are imputed to the defendant. When vicarious liability applies, the accused's conviction does not rest on anything done or omitted by him, but on the acts and mental state of another. Vicarious liability can therefore be distinguished from accessorial liability (see Chapter 17) where the defendant is liable for helping someone else commit a crime.

English law lacks a comprehensive and coherent set of rules on vicarious liability, and the report on the Draft Criminal Code says of the cases on the subject, 'there is no principle underlying these cases. Their existence is simply the product of statutory interpretation'. In *Seaboard Offshore* v. *Secretary of State for Transport* the House of Lords confirmed that whether vicarious liability can be relied upon depends on the wording of the statute and whether vicarious liability is necessary to give effect to legislation. Although usually vicarious liability operates where the offence is one of strict liability, it is not limited to such crimes (for example *Tesco* v. *Brent* and *Re Supply of Ready Mixed Concrete* (2)).

If the offence is found to be one where vicarious liability operates then the accused is responsible for anyone employed by her, or authorized to act on her behalf as an agent. An employer is only vicariously liable for an employee who is acting within the scope of her employment. For example, a chauffeur who uses his employer's vehicle as a getaway car for a robbery would be acting outside the scope of employment.

Why is there a need for vicarious liability? Why not merely prosecute the actor himself? There are many different reasons for wishing to prosecute the employer. The offence may be one which can only be committed by the employer, as for example where he is the holder of a licence and the offence is one which can only be committed by a licensee. It may also be very difficult to prove fault on the part of the employer, so the *actus reus* and *mens rea* of the employee are relied on. Or it may be that for policy reasons the employer is regarded as the appropriate target. *Coppen* v. *Moore*, for example, concerned the selling of goods under a false trade description (selling American ham as 'Scotch ham'). Lord Russell CJ held that the owner of a shop who had given express instructions that the ham was not to be sold under any specific name or place of origin was liable for the actions of his assistant:

> 'When the scope and object of the Act are borne in mind, any other conclusion would to a large extent render the Act ineffective for its avowed purposes . . . The appellant . . . carries on an extensive business as grocer and provision dealer, having, it appears, six shops or branch establishments, and having also a wholesale warehouse. It is obvious that, if sales with false trade descriptions could be carried out in these establishments with impunity as far as the principal [the appellant] is concerned, the Act would to a large extent be nugatory.'

This justification put forward by the Lord Chief Justice is similar to the claims of 'public interest' relied on by the judges in imputing strict liability (see Chapter 6.1 above). In a case such as the one just cited, the definition of the offence may include a word (such as 'sells' or 'uses') which seems to apply only to the employee. Here the courts hold that the act of the employee can be imputed to the employer; it becomes the employer's act. In *Coppen* v. *Moore*, Lord Russell said 'it cannot be doubted that the appellant sold the ham in question, although the transaction was carried out by his servants. In other words, he was the seller, although not the actual salesman'. In these cases, where the act of the employee or agent becomes that of the employer or principal, *mens rea* must be proved against the employer if it is required by the particular offence. It is only the act, and not the *mens rea*, that is imputed.

In another line of cases, the courts have been prepared to go further. In cases involving licences (for the sale of alcohol, for example) a different principle has been developed, based on delegation. Employers without any *mens rea* have been held liable on the basis of the *actus reus* and *mens rea* of the employee to whom authority has been delegated. If a licensee could escape liability by simply leaving the premises and putting an employee in charge, the licensing system would be largely ineffective. It has been stressed that vicarious liability on this basis will only operate if the delegation of management must be complete; the principle will not apply if the employee is merely 'acting behind the back of the licensee', according to Lord Parker CJ in *Winson**. In *Allen* v. *Whitehead*, the offence in question was 'knowingly permitting or suffering prostitutes to meet together on premises', in this case a refreshment house. The licensee was held to be liable although he did not know of the prostitutes' presence, because the manager who ran the house for him had the requisite knowledge. Lord Hewart CJ said:

'he had transferred to the manager the exercise of discretion in the conduct of the business, and it seems to me that the only reasonable conclusion is, regard being had to the purposes of this Act, that knowledge in the manager was knowledge in the keeper of the house.'

In *Vane* v. *Yiannopoullos*, some members of the House of Lords doubted this principle. Lord Reid referred to it as a 'long-standing anomaly' and refused to extend it to cases where the delegation of authority was only partial (in this case, a waitress had sold wine contrary to the conditions of a restaurant licence while the accused, the licence holder, was on the premises). Lord Donovan said that if the statutory offence contained the world 'knowingly', then actual knowledge on the part of the licensee should be required; the prosecution should not be able to rely on the knowledge of an employee to whom authority has been delegated. If this makes the statute difficult to enforce, Lord Donovan felt that 'the remedy lies with the legislature'. However, in *Winson* the principle was affirmed by the Court of Appeal in cases of complete delegation. Lord Parker CJ said that the doctrine of delegation had been applied in a number of licensing cases, and that:

'the principle of those cases was that a man cannot get out of the responsibilities and duties attached to a licence by absenting himself. The position of course is quite different if he remains in control. It would be only right that he should not be liable if a servant behind his back did something which contravened the terms of the licence. If, however, he wholly absents himself leaving somebody else in control he cannot claim that what has happened has happened without his knowledge if the delegate has knowingly carried on in contravention of the licence.'

The Law Commission's Draft Criminal Code abolishes this rule, in so far as it applies to *mens rea*. In the Draft Code, vicarious liability would only operate to impute to the accused the acts, and not the *mens rea*, of an employee or agent unless the statute defining an offence provided otherwise (Clause 33). The *mens rea* or fault element specified in the offence would have to be proved against the accused herself. The Code also states that vicarious liability applies where the other is 'acting in the scope of his employment or authority and the definition of the offence specifies the element in terms which apply to both persons' (Clause 29).

6.7   The Criminal Liability of Corporations

There has been increasing interest in recent years in finding companies guilty of crimes. This has been particularly so in the light of several large-scale disasters, for example the distressing number of railway crashes in recent years, the Zeebrugge ferry disaster, the King's Cross fire, and the Pipa Alpha explosion, to name but a few. In such cases awarding civil law damages (where possible) seems inadequate when gross misconduct by the company appears to warrant the censure of a criminal conviction. In some disaster cases the deaths may have occurred because of the way the company was structured and managed, and because of the company's general ethos towards safety, rather than the fault of any particular individual. In such a case, punishing the company itself seems more appropriate than punishing one or two of its employees.

There is, however, great difficulty in treating the company as a defendant within the traditional concepts that define a crime. The law recognizes that the company is a legal person, separate from its directors or shareholders, but the problem is in what way can we say that a company acts? Or has *mens rea*?

There are two possible solutions to this. The first is for Parliament to legislate specific criminal offences designed with companies in mind. One example is s.18 of the Theft Act 1968:

'(i) Where an offence committed by a body corporate under section 15, 16 or 17 of this Act is proved to have been committed with the consent or connivance of any director, manager, secretary or other similar officer of the body corporate, or any person who was purporting to act in any such capacity, he as well as the body corporate shall be guilty of that offence . . .'

The alternative approach is to try to manipulate current notions of *mens rea* and *actus reus* so that they can apply to companies. The courts have been attempting to do this, and various techniques have been proposed:

1.   Vicarious liability
As we have seen, this notion can mean that if an employee of the company,

acting within the terms of his employment, commits a crime then the company is criminally responsible for his actions. This is a useful doctrine as it avoids any difficulty in proving that a company has *mens rea* or has performed an *actus reus*. The key point in vicarious liability is that the *mens rea* and *actus reus* of another are assigned to the defendant. Although the doctrine makes the conviction of corporations easier it makes a company liable for the acts within the scope of employment of any employee, however junior or wayward. Some see this as extending corporate liability too far; others argue that it too easily enables a company to escape liability for the wayward actions of employees, by arguing that they were not acting within the scope of their employment.

2.   *Identification*

Under this doctrine, certain employees of the company are seen as having sufficient standing within the corporation to be identified as part of the corporation. Their actions and *mens rea* can be see as representing that of the company. In *Tesco* v. *Nattrass**, Lord Reid affirmed the principle:

> 'A corporation . . . must act through living persons, though not always one or the same person. Then the person who acts is not speaking or acting for the company. He is acting as the company and his mind which directs his acts is the mind of the company. There is no question of the company being vicariously liable. He is not acting as a servant, representative, agent or delegate. He is an embodiment of the company or, one could say, he hears and speaks through the persona of the company, within his appropriate sphere, and his mind is the mind of the company. If it is a guilty mind then that guilt is the guilt of the company.'

The last sentence of this passage makes it clear that the principle may be used even in cases where liability is not strict, and so may include liability as an accessory and for inchoate offences such as conspiracy. In such cases it must be shown that an individual representing the company had the *mens rea* required for the offence (*Attorney-General's Reference* (No. 2 of 1999)*).

Which officers of the company are to be regarded as the 'directing mind and will' of the company? Although Lord Reid held that this was a matter of law, the cases do not give very clear guidance. A recent House of Lords' case has suggested that the use of the identification theory depends on the interpretation of the particular statute. So in one statute it may be that only the acts of the board of directors could be seen as of sufficient seniority to count as the 'mind and will' of the company, while in another statute any full-time employee's acts might be attributed to a company (*Meridian*

Global Funds Management Asia Ltd v. *Securities Commission**). As Lord Hoffman stated:

> 'a court must fashion a special rule of attribution for the particular substantive rule. This is always a matter of interpretation: given that it was intended to apply to a company how was it intended to apply? Whose act (of knowledge or state of mind) was for this purpose intended to count as act etc. of the company? One finds the answer to this question by applying the usual canons of interpretation, taking into account the language of the rule (if it is a statute) and its content and policy.'

Even if the employee who performs the *actus reus* is not the 'mind and will' of the company, it may be that the company is still liable if the management (who are the 'mind and will' of the company) have failed to install adequate safety procedures and ensure that its employees abide by them (*Seaboard Offshore Ltd* v. *Secretary of State for Transport*). The identification theory works well where the company is very small. The one reported successful prosecution for corporate manslaughter has been that of a company, which was, in effect, a one-person company arranging canoeing holidays (*Kite and OLL Ltd*). It works less well when there is a large company where there is no one person that can be pointed to as having the necessary mental state for the crime. The next theory, the aggregation theory, tries to deal with this difficulty.

3. The aggregation theory

The theory is that the court can aggregate the mental states and actions of the employees of the company, and if together they provide sufficient *mens rea* for the crime then the company can be convicted, even though no one employee had the complete *mens rea*. This can be linked with the identification theory just discussed, to mean that only the acts and states of mind of those who are the 'mind and will' of the company can be aggregated. So, for example, if it could be shown that one director was aware that a particular piece of machinery was made of below-standard materials, another aware that there had been some near accidents with the machinery in the past, and yet another aware that the operators of the machinery often did not wear their protective clothing because it was too hot, then together these pieces of information may be sufficient to form a case of gross negligence manslaughter against the company if a worker was subsequently killed using the machinery, even though no one director had sufficient knowledge for a conviction. Although this theory has received some support among academics, the aggregation theory was rejected in *R* v. *HM Coroner for East Kent ex p Spooner*. Bingham LJ said that as the law does not permit the conviction of an individual person to be based on aggregating other people's *mens rea*, the same should be true for a company. This rejection of the aggregation theory was confirmed by the Court of Appeal in *Attorney-General's Reference* (No. 2 of 1999)*. So the present law requires a senior employee, representing the 'mind and will' of the company, to have the necessary *mens rea* for the crime if the company is to be convicted of the offence.

Hot Topic: Reforming Corporate Liability

Much controversy surrounds the criminal liability of companies. Some argue that the law adequately deals with corporate wrongdoing through regulation. That is, through inspections and investigations of executive regulatory bodies such as the Health and Safety Executive. These bodies tend to rely more on negotiation and persuasion than prosecution, and it is said such an approach can be more productive in raising safety standards than the combative criminal process. Others argue that the criminal law rests on the assumption that a defendant is a responsible agent and that a company itself cannot be seen as being morally responsible for its actions – it cannot itself change its behaviour. It is therefore argued that it is quite proper to punish individuals within the company who have behaved criminally, but to punish the company itself is to weaken the censuring function of the criminal law. Those who oppose criminal liability for companies stress the availability of civil actions that can be brought to obtain compensation for the victims of corporate wrongdoing.

However, these voices of opposition to corporate criminal liability are in a minority. Many commentators see the regulation procedure as an inadequate response to the number of deaths at the workplace, and argue for the need of the censure attached to a criminal conviction to be available to companies, at least when deaths have resulted. With public attention drawn to the issue through the large-scale disasters mentioned earlier, pressure has grown on the government to reform the law. The government has produced a document entitled *Reforming the Law on Involuntary Manslaughter: The Government's Proposals* (2000). The document has proposed a special crime of corporate manslaughter:

'(1) A corporation is guilty of corporate killing if
    (a) a management failure by the corporation is the cause or one of the causes of a person's death; and
    (b) that failure constitutes conduct falling far below what can reasonably be expected of the corporation in the circumstances.
(2) For the purposes of subsection (1) above –
    (a) there is a management failure by a corporation if the way in which its activities are managed or organised fails to ensure the health and safety of persons employed in or affected by those activities; and
    (b) such a failure may be regarded as a cause of a person's death notwithstanding that the immediate cause is the act or omission of an individual.'

It should be noted that this offence moves away from the identification doctrine and instead focuses on management. This means that it is not necessary to demonstrate that an individual has the *mens rea* necessary for a manslaughter conviction, what matters is the standard of the management and its structure.

Indeed there is no *mens rea* requirement at all. The offence is one of negligence. The court would ask whether the standards of safety shown by the defendant company were far below those that could be expected of a company working in a similar field. It would mean, for example, that the prosecution could argue the very fact that none of the managers was aware that the business was posing a danger to other people was in itself an indication that there was a management failure. It should also be noted that if a wayward individual employee behaves negligently and is to blame for causing the killing, it would still be open to argue that there was a management failure (for example, in not ensuring the employee was adequately supervised or trained). In relation to that example it should be noted that the management only needs to be a cause, not the cause of the killing. The causation requirement also demonstrates that even if a company's management is shown to have no regard to safety at all, it must still be shown that the management failure *caused* the killing. If in fact the killing would have occurred even in the best run company, the causal requirement would not be made out and the defendant company would have to be acquitted.

One key problem for corporate liability is the punishment. The proposals suggest a fine as most appropriate. Critics argue that a significant fine is likely to lead to loss of employment and wage cuts. No doubt the actual managers would be able to ensure they did not personally suffer greatly. Other possibilities such as 'capital punishment' for the company (closing it down) or 'imprisonment' (not allowing it to operate for a period of time) could have similar harmful effects on employees.

Summary

6.1 A strict liability offence is one where it is not necessary for the prosecution to prove any *mens rea*.

6.2 Judges have justified the imposition of strict liability by referring to public policy and effective enforcement of the law. Some strict liability offences are described as regulatory or quasi-criminal.

6.3 If it is not absolutely clear from the statute that an offence is to be one of strict liability, the courts will presume a *mens rea*. This *mens rea* will be that it will be a defence for the accused to demonstrate that he believed an element of the *actus reus* did not exist. In interpreting a statute and deciding whether the presumption of *mens rea* should be displaced and strict liability imposed, the courts will look to the words of the statute; the subject matter of the offence; whether the imposition of strict liability would make compliance to the statute more likely; and the public interest involved.

6.4 If Parliament wishes to create a strict liability offence it must make it absolutely clear in the wording of the statute that liability for the offence is to be strict.

6.5 As alternatives to strict liability, Parliament could pass a statute creating a negligence-based defence or alter the burden of proof.

6.6 Vicarious liability involves holding one person liable for the acts of another. The acts of an agent or an employee, acting within the scope of his employment, may be imputed to the principal or employer. If the offence requires *mens rea*, then the employer must be shown to possess the necessary state of mind, such as knowledge. In other cases, where there has been a complete delegation of authority, both the acts and the state of mind of the employee have been imputed to the employer.

6.7   Corporations are legal persons. They may be liable for any criminal offence that is punishable by a fine, and manslaughter. Corporations are subject to the rules of vicarious liability. In addition, a corporation will be liable for the acts of those employees of the company who are said to act as personifications of the company.

Case Notes

Attorney-General's Reference (No. 2 of 1999) [2000] Crim LR 475. Court of Appeal

The case concerned a train crash at Southall where seven people were killed and many injured. The operator of one of the trains was indicted for manslaughter, but the trial judge ruled that gross negligence manslaughter required a guilty mind and that an individual in the company had to be found with that guilty mind to secure a conviction for corporate manslaughter. The Court of Appeal confirmed that in order to secure a conviction for gross negligence manslaughter it was not necessary to show that the defendant had foreseen death. However in order to convict it was necessary to show an identifiable individual within the company who had the *mens rea* required for the offence.

B v. DPP [2000] Crim LR 403. House of Lords

The appellant was aged 15. He was convicted of inciting a girl under 14 to commit an act of gross indecency by persistently asked her to perform oral sex on him. The key issue was whether it would be a defence if the appellant believed the girl to be over the age of 14. The House of Lords noted that s.1(1) of the Indecency with Children Act 1960 was silent as the *mens rea* requirement. They stated that the starting point was that unless Parliament expressly or by necessary implication has indicated that there was to be no *mens rea*, there was a presumption that the offence had a *mens rea* requirement. There was nothing in the Indecency with Children Act to rebut this presumption. This meant that it would be a defence for the appellant if he honestly believed that the girl was over 14. He did not need to show that this belief was based on reasonable grounds.

R v. K 25 JULY 2001; [2001] UKHL 41. House of Lords

The appellant was charged with a sexual assault on a fourteen-year-old girl. He was unaware that she was fourteen and believed that she had consented to the sexual activities. The House of Lords held that it was a defence to a charge under s.14 Sexual Offences Act 1956 for the defendant to demonstrate that he honestly believed the victim to be over fourteen and that she consented. Such a belief did not need to be reasonable.

Lemon [1979] AC 617. House of Lords

The appellant was convicted of blasphemous libel. He was the editor of a magazine, *Gay News*, in which a poem had been printed, which was found to be blasphemous. The trial judge directed the jury that it was necessary for the prosecution to prove that the accused had intended to publish the poem, but that it was not necessary to prove that the accused had any intention to publish blasphemous material. The appellant argued that it was necessary to prove an intention to blaspheme: to outrage and insult the religious feelings of a Christian. The Court of Appeal and House of Lords dismissed the appeal. The House of Lords approved the direction of the trial judge that an intention to blaspheme was not a necessary part of the offence, as long as there was an intent to publish material which was in fact blasphemous.

Meridian Global Funds Management Asia Ltd v. *Securities Commission* [1995] 2 AC 500. Privy Council

Unknown to the board of directors, the chief investment officer and senior portfolio manager of an investment management company bought shares without giving notice as required by legislation. The Privy Council considered whether the individuals' acts could be attributed to the company and said, in deciding whose acts represented the 'mind and will' of the company, that the court should consider the company's constitution and company law. Sometimes the courts can consider the legislation in question and construe it to decide whose acts should be attributed to the company. In this particular case it was decided that the individuals' conduct could be attributed to the company, even though this would not generally be described as the 'mind and will' of the company, as to do so was necessary to give effect to the policy behind the legislation.

Sweet v. *Parsley* [1970] AC 132. House of Lords

The appellant was convicted of being concerned in the management of premises used for the purpose of smoking cannabis, contrary to s.5(b) of the Dangerous Drugs Act 1965. She had let rooms in a farmhouse to tenants; at first she also lived in the house, but after some time she ceased to do so. She did not know that cannabis was being smoked on the premises. Her conviction was quashed on the ground that this was not a strict liability offence: the word 'purpose' in the definition referred to the purpose of the management of the premises. There is a presumption that offences created by statute contain an element of *mens rea*, unless it appears that it must have been the intention of Parliament to create a strict liability offence.

Tesco v. *Nattrass* [1972] AC 153. House of Lords

The appellant company was convicted of an offence under the Trade Descriptions Act 1968. It relied on a statutory defence to the effect that the commission of the offence was due to the act or default of another person: in this case, the manager of the shop concerned. The magistrates took the view that the shop manager was not 'another person' within the meaning of the Act. The House of Lords allowed the appeal, on the ground that the manager of the shop could not be said to be acting as the embodiment of the company. Not all those who exercise some managerial discretion represent the company's directing mind and will, and speak and act as the company. The shop manager did not come within this category of superior officer: he was merely the servant or agent of the company and did not carry out the functions of management. There had been no delegation of control to him by the board of directors; he had to obey general directions and take orders. The company was therefore entitled to rely in its defence on the act or default of the manager as 'another person'.

Warner v. *Metropolitan Police Commissioner* [1969] 2 AC 256. House of Lords

The appellant was convicted of possessing unauthorized drugs contrary to s.1 of the Drugs (Prevention of Misuse) Act 1964. He had been found with two cases, one of which contained a quantity of amphetamine tablets and the other containing bottles of scent. He claimed that he had collected them from another man at a café, and thought that both cases contained bottles of scent. The jury was directed that lack of knowledge of the contents of the cases was no defence, if it was proved that the accused had control of the cases themselves. The House of Lords held that the jury had been misdirected, but dismissed the appeal on the ground that no miscarriage of justice had occurred as a properly directed jury would have been bound to find the appellant guilty. It was held that the offence under s.1 did not require any specific mental element. However, it did require possession, and it was not possible for a person to possess something when he did not know of its existence. Where the drugs were in a container, it was necessary to prove that the appellant possessed not only the case but also its contents. If the appellant had been completely mistaken as to the contents of the case then he could not be in possession of those contents, although ignorance as to the precise qualities of the contents would be no excuse. However, their Lordships thought that this exception did not assist the defendant in this case.

Winson [1969] 1 QB 371. Court of Appeal
The appellant was convicted of an offence under the Licensing Act 1964. He was the director of a company that owned a club, and the holder of a licence to sell alcoholic drinks at the club. Drinks were sold in breach of the terms of the licence. The club was run by a manager and visited from time to time by the appellant. His appeal was dismissed on the ground that he had delegated complete control to the manager and could not therefore rely on the claim that the breach of the licence was committed without his knowledge, as the knowledge of the manager was imputed to the appellant. If, however, he had remained in control and his servant then committed a breach of the licence without his knowledge, he would not have been liable.

Woolmington [1935] AC 462. House of Lords
See Chapter 2 case notes.

Further Reading

The leading work on corporate liability is Wells. The controversy over corporate liability is revealed by reading Braithwaite and Fisse, Clarkson, Gobert, Hawkins and Thomas, and Sullivan. Strict and vicarious liability is discussed in Ashworth and Blake, Honoré, Leigh and Richardson,

Ashworth and Blake, 'The Presumption of Innocence in English Criminal Law' [1996] *Criminal Law Review* 306.
Braithwaite and Fisse, 'The Allocation of Responsibility for Corporate Crime' (1988) 11 *Sydney Law Review* 468.
Clarkson, 'Kicking Corporate Bodies and Damning Their Souls' (1996) 59 *Modern Law Review* 557.
Gobert, 'Corporate Criminality: New Crimes for the Times' [1994] Criminal Law Review 722.
Hawkins and Thomas (eds), *Enforcing Regulation* (1984, Oxford University Press).
Hogan, 'Strict Liability' [1978] *Criminal Law Review* 593.
Honoré, 'Responsibility and Luck' (1988) 104 *Law Quarterly Review* 530.
Leigh, *Strict and Vicarious Liability* (1982, Sweet & Maxwell).
Richardson, 'Strict Liability for Regulatory Crime' [1987] *Criminal Law Review* 295.
Sullivan, 'Corporate Killing – Some Government Proposals' [2001] *Criminal Law Review* 31.
Sullivan, 'The Attribution of Culpability to Limited Companies' [1996] *Cambridge Law Journal* 515.
Wells, *Corporations and Criminal Responsibility* (2001, Oxford University Press).

PART II

OFFENCES AGAINST THE PERSON

7 Assaults

> **Key words**
>
> - **Assault** – the defendant intentionally or recklessly causes the victim to apprehend the application of some force.
> - **Battery** – the defendant intentionally or recklessly applies force to the victim.
> - **Actual Bodily Harm** – harm which is more than trifling or transitory.
> - **Grievous Bodily Harm** – really serious harm.

7.1 Common Law and Statutory Assaults

The criminal law of assault has developed in a piecemeal manner. It is a mixture of early common law (common law assault being derived from the medieval writ of trespass), statute (mainly nineteenth century) and more recent caselaw. The results can often appear illogical both in content and terminology, and the whole area, including sexual assaults, is ready for reform. Proposals for reform have been made by the Law Commission and in a Home Office paper. In this chapter we will examine the most important non-sexual assaults. Rape and indecent assault will be discussed in the next chapter.

The non-sexual statutory assaults are mainly to be found in the Offences Against the Person Act 1861. In the style of many nineteenth-century statutes, a large number of different offences were preserved in what was essentially a consolidating statute. The result is a collection of offences often of extreme specificity, which are rarely prosecuted, such as unlawfully and maliciously impeding a person in his endeavour to save himself or another from shipwreck, punishable with life imprisonment (s.17); or obstructing or assaulting a clergyman in the performance of his duties, punishable with two years' imprisonment (s.36). We will concentrate on the less colourful but more frequently used assaults.

7.2 Common Assault and Battery

The least serious of the assault offences is common assault and battery. In both common law and statute, the word 'assault' is used in two senses: first, as a generic name for the two common law offences of assault and battery; and second, as the specific offence of assault (often called 'common assault' or 'psychic assault'). The essence of an assault, in its narrow sense, is the causing of a victim to fear some immediate use of force against him. Battery is the direct application of such force to the victim. In *Fagan**, James J. brought out the dual meaning of 'assault':

> 'An assault is any act which intentionally – or possibly recklessly – causes another person to apprehend immediate and unlawful personal violence. Although "assault" is an independent crime and is to be treated as such, for practical purposes today "assault" is generally synonymous with the term "battery", and is a term used to mean the actual intended use of unlawful force to another person without his consent.'

Both assault and battery are triable summarily (punishable with six months' imprisonment or a fine, Criminal Justice Act 1988, s.39).

7.2.1 Common Assault

In order to convict the accused of an assault the following elements must be shown:

- The victim must apprehend immediate unlawful violence
- The defendant must intentionally or recklessly cause the victim to have this apprehension.

Actus reus

The *actus reus* of an assault involves the creation of an expectation (not necessarily fear) of immediate unlawful violence in the mind of the victim. So an assault may be committed by shaking a fist or brandishing a knife at someone, causing him or her to apprehend immediate violence. It is necessary to consider some of the elements of the *actus reus* in further detail.

1. The form of conduct

It used to be thought that it was impossible to assault someone by words alone, but it is now clear that an assault can consist solely of a verbal threat. In *Ireland**, a defendant was said to have committed an assault when he telephoned his victims a number of times and then remained silent. If silence alone can constitute an assault, then so can words, letters, e-mails and facial expressions. Indeed after *Ireland* it does not matter how the defendant has created the apprehension. Sometimes, on the other hand, words can belie the seriousness of the threat, as in the early case of *Tuberville* v. *Savage*, where Tuberville, in a quarrel with Savage, put his hand on his sword and said: 'If it were not assize-time, I would not take such language from you'. The words spoken so contradicted the gesture that they made it clear that the threat would not be carried out, and so the victim did not experience the necessary expectation of violence.

2. Apprehension of violence

There is no assault if the victim does not apprehend immediate violence. So if the victim does not see the defendant shake his fist (her back is turned, or she is asleep), or does not believe that the threat will be carried out, there is no assault. There can be an assault even if the defendant has no intention or means of carrying out the threat: in *Logdon*, a threat with an imitation gun was held to be an assault, because the victim believed that force was about to be inflicted upon her. The accused had apparently never intended to use force and indeed the gun was not loaded, but this was irrelevant. Common assault is not about a person being on the point of carrying out an attack, it is about creating the apprehension of immediate violence.

3. Immediacy

The threat must be of immediate violence or unlawful touching. A threat to injure someone in three weeks' time will not amount to an assault. Generally this requirement of immediacy will mean that for an assault, the actor and victim must be in each other's presence. However, looking in through the window of a woman's home with the intention of frightening her was held to be sufficiently direct to be an assault in *Smith* v. *Chief Superintendent of Woking Police Station*, even though there was no evidence that the accused was trying to enter the room. In *Ireland*, it was held that the silent phone calls could give rise to an apprehension of immediate harm because the victims did not know what the defendant was doing and that he could be on his way to their house. Lord Steyn suggested that saying 'I will be at your door in a minute or two' is sufficient to create a fear of immediate violence and the silent telephone call could be interpreted by the victims as having a similar message. This suggests that the immediacy requirement is not to be applied very strictly. Another recent case also indicates this. In *Constanza*, the defendant sent over 800 letters to the victim and generally harassed her. Two letters were particularly threatening and she suffered stress as a result. The court found that the defendant could be said to have committed an assault. The immediacy requirement was satisfied because after receiving the letters she was afraid that she might be attacked at any time, including the near future.

4. Apprehension that there may *be harm*

As Lord Steyn made clear, in *Ireland* it is enough if the victim fears that the defendant may use violence. It does not need to be shown that the victim fears that the defendant will use violence. This is useful for the prosecution in a case like *Constanza,* where the victim believes that the defendant may be on the point of attacking at any time in the future.

Mens rea

The *mens rea* of both assault and battery is intention or recklessness. In the passage from *Fagan* quoted above, James LJ referred to 'intentionally or possibly recklessly' causing the apprehension of violence. In the later Court of Appeal decision of *Venna* this doubt was resolved and it was decided that both assault and battery can be committed recklessly. James LJ said, giving the judgement of the court:

> 'We see no reason in logic or in law why a person who recklessly applies physical force to the person of another should be outside the criminal law of assault.'

Intention or recklessness applies to the *actus reus* of the offence. So for a common assault it is sufficient if the actor is reckless as to causing the victim to apprehend the use of force (for example, *Logdon*). *Spratt* and *Parmenter** (Court of Appeal) confirmed that it is *Cunningham* recklessness (see Chapter 4.6.1) which is the correct *mens rea* for these offences.

7.2.2   Battery

The offence of battery involves:

• Unlawful use of force against another person
• Intention or recklessness that force will be used against another.

Actus reus

The *actus reus* of battery, as we have seen, is the unlawful use of force against another person. Again we will examine some of the more controversial aspects of the actus reus.

1. There does not need to be any injury

To amount to a battery it does not need to be shown that the victim suffered an injury. Merely touching the other person would be enough, if done without the consent (express or implied) of the victim. Even touching a person's clothing seems to be sufficient (*Thomas* (1985)). Battery involves what might colloquially be known as 'invasion of personal space'.

2. Battery through objects
A battery can be committed with a weapon or object, as stated by James LJ in *Fagan*. He explained that a battery could be committed by the laying of a hand on another, or by using a stick, or even, as in that case, by intentionally allowing the wheel of a car accidentally driven onto the victim's foot to remain where it was. This was confirmed in *K* where a schoolboy put some acid in a hand-drier and another boy was splashed with the acid when he later used the drier. This was said to constitute a battery.

3. The touching must not be an everyday touching
The offence of battery does not include everyday touching, or 'generally acceptable standards of conduct', for example, bumping into someone on a crowded tube train, or tapping someone on the shoulder to point out that they have dropped something. It used to be thought that such conduct was not battery as the victim impliedly consented to it. However, this has not been followed by the courts and it is hard to imagine that someone in a crowded tube train could withdraw their implied consent by shouting out that no one is allowed to touch her. It is better explained on the ground that such conduct is simply excluded from the definition of a battery.

4. Does the touching need to be hostile?
There is some debate over whether there is a need to show hostility, in the sense of aggression, in order to establish a battery. In *Faulkner* v. *Talbot*, a woman took a boy to her bed and touched him in an indecent manner. It was said that there was a battery, even though the touching was not aggressive but rather 'affectionate'. In *Brown**, *obiter*, the House of Lords held there was a need to show that the battery was hostile, but only in the sense that it was not consented to. So the act must be hostile in the sense of not consented to, but not hostile in the sense of aggressive.

Mens rea

The *mens rea* for an offence is intentionally or recklessly using force against someone. Recklessly here refers to *Cunningham* recklessness (*Spratt* and *Parmenter**).

7.3   Assault Occasioning Actual Bodily Harm

Assault occasioning actual bodily harm (section 47 of the Offences Against the Person Act) is an aggravated assault, that is an assault with the additional element of actual bodily harm, making it more serious than common assault. It comprises of the following elements:

*   An assault (that is, a common assault or battery)
*   Occasioning
*   Actual bodily harm.

The *actus reus* of s.47 requires the commission of an assault or battery, and in addition that this assault or battery caused the actual bodily harm. For example, in the case of *Roberts* (1971)*, the accused had given the victim a lift in his car. He tried to pull off her coat and she jumped out of the car, suffering injuries. The defendant had committed an assault (in causing her to fear immediate violence by trying to pull off her coat) and this had caused actual bodily harm (the injuries she suffered in jumping out of the car) and so he was guilty of the offence under s.47.

The following terms require a little more explanation:

1. Assault
Assault here means either an assault or a battery. Both the *actus reus* and the *mens rea* need to be shown.

2. Occasioning
Occasioning here means the same as causing. It is not enough simply to show that the defendant assaulted the victim and that the victim suffered actual bodily harm. It must be shown that it was the assault that caused the actual bodily harm. This can be particularly problematic in a case like *Ireland* involving unpleasant phone calls. It must be shown that it was the fear of imminent unlawful violence that caused the psychological injuries. If the illnesses were caused by the general distress following the phone calls or fear that the defendant may telephone again, this would not be sufficient to establish a conviction under s.47. In other words, it is not enough just to show that there has been an assault and a battery and that the victim has suffered actual bodily harm. It must be shown that the actual bodily harm resulted from the assault or battery. If the defendant has subjected the victim to a campaign of assaults as a result of which the victim has suffered actual bodily harm, it is not necessary for the jury to decide which of the many assaults caused the harm as long as it is clear that one or more of them did (*Cox*).

3. Actual bodily harm

In *Donovan*, before the Court of Criminal Appeal, Swift J gave the 'ordinary meaning' of 'actual bodily harm' as:

'any hurt or injury calculated to interfere with the health or comfort of the [victim]. Such hurt or injury need not be permanent, but must, no doubt, be more than merely transient and trifling.'

In *Chan Fook**, it was confirmed that psychological illnesses could be included in the term 'actual bodily harm' as long as the harm was a medically defined illness and not a mere emotion, such as fear or panic. In *Ireland*, the House of Lords approved *Chan Fook*, and confirmed that medically recognized stress, for example, was capable of amounting to actual bodily harm.

4. Mens rea

The *mens rea* of s.47 is the *mens rea* of the assault or battery. It is not necessary for the accused to have foreseen that actual bodily harm would be caused to the victim as a result of his assault. It is only necessary to prove that the bodily harm was caused in fact and in law by the assault. This was recently confirmed by the House of Lords in *Parmenter*. This is one of the offences which is criticized by those who support the correspondence principle, discussed at Chapter 4.8.

7.4   Malicious Wounding

Section 20 of the Offences Against the Person Act is often referred to briefly as 'malicious wounding'. The offence can in fact be committed in two ways, either by wounding or by inflicting grievous bodily harm:

'Whoever shall unlawfully and maliciously wound or inflict any grievous bodily harm upon any other person, either with or without any weapon or instrument, shall be guilty . . . '

The offence is punishable with five years' imprisonment. The offence can be broken down into the following elements:

- Unlawfully
- Maliciously
- Wound or inflict any grievous bodily harm upon any other person

The *actus reus* here is an act which either causes a wound in the victim or which inflicts grievous bodily harm upon him. The *mens rea* is 'maliciousness'. It is useful to consider the elements of the offence separately.

1. Wound

A wound is any injury that breaks the skin and is more that a mere surface scratch (*JJC* v. *Eisenhower*). There is no need for the cut to be serious. It may seem rather odd that what may be a little cut is classified in the same offence as grievous bodily harm. The reason for this may be that in 1861 when the statute was enacted, all breaks of the skin were potentially serious without antiseptic treatment. The inclusion of wounding in this serious offence can also be seen as a deterrent against the use of knives.

2. Grievous bodily harm

The phrase 'grievous bodily harm' was defined by the House of Lords in *Smith* v. *DPP** as 'really serious bodily harm', and this was approved by the House in *Hyam* v. *DPP**. The Court of Appeal in *Saunders* and *Junjua and Choudury* has held that it was not a misdirection for a trial judge to omit the word 'really' and to describe grievous bodily harm as 'serious injury'. In deciding whether the injury was serious, the jury should be instructed to look at the injuries caused by the accused in total and so it may be that even though none of the injuries was sufficient itself to amount to grievous bodily harm, their combined effect was (*Grundy*). In deciding whether injuries are grievous, the jury asks whether an ordinary person would say that they were. The jury should not take into account whether the particular victim regarded them as grievous (*Brown and Stratton*). It has now been recognized that serious psychological injuries can constitute grievous bodily harm if they are really serious medically recognized conditions (*Burstow**).

3. Inflicting

There has been much debate over the correct meaning of the term 'inflict'. Particularly because in s.18 the word 'cause' is used. It used to be thought that the term 'inflict' required the direct application of force, while 'cause' meant to bring about grievous bodily harm in any way (*Wilson* (1984)*). However, this view was rejected by the House of Lords in *Burstow*. Lord Steyn accepted that the words did have different meanings, but did not say what he thought they were. However he thought the distinction insignificant for the purpose of the 1861 Act. Lord Hope thought the difference was that 'inflict' 'implies that the consequence of the act is something which the victim is likely to find unpleasant or harmful'; whereas '[t]he relationship between the cause and effect, when the word "cause" is used, is neutral. It may embrace pleasure as well as pain'. However, he explained, given that both sections only apply where the victim has suffered grievous bodily harm, this difference was irrelevant here and he said in effect that the words were 'interchangeable'. It is also notable in s.23 of the 1861 Act that the section refers to 'inflicting' injuries by poison. As poison does not normally cause injuries by using a direct application of force, it may well be that the wording of this section suggests that the drafters of the statute did not intend 'inflict' to have a particularly restrictive meaning. So although the position is still a little confused, it seems that there is no significant difference in meaning between 'cause' and 'inflict' in ss.18 and 20.

It might be thought strange if there was such a distinction, and some acts could be the *actus reus* for the more serious offence of s.18, but could not be the *actus reus* for the lesser offence of s.20. However, it has been suggested (by J. Gardner (1994)) that the fact that s.18 requires an intention to cause grievous bodily harm means that the law is willing to punish the defendant, however he causes the harm. By contrast, s.20 only requires recklessness as to some harm and so the offence (which would otherwise be very broad) is understandably slightly narrowed by requiring 'infliction' of harm.

For many years it was generally accepted that s.20, like s.47, required an assault. The leading authority was *Clarence**, in which Stephen J in the Court for Crown Cases Reserved, said: 'although the word "assault" is not used in the section, I think the words imply an assault and battery of which a wound or grievous bodily harm is the manifest, immediate and obvious result'. However, the House of Lords has now decided that s.20 does not necessarily require an assault, although it will very often involve one (*Burstow**, *Wilson**).

4. Maliciously

This is the *mens rea* of s.20. It is contained in the word 'maliciously', and its meaning is now well established. In *Parmenter*, in the House of Lords it was decided that 'maliciously' in this section meant that the accused must have foreseen that some harm might occur, that is *Cunningham* recklessness as to some harm. Lord Ackner stated, 'it is enough that he should have foreseen that some physical harm to some person, albeit of a minor character, might result.' It should be stressed that the accused does not need to have foreseen that grievous bodily harm may result from his actions; and that the accused need only foresee that some harm *might* occur, not that it would occur (*Rushworth*).

5. Unlawfulness

This requirement simply refers to the fact that the defendant will not be guilty if he can establish a defence, such as self-defence (see Chapter 15).

7.5   Wounding with Intent

Wounding with intent is the most serious of the statutory assaults and is punishable with life imprisonment. It is found in s.18 of the Offences Against the Person Act:

> 'Whosoever shall unlawfully and maliciously by any means whatsoever wound or cause any grievous bodily harm to any person, with intent to do some grievous bodily harm to any person, or with intent to resist or prevent the lawful apprehension or detention of any person shall be guilty . . . '

The *actus reus* of s.18 is similar to that required by s.20. The terms 'wound' and 'grievous bodily harm' carry the same meaning as they do for s.20 as just described. The word 'cause' is given its normal meaning (see Chapter 5). One difference in the *actus reus* of the offences in ss.18 and 20 may be of significance. Section 20 requires the injuries to be 'to any other person' whereas s.18 just states 'to any person'. This might suggest that you can be guilty of intentionally causing yourself grievous bodily harm contrary to s.18, but not inflicting grievous bodily harm upon yourself contrary to s.20.

The *mens rea* of s.18 is in two parts. First, as with s.20, there is the word 'maliciously'. In *Mowatt*, Lord Justice Diplock took the view that in s.18 'the word "maliciously" adds nothing', and that it is best ignored in directions to the jury on this offence. This is only partly true. Certainly, if the accused is charged with wounding or causing grievous bodily harm with intent to cause grievous bodily harm, then, as Lord Justice Diplock said, nothing further is added by requiring that the act be malicious. However, if the charge is of wounding or causing bodily harm with intent to resist or prevent the lawful apprehension or detention of any person, then it may be crucial to the case that the prosecution also has to prove that the accused acted maliciously in respect of the *actus reus*; that he either intended to cause or was reckless as to causing at least some harm to another person. Perhaps because of Lord Justice Diplock's dictum, there is little discussion of the exact meaning of malice in s.18, but there are no grounds for adopting a different definition of malice from that used for s.20 (that is, *Cunningham* recklessness as to some harm).

The second part of the *mens rea* of s.18 requires a specific intent, and gives three possibilities, any one of which may be used with either of the two possible forms of *actus reus*. The first possible intent is an intent to do some grievous bodily harm to any person. The wording ('any person') makes it clear that the doctrine of transferred *mens rea* will apply (see

Chapter 4.6), so that the accused need not intend to injure the person who is in fact injured.

The other two categories of specific intent are an intent to resist lawful apprehension and an intent to prevent the lawful apprehension of any other person. It is in these cases that particular attention should be paid to the additional requirement of malice (*Morrison*).

One question that has in the past caused some difficulty is whether a defendant who is charged with an offence under s.18 can be convicted of an offence under s.20 or s.47. The answer is now clear, and it is 'yes' (*Mandair*, *Wilson*).

7.6 Maliciously Administering Poison

If poisoning causes death it might be murder or manslaughter; if done with an intent to kill it may be attempted murder; or it may be an offence under s.18 if it causes grievous bodily harm and is done with the necessary intent. It may even constitute a battery or an offence against s.47. In addition, the Offences Against the Person Act 1861 has created two specific offences to deal with poisoning. The more serious, carrying a possible sentence of ten years' imprisonment, is s.23:

> 'Whosoever shall unlawfully and maliciously administer to or cause to be administered to or taken by any other person any poison or other destructive or noxious thing, so as thereby to inflict upon such person any grievous bodily harm, shall be guilty . . . '

Section 24, carrying a sentence of five years' imprisonment, does not require the consequence of endangering life or causing grievous bodily harm, but instead contains the additional *mens rea* element of a specific intent:

> 'Whosoever shall unlawfully and maliciously administer to or cause to be administered to or taken by any person any poison or other destructive or noxious thing, with intent to injure, aggrieve or annoy such person, shall be guilty . . . '

So s.23 focuses on the effect of the poison (endangering life), while s.24 focuses on the intention of the accused.

We will now examine in more detail some of the requirement of these offences.

1. Administer

Poison may be administered in the classic manner, by adding it to the victim's food or drink, but there are many other ways of achieving the same result. In *Cunningham**, a gas meter was ripped off a wall by the accused, releasing coal gas which injured the victim. In *Gillard*, CS gas was sprayed in his face. In *Cato**, the accused injected the victim with a syringe of heroin. The wording of both sections covers direct or indirect administration of the poison.

2. Poison

The courts have disagreed over the meaning of 'poison or other destructive or noxious thing'. In the early case of *Cramp*, Lord Coleridge CJ held that a poison was something 'injurious to health or life', and then said:

> 'There is hardly any active drug which taken in large quantities may not be so, and, on the other hand, there is hardly any poison which may not in small quantities be useful and salutary. It is therefore in each case a question of the quantity and the circumstances in which the drug is administered.'

In *Cato*, Lord Widgery CJ disagreed: 'an article is not to be described as noxious for present purposes, merely because it has a potentiality for harm if taken in an overdose'. More recently, the Court of Appeal has preferred the approach taken by Lord Coleridge. By noxious is meant 'something different in quality from and of less importance than poison or other destructive things' (*Marcus*). A substance can be noxious if it causes the victim to stay awake but only if the defendant administers it for malevolent reasons. In *Hill**, the defendant gave boys pills to keep them awake as he hoped to abuse the children. The pills would not have been deemed noxious if they had been given to the children so that they would be awake to meet their father returning home late. In *Marcus*, the court held that sleeping pills, administered in an ordinary dose, could be noxious. The jury must take into account the quantity of the drug administered, as well as its nature, in deciding whether it was noxious in the particular circumstances. This approach to the meaning of noxious leaves a great deal to the jury, and potentially widens the scope of the offences beyond the generally accepted idea of poison. If a drug were found to be innocuous in the quantity administered, but the *mens rea* were present, a conviction for attempt would be possible.

3. Maliciously

In s.23 the *mens rea* is supplied by the familiar word 'maliciously'. Again, there have been differing views over the meaning of the word in this context. In *Cunningham*, Byrne J approved a definition given by Professor Kenny, holding that 'maliciously' included intention to do the particular kind of harm that was done, or at least awareness of the risk of causing such harm. Byrne J then went on to hold that, applied to s.23, this had the effect of requiring the possibility of causing some injury to some other person. The unstated conclusion is that foresight of the risk of danger to life or grievous bodily harm would not be necessary: as in s.47 and s.20, the offence falls short of requiring full *mens rea* in respect of the precise injury caused.

Unfortunately the position has been confused by the decision of the Court of Appeal in *Cato*. In that case Lord Widgery distinguished *Cunningham* on the ground that in the earlier case the poison had been administered indirectly by removing the gas meter from the wall, whereas in *Cato* the heroin was administered directly, by injection. The Lord Chief Justice then went on to hold that in the case of direct administration of poison no foresight of any injury was required:

> 'The requirement of malice is satisfied if the syringe was deliberately inserted into the body of [the victim] as it undoubtedly was, and if Cato at the time when he so inserted the syringe knew that the syringe contained a noxious substance. That is enough, we think, in this type of direct injury case to satisfy the requirement of maliciousness.'

The result of this ruling, if it is followed, is that in 'direct injury' cases the section requires *mens rea* as to the first part of the *actus reus* (the administration of the noxious substance) only; the offence is one of strict liability with respect to the danger to life or grievous bodily harm. This is odd when one considers the more specific intent required by the statute for the less serious offence under s.24. There is no evidence that Byrne J had attributed any significance to that element of the case in *Cunningham* and it is not supported by the words of the section. In view of the unusual facts of *Cato*, and the comparative rarity of such a direct administration of poison, it is possible that the decision will be distinguished in future cases (as it was on a different point in *Marcus*).

4. Intent to injure aggrieve or annoy

Section 24, in addition to malice, requires a specific intent to injure, aggrieve or annoy the person to whom the poison is administered. It has been held by the House of Lords that an intent to injure means an intent to cause harm either by means of the substance itself or by enabling the accused to harm the victim in some other way (for example, by assaulting him while asleep, *Hill*). Unlike s.23, there is no room here for the operation of transferred *mens rea* (see Chapter 4.3).

It is also specifically an offence under s.22 Offences Against the Person Act 1861 to use any overpowering drug or substance with intent to enable the commission of an arrestable offence.

7.7   Consent

One of the most controversial issues on the law of offences against the person is the relevance of the law on consent. The following are the key questions.

7.7.1   Is the Consent of the Victim a Defence or is Lack of Consent an Aspect of the *Actus Reus*?

There is much dispute over whether consent should be seen as a defence to a criminal assault (the 'defence view') or whether absence of the victim's consent should be part of the definition of the *actus reus* (the '*actus reus* view'). According to the 'defence view', one person being violent towards another is a legal wrong, but a wrong which can in some circumstances be justified by the consent of the victim. According to the '*actus reus* view', if the assault is consented to no wrong of any kind has taken place, unless there are special reasons why the law wishes to render that conduct unlawful. The difference between the two views has important practical consequences. The evidential burden of proof will fall on the prosecution if consent is part of the definition of the offence, while it will fall on the defendant if consent is a defence.

The difference between the 'defence view' and the '*actus reus* view' is not just a technical one but reflects some profound philosophical disagreements. The '*actus reus* view' tends to be supported by those who adopt the traditional liberal view that prizes autonomy (see Chapter 1.5.2). The principle of autonomy emphasizes that each person should be able to live his or her life as he or she wishes, and the criminal law should only prohibit conduct that causes harm to others. If a person consents to the harm it should therefore not be criminalized and no legal wrong has taken place. Supporters of the '*actus reus* view' point to an example of two friends walking down the street holding hands as a gesture of friendship. To say in such a case that there is a legal wrong and a battery but fortunately the consent of the friend provides a defence, seems artificial. Surely the '*actus reus* view' that there is no battery because there is no legal wrong is more realistic.

The 'defence view' would be supported by legal moralists who argue that it is important for our legal system to protect and uphold the moral values that underpin our society. There is an important taboo that we should not hurt each other deliberately. If that principle is not upheld by the law, society may begin to unravel. The law should therefore see one person committing violence against another as *prima facie* unlawful, although there may be circumstances in which the victim's consent will provide a defence.

The majority of commentators who have written on this area have preferred the '*actus reus* view'. However, Simester and Sullivan suggest a compromise view. They suggest that some touchings are only harmful if there is no consent. For example, a handshake is only harmful if the victim does not consent. In such cases the '*actus reus* view' seems preferable. On the other hand some touchings are *prima facie* harmful, for example a punch in the face. These are *prima facie* illegal, but the law may wish to provide a defence in some cases if the defendant has consented (for example, as part of a boxing match). In such cases the 'defence view' seems preferable.

What have the courts had to say about the two views? In the House of Lords' case of *Brown** (1993), the majority (Lords Jauncey, Lowry and Templeman) saw consent as a defence to a charge of assault. They adopted the approach that violence against another is *prima facie* unlawful. More recently, Lord Hobhouse in *R* v. *K**, discussing the offence of indecent assault, took the opposite view and referred to absence of consent as an aspect of the *actus reus*. So no consistent approach has been adopted, but the 'defence view' seems to have greater support from the authorities and so consent will be referred to as a defence in the following discussion.

7.7.2 To What Crimes of Violence is Consent a Defence?

The consent of an adult provides a defence to an assault or battery (otherwise it would be unlawful for two consenting adults to kiss). However, consent to an act which causes actual bodily harm or a greater level of harm does not provide a defence unless the act falls within certain categories accepted by the law, or there are good public policy reasons why a new exempt category should be created (*Brown*). Although this is the approach adopted by the House of Lords in *Brown*, a more recent Court of Appeal case, *Wilson* (1996), has suggested that the question which should be asked in novel situations is 'does public policy or the public interest demand that the appellant's activity should be vested by the sanctions of the criminal law?' This seems clearly in conflict with the decision of the majority of their Lordships in *Brown*, which as a matter of precedent represents the present law.

There is no clearly stated list of the exempt categories in the caselaw, but there seems to be authority for the following as being situations where consent is a defence even though the victim has suffered actual bodily harm or worse:

(a) Sports and organized games

If in the course of an organized sport or game one player injures another, consent may provide a defence. The argument in favour of the exception is that the playing of sports and games is in the public interest: it improves the participant's health and provides enjoyment to many. These benefits justify permitting sporting activities even though, in the course of sports, injuries inevitably occur. However, if in the course of a game a player commits a breach of the rules which involves a level of force beyond that which might be expected in the game, then the fact that the victim consented to play the game appears to provide no defence to the defendant (*Bradshaw*). This can be explained on the basis that in playing a sport, a participant only consents to the kinds of injuries that might be expected during the sport. Those unexpected injuries caused by a player outside the rules of the game are simply not consented to and so not surprisingly there is no defence. Alternatively it may be that although there are public policy reasons to encourage people to play sports, even if incidentally harm may be caused, there is no public policy reason to encourage people to act outside the rules and cause injuries during sporting activities. This may explain why exception does not cover unorganized games, such as a fight in the street (*Attorney-General's Reference (No. 6 of 1980)**).

(b) Tattooing, ritual circumcision of males, ear piercing and personal adornment

This is a self-explanatory category. The Court of Appeal included within this category a man who burned his wife's buttocks with a hot knife to leave scars spelling out his initials, at her request (*Wilson* (1996)). Circumcision of women is prohibited by the Prohibition of Female Circumcision Act 1985. It is generally presumed that the circumcision of boys is lawful.

(c) Religious mortification

This covers cases where, as part of an act of religious repentance, the penitent asks another to inflict pain on him. This category was specifically mentioned by Lord Mustill in *Brown*.

(d) Rough horseplay

This seems to apply where children play rough games together (*Jones* (1986)). If this were not exempt there would be many hundreds of criminal offences committed in playgrounds across the country every day. However, it is important that rough horseplay and bullying are distinguished, although the courts have not yet been asked to clarify this distinction.

This exception has rather controversially been said to apply to members of the RAF who played a drunken game, setting each other alight while wearing their fireproof suits (*Aitken**). Such conduct, you might think, could legitimately be thought unacceptable and should be discouraged. Certainly had it been civilians acting in this way in a pub it is unlikely that the court would have taken the same approach. Not only have RAF officers been found analogous to children playing rough games, so too have students playing pranks on each other (*Richardson and Irvin*).

(e) Surgery carried out by a medically qualified person

(f) Dangerous exhibitions
This covers stunt shows and circus acts, for example. The Court of Appeal in *Attorney-General's Reference (No. 6 of 1980)* established the existence of this exception.

In *Brown*, the House of Lords appeared to suggest that any exception had to be supported on the basis that the activity was in the public interest. However, it will be apparent that these exceptions do not all seem to be situations where there is a positive public interest in the events being carried out; horseplay is one obvious example. In *Brown*, in the House of Lords it was decided that no new exception should be created for sado-masochistic acts which cause actual bodily harm or more serious injury. The majority held it could not be said that sadomasochistic acts were positively in the public interest and so no new exception could be created and the act were criminal. The majority were concerned by two factors in particular: that the conduct was immoral and degrading; and that the individuals needed protection from themselves, as the level of injury was unpredictable and there were concerns that young people may become involved. They were also concerned that the activities might lead to the spreading of AIDS. The majority has been criticized for not producing proof of these concerns, but they seemed to have taken the view that the burden lay on the defendants to allay these concerns. The minority argued that the acts could not be said to be against the public interest and so should be exempt. The minority judgements place weight on the right to respect for people's private life (see Chapter 19).

The majority's approach has been heavily criticized by commentators who have said insufficient weight was placed on the defendant's freedom of sexual expression. The case was taken to the European Court of Human Rights but the decision was upheld on the basis that it was arguably necessary in a democratic society to promote health (*Laskey, Jaggard and Brown v. UK*). The Court of Appeal has recently confirmed that the *Brown* ruling applies equally to heterosexual sadomasochistic activity (*Emmett*).

Some academics have asked whether there really is much difference between blows delivered in a boxing match or religious mortification, and beating as part of sadomasochistic sex, apart from the sexual element. Clarskon and Keating have explained the Law's approach:

'Violence in the playground or barrack-room is what is expected and normal in the male world; it is a "manly diversion". Two men expressing their sexuality together and in private are not doing the sort of thing real men do. It is an "evil thing" and "unnatural" and cannot be the subject of valid consent.'

If one was seeking to justify the present law, the best argument is that what the majority of the House of Lords were opposed to was the infliction of pain for the very purpose of inflicting pain or the enjoyment of pain, and not for an ulterior motive, for example the purpose of winning a boxing match or for personal adornment (as in *Wilson*). In all of the exceptions, if there was no pain the participants would still have regarded the activities as a success. In *Wilson,* for example, if Mrs Wilson had felt no pain, but still received the initials on her buttocks, she would have been very pleased. In *Brown*, if there was no pain the enterprise would have been a flop. Inflicting pain for the purpose of causing pain then is what the law here is designed to prevent. One exception would not be explained by this justification and that is the sport of boxing, where inflicting pain appears to the purpose of the sport. Lord Mustill in *Brown* explained that boxing, where the use of force is an inherent part of the game, was an anomalous exception which existed 'because society chooses to tolerate it'.

7.7.3   When Will Belief in Consent Provide a Defence?

So the consent of the victim will provide a defence in cases of assault or battery, but not in cases involving actual bodily harm or more serious injuries unless the activity falls into one of the exceptional categories. Even if the victim was not consenting, if the defendant believed she was and had she been that would have provided a consent, the defendant is not guilty (*R* v. *K**). So if Tom, a short-sighted man, sees Penelope whom he mistakes for his wife Nicole, and gives her a kiss, this would not be an assault despite the fact that Penelope did not consent. Surprisingly, it has even been held that a drunken belief that the victim consents will provide a defence (*Richardson and Irwin*).

But what of a case where the defendant believed that he was doing something which would only involve a battery and that the victim consented to it, but which in fact involved a more serious injury? Would this belief provide a defence? Two cases have discussed this issue. Both involved vigorous sexual activity, the participants consented to the acts performed and intended only to commit batteries upon each other; however, much more serious injuries resulted from their acts. In *Boyea*, it was held that if the more serious injuries were foreseeable (even if not foreseen) then the defendant could not rely on the victim's consent and the defendant could be convicted of an offence under s.47, Offences Against the Person Act 1861. However, in *Slingsby* it was said that the belief in consent would provide a defence, provided that the defendant did not actually foresee that his actions would cause more than actual bodily harm. Of these two cases *Slingsby* seems preferable as it fits in better with the general approach on assaults against the person, which require *Cunningham** subjective recklessness (see Chapter 7.2.1).

7.7.4 What is Consent?

There are two issues here. The first is who can give effective consent? In the case of children, consent to medical treatment or other actions that do not clearly harm the child (such as ear piercing) can be given by those who have parental responsibility for a child. A child who is sufficiently mature to understand what is involved may be able to give consent herself (*Gillick*). Adults are able to give effective consent unless they fall under the provisions of the Mental Health Act 1983.

The definition of consent in relation to offences against the person has largely followed the law defining consent in the context of rape. We will therefore discuss the notion of consent in greater detail in Chapter 8. There must be a positive act of consent by the victim. If the apparent consent is provided by a person who is mistaken as to the nature of the act, or as to the identity of the other individual involved, this may mean that the consent will not provide a defence. In *Richardson,* the 'victims' had been treated by a dentist who had been suspended from practice by the General Medical Council. The Court of Appeal confirmed that the patient's consent was effective unless there was a mistake as to the nature of the act or the identity of the individual performing the act. Here there was no deception as to the nature of the act because the treatment they received was the very treatment they expected. It might have been different if the treatment had been performed in an utterly negligent way. Further, there was no deception as to identity because she was the Richardson that the patients thought she was. It was true that the patients were mistaken as to whether she was a registered dentist, but that was a mistake as to attribute. This line of reasoning seems weak. If a person on leaving a hospital is told 'I am afraid there was a mistake, you were treated by Dr Jones not Dr Smith as you were told', they would probably not mind; but if told 'you have been treated by an unqualified person' they would be very concerned. In cases of medical treatment, the attribute of medical qualification is of far more importance than identity. In *Tabbussum*, the Court of Appeal held that a man who pretended to be medically qualified and so persuaded three women to let him give them a breast examination did commit an assault. This was because they were deceived as to the nature of the act: they thought the defendant was touching with medical motivations in mind, but in fact he was touching them with indecent motivations.

7.7.5   Reform of Consent

The Law Commission, in their Consultation Paper Number 139, suggested that consent should, subject to a few exceptions, only be a defence if the injury is less serious than a 'serious disabling injury'. They define serious disabling injury as injuries which:

'(1) cause serious distress, and
(2) involve the loss of a bodily member or organ or permanent bodily injury or permanent functional impairment, or serious or permanent disfigurement, or severe and prolonged pain, or serious impairment of mental health, or prolonged unconsciousness.'

This would greatly extend the kind of injuries to which the victim's consent would provide a defence.

7.8   Chastisement of Children

It is a defence for a parent charged with an offence of violence to prove that he was chastising his child. This defence is discussed in Chapter 19 as the topic is now dominated by the Human Rights Act.

7.9   Assault with Intent to Rob

This is an aggravated assault, provided for by s.8 Theft Act 1968 as a companion offence to robbery (see Chapter 12.1). Like robbery, the offence is punishable with life imprisonment. Assault here means an assault or battery. Intent to rob is not defined in the statute, but robbery involves theft, accompanied by the use of, or threat of the use of, force. The intent to rob must therefore involve an intent to steal (that is, to satisfy all of the elements of theft) and an intent to use force to assist in the robbery. The intent to rob must exist in the accused's mind at the time of the assault.

7.10 Assault with Intent to Resist Arrest

Under s.38 Offence Against the Person Act:

> 'Whosoever shall assault any person with intent to resist or prevent the lawful apprehension or detention of himself or of any other person for any offence, shall be guilty . . . '

This offence is punishable with a maximum of two years' imprisonment. It has been largely superseded by the offences of assaulting and obstructing a police constable in the execution of his duty (see below), but may, of course, be used where the person attempting to make the lawful arrest is not a police constable.

7.11 Assault with Intent to Rape

It is not at all clear whether this offence exists. In *P* (1990) it was suggested that there is no crime of assault with intent to rape, but in *J* it was held that there was such an offence. In many cases where a prosecutor may consider charging an assault with intent to rape, an attempted rape charge may be also available.

7.12 Assaulting, Resisting and Wilfully Obstructing a Police Constable

Section 89 of the Police Act 1996 creates three offences. Of these, it is the first, in subsection (1), which necessarily involves an assault, although the other two may also be committed by assault. Section 89 provides:

> '(1) Any person who assaults a constable in the execution of his duty, or a person assisting a constable in the execution of his duty shall be guilty of an offence . . .
> (2) Any person who resists or wilfully obstructs a constable in the execution of his duty, or a person assisting a constable in the execution of his duty, shall be guilty of an offence . . . '

These offences are triable summarily only (even though a common assault is triable on indictment, and the offence under s.89(1) is regarded as more serious than a common assault). The maximum penalty under s.89(1) is six months' imprisonment or a fine, and for s.89(2) one month's imprisonment or a fine. Because of their link with assault generally, they are briefly mentioned here, but they primarily relate to the topic of police powers, which is beyond the scope of this book.

The common element in all three offences is that the constable must be acting in the execution of his duty. This does not just mean that the constable must be on duty. It has not been decided whether a constable can be acting 'in the execution of his duty' even when 'off duty'. The general duties of the police include keeping the peace, preventing crime, detecting crime and bringing offenders to justice (per Lord Parker CJ in *Rice* v. *Connolly**). 'Duty' has been interpreted to include all those things that a constable is entitled to do and not just those things which he is bound to do. Whatever he does, a constable must act legally, and an action such as an unlawful arrest or a trespass cannot therefore be within the execution of his duty, and it cannot be an offence under s.89 to use reasonable force to escape (for example) from unlawful detention.

The assault required by s.89(1) is common assault. Resistance, in s.89(2), need not amount to a technical assault, although it frequently will do so. The interpretation of obstruction has given some difficulty. There is no positive general duty on the public to help the police, and yet unco-operative behaviour may be treated as an obstruction. For example, in *Ricketts* v. *Cox* the accused was approached by two policemen who tried to question him; he refused to stay and became abusive: a conviction for obstruction was upheld on appeal. This case is regarded as being at the limits of obstruction: in *Rice* v. *Connolly* it was held that there was no duty to answer police questions, so that a simple refusal to answer could not be an obstruction. However, it is clear that physical obstruction is not necessary, and it would be an obstruction to tell lies in response to police questioning. Other examples are informing an offender that the police are nearby, so that he can escape, or even warning other motorists of a police speed trap. In *Rice* v. *Connolly*, Lord Parker adopted a dictum of Lord Coleridge CJ from the much earlier case of *Hinchliffe* v. *Sheldon*: 'to "obstruct" in s.89(1) is to do any act which makes it more difficult for the police to carry out their duty'.

The *mens rea* under s.89(1) is limited to the *mens rea* of assault (see Chapter 7.2). There is no need to know that the victim is a constable, or that he is on duty: even a reasonable mistake will not excuse one from liability (*Forbes*). However, a mistaken belief that the constable was acting unlaw-fully may excuse, by rendering the accused's act a lawful act of self-defence and therefore not an assault (*Lee*, see *Williams (Gladstone)**; for further discussion of mistake and self-defence, see Chapter 15.3.1).

In s.89(2), the *mens rea* for resisting a constable seems also to be limited to an intent to resist. However, in the case of an obstruction, the statute specifies that the obstruction must be 'wilful'. This means not just that the obstruction is deliberate, but also that it is a defence to believe reasonably that the person obstructed is not a constable (*Ostler* v. *Elliott*). It is possible that such a belief, even if unreasonable, could also be a defence. It can be argued that there cannot be any 'obstruction of the execution of duty' without the accused at least being aware that the person being obstructed may be a constable; unlike assault, the status of the person obstructed is intrinsic to the obstruction. On the other hand, the element of wilfulness does not require any hostility towards the police; it may be that the accused is trying to be helpful (*Hills* v. *Ellis*). If his act is deliberate, does in fact obstruct a constable, and he knows that the person obstructed is a constable, he will be guilty.

Assault with intent to resist arrest (s.38 of the Offences Against the Person Act) is now less important than the offences under s.89 of the Police Act 1996 of assaulting, resisting or wilfully obstructing a constable in the execution of his duty. A constable's duty includes all those things which he is empowered to do, in particular those concerned with the prevention of crime, keeping the peace and the apprehension of offenders. Obstruction includes anything that makes the constable's task more difficult. The *mens rea* for assaulting or resisting a constable is limited to the intent to assault or resist. A belief that the victim is not a constable, or is not acting in the execution of his duty, will provide a defence, but not a mistake as to the law (for example, whether the arrest is lawful or whether the officer is acting in the course of his duty) (*Lee*). In the case of wilful obstruction, a reasonable belief by the accused that the person obstructed is not a constable will be a defence.

7.13   Protection from Harassment Act 1997

The Protection from Harassment Act 1997 was passed because it was felt that the criminal law failed to provide adequate protection to victims of stalking and sustained campaigns of violence. In fact the Act has been used to cover a far wider range of conduct than this: from neighbours disputing a boundary to someone writing threatening letters to a Member of Parliament. However, there are limits to the extent of the offence. The Act has been held not to apply to anti-vivisectionist protesters who campaigned outside the offices of a company who carried out experiments on animals.

Mr Justice Eady held that the Act was not intended to restrict the public's rights to protest reasonably about matters in the public interest (*Huntingdon Life Sciences Ltd* v. *Curtin*).

There are two key offences under the Act.

7.13.1   Harassment

Under section 1 of the Protection from Harassment Act 1997:

'(1) A person must not pursue a course of conduct –
  (a) which amounts to harassment of another; and
  (b) which he knows or ought to know amounts to harassment.
(2) For the purposes of this section the person whose course of conduct is in question ought to know that it amounts to harassment of another if a reasonable person in possession of the same information would think the course of conduct amounted to harassment of the other.
(3) Subsection (1) does not apply to a course conduct if the person who pursued it shows it was
  (a) pursued for the purpose of preventing or detecting crime;
  (b) that it was pursued under enactment or rule of law or to comply with any condition or requirement imposed by any person, under any enactment; or
  (c) in the particular circumstances, the pursuit of the course of conduct was reasonable.'

The offence can be broken down into the following four elements.

1. A course of conduct

There must be at least two incidents to establish a course of conduct. A single incident, however unpleasant, will not constitute the offence. Sometimes it can be difficult to tell whether there have been two incidents or one. In *Wass* v. *Director of Public Prosecutions*, the defendant followed the victim and tried to stop her entering a shop. He then confronted her when she left the shop a short time later. This was held capable of amounting to be two separate pieces of conduct and hence a course of conduct.

In order to amount to a course of conduct, the two incidents must be linked. The larger the number of incidents, the easier it will be to establish a course of conduct. The fewer there are, the harder. It would be wrong to say that there must be a 'campaign' against the victim, but there must be some connection between the pieces of conduct. In *Lau* v. *DPP*, the defendant slapped the victim and then four months later he threatened the victim's new boyfriend with violence. This did not constitute a course of conduct because of a combination of two factors: the length of time in-between the two incidents and the different nature of the events. The Divisional Court stressed that there could be a course of conduct if there was a lengthy gap of time between the events, but in that case there needed to be a close connection between the incidents. They gave the example of the same harassing conduct being performed each year on the victim's birthday. In *Hills*, the prosecution relied on two incidents of violence six months apart. Again there was no course of conduct, although much weight was placed on the fact that in-between the two incidents, the defendant and victim had had consensual sexual relations. This meant that the two were not sufficiently linked to indicate a course of conduct.

Conduct is defined widely in s.7(3) to include speech. It would therefore cover silent phone calls of the kind that were discussed in *Ireland*.

2. The course of conduct must amount to harassment

In s.7(2) it is explained that references to harassing a person include alarming the person or causing the person distress. In *Director Of Public Prosecutions* v. *Ramsdale* it was stressed that this reference is inclusive, not exhaustive; in other words, harassment includes alarming or distressing the victim, but there could be other ways of harassing someone. A wide range of conduct can amount to harassment and the courts have been unwilling to restrict the meaning of the word. The Home Office Circular 28/2001 stated that 'Harassment in any form is anti-social behaviour, which needs to be tackled'. This is not legally binding on the courts, but it is a remarkably wide definition.

The following points have been established by the courts:

(a) A person can be harassed by words communicated to a third party. In *DPP* v. *Kellett* the defendant contacted the victim's employer, complaining that the victim was not at work when she should have been and was defrauding her employer. These allegations were in fact untrue. It was held that the complaints could amount to harassment. The key finding was that it was foreseeable that the employer would ask the employee about the allegations and this would cause the victim distress. This was so even though the defendant had specifically requested that the victim be not informed of the allegations.

(b) The courts have been careful to distinguish acts where the defendant was essentially asking the victim whether she would be interested in a relationship and which do not amount to harassment, and acts which go beyond this (see Hot Topic below). In *King* v. *DPP* it was explained that offering a plant to the victim as a gift and writing one letter to the victim asking her whether she would be interested in a relationship would not amount to harassment. However such conduct could play an important part as the background against which other conduct could amount to harassment. In that case, the defendant subsequently searched through the victim's dustbins and removed some underwear. This could constitute harassment.

(c) A controversial issue is whether conduct about which the victim is unaware constitutes harassment. For example, in *King* v. *DPP*, unknown to the victim, the defendant had been filming the victim outside her house. This was held to amount to harassment. This might be surprising because if the victim does not know about the activity, she can hardly be alarmed or distressed (s.7(2)) nor anything like it. It is true that if she later found out she would then suffer distress and there would then be harassment. Of course, where such a case is brought, the victim will nearly always have found out about the conduct.

(d) There used to be difficulties in finding a course of conduct if the defendant used friends to take part in the harassment. This has been dealt with by the insertion of s.7(3A) into the Criminal Justice and Police Act 2001:

'A person's conduct on any occasion shall be taken, if aided, abetted, counselled or procured by another –
   (a) to be conduct on that occasion of the other (as well as conduct of the person whose conduct it is); and
   (b) to be conduct in relation to which the other's knowledge and purpose, and what he ought to have known, are the same as they were in relation to what was contemplated or reasonably foreseeable at the time of the aiding, abetting, counselling or procuring.'

The effect of this is that if the defendant does one act of harassment, and he then counsels someone else to do an act of harassment this can amount to a course of conduct.

3. The defendant must know or ought to know that the conduct is harassing
It should be noted that the test contains alternatives of either a subjective or objective *mens rea*. This is significant. It means that it is no defence for a defendant to claim, 'I thought I was expressing my love for the victim; I did not realize she would find this distressing" if it would be obvious to a reasonable person that the conduct was harassing. Further, if the defendant was acting in a way which he knew was harassing the victim, even if a

reasonable person would not realise the conduct was harassing he can still be convicted of the offence.

In *Colohan**, the defendant was a schizophrenic who wrote a number of threatening letters to his Member of Parliament. He argued that when considering whether a reasonable person would think the conduct amounted to harassment, the reasonable person should be given the characteristics of the victim (that is, in this case asking what a reasonable schizophrenic person would think). He sought to draw an analogy with the law on provocation (see *Smith,* Chapter 10.8.2). However the Court of Appeal rejected the argument and decided that the court should consider what a straight-forward reasonable person would think.

4. Defences to harassment

Section 1(3) sets out the statutory defences available to the section. The one that is likely to be relied upon the most is (c): that the conduct of the defendant is reasonable. The courts have made it clear that unlawful conduct will not be regarded as reasonable. In *Colohan*, discussed above, the defendant sought to argue that his conduct was reasonable, given that he was schizophrenic. The Court of Appeal rejected that his mental illness was a relevant factor when considering whether the conduct was reasonable.

7.13.2   Creation of Fear of Violence

Section 4 Protection from Harassment Act 1997:

'(1)   A person whose course of conduct causes another to fear, on at least two occasions, that violence will be used against him is guilty of an offence if he knows or ought to know that his course of conduct will cause the other so to fear on each of those occasions.

(2)   For the purposes of this section, the person whose course of conduct is in question ought to know that it will cause another to fear that violence will be used against him on any occasion if a reasonable person in possession of the same information would think the course of conduct would cause the other so to fear on that occasion.'

To establish a conviction it is not necessary to show that the victim was harassed, but it has to be shown that the accused has undertaken a course of conduct which on at least two occasions led to the victim having cause to fear that violence would be used against her. Seriously frightening the victim is not enough, the fear must specifically be of violence if the offence is to be made out (*Henley*). The court will consider the totality of the circumstances in deciding whether the victim was caused to fear that violence will be used against her. In *R* v. *DPP* there were two main incidents relied upon. First, the appellant brandished a knife and threatened to slash the victim's throat, and in the second he threatened to blow the victim's dog's brains out. The second threat, in the context of the first, could be regarded enough for the victim to fear for her own safety. Even though the threat was expressly made against the dog, the victim understandably believed that it implied a threat against her. In *Henley* it was stressed that it was not enough for the victim to fear for the safety of her family, she must fear violence against herself.

Given the relatively low maximum sentence for the s.1 offence (six months) and the difficulty of proving that the victim feared violence would (rather than might) be used against her for the s.4 offence (which has a maximum sentence of five years), prosecutors may still prefer to rely on charges under s.47 or s.20 of the Offences Against the Person Act 1861.

7.14 Racially Aggravated Assaults

There has been increasing concern over racially motivated crimes. The Crime and Disorder Act 1998 responded to these concerns by creating a new category of racially aggravated assaults. There are two elements that need to be shown:

1 The defendant has committed one of the listed assaults: a common assault; an offence contrary to s.20 or s.47 of the Offences Against the Person Act 1861; or offences contrary to s.2 or s.4 Protection from Harassment Act 1997. For other offences against the person a racial element may increase the sentence, even if there is not a specific crime.

2 The offence must be 'racially aggravated'. This is defined in s.28 Crime and Disorder Act 1998:

'(1) An offence is racially aggravated . . . if –
   (a) at the time of committing the offence, or immediately before or after doing so, the offender demonstrates towards the victim of the offence hostility based on the victim's membership (or presumed membership) of a racial group; or
   (b) the offence is racially motivated (wholly or partly) by hostility towards members of a racial group based on their membership of that group.
(2) In subsection (1)(a) above –

"membership" in relation to a racial group includes association with members of that group;

"presumed" means presumed by the offender.

(3) It is immaterial for the purpose of paragraph (a) or (b) of subsection (1) above whether or not the offender's hostility is also based to any extent, on –

    (a) the fact or presumption that any person or group of persons belongs to any religious group; or

    (b) any other factor not mentioned in that paragraph.

(4) In this section "racial group" means a group of persons defined by reference to race, colour, nationality (including citizenship) or ethnic origins.

The most difficult element for the prosecution for the offence may be that the defendant must have demonstrated his or her hostility based on the victim's race or that the defendant was motivated by racial hostility. The demonstration of racial hostility can easily be shown where the defendant utters racial insults as he attacks the victim. If nothing is spoken and the prosecution needs to rely on the defendant's motivation then the success of the prosecution will depend on how readily the jury will be to assume that the attack was racially motivated from the surrounding evidence.

Even if the defendant is not attacking the victim because of his or her race, if during the attack a racial hostility is demonstrated the offence will be made out (s.28(1)(a)). So, if there was an argument in a pub by a group of academic lawyers over the finer points of criminal law and an academic from one race attacked another academic of another race, and a racial insult was uttered during the attack, the offence could be established. This would be because racial hostility was demonstrated, even if the real cause of the fight was the dispute over the law. However in *DPP* v. *Pal* it was stressed that the mere fact that a racial insult is uttered prior to an attack does not necessarily prove that race was the motivation for the attack. In that case the court accepted that the attack on a caretaker was entirely due to the fact that he was demanding that some youth leave a community centre. Although a racial insult was made before the attack, the Divisional Court accepted that the attack was not racially motivated.

It should be noted that the offence includes 'presumed' membership of a group. So if a person attacks a victim believing that the victim belongs to a particular group, but in fact the victim does not, the offence is still made out. Also, as confirmed in *DPP* v. *Pal*, an attack may be racially motivated even if the defendant and victim are of the same race. The court gave the example of a white man attacking another white man because he was going out with a black women.

It is clear that the courts are not going to be sympathetic to arguments over the technical meaning of the term race. In *White*, an argument that the attack was motivated by the fact that the victim was African, but that African was not a race, was rejected. The court explained that the word 'race' was not to be interpreted restrictively and that African could be considered a race.

7.15   Reform of Offences Against the Person

The government has proposed reform of this complex area of the law. To replace the Offences Against the Person Act 1861, the draft Offences against the Person Bill includes the following key clauses:

'1(1) A person is guilty of an offence if he intentionally causes serious injury to another . . .

2(1) A person is guilty of an offence if he recklessly causes serious injury to another . . .

3(1) A person is guilty of an offence if he intentionally or recklessly causes injury to another . . .

4(1) A person is guilty of an offence if –
  (a) he intentionally or recklessly applies force to or causes an impact on the body of another, or
  (b) he intentionally or recklessly causes the other to believe that any such force or impact is imminent.

15(1): In this Act "injury" means –
  (a) physical injury, or
  (b) mental injury.

15(2) Physical injury does not include anything caused by disease but (subject to that) it includes pain unconsciousness and any other impairment of a person's physical condition.'

These reforms would do much to simplify and modernize the language used for these offences. However it can also be argued that the fine moral distinctions between different forms of assault are lost in the anodyne wording of the Bill. The Bill has not yet been presented to Parliament and such a long time has passed since the publication of the Bill that it may never be.

Hot Topic: The Limits of Preventing Harassment

There can be few more terrifying crimes than being stalked. For months or years the victim is aware that he or she may be being watched and at any moment the next incident in the campaign of intimidation will be sprung. It was because of a growing public concern with stalking, largely fuelled by the media, that the Protection from Harassment Act 1997 was passed. In fact the Act has only rarely been used to protect against stalking. Instead it has been used most often where after the break-up of a relationship, one party has behaved unpleasantly towards another. Indeed a Home Office Research Study (28/2001) found that by 2001 there had been 6000 convictions. It should, however, be noted that in the British Crime Survey 880,000 people suffered from persistent and unwanted attention from other people. This raises a difficult issue: at what point does the conduct of a person cross the line over legitimately seeking reconciliation or pursuing a friendship, and become an offence under the Prevention of Harassment Act 1997.

Consider these facts from *Woolford* v. *Director of Public Prosecutions*. These incidents occurred after the applicant (Mr Woolford) separated from his wife (Mrs Woolford):

' . . . x) During that night the applicant delivered a card to his wife's new, secret property addressed to the children. It read, Congratulations on your new house, love daddy.
xi) During the morning of 13 December 1997 the applicant returned to the former matrimonial home and gained entry to it. He removed the electric cooker which had been given to the couple by his parents.
xii) Later that day, 13 December 1997, the applicant left a message on his wife's mobile telephone saying that he had been to the house and forgotten to turn the electricity back on at the former matrimonial home and that she had better return to the former matrimonial home because of the food in the freezer.
xiii) Even later that same day the applicant left another message on Mrs Woolford's telephone saying, Welcome to the neighbourhood. My girlfriend lives around the corner.'

These facts demonstrate the difficulty. Mr Woolford at no point made any threats to his wife. Indeed his conduct could even be interpreted as kindly. However, the Queen Bench Division was willing to uphold his conviction under the Act. Given the context of the previous relationship between the parties, his conduct was reasonably interpreted by Mrs Woolford as threatening and harassing. The Court explained

'We felt that the applicant's actions over this period were skilfully aimed at Mrs Woolford by letting her know that he was superior to her, had inner sources of knowledge that enabled him to be one step ahead of her, indicated that he was prepared to violate her home (albeit that in law he was still a joint owner), and that he would still be around on a regular basis because she had moved into his girlfriend's neighbourhood, which by itself was a form of oppression.'

Some would rejoice that the court showed an enlightened awareness of the fear of violence that many women in Mrs Woolford's shoes feel. Others would be concerned that almost anything Mr Woolford did or said could be regarded as a threat. If the net of criminal liability is not to be thrown too widely, they would say, the criminal law should be restricted to overt threats.

A different kind of case where the Act has been used is where a person wishes to pursue a relationship which the other does not. What to one person can be seen as a plan to win over a beloved, to the beloved can appear as harassment. In *King* v. *DPP* the court had to consider whether the giving of a gift and sending of a letter could be regarded as harassment. The Court explained:

'Whilst I accept that the repeated offers of unwelcome gifts or the repeated sending of letters could well amount to harassment, nevertheless the single offer of a gift of modest value and the sending of one innocuous letter in the circumstances of this case cannot amount to harassment within the meaning of the 1997 Act. Nor could the letter and the gift be treated as the first stage or the first two stages of a course of conduct amounting to harassment.'

In fact in that case there was other conduct that could amount to harassment. But note that the court felt it needed to explain clearly that sending a letter and a gift did not amount to harassment. Some people will ask: have the lawyers gone mad? How can sending a letter declaring affection and sending a gift conceivably amount to harassment? Others respond that receiving unwelcome gifts and letters can in fact be extremely distressing, especially if the sender is not known to the victim. The victim may say to herself: 'this person does not know me and yet is sending me gifts and letter. They must be besotted, what will they do next?' Here there is a delicate balance to be struck between protecting the victim from this kind of fear and protecting the rights of the defendant who believes he is doing no more than expressing his love. The issue is further complicated by the requirement of the Human Rights Act 1998 (see Chapter 19) that criminal offences be defined with sufficient precision.

There is a further issue here. Are these kinds of cases suitable for the criminal law? Would it not be better to encourage these people to use family law. The victims could apply for injunctions against the defendant. These might be more effective than bringing in the full force of the criminal law, which might raise the ante between the two parties. In other words, would not these cases be better treated as a private dispute between the two parties, rather than a public one requiring the involvement of the criminal law? Interestingly, a Home Office Research Study on the operation found that over half of all convictions result in just a restraining order, identical to the order that would be granted if the case had been a civil one between the two parties.

The issue is controversial. Many argue that by treating these kind of cases as not criminal, the law is downplaying violent and threatening behaviour from which women in particular are likely to suffer. Others argue that seeking to downplay harassment is part of a wider approach which fails to take violence against women as seriously as violence against men.

Summary

7.1   The criminal law of non-sexual assaults is a combination of common law offences (assault and battery) and statutory assaults, mainly to be found in the Offences Against the Person Act 1861.

7.2   Common law assault consist of intentionally or recklessly causing another person to apprehend immediate and unlawful personal violence. It is now clear that words alone, or even silence, can amount to an assault. In an assault, the threat must be of immediate unlawful violence, and it must be a threat that is actually apprehended by the victim. It is immaterial that the accused may never intend to carry out the threat, as long as an apprehension is caused in the mind of the victim. A battery is the intentional or reckless direct application of unlawful personal violence. Violence includes any non-consensual touching and need not cause injury.

7.3 Assault occasioning actual bodily harm (s.47 of the Offences Against the Person Act) is an aggravated assault. Although the assault must be direct, the actual bodily harm may be caused indirectly, in accordance with the normal rules of causation. Bodily harm is an interference with the victim's health or comfort (including state of mind) and need not be permanent, and can include medically recognized psychological illnesses. *Mens rea* is only required in respect of the assault, and not the bodily harm caused.

7.4 Malicious wounding or inflicting grievous bodily harm (s.20 of the Offences Against the Person Act 1861) does not require an assault. Grievous bodily harm means serious injury, and a wound involves breaking the skin. The accused must either intend or foresee the possibility of some physical harm to another person, albeit of a minor character. An intent to frighten is not enough.

7.5 Wounding with intent (s.18 of the Offences Against the Person Act) is the most serious statutory assault. The *actus reus* is very similar to s.20. The *mens rea* includes malice, and in addition a specific intent: either the intent to cause grievous bodily harm or an intent to resist or prevent a lawful arrest.

7.6 Two offences in the Offences Against the Person Act deal with poisoning: s.23 and s.24. Both require the administration of a poison or destructive or noxious thing to another person. In deciding whether a substance is noxious, regard must be paid to the quantity and circumstances in which it was administered. The poison may be administered directly or indirectly. In s.24, a specific intent to injure, aggrieve or annoy is required. In the case of s.23, the administration of the poison must have the result of either endangering the life of the victim or causing grievous bodily harm, and the *mens rea* is limited to malice (which probably has the same meaning as in s.20).

7.7 The consent of the victim provides a defence to a charge of assault or battery. It is only a defence to charges involving a greater level of harm if the case falls into an exceptional category. Consent must be positive consent given by a competent victim, who is not suffering from a mistake as to the nature of the act nor as to the identity of the defendant.

7.8 A parent can rely on a defence of reasonable chastisement if he uses a reasonable level of force against his child.

7.9 Assault with intent to rob (s.8 of the Theft Act 1968) involves, in addition to an assault, an intent to steal and an intent to use or threaten to use force in order to steal, all of which must exist at the time of the assault. There is some doubt about whether or not there is the offence of assault with intent to rob.

7.10 It is an offence to commit an assault with intent to resist arrest.

7.11 It is an offence to commit an assault with intent to rape a victim.

7.12 There are a variety of offences involving resisting and obstructing police officers.

7.13 The Protection from Harassment Act protects victims from courses of conduct which harass the victim or cause the victim to fear immediate violence.

7.14 Racially aggravated offences are those where the defendant was motivated to attack the victim on the ground of the victim's race or during the attack racial hostility was revealed.

7.15 The Government has prepared a Bill which would reform the law on assaults, but it is unclear whether it will ever become law.

Case Notes

Aitken (1992) 95 Cr App Rep 304. Courts-Martial Appeal Court
Officers in the RAF were playing drunken games and set one another alight while wearing their fireproof outfits. The victim was seized by the appellants and set alight. He suffered serious burns. Their conviction under s.20 Offences Against the Person Act 1861 was overturned on the basis that the officers' belief in the victim's consent could be a defence as this was conduct that fell into the rough horseplay exception.

Attorney-General's Reference (No. 6 of 1980) [1981] 2 All ER 1057. Court of Appeal
The accused was charged with assault. He and another youth decided to settle a quarrel by fighting in the street. They fought with fists and the other youth suffered a nosebleed and bruises. The trial judge directed the jury that consent would be a defence if the accused had used 'reasonable' force, and the accused was acquitted. The Court of Appeal held that consent could not be a defence if actual bodily harm is intended or caused, as it was not in the public interest that people should try to cause each other actual bodily harm for no good reason. It is immaterial whether the act occurs in public or private.

Brown [1993] 1 AC 212. House of Lords
A group of sadomasochists committed violent acts towards each other and were convicted of assault occasioning actual bodily harm and unlawful wounding. They argued before the House of Lords that their consent was a defence to the charges. The majority of their Lordships argued that consent to injuries greater than batteries could only be a defence if the conduct fell into one of the accepted categories of exceptions or it could be shown it was in the public interest to create a new exception. The risk of infection by AIDS, the fact that participants might withdraw their consent or not really have consented, and the fear that young people may be involved, were cited as reasons why a new exception should not be created here. The minority of their Lordships focused on the accused's rights of privacy and argued that their consent should be an effective defence unless it could be shown that their conduct was harmful to the public interest.

Burstow [1997] 3 WLR 534. House of Lords
The accused had a social relationship with the victim. After she broke it off he harassed her over a lengthy period. This included making abusive telephone calls and sending unpleasant letters. As a result the woman suffered a severe depressive illness. The House of Lords, which heard the case along with *Ireland* (see below), argued that this conduct could amount to inflicting grievous bodily harm, as required by s.20 Offences against the Person Act 1861. There is no difficulty in saying a defendant inflicted psychological grievous bodily harm. Lord Steyn stated that the words 'cause' and 'inflict' were not exactly synonymous but that there is no 'radical divergence between the meaning of the two words'. Lord Hope thought the two words were interchangeable. Lord Steyn also confirmed that assault was not an element of the offence contrary to s.20.

Cato [1976] 1 All ER 260. Court of Appeal
The appellant was convicted of administering a noxious thing, contrary to s.23 of the

Offences Against the Person Act 1861, and of manslaughter. He had injected a friend with heroin. The Court of Appeal upheld his conviction on both counts, holding that heroin was a 'noxious thing' within s.23, because it is 'liable to injure in common use', even though the victim in this case had a high tolerance to heroin. The court also held that malice in s.23 did not imply any foresight on the part of the accused as to the likelihood of causing injury, where (as in this case) the injury was caused directly. (See also Chapter 10 case notes.)

Chan Fook [1994] 2 All ER 552. Court of Appeal
The appellant was convicted of an s.47 offence after assaulting the victim, whom he suspected of stealing a ring. The victim suffered psychiatric illnesses after being terrorized by the appellant. The Court of Appeal held that a psychiatric illness could constitute actual bodily harm if the illness is a recognized illness and more than fear, distress or panic.

Clarence (1888) 22 QBD 23. Court for Crown Cases Reserved
The appellant was convicted of offences under s.20 and s.47 of the Offences Against the Person Act 1861. He had had intercourse with his wife while suffering from a venereal disease, and had infected her. She would not have consented to the intercourse had she known that he had the disease. The court quashed the convictions on the grounds that there had been no assault on the wife, because she had consented to the act of intercourse, and the communication of a disease was not an assault; and (by a majority) that an assault was necessary for a conviction under s.20 as well as s.47.

Colohan [2001] EWCA Crim 1251. Court Of Appeal
The defendant was a schizophrenic who wrote a number of long letters to his Member of Parliament. The letters contained a measure of abuse and some material capable of being construed as threats of violence and/or death. The Member of Parliament gave evidence that the letters caused him to feel threatened and suffer from nightmares. The defendant was convicted under ss.1 and 2 of the Protection from Harassment Act. He appealed on two grounds. First, he argued that in deciding whether he had *mens rea* under s.1(2) the court should consider whether a reasonable person with his characteristics (namely schizophrenia) would have appreciated that his conduct was harassing. Second, he argued that when considering whether he had a defence on the basis that his conduct was reasonable under s.1(3)(c) the court should take into account the fact that he was a schizophrenic. Both of these arguments were rejected by the Court of Appeal which held that the defendant's schizophrenia was irrelevant in either of these cases.

Cunningham [1957] 2 All ER 412. Court of Criminal Appeal
The appellant was convicted of an offence under s.23 of the Offences Against the Person Act 1861. He had pulled a gas meter off the wall of a house with the intention of stealing money from the meter. In so doing, he broke the main supply pipe and released gas into the rest of the house, poisoning an old lady he knew to be living there. The trial judge directed the jury that 'malicious' in s.23 meant 'wicked'. The Court of Criminal Appeal allowed the appeal and quashed the conviction. Byrne J adopted the meaning of 'maliciously' given by Professor Kenny: 'in any statutory definition of a crime "malice" must be taken not in the old vague sense of wickedness in general, but as requiring either (i) an actual intention to do the particular kind of harm that in fact was done, or (ii) recklessness as to whether such harm should occur or not (i.e. the accused has foreseen that the particular kind of harm might be done, and yet has gone on to take the risk of it)'. Byrne J then held that in s.23, foresight of the risk of causing injury was sufficient.

Fagan [1969] 1 QB 439. Divisional Court
See Chapter 3 case notes.

Hill [1986] 83 Cr App Rep 386. House of Lords
The appellant was convicted of administering a noxious thing with intent to injure, contrary to s.24 of the Offences Against the Person Act 1861. He had given two teenage boys a number of tablets which were only available on prescription as an aid to slimming. The only issue at the trial was whether the appellant had administered the drugs with intent to injure. The Court of Appeal allowed the appeal on the basis that the trial judge had directed the jury that an intent to keep the boys awake could amount to an intent to injure. The House of Lords restored the conviction, holding that although an intent to keep the victim awake would not by itself amount to an intent to injure, the direction of the trial judge was not at fault. It had been made clear to the jury that an intent to cause physical injury was required.

Hyam v. *DPP* [1975] AC 55. House of Lords
See Chapter 9 case notes.

Ireland [1997] 3 WLR 534. House of Lords
The accused telephoned several women a number of times and simply remained silent. They suffered from a variety of psychiatric illnesses. Lord Steyn affirmed the interpretation of actual bodily harm in *Chan Fook* (see above). He stated that words alone and indeed silence could form the basis of an assault. He explained that the assault in this case could be said to have arisen because the victims would not have known what the accused was going to do next and may have feared that he was about to come around to their houses and attack them.

R v. *K* 25 JULY 2001; [2001] UKHL 41. House of Lords
See Chapter 6 case notes.

Martin [1881–5] All ER 699. Court for Crown Cases Reserved
The appellant was convicted of maliciously inflicting grievous bodily harm, contrary to s.20 of the Offences Against the Person Act 1861. He had left a theatre at the end of a performance, putting out the lights and blocking the exit door with an iron bar. The audience panicked and several people were injured by being crushed against the iron bar and the door. The court upheld his conviction, holding that he had done 'that which would certainly alarm and frighten a number of persons, and also obstruct their exit from the theatre' (per Lord Coleridge c J). The court did not state that Martin had committed an assault, and opinions on this differ.

Moloney [1985] AC 905. House of Lords
See Chapter 9 case notes.

Parmenter, Savage [1992] 1 AC 699. House of Lords
Mrs Savage had intended to throw beer over Miss Beal, her husband's former girl-friend, but the glass had slipped out of her hand and broken, injuring Miss Beal. Mr Parmenter had injured his child by rough handling, which he said he did not realize would harm his child significantly. These cases were brought before the House of Lords in order to determine the correct *mens rea* for s.47 and s.20. The House held that the *mens rea* for s.47 was that necessary for assault or battery. There was no need to prove a further *mens rea* as to the actual bodily harm. For s.20 the *mens rea* was foresight as to some harm, albeit not serious harm.

Rice v. *Connolly* [1966] 2 QB 414. Divisional Court
The appellant was convicted of wilfully obstructing a constable in the execution of his duty, contrary to s.51 (3) of the Police Act 1964. The constable had asked the appel-lant to give his name and address, and the appellant had refused. The court allowed

the appeal, holding (per Lord Parker CJ) that the obstruction was not 'wilful' as the appellant was under no legal obligation to disclose his name and address, and so had 'lawful excuse' for withholding the information; there is no general legal duty to assist the police. Lord Parker also said that the deliberate giving of false information would amount to an obstruction.

Roberts [1971] 56 Cr App Rep 95. Court of Appeal
See Chapter 5 case notes.

Smith v. *DPP* [1960] 3 All ER 161. House of Lords
See Chapter 9 case notes.

Williams (Gladstone) (1983) 78 Cr App Rep 276. Court of Appeal
See Chapter 15 case notes.

Wilson [1984] AC 242. House of Lords
The appellant was charged with maliciously inflicting grievous bodily harm, contrary to s.20 of the Offences Against the Person Act 1861. He was acquitted of that offence, and convicted of assault occasioning actual bodily harm, contrary to s.47 of the same Act. He appealed on the ground that a jury can only convict a defendant of an offence with which he is not charged, if the offence with which he is charged includes the elements of the other charge. He argued that the elements of an s.47 charge were not included in an s.20 charge. The Court of Appeal allowed the appeal, but on appeal to the House of Lords the House allowed the appeal and restored the conviction. It was held: (i) that s.20 does not require an assault, although the infliction of grievous bodily harm would usually be by means of an assault; (ii) (disagreeing with the Court of Appeal) that nevertheless an allegation of 'inflicting grievous bodily harm' did impliedly include an allegation of an assault, so that a conviction under s.47 was possible even where not expressly included on the indictment.

Further Reading

A discussion on the law on assaults and harassment is found in Gardner (1998), Herring and Wells. Reform of the law on offences against the person is found in Gardner (1994) and Horder (1994 and 1998). The role of consent in the criminal law is found in Bamforth, Kell, Roberts and Shute.

Bamforth, 'Sado-Masochism and Consent' [1994] *Criminal Law Review* 661.
Gardner, 'Rationality and the Rule of Law in Offences Against the Person' [1994] *Cambridge Law Journal* 502.
Gardner, 'Stalking' (1998) *Law Quarterly Review* 33.
Herring 'The Criminalisation of Harassment' (1998) *Cambridge Law Journal* 10.
Horder, 'Rethinking Non-fatal Offences Against the Person' (1994) 14 *Oxford Journal of Legal Studies* 335.
Horder, 'Reconsidering Psychic Assault' [1998] *Criminal Law Review* 392.
Kell, 'Social Disutility and Consent' (1994) *Oxford Journal of Legal Studies* 121.
Law Commission Consultation Paper Number 139.
Roberts, 'The Philosophical Foundations of Consent in the Criminal Law' [1997] 17 *Oxford Journal of Legal Studies* 389.
Shute, 'Something Old, Something New, Something Borrowed . . .' [1996] *Criminal Law Review* 684.
Wells, 'Stalking: the Criminal Law Response' [1997] *Criminal Law Review* 463.

8   Sexual Offences

8.1   The Scope of Sexual Offences

The scope of sexual offences is always controversial and raises the question of what purpose the criminal law serves in this area. J. Temkin has written 'the overriding objective which . . . the law . . . should seek to pursue is the protection of sexual choice, that is to say the protection of a woman's right to choice whether, when and with whom to have sexual intercourse'. Whether it achieves this end or whether the law is so concerned about protecting the position of a potential defendant that it condones many cases of sexual violence against women is a matter of much controversy. As well as protecting or undermining sexual choice, the law can also be seen as a means of defending the sexual morality of a particular society (see Chapter 1.2).

There is also debate over whether it is appropriate to consider sexual offences as a separate category of offences from other violent assaults. Some argue that the seriousness of sexual offences is belittled by being seen as 'sexual' offences, rather than a form of violent offence, especially as violence is often an aspect of rape. Others argue that it is crucial to emphasize that as well as the violence usually involved, sexual offences include a unique element. This unique wrong in sexual offences can be difficult to put into words. One suggestion is that in the same way that sexual contact can be used as the highest form of intimacy and the ultimate expression of love, misuse of such acts is a uniquely harmful invasion of privacy and damage to a person's identity. This is in addition to the infringement of the victim's sexual autonomy. Being able to choose with whom to have sexual relations is regarded by many as a fundamental freedom.

It is important to appreciate that the popular perception of rape is misleading. The traditional image of rape being a crime launched by a stranger against a woman out walking alone at night belies the fact that studies indicate that about two-thirds of victims are raped by people they know. This fact causes particular problems for prosecutors who need to show beyond all reasonable doubt that the victim did not consent to the sexual intercourse. The difficulty over proof of the victim's consent reveals the ever-present conflict between the interests of the victim and those of the accused, and is particularly visible in the procedural difficulties raised by the proof of these offences. Reform of sexual offences tends to centre around issues which illustrate these conflicts of interest: the question of consent; the appropriate *mens rea* for sexual offences; and whether acts committed by consenting adults in private should be penalized. The offences covered in detail here (rape, indecent assault and unlawful sexual intercourse) illustrate these issues well. We start with the most serious and perhaps the most controversial: rape.

8.2   Rape

The Sexual Offences Acts 1956 s.1(1) merely provides, 'It is an offence for a man to rape a woman or another man'. The Act provides a definition of rape in s.1(2) and (3), as amended by Sexual Offences (Amendment) Act 1976 and Criminal Justice and Public Order Act 1994:

'(2) A man commits rape if –
    (a) he has intercourse with a person (whether vaginal or anal) who at the time of the intercourse does not consent to it; and
    (b) at the time he knows that the person does not consent to the intercourse or is reckless as to whether that person consents to it.
(3) A man also commits rape if he induces a married woman to have sexual intercourse with him by impersonating her husband.'

This can be broken down into the following elements:

- Sexual intercourse
- Absence of the victim's consent
- Knowledge or recklessness as to the offence.

8.2.1   Sexual Intercourse

'Sexual intercourse' is to be given its normal meaning. There must be some penetration of the vagina or anus by the defendant's penis, although there does not need to be ejaculation. Penetration with other parts of the defendant's body or penile penetration of other bodily orifices do not amount to sexual intercourse, although they may be the basis of a charge of indecent assault. In principle, this means that a woman cannot be guilty of rape, although she can be guilty of aiding, abetting, counselling or procuring a rape (*DPP* v. *R and B*; see Chapter 17). It used to be that a boy under fourteen could not be capable in law of engaging in sexual intercourse. Section 1 Sexual Offences Act 1993 abolished this rule and it is no longer part of the law.

It used to be thought that sexual intercourse would only be 'unlawful' if the man and woman were unmarried. In other words a husband could not be guilty of raping his wife. This was based on the writing of the jurist Hale, who argued that a wife, by her wedding vows, gave to her husband her irrevocable consent to intercourse at any time during the marriage. A more modern argument was that marital rape was not suitable for the ministrations of the criminal law and should be left as a 'family law issue'. However, the House of Lords in *R* (1992) stated that the common law had to develop in line with the times. The old law was 'quite unacceptable' and so the common law should be restated so that a husband could be guilty of raping his wife without her consent. This decision was given statutory effect in the Criminal Justice and Public Act 1994 by removing the requirement that the sexual intercourse be unlawful. There will still be a slight difference in the treatment of cases involving husbands alleged to have raped their wives, in that a husband may more easily be able to persuade a jury that he believed that his wife was consenting, than if he had had intercourse with a stranger.

A second significant change introduced by the 1994 Act is that rape now covers anal and vaginal intercourse. There are two consequences of this. Firstly, it means that a man can be the victim of rape. Secondly, a man who has anal intercourse with a women against her consent commits the offence of rape.

Under s.44 of the 1956 Act, sexual intercourse is 'deemed complete upon proof of penetration only'. This must be read in the light of *Kaitamaki*, in which the Privy Council held that although the offence of rape is committed on penetration, it continues until withdrawal, and so it is not necessary for the act of penetration itself to be without consent. Even if the victim consents to the penetration, the defendant would be guilty of rape if he continues intercourse after becoming aware that the victim is no longer consenting (*Cooper and Schaub*). The decision is clearly correct. A victim's sexual autonomy includes not only controlling whether a person penetrates them, but also whether the person remains in them.

8.2.2 Lack of the Victim's Consent

The second element of the *actus reus* of rape is that the victim did not positively consent to the sexual intercourse. If the victim did consent to sexual intercourse then even if the defendant thought she did not consent there can be no rape (although there would be an offence of attempted rape). Lack of consent is an active state of mind and does not depend on an outward manifestation of dissent. The requirement that the victim positively consents to sexual intercourse means that intercourse with a woman who is asleep (*Lartner and Castleton*) or so drunk that she is unaware of what is happening to her (*Malone*) constitutes the *actus reus* of rape. Indeed it was held in *McFall* that the victim did not consent where she pretended to have an orgasm because of her fear of the attacker. She may have appeared to consent to an outside observer, but it was clear from all the evidence that subjectively she did not consent. Although this is the law, a lack of consent is notoriously difficult to prove beyond reasonable doubt unless there is clear evidence of dissent (for example, evidence of a struggle or violence).

If the victim lacks the capacity to give her consent then the *actus reus* of rape will be made out. So if the victim lacks sufficient understanding to be able to consent to sexual intercourse because of age (*Howard*) or mental deficiency (*Barratt*) then there is no true consent. Similarly if the victim is so drunk she is unable to consent, the *actus reus* of rape is made out. In all these cases the defendant may, of course, argue that he lacked the *mens rea* required, in that he was unaware of the victim's lack of capacity and believed that she was consenting.

Those cases which have caused the courts greatest difficulty are where the victim appears to consent but the reality of the consent is in question because the victim was acting out of fear or under a mistake. In *Olugboja**, Dunn LJ in Court of Appeal held that there was an important distinction to be drawn between consent and submission:

'It is not necessary for the prosecution to prove that what might otherwise appear to have been consent was in reality merely submission induced by force, fear or fraud, although one or more of these factors will no doubt be present in the majority of cases of rape . . . [T]he dividing line . . . between real consent on the one hand and mere submission on the other may not be easy to draw. Where it is to be drawn in a given case is for the jury to decide, applying their combined good sense, experience and knowledge of human nature and modern behaviour to all the relevant facts of that case.'

The courts have established different rules for those cases which involve fear and those which involve mistakes, and it is necessary to consider these issues separately.

1.   Where the victim appears to consent, but does so out of fear.
It is clear that in some circumstances threats can negate a victim's apparent consent and so the accused can be found guilty of rape. Where the issue of the victim's consent is raised, the jury has to decide whether the victim has reluctantly acquiesced and so consented, or submitted and so did not consent. In *Olugboja*, Dunn LJ took the view that this would be a question for the jury in each case 'applying their combined good sense, experience and knowledge of human nature and modern behaviour to all the relevant facts of that case.' Therefore the jury has to consider the effect of the threat on the particular victim in each case. The same threat that negates the consent of one victim in one case may not negate the consent of a different victim in another case. It all depends on the victim's character and the circumstances of the case. What matters is not the nature of the threat, whether it is a threat of violence or not, but the effect of the threat. No doubt where the threat is of death or grievous bodily harm, the jury will readily find that the victim did not truly consent. But there may be cases where threats not involving violence will negate the consent of the victim. Imagine a defendant who threatens to tell the victim's father that she has been seeing him unless the victim has sexual intercourse with him, and the victim fears that her father will react by ostracizing her from her family and that she will have nowhere to live. The 'consent' in such a case could be regarded as not true consent, but submission.

It is sometimes suggested that a victim who agrees to sexual intercourse following a promise of a benefit will not be rape. A popular example is an actress who consents to sexual intercourse with a director after he promises her a part in his film. Consent it is said can only be vitiated by a threat, not by a promise of a benefit. Others argue that this is not necessarily a useful distinction. Should the actress case be seen that differently if the actress had been given a part in the film and the director threatened to sack her unless she agreed to sexual intercourse? The better view, it is suggested, is that although a jury is far more likely to find consent vitiated by a threat rather than an offer of a benefit, there may be cases where the offer of the benefit could negate consent. If a man finds a homeless woman on a cold night and offers her shelter if she agrees to sexual intercourse and reluctantly she consents, is it not reasonable that this could be classified as rape?

Remember that the question of the victim's consent is subjective to the victim. This means that what is crucial here is the fear of the victim, not the threat made. Indeed the defendant may issue no threat, but if the victim fears that he will be violent towards her unless she consents to sexual intercourse, there may be no true consent.

It is important to note that it is a separate offence to procure a woman, by threats or intimidation, to have sexual intercourse in any part of the world with the accused or a third party (s.2 of the Sexual Offences Act 1956). In those cases where the defendant has threatened or intimidated the woman but the jury decides that the victim did consent, the defendant may still have committed an offence contrary to s.2. It must be shown that the woman would not have engaged in sexual intercourse with the defendant had the threats or intimidation not been issued (*Christian*). The offence is only available where the victim is a woman, but it can be committed by a person of either sex.

2. *Where the victim appears to consent, but does so under a mistake*
Difficulties also arise in cases where the victim's consent to sexual intercourse is based on a mistake, maybe induced by a fraud or deceit of the defendant. In *Clarence**, which concerned a husband infected with venereal disease prosecuted for inflicting grievous bodily harm on his wife, Stephen J said that

'the only sorts of fraud which so far destroy the effect of a women's consent as to convert a connection consented to in fact into a rape are frauds to the nature of the act itself, or as to the identity of the person who does the act.'

Examples of fraud as to the nature of the act include *Flattery*, where the defendant told the victim that the sexual intercourse was a form of medical treatment, and *Williams* (1923), where a singing teacher told his student that sexual intercourse was a 'breathing treatment'. Notably both these cases are over eighty years old, and improved sex education means that such cases are unlikely to arise in the future.

In *Papadimitropoulos*, it was held by the High Court of Australia that fraud as to whether the parties had undergone a ceremony of marriage did not affect the consent:

'rape is carnal knowledge of a woman without her consent: carnal knowledge is the physical fact of penetration; it is the consent to that which is in question; such a consent demands a perception as to what is about to take place, as to the identity of the man and the character of what he is doing. But once the consent is comprehending and actual the inducing causes [for example, that there has been a valid marriage] cannot destroy its reality and leave the man guilty of rape.'

In *Linekar**, the deception related to whether or not the defendant was going to pay for the sexual intercourse. The defendant led the victim (a prostitute) to believe he would pay, but ran off without paying. The Court of Appeal held that this was not a deception as to the nature of the act and so was not rape. The argument that the Court of Appeal accepted was that the act of sexual intercourse was exactly what both parties expected and the deception only related to what would happen after the intercourse (that is, whether there would be payment). One might have thought that for a prostitute there is a significant difference in the nature of unpaid sexual intercourse (for example, with her partner) and paid intercourse (for example, with a client) and so there is a deception as to the nature of the act, but the court did not accept this argument.

The law in this area has been thrown into some confusion by a decision of the Court of Appeal in relation to indecent assault. In *Tabussum*, three women permitted the defendant to examine their breasts after he said (untruthfully) that he was medically qualified. The Court of Appeal explained (uncontroversially) that the law on the meaning of consent was the same in relation to indecent assault as it was in relation to rape. It was held that although the women had consented to the nature of the acts, they had not consented to their quality. The Court of Appeal did not make crystal clear precisely what was meant by this. One explanation is that the women were deceived as to the quality of the act because they were deceived as to the purpose of the defendant's examination. It was not for medical purposes but for other reasons (presumably sexual). Might it then be that a woman who agrees to sexual intercourse after a man untruthfully tells her that he loves her has been mistaken as to the quality of the act? Is the quality of loving sexual intercourse different from that where sexual intercourse is entered into for purely carnal motivations?

One issue, which is yet to be resolved by the court, is the position where the victim consents to sexual intercourse *per vaginam*, but the defendant has sexual intercourse *per anum*. It is submitted that the consent must be to the specific act that the defendant performs. No doubt, in such a case, the *mens rea* of the defendant will be crucial.

So far we have been looking at mistakes as to the nature of the act. What about mistakes as to the identity of the defendant? The Sexual Offences Act 1956 s.1(3) states that: 'A man also commits rape if he induces a married woman to have sexual intercourse with him by impersonating her husband'. In *Elbekkay**, a case decided before s.1(3) was added to the Sexual Offences Act, the Court of Appeal stated that impersonation of a regular sexual partner could vitiate the apparent consent of the victim, as well as impersonation of a husband. Indeed it was stated that impersonating 'a husband or another' could vitiate consent and so it may be that later cases will confirm that impersonation of anyone known to the victim may negate consent. There is a possible argument that because the Act expressly mentions impersonating husbands but not others, it impliedly repeals *Elbekkay*. However, the statute's wording does not compel such a conclusion. It certainly does not say that impersonation of people other than husbands does not negate consent. As there is much to be said in favour of the *Elbekkay* approach on policy grounds, it is suggested that it should be held to still represent the law.

Again it should be stressed that the question of consent is subjective to the victim. So if the victim is mistaken as to the nature of the act or the identity of the defendant this will negate her consent, even if that mistake was not caused by anything done or said by the defendant. This is demonstrated in *Elbekkay* where the defendant entered the victim's bedroom late at night. The victim assumed he was her boyfriend and this mistake negated her consent, even though the defendant never said he was her boyfriend.

Section 3 of the 1956 Act creates a separate, less serious offence of procuring a woman by false pretences or false representations to have sexual intercourse in any part of the world. The offence is only available if the victim is a woman.

To summarize the law on mistakes and consent, the present law is that a deception as to the nature of the act, or impersonation of a husband or regular partner, can negate consent. S. Gardner (1997) has suggested that this approach, focusing on the kind of deception used, overlooks the fact that different deceptions will affect different victims in different ways. As we have seen, the Court of Appeal in the leading case of *Olugboja* stressed that the question of whether the victim's consent is invalidated by the threat or use of force is not based on the form of threat or outward appearances, but on the reality of the victim's consent. He suggests that a similar approach should be taken in relation to mistakes, and whether the victim consents should not depend on the nature of the fraud but on the 'victim's perception of her own interests'. Thus to one victim a mistaken belief that she was married to the defendant may be hugely important and negate her apparent consent. But to another victim that mistake may be of little significance and have no effect on her consent. Indeed the present law on mistakes on consent does appear rather unsophisticated when compared with the *Olugboja* test, although it is easier for a jury to use.

8.2.3 The *Mens Rea* of Rape

The *mens rea* for rape is twofold. The first aspect is that the defendant must intend to engage in sexual intercourse. It would only be in the most unusual of circumstances that the defendant had sexual intercourse with the victim but did not intend to do so. Although the courts are yet to address the question, a defendant would probably be entitled to introduce evidence of his drunkenness as evidence that he did not intend to commit sexual intercourse, because the intention here is a specific intent (see Chapter 15.3.2).

The *mens rea* of rape is now defined in s.1(1)(b) Sexual Offences (Amendment) Act 1976: the accused must either know that the victim is not consenting, or be reckless as to whether or not she is consenting. This provision gives statutory effect to the decision of the House of Lords in *Morgan**, and followed a report by an advisory group (the Heilbron Report (Cmnd 6352)). In *Morgan*, the House of Lords held that a mistake as to whether the victim was consenting, even an unreasonable mistake, negates *mens rea* and is a defence to a charge of rape. Lord Hailsham held:

'The minimum *mens rea* or guilty mind in most common law offences, including rape, is the intention to do the prohibited act . . . The only qualification I would make . . . is the refinement . . . that if the intention of the accused is to have intercourse *nolens volens*, that is recklessly and not caring whether the victim be a consenting party or not, that is equivalent on ordinary principles to an intent to do the prohibited act without the consent of the victim.'

Lord Halisham went on to point out that if the defendant claims to have believed that the victim consented, but this seems unreasonable on the facts of the case, the unreasonableness of the belief may lead the jury to disbelieve the defendant. This point has been put into statutory form in s.1(2) Sexual Offences (Amendment) Act 1976:

'It is hereby declared that if at a trial for a rape offence the jury has to consider whether a man believed that a woman was consenting to sexual intercourse, the presence or absence of reasonable grounds for such a belief is a matter to which the jury is to have regard, in conjunction with any other relevant matters in considering whether he is so believed.'

Section 1(1)(b) makes it clear that the key to the *mens rea* of rape is the recklessness of the defendant. But as noted in Chapter 4 the meaning of recklessness is far from settled. The caselaw is confused as to the precise *mens rea* required for rape, but has moved away from simply considering whether the *mens rea* is *Cunningham* or *Caldwell* recklessness and has sought a definition of recklessness which is unique to rape.

The cases suggest that a defendant is guilty of rape if he knows the victim was not consenting, believes that the victim might not be consenting, or did not care (was indifferent to) whether or not she was consenting (*Taylor*, *Pigg* and *Thomas* (1983)). As Lord Lane put it:

> 'A man is reckless if either he was indifferent and gave no thought to the possibility that the woman might not be consenting, in circumstances where, if any thought had been given to the matter, it would have been obvious that there was a risk she was not, or, he was aware of the possibility that she might not be consenting but nevertheless persisted, regardless of whether she consented or not . . .'

An alternative way of expressing this, and one that may be easier for juries to understand, is to state that the defendant is guilty unless he positively believed that the woman was consenting (*Satnam and Kewal** and *Gardiner*). As Bristow J in *Satnam and Kewal* suggested:

> 'If [the jury] thought he might genuinely have believed that she [the victim] did want to, even though he was mistaken in his belief, they would find him not guilty . . . If . . . they were sure he had no genuine belief that she wanted to, they would find him guilty.'

What if a defendant believed that the victim consented to sexual intercourse because he was drunk? The Court of Appeal in *Fotheringham* held that if a drunken defendant mistakenly believes that the victim is consenting, and had he been sober he would not have made this mistake, then his drunken belief affords no defence. This is in line with the attitude towards drunkenness shown by offences requiring recklessness (see Chapter 4.6).

The law on the *mens rea* for rape has been criticized by commentators. The law that a man, who honestly but unreasonably believed that a women was consenting, has a defence has been condemned. It has been argued that the defendant could easily have had reasonable grounds for his belief that the victim consented. He could, for example, have asked her whether she consented if there was any doubt over the issue. Given the seriousness of the consequences if he is mistaken over her consent, and the ease with which a defendant could have reasonable grounds for his belief, it does not seem unreasonable for the law to require a defendant to have reasonable grounds for his belief. Despite these arguments, *DPP* v. *B* and *R* v. *K* indicate that the House of Lords seem wedded to the idea that a defendant has a defence if he honestly believes an aspect of the *actus reus* is not present.

8.3   Indecent Assault

Indecent assault is an aggravated form of common assault and is found in the Sexual Offences Act 1956 s.14 (against a woman) and s.15 (against a man). It is subject to a maximum of ten years' imprisonment, whether the victim is a man or woman. In order to obtain a conviction it is necessary to show that the defendant committed an assault or battery upon the victim in circumstances that were indecent. There are three elements of the offence:

- An assault
- In indecent circumstances
- Intent to commit the indecent assault.

8.3.1   An Assault

In order for there to be an indecent assault there must be proof of an assault or battery. Both the *actus reus* and *mens rea* of the assault must be shown. These terms are to be given the meaning found in Chapter 7. In *Fairclough* v. *Whipp* it was held that an invitation by a man to a child to touch his penis was not an assault. The man did not touch the child and the child had no fear of immediate force. Therefore, despite the indecent circumstances, the offence of indecent assault was not made out. In *DPP* v. *K*, this case was described as revealing 'a gap in the protective net of the Act of 1956'. However, in such circumstances a charge involving gross indecency with or towards a child under 16 contrary to s.1(1) Indecency with Children Act 1960 may be appropriate. *Faulkener* v. *Talbott* has been interpreted by some commentators to mean that if a woman has sexual intercourse with a boy under 16 there is no indecent assault if she is a 'passive participant' and she would only commit the offence if she deliberately touched him in some way. An alternative view is that sexual intercourse inevitably involves both people touching each other (it is not something a man 'does' to a woman).

It is possible for there to be an indecent assault without the victim being aware of it. As has been explained by the Court of Appeal:

'The offence of indecent assault included both a battery, or touching, and psychic assault without touching. If there was touching, it was not necessary to prove that the victim was aware of the assault or of the circumstances of indecency. If there was no touching, then to constitute an indecent assault the victim must be shown to have been aware of the assault and of the circumstances of indecency' (*Court**).

A major element in the offence of indecent assault is, as with rape, a lack of consent. If the victim consents to the acts then there is no assault, and so no indecent assault. The law governing consent is the same for indecent assault as it was for rape (*McAllister*). But this is subject to the special statutory provisions which protect those who are thought to be particularly vulnerable to indecent assault: under s.14(2) and s.15(2), a girl or boy under sixteen cannot in law give the necessary consent; and under s.14(4) and s.15(3), a 'defective' cannot consent in law. However, one case (*Sutton*) suggests that subsections 14(2) and 15(2) only prevent children from consenting to indecent touching that is inherently indecent. In that case a man touched boys on their arms, showing how he wished them to pose for nude photographs. The touching was not inherently indecent and so the children could consent, and therefore there was no assault and no offence at all was made out (*Sutton*). However, another case suggests that children can never consent to an assault, including touching, in indecent circumstances (*Goss*), and this seems a preferable approach. Following *R*, a husband cannot rely on an argument that his wife is deemed to consent to his indecent acts by their marriage.

In order for the *mens rea* of an assault to be established it has to be shown that the defendant was aware that the victim was not consenting. What of those victims who cannot consent in law? When the victim is under sixteen or is 'a defective', it must be shown that either the defendant was aware the victim was not consenting or that she was either under 16 (*R* v. *K**) or a defective (s.14(4) and s.15(3); (*Hudson*)). These beliefs do not have to be reasonable, only genuinely held (*R* v. *K*). Although, as in rape, the more unreasonable the belief, the harder it will be for the defendant to prove that he genuinely believed that the victim did genuinely consent. Where, however, the victim is under thirteen there is no defence for a defendant to prove that he was not aware the victim was under sixteen (s.5 Sexual Offences Act 1956; *R* v. *K*).

8.3.2   The Circumstances were Indecent

The assault or battery must be in circumstances which are indecent. The House of Lords in *Court* has considered the definition of indecency and it is now necessary to distinguish three cases:

1 If reasonable people would describe the circumstances of the assault as clearly indecent then it is indecent. This is so even if in fact the defendant does not see it as indecent. An example of such conduct was given in *Court** of a man removing all of a woman's clothes in public. This

would be indecent even if the defendant acted in order to embarrass the victim, rather than for indecent motives.

2 If reasonable people would describe the situation as ambiguous – it might be indecent or it might not – then it is necessary to consider whether the defendant found it was indecent. If he did, then it is indecent; if he did not, then it is not. An example of this was found in the facts of *Court* itself. A shopkeeper spanked a twelve-year-old girl on her clothed bottom. The House of Lords suggested that this was an ambiguous act but the defendant was rightly convicted when he admitted that he spanked her because of a 'buttock fetish'.

3 If reasonable people would not think the situation indecent then it is not indecent, even if the defendant found it so. An example of this was *George* where a man removed a woman's shoe because he had a 'foot fetish'. He was acquitted as a reasonable person would not think removing a shoe indecent.

The act of the defendant itself need not be indecent if the circumstances of the assault are indecent. This was recently taken a little further in *Sargent* where a defendant threatened a fifteen-year-old boy with violence unless the boy masturbated into a condom. Although there was an assault followed by an indecent incident, it is unclear that the circumstances of the assault were themselves indecent.

8.3.3   The Defendant must be Aware that the Circumstances are Indecent

The defendant must be shown to be aware that the circumstances of the assault were indecent. If the situation is as **1** above, then what needs to be shown is that the defendant is aware that most right-thinking people would regard the circumstances as indecent. If the situation is as **2** above, then it is sufficient that the defendant is acting from indecent motivations. It should be explained that there is confusion because Lord Ackner in *Court* stated that it must be shown the defendant intended the assault to be indecent. The Court of Appeal in *C* explained that where the act is in category **1**, it is not necessary to show that the defendant intended the act to be indecent; recklessness (or knowledge that the act would be regarded by right-thinking people as indecent) is sufficient.

8.4   Unlawful Sexual Intercourse

We have already noted that it is an offence to procure a woman to have sexual intercourse by threats or intimidation (Sexual Offences Act s.2) or false pretences or false representations (Sexual Offences Act s.3). Section 4 of the Act provides that:

> 'It is an offence for a person to apply or administer to, or cause to be taken by, a woman any drug, matter or thing with intent to stupefy or overpower her so as thereby to enable any man to have unlawful sexual intercourse with her.'

This offence can be committed by a man and a woman but the victim must be a woman. It should be noted that the s.4 offence can be committed even if in fact sexual intercourse never takes place.

Sexual intercourse with a girl under sixteen is an offence under the Sexual Offences Act 1956, although the law makes a distinction between girls under thirteen (s.5, punishable with life imprisonment) and those between thirteen and sixteen (s.6, punishable with two years' imprisonment). These offences are committed even if the victim consents to the sexual intercourse. The 'age of consent' for heterosexual intercourse is therefore sixteen (note that for homosexual acts between men, the 'age of consent' has recently been reduced to sixteen, Sexual Offences (Amendment) Act 2000; and between women it is sixteen, s.14 Sexual Offences Act 1956). The girl under sixteen is regarded as the victim, even if she in fact consents to the intercourse, and she will not be guilty of any offence (see Chapter 17.11).

The House of Lords in *R* v. *K* has recently confirmed that there is no requirement that the accused knew that the girl was under sixteen or under thirteen. However, there is a specific provision in s.6 relating to girls between thirteen and sixteen: a man under twenty-four charged with an offence under this section will have a defence if he reasonably believed the girl to be over sixteen, and he has not previously been charged with a like offence. Note that this defence does not apply to indecent assault, and an accused to whom this provision applies could therefore be convicted of the latter offence.

It should be noted that a woman who has intercourse with a boy under sixteen may be guilty of indecent assault, but is not guilty of unlawful intercourse.

8.5   Sexual Offences (Amendment) Act 2000

A new offence of engaging in sexual activity with a person below the age of 18 in breach of trust was created by s.3 Sexual Offences (Amendment)

Act 2000. The maximum sentence is five years' imprisonment. The offence
is described as follows:

'(1) . . . it shall be an offence for a person aged 18 or over –
     (a) to have sexual intercourse (whether vaginal or anal) with a
     person under that age; or
     (b) to engage in any other sexual activity with or directed towards
     such a person, if (in either case) he is in a position of trust in rela-
     tion to that person.'

Some of these terms require further clarification:

1.   Sexual activity
Section 3(5) provides a definition of sexual activity. It

'(a) does not include any activity which a reasonable person would
     regard as sexual only with knowledge of the intentions, motives or
     feelings of the parties; but
 (b) subject to that, means any activity which such a person would
     regard as sexual in all the circumstances.'

What this means is that an activity is sexual if a reasonable person, looking
at what was happening, but without knowing the thoughts or feelings of the
parties, would regard it as a sexual activity. So, if the parties were simply
looking at each other, this would not be a sexual activity even if their minds
were full of lustful thoughts. Similarly if the parties were naked and touching each other, this would probably be a sexual activity, then even if there
were no indecent thoughts (for example, a teacher and a pupil are 'playing'
during a nude swim on a school holiday).

2.   Position of trust
This is defined in s.4. The list is a detailed one and includes a number of
different situations. It includes where the defendant is looking after children in a young offender's institution, hospitals, children's homes and
where the victim is accommodated in an institution. It notably includes
teachers of under-eighteen-year-olds and pupils at that teacher's school.
Inevitably the list does not cover some vulnerable children. For example,
youth club leaders, supply teachers and nannies are not covered. It should
be noted that although the aim of the statute is to protect vulnerable children, from a different perspective it limits children's freedom to enter into
sexual relationships. If a seventeen-year-old wishes to have sexual rela-

tionships with a teacher, should he or she be free to do so? The Act prefers to protect vulnerable children from potential abuse, rather than encourage children's sexual freedom.

3. Defences
Section 3(2) sets out various circumstances in which a defendant will have a defence:

> 'Where a person ("A") is charged with an offence under this section of having sexual intercourse with, or engaging in any other sexual activity with or directed towards, another person ("B"), it shall be a defence for A to prove that, at the time of the intercourse or activity –
> (a) he did not know, and could not reasonably have been expected to know, that B was under 18;
> (b) he did not know, and could not reasonably have been expected to know, that B was a person in relation to whom he was in a position of trust; or
> (c) he was lawfully married to B.'

8.6   Other Sexual Offences

It is an offence to commit an act outraging public decency if the act is committed in public and it is visible to more that one person. The act is in public if it is visible to the public even if the defendant is on private land and even if it is not actually seen. A common form of committing this offence is indecently exposing the body. It is not necessary to show anyone was actually disgusted or shocked. Nor is it necessary to show sexual motive for the exposure. A nude sunbather could therefore commit the offence (*Crunden*). There is a separate offence for men who indecently expose themselves, under s.4 Vagrancy Act 1824. The offence of gross indecency involves an act of gross indecency between two people in public.

Incest occurs when a man has vaginal sexual intercourse with a woman he knows is his daughter, granddaughter, sister or mother. In these cases if the woman is over sixteen she also commits the offence. The offence can be committed by two adults but is normally charged when one of the parties is under sixteen. The offence is contained in ss.10 and 11 Sexual Offences Act and is punishable with life if the victim is under thirteen, and seven years if the victim is over thirteen. The offence is seen as particularly serious as it involves a breach of trust by the adults concerned, who are meant to be the very people whom the child can depend upon for safety and support. In cases of incest there is nothing to stop the prosecution from relying on the charges of rape or indecent assault.

The government has carried out a major review of sexual offences in a document entitled *Setting the Boundaries: Reforming the Law on Sex Offences*. Some of the proposals were implemented in the Sexual Offences (Amendment) Act 2000, discussed above. Other proposals were to create an offence of sexual penetration (involving, for example, penetration of victims with objects) and extending rape to include forced oral intercourse.

Hot Topic: "Date Rape"

Most cases of so-called 'date rape' are in fact violent attacks on women after a night out and undoubtedly rape. It is unfortunate that such incidents are called 'date rape' by the media, somehow implying that they are not 'proper rapes'. Although rare, there are occasionally more difficult cases which concern intercourse after a date. Imagine this scenario. Albert is inexperienced in sexual matters. He is excited by the way that his relationship with Brenda is progressing. One night he decides to seek to seduce Brenda. He buys her an expensive dinner and Brenda agrees to return to his flat for coffee. Albert believes that this indicates that Brenda is willing to have sexual intercourse. In fact Brenda is not ready for sexual relations with Albert. When Albert suggests sex, Brenda is hesitant, but says she would like Albert to kiss her. Although Brenda is unsure whether she wants sexual intercourse, sexual intercourse takes place. The next day Brenda is unhappy about what happened. She admits that she never said she did not want sexual intercourse, and indeed she was, in fact, unsure if she wanted sexual intercourse or not. However she never gave consent to it. Albert says he assumed that when Brenda agreed to come to his flat for coffee after the meal and then asked for a kiss that she was willing to engage in sexual intercourse. This, he says, was reinforced by the fact that she did not say she did not want sexual intercourse.

If we were to apply the present law it is likely that Albert would be acquitted of rape. The *actus reus* would be made out, because although Brenda did not object to the intercourse she did not positively consent (*Malone*). However Albert would be acquitted because he honestly (even if unreasonably) believed that Brenda consented and so lacked the *mens rea* for rape (*Morgan*).

Both of these are controversial. Is it correct that the *actus reus* of rape took place? We are told that Brenda was hesitant and not sure whether she wanted sexual intercourse; is this enough to amount to the *actus reus* of rape? Some commentators have suggested that it is common for both men and women to be hesitant and unsure about sexual intercourse, especially if they lack experience in sexual matters. For the law of rape to cover such cases is to stretch the definition of rape. Others argue strongly that if we take the right to sexual autonomy seriously, only if there is positive consent is sexual intercourse permissible. We would not accept being hesitant or unsure as sufficient consent to a doctor who has amputated a patient's leg.

What about the *mens rea* issue? Again there is a division of opinion. Clearly those who support the *Morgan* rule would be happy with the result. However, there may be a division of opinion among those who disagree with *Morgan*. As indicated above, many commentators have argued that the defendant should be convicted unless he has reasonable grounds for his belief that the victim was consenting to the intercourse. Here Albert should have ensured that Brenda was consenting by asking her. Some commentators would argue that a defendant can rely on 'social understandings' to communicate consent. People are often embarrassed to talk openly about sexual matters and often rely on unspoken communication. It was therefore reasonable for Albert to assume that after he and Brenda had been going out for a while, she had agreed to come to his flat after a meal and then asked him to kiss her, that this amounted to implied consent to sexual intercourse. To require parties to gain explicit consent to every stage of sexual intercourse would rob lovemaking of any spontaneity and passion, they argue. The criminal law must be realistic, it is said. Maybe couples should be able to talk more openly about sexual matters, but the criminal law is not the way to force them to do so. There is much force in this argument. However, the embarrassment to talk about sexual matters (if that is the cause of the problem) is working to the significant disadvantage of men. Where the woman gets the wrong end of the stick, there may be embarrassment, but normally no more; where men do, unwanted sexual intercourse often results. Why is this?

Summary

8.1 The scope of sexual offences is controversial and presents special problems of proof connected with the inevitable conflict of interest between the victim and the accused. The law is concerned in protecting freedom of sexual choice as well as punishing the especial harm that sexual invasion can occasion.

8.2 The *actus reus* of rape involves unlawful sexual intercourse without the consent of the victim. Submission induced by force or the fear of force is not consent. Consent induced by fraud can be vitiated if the fraud relates to the nature of the act of sexual intercourse itself or the identity of the accused. The *mens rea* of rape involves proof that the man did not positively believe that the victim consented. An honest mistake as to consent, even if unreasonable, will entitle the accused to an acquittal.

8.3 Indecent assault on a man or a woman involves a common assault or battery, accompanied by circumstances of indecency. Certain categories of person cannot consent in law to conduct that would amount to an indecent assault: children under sixteen and defectives. The accused must know or be reckless that the victim was not consenting and must be aware of the circumstances of indecency. A reasonable mistake as to the age of the victim will not excuse. However, if the victim is a defective, the accused, to be liable, must know or have reason to suspect this.

8.4 Sexual intercourse with a girl under sixteen is an offence; it is a more serious offence if the girl is under thirteen. The girl herself does not commit any offence even if she consents in fact to the intercourse. Consent in fact is irrelevant to the guilt of the accused as a girl under sixteen cannot in law consent to sexual intercourse.

8.5 The Sexual Offences (Amendment) Act 2000 aims to prohibit those who are in a position of trust in relation to children to engage in sexual relationships with those in their care.

8.6 Incest is a particular criminal offence that outlaws sexual relations between close relatives. Various other sexual offences exist, mainly covering indecent acts in public.

Case Notes

Caldwell [1982] AC 341. **House of Lords**
See Chapter 4 case notes.

Clarence (1888) 22 QBD 23
See Chapter 7 case notes.

Court [1989] AC 28. **House of Lords**
The appellant was convicted of indecent assault. He was a shop assistant who had seized a twelve-year-old girl and, pulling her across his knees, had struck her across the buttocks. He admitted the assault, but denied that it was indecent, although in an interview with the police he had given 'buttock fetish' as an explanation for his conduct. The House of Lords distinguished between an act that a reasonable person would say is clearly indecent, one that is clearly not indecent, and one that is ambiguously indecent. If the act is clearly indecent, then whatever the defendant's motive the act is indecent; if clearly not, then it is not; and if ambiguous, it depends on the defendant's motive.

Elbekkay [1995] **Crim LR 163. Court of Appeal**
The accused had intercourse with the victim, who was sleepy and intoxicated, and she believed that he was her boyfriend. The Court of Appeal suggested that consent based on the mistaken belief that the man was her husband 'or another' could vitiate the victim's consent. The appellant's appeal against his conviction was therefore dismissed.

R v. K 25 JULY 2001; [2001] UKHL 41. **House of Lords**
See Chapter 6 case notes.

Linekar [1995] QB 250. **Court of Appeal**
The accused agreed to pay £25 for sexual intercourse, but ran off without paying. The Court of Appeal held that only deceptions as to the nature of the act or the identity of the accused could vitiate consent. Here the deception concerned whether the victim would be paid for the sexual intercourse, not over the nature of the act itself, and so the mistake could not vitiate the victim's consent. The appellant's conviction was overturned.

Morgan [1976] AC 182. **House of Lords**
The appellant was convicted of aiding and abetting the rape of his wife. He had encouraged three friends to have sexual intercourse with his wife, telling them that any resistance on her part was a pretence and in fact a sign of her enjoyment. The other three men were convicted of rape. The trial judge directed the jury that a belief that the victim was consenting was no defence to rape, unless the belief was based on reasonable grounds. The Court of Appeal dismissed the appeals, and on appeal to the House of Lords the appeals were also dismissed. However, the House of Lords held that the trial judge had misdirected the jury on the mental element of rape. A genuine belief that the victim was consenting was inconsistent with the *mens rea* of rape, which was an intention to have sexual intercourse with a woman without her consent.

Olugboja [1982] QB 320. **Court of Appeal**
The victim did not struggle or resist while the accused had intercourse with her, as she was terrified following another rape by the defendant's friend. The Court of Appeal said whether the victim consented, albeit reluctantly, or whether she was submitting was a question for the jury, bearing in mind all the circumstances. The appellant's convictions were dismissed.

Satnam and Kewal (1983) 78 Cr App Rep 149. Court of Appeal
The appellants were both convicted of rape, being reckless as to the consent of the victim. The trial judge directed the jury that if it would have been obvious to an ordinary observer that the victim was not consenting, then the appellants were guilty of rape. The court allowed the appeals on the ground that this was a misdirection. Following *Morgan*, the jury should have been told that a genuine mistaken belief in consent, however unreasonable, should lead to an acquittal. The decision in *Caldwell* has not changed this. An accused who does not have a genuine belief in the victim's consent, but does not care whether she is consenting or not, is reckless.

Further Reading

For theoretical issues relating to rape see Gardner and Shute, Mitra and West. The Sexual Offences (Amendment) Act 2000 is discussed in Burnside. The present law on sexual offences is discussed in Gardner, Horder and Temkin. Reform of the law is analysed in Lacey.

Burnside, 'The Sexual Offences (Amendment) Act 2000' [2001] *Criminal Law Review* 425.

Gardner, 'Reckless and Inconsiderate Rape' [1991] *Criminal Law Review* 172.

Gardner, 'Appreciating *Olugboja*' (1997) *Legal Studies* 175.

Gardner and Shute, 'The Wrongness of Rape' in Horder (ed.), *Oxford Essays in Jurisprudence* (4th Series).

Horder, 'How Culpability Can, and Cannot, be Denied in Under-age Sex Crimes' [2001] *Criminal Law Review* 15.

Lacey, 'Beset by Boundaries: The Home Office Review of Sex Offences' [2001] *Criminal Law Review* 3.

Mitra, 'For She has no Right or Power to Refuse her Consent' [1979] *Criminal Law Review* 558.

Temkin, *Rape and the Legal Process* (1987, Sweet & Maxwell).

West, 'A Comment on Consent, Sex and Rape' (1996) 2 *Legal Theory* 233.

9 Murder

Key Words

- **Death** – the medical definition of the end of life.
- **Intention** – the aim or purpose of the defendant.

9.1 Homicide

There is general agreement that causing another person's death in a culpable way is the most serious of criminal offences. This reflects the high value society puts on each individual's life and the fact that to kill someone is the most permanent of injuries. As Professor Ashworth has written:

'. . . death is final. This finality makes it proper to regard death as the most serious harm that may be inflicted on another, and to regard a person who chooses to inflict that harm without justification or excuse as the most culpable of offenders'.

However, the law does not treat all killings in the same way. It is perhaps best to see manslaughter as the basic charge in respect to a homicide and murder as an aggravated crime of killing – a killing with an intent to kill. Given the seriousness of the consequence (that is death), only a low level of blame is necessary for a manslaughter conviction. As G. Fletcher has written, 'In the law of homicide the formal point is neither the act nor the intent, but the fact of death. This overpowering fact is the point at which the law deigns to draw the radius of liability'.

Murder is the most serious type of homicide, requiring an intention to kill or cause grievous bodily harm. Manslaughter includes cases of homicide where the *mens rea* of murder is lacking. However there are cases where even though the defendant has the *mens rea* for murder, the presence of an additional factor reduces what would otherwise be murder to manslaughter. The most important of these are manslaughter by provocation and manslaughter by reason of diminished responsibility (a form of mental abnormality).

So, key to the distinction between murder and manslaughter is the intention of the defendant. The definitions of murder and manslaughter take no account of other factors, such as the method of killing (for example, whether or not a gun was used), or the context of the offence (was it in the course of a robbery, rape, or terrorist attack, or was it a domestic killing? was it part of a series of killings by the same defendant?), or the identity of the victim (a policeman or a child, for example). These factors are considered by the court only after conviction, at the sentencing stage. In the case of murder, moreover, the extent to which they can be taken into account in sentencing is very limited, as the offence is subject to a compulsory sentence of life imprisonment and the trial judge merely has the power to recommend that the offender should serve a minimum number of years in prison before being released on licence. In sentencing for manslaughter, the judge has greater powers as the maximum sentence is life imprisonment, but the judge can impose a more lenient sentence, such as a shorter term of imprisonment, or even a community-based sentence or absolute discharge.

The existence of the mandatory life sentence is capable of producing apparent injustices. For example, in *Cocker* a man had been caring for his terminally ill wife for years. She had continually pleaded with him to kill her. After many sleepless nights he placed a pillow over her head and she died. Whatever one's views on the rights and wrongs of euthanasia, to give a life sentence in such a case seems inappropriate, but the Court of Appeal stated that there was no alternative following his conviction for murder but to impose a life sentence. Cocker had an intention to kill her and he could not plead provocation. The Court of Appeal could not reduce his conviction to one of manslaughter simply because it was sympathetic to him or thought a life sentence inappropriate. Such cases have led many, such as Lord Kilbrandon in *Hyam* v. *DPP**, to suggest that the distinction between murder and manslaughter should be abolished, and with it the compulsory life sentence for murder.

What constitutes murder or manslaughter is a reflection of a certain set of values. The present law focusing on intention is only one way in which the law could draw the distinction between murder or manslaughter. An alternative would be to focus on the motive of the defendant or whether the victim was a child, for example. It is also a political choice that certain killings fall outside murder and manslaughter. A notable example of this is killing by motor car, which is covered by a separate statute: causing death by dangerous driving (see Chapter 10.5), an offence under s.2A Road Traffic Act 1988, with a maximum sentence of two years. There is no justification for separate treatment of this kind of killing except that prosecutors have reported difficulties in persuading juries to convict in cases of car killing, even in clear cases of recklessness. Juries, it appears, are sympathetic to those who kill while driving. Similarly, killings that are 'accidents at work' tend not to result in homicide convictions, but are dealt with by regulatory bodies concerned with health and safety at work (see Chapter 6). Whether the way in which the law operates in relation to killings in car accidents and at work is consistent with the Human Rights Act is discussed in Chapter 19.

The nature and frequency of murder is often misunderstood. There were only 761 homicide convictions in the year 1999/2000, probably similar to the number of killings viewable on television dramas and in films over a weekend. It is interesting to note that most murder convictions involve people known to each other, and the most dangerous age for becoming a victim of homicide is under one year old. This indicates that the popular view of murder portrayed on television and in films is not the most common kind of homicide found in the courts. It may be that much of the development on the law of murder and manslaughter has been based on an image of murder which is in fact quite exceptional. The killing of babies, those in road accidents and at work is more common, but has received little attention from the courts or criminal lawyers.

This chapter will focus on the law of murder. Chapter 10 will discuss the crime of manslaughter. First it is appropriate to draw the line between murder and other criminal offences such as child destruction and abortion. These distinctions are found in the definition of the *actus reus*.

9.2   The *Actus Reus* of Murder

The *actus reus* of murder is unlawfully causing the death of another person. These elements requires further discussion.

9.2.1   Unlawfully

As with other criminal offences, the element of 'unlawfulness' indicates the absence of a valid defence, such as self-defence, or the killing with lawful authority (for example, killing under orders in time of war). It should be noted, however, that the consent of the victim does not provide a defence to murder. If the victim has asked the defendant to kill him or her, this will still be murder, provided that the defendant has the necessary *mens rea*. This is discussed in greater detail in the *Hot Topic* of Chapter 4.

9.2.2   Causing a death

It must be shown that the defendant caused the death of the victim. The normal rules of causation, discussed in Chapter 5, will be applied. There are a couple of topics that require a little more analysis.

What about those cases in which a doctor decides to withdrawing life-saving treatment for a very ill patient? Lord Goff in *Airdale NHST* v. *Bland* has recently summarized the position:

> 'the law draws a crucial distinction between cases in which a doctor decides not to provide, or to continue to provide, for his patient treatment or care which could or might prolong his life, and those in which he decides, for example by administering a lethal drug, actively to bring his patient's life to an end.'

This subject is discussed in detail in the *Hot Topic* in Chapter 4.

There used to be a rule that for murder, the death of the victim had to occur within a year and a day from the action of the accused. However, this rule has now been abolished. The original reason for the rule was that it could never be conclusively proved that the defendant's act had caused the victim's death if the death occurred over a year after the defendant's act. With the advance of forensic science this has become a less significant consideration, but the rule has another justification: it is felt to be unreasonable to subject a person who has seriously assaulted another to the indefinite risk of prosecution for murder or manslaughter, should the victim die years later. A limit of a year seemed practical and fair. However, the Law Reform (Year and a Day Rule) Act 1996 has abolished the rule as it applies to all acts that are committed after 17 June 1996. If more that three years have elapsed since the act that was said to have caused the death then the consent of the Attorney-General is required for a prosecution.

9.2.3 Causing the Death of a Person

The victim of murder must be a human being who was alive when the accused caused his or her death. This may lead to problems of definition both at the beginning and end of life.

When does life begin?

The unborn child is protected elsewhere within the criminal law, but not by the law of murder (*Attorney-General's Reference (No. 3 of 1994)**). The destruction of a foetus will be punishable as a crime unless it falls within the provisions of the Abortion Act 1967. If the foetus is 'capable of being born alive' then it is protected by the offence of child destruction, under the Infant Life (Preservation) Act 1929. If the foetus is not 'capable of being born alive' then the offence will be of procuring a miscarriage under s.58 Offences Against the Person Act 1861.

In order to be the victim of murder (or manslaughter), the child must be fully born (that is, completely outside her mother) and have an existence independent of his or her mother, if only for the briefest of moments (*Crutchley*). This is taken to mean that the child must have started breathing and have independent circulation. This rule does not mean that no account can be taken of injuries inflicted on a child while still in the womb in a case of murder or manslaughter. If the defendant injures the unborn child who is subsequently born alive but then dies from his or her injuries, this would amount to the *actus reus* of murder or manslaughter. The most likely offence would be manslaughter. If the defendant has committed a dangerous criminal act against the mother, foetus or some other person which causes the death of a child then a conviction can follow using the law of constructive manslaughter (*Attorney-General's Reference (No. 3 of 1994)**). In the unlikely event that the defendant intended that the foetus be born alive and then die as a result of his act this would be murder.

When does life end?

Discussion of the legal test of death has recently been renewed with the development of medical technology (such as life-support machines). The traditional tests of breathing, heartbeat and blood circulation are no longer adequate, but they have not yet been definitively supplanted by new tests in the courts. The medical profession has developed its own tests for 'brain death', and it is obviously important that doctors should be able to rely on the legality of these procedures when switching off life-support machines or performing transplant operations. *Re A (a minor),* a civil case, accepted that 'brain death' was the correct test of death. It is likely that a criminal court would accept this medical definition of death. Certainly, the Court of Appeal has refused to countenance the argument that the action of a doctor in switching off a life-support machine can break the causal link between the injuries inflicted by the accused and the death of the victim (*Malcherek and Steel**).

9.3   The *Mens Rea* of Murder

The *mens rea* of murder is known as 'malice aforethought', but this is a misleading term in that the state of mind referred to is not 'malice' in its ordinary meaning, and there is no need for the premeditation which the word 'aforethought' implies. The *mens rea* of murder is an intention to kill or cause grievous bodily harm to the victim (*Cunningham*; *Attorney-General's Reference (No. 3 of 1994)**). If the defendant intended to kill someone other than the victim but in so doing caused the victim's death, then the doctrine of transferred *mens rea* (see Chapter 4.6) operates to enable the accused's conviction for murder of the victim. If the defendant commits an act intending to kill anyone who happens to be in the area (for example, a terrorist bomber who places a bomb in a city centre) this is known as 'general malice' and is sufficient for the *mens rea* of murder (*Attorney-General's Reference (No. 3 of 1994)**).

The intention to kill is sometimes referred to as 'express malice' and the intention to cause grievous bodily harm as 'implied malice'. At common law, a further form of *mens rea* was developed, known as 'constructive malice', but this has now been abolished. 'Constructive malice' was used when the accused was killed in the course of committing another serious offence involving violence, such as rape or robbery. In such cases the only *mens rea* which was required was the *mens rea* for the other offence, for example the rape or the robbery. This form of liability still exists within manslaughter, but was abolished in relation to murder by the 1957 Homicide Act, which provides in s.1(1):

'Where a person kills another in the course or furtherance of some other offence, the killing shall not amount to murder unless done with the same malice aforethought (express or implied) as is required for a killing to amount to murder when not done in the course or furtherance of another offence.'

The convoluted wording is the result of an unwillingness on the part of Parliament to define precisely what express and implied malice actually mean, and this failure has resulted in considerable uncertainty in the years since 1957.

Almost immediately a problem arose over implied malice. It was argued in the case of *Vickers** that the 1957 Act had in fact abolished implied malice as well as constructive malice. The contention was that the intention to cause grievous bodily harm (implied malice) was the *mens rea* of another offence, namely causing grievous bodily harm with intent contrary to s.18 Offences Against the Person Act 1861 (see Chapter 7.5). It was therefore no more than a form of constructive malice, and as such had been abolished by the 1957 Act. This ingenious argument failed to convince the Court of Appeal in *Vickers*, and has not been much more successful in subsequent cases. Lord Chief Justice Goddard, giving the judgement of the court in *Vickers*, said that implied malice had been preserved by the wording of s.1(1):

'If a person does an act on another which amounts to the infliction of grievous bodily harm he cannot say that he did not intend to go so far . . . he must take the consequences. If he intends to inflict grievous bodily harm and that person dies, that has always been held in English law, and was at the time when the Act of 1957 was passed, sufficient to imply the malice aforethought which is a necessary constituent of murder.'

The point was raised again in *Hyam* v. *DPP**, and two of the judges, Lord Diplock and Lord Kilbrandon, were of the opinion that murder should be restricted to cases where there is an intent to kill, or, at the very least, to endanger life. However, two further judges (Lord Hailsham and Viscount Dilhorne) held that *Vickers* was correct and that implied malice had always been and was still a part of malice aforethought. The fifth judge, Lord Cross, was undecided but unwilling to overrule *Vickers*, and so formed a majority in favour of the retention of implied malice for murder. Largely because of the equivocal position taken by Lord Cross, the question was raised yet again, in *Cunningham* (1982)*, and this time the House of Lords gave a clear ruling that an intention to cause grievous bodily harm remained part of the *mens rea* of murder. Lord Hailsham, giving the leading judgement, based his decision not only on historical arguments from early caselaw and writers on the criminal law, but also on policy. The argument is really about the proper scope of murder, and Lord Hailsham relied on 'the increased lethal characteristics of modern weaponry' as well as recent examples of violence on the streets of Britain. So now it is quite clear that the *mens rea* of murder is an intent to kill or cause grievous bodily harm.

What is grievous bodily harm? It means a really serious harm (*DPP* v. *Smith*; for further discussion see Chapter 6). Notably an injury may amount to grievous bodily harm even though it does not endanger a person's life. For example a terrorist may shoot a victim in the knee; if unexpectedly the wound becomes infected and the victim dies, the defendant could be guilty of murder, even though it was not foreseeable that his act would lead to the victim's death. The rule that intention to commit grievous bodily harm is sufficient for the *mens rea* of murder has been recently confirmed, albeit reluctantly by the House of Lords (*Attorney-General's Reference (No. 3 of 1994)**). Lord Mustill commented that the 'rule is an outcropping of old law from which the surrounding strata of rationalisations have weathered away'. Similar criticisms are to be found in Lord Styen's judgment in the House of Lords' decision in *Powell and English** where he suggested that a person convicted of murder having only an intent to cause grievous bodily harm was not 'in truth' a murderer. Despite these criticisms it is unlikely that the House of Lords will overrule the grievous bodily harm rule which is now well established. It will be up to Parliament to change the law.

The Draft Criminal Code suggests slightly modifying the grievous bodily harm test to define murder as follows:

'(1) a person is guilty of murder if he causes the death of another
    (a) intending to cause death; or
    (b) intending to cause serious personal harm and being aware that he may cause death' (Clause 54).

This proposal has received the support of Lord Steyn in *Powell and English* and would be supported by those who promote the "correspondence principle" (see Chapter 4.8).

So, it is clear that the *mens rea* of murder is an intent to kill or cause grievous bodily harm. But what does 'intent' mean in this context?

9.4 Intention in Murder

In Chapter 4 we considered in detail the meaning of intention. Notably it is in the context of murder that the definition of murder has received the greatest intention. This is because if there is no intent to kill or cause grievous bodily harm, the defendant cannot be guilty of murder but may be guilty of manslaughter. Five times in recent years the issue has been addressed by the House of Lords: *Smith* v. *DPP*, *Hyam* v. *DPP**, *Moloney**, *Hancock and Shankland** and *Woollin**. These concepts have been discussed in greater detail in Chapter 4, but will be summarized here. The House of Lords has declined to give a definition of intention, apart from saying that intention is a word which should be given its normal meaning. Indeed in most cases the judge should not address the jury on the meaning of intention. In the rare cases where it is necessary to direct the jury, two questions should be asked:

(i)   Was the victim's death or grievous bodily harm virtually certain?
and
(ii) Did the defendant realize that the victim's death or grievous bodily harm was virtually certain?

If the answer to both questions is 'yes' then the jury are entitled to find that the defendant intended death or grievious bodily harm (*Woollin*).

The restrictive meaning of intention means that the violent risk-taker, the person who is willing to take risks with other people's lives, will not be convicted of murder. In *Hancock and Shankland*, Lord Scarman describes the problem:

'crimes of violence where the purpose is by open violence to protest, demonstrate, obstruct, or frighten are on the increase. Violence is used by some as a means of public communication. Inevitably there will be casualties, and inevitably death will on occasion result. If death results, is the perpetrator of the violent act guilty of murder? It will depend on his intent.'

Only if the perpetrator intends to kill or cause grievous bodily harm will he or she be guilty of murder. If the perpetrator simply could not care less whether a person is killed during his or her actions, he or she will be guilty of manslaughter, but not murder. Whether it is acceptable that such wicked indifference does not amount to murder is a matter of much dispute. When considering that issue it should be remembered that it is still possible to impose a life sentence on a person convicted of manslaughter.

9.5   The Relevance of the Mandatory Life Sentence

The development and understanding of the law of murder has been strongly influenced by the mandatory life sentence for murder. As already mentioned, if a person is convicted of murder then the court has no discretion but to impose a life sentence of imprisonment. This is highly controversial. The main justification for the present position is that the sentence marks the fact that murder is the most heinous offence. However others reject this argument, pointing to the breath of the offence. As Lord Hailsham has explained:

'Murder, as every practitioner of the law knows, though often described as one of the utmost heinousness, is not in fact necessarily so, but consists in a whole bundle of offences of vastly differing degrees of culpability, ranging from brutal, cynical and repeated offences like the so-called Moors murders' (*R* v. *Brady and Hindley*, 6 May 1966, unreported) 'to the almost venial, if objectively immoral, 'mercy killing' of a beloved partner' (*Howe**).

The existence of the mandatory life sentence might explain why intention can only be found from foresight of circumstances as virtually certain (see *Woollin*). The cases on the meaning of intention can be interpreted as seeking to limit the offence of murder to the most serious of circumstances, the kind in which a mandatory sentence is appropriate. On the other hand the existence of the mandatory life sentence is used by those seeking to reform the *mens rea* for murder, either by restricting further the definition of intention, or by rejecting the law that an intention to cause grievous bodily harm is sufficient to amount to the *mens rea* for murder (see, for example, Lord Steyn in *Powell and English**).

The mandatory life sentence may also explain the existence of the partial defences to murder, such as provocation or diminished responsibility. These partial defences will reduce the conviction from murder to manslaughter, and thereby give the court discretion as to sentence. It is certainly possible that if there were a wide discretion as to the sentence in murder, there may be no need to have these defences.

Hot Topic: The Legal Status of The Unborn Child

This is not the place to discuss the moral status of foetuses or unborn children (see Further Reading) or how the law should treat them. What shall be discussed here is how the criminal law treats the foetus.

It is clear that the criminal law does not regard the foetus or unborn child as a full human being. The death of the unborn child is not regarded as murder or manslaughter. It is only once the child has been born that the child is regarded as a human being for the purposes of the criminal law. However, the criminal law does not treat the foetus as 'a nothing', not worthy of the protection of the law. The foetus is protected by the offences of procuring a miscarriage under s.58 Offences Against the Person Act 1861 and the offence of child destruction under the Infant Life (Preservation) Act 1929. It is not possible to explain these offences as in reality protecting the interests of the mother rather than the foetus, because the mother can be convicted of these offences. Further the very fact that abortion is only available if the requirements set out in the Abortion Act 1967 are satisfied indicates that the law regards something that needs protection. So then, although not a person, the law does recognise that the foetus has some interests that are worth protecting.

The status of the foetus in the criminal law was given some attention in *Attorney-General's Reference (No. 3 of 1994)**). The Court of Appeal argued:

'In the eyes of the law the foetus is taken to be a part of the mother until it has an existence independent of the mother. Thus an intention to cause serious bodily injury to the foetus is an intention to cause serious bodily injury to a part of the mother just as an intention to injure her arm or her leg would be so viewed.'

This view was forcibly rejected by Lord Mustill in the House of Lords and his judgement is worth quoting at length, as it is the clearest explanation of the criminal law's approach to the foetus:

'I must dissent from [the Court of Appeal's view] for I believe it to be wholly unfounded in fact. Obviously, nobody would assert that once M [the mother] had been delivered of S [the child], the baby and her mother were in any sense "the same." Not only were they physically separate, but they were each unique human beings, though no doubt with many features of resemblance. The reason for the uniqueness of S was that the development of her own special characteristics had been enabled and bounded by the collection of genes handed down not only by M but also by the natural father. This collection was different from the genes which had enabled and bounded the development of M, for these had been handed down by her own mother and natural father. S and her mother were closely related but, even apart from differing environmental influences, they were not, had not been, and in the future never would be "the same." There was, of course, an intimate bond between the foetus and the mother, created by the total dependence of the foetus on the protective physical environment furnished by the mother, and on the supply by the mother through the physical linkage between them of the nutrients, oxygen and other substances essential to foetal life and development. The emotional bond between the mother and her unborn child was also of a very special kind. But the relationship was one of bond, not of identity. The mother and the foetus were two distinct organisms living symbiotically, not a single organism with two aspects. The mother's leg was part of the mother; the foetus was not.

The only other ground for identifying the foetus with the mother that I can envisage is a chain of reasoning on the following lines. All the case law shows is that the child does not attain a sufficient human personality to be the subject of a crime of violence, and in particular of a crime of murder, until it enjoys an existence separate from its mother; hence, whilst it is in the womb it does not have a human personality; hence it must share a human personality with its mother. This seems to me an entire *non sequitur*, for it omits the possibility that the foetus does not (for the purposes of the law of homicide and violent crime) have any relevant type of personality but is an organism *sui generis* lacking at this stage the entire range of characteristics both of the mother to which it is physically linked and of the complete human being which it will later become . . . I would, therefore, reject the reasoning which assumes that since (in the eyes of English law) the foetus does not have the attributes which make it a "person" it must be an adjunct of the mother. Eschewing all religious and political debate I would say that the foetus is neither. It is a unique organism.'

This view that the foetus is separate from the mother, not fully human, but worthy of protection under the law has given rise to some concern. Could it be argued that a mother could be convicted of causing grievous bodily harm if she takes drugs during her pregnancy, thereby harming the unborn child, who is subsequently born disabled? If drug-taking when pregnant becomes a criminal offence, what about other activities that could damage the unborn child: smoking or eating soft cheese for example? Even fathers may not be exempt. A father who smokes around the pregnant women could be said to harm the child. The approach of the Court of Appeal in *Attorney-General's Reference (No. 3 of 1994)**, seeing the mother and foetus as one, would seem to prevent a conviction in such cases (at least in the case of the mother). But after the House of Lords' decision in *Attorney-General's Reference (No. 3 of 1994)** it is not clear why such a charge would not lie. If therefore the defendant stabbing the pregnant woman so that the child was born alive and then died could amount to manslaughter, would not the same be true if the mother took drugs with the same effect?

No such case has come before the English courts. In *St George's v. S* it was held that where a competent mother refused to have a Caesarean Section operation, even though it was feared that without it both she and the unborn child would die, it would be unlawful for the doctors to perform the operation. The Court of Appeal explained that the mother's right to bodily integrity could not be overridden in the name of saving the foetus (nor the mother herself). This indicates that the courts would be reluctant to use the interests of the foetus (even at the point of birth) to interfere with the basic rights of the mother. It cannot be long before the courts will be asked whether 'the right to take illegal drugs' is stronger than the interests of the foetus. The court will, no doubt, have to consider the practical consequences of any development of the law in this area. If taking drugs while pregnant becomes, in effect, a criminal offence, will such women simply avoid seeking any medical treatment, fearful of the consequences? And what would be the punishment? Imprisoning the pregnant mother might not in the long run promote the child's interests. As can be seen, the issue is far from straight-forward.

Summary

9 .1 Murder is the most serious form of homicide, and carries a compulsory sentence of life imprisonment. Murder is distinguished from manslaughter by its *mens rea*, malice aforethought. It is a common law offence.

9.2 The *actus reus* of murder is the unlawful killing of the victim. It has to be proved that the accused caused the death of the victim. A new-born child is protected by the law of murder once he or she has an existence independent of her mother. The legal test of death has in the past been determined by heartbeat and breathing, but in some cases where a life-support machine is used these tests are now questionable. It is probable that the courts will adopt the medical tests for 'brain death'. The courts have placed much emphasis on the act/omission distinction in order to distinguish murder and acceptable medical treatment of the dying.

9.3 The *mens rea* of murder is malice aforethought. This includes an intent to kill (express malice) and an intent to cause grievous bodily harm (implied malice). Grievous bodily harm is defined as serious bodily harm, which need not endanger life.

9.4 Both express and implied malice require intention, which is tested subjectively. Foresight by the accused that the result will almost certainly occur is evidence that he intended the result. The courts have had difficulty in deciding whether violent risk-takers should be guilty of murder; the present position leaves much to the discretion of juries, as intention is largely undefined. The defendant must intend to cause death or grievous bodily harm to the victim or a group of people including the victim, although the prosecution can also rely on the doctrine of transferred *mens rea*.

9.5 If convicted of murder, the judge must impose a mandatory life sentence on the defendant. If the conviction is for manslaughter, the judge has a wide range of possible sentences. The sentencing consequences may have affected the development of the law on murder and manslaughter.

Case Notes

Re A (Children) **[2000] 4 All ER 961. Court of Appeal**
See Chapter 9 case notes.

Arthur **(unreported), see [1985] Crim LR 705**
Dr Arthur, a paediatrician, was charged with the murder of a child who was suffering from Down's syndrome and who died when a few days old. During the trial the charge was reduced to attempted murder as a result of evidence that the death could have been caused by inherent defects rather than, as had been alleged, a drug adminis-

tered on the instructions of Dr Arthur. The trial judge directed the jury that there was a difference between an action which causes the death of a child (such as the administration of a drug) and an omission to perform an operation, thereby allowing the child to die. Dr Arthur was acquitted.

Attorney-General's Reference (No. 3 of 1994) [1997] 3 WLR 421. House of Lords

The defendant punched his girlfriend, who was pregnant, intending to cause injury to the unborn child. The baby was in due course born, but died shortly after its birth owing to the injuries suffered as a result of the defendant's actions. The Court of Appeal stated that although at the time the accused hit the mother the foetus was not a person in law, the foetus could be seen as part of the mother. He therefore intended to cause injury to the mother and caused the death of the child once it was born, and using the doctrine of transferred malice the defendant could be convicted of the murder of the child. The House of Lords disagreed and stated that the foetus was an organism *sui generis* and not just part of the mother. The doctrine of transferred malice could not be relied upon as it involved a double fiction – that the intention directed to the mother be transferred to the foetus and that the foetus be deemed to be born so that it could be a person for the purposes of the law. However, the death could be seen as manslaughter using the offence of constructive manslaughter as there was an unlawful act (the stabbing of the mother) which was dangerous (to the mother) and it caused the death of someone (the foetus).

Cunningham [1982] AC 566. House of Lords

The appellant was convicted of murder. He struck the victim on the head with a heavy chair, and the victim died from a fractured skull. He denied that he had intended to kill the victim. The trial judge directed the jury to convict of murder if it was sure that the accused intended to do the victim really serious harm. Both the Court of Appeal and the House of Lords upheld the conviction on the ground that malice aforethought could be implied where the accused intended to inflict grievous bodily harm. Lord Hailsham held that the law on this point had been laid down by *Vickers* and *Hyam* v. *DPP*, and there was no reason to change the law.

Hancock and Shankland [1986] AC 455. House of Lords

The appellants were convicted of murder. They had pushed two blocks of concrete over the parapet of a motorway bridge onto a taxi that was taking a miner to work during the 1985 miners' strike. The appellants said that they had intended merely to block the road and not to injure anyone. The trial judge based his direction on the guidelines given by Lord Bridge in *Moloney*: that the jury was entitled to infer an intention to kill or inflict grievous bodily harm if the accused had foreseen those consequences as natural consequences of their acts. The Court of Appeal allowed the appeal, substituting manslaughter convictions, on the ground that the guidelines were misleading. The House of Lords agreed with the Court of Appeal. It was held (per Lord Scarman) that *Moloney* had clarified the law in several ways, especially that foresight was merely evidence of intention, although intention may be inferred from foresight of consequences. However, it was misleading to refer to 'natural' consequences and to omit any reference to the probability of those consequences.

Howe [1987] 1 AC 417. House of Lords

See Chapter 16 case notes.

Hyam v. *DPP* [1975] AC 55. House of Lords

The appellant was convicted of murder. She had set fire to a house by pouring petrol through the letterbox and setting light to it. Two children died in the fire. The appellant claimed that she had only intended to frighten the occupant of the house into leaving the neighbourhood, and had not intended to cause death or grievous bodily harm. The trial judge directed the jury to convict if it was satisfied that the appellant knew when she set fire to the house that it was highly probable that it would cause death or serious bodily harm. The appeal was dismissed by the Court of Appeal and the House of Lords. The majority of the House held that an intention to inflict serious bodily harm was a type of malice aforethought. It was also held (Lord Hailsham disagreeing) that if the accused foresaw that death or serious bodily harm were likely or highly probable, this was equivalent to intending those consequences.

Malcherek and Steel [1981] 2 All ER 422. Court of Appeal
See Chapter 6 case notes.

Moloney [1985] AC 905. House of Lords
The appellant was convicted of murder. He had shot his stepfather with a shotgun in the early hours of the morning. Both the appellant and the victim had been drinking and had started an argument as to which one was faster at loading and shooting a shotgun. The appellant claimed that he had not intended to injure the victim. The trial judge directed the jury that in law a man intends the consequence of his act where he desires it to happen; or where he foresees that it will probably happen, whether or not he desires it. An appeal against conviction was dismissed by the Court of Appeal, but on appeal to the House of Lords the conviction was quashed, and a conviction for manslaughter substituted. Lord Bridge recognized that the decision in *Hyam* v. *DPP** had caused some confusion in the law. He held that, as a general rule, the jury did not need to be directed on the meaning of intention, but that in cases where some reference to foresight of consequences was necessary, it must be made clear that such foresight is not equivalent to intention, but is evidence from which intention may be inferred. A jury would be entitled to infer intention in a case where the consequence was 'natural' in the sense that 'in the ordinary course of events a certain act will lead to a certain consequence unless something unexpected supervenes to prevent it'. Lord Bridge also rejected the suggestion of Lord Hailsham in *Hyam* v. *DPP* that in cases of murder the act of the accused must be aimed at a specific person.

Nedrick [1986] 3 All ER 1. Court of Appeal
The appellant was convicted of murder. He had set light to a house by pouring paraffin through the letterbox and setting fire to it. A child died in the fire. The appellant claimed that he had only intended to frighten the woman who lived in the house. The trial judge's direction to the jury followed *Hyam* v. *DPP* and was in the form disapproved of in *Moloney*. The Court of Appeal allowed the appeal and substituted a conviction for manslaughter. Lord Lane held that in cases in which some explanation of intention is needed, the jury should be told that a person may intend a consequence which is not desired. It should consider how probable the consequence was, and whether it was foreseen by the defendant. The jury may infer intention if it is sure that the defendant realized that the consequence was a virtual certainty.

Powell and English [1999] AC 1. House of Lords.
See Chapter 17 case notes.

Vickers [1957] 2 QB 664. Court of Criminal Appeal
The appellant was convicted of murder. He had broken into a shop, intending to steal, and had attacked an elderly lady who died as a result. He appealed against conviction on the ground that s.1(1) Homicide Act 1957 had abolished implied malice aforethought (intention to inflict grievous bodily harm). The court dismissed his appeal, holding that implied malice was preserved by s.1(1) and that murder is committed where the accused causes death by a voluntary act which is intended to cause grievous bodily harm to the victim.

Woollin **[1999] AC 82. House of Lords**
See Chapter 4 case notes.

Further Reading

For readings on intention see Further Reading in Chapter 4 and Goff. The structure of the law of murder is examined in Wilson. On the meaning of death see Devlin and Dickens. On the legal and moral status of the foetus there is a huge volume of material, including Dworkin, Herring and Kaufman. On the life sentence for murder see Criminal Law Revision Committee and House of Lords.

Criminal Law Revision Committee: *14th Report, Offences Against the Person* (1980, Cmnd 7844).

Devlin, *Easing the Passing* (1986, Oxford University Press).

Dickens, 'Death' in Kennedy and Grubb (eds), *Principles of Medical Law* (1998, Oxford University Press).

Dworkin, *Life's Dominion* (1993, HarperCollins).

Goff, 'The Mental Element in the Crime of Murder' (1988) *Law Quarterly Review* 30.

Herring, 'The Caesarean Section Cases and the Supremacy of Autonomy' in Freeman and Lewis (eds), *Law and Medicine* (2000, Oxford University Press).

House of Lords, *Report of the Select Committee on Murder and Life Imprisonment* (Session 1988–1989).

Kaufman, 'Legal Recognition of Independent Fetal Rights' (1997) 17 *Children's Legal Rights Journal* 20.

Wilson, 'Murder and the Structure of Homicide', in Ashworth and Mitchell (eds), *Rethinking English Homicide Law* (2000, Oxford University Press).

10   Manslaughter

Key words

- **Voluntary manslaughter** – the defendant would be guilty of murder but has successfully raised a defence such as provocation or diminished responsibility.
- **Involuntary manslaughter** – the defendant lacks the mental element required for murder, but can be convicted on the basis of constructive or gross negligence manslaughter.
- **Provocation** – the defendant killed having reasonably lost his self-control.
- **Diminished responsibility** – the defendant was suffering an abnormality of mind which lessened his responsibility for the killing.

10.1   Distinguishing Voluntary and Involuntary Manslaughter

There are two basic types of manslaughter, usually referred to as voluntary and involuntary manslaughter. In the case of involuntary manslaughter the accused lacks malice aforethought, the *mens rea*, for murder. Voluntary manslaughter is different: it arises in cases where both the *actus reus* and *mens rea* of murder exist, but an additional factor is present which operates as a partial defence to murder, reducing it to manslaughter. At common law there is only one such factor: provocation. The Homicide Act 1957 created two further categories (diminished responsibility and suicide pact) as well as amending the common law on provocation. These special defences fall between ordinary defences (such as self-defence) which exonerate completely, and mitigating factors which make no difference to criminal liability (legal guilt or innocence), but which can be taken into account by the judge at the sentencing stage. They are needed in the case of murder because murder is an offence with a mandatory sentence of life imprisonment and therefore no sentencing discretion is available to the judge. It is not only the question of sentence that is important: voluntary manslaughter also removes the stigma of a conviction of murder.

There are three forms of voluntary manslaughter: constructive manslaughter; gross negligence manslaughter; and reckless manslaughter. We shall consider these first.

10.2   Constructive Manslaughter

Constructive manslaughter arises in cases where the accused lacks the *mens rea* of murder but kills the victim in the course of committing an unlawful and dangerous act. It is called constructive manslaughter as the offence is constructed from a less serious crime. The House of Lords in *Attorney-General's Reference (No. 3 of 1994)** has set out the four requirements for constructive manslaughter. Lord Hope explained:

> 'The only questions which need to be addressed are (1) whether the act was done intentionally, (2) whether it was unlawful, (3) whether it was also dangerous because it was likely to cause harm to somebody and (4) whether that unlawful and dangerous act caused the death.'

We will now consider these requirements separately.

10.2.1   Intentional Act

It is necessary to show that the defendant intended to do the act that is the basis for the constructive manslaughter conviction. That is, that the defendant's act was voluntary and not accidental (see Chapter 5).

10.2.2   Unlawful Act

What is an unlawful act for these purposes? In the past there was some doubt over whether the act needed to be criminally unlawful or whether it was sufficient for the act to be contrary to the civil law (for example, a breach of contract). It is now clear that the act does need to be criminal. In *Lamb**, Lord Justice Sachs said that the act must be unlawful 'in the criminal sense of that word'. In *Andrews* v. *DPP**, Lord Atkin held that the unlawful act must be a criminal one which requires more than negligence on the part of the accused. This was in order to preserve a distinction between constructive manslaughter and gross negligence manslaughter. So a negligence-based or strict liability crime is not sufficient as the basis of a constructive manslaughter conviction. Neither is a crime to which a defendant has a defence (for example, self-defence as in *Scarlett*). The unlawful act need not be a serious criminal offence: a common assault will do. This can combine with the rules of causation, such as the 'thin skull' rule (see Chapter 5.4.2), to produce liability for manslaughter in cases where death was unforeseen and was not even reasonably foreseeable by the accused.

Some commentators take the view that constructive manslaughter is limited to criminal actions and does not include omissions. There is some authority for this in *Lowe*, and indeed cases where death is caused by an omission are usually charged as gross negligence manslaughter (see Chapter 10.3 below). That said, there seems no reason in principle why death caused by an unlawful omission should not lead to a charge of constructive manslaughter.

Some cases are problematic as the courts have not clearly identified the precise offence that caused the death. In the House of Lords decision in *Newbury and Jones** the accused had thrown a paving-stone off a railway bridge, hitting a train and killing the guard. Unfortunately it is not clear from the judgements in the House of Lords exactly what form the unlawful act took: it was merely assumed that the accused had committed an unspecified unlawful act. However defenders of the decision in *Newbury and Jones** point out that the existence of an unlawful act was not an issue disputed before their Lordships and it would not have been too difficult to find offence on the facts (for example, offences contrary to the Criminal Damage Act 1971).

The House of Lords in *Newbury and Jones** held that it was not necessary for the accused to have foreseen the risk of causing harm to any person as a result of his unlawful act. This does not mean that constructive manslaughter has no *mens rea* at all. In order to prove the unlawful act it is necessary to prove both the *mens rea* and *actus reus* of the offence (*Jennings*). In the case of *Lamb*, for example, the accused had pointed a revolver at his friend and pulled the trigger. He did not understand the mechanism of the gun, and thought that it would not fire as there was no bullet opposite the trigger. In fact the gun's cylinder rotated when the trigger was pulled and the gun fired, killing his friend. The Court of Appeal held that there had been no unlawful act because the accused lacked the *mens rea* for assault: he did not even intend to frighten the victim. There is a slight question mark over this requirement in light of *Attorney-General's Reference (No. 3 of 1994)* as Lord Hope at one point in his judgement stated, 'manslaughter is one of those crimes in which only what is called a basic intention need be proved – that is, an intention to do the act which constitutes the crime'. This seems to suggest that the *mens rea* for the crime is unnecessary and all that is needed is an intent to do the act which forms the *actus reus* for the crime. However, Lord Hope did not explicitly state that *Jennings* and *Lamb* were wrong, and when considering the facts of the case before him Lord Hope stated: 'it is plain that it was [an] unlawful [act] as it was done with the intention of causing her injury'. This does seem to imply that the *mens rea* for the unlawful act needs to be proved, which seems the best interpretation of his judgment and of the present law.

10.2.3   Dangerous Act

The unlawful act must be objectively dangerous. It does not need to be shown that the act might cause the death of the victim, it is enough if it might cause an injury to the victim. The defendant does not need to realize that his act is dangerous if a reasonable person would have done so. In *Larkin*, Humphreys J explained that there must be 'a dangerous act, that is, an act which is likely to injure another person'. The classic statement of this rule is found in *Church**, where Lord Edmund-Davies said:

> 'an unlawful act causing the death of another cannot, simply because it is an unlawful act, render a manslaughter verdict inevitable. For such a verdict inexorably to follow, the unlawful act must be such as all sober and reasonable people would inevitably recognise must subject the other person to, at least, the risk of some harm resulting therefrom, albeit not serious harm.'

'Harm' in this context was defined by the Court of Appeal in *Dawson, Nolan and Walmsley** to be limited to actual physical injury and not include terror. However, this was before the House of Lord's interpretation of actual bodily harm in the Offences Against the Person Act as including psychological illnesses (*Ireland and Burstow*). Whether *Dawson, Nolan and Walmsley** must now be reconsidered on this question is a matter of debate.

The other issue raised by *Dawson, Nolan and Walmsley* was: whose perspective should be used when deciding whether the act was objectively dangerous? In this case the defendants had committed an armed robbery against the victim, who had a weak heart. Knowing that the victim had a weak heart, the act of subjecting him to an attempted armed robbery was clearly dangerous. However, the court said that the dangerousness of the act had to be judged from the viewpoint of a reasonable bystander, not someone having any special knowledge. Thus the jury could have decided that the robbery here was not dangerous, that it did not involve a risk of harm. In a later case, *Watson*, the defendant broke into an elderly man's house, who later died from a heart attack. This time the court said that the act of burglary became dangerous as soon as a reasonable person in the defendant's shoes (note, not a bystander) would have realized that the act was dangerous. So in that case the act was presumably dangerous as soon as the accused should have realized that the resident was an elderly person. The court added that if the defendant had special knowledge which would not have been known to the reasonable person in the defendant's shoes (that is, if he had been told by a friend that an elderly person lived in that flat) then that knowledge was to be given to the reasonable person in deciding whether the reasonable person would think the act dangerous. In *Ball*, the test was developed further. There the defendant fired a gun at the victim, which he thought he had loaded with blank bullets. The court held that the defendant's mistaken belief should not be attributed to the reasonable person in these circumstances. A reasonable person would have realized that the bullets that he had loaded were live (they were of a different weight) and so firing the gun was a dangerous act. So the present position seems to be that in deciding whether the act was dangerous, the jury should consider whether a reasonable person in the defendant's shoes, with any special knowledge that the defendant had, but without any unreasonable mistakes that the defendant had made, would think the act dangerous.

In *Dalby*, Lord Justice Waller suggested that the unlawful and dangerous act must be 'directed at the victim', and quashed a conviction of manslaughter on the grounds that the act of supplying the victim with a drug was not so directed. However, the 'aimed at' requirement is not part of the law in the light of *Attorney-General's Reference (No. 3 of 1994)* which stated that there is no need for the unlawful act to be dangerous to the victim, as long as the act is dangerous to someone. In that case it was sufficient for constructive manslaughter that the unlawful act was dangerous to someone (the mother), even if it caused the death of someone else (the child).

10.2.4   Act Caused the Death

The unlawful and dangerous act must cause the death of the victim. This is a straightforward question of causation using the normal rules (see Chapter 5). As we have just noted, there is no need to establish that the actual victim was the intended victim nor that the victim was the person to whom the act was dangerous.

In *Cato**, Lord Widgery in the Court of Appeal appeared to go further and to hold that it is not necessary for the act which causes the death to be a criminal offence at all, as long as the defendant had performed a criminal act shortly before the death. The accused had injected the victim with heroin which was illegally in his possession, and this act of possession was said by Lord Widgery to be a sufficient unlawful act, as the administration of heroin was not in itself a criminal offence. The problem is that it was not the possession which caused the death, but the administration. The court seemed to suggest that there was a taint of illegality over the whole affair and this was sufficient to satisfy the requirement for an unlawful act for constructive manslaughter. This statement was not an essential part of the judgement, and *Cato* is not a strong authority. In light of the implicit reaf-

firmation in *Attorney-General's Reference (No. 3 of 1994)** of the requirement of an unlawful act, *Cato* seems clearly wrong on this point.
Unfortunately the issue is still in doubt because the Court of Appeal in the
controversial decision of *Kennedy* (see Chapter 5.4.2) approved *Cato*,
although not explicitly on this issue.

10.3   Gross Negligence Manslaughter

The second form of manslaughter is gross negligence manslaughter. This
was recently considered by the House of Lords in the case of *Adomako**. It
had previously been thought that the *mens rea* for this kind of manslaughter was *Caldwell** reckless. It is now clear that this is not so. There is no
offence of '*Caldwell* recklessness manslaughter'. Gross negligence
manslaughter can involve a wide range of cases from the master of a
schooner alleged to be sailing unsafely and so causing the ship to founder
(*Litchfield*) to a landlord not maintaining the proper repair of gas fires in his
flats. The test for gross negligence manslaughter requires proof of the
following:

* A duty of care
* A breach of the duty
* The breach of the duty caused the death; and
* The breach of the duty was so gross as to justify a criminal conviction.

These will be now examined separately.

10.3.1   A Duty of Care

The requirement of a duty of care is essentially a civil law concept found
in the law of tort. We owe a duty of care not to injure anyone that we could
reasonably foreseeably injure. Applying that to this context, there will be a
duty of care if there was a risk that an act or omission of the defendant
might kill the victim. As the concept of a 'duty of care' is a legal concept
it is surprising that the Court of Appeal in *Khan and Khan* held that it was
for the jury to decide whether a duty of care existed, although the judge
could withdraw that question from the jury if the facts were not capable of
supporting such a conclusion. More convincing is the approach of the Court
of Appeal in *Singh* which assumed it was for the judge to decide whether a
set of facts gave rise to a duty of care.

10.3.2   A Breach of the Duty

The second requirement, breach of the duty, requires that the defendant acted in a way that a reasonable person would not have acted. If the defendant is purporting to exercise some special kind of skill then the defendant must act as a reasonable person possessing that skill. For example, in *Adomako* the question was whether a reasonably qualified anaesthetist (not an ordinary person) would have realized what was wrong with the patient and have intervened to help him. The test is therefore objective. Adomako's defence that his training was inadequate and that he was exhausted from overwork was irrelevant in deciding whether he had breached a duty. He had not acted as a reasonable anaesthetist would have done and that was that.

The breach of duty could arise through an act or omission of the defendant, although in the case of an omission it would have to be shown that there was a special duty to act as required generally concerning omissions (*Khan and Khan;* see *Hot Topic*, Chapter 4). The duty may require the defendant to summon expert help if it is a situation where that is what a reasonable person would do. In *Singh*, the defendant was responsible for some flats and was told by the tenants that the gas fires were not working properly. It was held that the reasonable landlord in such circumstances would have called in an expert to ensure the fires were working properly.

10.3.3   The Breach of the Duty caused the Victim's Death

The third requirement is that the breach caused the death. This involves applying the normal rules of causation. It must be stressed that it is not enough to show that the defendant caused the death of the victim, it must be shown that his negligence did. So, in *Singh*, it was not enough to show that the defendant had acted negligently in not summoning expert help to ensure that the gas fires were working properly and that the gas fires' malfunctioning caused the victim's death. It had to be shown that had the defendant not acted negligently (had he summoned help) the victims would not have died.

In the majority of cases, if the defendant had done an act that caused someone else's death then the first three requirements will be made out. Almost always there will have been a duty of care owed to the victim and a breach of that duty. Therefore much weight is placed on the fourth requirement.

10.3.4   The Defendant's Negligence was Gross

This fourth requirement is satisfied if the jury decides that the negligence was sufficiently gross as to justify a criminal conviction. As Lord Mackay, in *Adomako*, put it:

> 'The essence of the matter . . . is whether having regard to the risk of death involved, the conduct of the defendant was so bad in all the circumstances as to amount in their judgment to a criminal act or omission.'

Essentially this leaves the jury with a discretion: to decide in its judgment whether the defendant deserves a conviction for manslaughter. So what kind of factors will a jury be likely to take into account when considering whether the negligence is gross or not. Of course, the issue is entirely up to the jury but these are some of the factors the jury is likely to take into account:

1 How far below the standard of the reasonable person was the defendant's conduct?
2 Had the defendant foreseen the risk of death?
3 Did the defendant have a good explanation for his behaviour?
4 Had the victim put his trust in the defendant to exercise special skill?

There were some ambiguous phrases in Lord Mackay's judgement in *Adomako* which suggested that it had to be shown that the defendant was aware of the risk of death. However the Court of Appeal in *Attorney-General's Reference* (No 2. of 1999) has since made it clear that the jury is entitled to convict a defendant of gross negligent manslaughter even though he had not foreseen that the victim would be killed, or even injured. Clearly in considering whether the negligence is gross, the jury will consider whether the defendant foresaw that the victim might die or be seriously injured as a result of his or her act (*Attorney-General's Reference* (No 2. of 1999)). That said, the jury might be reluctant to convict a person of gross negligence unless the defendant at least foresaw the possibility of death. It should be recalled that in order to establish a breach of duty of care it must be shown that death was foreseeable.

10.4   Reckless Manslaughter

We have already noted that following *Adomako* there is no offence of *Caldwell* reckless manslaughter. There may be a crime of *Cunningham* reckless manslaughter, that is where the defendant causes the death of the victim, aware that there is a risk that the victim might die. In such cases the defendant would be guilty of constructive manslaughter or gross negligence manslaughter. It is because of this that *Cunningham* reckless manslaughter has not been directly referred to by the courts in a reported case. There is therefore doubt whether it exists, but if it does, the offence is primarily of academic interest only. Notably, reckless manslaughter was not mentioned in Lord Hope's thorough analysis of the different forms of manslaughter in *Attorney-General's Reference (No. 3 of 1994)*.

10.5   Killing while Driving

If someone kills another by driving a car, there is nothing to stop her being charged with manslaughter (*Jennings* v. *US Government*). However, juries tend to be very reluctant to convict people who kill in driving 'accidents'. Maybe they can relate more easily to a driver than other kinds of killers and there is a sense of 'there but for the grace of God go I'. As a result of the low rate of conviction of killers while driving, Parliament enacted legislation to create a special offence of killing while driving dangerously. A manslaughter or murder conviction is only likely to be sought where a defendant has used the car in effect as a weapon and driven deliberately into someone.

The offence of killing by dangerous driving is found in s.2A Road Traffic Act 1988 and reads:

'A person who causes the death of another person by driving a mechanically propelled vehicle dangerously on a road or other public place is guilty of an offence.'

Dangerousness here is an objective requirement and the question is simply whether the conduct falls below the standard of the ordinary careful and competent driver. There is no *mens rea* requirement. There is no need to show that the defendant was aware she was driving dangerously. The driver can be convicted even if the accident occurs because of a sudden illness (in contrast to the old offence of causing death by reckless driving, discussed in *Reid*). However a defendant would have a defence if he can show that he was an automaton and hence not 'driving' (see Chapter 3.6). The offence is interesting for two particular reasons. Firstly, it shows the significance that the law can attach to the consequences of an action. Dangerous driving that does not cause death is a relatively minor crime and often goes unpunished. The fact that it causes death dramatically increases the potential sentence, without there being any increase in the blame attached to the defendant. Secondly, as we have already mentioned, the existence of the offence shows the effect that society's attitudes can have on the criminal law. Car crimes are generally seen as less serious than equally dangerous and blameworthy conduct involving say, guns or knives.

There are also special offences of causing death by careless driving or while driving under the influence of illegal drugs or alcohol, which are not covered in this book.

10.6   Criticisms of and Reform of Involuntary Manslaughter

The present law on involuntary manslaughter has come under heavy criticism. There are four particular complaints. First, manslaughter can be committed with the defendant having only a low level of *mens rea*. If the defendant lightly punches the victim on the nose, who then falls over and bangs his head and dies, the defendant may be guilty of constructive manslaughter. For gross negligence manslaughter, it does not need to be shown that the defendant foresaw death, or even any harm at all to the victim (*Attorney-General's Reference* (No. 2 of 1999)). The defendant's state of mind is only relevant for the jury when deciding whether his behaviour was gross enough to justify criminal liability (*Attorney-General's Reference* (No. 2 of 1999)). An interesting aspect of this argument is that in *Adomako*, had the victim survived with brain damage, it is possible that Dr Adomako would not have been guilty of an offence, that is unless it could be shown there was intention or *Cunningham* recklessness. Allen has asked:

> 'Why should the chance occurrence of death, something outside his control, result in liability for one of the most serious offences in the criminal calendar, whereas survival of the patient in a condition which many would characterise as a 'living death' results in no criminal liability if *mens rea* cannot be proved?'

The second and linked point is that the label 'manslaughter' covers a wide range of killings, from a defendant who only just falls outside the band of murder, to an act which may be regarded as little more than a careless accident. The present distinction between constructive manslaughter and gross negligence does not help in dividing the offence into less serious and more serious forms. It is not possible to state whether a constructive manslaughter is necessarily more serious than a gross negligence manslaughter.

The third complaint is that gross negligence manslaughter does not take account of the defendant's capacity to abide by the standard of the reasonable person. It would be possible (although unlikely) for a jury to convict someone who fell below the standard of conduct required for the reasonable person, even though she was not capable of meeting that standard. For example in *Stone and Dobinson** the defendants were convicted of manslaughter, having failed to provide their relatives with the care expected of a reasonable person, even though the defendants suffered from various mental infirmities and there were grave doubts about whether the defendants were in fact capable of meeting the standard expected.

A fourth point applies particularly to gross negligence manslaughter. That is, the definition of the offence is too uncertain because so much emphasis is placed on whether the jury believes that the victim deserves a manslaughter conviction. Lord Mackay himself admitted that the test is circular – what conduct leads to a manslaughter conviction? That conduct that deserves to lead to a manslaughter conviction. However, he believed this was the best test to be used; although it must be admitted that it gives the jury little guidance as to which criteria it should be using. The uncertainty involved might lead to inconsistent verdicts, for example some juries might be sympathetic to an overworked junior doctor who makes a careless mistake which kills someone, another jury might not. Another consequence of the lack of certainty of the definition of the offence is that *Adomako* provides little guidance for the Crown Prosecution Service. Many unnatural deaths could potentially result in a gross negligence manslaughter conviction and the Crown Prosecution Service must decide whether or not to prosecute based on its predictions of how it thinks the jury will react to a case. So, it is not surprising that a subsequent Law Commission Report has noted that the Crown Prosecution Service faced difficulties in deciding whether to prosecute for gross negligence manslaughter. Also there have been an increasing number of applications by relatives of people who have died following accidents, for judicial review of decisions not to prosecute for gross negligent manslaughter (see, for example, *R* v. *DPP ex p Jones*).

In light of these objections, the Law Commission has suggested that the present law on involuntary manslaughter should be replaced by two offences. The first is reckless killing:

'A person who by his conduct causes the death of another is guilty of reckless killing if
(a) he is aware of a risk that his conduct will cause death or serious injury; and
(b) it is unreasonable for him to take that risk having regard to the circumstances as he knows or believes them to be.'

The second, less serious, is killing by gross carelessness:

'(1) A person who by his conduct causes the death of another is guilty of killing by gross carelessness if
(a) a risk that his conduct will cause death or serious injury would be obvious to a reasonable person in his position;
(b) he is capable of appreciating that risk at the material time; and
(c) either
  (i) his conduct falls far below what can reasonably be expected of him in the circumstances; or
  (ii) he intends by his conduct to cause some injury or is aware of, and unreasonably takes, the risk that it may do so.
(2) There shall be attributed to the person referred to in subsection (1)(a) above
(a) knowledge of any relevant facts which the accused is shown to have at the material time; and
(b) any skill or experience professed by him.'

The benefits of these proposals are that they distinguish between less serious and more serious forms of manslaughter, reckless killing being the more serious. The offence of gross carelessness also ensures that a defendant is only liable if he had the capacity to commit the offence.

10.7 Voluntary Manslaughter

The special nature of voluntary manslaughter has an important result. Because it is only relevant where the *actus reus* and *mens rea* of murder are present, it cannot be charged as a separate offence by the prosecution. The charge must be for murder, and then the accused may put forward a plea of guilty to manslaughter on the ground of (for example) provocation. This plea will either be accepted by the prosecution, in which case there is no trial and the judge will proceed to sentence, or it will be rejected, in which case the trial for murder will continue, with the accused putting in evidence of provocation to be considered by the jury. In the case of diminished responsibility, the plea will often be accepted by the prosecution, and so not contested before the jury. However, the prosecution may refuse to accept the plea and counter with its own evidence that the accused is severely mentally ill, so as to come within the legal definition of insanity, or that the accused is not suffering from any kind of illness at all and should be convicted of murder.

10.8 Provocation

Provocation is only a defence to murder, and if successful, reduces the charge to manslaughter. Therefore if a defendant has a choice it is better for her to rely on self-defence, which if successful leads to a complete acquittal. If the defendant raises the defence of self-defence, but there is evidence that she was provoked, then the judge should direct the jury to consider whether either defence is available. Provocation is available to someone charged as an accessory to murder (*Marks**); but not to a charge of attempted murder (*Bruzas*). In relation to offences other than murder, provocation is not a defence, but it can be taken into account at the sentencing stage.

Section three of the Homicide Act 1957 states:

> 'Where on a charge of murder there is evidence on which the jury can find that the person charged was provoked (whether by things done or by things said or by both together) to lose his self-control, the question whether the provocation was enough to make a reasonable man do as he did shall be left to be determined by the jury; and in determining that question the jury shall take into account everything both done and said according to the effect which, in their opinion, it would have on a reasonable man.'

This provision makes clear the respective roles of the judge and jury. First, the judge should determine whether or not there is evidence on which the jury can find that the accused was provoked. Unless the accused supports the allegation of provocation with some legally relevant evidence, the judge will direct the jury to ignore the issue of provocation altogether (see Chapter 2.2). Once this preliminary point has been decided, the issue of provocation will be left to the jury. It will be faced with two distinct questions:

1 Had the defendant lost her self-control as a result of something said or done?
2 Was the provocation enough to make a reasonable person do as the defendant did?

These questions will now be examined in greater detail.

10.8.1 Had the Defendant Lost her Self-control as a Result of Something Said or Done?

This is essentially a factual question about the defendant's state of mind. The question is not about whether the defendant should have lost her self-control, but whether as a matter of fact at the time of the killing the defendant had lost her self-control. In deciding whether or not this was so, the jury can take all the evidence into account. It should be stressed that this requirement means that provocation will not apply to a defendant who is a particularly laid back individual who in the face of a highly provocative incident does not lose his cool, but instead carefully plans his revenge.

The question appears straightforward but there are a number of complex issues here:

1.   What is 'loss of self-control'?
It should be stressed that the defence of provocation is only available when a charge of murder is otherwise appropriate. Hence the defendant must have been found to have intended to kill the victim or cause him grievous bodily harm. This means that loss of self-control cannot mean that the defendant was so angry that she was completely unable to control her movements or was unaware of what she was doing, because if either of these were so she would not be able to have the *mens rea* for murder. Instead, a defendant loses self-control when he is so overcome with emotion that it is very difficult to stop himself performing the action (*Richens*).

In *Cocker*, a man smothered his wife with a pillow following her persistent pleas that he kill her as she was suffering from a painful fatal illness. The court decided that his acts in placing a pillow over her face were fully controlled and so he could not use the defence of provocation. This seemed to limit the concept of loss of self-control to a loss of physical self-control, an uncontrolled flailing around. An alternative vision of loss of self-control would see it as involving a lack of self-restraint, a lack of 'moral check' over one's actions. Seen in this light, *Cocker* may have succeeded in using the defence. A later case (*Richens*) referred to self-control as involving 'loss of self-restraint', but it is perhaps reading too much into this comment to believe that the Court of Appeal would reach a different conclusion if a case with the facts of *Cocker* were to come before it again.

2.   The loss of self-control must be caused by something said or done
There is no need for the defendant to be provoked by the victim as long as he was provoked by someone or something. In one case a man was provoked by the acts of his wife's lover to kill his wife (*Davies*). There must, however, be something 'said or done' that led to that loss of self-control (*Acott*). In *Acott* there was evidence that the defendant had lost his self-control, but there was no evidence that anything had been said or done to cause this. In colloquial terms, he 'suddenly flipped'. It was therefore impossible for him to use the defence of provocation. So a defendant cannot claim that being stuck in a traffic jam or having his picnic spoiled

by rain is sufficient to amount to a provocative act for the purposes of the section. In contrast, a baby's incessant crying was sufficient because it was something 'said or done' (*Doughty*).

3. The loss of self-control must be 'sudden and temporary' (Duffy)
It used to be thought that this requirement meant that the defendant had to kill immediately after the provocative act. However it was reinterpreted in *Ahluwalia**, where the Court of Appeal explained that the longer the gap in time between the provocative act and the killing, the less likely the jury is to believe that the defendant had lost her self-control at the time of the killing as a result of that provocation. But the court did not rule out the possibility of a 'slow burn' reaction, where the defendant suddenly 'snaps' some time after the provocation has taken place. It still appears that the loss of self-control was sudden. This might mean that a defendant who gradually gets more and more angry over a long period of time cannot use the defence. Presumably he should realize he is losing his self-control and seek help.

4. Must the loss of self-control be produced by anger?
The loss of self-control is normally through anger, although there is nothing in s.3 that would limit the defence to those who lose their self-control through anger. In *Cocker*, for example, the alleged loss of self-control was through compassion, but this was not mentioned as a reason why the defence was unsuccessful. However, Lord Steyn, in the House of Lords, has stressed that the loss of self-control must be provoked, and not arise, say, as a result of a panic (*Acott*). So, although a provoked loss of self-control through grief or compassion could amount to provocation there may be difficulties in satisfying the second question, the reasonableness requirement, which we will now consider.

10.8.2 Was the provocation enough to make a reasonable person do as the defendant did?

This part of the test is largely objective and requires consideration of whether the defendant's reaction can be said to be reasonable. The courts have had great difficulty in deciding on the relevance of the defendant's characteristics when considering the reasonableness of the defendant's reaction. In other words, should the jury consider how a reasonable person would react, or how a reasonable person with the defendant's characteristics would react? It has become clear that simply asking how the reasonable person would react is unworkable. This is demonstrated by two cases.

In *Bedder*, an impotent man visited a prostitute, who taunted him about his impotency. He flew into a rage and killed her. The House of Lords held that the jury had to consider how a reasonable person (without any of the defendant's characteristics) would react to a provocation of that gravity. In other words, the jury had to consider how a potent man would react to taunts about being impotent. The ruling in *Bedder* is highly artificial. To taunt an impotent man about being impotent is clearly a different kind of taunt from telling a potent man that he was impotent. The case of *Bedder* was prior to the Homicide Act 1957 and was held no longer to be law by the House of Lords in *Camplin*. So if the facts of *Bedder* were to occur now the jury would be directed to consider how grave an impotent man would judge taunts about his impotency to be.

In *Camplin*, a fifteen-year-old boy was raped by a man who then taunted him. The boy lost his self-control and killed the man with a chipati pan. The House of Lords held that one could not expect 'old heads on young shoulders'. This meant that the defendant could only be expected to show the level of self-control of someone of his age.

These cases demonstrate that there are two separate reasons why a jury should be directed to consider a reasonable person with some of the defendant's characteristics: to make sense of the provocation and to take account of characteristics which may affect the level of self-control to be expected. Does this mean that the jury should consider a reasonable person with every characteristic of the defendant? This is an issue that has troubled the courts greatly.

Lord Goff in *Morhall**, following *Camplin*, suggested that the jury should consider:

'a hypothetical person having the power of self-control to be expected of an ordinary person of the age and sex of the defendant, but in other respects sharing such of the defendant's characteristics as they think would affect the gravity of the provocation to him.'

This required the jury to consider how a reasonable person of the age and sex of the defendant would react to a provocation of the gravity perceived by the accused. However this distinction between characteristics that affect the level of self-control and those that affect the gravity of the provocation proved impossible to maintain. Take *Dryden,* which involved a defendant who was eccentric and had an obsessive personality. The Court of Appeal, following *Morhall*, explained that his eccentricity could be considered as a factor in considering the gravity of the provocation, but not as affecting the expected level of self-control. But is not seeing minor provocation as grave because of your obsessive personality in effect having a low level of self-control, but in another way? The Court of Appeal became increasingly dissatisfied with the distinction drawn in *Camplin* and it was inevitable that the House of Lords would have to consider the issue again.

The House of Lords, in *Smith**, was required to undertake a major re-evaluation of the reasonable person test in provocation. The case now represents the law on provocation. The House of Lords divided three to two. The majority decided that rather than setting down a hard and fast rule as to which characteristics could or could not be given to the reasonable person, it should be left to the discretion of the jury to decide which characteristics were relevant. Further, that the jury should not be instructed to distinguish between characteristics affecting the gravity of the provocation and those affecting the level of self-control expected. On the facts of *Smith* itself, the trial judge had been wrong to tell the jury that it could not take into account the respondent's depression as it affected his level of self-control. Instead, it should have been left to the jury to decide whether it wished to take his depression into account. The jury simply had to decide whether the respondent had measured up to the standard of self-control that ought reasonably to have been expected of him. Lord Hoffman suggested that it may assist the jury to consider the question without reference to the reasonable person:

'the fact that something caused him to lose self-control is not enough. The law expects people to exercise control over their emotions. A tendency to violent rages or childish tantrums is a defect in character rather than an excuse. The jury must think that the circumstances were such as to make the loss of self-control sufficiently excusable to reduce the gravity of the offence from murder to manslaughter. This is entirely a question for the jury. In deciding what should count as a sufficient excuse, they have to apply what they consider to be appropriate standards of behaviour; on the one hand making allowance for human nature and the power of the emotions but, on the other hand, not allowing someone to rely upon his own violent disposition. In applying these standards of behaviour, the jury represent the community and decide, as Lord Diplock said in *Camplin* [1978] AC 705, 717, what degree of self-control "everyone is entitled to expect that his fellow citizens will exercise in society as it is today".'

In a pithier statement Lord Slynn, agreeing with Lord Hoffman, suggested that the jury should consider whether the defendant had 'exercised the degree of self-control to be expected of someone in his situation?' It must be emphasized that the result of the decision in *Smith* is *not* that the jury should consider a reasonable person with all of the defendant's characteristics. It is quite open to the jury to decide that the defendant's short-temper, drunkenness, racial prejudice and obsessive personality are not relevant. Indeed, Lord Hoffman went further and suggested that a judge should recommend that a jury does not take into account male possessiveness, jealousy or obsession. However, throughout his judgment he stresses that at the end of the day the issue is ultimately one for the jury. It should, here, be remembered that if the judge decides that the evidence is insufficient for any jury to be persuaded that the defendant was provoked to lose his self-control, she can withdraw the case for the jury.

The two dissenting judges, Lords Hobhouse and Millet, argued that on the facts of this case, to say that the jury had to consider how a reasonable person with depression would react to the provocation was to create an unacceptable blurring between provocation and diminished responsibility. If it was his mental state that caused his loss of self-control, the case was better classified as diminished responsibility. The majority saw the force of this argument but thought that it was better to have this blurring between the two defences than to seek to draw a sharp distinction between characteristics which could or could not affect the level of self-control expected. Lord Slynn argued that a sharp distinction between provocation and diminished responsibility could be drawn on the basis that provocation results from a factor external to the defendant (something said or done), while diminished responsibility results from a factor internal to the defendant (an abnormality of mind).

There are three other aspects of the reasonable person test which need to be discussed. First, if the defence is to succeed, the jury must decide that the reasonable person would have killed the victim in the same way (that is, by using the same method of killing) that the defendant did (*Clarke* (1991)). So if the defendant understandably loses his self-control, but then kills in a bizarre way, the defence may not be available.

Second, it is not uncommon, especially where the provocation is an act of violence directed at the accused, for the provoking act itself to have been provoked by some action or words of the accused. It used to be thought that provocation could only be available where the victim's response (the provoking act) was an unexpected result of the defendant's acts. In other words, the defendant could not say that he was provoked by a foreseeable response of the victim to the accused's own acts (*Edwards*). However, the Court of Appeal has now made it clear that the question is simply whether the defendant's response was reasonable in all of the circumstances, including that the provocation was self-induced (*Johnson* (1989)).

Third, if the defendant mishears a remark made by the victim and believes that he has been insulted, when in fact he has not, the jury must consider what would be a reasonable response to the provocation as understood by the defendant (*Letenock*). So, if a husband on returning home late from work says 'I am late because I had a cup of tea', but this is misheard by his wife as 'I am late because I had adultery' and she loses her self control and kills, the jury should consider how a reasonable person would react to the adultery comment, not the comment about tea. This may even be true if the defendant mishears because he or she was drunk (*Letenock*).

10.8.3 Why is Provocation a Defence?

There has been much debate over whether the defence of provocation is best seen as a partial justification or as an excuse. The difference between a justification and an excuse is explained in Chapter 16.1. Those who see it as an excuse argue that the fact that the defendant had lost her self-control meant that the killing was not a true choice and the individual is not morally responsible for his or her acts (see Chapter 1.4.3). The problem with this theory is that it does not explain why there is a reasonableness requirement. If a person has unreasonably lost her self-control, has she not as little choice in reacting as a person who has reasonably lost her self-control? There may be three responses to this. It may be that the reasonableness requirement is really an evidential requirement, ensuring that the defendant really did lose her self-control; but that is not how it operates in the law. Secondly, it may be that, although theoretically the defence would be available to all that lose self-control, there are policy reasons for requiring reasonable self-control and encouraging self-restraint. Lord Hoffman, in *Smith*, suggested that the objective requirement played the role of protecting the public from exceptionally ill-tempered people. Thirdly, the reasonableness requirement could be seen as an example of the defendant being denied an excuse if she is at fault in bringing about the circumstances of the defence (see a similar situation in relation to duress in Chapter 16.2.2).

Others argue that provocation is a partial justification, in that the victim brought the attack upon himself by his provocative conduct. This is hard to accept now that third parties can provoke (*Davies*), and also in cases such as *Doughty* where the victim was a crying baby. An alternative argument for provocation being a justification is that when faced with grave insults it is right that a display of righteous indignation be made. If a man informed a mother that he had abused her child, for the parent not to display any shock and anger would be immoral in a sense – some display of righteous anger is appropriate (J. Horder). It is true that the killing is an inappropriate display of righteous anger, but that is why it is only a partial defence.

This debate over the basis of the defence is reflected in the difficulties that the courts have had in deciding which characteristics of the accused to attribute to the reasonable person. If the defence is seen as a partial justification then few (if any) of the defendant's characteristics should be considered. If seen as an excuse then it will be more appropriate to consider the defendant's characteristics when looking at the objective requirement.

10.9   Diminished Responsibility

Diminished responsibility is only available to a charge of murder. It does not provide a defence to any other charge. The defence has the effect of reducing murder to manslaughter, thereby enabling the trial judge to exercise discretion in sentencing (a discretion that the judge does not possess on a conviction of murder, where the mandatory life sentence applies). In the case of attempted murder there is a peculiarity. If a defendant attempts to kill the victim while suffering from diminished responsibility, she will be convicted of attempted murder, even though had she succeeded she would have been convicted of manslaughter. This is an oddity, but the wording of the 1957 Homicide Act s.2 is based on the clear presumption that the offence applies to murder, but not attempted murder (*Campbell*).

Diminished responsibility is a popular defence for those charged with murder. The prosecution will often accept a plea of guilty to manslaughter on the basis of diminished responsibility. It is only in cases where the prosecution either refuses to accept the plea of diminished responsibility or counters with evidence of insanity that the scope and application of diminished responsibility will be argued before the court. Diminished responsibility must be proved on the balance of probability by the party raising it.

10.9.1   What is Diminished Responsibility?

Section 2 Homicide Act 1957 defines diminished responsibility:

'(1) Where a person kills or is a party to the killing of another, he shall not be convicted of murder if he was suffering from such abnormality of mind (whether arising from a condition of arrested or retarded development of mind or any inherent causes or induced by disease or injury) as substantially impaired his mental responsibility for his acts and omissions in doing or being a party to the killing.'

The burden of proof rests on the defence (s.2(2)). The section can be broken down into three separate requirements:

- Abnormality of the mind
- Caused by one of the listed factors
- Substantial impairment of responsibility.

1. Abnormality of mind

It needs to be shown that the defendant was suffering from an abnormality of mind at the time of the incident. The concept of abnormality of mind has been widely interpreted, to include depression, morbid jealousy and the anguish suffered by someone watching a loved one in an agonizing illness (*Dix*). The definition of the term given by Lord Parker in *Byrne** was formulated in non-medical language, and in terms of the reasonable person:

> 'Abnormality of mind . . . means a state of mind so different from that of ordinary human beings that the reasonable man would term it abnormal. It appears to us to be wide enough to cover the mind's activities in all its aspects, not only the perception of physical acts and matters and the ability to form a rational judgement whether an act is right or wrong, but also the ability to exercise will-power to control physical acts in accordance with that rational judgement. The expression "mental responsibility for his acts" points to a consideration of the extent to which the accused's mind is answerable for his physical acts which must include a consideration of the extent of his ability to exercise will-power to control his physical acts.'

This passage also makes it clear that an irresistible impulse is capable of amounting to diminished responsibility. It also makes it clear that a defendant may be fully aware of what he is doing, yet be suffering from an abnormality of the mind, if, for example, it was very difficult for him to restrain himself. In *Seers*, the trial judge suggested that the jury had to find a state of mind that was 'on the borderline of insanity'. The Court of Appeal held that this was a misdirection.

2. The cause of the abnormality

The second requirement is that the abnormality must be caused by 'a condition of arrested or retarded development of mind or any inherent causes or induced by disease or injury'. This is a wide list and makes it clear that the abnormality can be the result of organic or physical causes. It is in practice essential to introduce medical evidence to support the defence to establish the necessary cause (*Dix*).

A defendant suffering from post-natal depression or pre-menstrual tension has been able to rely on diminished responsibility (*Reynolds*). However, a temporary abnormality caused by the taking of alcohol or drugs (even legal ones) cannot form the basis of a plea of diminished responsibility (*O'Connell*). This is because an abnormality produced by alcohol or drugs cannot be regarded as injury (*O'Connell*).

3.   *Substantial impairment of responsibility*

It must be shown that the abnormality was such as to 'substantially impair the defendant's responsibility for her actions'. 'Substantially' here means that the impairment was not a trivial or minimal one. The requirement does not mean that the defendant must be not at all responsible for his or her actions (*Lloyd* (1967)). What must be shown is that because of the abnormality, the defendant finds it substantially harder not to kill in the particular set of circumstances than other people would. This may appear unduly generous to the defendant, but remember that the defendant is not to be completely acquitted and is still guilty of manslaughter.

10.9.2   Diminished Responsibility and Intoxication

In the caselaw there has been some difficulty in dealing with voluntarily intoxicated defendants who claim that they suffer diminished responsibility. The test for the jury seems to be:

'Has the defendant satisfied you on the balance of probabilities that, if he had not taken drink (i) he would have killed as he did and (ii) he would have been under diminished responsibility when he did so?' (*Egan*).

If the answer to both of these questions is 'yes' then the defendant can rely on the defence of diminished responsibility. But if the answer to either question is 'no' then the defence is not available (*Dietschmann*). There are two exceptions to this. The first is where the defendant is an alcoholic. In this case if every drink in the drinking spree that led to the intoxication was involuntary, in the sense that it was compelled by the disease, then the court will see the alcoholism as the cause of the lack of responsibility for the purpose of s.2. As alcoholism can be regarded as a disease of the mind, the defence will be available (*Tandy*). The second is where the alcohol intake has actually damaged the brain (*Dietschmann*).

10.9.3   Why is Diminished Responsibility a Defence?

The justifications for the defence of diminished responsibility have been challenged. There are two main grounds of complaint. The first is that the defence exists simply because of the mandatory life sentence for murder. This is to some extent true, but given the existence of the life sentence it makes sense to have this defence, to avoid what may otherwise be an inappropriate life sentence. The second and more substantial criticism is that it either is or is not true that the defendant acted the way he did because of his illness or condition. If the defendant would still have killed had he not been suffering from the abnormality then the abnormality should have no effect on his liability. However, if the defendant would not have killed had he not suffered from the abnormality then the defendant should be seen as blameless. In other words, the defence should either be complete and be available for all offences, or not exist at all. This criticism argues that the present law on diminished responsibility is an illogical halfway house.

10.9.4   Reform of Diminished Responsibility

The Law Commission's proposals on diminished responsibility are that the defence should be available to a defendant 'if, at the time of his act, he is suffering from such mental abnormality as is a substantial enough reason to reduce his offence to manslaughter' (Clause 56). 'Mental abnormality' is defined as 'mental illness, arrested or incomplete development of mind, psychopathic disorder, and any other disorder or disability of mind except intoxication'. This proposed redefinition would make two important changes to the law. The first is that any kind of mental abnormality can form the basis for the defence. The second is that the defendant's responsibility is not just diminished but is diminished sufficiently to reduce liability to manslaughter. This makes explicit what the jury should ask itself under the present law.

10.10   Suicide Pact

It is not a defence to a charge of murder that the victim has asked the accused to kill her. Hence voluntary euthanasia is classed as murder or manslaughter (see *Hot Topic*, Chapter 4). However, if the defendant killed the victim intending to go on and kill herself as part of a suicide pact then it is possible for the defendant to plead the defence of suicide pact to a charge of murder (s.4 Homicide Act 1957). If successful, the defence will reduce the charge to manslaughter, and open up the discretion in sentencing that is appropriate in such sad cases. The onus of proof in establishing the defence is on the defendant. It should be added that if the defendant did not herself actually kill the other party to the pact, she may be found to have aided or abetted their suicide which is an offence under s.2(1) Suicide Act 1961.

10.11   Infanticide

Infanticide is an offence that can be charged when a mother kills her recently born child. It is also a defence that such a woman can raise if she is charged with murder. Its requirements are set out in s.1(1) Infanticide Act 1938. Infanticide is available where:

1 the mother has killed her own child;
2 the child is under the age of twelve months;
3 the mother does not have a younger child;
4 and if 'the balance of her mind was disturbed by reason of her not having fully recovered from the effect of giving birth to the child' or by reason of the effects of lacerations consequential upon the birth.

The maximum sentence is life, but the most common sentence is a probation order. The offence has been criticized for only allowing the mother to rely on a disturbance of mind resulting from the birth or resultant lacerations, but not on the social and economic consequences that may follow a birth. This restriction may reflect the law's general refusal to permit a defendant's socio-economic background to be considered. It should be added that the reference to lacerations is based on a now discredited medical opinion as to the causes of post-natal depression.

At one time the defence was thought to be justified on the basis of the argument that to kill a child less than one year old was less serious than to kill an older child. Nowadays the defence is seen as analogous to diminished responsibility. The mother who kills her child, suffering from post-natal depression, is less culpable than a person who calmly plans the killing.

Some commentators argue that a father should be able to use the defence. However, it seems more appropriate for him to use diminished responsibility, as it is unlikely that he would suffer any form of mental illness directly linked to the birth rather than related to social problems or a pre-existing mental condition.

Hot Topic: Battered Women

In recent years, women who have killed their abusive husbands or partners have struggled to find a defence to a charge of murder. Before looking at the particular difficulties these defendant have faced, it is interesting to note that the vast majority of murders by women are committed by those who have killed their abusive partners. The fact that they have not neatly fallen into an established defence lends force to the arguments of feminist commentators who have complained that the law has been based on a male norm. In other words, the offences and defences are built up with men rather than women in mind. We will return to this point at several times in this discussion.

In the past decade, the courts have sought to develop the established defences to enable a battered women to have access to a defence. The courts have been particularly influenced by medical evidence of 'battered women's syndrome'. This 'syndrome' is caused by lengthy experience of abuse and produces a variety of symptoms, including a feeling of helplessness so that the option of leaving the relationship does not appear viable and sudden outbursts of desperate violence can occur. Interestingly, in *Hobson*, a conviction of a battered women many years ago was overturned because there was a lack of awareness of battered women's syndrome at that time.

So, let us imagine a woman, Eve, who has suffered months of abuse and mistreatment at the hands of her husband. One night, while he is asleep, she pours petrol over him and sets it alight, killing him. Is this a clear case of murder, or can Eve raise any defences?

1. Provocation

In a number of cases, battered women have killed their abusing partners and have sought to use provocation. Eve will face four main problems:

(a) The first is that Eve must show that she suffered a loss of self-control. The case of *Cocker*, although on very different facts, illustrates the potential problem. As mentioned above, Mr Cocker was thought by the Court of Appeal not to have lost his self-control, but to have acted in a calm and deliberate way. The prosecution would argue that finding petrol, pouring it and setting it alight was just like the calm conduct of Mr Cocker in placing the pillow over his wife's face. Hence it could not be said that when Eve set her husband alight she was suffering a sudden and temporary loss of self-control.

(b) The loss of self-control needs to be sudden and temporary. This was originally interpreted by the courts to mean that the killing must happen immediately after the provocative words or conduct. This was said by some commentators to represent a male notion of anger and loss of self-control. They argued that women are more likely to feel 'slow burn' anger, with the anger not being expressed until some time after the provocation. In particular, women faced with a threatening abusive partner will not respond immediately because to do so would be very dangerous to them. To some extent these concerns are met by the Court of Appeal's decision in *Alhuwalia*, which held that there was no need for the loss of self-control to follow immediately on the provocation, although it must be caused by the provocation and be sudden and temporary.

(c) Eve must point to something said or done that caused her to lose her self-control (*Acott*). It is not possible for her to allege that she simply snapped because of the pressure caused by the months of abuse. Given the point in (b), she will probably need to point to something said or done by her husband shortly before he fell asleep, which caused her to lose her self-control. Eve will be assisted here by *Thornton (No. 2)* and *Morhall*, which stressed that in considering the provocative conduct the jury can consider the entire history of the relationship. In light of such evidence, what might otherwise appear to be a minor provocation can be seen as the significant provocation that it was. This means that if Eve can point to words said or things done shortly before her partner fell asleep, she may be able to argue that its gravity should be seen in the light of the months of abuse beforehand and so as a grave provocation.

(d) The fourth problem concerns battered-women's syndrome itself. Before *Smith* in the House of Lords, the courts were reluctant to accept that battered women's syndrome could affect the level of self-control expected (*Thornton (No. 2)*). After *Smith*, it is clear that it can be taken into account by the jury if it decides that it is relevant. This should make it much easier for defendants such as Eve to persuade a jury that she acted reasonably.

Before leaving provocation, it should be emphasized that provocation is only a defence to murder and so will provide no assistance to a battered women who injures, rather than kills, her partner. Also the defence is only partial and so if it succeeds, the defendant will still be convicted of manslaughter.

2. Diminished responsibility

Like provocation, diminished responsibility is only a defence to murder and is only a partial defence. Diminished responsibility has a higher chance of success, especially if Eve can introduce medical evidence that she suffered from battered-women's syndrome. It appears to be now generally accepted that a defendant who kills while suffering from battered-women's syndrome will be able to use diminished responsibility (*Ahluwalia*; *Thornton (No. 2)*). That said, to rely on diminished responsibility may appear demeaning to Eve. Far from reacting in a mentally disordered way, she may feel she acted in a reasonable way, under the appalling circumstances.

3. Self-defence

Self-defence will provide a complete defence and so will lead to an absolute acquittal. It is therefore an attractive defence. However, Eve will face severe difficulties in using this defence. First, it must be shown that she was facing an imminent threat (see Chapter 15.3.1). Eve will not be able to show that she was facing such a threat, because her husband was asleep when she attacked him. Second, it needs to be shown that the use of force was necessary and reasonable. A jury may feel that a battered women could escape the violence by leaving her husband and that killing could not be seen as necessary or reasonable. The second point could be resolved by a reference to *Gladstone Williams* and battered women's syndrome. *Gladstone Williams* stresses that whether the defendant's response was reasonable and necessary must be assessed on the facts as the defendant believed them to be. As explained earlier, battered women's syndrome can lead a sufferer to believe that escape is impossible and to see no way out of the violence. On that version of the facts, the attack could be seen as reasonable.

Some argue in favour of a change in the law on self-defence. It is argued that if the battered woman can only use force to protect herself when facing an imminent attack, the defence is of little use because in the face of her abuser she is physically unable to defend herself or prevent the attack. It is only when she is not under attack, for example when the abuser is asleep, that she has an opportunity to prevent the abuse continuing.

4. No mens rea

Eve could claim that she lacked the *mens rea* for murder (an intent to kill or cause grievous bodily harm). Such a defence may succeed where the defendant acted in a frenzied way. In Eve's case it is unlikely that she can successfully deny that she had the relevant intention.

5. Creation of a new defence

Some commentators have suggested that there should be a new defence created to deal specifically with battered women who kill. For example, McColgan suggests a defence where a person kills for the purpose of sustaining his or her autonomy while facing the unlawful and brutally oppressive conduct of another.

Summary

10.1 Voluntary manslaughter exists where the accused has committed the *actus reus* of murder, with malice aforethought, but an additional factor operates to reduce liability to manslaughter. There are three of these factors: provocation, diminished responsibility and suicide pact, the latter two created by the Homicide Act 1957.

10.2 Constructive manslaughter is a common law offence. It consists of causing the death of the victim by an unlawful and dangerous act. The unlawful act should be a crime but it probably need not be directed at another person. The accused need not know that the act is unlawful, but if the unlawful act requires *mens rea* then this must be proved by the prosecution. 'Dangerous' means that an ordinary person in the defendant's shoes would appreciate the risk of causing some physical injury to another. There is no need for the accused to foresee the risk of injury; negligence as to causing injury is sufficient.

10.3 Gross negligence manslaughter is established when it can be shown that the defendant owed the victim a duty of care and broke that duty in a way which caused the victim's death, and the jury thinks that the defendant's conduct was sufficiently serious to justify a criminal conviction.

10.4 *Cunningham* reckless manslaughter may exist but it has never been used in a reported case. Any defendant who is guilty of *Cunningham* reckless manslaughter would also be guilty of either constructive or gross negligence manslaughter.

10.5 Causing death by dangerous driving is a statutory offence, now found in s.1 Road Traffic Act 1988. The requirement for dangerousness is entirely objective.

10.6 The Law Commission has suggested that the present law be replaced with two new offences: killing by gross carelessness and reckless killing.

10.7 Voluntary manslaughter occurs where the defendant has the *mens rea* for murder, but the defendant introduces evidence of provocation or diminished responsibility, for example.

10.8 The defendant can establish the defence of provocation if he can show that he killed having lost his self control as a result of something said or done and that a reasonable person would have acted in the same way in the face of the provocation. When considering whether the reasonable person would have acted in the same way, the jury can take into account any of the accused's characteristics which it thinks relevant. Provocation is only a defence to a charge of murder and if successful, reduces the charge to manslaughter.

10.9 Diminished responsibility is only available to murder. It has the effect of reducing the charge of murder to manslaughter. It is based on an abnormality of mind causing a substantial impairment of mental responsibility. This may include an inability to exercise will-power to control physical actions.

10.10 If the defendant killed someone as part of a suicide pact, this will provide a defence to murder, but the defendant may still be guilty of manslaughter.

10.11 A mother who kills her child (under one year old) as a result of a disturbed mental state, caused by the birth, may be able to rely on the defence of infanticide. The mother will still be liable to be sentenced as if convicted of manslaughter.

Case Notes

Adomako [1995] 1 AC 171. House of Lords
The appellant was an anaesthetist, who failed to notice that a patient's tube had become disconnected during an operation and as a result the patient died. The House of Lords, dismissing the appellant's appeal against his conviction, referred back to the test for negligence in *Andrews* v. *DPP* and confirmed that it represented the law. Lord Mackay confirmed that it was necessary to show that there had been a duty of care owed by the accused to the victim, that the duty had been breached, that the breach had caused the victim's death, and that the breach had been gross enough to justify a criminal conviction. His speech also made it clear that there had to be a risk of death from the accused's acts if a conviction was to be established. He suggested that a trial judge could direct a jury to consider whether the defendant was 'reckless' in the normal sense of the word, but that it would be inappropriate to attempt to give a full legal definition of that word.

Ahluwalia [1992] 4 All ER 889. Court of Appeal
The accused had entered an arranged marriage with her husband, who abused her over several years. One night she poured petrol over him while he was asleep and lit it, causing a fire that killed him. The court stated that it was necessary to show that she had suffered a sudden and temporary loss of self-control although it was not necessary to show that the killing had been immediate upon a provocative act. The court also confirmed that battered-women's syndrome was a relevant characteristic that could be given to the reasonable person when considering how a reasonable person would have reacted. Battered-women's syndrome could also form the basis of a manslaughter verdict on the basis of diminished responsibility, and it was on this ground that the accused's murder conviction was overturned and replaced with a manslaughter conviction.

Andrews v. *DPP* [1937] AC 576. House of Lords
The appellant was convicted of manslaughter and his appeal against conviction was dismissed by both the Court of Appeal and the House of Lords. He had killed a pedestrian while driving his van. Lord Atkin in the House of Lords held that for manslaughter a very high degree of negligence was required. 'Reckless' was an appropriate description, suggesting an indifference to risk, but manslaughter also covered the person who appreciated the risk and intended to avoid it, but showed a high degree of negligence in the means adopted to avoid the risk. The simple lack of care sufficient for civil liability was not enough, and manslaughter cannot be based on an unlawful act requiring simple negligence, such as driving without due care and attention.

Attorney-General's Reference (No. 3 of 1994) [1997] 3 WLR 421. House of Lords
See Chapter 9 case notes.

Byrne [1960] 3 All ER 1. Court of Criminal Appeal
The appellant was convicted of murder. He had strangled a young woman. His only defence was that he was suffering from diminished responsibility, and there was uncontradicted medical evidence that the appellant was a sexual psychopath: that is, he suffered from violent perverted sexual desires which he found difficult or impossible to control. The trial judge directed the jury that diminished responsibility, as defined in s.2 Homicide Act 1957, did not include an inability to control one's actions. The Court of Criminal Appeal allowed the appeal and substituted a verdict of manslaughter, leaving the sentence of life imprisonment unchanged. The court held that diminished responsibility, unlike insanity, did cover an inability to exercise will-

power to control one's physical actions, as well as the inability to form a rational judgement. Whether the accused was suffering, at the time of the killing, from an 'abnormality of mind' which substantially impaired his mental responsibility for his actions is a matter for the jury. The jury should take into account all the evidence, including any medical evidence, and decide on the balance of probabilities.

Caldwell [1982] AC 341. House of Lords
See Chapter 3 case notes.

Cato [1976] 1 WLR 110. Court of Appeal
The appellant was convicted of manslaughter. He had injected the victim, a friend of his, with heroin; the victim became unconscious and died as a result. The trial judge had left the charge to the jury on the alternative bases of (i) the unlawful act of injecting the heroin and (ii) that the injection of heroin had been done with recklessness or gross negligence. The Court of Appeal dismissed the appeal against conviction, holding that the injection of heroin was an unlawful act in itself as the heroin was unlawfully in the possession of the accused; it was also an offence under s.23 Offences against the Person Act 1861. Lord Widgery CJ also held that in considering whether the accused had been reckless, his knowledge of the potentiality of heroin to kill or cause grievous bodily harm would be relevant; but recklessness was a simple word in common use and its meaning did not need to be explained in detail to a jury. (See also Chapter 7 case notes.)

Church [1966] 1 QB 59. Court of Criminal Appeal
The appellant was acquitted of murder, but convicted of manslaughter. He had a fight with the victim, knocking her unconscious. He concluded that she was dead, and put her in a river; she died as a result. The Court of Criminal Appeal dismissed the appeal. Edmund Davies J held that in a manslaughter case, it was not enough merely to prove that the accused had committed an unlawful act that caused the death. The unlawful act must have been such that all reasonable people would inevitably realize that the victim was subjected to the risk of at least some harm, albeit not serious harm.

Dawson, Nolan and Walmsley [1985] 81 Cr App Rep 150. Court of Appeal
The appellants were convicted of manslaughter. They had attempted to rob a petrol filling station using a replica gun. The attendant had pressed the alarm button, and the appellants fled, but the attendant had then collapsed and died of a heart attack. The trial judge ruled that in the context of the test laid down by Edmund Davies J in *Church* (see above), 'harm' included emotional or physical disturbance. The Court of Appeal allowed the appeal and quashed the convictions, holding that emotional disturbance alone cannot constitute 'harm'. However, the test would be satisfied if all sober and reasonable people would have realized that the accused's act would cause emotional disturbance or shock, and that the shock would cause physical injury.

Ireland and Burstow [1998] AC 147. House of Lords
See Chapter 6 case notes.

Lamb [1967] 2 QB 981. Court of Appeal
The appellant was convicted of manslaughter. He had pointed a revolver at his friend as a joke and pulled the trigger; the gun fired and the friend was killed. The appellant had thought that the gun would not fire, as he did not understand the mechanism of a revolver. The trial judge directed the jury that firing the gun was an unlawful act, even if there was no intent to harm or frighten the victim. The Court of Appeal allowed the appeal and quashed the conviction. The act of the appellant could not be unlawful in this context unless there was an assault, and this required proof of the *mens rea* of assault: an intent to frighten. With respect to gross negligence or reckless

manslaughter, Sachs LJ held that the jury would need to consider whether the appellant thought that what he was doing was safe, and whether this view was formed in a 'criminally negligent way'.

Marks [1998] Crim LR 676. Court of Appeal

The appellant and his friend (P) went to visit the deceased. An argument broke out when the appellant shouted 'wet him' as a result of which P shot the deceased dead. At the trial there was much dispute over whether 'wet him' meant throw water over him or shoot him. The jury must have thought the latter as it convicted the appellant as an accessory to murder. The Court of Appeal confirmed that the defence of provocation was available to a person who as a result of provocation had aided, abetted, counselled or procured murder; although on the facts of the case there was no evidence that the appellant had been provoked to lose his self control.

Morhall [1996] 1 AC 90. House of Lords

The appellant was teased about his glue sniffing and killed his taunter. He was convicted of murder and he appealed on the ground that, when considering the defence of provocation, the jury should have been directed to consider how a reasonable glue sniffer would have reacted to the taunts. The Court of Appeal stated that glue sniffing was not a characteristic that could be endued to the reasonable person because it was a discreditable characteristic. The House of Lords rejected this approach and said that any characteristic that affected the gravity of the provocation to the accused could be taken into account (except drunkenness, unless the taint related specifically to drunkenness), but only the characteristics of age and sex could affect the gravity of the provocation to the accused. The House of Lords therefore quashed the conviction for murder and substituted a conviction for manslaughter.

Newbury and Jones [1977] AC 500. House of Lords

The appellants were convicted of manslaughter. They had pushed a piece of pavingstone over a railway bridge onto a train passing underneath. The stone hit and killed the guard of the train. Both the Court of Appeal and the House of Lords dismissed their appeal. The House of Lords held that in the case of manslaughter by an unlawful and dangerous act, it is unnecessary for the accused to foresee that his act might cause harm to another. The test of dangerousness is objective: it depends on whether a reasonable person would recognize the risk of harm to another, and not on the foresight of the accused.

Smith [2000] Crim LR 1004 House of Lords

The respondent was an alcoholic and suffered from depression. He had an argument over some carpentry tools with the victim as a result of which he stabbed the victim. The trial judge directed the jury that when considering provocation, it should consider the mental impairment of the defendant as it affected the gravity of the provocation, but not so as to alter the expected level of self-control. The House of Lords, by a three to two majority, rejected this, arguing that the jury could consider whichever characteristic of an accused it believed relevant and decide whether the respondent had measured against the level of self control to be expected of him. The dissenting judgement sought to follow *Camplin* and stress that only age and sex were reasons for exercising a lower level of self-control than that expected of the reasonable person.

Stone and Dobinson [1977] QB 354. Court of Appeal

Stone (who was nearly blind and of low intelligence) and Dobinson (who was 'ineffectual and inadequate') were convicted of manslaughter and appealed. Stone's sister lived in the appellants' house, and suffered from anorexia nervosa. She refused to see a doctor or to leave her room, and eventually died of toxaemia. The appellants made some effort to help her by trying to trace her doctor, and by washing and feeding her, but failed to make contact with her doctor. The appellants argued on appeal (i) that there was insufficient evidence that they had undertaken the care of the victim, and (ii) that the jury had been misdirected on the recklessness required for manslaughter which, it was argued, involves foresight of the possibility of death or serious injury. It was held (i) that they had been under a duty to summon medical help for the victim if they could not care for her themselves; there was evidence on which the jury was entitled to find that a duty of care had been assumed by them, and that they had failed to discharge this duty; (ii) 'that indifference to an obvious risk and appreciation of such risk, coupled with a determination nevertheless to run it, are both examples of recklessness'. However, mere inadvertence is not enough: there must be a 'reckless disregard of danger to the health and welfare of the infirm person'. Their appeals were therefore dismissed.

Further Reading

Reform of involuntary manslaughter is discussed in Clarkson and Keating. The defence of provocation is analysed in Ashworth, Dressler, Gardner and Macklem, Horder, Nicholson and Sanghavi, and Wells. Diminished responsibility is examined in Griew, Mackay and Sullivan. Defences available to battered women are considered in McColgan and Wells. The concept of a partial defence is analysed by Lacey.

Ashworth, 'The Doctrine of Provocation' [1976] *Cambridge Law Journal* 292.

Clarkson, 'Context and Culpability in Involuntary Manslaughter: Principle or Instinct?', in Ashworth and Mitchell (ed.), *Rethinking English Homicide Law* (2000, Oxford University Press).

Dressler, 'Provocation: Partial Justification or Partial Excuse?' (1988) 51 *Modern Law Review* 467.

Gardner and Macklem, 'Compassion without Respect? Nine Fallacies in R v. Smith' [2001] *Criminal Law Review* 623.

Griew, 'The Future of Diminished Responsibility' [1988] *Criminal Law Review* 75.

Horder, *Provocation and Responsibility* (1992, Oxford University Press).

Keating, 'The Restating of a Serious Crime' [1996] *Criminal Law Review* 535.

Lacey, 'Partial Defences to Homicide', in Ashworth and Mitchell (ed.), *Rethinking English Homicide Law* (2000, Oxford University Press).

McColgan, 'In Defence of Battered Women who Kill' (1993) 13 *Oxford Journal of Legal Studies* 508.

MacKay, *Mental Condition Defences* (1995, Oxford University Press).

Mackay, 'The Abnormality of Mind Factor in Diminished Responsibility' [1999] *Criminal Law Review* 117.

Nicholson and Sanghavi, 'Battered Women and Provocation' [1993] *Criminal Law Review* 728.

Sullivan, 'Intoxicants and Diminished Responsibility' [1994] *Criminal Law Review* 156.

Wells, 'Battered Women Syndrome and Defences to Homicide: Where Now?' (1994) *Legal Studies* 266

Wells, 'Provocation: The Case for Abolition', in Ashworth and Mitchell (ed.), *Rethinking English Homicide Law* (2000, Oxford University Press).

PART III
OFFENCES AGAINST PROPERTY

11   Theft

> **Key words**
> - **Appropriation** – the assumption by the defendant of one of the owner's rights over a piece of property.
> - **Dishonesty** – the defendant acts in a way regarded as dishonest by the standards of the community, and he or she is aware of that.

11.1   Property Offences

Property offences are some of the most complex in the criminal law. Initially this is surprising – property offences are less serious than offences against the person, so we need be less concerned about careful gradations of liability. However, there are two particular reasons why this area has caused so many problems.

The first is that the criminal law on property offences has to interact with the civil law on ownership of property (for example, the law of contract). For instance, many commentators believe that it would be unsatisfactory if the civil law were to say *A* has validly transferred this property to *B*, but the criminal law were to say *B* has stolen this property from *A*. The problem is that different principles underlie these different areas of the law. Expediency and certainty carry greater weight in civil law than in criminal law. Yet an interaction between the two areas of the law is inevitable. The property offences forbid the harming or taking of property 'belonging to another', and it is largely the complex civil law that determines whether property belongs to another.

The second problem is the structuring of property offences. The offences against the person are generally distinguished on the basis of the severity of the harm caused to the victim (for example, distinguishing death, grievous bodily harm and actual bodily harm). However, this approach is not entirely suitable for property offences. The value of the property lost does not necessarily reflect the severity of the offence: stealing a pensioner's life savings of a few hundred pounds may be thought more serious than stealing several thousand pounds from a millionaire. So property offences tend to focus not on the severity of the loss, but on the way that the loss was caused, for example be it by force, deception or subterfuge.

The offences against property are largely in statutory form, the major statutes being the Theft Act 1968, amended and supplemented by the Theft Act 1978, and the Criminal Damage Act 1971. These statutes have replaced a great deal of earlier legislation and the common law, which had grown very complex. They were an attempt to get rid of the fine distinctions and legalisms that bedevilled the common law – to draft legislation and define criminal offences in clear uncomplicated language that would be accessible to the non-expert. However, the caselaw since 1968 has demonstrated the difficulty of achieving this in the area of offences against property: for example the notion of 'property' itself is essentially legal and unavoidably complex. Indeed the law has become so complex that the Court of Appeal has called for further reform of the law (*Hallam and Blackburn*).

11.2   The Definition of Theft

Theft is the central offence against property and its definition occupies the first six sections of the Theft Act 1968. It is subject to a maximum sentence of seven years' imprisonment. In drafting the Theft Act 1968 a decision was taken to change the basis of theft from 'interference with possession' to 'interference with ownership'. 'Ownership' is a wider concept more suitable for dealing with intangible property and the different types of interest in property, but it is also a more technical concept.

The basic definition of theft is found in s.1 Theft Act 1968:

'(1) A person is found guilty of theft if he dishonestly appropriates property belonging to another with the intention of permanently depriving the other of it; and "thief" and "steal" shall be construed accordingly.

(2) It is immaterial whether the appropriation is made with a view to gain, or is made for the thief's own benefit.

(3) The five following sections of this Act shall have effect as regards the interpretation and operation of this section . . .'

The offence of theft can then be divided into five elements, the first three making up the *actus reus*, the last two being the *mens rea*:

- Appropriation
- Property
- Belonging to another
- Dishonesty
- The intention of permanently depriving another property.

11.3 Appropriation

We start with the definition of appropriation given in s.3(1) Theft Act 1968:

'Any assumption by a person of the rights of an owner amounts to an appropriation, and this includes where he has come by the property (innocently or not) without stealing it, any later assumption of a right to it by keeping or dealing with it as owner.'

Appropriation is therefore an assumption by a person of the rights of an owner. Taking possession of another's property is a common form of appropriation, and perhaps the most obvious 'assumption of the rights of an owner', but there are other ways of appropriating property. Destroying property is an appropriation (as well as an offence under the Criminal Damage Act 1971), and so is selling property (as in *Hircock**, where the accused dishonestly sold a car that was the subject of a hire-purchase agreement). Offering another person's property for sale amounts to an appropriation, even though the accused never takes possession of the property (*Pitham and Hehl**). This broad definition of the *actus reus* indicates that the Theft Act 1968 has moved beyond preventing one person taking another's property to a more general notion of interference with the enjoyment of the property.

The latter half of s.3(1) makes it clear that it is possible for the thief to appropriate property already in his possession as long as it came into his possession without stealing. If it were not for this proviso, a thief would commit endless offences of theft every time he dishonestly used the stolen property. In *Hircock*, for example, the accused appropriated a car by selling it; the car was already lawfully in his possession as he had obtained it (by deception) under a hire-purchase agreement. Because of s.3(1) he could be held to have appropriated the property.

The courts have been troubled by a number of key questions about the notion of appropriation and we will consider these now.

11.3.1 Is it Necessary for a Defendant to Appropriate All of the Owner's Rights?

Appropriation of the rights of the owner involves usurpation of an owner's rights. This means that the defendant is doing something that the owner is entitled to do. The House of Lords has held in *Morris** that property is appropriated when any *one* of the owner's rights is assumed. It is not necessary to show that all of the owner's rights have been assumed. A piece of property may, then, be appropriated even though it is still in the victim's hands. Changing the price label on goods in a shop was held to be an appropriation because the right to put labels on items for sale is one of the owner's rights. Indeed, in the same way, merely touching the item would be to appropriate it, because one of the rights of the owner of a piece of property is to touch it. This means that there is a huge range of methods of appropriating property. An owner has the right to touch, move, sell, lend, use, destroy or consume his or her property. Doing any of these will amount to appropriation; although, of course, there will be no theft unless the other elements of the offence are made out.

The benefit of this interpretation is that it enables the court to convict a defendant who manipulates a victim's property rights, without ever fully possessing the property. For example, if a defendant offered his neighbour's car to a friend as a gift, and the friend drove it away, the defendant can be convicted of the theft of the car, even though he never fully possessed the car, or even touched it. Critics of this aspect of the decision in *Morris* argue that it has stretched the meaning of theft too widely. Smith points out that s.3(1) talks about 'the rights' not 'a right'. Consider Ben who sees a car that he is interested in stealing and then puts his hand on the door handle, but then runs off because he sees the owner approaching. Ben's touching would amount to theft, although most people would regard this as more naturally labelled attempted theft. More than this: is the touching of the car door handle properly regarded as a harm of sufficient seriousness to justify the intervention of the criminal law (see Chapter 1.4.1)?

11.3.2   Is it Possible to Appropriate by Omission?

Consider the following: while in a supermarket, Emma's toddler (Andrew) picks up an item and, unknown to Emma, Andrew hides the item, which as a result is not paid for. Once Emma arrives home, she discovers what Andrew has done but decides to keep the item. Is this theft, assuming it is dishonest? There is little doubt that if Emma in any sense touches the item or uses it this will amount to appropriation and so a charge of theft could lie. But what if once she has discovered what has happened she does nothing with the item? The law is unclear. One view is that she is under a duty to return the item to the shop (a *Miller*-type reasoning could be used, see Chapter 3) and in the light of this duty the omission could be liable to criminal punishment (see the New Zealand case of *Subrizky*). An alternative view is that if no act is done there can be no appropriation (*Broom* v. *Crowther*).

11.3.3 Is it Possible to Appropriate Property Honestly?

The issue behind this question is whether the notion of appropriation in effect contains an element of *mens rea*. Lord Roskill in *Morris* appeared to suggest that the notion of appropriation did involve an element of *mens rea*. He stated that a practical joker who switched labels on goods in a supermarket would not have appropriated the items, although if a rogue did the same things, hoping to profit from so doing, he would have appropriated the property. In *Gomez*, Lord Keith rejected this conclusion. He explained that both the joker and the rogue had assumed the rights of the owner and had therefore appropriated the goods. Their different motivations were relevant to the question of dishonesty, but not to appropriation. Their Lordships in *Gomez* saw appropriation as a neutral concept, not necessarily indicating wrongdoing, but just a word describing an act of the accused.

11.3.4 Can Appropriation only Involve the Defendant Acting without the Consent of the Owner?

The definition of appropriation in the Theft Act 1968 does not contain words to the effect that the appropriation must be without the owner's consent, as the previous definition of theft had done. However, the conception of theft among the general public would involve acts which take place without the owner's consent. The lack of precise words in the statute has generated a confused series of cases. The arguments have centred on whether the act of appropriation had to be unauthorized by the owner; or whether an outwardly innocent act, performed with the consent of the owner, could be transformed into an appropriation, and therefore theft, if done with dishonest intent. For example: a person in a supermarket takes a wire basket provided by a shop and puts several items into the basket. Overtly, nothing has been done to which the supermarket manager would take exception. Suppose, however, that when putting the items in the basket, the shopper intended to avoid paying for them: is this act an appropriation and does this dishonest intent turn the otherwise lawful act into an offence of theft before the shopper has even left the shop?

The question resulted in conflicting decisions in the House of Lords: *Lawrence**, which suggested that an act could constitute appropriation even if it was consented to; and *Morris*, which said it could not. The Court of Appeal thereafter issued a large number of conflicting decisions, some following *Lawrence*, some *Morris*, and others seeking to reconcile the two decisions. However, the issue has now been settled by the House of Lords in *Gomez**: an act can amount to appropriation even if it has been consented to or authorized by the victim. This means that any customer in a supermarket who touches an item will thereby appropriate the property (the customer is assuming a right of the owner by touching it), however, she will not be guilty of theft unless she dishonestly intends to permanently deprive the owner of it. In so deciding, the majority judgement in *Gomez* did not rely on key legal principles, but simply stated that *Lawrence* was binding and the statement in *Morris* requiring an unauthorized act was *obiter*.

Although *Gomez* has resolved the uncertainty in the law, it has been strongly criticized by some commentators. There are three main grounds of complaint:

1 The first is that relied upon by Lord Lowry in his dissenting judgement in *Gomez*, namely that the majority decision is not in line with the view of the Criminal Law Revision Committee, whose report formed the basis of the Theft Act 1968. Supporters of *Gomez* may reply that the House of Lords is in no way bound to accept the interpretation of a statute given by a committee, especially if, as the majority suggested, that interpretation would be unworkable.

2 The second ground of complaint is that as a result of the decision in *Gomez*, the offences in s.1 (theft) and s.15 (obtaining property by deception) of the Theft Act 1968 now significantly overlap. If a defendant deceives a victim into handing over her property then this, after *Gomez*, can be a theft. The receiving of the property will be an appropriation and the fact that the victim willingly handed over the property is irrelevant to the question of appropriation. The only significant exception relates to land and the other types of property referred to in s.4(2), (3) and (4), which can be obtained by deception but not stolen. Opponents of *Gomez* argue that it is wrong to have such an overlap between two offences when they were intended to be distinct. Supporters of *Gomez* point out that all robberies and burglaries (where the intention is to steal) involve theft (S. Gardner). They are offences of aggravated theft – that is theft plus use of force or trespass. Similarly s.15 can be seen as aggravated theft – theft plus deception – and the higher sentence for an s.15 offence reflects this. Opponents disagree and argue that there is a fundamental moral distinction between the two offences in that deception involves manipulating the mind of the victim and persuading her to hand property over, rather than taking property from her. Therefore it is said deception involves a different invasion of the victim's personal autonomy from that of theft, and so obtaining property by deception is not just a serious kind of theft but a different kind of property offence all together. Supporters of *Gomez* would reply that it is not clear that this distinction is watertight as many thefts involve a deception (and manipulation of the victim's

mind) in order to enable the theft to occur (for example, lying to the victim in order to distract his attention so that the defendant can steal from his pocket).

3 The third complaint is that as a result of *Gomez*, theft is committed when there is no outwardly wrong act. For example, it is said, it would be harsh to convict defendants, such as those in *Eddy* v. *Niman*, who had picked up items from a supermarket shelf intending to steal them, but changed their minds and left the items in the shop and ran off, as they had not clearly demonstrated their intention to do wrong. However, on the other side of the argument, *Gomez* does enable the police to intervene at an early stage and protect the victim's property. In the case of international financial frauds where money in bank accounts can be transferred abroad in seconds this may be very important.

Turning to the arguments in favour of Gomez, perhaps the strongest is the difficulty in finding any alternative test. Suggestions have included distinguishing consent and authorization (*Dobson*), or between voluntary and involuntary acts of the victim (S. Shute and J. Horder), or by asking whether the act was 'manifestly thefteous' (G. Fletcher); but all of these distinctions could be very difficult for juries or magistrates to draw. *Gomez* is certainly easy to understand and apply. It also avoids having to acquit a defendant simply because he has been charged with an offence under s.1 rather than s.15 or vice versa. The decision in *Gomez* also helps in cases where a director is alleged to have stolen from a company. Under the *Morris* approach, it could have been argued that there was no appropriation as the company, through its directors, authorized the act. After *Gomez* such consent would be irrelevant.

Perhaps because of the opposition it has faced, the Court of Appeal in some subsequent cases has been unwilling to interpret *Gomez* literally. In *Gallasso*, a nurse took a mentally ill patient's cheque and placed it in a bank account that she had opened in the patient's name. However, she did so intending at some later point to take the money for herself, but before she could she was arrested. *Gomez* would suggest that she had appropriated the money by placing the cheque into the account. The fact that she was permitted to do this by the patient was irrelevant as she had the necessary *mens rea*. However, the Court of Appeal overturned her conviction, arguing that to establish an appropriation it was necessary to show there had been a 'taking', and as there was no such taking her conviction was overturned. The requirement of 'taking' seems clearly contrary to the authority of *Gomez,* and *Gallasso* should be regarded as being wrongly decided.

As we shall see shortly, the House of Lords in *Hinks* has recently reconfirmed its decision in *Gomez*. Therefore, despite its critics, *Gomez* represents the law unless Parliament decides to change the law.

11.3.5 Can there be Appropriation where the Transaction Constituted a Valid Gift?

The House of Lords was required again to consider the nature of appropriate in *Hinks**. The case concerned a gullible man of limited intelligence who had been befriended by the appellant and had handed over large sums of money to the appellant. It could not be shown that there was duress or undue influence and so it appeared the gifts were valid gifts in law. Could the appellant be convicted of theft in such a case? Could there be an assumption of the rights of the owner, where the owner entered into a transaction regarded as effective under civil law?

The majority of the House of Lords, by three to two held 'yes', if the defendant was acting dishonestly. The majority rejected an argument that the reasoning in *Gomez* (that there could be an appropriation even if the owner of the property consented to the defendant's actions) applied to cases where the victim's consent was obtained by deception and did not apply to where the consent was obtained by duress or undue influence. Lord Steyn, for the majority, applied Gomez in the most straight-forward of ways:

'It is true of course that the certified question in *Gomez* referred to the situation where consent had been obtained by fraud. But the majority judgments do not differentiate between cases of consent induced by fraud and consent given in any other circumstances. The ratio involves a proposition of general application.'

In *Hinks*, the fact the victim consented to the handing over of the property was irrelevant to the issue of appropriation. It is important to note that s.2 (as we shall see) states that a defendant who believes he has a right in law to appropriate the property or believes that the owner is consenting to the appropriation will not be regarded as dishonest. Therefore if the defendant is given a gift by someone and the defendant believes she is entitled in law to the gift, it will not be dishonest for her to take it.

If *Gomez* received a torrent of criticism, *Hinks* has received a waterfall. Here are some of the main criticisms:

1 The decision sets up a conflict between the criminal law and the civil law. In the eyes of contract law, the gifts are regarded as valid and the appellant can keep the property. While in the eyes of the criminal law, the transaction is regarded as a criminal offence. This is a strong argu-

ment, but there are responses. The response given by Lord Steyn was that if there is a conflict between contract law and criminal law it is the fault of contract law. If contract law allows someone to obtain property through dishonesty from vulnerable people then it is contract law that has got things wrong, not criminal law. Critics of *Hinks* reply that it is the role of criminal law to protect property rights. Property rights are to be determined by civil law. It is meaningless to say that criminal law should seek to protect property rights that do not exist in civil law. An alternative response is that it is arguable that the aims and justification of criminal law and contract law are different. Contract law may be more concerned to ensure that there is certainty as to who owns which property and to uphold contracts whenever possible; whereas criminal law may be far more concerned with protecting vulnerable victims from dishonest offenders. A third response, but one that cannot be dealt with here, is that civil law in fact would not accept the gift as valid whenever there is dishonesty, relying on the notion of unconscionability.

2 The case leads to some highly undesirable results. Lord Steyn considers the following example:

> 'P sees D's painting and, thinking he is getting a bargain, offers D £100,000 for it. D realises that P thinks the painting is a Constable, but knows that it was painted by his sister and is worth no more than £100. He accepts P's offer. D has made an enforceable contract and is entitled to recover and retain the purchase price.'

Lord Steyn appears to accept that following *Hinks*, D could be convicted of theft if the jury decides that D has been dishonest. The difficulty is that if this is correct, what are the limits of the criminal law? Must double-glazing companies ensure that people are paying a fair price for their products? Must lawyers ensure they are not presenting clients with excessive fees? And must pop stars ensure their concert tickets are not being charged at too high a rate? In all these cases, if the jury decides there is dishonesty then a conviction of theft could follow. Supporters of *Hinks* would reply that the Crown Prosecution Service can be relied upon to ensure that the offence is only charged in reasonable cases.

3 There are serious difficulties in deciding how it can be said that at the time of the appropriation the property belonged to another. If receiving the gift was the act of the appropriation, and the gift was a valid one under civil law at the receiving of the gift, did not the property cease to belong to another? The position seems to be that at exactly the same time there was appropriation and the ownership changed hands. The majority seemed willing to accept that if the appropriation took place at the

moment ownership changed hands, this is sufficient to amount to appropriation of property belonging to another.

In the light of the opprobrium, can anything be said in favour of *Hinks*? This would be what supporters of *Hinks* might say:

1 The key argument in favour of *Hinks* is that conduct that was found by the jury to be dishonest was punished. Quite simply, the result was right. Lord Steyn argued that if a narrow understanding of appropriation was accepted, this would lead to the acquittal of defendants who were undoubtedly dishonest. This argument has been strongly criticized by Simester and Sullivan: 'It is wrong, a profound violation of the Rule of Law, to reinterpret the law in order to convict a particular defendant who deserves the label of criminal'. Lord Hobhouse, dissenting, made a similar point. But we have seen in the discussion of *R* v. *R* that the House of Lords is willing to ensure that criminal law must move with the times. Wives must be protected from husbands who wish to have sexual intercourse without their consent. In *Hinks*, their Lordships offered protection to the elderly and vulnerable from those who seek to dishonestly deprive them of their property.

2 The effect of *Hinks* is that the key question in cases of this kind is whether the defendant is dishonest. Supporters of *Hinks* will argue that asking the jury to consider whether there is dishonesty will produce better justice than asking whether the gift was valid under civil law. The dishonesty approach is easier for juries to apply, will lead to quicker and cheaper trials, and will focus the jury's mind on the important question (was there dishonesty?), rather than the less significant question for criminal lawyers of the civil law effect of the transaction. As indicated above, the main (some would say only) benefit of *Gomez* is its ease of use. Had *Hinks* been decided differently, this advantage would have been lost.

11.3.6   Does a Defendant Continue to Appropriate Property whenever He Assumes the Rights of an Owner?

Another question that has received conflicting answers from the courts is whether appropriation can be a continuing process or whether appropriation is a one-off occurrence. In *Atakpu*, the most recent case on the topic, it was recognized that one can appropriate an item any number of times until all of the ingredients of theft occur together, at which point the offence of theft is committed, and after that there can be no more thefts or appropriations. For example if a defendant absent-mindedly picks up a toenail clipper and walks out of a shop with it without paying, lacking the *mens rea* of theft he is seen as continuing to appropriate it, although there is no theft. If sometime later when using the clippers he realizes what he has done but decides to keep the item, then at that point the *mens rea* comes into existence and he commits theft. But he only commits theft at that point in time, and he does not continue to appropriate or steal the clipper every time he clips his toenails.

11.3.7 Does a Purchaser of Stolen Property Appropriate it?

Section 3(2) of the Theft Act 1968 provides that a person who buys stolen property for value in good faith will not be said to appropriate the property when he realizes that the property is stolen:

> 'Where property or a right or interest in property is or purports to be transferred for value to a person acting in good faith, no later assumption by him of rights which he believed himself to be acquiring shall, by reason of any defect in the transferor's title, amount to theft of the property.'

This subsection only applies where the transferee has given 'value'. This does not mean that the true market value must have been paid, merely that the property must not have been received as a gift. The subsection thus protects from liability for theft the figure familiar to property lawyers, the '*bona fide* purchaser without notice' (*bona fide* meaning good faith).

It is worth noting, however, that the protection only extends to theft; if the transferee decides to sell the goods once he has discovered that he does not have a good title to them, and does not inform the buyer of that fact, he will probably be guilty of obtaining any money he receives by deception. If he does inform the buyer that he does not have good title, the buyer will probably be guilty of receiving stolen goods and the original transferee will then become an accessory to that offence (see the discussion of *Bloxham** in Chapter 12.5). The protection of s.3(2) is therefore only of real value if the transferee merely keeps the property.

11.4 Property

There are two issues here. The first is the definition of the term 'property' and second the requirement that the indictment with which the defendant is charged specifies which property it is alleged that the defendant has stolen.

Normally there is little difficulty with the property requirement. It is usually obvious that what the defendant has taken is property. Where there is a dispute over the issue, a defendant may seek to raise an argument either that the item is not regarded as property in the eyes of the law; or that even if it is regarded as property it is excluded from the ambit of theft by s.4. These arguments will be considered separately.

11.4.1   The Item is Not Property in the Eyes of the Law

Property is defined in s.4 Theft Act 1968 as including 'money and all other property, real or personal, including things in action and other intangible property'. Some of these terms require explanation:

- 'Real property' includes buildings and land, but there are special provisions relating to land in s.4(2).
- 'Personal property' (that is, property other than real property) may be tangible or intangible (that is, things that can or cannot be touched physically).
- A 'thing in action' is intangible property which gives rise to a right to sue someone in the courts: for example a copyright, a debt or a bank credit (*Hilton*). Such things cannot be touched but are regarded as property and can be stolen.

The way that the law deals with property offences involving cheques, credit cards and bank accounts is particularly intricate and will be dealt with separately as the *Hot Topic* at the end of Chapter 13. That complex area is best understood once the basics of the different offences have been grasped.

So what is not regarded as property in the eyes of the law. Clearly a complete list cannot be given, but here are some of the items which have come before the criminal courts and found not to be property.

1.   Information
It was held in *Oxford* v. *Moss* that information itself is not capable of being stolen, so that borrowing an examination paper to look at the contents could not be theft of the information on the paper. It was fortunate for the student that he returned the examination paper, because this meant that he could not be guilty of stealing the piece of paper on which the examination was printed because he was able to argue that he had no intention to permanently deprive the university of the piece of paper itself.

2.   Electricity
It has also been held that electricity is not property and so cannot be stolen (*Low* v. *Blease*). However a specific offence of unauthorized and dishonest abstraction of electricity deals with this in s.13 Theft Act 1968.

3. Bodies

A body cannot be stolen and that is true whether the person is dead or alive, although in certain circumstances a part of a body can be stolen. This is discussed in greater detail in the *Hot Topic* at the end of this chapter.

4. Services

Services cannot be property; you cannot steal a haircut or a train ride. Section 1 Theft Act 1978 (see Chapter 13.4) deals with the obtaining of services by deception.

11.4.2 Where an Item is Property but Cannot be Stolen because of Section 4

Section 4 provides that two kinds of property are not property for the purposes of the 1968 Theft Act.

1. Land

Parliament decided that it should not be possible to steal land, partly because of the difficulties this may cause for land law. So s.4(2) provides that land (or things forming part of land and severed from it, such as trees or minerals) can only be stolen in certain limited circumstances:

(a) Where a trustee, a personal representative, a person authorized under a power of attorney, or a liquidator appropriates the land 'by dealing with it in breach of the confidence reposed in him' (s.4(2)(a)). Thus a trustee, who is the legal owner of the trust property, will be guilty of theft if he dishonestly sells land that was subject to a trust.

(b) When a person in possession of the land under a tenancy appropriates a fixture (for example, taking a kitchen sink away from a flat), this will be theft of the fixture. The technical definition of land includes fixtures on the land. It is, of course, theft for anyone to steal a movable object on the land (for example, a table).

(c) The Act deals with things forming part of land and which may be severed from it, such as plants, trees or minerals. If a person who is not in possession of land cuts down trees or digs up plants or bushes then this can be theft (s.4(2)(b)). However, merely picking apples, fruit or foliage from plants growing wild on someone else's land is not theft unless it is done for a commercial purpose (s.4(3)). So it would not be theft to pick blackberries from a hedgerow unless the fruit were to be sold in a local market. The same rule applies to mushrooms. What the law is seeking to do here is to distinguish casual picking (for example, picking a wild strawberry while out on a walk) from commercial picking or the digging up of plants.

2.   Wild animals

Section 4 also deals with 'wild creatures, tamed or untamed'. These are property but cannot usually be stolen as they do not 'belong to' anyone (s.4(4)). However, if the wild creature is ordinarily kept in captivity then it can be stolen. Likewise, if the creature has 'been reduced into possession' (caught) by another person, and possession has not since been lost (the animal has not escaped), then the creature can be stolen from that person.

A tame animal, such as a cat or a dog, is the property of its owner (as are domesticated animals such as horses, cows and sheep) and a dishonest appropriation will be theft. The aim of the law here is to avoid treating poaching as theft, as poaching is governed by separate statutes, for example the Night Poaching Act 1828. However the taking of pets or farm animals is to be regarded as theft.

11.4.3   Specifying the Property in the Indictment

The indictment must identify the piece of property which it is alleged the defendant stole. It is not necessary to show the exact quantity of what the defendant stole. So an indictment alleging that the defendant stole 'a quantity of ugli fruit' would be sufficient, but a defendant should not be charged with stealing 'something worth £5'.

11.5   Belonging to Another

Normally there is little dispute about whether the property belonged to another. In a typical shoplifting case the defendant is unlikely to dispute that the items belonged to the supermarket. Any dispute over whether property belonged to another should be resolved by applying the rules of contract and property law (*Marshall*). However the requirement can give rise to some difficult issues in the following cases:

11.5.1   The Property Belongs to No One

The definition of theft provides that the property must belong to another at the time of the appropriation. It is possible to convict an accused of theft even though it is impossible to ascertain who owned the property as long as it is clear that it was someone other than the defendant. It is not necessary to show that any victim has suffered a financial loss as the result of the theft

(*Chan Man-sin*). Some property cannot be stolen, because no one has any proprietary interest in it. This is true, under the common law, of a corpse (*Sharpe*), and also arises where property has been truly abandoned (and not merely lost) by its owner. Property left out for the dustman is not abandoned (*Williams* v. *Phillips*). Property dumped in a remote place may be regarded as abandoned and owned by no one.

11.5.2 Where the Victim has a Right of Possession or Control

It is crucial to appreciate that it is not necessarily a defence for an accused to demonstrate that he owned the property in question. The issue is whether it belonged to another. The significance of this way of putting it is that sometimes the law recognizes that the defendant owned the property, but that it also belonged to another.

The phrase 'belonging to another' is defined in s.5(1):

'Property shall be regarded as belonging to any person having possession or control of it, or having in it any proprietary right or interest (not being an equitable interest arising only from an agreement to transfer or grant an interest).'

There are three concepts here: possession, control and proprietary interest. For property to 'belong to' a person, he or she need only have one of these – possession alone would be enough, for example. The meaning of 'proprietary interest' will be discussed below.

The significance of the fact that property is treated as belonging to a person having possession or control of it is that the owner of a piece of property can appropriate and indeed steal that property if he takes it from a person who possesses it. In *Turner (No. 2)**, the accused was convicted of stealing his own car; he had left his car at a garage to be repaired but later drove the car away without paying for the repairs that the garage had carried out. Lord Parker CJ held:

'there is no ground whatever for qualifying the words "possession or control" in any way. It is sufficient if it is found that the person from whom the property is taken ... was at the time in fact in possession or control.'

The Court of Appeal did not decide whether the possession or control must be lawful. However, in a later case, *Meredith*, the court held that an owner, who took his car from someone who had no right to retain possession of it as against the owner, was not guilty of theft. This case can therefore be distinguished from *Turner (No. 2)**, where the garage had a right to possess the car as against the owner until he paid the bill.

Possession and control are not synonymous: property may be in the possession of one person while being in another person's physical control. For example, if you invited a friend around for a cup of tea, your friend for a while may control the tea cup, even though it will remain in your possession. It is therefore possible for the person in control to steal from the person in possession, though it is difficult to imagine cases where there would be the necessary dishonesty. In general in the criminal law, possession is taken to require some degree of knowledge: the possessor must know that he has something in his possession (see Chapter 14.5 and *Warner* v. *Metropolitan Police Commissioner**). It has been held that control does not require such knowledge: the occupier of a disused factory surrounded by fencing to exclude trespassers was in control of scrap metal on the site because he was in control of the whole site, even though he did not know that the scrap was there, and so someone who took the metal was held to steal from the occupier of the factory (*Woodman*). The advantage of this wide definition of 'belonging to another' is that there is no need to specify who actually owned the goods, which may be hard to ascertain, for example if goods are stolen from a lorry on its way from one factory to another.

11.5.3   The Victim has a Proprietary Right or Interest

Section 5(1) explains that property is treated as belonging to a person who has proprietary right or interest in it. This means that not only will the legal owner be regarded as owning the property, but so will those who have an equitable interest (for example, a right of a beneficiary under a trust).

Section 5(1) makes an exception of 'an equitable interest arising only from an agreement to transfer or grant an interest'. This is a reference to the equitable interest of a person who has agreed by contract to buy, for example, land or shares; in both cases the buyer may enforce the specific performance of the contract against the seller. If the seller dishonestly sells the property to a third party, this will be a breach of contract, but not a theft from the buyer. So if Richard enters a contract to sell to Cedric his hot air balloon but decides not to fulfil the contract and instead sells it to Al, this is not theft.

11.5.4   The Victim is a Company, Partnership or Trust

What about property owned by a partnership or a company? In the case of a partnership, each partner has a sufficient proprietary interest in the partnership property, so that one partner can steal from the others (*Bonner*). In the case of a company, even where the directors are the sole shareholders, it has been held that the directors can steal from the company (which has a separate legal personality) if they dishonestly appropriate company property (*Attorney-General's Reference (No. 2 of 1982)*).

Section 5(5) provides for a certain unusual type of corporation, the corporation sole, which concerns certain offices (such as the Crown or a Bishop) which possess a legal personality distinct from that of the person who happens to be the holder of the office at any particular time. This legal personality continues uninterrupted during periods when the office is not filled and the subsection provides that 'property of a corporation sole shall be regarded as belonging to the corporation notwithstanding a vacancy in the corporation'.

Section 5(2) deals with trust property and provides, for the avoidance of doubt, that property belongs to any person who has a right to enforce the trust, such as a beneficiary. In cases of charitable trusts, this would be the Attorney-General.

11.5.5 Where Ownership Passes in Dishonest Circumstances

Many of the difficulties that have arisen in the interpretation of the phrase 'belonging to another' result from the requirement that 'the appropriation', 'dishonesty' and 'property belonging to another' must all coincide in time. In cases where the ownership of property passes from the victim to the thief, it will often be crucial to know and be able to prove precisely when the rights in the property were transferred and when the dishonest appropriation took place. If the former occurs before the latter (as in *Edwards* v. *Ddin**) then there will be no theft.

As we have seen, a thief may steal from another person who has possession, control or a proprietary interest in property (even though that interest might be a lesser interest than ownership). However, if the owner divests herself of possession, control and all proprietary interests (for example, by selling the property) then the property no longer belongs to her and cannot be stolen from her. This may cause problems if the 'buyer' is dishonest and does not intend to pay for the property; he cannot be convicted of theft because the property does not 'belong to another' once ownership, possession and control have passed to him. If there is evidence of dishonesty at the outset before ownership, possession and control pass to him then it may be possible to convict of theft on the basis of his initial appropriation (*Lawrence*), and it would often also be possible to charge with obtaining property by deception (the more natural charge in these circumstances; see Chapter 12). However, there may be no external evidence (and therefore proof) of the buyer's dishonesty until too late: in *Edwards* v. *Ddin*, for example, the accused, having asked the attendant to put petrol in the tank, drove away from a garage without paying. The prosecution could only prove dishonesty at the time when he had driven away, but by that time he was the owner of the property and it was not 'belonging to another'. The court took the view that the garage does not retain any right to dispose of the petrol once it has been put into a motorist's car and mixed with the petrol already there and so, under the Sale of Goods Act 1893, ownership passes to the motorist together with possession and control. The consumption of food in a restaurant is another example of such a transaction: ownership as well as possession and control pass to the customer before payment (*Corcoran* v. *Whent*). The reason for this is that once the petrol has been put into the car or the food eaten, it is not readily returnable to the original owner, and so ownership must pass at the point of consumption and not at the time of payment. In ordinary sales of goods in shops, ownership does not pass until payment, even when goods are delivered into the buyer's possession before payment (as is often the case in a shop), and so the seller retains the 'proprietary right' of ownership until she is paid. Unfortunately, even an ordinary shop transaction can cause difficulty, as the facts of *Kaur** reveal. It has proved necessary to create a new offence, 'making off without payment', to fill the gap in the law revealed by *Edwards* v. *Ddin* and other cases of 'bilking' (s.3 Theft Act 1978; see Chapter 13.6).

Fortunately there are few situations where the difficulties outlined above cause problems. If *A* transfers ownership of property to *B* in circumstances of dishonesty, there are four ways the law may still convict *B*:

(a) *B* may be guilty of theft if he is under a personal legal obligation with respect to the property transferred, in which case the property is deemed to belong to another for the purpose of the law of theft under s.5(3) which provides:

> 'Where a person receives property from or on account of another, and is under an obligation to the other to retain and deal with that property or its proceeds in a particular way, the property or proceeds shall be regarded (as against him) as belonging to the other.'

The obligation referred to must be a legal obligation (*Gilks*); a purely moral obligation will not be enough. In cases of this sort, where one person receives property on behalf of another, the property is frequently money. The subsection will only apply where the obligation is to retain that money and deal with it in a particular way; it does not apply where the obligation merely creates a creditor/debtor relationship between the parties. For example, in *Hall* (1972) it was held that s.5(3) did not apply to a travel agent who received money from clients for air tickets. The obligation was to produce the air tickets. There was no obligation to use the actual money given by the clients in a specific way. By contrast, in *Davidge* v. *Bunnett* the accused had an agreement with her flatmates to share the gas bills; she spent the money received from them on other things, and her conviction for theft was upheld by the Divisional Court. Section 5(3) did apply: the accused's flatmates had given her cheques on the understanding that she would use the proceeds of the cheques to pay the bills. In *Brewster*, the Court of Appeal held that s.5(3) could apply in the case of an insurance broker who acted as an agent collecting premiums for insurance companies, and then used the premiums to finance his own business. Under the terms of the contracts between the accused and the companies, he was under an obligation to retain the money collected and to account for it regularly to the companies concerned. This legal obligation was not affected by the 'indulgence' granted by the companies whereby it was accepted that the agent would use the money collected for his own purposes and account for an equivalent amount to the companies; the indulgence would not extend to a dishonest use of the money. It is also clear that the obligation to deal with the money need not be to the 'victim' as long as the defendant is under an obligation to someone to deal with the money in a particular way (*Floyd* v. *DPP*)

(b) *B* may be guilty of theft if he is obliged in law to return the money to *A*, that is, if s.5(4) applies. This states:

> 'Where a person gets property by another's mistake, and is under an obligation to make restoration (in whole or in part) of the property or its proceeds or of the value thereof, then to the extent of that obligation the property or proceeds shall be regarded (as against him) as belonging to the person entitled to restoration, and an intention not to make restoration shall be regarded accordingly as an intention to deprive that person of the property or proceeds.'

This subsection was included in order to deal with the situation that arose in *Moynes* v. *Cooper*, decided before the Theft Act 1968, in which an employee, overpaid by a wages clerk and not discovering the mistake until later, kept the overpayment, and was held to have committed no offence by the Divisional Court. In a case with similar facts (wages were paid by direct debit into the accused's bank account in error), the Court of Appeal held that s.5(4) should apply (*Attorney-*

General's Reference (No. 1 of 1983)* and the accused was convicted. The overpaid employee was under an obligation to restore to her employer the value of the 'thing in action' (the overpayment in her bank account) as soon as she realized that a mistake had been made. However, the Court of Appeal also felt that 'such cases should normally be resolved without resort to the criminal courts'. There is some (unintended) irony in this, as it is becoming increasingly clear that such cases of overpayment of money are almost the only cases that do fall within the subsection. An obligation to make restoration of other types of property only arises very rarely. Glanville Williams has even said that use of the word 'property' in s.5(4) was a mistake: 'it should have been "money" because that is the only form of property in respect of which the subsection has any practical operation' (Williams, 1983).

(c) It may be that *B* does not in fact receive ownership of the property and it still belongs to *A*, therefore he is guilty of theft. This would occur where the contract, which was to transfer the property from *A* to *B*, is void. If the contract is void there is no difficulty in saying the property belongs to *A*; it does and always had. For example, in *Williams* (1980)* the accused exchanged some obsolete Yugoslav banknotes at a bureau de change and received sterling in return. In the view of the Court of Appeal, it was not necessary to rely on s.5(4); the mistake made by the bureau de change (that the obsolete notes were valid currency) was so fundamental that there was no valid contract between the accused and the bureau. The bureau did not part with ownership of the sterling currency, which therefore belonged to another (that is, the bureau) when it was appropriated by the accused. The circumstances in which a contract is void involve complex aspects of contract law and cannot be explained here.

(d) It may be that although *B* becomes the owner of the property in common law he has to hold it on trust for *A*. This would usually be a special kind of trust called a constructive trust. The law on constructive trusts is still being developed by the courts and it is not clear when they will arise. Lord Browne-Wilkenson has stated: '. . . when property is obtained by fraud equity imposes a constructive trust on the fraudulent recipient' (*Westdeutsche Landesbank* v. *Islington*). If a constructive trust is imposed, this will mean that s.5(2) can apply as *A* will still have an equitable interest in the property. If *B* spends the money he could be guilty of theft. There is a suggestion in *Attorney-General's Reference (No. 1 of 1985)* that an interest under a constructive trust is insufficient to count as 'property belonging to another', but *Shadrockh-Cigari* seems to suggest that it is sufficient and there seems no reason in principle why a beneficiary under a constructive trust should be treated differently from a beneficiary under any other kind of trust for the purposes of s.5(2).

In many of the cases discussed under this heading, a charge based on deception would be more appropriate, although it would not always be easy to prove the necessary deception. For example, it is debatable whether *Kaur* was guilty of a deception merely by offering the wrongly marked shoes to the shop assistant.

11.6 Dishonesty

The *mens rea* of theft, the state of mind that must accompany the appropriation, has two parts: dishonesty; and the intention of permanently depriving the owner of the property. There are two elements of the law's understanding of dishonesty: s.2 Theft Act 1968; and the well-known *Ghosh* direction on dishonesty which applies when s.2 does not cover the case.

11.6.1 Section 2(1) Theft Act 1968

Section 2 does not contain a definition of dishonesty. Instead s.2(1) provides three examples of states of mind which are not to be regarded as dishonest. Section 2(1) reads:

'A person's appropriation of property belonging to another is not to be regarded as dishonest

(a) if he appropriates the property in the belief that he has in law the right to deprive the other of it, on behalf of himself or of a third person; or

(b) if he appropriates the property in the belief that he would have the other's consent if the other knew of the appropriation and the circumstances of it; or

(c) (except where the property came to him as trustee or personal representative) if he appropriates the property in the belief that the person to whom the property belongs cannot be discovered by taking reasonable steps.'

The three subsections will be considered separately.

1.   *Claim of right: section 2(1)(a)*

Section 2(1)(a) incorporates what is known as the 'claim of right' defence. The accused is not dishonest if he believes that he has a better legal right to the property than the other person. He may believe that he is the owner or that in law he has a right to take the property from the victim. For example, in *Robinson* (1977) a belief that the accused was entitled to take from the victim a sum of money which the victim owed him was held to excuse, as a claim of right. There appears to be no requirement that the belief be a reasonable one, as long as it is honestly held (*Holden*). But the belief must be a belief in a legal, as opposed to a moral, right to the property. This is one of the rare circumstances in which a mistake of law can provide a defence. The explanation is that the essence of theft is the interference with the owner's legal property rights; if the defendant is unaware that he is interfering with these rights then the defendant would be said (at least by subjectivists) to lack *mens rea*.

Lord Hutton, one of the dissentients in *Hinks,* argues that s.2(1)(a) necessarily implied that where the defendant in fact has a claim of right he or she cannot be dishonest. This was rejected by the majority. So if a defendant in fact has a 'claim of right' but does not realize this then he can still be regarded as dishonest by the jury. This means that it can be dishonest to assert one's legal rights, which is another surprising result of the decision in *Hinks*.

2.   *Belief in consent: section 2(1)(b)*

Section 2(1)(b) explains that a defendant who believed that the owner consented to what he was doing would not be dishonest. So borrowing your brother's clothes is not dishonest if you believed he had or would have consented. Again, the subsection requires a belief in a true consent, honestly obtained (*Attorney-General's Reference (No. 2 of 1982)*). Such a belief need not be a reasonable one, but must be a genuine one.

3.   *Inability to discover owner: section 2(1)(c)*

Under s. 2(1)(c), believing that you cannot discover the owner of a piece of property by reasonable means is a defence. Again there is no requirement that such a belief be based on reasonable grounds. If therefore Lucy after a party finds a toothbrush in her bathroom and decides to keep it because she cannot reasonably find out whose it is she will not commit theft. If, however, a week later Alex tells her that he has lost his toothbrush, but Lucy decides not to mention her discovery and to keep his toothbrush then she may be guilty of theft. There may be appropriation relying on s.3(1) (see Chapter 11.3 above) and the jury may decide she is dishonest, relying on the *Ghosh* test (see Chapter 11.6.3 below).

In *Small*, the Court of Appeal held that an honest belief that property has been abandoned is a defence to theft, even if the belief was not a reasonable one. The court treated this belief as a denial of dishonesty, although as Professor Smith points out, it is perhaps more obviously a denial of the intention of permanently depriving another person of the property (see Chapter 11.7 below).

11.6.2 Section 2(2) Theft Act 1968

Section 2(2) Theft Act 1968 states:

'A person's appropriation of property belonging to another may be dishonest notwithstanding that he is willing to pay for the property.'

This subsection does not provide a definition of dishonesty. Instead it prevents a line of argument that a defendant may seek to raise. It is no defence to a charge involving dishonesty that one intended to pay for the item. Thus taking a neighbour's garden gnome and pushing a cheque through her door for its value does not negate dishonesty. Such a case would need to be resolved by the *Ghosh* test, to which we now return.

11.6.3 The Common Law Interpretation of Dishonesty

If the defendant is not dishonest because he or she falls under s.2(1) then that is the end of the case: the defendant is not dishonest. But if the case does not fall under s.2(1), the judge must give further guidance to the jury. The present position is summarized in the leading cases of *Feely** and *Ghosh**. In the judgement of Lord Lane CJ in *Ghosh**:

'In determining whether the prosecution has proved that the defendant was acting dishonestly, a jury must first of all decide whether according to the ordinary standards of reasonable and honest people what was done was dishonest. If it was not dishonest by those standards, that is the end of the matter and the prosecution fails. If it was dishonest by those standards, then the jury must consider whether the defendant himself must have realized that what he was doing was by those standards dishonest . . . It is dishonest for a defendant to act in a way which he knows ordinary people consider to be dishonest, even if he asserts or genuinely believes that he is morally justified in acting as he did.'

This direction can be broken down into two stages:

1 First the jury must decide whether in all the circumstances of the case, including the defendant's motives and beliefs, he is dishonest judged by the standards of reasonable and honest people. If the jury decides that the defendant is not dishonest then this resolves the issue: the defendant is not dishonest. If the jury decides that the defendant was dishonest by the standards of ordinary people then the jury must move on to the second stage.

2 The jury must decide if the defendant was aware that his conduct was dishonest by the standards of ordinary people. If the defendant was so aware then he will be dishonest; if he was not aware then he will not be dishonest.

The test is therefore neither entirely subjective nor objective. This is demonstrated by the following examples:

1 Grace, a particularly virtuous woman, regards her conduct as dishonest, but most people would not. Applying the *Ghosh* direction, Grace would not be regarded as dishonest.

2 Tom, an anti-fur protester, takes fur coats from a shop. He gives evidence, believed by the jury, that he thought a majority of people are anti-fur and so would not regard his conduct as dishonest. Applying the *Ghosh* direction, Tom would not be regarded as dishonest.

3 Brian, an anti-fur protester, also takes fur coats from a shop. He gives evidence, accepted by the jury, that he believes he was acting honestly, although he accepts that most people would not agree with him. Applying the *Ghosh* direction, Brian would be dishonest (assuming that the jury found taking the coats to be contrary to the standards of honesty of ordinary people). It should be noted that the jury in this case must not ask itself whether as individuals they believe Brian's conduct is dishonest, but rather what ordinary people would think. So an anti-fur juror may himself or herself approve of Brian's conduct, but the juror should ask what ordinary people would think.

The Court of Appeal in *Ghosh* explicitly rejected an argument that the defendant's honesty should be tested by his own subjective standards. The justification for this rejection is that to apply the accused's own standards would be to acquit those who had little or no sense of their own wrongdoing. As it was put by the trial judge in *Greenstein*, in a passage that was expressly approved in the Court of Appeal:

'It is no good, you see, applying the standards of anyone accused of dishonesty otherwise everyone accused of dishonesty, if he were to be tested by his own standards, would be acquitted automatically, you may think.'

But the test does involve a subjective element – not the accused person's own standards of honesty but his awareness of the standards of ordinary people. If the defendant believes that his conduct was not dishonest according to the standards of ordinary people then he is not dishonest. One difficulty with this approach is that it assumes that a potential defendant will go through the unlikely thought process of acknowledging that he is not an 'ordinary' person because his standards differ from the norm. It is much more likely that the defendant will merely assert that he was not aware that his standards were different from the norm, and much will then depend on his credibility (see also *Hot Topic*, Chapter 14, for another example of this kind of uncertainty).

There is no need for the judge to give the *Ghosh* direction in every case. It is not necessary if the conduct is obviously dishonest (*Forrester*) and there is no need to use it if the defendant does not raise the possibility that he thought the conduct was honest (*Brennan*). In these cases it is enough simply to ask the jury to consider whether the conduct was honest according to the standards of ordinary people. However, the Court of Appeal has confirmed that the *Ghosh* test should be applied, if necessary, whenever the concept of dishonesty is used in the criminal law. This includes, for example, deception offences under the Theft Acts 1968 and 1978, the common law offence of conspiracy to defraud, and other offences involving fraud (*Lockwood*).

Following the decisions of the House of Lords in *Gomez* and *Hinks*, the *actus reus* requirement for theft has been greatly reduced. Much weight will therefore be thrown onto the *mens rea*, and especially the *Ghosh* test for dishonesty. Whether the *Ghosh* test will be able to play the crucial role it is now expected to play, time will tell. The test has attracted considerable criticism from commentators who dislike the resulting uncertainty. Indeed inconsistent verdicts may occur with different juries disagreeing over the standards of 'reasonable and honest people'. This would not be surprising when many doubt that, given the variety of religious, cultural and moral values in our society, there are such things as 'generally accepted standards'. Malcolm, a homeless person, has not eaten for three days and is extremely hungry. Passing by an expensive restaurant he sees a loaf of bread sitting on a window ledge and takes it. Is this dishonest? It is not hard to imagine reasonable people disagreeing on this. Indeed it might even be that juries in different parts of the country would reach different conclusions on issues like these. One of the difficulties is that it is virtually impossible to correct wrong decisions, as Professor Griew (1985) has pointed out in this context:

'A jury without stars or compass cannot be accused of bad navigation. The direction it takes may be deplorable but cannot be wrong.'

Despite these concerns is clear that any change in the definition of the meaning of dishonesty would require legislation or a decision of the House of Lords, which has not yet been asked to rule on the question. Reform of the definition of dishonesty could be spurred by the argument that its uncertainty infringes article 7 of the European Convention of Human Rights (see Chapter 19)

11.7   Intention of Permanently Depriving

As well as dishonesty, the other part of the *mens rea* of theft is an intention of permanently depriving the owner (or other person to whom the property 'belongs' within s.5 of the 1968 Act) of the property. This means that borrowing is not theft. Borrowing a friend's dress, intending to return it the next day, even knowing that she does not consent, will not amount to theft. This is a controversial position for the law to take. Borrowing property can cause the owner great inconvenience and can be seen as a clear infringement of the owner's property rights. Imagine if someone took all your criminal law books and notes and returned them to you after you had sat your criminal law exam. However Parliament has taken the view that borrowing property is too minor a harm to justify the full force of the criminal law and that remedies in civil law are sufficient.

This is not to say that no borrowing can be theft. There are some statutes which make specific forms of borrowing a criminal offence: taking and driving away a conveyance without the owner's consent (s.12 Theft Act 1968, see Chapter 14.3), and the removal without lawful authority of articles kept for display in places open to the public (such as museums and stately homes; s.11 of the 1968 Act), for example.

It will usually be clear whether or not a person has an intention of permanently depriving. A jury will be very unlikely to believe a pickpocket who claims that he was going to return the wallet had he not been arrested by the police. There are however some cases where the issue is less obvious. We will now discuss two of these.

11.7.1   Borrowing Money

Taking money belonging to another, intending to repay, will involve an intention of permanently depriving the other of the particular notes and coins that were taken and so will be theft (*Velumyl*). Such a taking will be theft if it is dishonest. In considering dishonesty in such a case, it should be born in mind that s.2(2) explains that paying for the item taken will not negate dishonesty (see Chapter 11.7 above); although if the defendant believes that the victim would have consented to the taking, this may negate dishonesty under s.2(1)(b).

11.7.2 Conditional Intent

Imagine Nigel is found rifling through Rosie's handbag. By touching the bag and its contents he appropriates them. However he may believably claim that he had not formed an intent to permanently deprive Rosie of any particular item. In such a case it is necessary to distinguish three possible states of mind:

(i) There is no difficulty if it could be shown that Nigel was looking for a particular piece of property, for example a credit card. He could be charged with theft of the credit card or an attempt to steal the credit card if he had not managed to appropriate it (see *Hot Topic*, Chapter 13).

(ii) If Nigel had not yet decided whether or not to take anything, it seems he must be acquitted. Lord Scarman has said (in *Nock*), 'if a man be in two minds whether to steal or not, the intention required by the statute is not proved'.

(iii) If Nigel had decided to take anything that was of value, this is known as 'conditional intent'. The phrase was defined by the Law Commission:

'Conditional intent . . . means that the accused does not know what he is going to steal but intends that he will steal whatever he finds of value or worthwhile stealing.'

A person with conditional intent can be charged with attempted theft or burglary, although the prosecution will have to exercise care in drafting the indictment. An allegation of an intent to steal specific named property will fail because it cannot be proved that the accused had the intent to steal that property. In the case of *Husseyn*, for example, the accused and a friend were found trying to get into a van which contained sub-aqua equipment, and the indictment charged them with attempting to steal this sub-aqua equipment. Their conviction was quashed by the Court of Appeal, as it was not shown that they intended to steal sub-aqua equipment. In *Easom**, the accused had picked up a handbag, examined its contents and put it down, having discovered that it contained nothing of value. He was charged with theft of the handbag and certain identified contents. His conviction was quashed. In *Attorney-General's References (Nos 1 and 2 of 1979)**, Lord Justice Roskill explained these decisions on the basis of the over-precise wording of the indictment. In both cases the accused had a general intention to steal and this would be sufficient provided the indictment did not refer to specific objects. Roskill LJ said:

'we see no reason in principle why . . . a more imprecise method of criminal pleading should not be adopted . . . as for example attempting to steal some or all of the contents of a car or some or all of the contents of a handbag.'

This solution has been criticized by some writers (see, for example, Williams (1980)) as a purely procedural device which does not go to the root of the problem of conditional intent. Certainly there is little evidence in the judgements of Lord Edmund Davies in *Easom* and Lord Scarman in *Husseyn* that it was this precise wording of the indictment that was at fault. In reality, those cases decided that conditional intent was not sufficient for theft or attempted theft. The *Attorney-General's References (Nos 1 and 2 of 1979)*, in order to avoid repudiating them entirely, limits their effect to cases where the indictment is drafted in specific terms.

Lord Justice Roskill said that his guidance would apply to all offences which require an intent to steal (an intention of permanently depriving another of his property), but there is in fact a difficulty with theft itself. If the *actus reus* of theft requires the appropriation of property belonging to another, it is difficult to see how the indictment can avoid specifying which property has been appropriated. This is a minor problem because it will always be possible to charge with attempted theft where an appropriation does not need to be proved (*Bayley and Easterbrook*).

11.7.3   Borrowing and Returning Property in a Less Valuable State

We mentioned earlier that borrowing something is not theft and gave the example of borrowing a friend's dress for the evening. But what if the dress was returned damaged, would this alter the position? This situation is dealt with in s.6 Theft Act 1968, which reads:

'(1) A person appropriating property belonging to another without meaning the other permanently to lose the thing itself is nevertheless to be regarded as having the intention of permanently depriving the other of it if his intention is to treat the thing as his own to dispose of regardless of the other's rights: and a borrowing or lending of it may amount to so treating it if, but only if, the borrowing or lending is for a period and in circumstances making it equivalent to an outright taking or disposal.

(2) Without prejudice to the generality of subsection (1) above, where a person, having possession or control (lawfully or not) of property belonging to another, parts with the property under a condition as to its return which he may not be able to perform, this (if done for purposes of his own and without the other's authority) amounts to treating the property as his own to dispose of regardless of the other's rights.'

Section 6 is designed to elucidate the meaning of the phrase 'intention of permanently depriving', but is so obscure that it may be more of a hindrance than a help. This section has been described by Lord Chief Justice Lane as 'abstruse' and by J. R. Spencer as a provision which 'sprouts obscurities at every phrase' (Spencer, 1977). It is perhaps reassuring, then, that the section is hardly ever needed. Lord Chief Justice Lane takes the view that 's.6 should be referred to in exceptional cases only. In the vast majority of cases it need not be referred to or considered at all' (*Lloyd, Bhuee and Ali**). Soon after the Theft Act 1968 came into force, Edmund Davies LJ warned that s.6 must not be interpreted as in any way 'watering down' the definition of theft, which includes the intention of permanently depriving; it merely gives illustrations of such an intention, and clarifies its meaning (*Warner*). This approach has been broadly adopted by other judges; Lord Lane in *Lloyd, Bhuee and Ali* summed up the section by saying 'it must mean, if nothing else, that there are circumstances in which a defendant may be deemed to have the intention permanently to deprive, even though he may intend the owner eventually to get back the object which has been taken'.

So, how does the section help in cases where the defendant is returning damaged property? It should be noted that s.6 appears to draw a distinction between 'property' and 'the thing itself'. This distinction is not explained in the Act, but means that there will be occasions where 'the thing itself' is returned to the owner in such an altered form that the 'borrowing' is treated as 'equivalent to an outright taking' of the property. In a debate in Parliament, the Government Minister gave the example of a person who 'borrows' a season ticket and uses it: he is guilty of theft (if dishonest) because he is acting as owner of the ticket; it will make no difference that he intends to return the ticket ('the thing itself') after it has expired. As far as the owner is concerned, the property has been deprived of all its virtue and is therefore 'equivalent to an outright taking'. Lord Lane said:

'Borrowing is "ex hypothes" not something which is done with an intention permanently to deprive. This half of the subsection, we believe, is intended to make it clear that a mere borrowing is never enough to constitute the necessary guilty mind unless the intention is to return the "thing" in such a changed state that it can truly be said that all its goodness or virtue has gone.'

An attempt was made in *Lloyd, Bhuee and Ali* to apply the 'using up' principle to video piracy, but the Court of Appeal held that the borrowing of the films in order to make illegal copies of them had not deprived the films of their intrinsic value: they could still be shown to paying audiences. This case illustrates well the restrictive approach of the courts. A freer interpretation of 'an intention to treat the thing as his own to dispose of regardless of the other's rights' might well have included the copying of film tapes in breach of copyright.

Examples of the use of s.6 given in *Lloyd, Bhuee and Ali* include the taking of a railway ticket, intending that the ticket should be returned after use (when its value has gone), and the taking of an electric battery, such as a torch battery, intending to return it only when all its power has been used up. It is unclear whether in order for s.6 to be available it is necessary for the item to lose all of its virtue – would the offence be committed where the defendant took a season train ticket and used all bar a few days? Lord Lane suggested *obiter* in *Lloyd, Bhuee and Ali* that all the value needed to be removed and this seems correct if the phrase 'equivalent to outright taking' is interpreted strictly; but we need further caselaw before we can answer this question for certain.

Another issue yet to be resolved by the courts is whether the test of value is to be subjective to the victim. If the victim's wedding dress is stolen the day before the wedding and returned the day after, could it be argued that to the victim the dress has lost 'all its goodness'? Or is the answer that it still has the same monetary value as when it was taken and therefore s.6 does not enable a theft conviction.

11.7.4   Treating Property as Your Own

According to s.6, a defendant is treated as having an intention to permanently deprive the victim of their property if he has an intention 'to treat the thing as his own to dispose of regardless of the other's rights'. A remarkably broad definition of this phrase was given by the Divisional Court in *Lavender*. There the defendant moved the victim's door from part of the victim's building to another. This was seen as the defendant treating the door as his own to dispose of regardless of the victim's rights. It is surprising that moving the door was regarded as 'disposing' of the door. If this is correct, it is hard to see why any moving of the victim's property could not similarly be regarded as treating it as the defendant's own. In which case, there is really no problem with the borrowing cases and most appropriations can be regarded as treating the property as her own. It is hard to believe that *Lavender* can be interpreted so widely, especially given the view of the Court of Appeal in *Lloyd, Bhuee and Ali* that s.6 should have a minimalist role. A similarly wide interpretation of the phrase can also be found in *Fernandes*, where a solicitor put a client's money into an unauthorized risky investment. It was held that this could count as 'treating the property as his own' for the purpose of s.6. In short, it is hard to predict what conduct a court might interpret as treating 'the thing as his own to dispose of regardless of the other's rights'.

11.7.5 'Kidnapping' Property

This heading deals with what is colloquially but inaccurately described as 'kidnapping' property. What if a defendant takes the victim's dog and then tells the victim that he can have his dog back if he pays the defendant £100? Is this theft of the dog? Can the defendant claim he never intended to permanently deprive the victim of his dog because he intended the victim to pay the ransom demand and to return the dog? Lord Lane explained in *Lloyd, Bhuee and Ali* that s.6 covered such a case:

'[the] first part of s.6(1) seems to us to be aimed at the sort of case where a defendant takes things and then offers them back to the owner for the owner to buy if he wishes. If the taker intends to return them to the owner only on such payment, then, on the wording of s.6(1), that is deemed to amount to the necessary intention permanently to deprive.'

This is sometimes referred to as the 'ransom' principle, and covers not only straight-forward ransom cases but any case in which the taker makes his own terms and conditions for the return of the property, whether these are known to the owner or not. In *Scott*, for example, the accused took a pair of curtains from a department store without paying for them, and then returned them, alleging that he had bought them the previous day and asking for a refund. He was treating the property as 'his own to dispose of regardless of the other's rights' and was guilty of theft.

11.7.6 Gambling or pawning another's property

Section 6(2) deals with the situation where a person borrows another's property and gambles with it or pawns it. Section 6(2) explains that such a person cannot claim he or she had no intent to permanently deprive because they intended to win the gamble or intended to buy back the pawned property.

Hot Topic: Stealing Bodies

Is it possible to steal someone's body or parts of the body? When discussing this question, it is necessary to distinguish between the bodies of people who are alive and those who are dead. The traditional response is that it is not possible to steal bodies or parts of the body. It is not clear why the established common law took this view. It may be because the body and parts of the body were not seen as property. Or that even though the body was property, it could not be owned by anyone and so could not be regarded as 'property belonging to another' (*Williams* v. *Williams*).

Recently the courts have been willing to accept that it is possible to steal bodies or their parts. They have been able to do this in three ways:

1 They have accepted that there is a right to possession of a corpse, even if it is not possible to own it (*Dobson* v. *North Tyneside HA*). As the definition of property belonging to another in ss.4 and 5 Theft Act 1968 includes property to which someone has a right of possession, it is possible to conclude that bodies and parts of bodies can be stolen. So in what circumstances does a person have a right to possession of a body or part of a body? The following are the two most important examples:

    (a) A right of possession is given to enable relatives or hospitals to arrange for the proper burial or disposal of the body (*Dobson* v. *North Tyneside HA*). In *Williams*, Kay J explained: 'the law in this country is clear, that after the death of a man, his executors have a right to the custody and possession of his body (although they have no property in it) until it is properly buried'. As this *dictum* indicates, it is well established that a buried corpse cannot be stolen (*Foster* v. *Dodd*).

    (b) A right of possession is also given in respect of a corpse or a body part upon which someone has exercised work or skill (for example, dissection or embalming)(*Kelly*). This will include bodies or parts of bodies taken as medical specimens for research or teaching; also parts of bodies or bodies kept as specimens in museums. So far the cases under this heading have involved dead bodies. It is arguable that if a person has exercised special skill on his own body (for example, by tattooing it) that part becomes property over which he has a proprietal right.

2 Courts have been willing to find theft of parts or products of a live body. In *Herbert*, a man was convicted of theft of a woman's hair, having cut a piece off. It should be noted that this case could also be seen as one of battery (see Chapter 7.2). In *Welsh*, a man was convicted of stealing his urine having handed over a sample to a police office. Although *Herbert* is seen as controversial, there can be little doubt that a person can enter a contract to sell his or her hair (for example, to a wig maker); this has been happening for centuries. Therefore it is hard to deny that hair is property.

3 Following advances in technology, and particularly medical advances, there are a whole range of issues where a person may make a claim that is similar to a property right. Consider these scenarios:

(a) A patient is top of the queue for a transplanted kidney and one becomes available. A doctor takes the kidney and implants it into his brother who also needs one.

(b) A patient is found to have a highly unusual and very useful genetic make-up. His doctor sells his genetic code to a pharmaceutical company for a large sum of money.

(c) A husband and wife have fertility difficulties. Using assisted reproductive techniques, three embryos are produced and stored in a hospital. Both husband and wife are killed in a car crash. The husband's brother and the wife's sister, both of whom also suffer from infertility, claim they are entitled to inherit the embryos.

(d) A prostitute is visited by a well-known personality. She is able to store some of his sperm and offers it for sale on the internet.

So, we are in the position that some parts of the body in some circumstances can be stolen. The exact boundary between what can and what cannot be stolen is far from clear. As these cases indicate, the question of ownership of the body and its parts is far from resolved and will trouble the courts for many years to come. It should of course be noted that misuse of other's bodies is protected by other offences, apart from theft. The most obvious are the offences against the person. Less obviously, there is a specific common law offence of preventing the lawful burial of a body.

Summary

11.1 The basic definition of theft is found in s.1 Theft Act 1968. An attempt was made to use clear and uncomplicated language but the complexities of the law of property and contract create inevitable difficulties in defining the scope of theft. Many of the concepts that are used in theft appear in other property offences.

11.2 The offence of theft is made up of five core elements: appropriation; property; belonging; dishonesty; and intention to permanently deprive.

11.3 Appropriation is defined in s.3 Theft Act 1968 and includes any assumption by a person of any one of the rights of an owner in the sense of an adverse interference with or usurpation of the owner's rights. Section 3(2) protects a person who buys stolen property in good faith: no later use of the property will amount to theft. Whether the owner consents to the act of usurpation is irrelevant in deciding whether or not there is appropriation.

11.4 Property is defined very widely in s.4 Theft Act 1968 and includes 'things in action' such as a credit balance in a bank account. 'Land' is property that can only be stolen in certain very limited circumstances. Confidential information is not property within s.4.

11.5 The property must belong to another at the time of the appropriation. Property belongs to any person having possession, control, or any proprietary right or interest (s.5(1)). The timing can cause difficulty, particularly if property rights pass as a result of the transaction. If all proprietary rights, as well as possession and control, pass before the act of appropriation, there can be no theft. A new offence has been created (s.3 Theft Act 1978) to deal with 'bilking' cases. The requirement of belonging to another has been given an extended meaning in s.5. Section 5(3) applies where all rights in property are transferred to the thief but he is under a legal obligation to retain and deal with the property in a particular way. Section 5(4) applies where property has been handed over under a mistake and there is a legal obligation to return the property.

11.6 Dishonesty is an important part of the *mens rea* of theft. Section 2 Theft Act 1968 gives some guidance on the meaning of dishonesty but the concept is not defined and it has been held to be primarily a matter for the jury or magistrates. The jury should ask itself two questions. First, was the conduct dishonest according to the standards of reasonable and ordinary people? Second, was the accused aware that what he was doing was, by those standards, dishonest?

11.7 The other element of *mens rea* in theft is an intention of permanently depriving another of property. Borrowing property is not theft. There is no bar to conviction for attempted theft in cases where the accused intends to steal anything of value but is arrested before finding anything to steal (even if in fact there is nothing to steal), as long as the indictment is worded in sufficiently general terms. An attempt is made in s.6 Theft Act 1968 to clarify the meaning of the phrase 'intention of permanently depriving'. The section is difficult to construe, and in most circumstances will be redundant. It covers 'ransom' cases, where the accused is only prepared to return the property of another on the performance of some condition. It also covers the cases of 'using-up', where the property is returned to the owner, but in circumstances such that its value has completely gone. In these cases, even though the accused may intend to return the 'thing itself', he is deemed to have an intention of permanently depriving the owner of the property.

Case Notes

Attorney-General's References (Nos 1 and 2 of 1979) [1979] 2 All ER 143. Court of Appeal

Two questions were referred to the Court of Appeal arising out of two cases in which the trial judge had directed an acquittal. The Court of Appeal was asked whether the accused's intention of stealing anything of value which he might find in a building amounted to an intention of stealing necessary for a conviction of burglary or attempted burglary. The Court of Appeal held that this intention was sufficient, as long as the indictment did not allege that the accused intended to steal specific items. The same principles would apply to theft and attempted theft.

Attorney-General's Reference (No. 1 of 1983) [1984] 3 All ER 369. Court of Appeal

The accused received an overpayment of wages by direct transfer of money from her employer (the Metropolitan Police). She knew of the overpayment but did nothing. She was charged with theft of the overpayment. The trial judge directed an acquittal, but it was held in the Court of Appeal that this was a case where s.5(4) Theft Act 1968 applied. The overpayment, in the accused's bank account, was a debt and a thing in action; she was under an obligation to make restoration of the value of that thing in action when she found that the mistake had been made. The property therefore notionally belonged to another person.

Bloxham [1982] 1 AC 109. House of Lords
See Chapter 13 case notes.

Easom [1971] 2 All ER 945. Court of Appeal
The appellant was convicted of theft of a handbag and its contents. He had taken the bag in a cinema, looked through it, and finding nothing of value, had put it back by the

owner. His appeal was allowed, and the Court of Appeal held that he could not in those circumstances be convicted of theft or attempted theft because there was no evidence that he had an intention of permanently depriving the owner of the specific property named in the indictment.

Edwards v. *Ddin* [1976] 1 WLR 942. Divisional Court

The accused was charged with theft of petrol from a garage. He had asked the garage attendant to fill the tank of his car with petrol and had then driven away without paying for it. The magistrates held that this was not appropriation of property belonging to another because ownership of the petrol transferred to the accused when it was put into his car. The Divisional Court upheld this decision on the ground that under the Sale of Goods Act 1893 this was a contract where ownership in goods passed to the buyer before payment. When the accused drove away from the garage, therefore, the petrol in his car belonged to him and not to the garage.

Feely [1973] 1 All ER 341. Court of Appeal

The appellant was convicted of theft of a sum of money from his employers. He had taken about £30 out of the till, leaving an IOU. He said that his employers owed him about £70 and that he had intended to pay the money back. The jury was directed that his intention to pay back the money was irrelevant to the question of dishonesty in theft. The court allowed the appeal, holding that dishonesty related to the state of mind of the accused; whether or not a person was dishonest was a question of fact for the jury, and the jury should apply the current standards of ordinary decent people.

Ghosh [1982] QB 1053. Court of Appeal

The appellant was convicted of obtaining money by deception contrary to s.15 Theft Act 1968. He was a surgeon who had allegedly claimed payment for operations carried out either by another person or under the National Health Service. The court held that there had been a misdirection on the meaning of dishonesty, but dismissed the appeal, applying the proviso to s.2(1) Criminal Appeal Act 1968. It was held that dishonesty was a state of mind of the accused. The jury should first ask itself whether what was done by the accused was dishonest by the ordinary standards of reasonable and honest people, and then whether the accused realized that it was dishonest by those standards.

Gomez [1993] AC 442. House of Lords

The accused was employed as the assistant manager of a shop. He persuaded the manager of the shop to accept two building society cheques from a customer in exchange for some electrical goods. He was aware that the cheques were worthless but told the manager that they were 'as good as cash'. He was convicted of theft of the goods. He appealed to the House of Lords, arguing that if the victim authorized the handing-over of property there could be no appropriation. The House of Lords, by a four to one majority, held that the fact that the manager had authorized the handing-over of the goods was irrelevant to the issue of appropriation. All that needed to be shown for an appropriation was an assumption of any of the rights of the owner, and so the conviction was upheld.

Hinks [2000] 3 WLR 1590. House of Lords

The appellant befriended John Dolphin, a naive, gullible 53-year-old man of limited intelligence. It was alleged that the defendant had persuaded Dolphin to hand over £60,000 from his building society account and some other property. The appellant claimed that the man had voluntarily handed over the property as valid gifts or loans. The majority of the House of Lords held that even if the transfers were valid gifts under contract law, they were appropriations. If they were dishonest, they could be the basis of a conviction of theft. The minority believed that this created an unacceptable conflict between the civil and the criminal law.

Hircock (1978) 67 Cr App Rep 278. Court of Appeal

The appellant was convicted of obtaining a car by deception (contrary to s.15 Theft Act 1968) and of theft of the same car. He had obtained the car on hire purchase, using a false name, and had then sold it. The convictions were upheld by the court, which held that when the appellant obtained the car, this was not a theft, as the owner had consented. There was therefore no bar to his conviction for theft on the basis of the later dishonest selling of the car.

Kaur [1981] 1 WLR 578. Divisional Court

The appellant was convicted of theft of a pair of shoes. She had taken them from a rack in a shop and noticed that the shoes were each marked with a different price. The higher price was the correct one. She presented them to the cashier without mentioning this difference, and was charged the lower price, which she paid. On leaving the shop with the shoes she was arrested and charged with theft. The court allowed the appeal, holding that at the time when she walked out of the shop and appropriated the shoes, they were her own. She had paid for them, and the mistake as to the price was not sufficiently fundamental as to render the contract of sale void *ab initio*.

Lawrence [1972] AC 626. House of Lords

The appellant was convicted of theft of £6. He was a taxi driver who, when offered £1 for a 10s 6d fare, told the victim, who was an Italian on his first visit to England, that it was not enough and took a further £6 out of his wallet. The victim did not object to this money being taken, but there was no evidence that he intended to pay the appellant more than the correct fare. The appellant argued on appeal that the victim had consented to the taking of the money, and that this consent had operated to transfer ownership of the money to the appellant, so that when the appellant took the money it no longer belonged to the victim. These arguments were rejected both by the Court of Appeal and the House of Lords. Viscount Dilhorne in the House of Lords held that there was no reason to add the words 'without the consent of the owner' to s.1 Theft Act 1968. He also held that the money belonged to the victim at the time when the appellant appropriated it, even though the act of appropriation itself may have transferred the ownership. It was also held that s.1 and s.15 Theft Act 1968 are not mutually exclusive, and conduct which falls within s.15 may also amount to theft within s.1.

Lloyd, Bhuee and Ali [1985] 2 All ER 661. Court of Appeal

The appellants were convicted of conspiracy to steal. They had taken video-tapes of films from the cinema in which Lloyd worked, in order to make pirated copies of the films for sale. The films were returned promptly to the cinema in order to avoid detection. The appellants appealed against conviction on the ground that the trial judge should not have directed the jury in terms of s.6(1) Theft Act 1968. The appeal was allowed and the convictions quashed. It was held that s.6 should be referred to in exceptional cases only. It was designed to deal with two kinds of case: (1) where the accused takes property intending to offer it back to the owner for payment; (2) where the accused intends to return the 'thing' in such a changed state that all its goodness or virtue has gone. In this case, the planned copyright swindle would adversely affect the commercial interests of the owners but would not affect the value of the films themselves, which could still be shown to paying audiences.

Morris [1984] AC 320. House of Lords

The appellant was convicted of theft of goods from a supermarket. He had changed the price labels on the goods for labels showing a lesser price, paid the lower price at the checkout, and was then arrested. In a second case which was consolidated on appeal (*Anderson* v. *Burnside*), the facts were similar although the appellant was detected at the checkout before paying the lower price. It was argued on appeal that dishonest label switching did not in itself amount to an act of appropriation. The House of Lords dismissed the appeals on the ground that the label switching was a sufficient appropriation: it amounted to an assumption of one of the rights of the owner, which was to determine the price at which goods should be sold. Lord Roskill held that an appropriation in theft required an adverse interference with, or usurpation of, one of the owner's rights.

Pitham and Hehl (1976) 65 Cr App Rep 45. Court of Appeal
See Chapter 12 case notes.

Turner (No. 2) (1971) 2 All ER 441. Court of Appeal
The defendant left his car at a garage for repairs. Once the repairs were complete, but not paid for, the defendant drove the car away. The court held that the garage were possessors of the car and so even though the defendant was the owner of the car, he could be held guilty of theft. The decision is rather unfortunate as it was not clear on the basis of the right to possession. The court said that it was not necessary to discuss the lien (a form of property right, which would have arisen following the performance of work on the car until payment), but this seems the best explanation of the right of possession. The alternative was to rely on bailment but this could have been ended by the solitary act of the owner.

Warner v. *Metropolitan Police Commissioner* [1969] 2 AC 256. House of Lords
See Chapter 6 case notes.

Williams [1980] Crim LR 589. Court of Appeal
The appellant was convicted of theft. He had exchanged obsolete Yugoslav banknotes at a bureau de change in a department store for sterling currency, and had been charged with theft of the sterling as well as obtaining the currency by deception. The trial judge ruled that there was insufficient evidence of the false representations alleged to support the charge of obtaining by deception, but he was convicted of theft, the jury having decided that the appellant was dishonest. On appeal it was held that the appellant had, by offering the obsolete banknotes for sale at a bureau de change, represented that they were valid currency. The theft conviction was upheld on the ground that there had been no sale of the sterling currency to the appellant. His fraud rendered any such contract void, and the sterling therefore remained throughout the property of the bureau de change.

Further Reading

On the nature of appropriation read Beatson and Simester, Gardner, and Shute and Horder. Elliot, Griew and Halpin discuss dishonesty. Issues surrounding what is property for the purposes of theft are considered by Cross, Harris and A. Smith. Permanent deprivation is examined in Spencer and Williams.

Beatson and Simester, 'Stealing One's Own Property' (1999) 115 *Law Quarterly Review* 372

Cross, 'Protecting Confidential Information under the Criminal Law of Theft and Fraud' (1991) 11 *Oxford Journal of Legal Studies* 264.

Elliot, 'Dishonesty in Theft: A Dispensable Concept' [1982] *Criminal Law Review* 395.

Gardner, 'Appropriation in Theft: the Last Word' (1993) *Law Quarterly Review* 195.

Gardner, 'Property and Theft' [1998] *Criminal Law Review* 35.

Griew, 'Dishonesty: The Objections to *Feely* and *Ghosh*' [1985] *Criminal Law Review* 341.

Halpin, 'The Test for Dishonesty' [1996] *Criminal Law Review* 283.

Harris, 'Who Owns My Body' (1996) 16 *Oxford Journal of Legal Studies* 55.

Shute and Horder, 'Thieving and Deceiving: What is the Difference?' (1993) 56 *Modern Law Review* 548.

A. Smith, 'Stealing the Body and its Parts' [1976] *Criminal Law Review* 622.

J. Smith, 'Stealing Tickets' [1998] *Criminal Law Review* 723.

Spencer, 'The Metamorphasis of Section 6' [1977] *Criminal Law Review* 653.

Wiiliams, 'Three Rogue Charters' [1980] *Criminal Law Review* 263.

Williams, 'Temporary Appropriation should be Theft' [1981] *Criminal Law Review* 129.

12 Offences Connected to Theft

Key words

- **Robbery** – the use of force combined with the offence of theft.
- **Burglary** – entering a building as a trespasser either with intent to commit certain offences or having so entered committing certain offences.

12.1   Robbery

All the offences discussed in this chapter are broadly connected to the offence of theft and are found in the Theft Act 1968. The first to be considered is robbery. Robbery is a from of aggravated theft. It involves theft combined with the use of force. The offence covers a wide range of conduct: from 'bag snatching', to an armed gang forcing cashiers at a bank to hand over large sums of money. It is subject to a maximum punishment of life imprisonment, in contrast to a maximum of seven years for theft.

Section 8 Theft Act 1968 describes the offence of theft:

'(1) A person is guilty of robbery if he steals, and immediately before or at the time of doing so, and in order to do so, he uses force on any person or puts or seeks to put any person in fear of being then and there subjected to force.

(2) A person guilty of robbery, or of an assault with intent to rob, shall on conviction on indictment be liable to imprisonment.'

The essence of robbery is the combination of two elements:

12.1.1   Theft.

Unless every element of theft is made out, a conviction of robbery is impossible; this includes the *mens rea* of theft. It will therefore be a defence to robbery to argue lack of dishonesty for one of the reasons set out in s.2(1) Theft Act 1968, such as the claim of right. It is not necessary for the accused to believe that he had the right to take the property by force (*Robinson*), as long as he honestly believed that he had a legal right to the property. Therefore the dishonesty question is linked to the appropriation, not the use of force. It is tested, in the absence of one of the states of mind specified in s.2(1), by the test laid down in *Ghosh** (see Chapter 11.6.3).

12.1.2   Force

The defendant must have used or threatened to use force. The courts have left the definition of force to the jury, making it clear that a relatively small degree of force may be enough – there is certainly no need for actual injury, but presumably there must be more than a mere touching. In *Hale**, it was said that 'the jury were at liberty to find the appellant guilty of robbery relying on the force used when he put his hand over [the victim's] mouth to restrain her from calling help'. In *Dawson*, the jury decided that jostling the victim in order to pick his pocket was capable of amounting to force and the Court of Appeal thought the jury was entitled to take that view. The force or threat of force need not be directed at the victim of the theft (the person to whom the property belongs): it may be used on a bystander, a hostage or a security guard, for example. Nor does it matter whether the force is applied to a piece of property rather than aimed at a person (*Clouden*). This is a surprising decision as it blurs the division between theft and robbery. The decision could be supported on the basis that if the defendant is aggressively tugging on a piece of property, this will often put the victim in fear of violence. It will be noted that a threat of force is sufficient. So an accused who passes a note to a bank cashier threatening violence unless money is handed over may be convicted of theft if the money is indeed handed over.

The force (or threat of force) must be used in order to steal. It will normally be possible to infer from the fact that the use of force assisted the theft that the force was used in order to steal. The force may take the form of snatching the property from the victim or distracting the victim to enable the theft to take place. The timing of the force is important: it must occur at the time of the theft itself or just before it. So it will not be robbery to use force in order to escape after the theft is over (although the separate offences of theft and assault may be charged in such a case). Nor would it be robbery if the defendant assaulted the victim and then noticed the victim's watch and took it. It is therefore important to know when the theft is complete, and this will depend on the understanding of appropriation (see Chapter 11.3). The attitude of the courts has been flexible: on the one hand, it has been held that the theft was complete, and robbery committed, on the basis of a momentary appropriation. For example, in *Corcoran* v. *Anderton*, the two accused attacked a woman, pulling at her handbag so that she dropped it. They then ran away, leaving the handbag on the ground, but it was held that the appropriation, the 'assumption of the rights of an owner' (s.3 Theft Act 1968) had occurred by tugging the handbag and so they were guilty of theft. On the other hand, in *Hale**, Eveleigh LJ in the Court of Appeal said that although a theft had been committed when the accused seized a jewelry box, 'the act of appropriation does not suddenly cease. It is a continuous act and it is a matter for the jury to decide whether or not the act of appropriation had finished'. In this case, the theft was held still to be continuing when the accused tied the victim up after seizing the jewelry box and so the conviction was upheld. Recently the Court of Appeal has suggested that the appropriation continues while the accused can be said to still 'be on the job', but once the theft is complete there can be no further thefts of that piece of property by the defendant (*Atakpu*).

The *mens rea* of robbery includes the requirement that the force was used for the purpose of enabling theft. So a defendant who accidentally used force while stealing would not commit the offence of robbery.

12.2 Assault with Intent to Rob

As implied in s.8(2) Theft Act 1968, it is an offence to assault with intent to rob. This offence is also punishable with life imprisonment. It involves proof of an assault, performed with an intent to commit robbery. As robbery itself has not been committed it is surprising that no distinction is made in the sentence.

12.3 Burglary

Burglary is regarded as a particularly unpleasant crime as it typically involves an invasion of a home, a place where people are meant to feel secure and safe. The definition of burglary is in fact wider than commonly perceived as it is not limited to dwelling houses nor to offences involving stealing. In fact, burglary is a complicated offence because it can be committed in so many different ways.

12.3.1 The Essence of Burglary

The essence of burglary is trespass into a building (such as a private house or a factory) for some criminal purpose. Section 9 Theft Act 1968 provides:

'(1) A person is guilty of burglary if –
   (a) he enters any building or part of a building as a trespasser and

with intent to commit any such offence as is mentioned in subsection (2) below; or

(b) having entered any building or part of a building as a trespasser he steals or attempts to steal anything in the building or that part of it or inflicts or attempts to inflict on any person therein any grievous bodily harm.

(2) The offences referred to in subsection (1)(a) above are offences of stealing anything in the building or part of a building in question, of inflicting on any person therein any grievous bodily harm or raping any women therein, and of doing unlawful damage to the building or anything therein.'

The maximum punishment for burglary is fourteen years if the building involved was a dwelling, and ten years if it was any other kind of premises (for example, a factory). In addition there is an aggravated offence of burglary with a firearm, which is subject to life imprisonment (s.10 Theft Act 1968).

12.3.2   The Two Kinds of Burglary

There are essentially two kinds of burglary. Both involve proof that the defendant entered a building or part of a building as a trespasser, but the requirements differ:

1 Section 9(1)(a) requires that the defendant entered with intent to commit one of the offences listed in s.9(2). There is no need for the defendant actually to commit any of the offences.
2 Section 9(1)(b) requires that the defendant actually committed theft or inflicted grievous bodily harm. The purpose of s.9(1)(b) is to cover the defendant who enters a building not intending to commit any offence but once inside the building decides to do so.

The elements of the offence are as follows:

- Entry
- A building
- As a trespasser
- Awareness of being a trespasser
- Intent to commit a crime (s.9(1)(a)) or commission of crime (s.9(1)(b)).

These factors will now be considered separately.

12.3.3 Entry

The leading case on burglary is *Collins**. The accused climbed naked up a ladder to the bedroom window of a girl he knew slightly, intending to have sexual intercourse with her. It was the middle of the night and the girl was asleep in bed, but when she saw the accused at the window she jumped to the conclusion that he was her boyfriend and invited him into the room. They then had sexual intercourse. Collins was convicted of burglary with intent to rape, under s.9(1)(a). His appeal was allowed on the basis of the uncertainty over whether he had entered as a trespasser: if the victim had invited him into the room before he had entered it then, according to the court, he would not have been a trespasser. If, however, he had entered the room before the invitation then he would have committed the offence.

The key issue in *Collins* was the meaning of the term 'entry'. Lord Justice Edmund Davies said that the entry must be 'effective and substantial'. In *Brown* (1985), the Court of Appeal preferred to use just the word 'effective' and refused to interpret this to mean that the whole of the body must be in the building. It has recently been held that putting an arm and head through a window amounted to 'entry' (*Ryan*). It might be thought that the use of the word 'effective' means that it is necessary to show that enough of the body was inserted into the building to enable the theft to be carried out. However in *Ryan* this interpretation was rejected. In *Ryan*, although the defendant had not put enough of himself into the building to enable him to steal, he was still found to have entered. So we are left with the conclusion that the entry must be effective, but it is not clear what effective means.

It is possible to use an innocent agent (for example, a young child) to burgle (*Wheelhouse*) and presumably it could be burglary to insert an object though a window to remove an item.

12.3.4 Building or Part of a Building

The word 'building' is not defined, although inhabited vehicles and vessels are expressly included by subsection (3). 'Building' is to be given its ordinary meaning, but it requires a construction that has a degree of permanence. The word is not restricted to homes, but can include offices, factories and outbuildings (*B and S* v. *Leathley*). Vehicles do not count as buildings unless they are inhabited (for example, a houseboat). This is made clear in s.9(4).

Burglary can be committed where either a building or part of a building is entered by a trespasser. This is significant where buildings, such as banks and shops, are generally open to the public but have sections reserved to those with express permission to enter. Entering one of those private parts will be entry into part of a building as a trespasser, even where entry into the building itself is permitted. What amounts to a separate part of a building will be a question of fact for the jury. In *Walkington**, it was held that an area of a shop floor behind a three-sided counter was a separate part of the building, from which the public was excluded. It is the absence of any authority to enter which sets this 'part' of the building apart from the public area, although as Geoffrey Lane LJ accepted, the physical characteristics of the building were also relevant. There needs to be some visible sign or marking that separates the part of the building not open to the public; for example, a 'no entry' sign would be sufficient.

12.3.5   As a Trespasser

The concept of entry 'as a trespasser' has proved to be one of the most controversial aspects of burglary. Trespassing is a civil law concept, but is adopted as part of the criminal law definition of burglary. A trespasser is a person who lacks authority for his presence – he lacks either express or implied permission from the owner to enter. It is crucial to the offence that the accused must *enter* the building (or part of the building) as a trespasser. It is not enough to enter with permission but become a trespasser at some later stage (for example, on being asked to leave), unless he then enters a separate part of the building.

There may in some cases be doubt over who is entitled to give the permission to enter. In *Collins*, one issue was whether the daughter of the owner could give the permission. The court found no difficulty in deciding that she could, but it might have been harder if the girl had been the owner's *au pair*.

If the permission to enter is obtained by a misrepresentation then the permission may be seen as invalid, but it is unclear when this is so. It may be that mistakes as to identity negate the effectiveness of permission. The question was not properly addressed in *Collins*, but may depend on the court's interpretation of the facts – was the invitation issued to her boyfriend or the man standing on the windowsill?

12.3.6   Awareness of Being a Trespasser

It was held in *Collins* that trespass contains within it a *mens rea* element. This is not made explicit in the statute and is not required for trespass in the civil law, but may be implied from the general presumption in the criminal law in favour of *mens rea* (*B* v. *DPP*). Edmund Davies LJ said:

'In the judgement of this court, there cannot be a conviction for entering premises "as a trespasser" within the meaning of s.9 of the Theft Act 1968 unless the person entering does so knowing that he is a trespasser and nevertheless deliberately enters, or, at the very least, is reckless whether or not he is entering the premises of another without the other party's consent.'

This statement appears to require that the defendant was aware that when entering the building he was a trespasser. This does not mean it must be shown that the defendant was aware that he fell into the legal category of a trespasser, but rather that he knows the facts which render him a trespasser at law.

It is unfortunate that in a subsequent case the importance given to the *mens rea* of trespass in *Collins* has been expanded so much that the mental element threatens to take over the concept of trespass altogether. In *Smith and Jones**, two boys decided to steal two television sets from the house of the father of one of the boys. The Court of Appeal held that the very fact that they had entered the house with the intention of doing something which they knew they had no authority to do (stealing the television sets) made them trespassers. James LJ said that a person would be a trespasser for the purposes of s.9:

'if he enters the premises of another knowing that he is entering in excess of the permission that had been given to him, or being reckless as to whether he is entering in excess of the permission that has been given to him to enter, providing the facts are known to the accused which enable him to realise that he is acting in excess of the permission given or that he is acting recklessly as to whether he exceeds that permission.'

It has been argued that this decision, although it purports to follow *Collins*, is in fact inconsistent with it. Applying the *Smith and Jones* doctrine, *Collins* would still have been a trespasser in spite of the invitation, because the accused's intent to rape was certainly 'in excess of the permission given', and he must have known this. If this is correct, there was no need for the court to spend so much time considering whether Collins had entered. Some argue that Collins may have thought the invitation indicated that she was consenting to sexual intercourse. This interpretation, although a possible reading of the facts, was not mentioned by the Court of Appeal and so clearly it could not have seen this as important.

The possible conflict with *Collins* gives some support to those who dislike the implications of the decision in *Smith and Jones* and would like to see it overruled. Applied rigorously, the decision would mean that every person who enters a building with what Glanville Williams calls 'burglarious intent' (an intent to commit one of the offences listed in s.9(2)), automatically becomes a trespasser and so guilty of burglary under s.9(1)(a). The would-be shoplifter, who enters a shop with the intention of stealing therein, becomes a trespasser and therefore a burglar (see Pace, 1985). This would widen the scope of the offence enormously and unnecessarily. In effect it is punishing people for their thoughts, because without their 'burglarious intent' there would be no crime. It has also been argued that the particular evil of burglary, invading someone's home, is not present when they have been invited in. *Smith and Jones* is also not easily reconcilable with the subsequent decision in *Walkington*. There Geoffrey Lane LJ stressed the fact that the accused had entered a separate part of the shop which the public had no general permission to enter, and it was that which rendered him a trespasser. However his Lordship need not have stressed this if the accused's intention to steal had made him a trespasser when entering the shop, as *Smith and Jones* seems to imply.

In spite of these criticisms there has been no direct judicial disapproval of *Smith and Jones*, and the conflict with *Collins* (an earlier case) and *Walkington* (a later case) is implicit rather than explicit. *Smith and Jones* must therefore be treated as good law until the Court of Appeal addresses the issue again directly. Indeed, there are some arguments that can be put forward on behalf of *Smith and Jones*. It makes the law easier to use in that the focus is entirely on the mental state of the defendant rather than trying to draw lines between what does and does not count as permission, which can involve some complex issues. Further it might be thought that we need have little sympathy for those who enter buildings with intent to commit crimes, whether they appear to have the owner's permission or not.

12.3.7   The Intent to Commit a Crime: Section 9(1)(a)

For a conviction under s.9(1)(a) it must be shown that on entering the building, the defendant intended to commit one of a number of offences specified in s.9(2). The most common form of burglary under s.9(1)(a) involves an intent to steal. The offence is complete as soon as the accused entered the building; it is irrelevant that he had not been able to do anything to further his intent, and it is also irrelevant that the property he would have liked to steal is not in the building (*Walkington*).

For a time, the problem of conditional intent bedeviled burglary under s.9(1)(a) as well as theft (see Chapter 11.7.2). There were several acquittals of alleged burglars who could not be said to intend to steal a specific piece of property, because they intended to steal anything they might find in the building that was worth stealing. Following two such acquittals, the

Attorney-General made two references to the Court for Appeal on the question of whether or not a conditional intent was sufficient for burglary under s.(9)(1)(a). The Court of Appeal ruled that if the indictment alleged an intent to steal specific items, an intent to steal those items would need to be proved. However, there was no objection to drafting the indictment more widely without stating specific items (for example, 'entering as a trespasser with intent to steal'). In such a case, so-called conditional intent is no bar to a conviction for burglary (*Attorney-General's References (Nos 1 and 2 of 1979)**; see Chapter 11.7.2, for a more detailed discussion of conditional intent).

There is still some doubt over an accused who enters a house with the intent to steal a specific item under a certain condition: for example an intent to steal a painting if it is not alarmed. In such a case the defendant may be said not to have the *intention* to permanently deprive the owner of the item at the time of entering the house. It is unlikely that a court would be sympathetic to such an argument.

12.3.8   The Commission of a Crime: Section 9(1)(b)

For a commission of an offence under s.9(1)(b) it must be shown that the defendant entered a building as a trespasser. These requirements are as discussed above. Unlike s.9(1)(a), where the burglary is complete as soon as the accused has entered the building with the necessary *mens rea*, under s.9(1)(b) a further element of *actus reus* is required. The accused must either steal or attempt to steal something in the building, or inflict or attempt to inflict grievous bodily harm on any person in the building.

The infliction of grievous harm in s.9(1)(b) does not in itself refer to a specific offence under s.18 or s.20 Offences Against the Person Act 1861. But it is very likely that grievous bodily harm would be interpreted in line with ss.18 and 20 to mean serious bodily harm. It has been held (*Jenkins**) that 'inflict' does not necessarily imply assault, although in practice an assault will usually be involved. It is not clear what, if any, further *mens rea* is required, but it is likely that *Cunningham* recklessness as to inflicting grievous bodily harm would be needed. It seems a little odd that a defendant who enters a building without an intent to commit a crime but then commits criminal damage or rape is not guilty of burglary, although the defendant would still be guilty of plain criminal damage or rape.

The difference between the *actus reus* of s.9(1)(a) and s.9(1)(b) has an important consequence for the timing of the *mens rea*. Since the offence under s.9(1)(a) is complete on entry into the building, the *mens rea*, both the knowledge that the accused is a trespasser and the further intent, must exist at the time of entry. In the case of s.9(1)(b), although the accused must actually be a trespasser on entry, it will normally be sufficient if the accused realizes that he is a trespasser by the time the further offence is committed (the theft or infliction of grievous bodily harm). However, if the accused is only a trespasser by virtue of the *Smith and Jones* doctrine, he must have *mens rea* from the moment of entry into the building or part of the building, since it is this *mens rea* that makes him a trespasser and without it he will not have 'entered as a trespasser'.

12.4 Aggravated Burglary

Aggravated burglary is a more serious form of burglary (burglary under s.9(1)(a) or s.9(a)(b)). Under s.10 Theft Act 1968, aggravated burglary is punishable with life imprisonment if, at the time of the burglary, the accused has with him a firearm, imitation firearm, or weapon of offence or explosive. It is worth noting that 'weapon of offence' is defined in s.10(1)(b) as 'any article made or adapted for use for causing injury to or incapacitating a person *or intended by the person having it with him for such use*' (emphasis added). An 'innocent' object such as a screwdriver could therefore be regarded as a weapon of offence, depending on the intent of the accused. In *Kelly* (1992), the accused had a screwdriver and used it to open a window and to later poke the victim. He was found guilty of an offence under s.10(1)(b). There is no need to show that the defendant intended to use the innocent item in a particular burglary as long as he had it with him as a weapon to use against someone at some time (*Stones*). It is also sufficient if the accused intended to use the weapon should the need arise (*Kelly* (1992)).

The difference between the *actus reus* of s.9(1)(a) and s.9(1)(b) is important for aggravated burglary, as it affects the time at which the firearm or weapon must be in the possession of the accused: in the case of s.9(1)(a) it will be the time of the entry; whereas for s.9(1)(b) it will be the time at which the further offence is committed. Thus in *O'Leary*, the accused entered a house and found a knife in the kitchen. He later used it to threaten the occupant during a theft. As he used the knife in the course of a stealing this was sufficient, even though he did not have the knife at the point of entry to the building. Had he never actually used it during the burglary he would not have committed aggravated burglary. In *Francis*, a conviction under s.10 was quashed on these grounds; the prosecution, having alleged an s.9(1)(b) type of burglary, had not proved that the accused had the weapons of offence (sticks) with them when they stole (they had discarded them at the door of the house).

Connected with aggravated burglary is the offence under s.25 of the Act that a defendant has with him, not at his place of abode, 'any article in connection with any burglary, theft or cheat'. There is no need to show that the accused was on her way to commit a specific crime and *Ellames* suggested that it is sufficient if the accused possessed the articles for future use by another. The article could be anything that may assist in a crime – the cases have included a sliced loaf and a bag of tomatoes used to defraud an employer (*Rashid*) and a pair of gloves to prevent fingerprints (*Ellames*). The *mens rea* for the offence is knowledge that one possesses the item and an intention to use it, or let it be used, in one of the listed crimes.

12.5 Handling Stolen Goods

The offence of handling stolen goods is concerned with those who help thieves dispose of stolen property. The offence is justified on the basis that 'there would not be so many thieves if there were no receivers' (*Battams*). It is because people are willing to buy stolen goods that theft and burglary are so prevalent. Section 22(1) Theft Act 1968 provides:

'A person handles stolen goods if (otherwise than in the course of the stealing) knowing or believing them to be stolen goods he dishonestly receives the goods, or dishonestly undertakes or assists in their retention, removal, disposal or realisation by or for the benefit of another person, or if he arranges to do so.'

Handling stolen goods is subject to a maximum sentence of fourteen years. It is therefore seen as at least potentially more serious than theft. This is understandable when one considers that some handlers operate on a very large scale, sometimes 'commissioning' thieves to work for them. Indeed the report to the Criminal Law Revision Committee proposing the creation of this offence suggested that punishment of handlers might deter theft, by making that crime less profitable.

The following elements make up the offence:

12.5.1 Goods

'Goods' is widely defined by s.34(2)(b) Theft Act 1968. The term excludes land but includes money and every other description of property (including things severed from land (such as timber or minerals)). In *Attorney-General's Reference (No. 4 of 1979)* it was stated that things in action could be included in this definition of goods for the purposes of this offence.

12.5.2   Stolen

The goods at the time of the handling must be 'stolen', although this is given a wide definition in the Act. There are three situations in which the goods will be considered 'stolen':

1.   Goods that have actually been stolen
The difficulty for the prosecution is often in proving beyond reasonable doubt that the goods have been stolen. The prosecution can prove this in several ways. The most obvious is to show that someone else has already been convicted of stealing the goods (s.74 Police and Criminal Evidence Act 1984; it is not usually possible for the thief to be a handler, as we will see). Failing a previous conviction, the prosecution could rely on circumstantial evidence that the goods handled by the accused were in fact stolen. It is important not to allege that the goods must have been stolen just because the handler thought that they were (*Overington*). There needs to be evidence independent of the accused's own beliefs, such as the circumstances in which the accused came by the goods, their price, or evidence of goods of the same description having been reported stolen (*McDonald*). The definition of stolen goods also includes goods stolen outside England provided that the stealing was either an offence under the Theft Act 1968 or amounted to an offence where, and at the time, the goods were stolen.

2.   Goods obtained by robbery, burglary and deception under s.15(1) Theft Act 1968, and goods obtained by blackmail (s.21 Theft Act 1968)

3.   The proceeds of the goods falling into 1 or 2
This means that if the thief sells the stolen goods (for example a car) the money he receives in exchange for the car will also be considered stolen. If the thief passes the money on to another person that person could be convicted of handling the 'stolen' money. In order for proceeds to become stolen goods under s.24(2), two conditions must be fulfilled:

(a)   First, the proceeds must be in the hands of either the thief or a handler. This means that proceeds which have been through innocent hands cannot be stolen goods. For example, if Ronnie steals a Rolls-Royce and sells it to Andrew for £2000 but tells Andrew to pay the money to his grandmother then, if the grandmother knows nothing about the stealing of the Rolls-Royce, the money is not stolen in her hands. Even if the grandmother later gives the money to her friend, Charles, who knows all about the source of the money, it is still not stolen property in Charles' hands. This is because the money has passed from an innocent person's hands and therefore cannot be stolen property.

(b) The second requirement is that the proceeds must represent directly or indirectly the original stolen goods. So if Ronnie sells the stolen Rolls-Royce for £2000, uses the £2000 to buy shares and later sells the shares and buys a Rover car, then the Rover would be stolen goods, as one could trace the Rover back to the stolen Rolls-Royce through the shares. The result of these rules could be that from one stolen item there might be several pieces of property that are 'stolen' for the purposes of the statute. For example if Ronnie sells the stolen Rolls-Royce to Andrew for £2000, who sells it to Imogen for £2400, all of them aware of the origin of the car, then the £2000 in Ronnie's hands, the £2400 in Andrew's hands and the Rolls-Royce in Imogen's hands are all deemed 'stolen property'.

Let us now suppose that Andrew had written Ronnie a cheque for £1000 in exchange for the stolen Rolls-Royce, and Ronnie, after depositing the cheque, drew out of his account the sum of £500 and gave it to his girlfriend. Is the £500 now stolen goods by virtue of s.24(2)? This question was faced in *Attorney-General's Reference (No. 4 of 1979)* and the Court of Appeal said that in order to prove that money drawn out of a bank account (in our example, the £500) was stolen, two things would have to be proved: first that the bank account was made up, at least in part, of stolen goods; and second that the sum drawn out of the account was at least in part made up of proceeds of these stolen goods. If, for example, when Ronnie paid the £1000 into his account, there was only £100 already in the account, then it must be that the £500 he later drew out at least in part represented the stolen £1000 paid in. If, however, Ronnie's account already contained several thousand pounds, it would be difficult to prove that the sum later withdrawn must have represented the stolen £1000. It could have represented the money that was originally in the account. The court made it clear that the belief of the receiver of the money (the girlfriend in our example) was irrelevant, but left open the question of whether it would be possible to rely on the intentions of the account-holder: if it could be shown that the account-holder intended the withdrawn money to represent particular stolen money paid into the account on an earlier occasion, this may be sufficient evidence to satisfy a jury that the withdrawn money was stolen.

A separate difficulty concerns the possibility of stolen goods ceasing to be 'stolen' for the purposes of s.22. This is covered by s.24(3), which provides that goods will no longer be regarded as stolen once they have reached either (i) the original owner, (ii) an innocent person or (iii) lawful custody (for example, the police). This last category can be difficult to define, especially if the police discover some stolen property, but while they are making inquiries someone takes the property away. Whether goods are in the custody of the police often depends on the intentions of the police officers involved (*Attorney-General's Reference (No. 1 of 1974)**). It will not always be easy to draw the line between an investigation of the goods and a decision by the police to take charge of the goods.

Goods will also cease to be stolen under s.24(3) where the person from whom they were stolen loses any right to restitution of the goods. This is a matter of civil law and rarely arises. It is most likely to occur when the goods were originally obtained by deception, and the owner on discovering the deception nevertheless decides to ratify the disposal of the goods: this was the example given by the Criminal Law Revision Committee in its Eighth Report (Cmnd 2977).

12.5.3   The Different Ways of Handling Stolen Goods

The definition of handling stolen goods in s.22 specifies 18 different ways of handling. It is easiest to list these:

(1) receiving stolen goods;
(2) undertaking the retention of stolen goods for the benefit of another;
(3) undertaking the removal of stolen goods for the benefit of another;
(4) undertaking the disposal of stolen goods for the benefit of another;
(5) undertaking the realization of stolen goods for the benefit of another;
(6) assisting in the retention of stolen goods by another;
(7) assisting in the removal of stolen goods by another;
(8) assisting in the disposal of stolen goods by another;
(9) assisting in the realization of stolen goods by another;
(10–18) arranging to do any one of the above.

When the indictment is drafted, the prosecution is not expected to specify exactly in which one of the eighteen ways the accused is alleged to have handled the goods. The crucial requirement is that the accused knows in enough detail the case he has to meet, in order to prepare his defence. The large number of ways it is possible to commit the offence indicates that the section is casting a wide net to make it as difficult and less profitable as possible to dispose of stolen property (*Tokeley-Parry*).

In the important case of *Bloxham*, Lord Bridge said that s.22 creates in essence two offences: one of receiving (or arranging to receive); and the other covering all the other forms of handling. All offences except receiving need to be carried out 'by or for the benefit of another person'. Most of the forms of handling are self-explanatory – retaining, removing, disposing, realizing, undertaking and assisting. These words are to be given their normal meaning. However, something needs to be said here about the terms 'receiving', 'assisting' and 'by or for the benefit of another'.

1. *'Receiving'*

'Receiving' takes place when the goods are taken into the possession or control of the accused. This means that the accused must be aware that she has possession or control of the items (*Hobson* v. *Impett*). No offence will be committed if at the time of receiving, the accused lacks *mens rea* for handling (defined below) at the moment of receipt. A subsequent discovery that the goods are stolen will not turn the receiver into a handler. Likewise the goods must be stolen at the time of receipt, and it is worth noting that this applies also to arranging to receive stolen goods: the goods must already be stolen at the time when the arrangement is made. If they are not yet stolen, the 'arrangement' will amount to a conspiracy to handle stolen goods, but not the complete offence of handling.

2. *'Assisting'*

'Assisting' has been held to involve an element of help or encouragement. It was not enough in *Sanders* for the accused merely to use the stolen property left in his father's garage. The use did not help or encourage the person retaining the goods. Also, in *Brown* (1970), it was held that a failure to inform the police of the presence of stolen goods in the accused's flat did not by itself amount to assisting in the retention of the goods. However, there was evidence that the accused had 'provided accommodation' for the goods, and this was sufficient to be assistance. If the police ask an accused about the presence of stolen goods and the accused tells lies about the existence of the goods then she may be guilty of assisting in the retention of stolen goods. But she will not have committed an offence by keeping silent or refusing to answer questions (*Kanwar*).

3. *'By or for the benefit of another'*

If the defendant is not alleged to have received the property, and one of the other forms of handling is relied upon, it must be shown that the defendant acted for the benefit of another. In *Bloxham*, it was held by the House of Lords that selling goods did not amount to a disposal 'for the benefit of' the buyer. The accused had bought a stolen car, without realizing that it was stolen. On becoming certain that it was stolen, he sold the car to an innocent third party. He was charged with handling the car by undertaking its disposal or sale for the benefit of another person (the innocent third party). Lord Bridge supported the common-sense view that a sale is undertaken by the seller primarily for his own benefit. People rarely sell property for altruistic reasons. A sale could only be regarded as for the benefit of another if it was carried out on behalf of someone else. This might arise where a defendant is acting as the agent of someone who has stolen the property. This means that a '*bona fide* purchaser' such as *Bloxham* cannot be charged either with receiving or handling by disposal. He cannot be charged with theft either, as a result of s.3(2) Theft Act 1968 (Chapter 11.3). However, as Lord Bridge pointed out, if the *bona fide* purchaser sells the stolen goods once he discovers that they are stolen, as *Bloxham* did, he will almost certainly be guilty of an offence: either obtaining the purchase price by deception (if he does not inform his purchaser that the goods were stolen), or being an accessory to the receiving offence committed by his purchaser (if he does enlighten him).

It is not clear from Lord Bridge's judgement whether or not the *Bloxham* principle applies only to those who sell the goods on to another. Could it be said that a person who gives away stolen goods does so for the benefit of the recipient? It is arguable, although it does not seem right, to distinguish between the person who gives away the goods and the person who asks a very low price.

12.5.4   Dishonesty

There are two *mens rea* elements in handling stolen goods: the act of handling itself must be dishonest; and the accused must, at the time of that act, know or believe that the goods are stolen. There has been little discussion of the meaning of dishonesty in s.22, largely because it will be unusual for a person to know or believe the goods to be stolen and yet not be dishonest. In fact, in *Roberts* (1987) it was held that a person who receives stolen goods knowing that they are stolen and then sells them must be dishonest. The requirement of dishonesty seems to add little, although lack of dishonesty may provide a defence to a person who knowingly receives stolen goods, intending to return them to the owner or to lawful custody such as the police. It is clear from *Roberts* (1987) that the *Ghosh* test for dishonesty applies to s.22, although it was held that the full *Ghosh* for direction (see Chapter 11.6.3) need not be given unless the issue of dishonesty is raised on the facts, or by the accused.

12.5.5   Knowledge or Belief that the Goods are Stolen

The requirement of knowing or believing the goods to be stolen has given rise to a large number of cases going to appeal. The law is still not completely certain, partly because the courts have been content to leave the definition of knowledge and belief to the 'common sense of the jury' (Waller LJ in *Reader*). Guidelines have been largely restricted to a series of statements of what knowledge and belief are not. The best that can be said is that knowledge and belief should be given their normal meanings (*Forsyth*). Certain points are clear, however:

1 The knowledge or belief of the accused is tested subjectively (*Atwal* v. *Massey*). It is a question of the accused's actual state of mind, not what he or she ought to have known, or what a reasonable person would have believed in the circumstances.

2 While belief must fall short of knowledge (otherwise there would be no point in the statute using both words), belief is not the same thing as suspicion. Nor is 'turning a blind eye' equivalent to a belief that the goods are stolen (see, for example, *Bellenie* and *Moys*). Something approaching more useful guidance has now been given by the Court of Appeal in *Hall**. Lord Lane CJ held that a person would 'know' goods were stolen when told that they were by a person with first-hand knowledge, such as the thief. Belief, on the other hand, could be said to be the state of mind of a person who says to himself: 'I cannot say I know for certain that those goods are stolen, but there can be no other reasonable conclusion in the light of all the circumstances of all that I have heard and seen'. This supports Glanville Williams's view that belief amounts to being 'virtually certain', adding very little to actual knowledge.

3 The jury is entitled to infer knowledge or belief from the fact that the accused was in possession of goods which had recently been stolen. This is the so-called doctrine of recent possession, but it is important to realize that it is only one factor which the jury may take into account; it is in no sense a conclusive proof of *mens rea*, which must be based on the actual state of mind of the accused.

12.5.6 Handling and Theft

Is it possible to steal property which has already been stolen? Property which has been stolen can be stolen again, though not by the original thief (see s.3(1) Theft Act 1968; and Chapter 11.3). The statute states that the handling must be otherwise than in the course of the stealing and this has been held to mean the original theft (*Sainthouse* and *Devall*). Many acts of handling, such as receiving, will also amount to an appropriation of property belonging to another, and so a new theft. There is nothing to prevent two counts, alleging theft and handling respectively, on the indictment, although the Court of Appeal has said that a jury should be directed not to convict for both theft and handling (*Shelton**).

Not all acts of handling will be theft: some types of handling may not amount to an appropriation (such as arranging to receive). If the goods are 'stolen' by virtue of having been obtained by deception, or because they are proceeds, ownership of the goods may be transferred to the handler. This does not affect liability for handling, but it does mean that the goods no longer belong to another, a requirement for theft. In both these cases, an element of the *actus reus* of theft is missing. However, it will be very unusual for a person to possess the *mens rea* of handling but lack the *mens rea* of theft.

The original theft will not be an act of receiving because of the requirement in s.22 that the handling must be 'otherwise than in the course of the stealing'. While 'the stealing' is still occurring, no handling can take place. Only once the theft is completed can the goods become stolen and then the subject of a handling charge. Following the wide interpretation of appropriation in *Gomez* (see Chapter 11.3) and the fact that a piece of property once stolen by a defendant does not continue to be stolen every time an item is appropriated (see *Atakpu*, and Chapter 11.3) means that handling can take place very shortly after the thief first touched or dealt with the property (*Pitham and Hehl**). To summarize, this rule, that the handling must be otherwise than in the course of the stealing, means that the thief cannot be guilty of handling unless an act of handling is committed once the stealing is over.

Hot Topic: Why is Burglary a Specific Offence?

Here we will discuss why burglary is a specific offence. Although burglary is a well-established criminal offence, its justification is not straight-forward. There are two separate issues, depending on the kind of burglary involved. First, s.9(1)(a): entering a building as a trespasser with intent to commit one of the listed criminal offences. Here the question is why is an intention to commit theft suddenly a serious offence if it is held while entering a building as a trespasser? We do not normally punish intentions to commit crimes, unless the defendant has gone so far as to commit an attempt (see Chapter 18). Why not just rely on the civil law on trespass and the law on attempts to deal with the situation? It is notable that entering a building intending to commit theft (that is, burglary) carries a higher maximum sentence than actual theft. This is surprising when it is remembered that simply entering a building as a trespasser is not a criminal offence and that in this form of burglary no theft need have actually taken place.

Second, s.9(1)(b): committing one of the listed offences while being a trespasser in a building. Here the question is why is burglary not treated simply as a form of theft or inflicting grievous bodily harm? We do not have special offences of shoplifting or pickpocketing. These offences are simply regarded as forms of theft. So why single out burglary as a particular kind of theft. This issue is part of a much wider debate about how precisely we should define criminal offences (see Chapter 1.4).

Some commentators such as Simester and Sullivan seek to justify both these offences with an overarching explanation. They can be conceived of as an invasion of a person's private and family life. To many people what makes a home is not so much the building and the possession in it, but the sense of security and peace that is offered there. It is this sense of security and peace that to many is extremely important. Therefore an uninvited person entering a home and committing a crime or intending to commit a crime destroys the one place where people find security and peace. Simester and Sullivan explain:

> 'It is hardly surprising that house burglary, in particular, causes victims great distress even if they were absent at the material time. The victim of such a burglary is unable to live assured of her safety even in her own home. Most people, when their safety cannot be taken for granted, are no longer free. One of the foundations of autonomous life is destroyed.'

Such an explanation is convincing, but not unproblematic. First, it presents a rather 'home-made apple pie' image of a home. Victims of domestic violence and parents caring for constantly screaming babies or rebellious teenagers might not recognize the description of a home as a haven of peace but rather see home as a prison. Indeed there is strong evidence that women are more likely to face violence in the home than outside it. Nevertheless, that image of home is one shared by many, even as an ideal if not in reality. Secondly, it does not explain why invasion into office buildings and garden sheds are regarded as burglaries. It is, however, noticeable that in sentencing, burglaries of homes are not treated as more serious than burglaries of commercial premises.

Another explanation for the existence of the offence of burglary is that it is more likely to lead to violence. A person who finds a burglar in his home may well resort to violence (see the controversial case of *Tony Martin*), and is more likely to do so than in a case of pickpocketing for example. In particular, in burglary the victim has nowhere safe to run to, to escape from any feared attacker. This argument would then be that this is a form of conduct that is particularly likely to lead to serious violence and for that reason should be prohibited.

Summary

12.1 Robbery is theft accompanied by the use or threat of force. The force must occur at the time of, or immediately before, the theft, and for the purpose of stealing.

12.2 Assault with intent to rob is also an offence. There must be an assault or battery made with the intent to commit robbery.

12.3 There are two main types of burglary. Both require entry into a building as trespasser. A person who enters without authority is a trespasser. It has been held that a person is a trespasser who enters a building for a purpose that is outside the scope of the permission given, expressly or impliedly, by the owner. The accused must know or be reckless that he is a trespasser. One type of burglary requires that the accused entered the building with the intention of committing a further offence, such as stealing something in the building. The offence was complete as soon as the building was entered with the necessary intent.

Burglary may also be committed by stealing or inflicting grievous bodily harm once inside the building. In this case the offence is not complete until the further act has been committed.

12.4 It is aggravated burglary to commit burglary with a firearm, explosive or weapon of offence.

12.5 Handling stolen goods requires that the goods be stolen at the time of the act of handling. 'Stolen' means appropriated by theft, or obtained by deception or blackmail. Goods are also 'stolen' if they are the proceeds of stolen goods and have represented the stolen goods in the hands of the thief or a handler. Goods may cease to be stolen if they are returned to their owner or other lawful custody. There are two main ways of handling stolen goods: handling by receiving; and handling by retaining, removing, disposing or realizing the goods. The second form of handling must be done to assist, or for the benefit of, another. A sale of stolen goods is not undertaken for the benefit of the buyer. An act of handling cannot be committed at the same time as the original theft, but may amount to a separate theft in respect of the same goods. All forms of handling require dishonesty and the fact that the handler knew or believed the goods to be stolen. Belief is not the same as suspicion; it amounts to being virtually certain that the goods are stolen. If the accused has a recent conviction for theft or handling, this can be used to prove knowledge or belief that the goods were stolen.

Case Notes

Attorney-General's Reference (No. 1 of 1974) [1974] 2 All ER 899. Court of Appeal

The accused was acquitted of handling stolen goods at the direction of the trial judge. A police officer had found an unlocked car containing clothing that he suspected was stolen. He immobilized the car and waited until the accused returned and tried to start the engine. He then questioned the accused and arrested him, as he was not satisfied with his explanation. At the trial the judge accepted the defence submission that the clothing was no longer stolen at the time of the act of handling, since it had been taken into lawful custody by the officer. The Court of Appeal was asked for its opinion as to whether goods are restored to lawful custody when a police officer suspects them to be stolen and keeps them under observation with a view to tracing the thief or handler. The court held that goods would cease to be stolen once they had been taken into the possession of a police officer acting in the execution of his duty. If the officer was merely watching the goods, and was of an open mind as to whether he would take them into possession, they would remain stolen. This would depend primarily on the intention of the officer. The issue should therefore be left to the jury to determine.

Attorney-General's References (Nos 1 and 2 of 1979) [1979] 2 All ER 143. Court of Appeal

See Chapter 11 case notes.

Bloxham [1983] 1 AC 109. House of Lords

The appellant was convicted of handling stolen goods. He had bought a car from an unidentified third party without realizing that it was stolen. When the seller disappeared without producing the registration papers, the appellant realized that the car was stolen; he then sold the car to another person who was prepared to buy it without registration documents. The appellant argued at the trial, and on appeal, that his disposal of the car had been for his own benefit and not for the benefit of 'another person' as required by s.22(1) Theft Act 1968. The House of Lords agreed with this argument and allowed the appeal. Lord Bridge held that a purchaser of stolen goods was not 'another person' for whose benefit the seller acted.

Collins [1973] QB 100. Court of Appeal

The appellant was convicted of burglary contrary to s.9(1)(a) Theft Act 1968. It was alleged that he had entered, as a trespasser and with intent to rape, the bedroom of a girl that he knew slightly. His appeal was allowed on the basis that it was unclear whether or not he was in fact a trespasser when he entered the room. There was evidence that the girl, mistaking him for her boyfriend, had invited him into the room before he entered it. It was also held that being a trespasser requires an element of knowledge or at least recklessness on the part of the accused, as to whether or not he is entering the building without permission.

Ghosh [1982] QB 1053. Court of Appeal

See Chapter 11 case notes.

Hale (1978) 68 Cr App Rep 415. Court of Appeal

The appellant and another were convicted of robbery, contrary to s.8 Theft Act 1968. They had entered the victim's house and the appellant had taken a jewelry box while his companion tied the victim up. It was argued on appeal that the force was used on the victim after the theft was complete, and was not therefore immediately before or at the time of the theft, as required by s.8. The appeal was dismissed, on the ground that an appropriation may continue over a period of time. It is for the jury to decide whether the appropriation has ceased.

Hall (1985) 81 Cr App Rep 260. Court of Appeal

The appellant was convicted of handling stolen goods. He was an antique dealer and had been found with the goods, in company with two other men who later pleaded guilty to burglary. He claimed that he had not been told by the other two men that the goods were stolen, but had become very wary and refused to purchase them. He appealed against conviction on the ground that the trial judge had not sufficiently emphasized the distinction between belief and suspicion. His appeal was dismissed on the ground that the trial judge had not misled the jury by confusing belief and suspicion. The court held that 'belief' fell short of knowledge – it was the state of mind of a person who was not certain that goods were stolen, but who felt that there was no other reasonable conclusion in all the circumstances. However, mere suspicion was not enough to amount to 'knowledge or belief'.

Jenkins [1984] AC 242. Court of Appeal

The appellant and others were charged with burglary, contrary to s.9 (1)(b) Theft Act 1968 (entry of a building as trespassers and inflicting grievous bodily harm on a person in the building). The jury, after a direction from the trial judge, acquitted the appellants of burglary, but convicted them of assault occasioning actual bodily harm. They appealed against conviction and the appeals were allowed on the basis that 'inflict grievous bodily harm' in s.9 Theft Act 1968 had the same meaning as in s.20 Offences against the Person Act 1861.

Pitham and Hehl (1976) 65 Cr App Rep 45. Court of Appeal

The two appellants were convicted of handling stolen goods. They had agreed to buy some furniture from a third man. The appellants were aware that the third man was not the true owner of the goods (who was in prison). They went to the victim's house in a furniture van. They appealed against conviction on the ground that their alleged act of handling had been committed 'in the course of stealing'. The appeals were dismissed. It was held that the third man had stolen the furniture by offering to sell it to the appellants and this was an assumption of the rights of the owner; the appropriation was then complete. Any later dealing by the appellants was therefore not 'in the course of stealing'.

Shelton (1986) 83 Cr App Rep 379. Court of Appeal

The appellant was convicted of theft and obtaining by deception. He had obtained money on cheques taken from a chequebook that had been stolen that day. He had also been charged with handling, and had submitted at the trial that he should be acquitted of both theft and handling if the jury was not sure which offence he had committed. The trial judge directed an acquittal on the handling charge and left the theft charge to the jury. The appeal was dismissed. The Court held that it was proper to charge with both theft and handling in the alternative, but the jury should be told that the accused could not be convicted of being both a thief and a handler in respect of the same transaction. A conviction for theft may be based on the original appropriation from the victim, or on a later appropriation by the accused from someone else, if the indictment is sufficiently widely drafted.

Smith and Jones [1976] 3 All ER 54. Court of Appeal

The appellants were convicted of burglary contrary to s.9(1)(b). They had entered the house of Smith's father and taken two television sets. They appealed against conviction on the basis that Smith had general permission to enter his father's house, and could not therefore be a trespasser. The appeals were dismissed. The court held that it was trespass to enter a building for a purpose that is outside the permission given, if the accused realized or was reckless as to whether he was entering outside that permission.

Walkington [1979] 2 All ER 716. Court of Appeal

The appellant was convicted of burglary, contrary to s.9 (1)(a) Theft Act 1968. He had gone behind a three-sided counter in a department store and attempted to steal money from the till, which was open but empty. At the trial, the accused submitted that there had been no trespass, but the trial judge ruled that if the jury were satisfied that the area behind the counters was prohibited to customers, and that the accused realized this, then this was a trespass. The appeal was dismissed. The court held that the question of trespass was rightly left to the jury; it was a question of fact whether the public was excluded from the area behind the counters. It was also held that the fact that the till might be, and was, empty did not affect the appellant's intention to steal money from it if he could.

Further Reading

Pace discusses burglary, while the other three articles consider aspects of the law on handling stolen property.

Pace, 'Burglarious Trespass' [1985] *Criminal Law Review* 716.
Spencer, 'Handling and Taking Risks – A Reply to Professor Williams' [1985] *Criminal Law Review* 440.
Spencer, 'Handling, Theft and the *Mala Fide* Purchaser' [1985] *Criminal Law Review* 92.
Williams, 'Handling, Theft and the Purchaser who takes a Chance' [1985] *Criminal Law Review* 432.

13 Deception Offences

> **Key words**
>
> - **Deception** – an untruthful representation.
> - **Forgery** – the making of a document that lies about itself with intent to persuade others to accept the document as true and as a result suffer a loss.

13.1 The Deception Offences

Why has the law treated offences where a defendant has acquired another's property by deception differently from cases where the defendant has taken the victim's property? Indeed in Chapter 11.3 it was noted that following the House of Lord's decision in *Gomez*, nearly all cases of obtaining property contrary to s.15 now could be charged as theft. Could not theft and the deception offences all be treated as examples of wrongful interference with a person's property interests? It is submitted that there is a strong case for regarding deception offences as different from theft and the taking of property. First, a deception involves not only the interference with the defendant's property but also a manipulation of the victim. By the deception, the defendant has persuaded the victim to hand over his property or perform a service. In a way, the defendant has treated the victim as a puppet, and has certainly infringed his autonomy in a manner that does not take place in a theft. Second, the ownership of property and the free transfer of property by buying, selling, giving and receiving is an important aspect of our society. In acquiring property or services by a deception, the defendant is undermining this crucial aspect of our society. The deception offences are therefore there to protect society, as well as to highlight the special harm that the victim has suffered as a result of the deception. Whether the special harm means that deception offences should be regarded as a particularly bad kind of theft or something morally quite distinct from theft is a matter of debate (see Chapter 11.3).

The deception offences are an important group among the offences against property. They are now found in the Theft Act 1968 and the Theft Act 1978. In addition, the common law offence of conspiracy to defraud (see Chapter 18.3.1) has close links with the statutory deception offences.

Under the original scheme in the 1968 Act, there were two major deception offences: obtaining property by deception under s.15 and obtaining a pecuniary advantage (essentially the avoidance of debt) by deception under s.16. But s.16 proved to be unworkable as it stood, and one concisely worded subsection – s.16(2)(a) – caused such difficulty that it had to be repealed and replaced by a number of more specific offences in the Theft Act 1978. We now need to discuss six offences instead of two, but there are several common elements among them. The 1968 Act also covers other frauds, such as false accounting and false statements by company directors, which are outside the scope of this book.

The six deception offences which will be covered here are:

- Obtaining property by deception, s.15 of the 1968 Act;
- Obtaining a pecuniary advantage by deception, s.16(2)(b) and (c) of the 1968 Act;
- Obtaining services by deception, s.1 of the 1978 Act;
- Securing the remission of a liability by deception, s.2(1)(a) of the 1978 Act;
- Inducing a creditor, by deception, to wait for or forgo payment, s.2(1)(b) of the 1978 Act;
- Obtaining exemption, by deception, from liability to make a payment, s.2(1)(c) of the 1978 Act.

There is a certain amount of overlap between these offences themselves and, as we have already noted, between the deception offences and theft. Where there is an overlap, the prosecuting authorities will often prefer to include a charge of theft (see, for example, *Williams* (1980)*) because of the difficulty in proving, in the case of s.15, the element of deception and a causal link between the deception and the obtaining. These elements, together with dishonesty, are found in each of the deception offences covered in this chapter, and we will look at them in more detail in the context of s.15.

13.2   Obtaining Property by Deception

Section 15 Theft Act 1968 provides:

> '(1)   A person who by any deception dishonestly obtains property belonging to another, with the intention of permanently depriving the other of it, shall on conviction on indictment be liable to imprisonment for a term not exceeding ten years.
>
> (2)   For purposes of this section a person is to be treated as obtaining property if he obtains ownership, possession or control of it, and

"obtain" includes obtaining for another or enabling another to obtain or retain.

(3) . . . [not relevant to this chapter]

(4) For purposes of this section "deception" means any deception (whether deliberate or reckless) by words or conduct as to fact or as to law, including a deception as to the present intentions of the person using the deception or any other person.'

The offence can be broken down into the following elements:

1. A deception

A deception is a representation which is untrue. Even if the defendant believes the statement to be false, if in fact it is true the defendant is not guilty under s.15, although she may be liable for attempted deception. The deception may be by words or conduct, and can be express or implied. The representation can concern facts or law. Most deceptions will involve untruthful statements made by the accused. However sometimes the deception is not straightforward. Here are some of the other ways in which a deception can be made:

(a) Deception by conduct

A deception by conduct may arise, for example, where a defendant wears a uniform and so purports to be an authorized official. In *Barnard*, a man dressed in a university cap and gown and was granted credit facilities. It was held that by wearing this garb he was representing that he was a member of Oxford University. The deception by conduct need not involve a disguise. If a person went to a wedding reception to which he had not been invited and ate the food, the very act of walking into the room where the reception was taking place and eating the food may be taken as representing that he was an invited guest. In *Ray*, the House of Lords held that the accused, who remained seated in a restaurant after having finished a meal, thereby represented that he was an honest customer who intended to pay for his meal before leaving. The accused had apparently intended to pay at the outset, but had changed his mind; the continuing representation became a deliberate deception. This case indicates that the courts can be quite creative in deciding whether there is a deception by conduct.

(b) Implied deceptions

If the defendant makes a statement which is literally true, but implies a statement which is untrue then this may amount to a deception. An example of an implied deception is *Williams* (1980), where it was said that the presentation of obsolete Yugoslav banknotes at a bureau de change involved an implied representation that the notes were valid currency. The deception may be implied from the surrounding circumstances as well as the conduct of the accused. The jury should ask itself how a reasonable person in the victim's shoes would have understood the defendant's statements. In *Silverman* it was held that in giving a quotation for work, the accused was impliedly representing that the quotation was fair and reasonable. However this was only because the quote was given in 'circumstances of mutual trust' (the victims were elderly and had employed the accused to do work for them on several occasions in the past). If there had been no relationship between the builders and the 'victims', the court indicated that a quotation for work would not include the implied representation that the quote was reasonable.

(c) Statement of opinion or intentions as deceptions

A statement of opinion can be deceptive if what is said is not truly the speaker's opinion. In some circumstances a statement of opinion may include an implication that a speaker has grounds for her belief, particularly where the victim is relying on the expertise or special knowledge of the accused (*King and Stockwell**). In *King*, the car dealer stated that the odometer reading 'may not be correct'. This implied that he was not sure whether it was correct. In fact he knew it was incorrect and so the statement of opinion amounted to a misrepresentation. A similar point can be made about representations concerning intentions. But it should be stressed that the fact that the speaker changes her mind and so does not carry out her intention does not make the original statement of intent itself untrue and therefore deceptive.

(d) Silence as a deception

Whether silence alone can amount to a deception is a controversial issue. One might think that silence cannot be 'words or conduct' as required by the definition in s.15(4) but, where there is a duty to speak, silence can amount to a deception, in line with the law's general approach to omissions. Here are some of the circumstances in which silence may amount to a deception:

(i) Where there is a legal duty to reveal information (for example, because of a contract between the victim and the defendant, as in *Firth*) and the defendant fails to reveal it.

(ii) Where there is a special relationship of trust between the victim and the defendant which leads the victim to believe that the defendant is providing all the relevant information (*Silverman*). A similar obligation arises if the defendant has special knowledge upon which the victim is relying (*Whiteside and Antoniou*).

(iii) Where the defendant has made a statement that although true at the time has become untrue, the failure to correct the statement can amount to a representation. For example, in *Rai* the defendant applied to a City Council for a grant to install a downstairs bathroom in his house for his elderly and ill mother who was living with him. He was told the grant was approved, but shortly after his mother died. He did not tell the Council that she had died and the builders carried out the work. He was convicted of obtaining property by deception because although he initially made a truthful statement, this had become untrue and so the defendant was under a duty to correct his statement.

2. *Obtaining property belonging to another*

Turning now to the question of what is obtained under s.15: the property belonging to another. There is no need to show that the property was of any value. Obtaining a passport by deception would amount to an offence under s.15 for example (*Ashbee*). Section 34(1) Theft Act 1968 provides that s.4(1) shall apply to the understanding of property belonging to another in s.15, but the rest of s.4 does not. This means that land, for example, can be obtained by deception, even though it cannot be stolen. The concept of 'belonging to another' is similar to that for theft, as s.5(1) applies to the meaning of 'belonging to another, under s.15(1).

By s.15(2), 'obtaining' means acquiring ownership, possession or control. So, as with theft, it is possible for an owner of property to obtain it by deception from another who has possession of it as long as the *mens rea* requirements are satisfied. So in *Turner (No. 2)*, had the owner of the car untruthfully told the garage owners that he needed the car urgently to take his wife to hospital, and so persuaded them to let him drive the car away without paying for the repairs, an offence under s.15 would have been committed.

It should be added that there is no need to show that *the defendant* obtained the property belonging to another, although this will usually be the case. The accused will also have committed the s.15 offence if as a result of his deception *someone else* obtains property that belonged to another.

3. *Causation*

There must be a causal link between the deception and the obtaining of the property. In other words, the obtaining of the property must have occurred because the deception was made. This has several implications. First, the deception must take place before the property is obtained. In *Collis-Smith*, the accused asked for petrol to be put into his car, and when it was in the tank he made a false representation that he was using the car on his employer's business and that the cost of the petrol could be added to his employer's account. He was convicted of obtaining the petrol by deception, but the conviction was quashed on appeal as the deception had occurred after the accused obtained the petrol. He could now be convicted of an offence under s.2 Theft Act 1978.

Second, it must be proved that the deception was effective – that the victim actually was deceived. If he was not, the complete offence was not committed, even if the victim still handed the property over to the accused. If therefore the defendant pretended that he needed money to get a bus home, but the victim realized that this was not true and that the defendant was really going to use the money to buy alcohol, there would be no s.15 offence. In such a case, the defendant could be convicted of an attempted s.15 offence. Because of this requirement that the victim must be made to believe something untrue, it seems that one cannot deceive a machine (*Goodwin*). If one did use dishonest means to acquire property from a machine, the correct charge would be theft. There are special rules in deciding whether the accused has deceived a company – it is necessary to show that the people deceived were authorized to deal with the transaction in question and were not parties to the fraud (*Rozeik*).

Third, it must be proved that the deception was operative – that it was the deception that caused the victim to hand over the property. In *Laverty*, for example, there was an undoubted deception by the accused that a stolen car that he had sold to the victim bore its original number plates. However, the conviction was quashed by the Court of Appeal on the ground that there was insufficient evidence that this particular deception had induced the victim to buy the car. The evidence was that the victim had bought the car because he believed the accused to be the owner and entitled to sell the car. The statement about the number plates had not influenced his decision to buy the car. The fact that the victim was influenced by other factors as well as the deception need not be fatal to the prosecution, as long as the deception was sufficiently influential on the victim. It seems sufficient to show that the victim would not have acted as he did but for the deception. This requirement is also relevant where the victim checks up on what the defendant states. So if an antique dealer falsely states that a chair is two hundred years old, but the victim seeks a second opinion from an (unreliable) friend who confirms what the antique dealer has said, a jury may take some convincing that it was what the antique dealer said, rather than what the friend said, that caused the victim to buy the chair. It should be added that it is no defence for the defendant to claim that most people would not have been affected by the deception or that the victim should not have been influenced by the deception, if the victim actually was (*Talbott*).

In some cases, the courts have formulated the test in the form of a question: if the victim had known of the true facts, would he have still been willing to conclude the transaction? On this test, the conviction in *Laverty* should probably have been upheld. In *Doukas**, the accused was a waiter in a hotel and was found with bottles of wine which he had bought, intending to substitute them for the hotel's own carafe wine. The question before the Court of Appeal was whether the hotel guests would have been induced to buy the wine by his deception. Geoffrey Lane LJ said:

> 'Certainly as far as the wine is concerned, we have no doubt at all that the hypothetical customer, faced with the waiter saying to him: "This of course is not hotel wine, this is stuff which I imported into the hotel myself and I am going to put the proceeds of the wine, if you pay, into my own pocket", would certainly answer, so far as we can see, "I do not want your wine, kindly bring me the hotel carafe wine" . . . The hypothetical customer must be reasonably honest as well as being reasonably intelligent and it seems to us incredible that any customer, to whom the true situation was made clear, would willingly make himself a party to what was obviously a fraud by the waiter on his employers.'

Doukas is often contrasted with *Rashid*, where the Court of Appeal was not prepared to assume that a passenger on a British Rail train would refuse to buy a sandwich which was prepared by a guard using his own bread and butter rather than being an official British Rail sandwich. It is not easy to see why a hotel guest should be any less willing to assist an employee to defraud his or her employer than a British Rail passenger. That is unless one accepts that people will do anything to avoid eating an official British Rail sandwich!

In *Ray*, like *Doukas*, the House of Lords were prepared to infer that the deception was operative in the absence of direct evidence. Lord Morris said:

> 'if the waiter thought that if he left the restaurant to go to the kitchen the [accused] would at once run out, he (the waiter) would not have left the restaurant and would have taken suitable action. The waiter proceeded on the basis that the implied representation made to him (i.e. of an honest intention to pay) was effective. The waiter was caused to refrain from taking certain courses of action which but for the representation he would have taken.'

This reasoning is a little strained as it is unlikely that the waiter was aware of the implied deception that the House of Lords held the customer was making and, certainly, the implied deception did not cause the waiter to leave the eating area and so enable the customers to escape. In *Miller*, a defendant pretended to be an authorized taxi driver and then charged customers an exorbitant rate. Unfortunately for the prosecution, the victims gave evidence that by the time the journey was over they had realized that the driver was not an official taxi driver, but they paid the amount requested, because they felt pressurized. In the light of these facts it appears that the obtaining was not caused by the deception. The Court of Appeal was able to get around this difficulty by arguing that looking at the incident as a whole, the deception had caused the obtaining: had the victims not been deceived into thinking that this was a proper taxi they would not have got on board and would not have later felt pressurized into paying. These cases suggest that the courts are on occasion rather lax about this causation requirement, particularly where it is clear that a dishonest deception has been made as a result of which the defendant has acquired property. A similar point can be made in the cases involving cheques, which we will be considering later.

4.   The deception must be deliberate or reckless.

As s.15(4) indicates, the s.15 offence requires an element of *mens rea* in that the deception must be 'deliberate or reckless'; a negligent deception will not be enough. In *Staines*, James LJ said, 'this Court accepts . . . that in this section "reckless" does mean more than being careless, does mean more than being negligent, and does involve an indifference to or disregard of the feature of whether a statement be true or false'. This suggests that the *mens rea* is not limited to *Cunningham* recklessness, but can include a defendant who could not care less whether the representation he made was true or not. However it is clear that a defendant who honestly, even if unreasonably, believes that the representation she has made is true will not have made a deception.

5.   Dishonesty

It must be shown that the defendant was dishonest. Dishonesty possesses the same meaning as in theft, except that s.2 Theft Act 1968 does not apply to s.15. That said, in practice it is very unlikely that a jury would find a defendant who fell within the terms of s.2(1) dishonest (*Wood*). The leading case on dishonesty is *Ghosh** (see Chapter 11), and this case in fact concerned a conviction for obtaining property (money) by deception. As Lord Lane pointed out in that case, usually there does not seem to be much that dishonesty can add to the *mens rea* requirement, at least where it is alleged that the deception was deliberate:

> 'if a person knows that he is not telling the truth he is guilty of dishonesty. Indeed deliberate deception is one of the . . . most obvious forms of dishonesty. One wonders therefore whether "dishonesty" in s.15(1) adds anything, except in the case of reckless deception.'

However, one effect of the requirement of dishonesty is that an accused may rely on a 'claim of right' where, for example, he uses a deception to obtain property to which he believes he has a legal right. It is probable that a jury would regard a deception in some other circumstances as compatible with the current standards of honesty of 'ordinary decent people'.

6. *Intention to permanently deprive*
The *mens rea* for s.15 includes the intention of permanently depriving the victim of the property, which is also necessary for theft. Section 15(3) specifically provides that s.6 shall apply, although as we have seen in relation to theft, it is of limited use in helping to define what is meant by an intention of permanently depriving (see Chapter 11.7).

13.3   Obtaining a Pecuniary Advantage by Deception

The scope of this offence (s.16 Theft Act 1968) has been greatly reduced by its partial repeal and replacement by the Theft Act 1978. It is an offence to obtain, dishonestly and by deception, any pecuniary advantage (a financial gain). However, the scope of pecuniary advantage is very limited and is exhaustively defined in s.16(2):

'The cases in which a pecuniary advantage within the meaning of this section is to be regarded as obtained for a person are cases where
(a)   [repealed]
(b)   he is allowed to borrow by way of overdraft, or to take out any policy of insurance or annuity contract, or obtains an improvement of the terms on which he is allowed to do so; or
(c)   he is given the opportunity to earn remuneration or greater remuneration in an office or employment, or to win money by betting.'

Section 16 is therefore restricted to only the following kinds of pecuniary advantage obtained dishonestly by a deception:

1. *'Being allowed to borrow by way of overdraft'*
This applies where a person writes a cheque or uses a credit card to exceed the agreed overdraft or credit limit. It has been held that a person is 'allowed to borrow by way of overdraft' if he uses his cheque card to run up an overdraft without the bank's prior permission (*Waites** and *Bevan*). It is therefore no defence for an accused to say to her bank: 'you did not allow me to have the overdraft, in fact you had forbidden me to have one!' The deception here will be made to the provider of the goods or service for

which the cheque or credit card is used to pay. As a result of the deception and the agreement between the bank and the provider, the overdraft is created. (See, further, *Hot Topic*, at the end of this chapter.)

2. *Taking out a policy of insurance or annuity contract, or obtaining an improvement of the terms on which he is allowed to do so*

This would cover the case where in order to get a cheap car insurance, an accused falsely states that he has not been involved in any accident in the past five years. There is, in fact, a difficulty here because in civil law the insurance policy may be void if it is obtained by deception, and that would mean that in civil law the insurance policy never existed. However, it has been held in these circumstances that the accused is still 'allowed to take out a policy of insurance' and so the offence has been committed (*Alexander*).

3. *Being given the opportunity to earn remuneration or greater remuneration in an office or employment*

This would arise where the defendant lies about his qualifications in order to get a job, for example. The provision is carefully worded. Consider the following example. If a workman untruthfully tells a homeowner that her roof needs repairing and she agrees to employ him to do the job, then when she pays him at the end of the job it may be thought that the payment is more directly caused by the completion of the job than by the deception. This may be so, but the s.16 offence talks about being given the *opportunity* to earn remuneration and certainly the workman has done that. That said, in *King and Stockwell* the Court of Appeal upheld a conviction under s.15 of attempting to obtain by deception payment for work that the victim agreed should be done, following a deception from the defendant. The court said that it was for the jury to decide whether the deception had been the operative cause, bearing in mind all the circumstances of the case.

4. *'Being given the opportunity . . . to win money by betting'*

This might arise where a betting event is only available to certain people. For example, if a Student Union at a University held a raffle which was only open to members of the university, but the defendant falsely represented he was a member and was therefore allowed to buy a ticket, he would have committed the s.16 offence. It should be noted that he does not even have to win anything in the raffle to be convicted; it was enough he had the opportunity to win.

13.4   Obtaining Services by Deception

Section 1 Theft Act 1978 provides:

'(1)   A person who by any deception dishonestly obtains services from another shall be guilty of an offence.

(2)   It is an obtaining of services where the other is induced to confer a benefit by doing some act, or causing or permitting some act to be done, on the understanding that the benefit has been or will be paid for.

(3)   Without prejudice to the generality of subsection (2) above, it is an obtaining of services where the other is induced to make a loan, or to cause or permit a loan to be made, on the understanding that any payment (whether by way of interest or otherwise) will be or has been made in respect of the loan.'

This section makes it clear that it is necessary to prove that the deception caused the obtaining of the benefit. The definition of 'conferring a benefit' is wide. It includes doing something for somebody (for example, cutting hair, teaching someone to play the piano, delivering goods) as well as allowing somebody to do something (for example, to use sporting facilities, or allowing someone to look around a country house). There are however three important limitations on what counts as a benefit:

1 The benefit must be provided 'on the understanding that the benefit has been or will be paid for.' This means that lying in order to get a gratuitous service will not constitute an offence. So, James would not commit an offence if he persuaded his neighbour Elizabeth to weed his garden, after untruthfully saying that he has injured his back. Similarly, if Guy persuaded a barber to give him a free cut, claiming untruthfully that he was an impoverished actor, he would commit no offence under s.1 (although it may be an offence under s.2 Theft Act 1978). The requirement that the offence must be provided on the expectation that it will be paid for means that the offence can be committed even though the accused pays for the service as expected. For example, a seventeen-year-old who tells a cinema that he is nineteen in order to get into an 18-rated film is guilty of the offence, as long as dishonesty is made out. This is so, even though the cinema has not suffered a loss. An issue, yet to be addressed by the courts, is whether a service provided on the understanding that another service will be provided is 'paid for'. Simester and Sullivan give the example of a defendant who tricks the victim into writing a criminal law essay for him by promising to have sexual inter-

course in return. Will the promise of sexual intercourse be sufficient to 'pay for' the essay writing?

2 Section 3(2) requires proof that the victim did some act or permitted some *act* to be done as a result of the deception. This may suggest that if a passenger on a train untruthfully tells a guard that he has paid for a valid ticket, there may be no *act* which provides a benefit that has been caused by the deception.

3 There is some debate over the use of the word 'benefit'. Could the seventeen-year-old who has seen the 18-rated film claim that the film was harmful to him and so not a 'benefit'? Professor Griew has suggested that the word 'benefit' simply refers to the thing that has been paid for, and does not limit the offence to obtaining beneficial services. However, Professor Smith has suggested the word must have some meaning, and that 'benefit' indicates the services must at least have been lawful. In which case, a man who deceives a prostitute into letting him have sexual intercourse with her may not commit this offence.

Subsection (3) was added by the Theft (Amendment) Act 1996, reversing the case of *Halai**, which suggested that obtaining a mortgage or loan might not be a service. *Halai* also suggested that paying money into a bank account or writing a cheque may not be a service, as it is not normally paid for directly. This aspect of the case is not reversed by the statute but the Court of Appeal in *Graham*, *Cummings-John* and *Naviede* has suggested that *Halai* was wrongly decided and so is no longer a sound authority.

The *mens rea* for the s.3 offence is twofold: that required for the deception (see Chapter 11.6) and dishonesty.

13.5   Evasion of Liability by Deception

Section 2 Theft Act 1978 provides:

'(1) Subject to subsection (2) below, where a person by any deception -
  (a) dishonestly secures the remission of the whole or part of any existing liability to make a payment, whether his own liability or another's; or
  (b) with intent to make permanent default in whole or in part on any existing liability to make a payment, or with intent to let another do so, dishonestly induces the creditor or any person claiming payment on behalf of the creditor to wait for payment (whether or not the due date for payment is deferred) or to forgo payment;

(c) dishonestly obtains any exemption from or abatement of liability to make a payment; he shall be guilty of an offence.

(2) For purposes of this section "liability" means legally enforceable liability; and subsection (1) shall not apply in relation to a liability that has not been accepted or established to pay compensation for a wrongful act or omission.

(3) For purposes of subsection (1)(b) a person induced to take in payment a cheque or other security for money by way of conditional satisfaction of a pre-existing liability is to be treated not as being paid but as being induced to wait for payment.

(4) For purposes of subsection (1)(c) "obtains" includes obtaining for another or enabling another to obtain.'

13.5.1 Distinguishing the Different Offences in Section 2

Section 2(1) creates three separate offences in subsections (a), (b) and (c) (*Holt*). The section has been difficult to interpret but the courts have said that the wording of the section should be given its ordinary meaning (*Sibarte*). There is a close connection, and some overlap, between subsections 2(1)(a), 2(1)(b) and 2(1)(c).

It may be useful to consider a core example of each of the three subsections. The following examples are not designed to give a complete definition of each subsection, but to provide a flavour of the key idea covered by the subsections.

1 Subsection 2(1)(c) deals with a situation where by a deception the defendant obtains an exemption from having to pay for something. For example, where Toni visits a hairdresser and asks the hairdresser to give her a free haircut by untruthfully stating that she is an impoverished student.

2 Subsection 2(1)(a) covers the case where the defendant, by deception, persuades the victim to let the defendant off the debt or part of the debt. For example, where Toni receives the haircut and then asks the hairdresser to let her off the charge because she is an impoverished student (which she is not).

3 Subsection 2(1)(b) creates an offence where the defendant persuades the victim to let him or her off the debt or part of the debt. For example, where Toni is asked to pay and asks if she can pay next week because she is an impoverished student, but in fact Toni intends never to pay.

One way of distinguishing the subsections is to ask the following two questions.

1 At the time of the deception, did the defendant owe the victim money? If the answer is 'yes' the case could fall into subsection 2(1) (a) or (b), as in those subsections the deception is used as a way of avoiding a liability that is already in existence. Go to question **2** to decide which of 2(1)(a) or (b) should be used. If the answer is 'no' then subsection 2(1)(c) should be used.

2 As a result of the deception, is the debt extinguished (so that no money is now owed)? If the answer is 'yes' then subsection 2(1)(a) may apply. If the answer is 'no' then subsection 2(1)(b) should be used. Subsection 2(1)(b) covers cases where the creditor is induced to wait for payment. Under subsection 2(1)(b) the debtor is ostensibly merely 'buying time': the creditor does not agree to extinguish liability altogether. To answer this second question requires an understanding of the complex civil contract law.

The above might suggest that a clear distinction can be drawn between the three offences. In fact the wording of each subsection is ambiguous and there are difficulties in interpreting the exact extent of the offences. It is to these we now turn:

13.5.2   Subsection 2(1)(a)

As already noted, subsection 2(1)(a) only applies where there is an existing liability to pay money (for example, a debt). It does not apply where the defendant persuades the victim to give a service or a good free. Nor does the subsection apply if in fact the debt is not legally enforceable (*Gee*).

The difference between remitting liability in subsection 2(1)(a) and forgoing payment in subsection 2(1)(b) is unclear. Commentators have been ingenious in suggesting possibilities: for example, that remission involves the creditor agreeing to alter his legal rights; whereas a creditor who forgoes payment is merely induced not to enforce rights which themselves remain unchanged (J. Smith, 1977). As we shall see, the courts have not been eager to rely on these fine distinctions.

13.5.3   Subsection 2(1)(b)

This subsection has an extra *mens rea* requirement: the intent to make permanent default. This was included following considerable debate as to whether the 'stalling debtor', who uses a deception in order to postpone payment of a debt, should be criminally liable at all. Often people who owe money seek to buy extra time for payment. Lies such as 'the cheque is in the post' are all too common. The criminal sanction will not normally help (and may hinder) the creditor in recovering the debt, and there are strong arguments in favour of keeping this kind of behaviour outside the criminal law. A compromise solution is found here: a defaulting debtor will only be criminally liable under this subsection if he uses a deception and intends never to pay.

However, this *mens rea* element in subsection 2(1)(b) has the effect of obscuring the distinction between 'remission' of liability in subsection 2(1)(a) and 'waiting for' payment in 2(1)(b). Under both paragraphs it is likely that the creditor will never be paid what is owed. The only real difference is that in the case of subsection 2(1)(a), the creditor agrees to this (as a result of a deception), whereas in the case of subsection 2(1)(b), the creditor merely agrees to wait for payment.

It should be stressed that subsection 2(1)(b) only applies where the defendant deceives the victim into waiting for payment from the defendant or a person for whom the defendant is acting as agent. It does not apply where the defendant deceives the victim into waiting for payment for a third party (*Gee*).

13.5.4   Subsection 2(1)(c)

The difference between subsection 2(1)(c) and the other two offences is that it covers cases where the deception takes place at the outset, before liability to make a payment is incurred. The Criminal Law Revision Committee, in its 13th Report, gives the example of obtaining a rate rebate by making a false statement, or obtaining a service such as air travel at a reduced rate by pretending to be a student. However, subsection 2(1)(c) has been applied to a case where the deception took place after the liability to pay was incurred, although before payment was requested. In *Sibartie*, the accused was held to have been rightly convicted of an attempt to evade liability by deception under subsection 2(1)(c). He had tried to leave through a ticket barrier on the London Underground, holding up an inapplicable season ticket. By waving the season ticket he had represented that it was a valid ticket for that journey; this deception enabled him to avoid payment of the 'excess' fare which would otherwise be demanded by the ticket collector, thus obtaining an 'exemption from' the liability to make that payment.

13.5.5   The Overlap between the Section 2 Offences

We can be relieved that the courts have so far taken a sensible approach to the construction of s.2 as a whole and have refused to be drawn into an intricate discussion of the exact boundaries between the different offences.

They have not proved sympathetic to appeals based on allegations that the wrong part of s.2 has been charged. In *Holt and Lee*, for example, the accused were charged under subsection 2(1)(b) with an attempt to induce a restaurant to forgo payment of their bill. They had been overheard planning to pretend that the waitress had already taken £5 in payment. They were convicted and appealed on the ground that they should have been charged under subsection 2(1)(a): securing the remission of the liability. The Court of Appeal dismissed the appeal, dwelling on the common features between all three paragraphs in s.2. The unique element in subsection 2(1)(b) was the intent to make permanent default, and as that had been proved, the accused had been properly convicted.

It was accepted in *Jackson* (1983) that the three paragraphs of s.2 are not mutually exclusive, so that the same conduct could fall within more than one subsection. In fact, as we have seen, this will often be the case if the courts continue to give a wide and flexible interpretation to s.2. Professor J. Smith has suggested that this may be a case of legislative overkill (J. Smith, 1983), but the courts are keen to avoid creating for themselves the 'judicial nightmare' (in the words of Edmund Davies LJ) of the pre-1978 legislation.

13.6   Making off without Payment

This offence was created to fill a gap that had become apparent some years after the Theft Act 1968 was enacted. Conduct known as 'bilking' – leaving without paying for goods or services – did not easily fall within either theft or any of the deception offences. The difficulties arose where the defendant obtained ownership of the goods or provision of the services before she was obliged to pay (for example, she had eaten a meal before being presented with the bill). If then the defendant, after receiving the goods or services, decided not to pay, there was grave difficulty in obtaining a conviction. There was no theft as the dishonesty only existed once the ownership in the goods had passed and so at that point the goods were not 'property belonging to another'. Similarly, for a deception offence it could not be said that the goods or services had been obtained by the deception (although see *Ray*, which shows that the courts were willing to go to some lengths to avoid this difficulty). The prosecution's job in such case is easier now because s.3 Theft Act 1978 creates a specific offence that requires neither a deception nor the appropriation of property belonging to another.

Section 3 Theft Act 1978 provides:

'(1) Subject to subsection (3) below, a person who, knowing that payment on the spot for any goods supplied or service done is required or expected from him, dishonestly makes off without having paid as required or expected and with intent to avoid payment of the amount due shall be guilty of an offence.

(2) For purposes of this section 'payment on the spot' includes payment at the time of collecting goods on which work has been done or in respect of which service has been provided.

(3) Subsection (1) above shall not apply where the supply of the goods or the doing of the service is contrary to law, or where the service done is such that payment is not legally enforceable.'

The offence can be separated into the following elements:

13.6.1 Goods Supplied or Service Done

There is no definition of 'service' but presumably the definition of 'services' in s.1(2) Theft Act 1978 would be used. By s.5(2) Theft Act 1978, the definition of 'goods' given in subsection 34(2)(b) of the Theft Act 1968 is used:

' "goods" except in so far as the context otherwise requires, includes money and every other description of property except land and includes things severed from the land by stealing.'

Probably the most common examples of the s.3 offence are people leaving restaurants, petrol pumps or taxis without paying the amount due. There is some doubt whether goods are *supplied* when an accused takes them from a self-service supermarket. Griew has argued that such goods are not supplied but 'exposed for sale' while Smith argues they are supplied in the sense that they are 'made available for sale'. In reality, most takings from supermarkets are easily charged using theft and so the question is unlikely to trouble the courts too much.

It will be noted that under subsection (3), the section only applies where 'the supply of the goods or the doing of the service is contrary to law, or where the service done is such that payment is not legally enforceable'. This requires reference to the law of contract. An example of a contract 'contrary to law' would be the sale of alcoholic liquor to a person under eighteen years old; an example of a contract which is not legally enforceable would be a wagering or gaming contract, or certain contracts with infants.

13.6.2   Payment on the Spot is Required or Expected

It is implied in s.3 that payment on the spot must not only be required or expected by the supplier, but actually legally due from the accused. A conviction under s.3 was quashed on this ground in *Troughton*. The accused, after a dispute with a taxi driver, apparently left without paying the fare. It was held that he was under no obligation to pay the driver because he had not been taken to the correct destination and the driver was therefore in breach of contract. The expectation of payment in the mind of the taxi driver was not enough.

The goods must be supplied or the goods provided on the understanding that there will be payment on the spot. Payment on the spot must be taken to include (though again this is not made explicit) cases where payment by cheque or credit card is acceptable. This is debatable because where there is payment by credit card, the restaurant (for example) will in fact only receive the money from the credit card company some time later. However, it is widely accepted that payment by cheque or credit card should be regarded as payment on the spot. If this were not so, the offence would be useless in practical terms since all establishments at risk from the 'bilker' are prepared to accept cheques and most will accept credit cards.

13.6.3   Makes Off

The accused must 'make off', and this has been held to mean that he must leave the spot where payment is required (*Brooks and Brooks*). Often in s.3 cases the defendant will try and leave the place surreptitiously, for example leaving a restaurant through a toilet window. However, this is not required by the offence. As the Court of Appeal explained, a making-off may 'be an exercise accompanied by the sound of trumpets or a silent stealing away after the folding of the tents'. So boldly walking out of a restaurant in full view of everyone will involve a making-off.

More difficult are cases where the victim has consented to the defendant leaving. Michael enjoys a pleasant meal at Moira's restaurant, but when presented with the bill he explains to Moira that he has left his wallet at home. He provides Moira with a false name and address, promising to return later that week to pay. Moira is taken in and waves him goodbye as he leaves the restaurant. Could it be said that Michael has 'made off'? The caselaw as yet does not provide an answer. However, J. R. Spencer has usefully suggested that 'making off' be defined as 'disappearing or leaving in a way that makes it difficult for the debtor to be traced'. If this definition was used, Michael could be said to have made off, although he could not if the address was correct.

The defendant must have made off from the spot where payment is expected. If therefore the defendant makes a dash for the door of the restaurant, but is apprehended by a waiter before he reaches it, he may not have committed the s.3 offence because payment would be expected anywhere inside the restaurant (*McDavitt*). In such a case, the correct charge would be an attempt to commit the s.3 offence. The Divisional Court has held that if the victim offers two places to pay – one where people are meant to pay and a second for anyone who forgot to pay the first time – it will only be once the second place is passed that the defendant will have gone past the spot where payment is expected or required (*Moberley* v. *Alsop*).

13.6.4   Without Having Paid as Required or Expected

The defendant must make off 'without having paid as required or expected'. It is interesting that the statute uses the word 'or' here. It may be that the law is concerned about someone who eats an unsatisfactory meal at a restaurant, and is so unhappy with it that he pays only half of his bill and walks out. If he is entitled under contract law to do this, he may have 'paid as required' (although not 'as expected') and so not have committed an offence. Where a defendant had by deception persuaded hotel owners to let him pay at some time in the future, he had not committed the offence because he had paid as expected (that is, he had paid nothing at the time of deception, as expected) (*Vincent*).

There is some doubt about whether a defendant who leaves a worthless cheque for payment can be said to have 'paid'. As such a defendant would commit an offence under subsection 2(1)(b) Theft Act 1978, the issue may be of limited significance. In *Hammond*, Morrison J suggested that a worthless cheque would be regarded as being payment, although he also suggested that counterfeit money would not. On the other hand, J. Smith (1977) argues that a worthless cheque is not payment 'as expected'.

13.6.5   Knowledge that Payment on the Spot is Required or
Expected

The *mens rea* for s.3 includes knowledge that payment on the spot is required or expected, and must coincide in time with the making off. So, there is no offence under s.3 if the defendant absentmindedly walks out of a restaurant, even if he remembers some time later that he forgot to pay, but does not return to the restaurant. At the time he made off he was not aware that payment was required or expected.

13.6.6   Dishonestly

This will be given its usual meaning in property offence (that is, as in the *Ghosh* direction, see Chapter 11).

13.6.7   Intent to Avoid Payment

There is an additional element to the *mens rea*: the intent to avoid payment of the amount due. Initially there was some doubt as to precisely what this phrase meant but the point has been resolved by the decision of the House of Lords in *Allen**. The accused left a hotel without paying a bill of over a £1000. He claimed that he genuinely expected to be able to pay the bill and intended to do so at some point. It was held in the House of Lords that an 'intent to avoid payment' means an intent to make permanent default, or never to pay, and not merely an intent to avoid payment on the spot or to defer payment. This interpretation of s.3 was supported by the 13th Report of the Criminal Law Revision Committee, which was referred to by the House of Lords in *Allen**. The decision is however controversial as it will be difficult for the prosecution to prove beyond reasonable doubt that the defendant did not intend to return to pay his bill. The decision also creates some overlap between s.3 and subsection 2(1)(b) Theft Act 1978.

13.7   Forgery

Some have argued that the offence of forgery is unnecessary. The deception offences and the law of attempts can be used to cover anyone seeking to use a forged document. However, the Law Commission (1973) has argued that the importance placed on the reliability of written documents is such as to justify a special offence.

The offence of forgery is contained in the Forgery and Counterfeiting Act 1981. The core concept is the use of a 'false instrument'. 'Instrument' is widely defined and includes documents, stamps, computer disks and bank notes (s.8). However, the Act only deals with instruments that lie about themselves (*More*). So, for example, if a man writes a letter to a conductor asking to perform at a concert and falsely claiming that he is a brilliant violinist who has made many recordings, the letter would not be a false instrument for the purpose of the Act: the letter tells no lies about itself, even if the letter does contain lies. If, however, the letter falsely purported to come from a well-known music critic, singing the violinist's praises, then it would be covered by the Act, as it would be telling lies about itself (that is, the authorship of the letter). Section 9 Forgery and Counterfeiting Act specifies the kinds of falsity covered by the Act. It includes lies as to who wrote the document, who amended it, the date the letter was written; and the circumstances in which it was written.

The *mens rea* for the offence has two elements:

1 The intention to induce someone to accept the instrument as genuine.
2 To induce someone to do or not to do an act to any person's prejudice as a result of accepting the document as genuine (*Ondhia*).

Prejudice here includes economic loss, but also includes causing a person to act 'in connection' with his employment or other official duties. The intention must be shown to exist at the time when the document was made (*Ondhia*)

Hot Topic: Offences Involving Cheques and Credit Cards

As mentioned earlier, the way in which the deception offences and theft deal with cheques, credit cards, and bank accounts is complex. It is an area of law that often confuses students. Four separate circumstances will be considered.

1. A dishonestly writes a cheque or uses a credit card to buy a car from B
If *A* is not authorized to use the cheque or credit card, then *A* can be seen as committing offences either against *B* or against *A*'s bank. Firstly let us consider offences that *A* has committed against *B*:

(a) *Obtaining the car by deception contrary to s.15 Theft Act 1968.* The House of Lords has stated that if a defendant writes a cheque, she represents that she is the person whose name appears on the cheque and that she believes that in the ordinary course of events the cheque will be honoured (*Charles**). If she uses a cheque guarantee card, she also represents that she has been authorized by the bank to use the card in this kind of transaction (*Charles*). If the defendant uses a credit card, she is held to represent that she is authorized to use the credit card (*Lambie**; *Nabina**). If any of these is untrue, when *A* writes the cheque or uses the credit card then *A* will be held to have deceived *B*.

In order to make out an offence against s.15 it must be shown that *A* obtained the car as a result of the deception. This causes a particular difficulty in cases involving cheque guarantee cards and credit cards, as when those are used the bank guarantees that the cheque or credit-card slip will be honoured as long as the shopkeeper performs various formalities. So, in fact, the shopkeeper may not really mind whether these representations are true or not, as long as he is confident that the bank has guaranteed payment. However, in two House of Lords cases, *Charles*, involving cheque guarantee cards, and *Lambie*, involving credit cards, their lordships were willing to assume that the victims could not have wanted to be involved in a fraud. So despite the victims' evidence that they were only concerned to ensure that the cheques or credit-card vouchers would be honoured by the bank, the House of Lords held in both cases that the deception of the defendant had caused the obtaining. This reflects the law's flexibility towards the causality requirement (see Chapter 13.2, above). So *B* will be

presumed to have relied upon *A*'s implied representation and, if those representations are false, the offence will be made out.

It should be added that these implied representations are rather artificial. Few
people are aware that they are making these representations when using cheques
or credit cards, and few shopkeepers realize such representations are being
made.

(b) *Offences against s.2 Theft Act 1978.* If *A* tells *B* a lie and so persuades him to
accept a cheque as payment for the car, rather than cash, then there may be an
offence under subsection 2(1)(b). This might arise where *A* untruthfully tells *B* he
has left his cash at home and only has his cheque book on him. Subsection 2(1)(b)
is concerned primarily with the defaulting debtor, and one obvious way of dishonestly obtaining more time to pay is by writing a cheque which the drawer knows
will 'bounce' because there are insufficient funds in his account to meet the
cheque. In the context of sale-of-goods law, a cheque is regarded as 'payment',
but s.2 provides that a person who is induced to take a cheque 'is to be treated
not as being paid but as being induced to wait for payment' (s.2(3)). We need to
be careful here. *A* must be induced to take the cheque as a result of the deception; if the creditor would accept a cheque in the ordinary course of dealing with
the accused then the deception may not be operative (*Andrews and Hedges*).
Also, under subsection 2(1)(b), it must be shown that *A* never intends to meet the
debt; if he is only 'buying time' by writing the cheque, this will not amount to an
offence.

Jackson (1983) is another example of how s.2 could be relevant here. The
accused used a stolen credit card to pay for petrol, and was charged under
subsection 2(1)(a). He claimed that the charge should have been brought under
subsection 2(1)(b), but the Court of Appeal held the possible application of
subsection 2(1)(b) was irrelevant here, as the conduct fell within the offence
charged: as a result of using the credit card, the seller of the petrol would look to
the bank issuing the card for payment rather than to the accused. The accused
had therefore secured the remission of an existing liability and so had committed
an offence under subsection 2(1)(a). So *Jackson* (1983) could be relied upon to
secure a conviction against *A* under subsection 2(1)(a) as well as under subsection 2(1)(b).

(c) *Theft of the car.* Normally a theft charge could not be made in this case. This
is because payment by cheque is effective payment for the price of goods; thus
ownership would pass from *B* to *A* and the car would belong to him by the time he
appropriates it by driving it away. Even if the cheque bounces, the cheque is still
payment for the car, although the seller can now sue the defendant on the basis
of the dishonoured cheque. If it could be shown that the parties specifically agreed
that ownership was not to pass until the cheque had been honoured then an
offence of theft may be made out.

Against the bank or credit-card company, *A* could be charged with the following:

(a) *Obtaining a pecuniary advantage by deception contrary to subsection 16(2)(b)
Theft Act 1968.* There is some authority for the view that by extending the overdraft
beyond agreed limits, *A* has by deception been 'allowed to borrow by way of overdraft' for the purpose of subsection 16(2)(b) (*Waites*). This is surprising, as it is not
a natural interpretation of the word 'allows' to say that a bank 'allows' someone to
exceed his overdraft to borrow money. Although there is no deception made
directly to the bank, the offence only requires the obtaining to be 'by a deception'
and here it could be said that the obtaining was caused by the deception to *B*.

(b) *Theft of money from the bank or credit-card company.* One might think that if the bank or credit-card company has to honour the cheque or credit-card voucher then *A* could be seen as having stolen that money from the bank. However, in those circumstances there is no direct appropriation of that money by *A*, as the money goes to the shop, and so there is no theft.

(c) *Section 1(3) Theft Act 1978.* It could be said that the loan of the money to *B* by the bank or credit-card company is a service which *A* has obtained by deception. Normally, to establish the offence of obtaining services by deception under s.1 Theft Act 1978 the service has to be one which is paid for, but s.1(3) specifically states that payment of interest on a loan may be sufficient to render the loan a service for the purposes of s.1. The phrase 'induces' rather than 'allows' is used in subsection 16(2)(b) and so seems more appropriate than the s.16 offence, although there again may still be some doubt over whether there is a deception made to the bank which causes the provision of the loan.

2. A dishonestly writes B a cheque in payment for services
Much of the discussion above is relevant to this scenario. Looking at the offences that *A* has committed against *B*, instead of theft or obtaining property by deception the most likely offence will be obtaining services by deception contrary to s.1 Theft Act 1978. In addition there will be the possibility of *A* committing an offence of making off without payment contrary to s.3 Theft Act 1978. The difficulty is that s.3 requires that *A* had not made payment as expected or required. Is the cheque not payment? There is an argument that the cheque is 'payment', whether or not the cheque will be honoured on presentation. This is because the cheque cancels the debt that arises following the provision of services, and creates a new debt (based upon the cheque) between *B* and *A*. The words 'as required or expected' refer to the fact that payment should be made on the spot, and not to the creditor's presumed expectation that the cheque will be honoured. This interpretation is supported by *Hammond*, where the accused wrote out cheques for car repairs knowing that there was no money in his bank account to meet the cheques. The trial judge ruled that the jury should acquit him of the charges under s.3 as the accused had not made off without payment.

In relation to offences that *A* has committed against his bank, the position is exactly as discussed in scenario 1.

3. A steals C's cheque book and forges a cheque from C's cheque book in payment for a car or services from B
The position is largely as discussed in **1** and **2** above except for the following. There is no doubt that if *A* forges a cheque, he has not paid and commits an offence under s.3, Theft Act 1978. This again is consistent with civil law, under which a forged cheque will not even conditionally discharge a debt. *A* would also be liable for the offence of forgery, as the cheque is lying about itself (that is, about who wrote it).

A can also be convicted of theft against *C*. The theft would be of *C*'s bank balance. In technical terms, *A* has not appropriated *C*'s money but the claim *C* had against his bank (a 'thing in action') for the balance in his account (*Chan Man-sin*). As this is how the law sees the situation, if *C*'s account had already reached its overdraft limit when *A* wrote the cheque, the bank would not be legally obliged to honour the cheque and so there would be no 'thing in action' to appropriate and so no theft (*Kohn*).

4. A dishonestly deceives B into writing a cheque in A's favour

The following offences could be said to have been committed by *A*:

(a) *Obtaining the cheque as a piece of paper by deception contrary to s.15 Theft Act 1968*. As a piece of paper, the cheque is clearly property (*Arnold*). The difficulty with seeing the offence as obtaining a cheque as a piece of paper by deception is that the cheque, when it is paid in by *A*, will be returned to *B*'s bank and can be collected by her. There is thus a difficulty in saying that there was an 'intention to permanently deprive' *B* of the piece of paper on which the cheque is written. One reply might be that although the cheque can be collected by *B*, it is now of a different character (a used-up cheque) and so there is permanent deprivation under the extended definition of that term in s.6.

(b) *Obtaining the cheque as a thing in action by deception*. This way of conceiving the offence will be ineffective. When *B* writes a cheque he creates a 'thing in action': a right to sue *B*. The problem is that this 'thing in action' in this cheque (the right of *A* to sue *B*) never belonged to another, it belonged to *A* from the moment when the cheque was signed. Therefore it cannot be obtained by deception contrary to s.15. This reasoning has been accepted by the House of Lords in *Preddy*.

(c) *Obtaining the money by deception*. Money can of course take many forms; as a credit balance in a bank account it is actually a 'thing in action': the account-holder is a creditor and the bank is under an obligation to repay the balance to the creditor, or to honour valid cheques drawn on the account in favour of third parties. In other words, an account-holder with £100 in her account technically does not own £100 but rather owns a 'thing in action' (a right to sue) against the bank for £100. This means that if part or the whole of the credit balance of an account is dishonestly appropriated, what is stolen is not the tangible 'money', but an intangible 'thing in action' – the right of the creditor/account-holder to enforce payment for that amount from the bank (*Kohn*; *Williams* (*Roy*)). But a thing in action is still property. The problem is that when the cheque is paid in and *B*'s bank balance is reduced and *A*'s bank balance is increased technically what leaves *B*'s bank account is not the same 'thing' that enters *A*'s bank balance. *B* has not gained what used to belong to *A*. It is just that *A*'s bank now owes him more and *B*'s bank owes him less. This is a very technical way of seeing things and most people would say that *A* has got *B*'s money, but in strict banking law terms this has not happened. Therefore *A* has not acquired property that belonged to *B* and so there can be no obtaining (or theft) of it (*Preddy*).

(d) *Obtaining a money transfer by deception, contrary to s.15A*. As a result of these difficulties, the Theft (Amendment) Act 1996 has inserted a new section 15A into the 1968 Theft Act:

'(1) A person is guilty of any offence if by a deception he dishonestly obtains a money transfer for himself or another.

(2) A money transfer occurs when
    (a) a debit is made to one account,
    (b) a credit is made to another, and,
    (c) the credit results from the debit or the debit results from the credit.'

This should overcome all the problems mentioned above and will be the most suitable charge in cases where a deception has caused a transfer from one account to another. This can be used whenever *A* gets money from *B*'s account by a deception, be it via a cheque, money transfer or standing order.

It is suggested that the above summary of the law reveals that there is a desperate need for a statute to deal specifically with this area. Making it an offence to knowingly (or recklessly) use a credit card or cheque book which you are unauthorized to use would remove the difficulties over proving the existence of a deception or that the deception was operative. It would also make the law easier to understand and explain!

Summary

13.1 There are a number of offences involving obtaining property or services, or the evasion of a liability, by deception. They are found in the Theft Acts 1968 and 1978. Obtaining property by deception may also amount to theft of the property. In each of the deception offences, there must be (1) a deception, (2) a causal link between the deception and the obtaining, and (3) dishonesty.

13.2 Deception may be by words or conduct; the surrounding circumstances can be taken into account in deciding whether there was a deception. The deception must be deliberate or reckless. There must be a causal link between the deception and the obtaining. This means that the deception must precede the obtaining, the victim of the deception must in fact be deceived, and the accused must obtain the property as a result of the deception. Dishonesty is a question for the jury, applying the test laid down in *Ghosh**; a deliberate deception will usually be dishonest. Where property belonging to another is obtained by deception, under s.15 Theft Act 1968 there must be an intention of permanently depriving the other of that property.

13.3 Obtaining a pecuniary advantage by deception is defined in s.16 Theft Act 1968. The scope of the offence is relatively narrow, but includes being allowed to borrow by way of overdraft, which covers an overdraft obtained as a result of unauthorized use of a cheque card. The offence also covers obtaining an insurance policy, and the opportunity to earn remuneration in an office or by employment, by deception.

13.4 Obtaining services by deception is defined in s.1 Theft Act 1978. A service is the conferring of a benefit on the recipient; gratuitous (free) services are not covered. The deception must be effective, and cause the victim to confer a benefit on the accused, but it need not relate to the payment for the service.

13.5 Section 2 Theft Act 1978 creates three offences of evading liability by deception, which overlap to some extent. It is an offence to secure the remission of a pre-existing liability, for example by using a stolen credit card to pay for goods. It is an offence to obtain an exemption from, or abatement of, a liability (for example, a reduced fare). It is also an offence to induce a creditor to wait for payment, or forgo payment, intending to make permanent default. Being induced to take a cheque instead of cash amounts to waiting for payment. A creditor is induced to forgo payment if, for example, the debtor deceives him into thinking that he has already been paid.

13.6 It is an offence under s.3 Theft Act 1978 to make off without payment for goods or services, knowing that payment on the spot is required or expected. The accused must intend never to pay, not merely to defer payment.

13.7 Forgery involves using a false instrument with intent that another person act against his prejudice. The instrument must tell lies about itself – for example, who wrote the document or when.

Case Notes

Allen [1985] AC 1029. House of Lords

The appellant was convicted of making off without payment. He had left a hotel without paying his bill of over £1000. He claimed that he had genuinely hoped to be able to pay the bill. His conviction was quashed by the Court of Appeal, and the House of Lords agreed with the decision of the Court of Appeal. It was held that the words 'with intent to avoid payment of the amount due' in s.3 Theft Act 1978 should be interpreted to mean with intent never to pay.

Charles [1977] AC 177. House of Lords

The appellant was convicted of obtaining a pecuniary advantage by deception: being allowed to borrow by way of overdraft contrary to subsection 16 (2)(b) Theft Act 1968. He had paid for gaming chips at a club with a cheque backed by a cheque card, knowing if the cheque were honoured his account would be overdrawn without authority. The manager of the club gave evidence that if a cheque card was used, he did not enquire as to the creditworthiness of the drawer of the cheque. The appeal was dismissed, on the ground that the appellant had impliedly represented that he was entitled to use the cheque card to back a cheque for that amount, and that the manager had been induced to accept the cheque by this false representation.

Doukas [1978] 1 All ER 1061. Court of Appeal

The appellant was convicted of having an article for use in connection with the obtaining of property by deception (s.25(1) Theft Act 1968). He was a hotel waiter who was discovered with bottles of wine in his possession, which were to be sold to hotel customers as the hotel's wine. The court upheld the conviction, holding that there was a causal link between the appellant's deception and the obtaining of the customer's money. The customers would not have paid for the wine if they had known that it belonged not to the hotel but to the appellant, who would pocket the proceeds. A reasonably honest customer would not be a party to the fraud on the appellant's employers.

Ghosh [1982] QB 1053. Court of Appeal

See Chapter 11 case notes.

Halai [1983] Crim LR 624. Court of Appeal

The appellant was convicted of several offences of obtaining services by deception and obtaining property (£100) by deception. He had applied for a mortgage with a building society and opened a savings account with a post-dated cheque; he then drew out £100 in cash from the account. He did not have sufficient funds in his bank account to meet the cheque, which was not honoured. His convictions as to the opening of the savings account and the attempt to obtain a mortgage advance were quashed. It was held that a mortgage advance was not a service; and that when an account was opened and money was paid into the account, no benefit was conferred on the customer, and so no service was obtained.

King and Stockwell [1987] 1 All ER 547. Court of Appeal

The appellants were convicted of attempting to obtain property by deception. They had falsely told an elderly widow that they were from a firm of tree surgeons, and that it was necessary to remove some trees in her garden to prevent damage to the foundations of her house. It was argued on appeal that any money paid by the victim would have been as a result of the work done by the appellants and not as a result of their representations. The appeal was dismissed, the court holding that the question of whether the deception was an operative cause of the obtaining of the money was a question of fact for the jury, and there was evidence on which the jury was entitled to come to the conclusion that the deception would have been operative in this case had the attempt succeeded.

Lambie [1982] AC 449. House of Lords
The appellant was convicted of obtaining a pecuniary advantage by deception. She had used a credit card to make purchases in a shop, although she knew that she was over the credit limit, and the issuing bank had asked her to return the card. It was argued on appeal that any representation she had made as to her authority to use the card was not operative, since the shop was guaranteed payment on the transaction as a result of the contract between the shop and the issuing bank. Her appeal was dismissed. The House of Lords followed *Charles* (above), and held that the jury was entitled to find that the manager of the shop would not have accepted the card had she known that the appellant had no authority to use it, and that the deception was therefore operative.

Nabina [2000] Crim LR 481. Court of Appeal
The defendant obtained a credit card after making an application in which he lied about his personal circumstances. This meant under contract law that he was authorized to use the card, but the credit-card company could end his authorization unilaterally by giving him notice that it was doing so. He used the card to obtain goods and was charged with obtaining property by deception. The Court of Appeal overturned the conviction on the basis that the jury had not been directed to consider whether he had represented that he had not used deceptions to the credit-card company in order to get the card, and that these representations had persuaded the suppliers to accept payment by credit card and hand over the goods.

Preddy [1996] 3 All ER 481. House of Lords
The appellants obtained a substantial number of mortgage advances after making several false representations in their applications. They claimed that they intended to repay the advances by selling the houses for a profit, as house prices were rising rapidly at that time, and therefore did not intend to permanently deprive the banks of the money. The mortgage advances were made by telegraphic transfer, CHAPS or cheque. The convictions were overturned by the House of Lords. *Duru* was not followed on the ground that if a cheque is written out to the accused it creates a brand new 'thing in action' in the accused's favour, and that cannot be said to have belonged to another. Further, the House held that when money is transferred from one account to another, in reality the credit to one account is not the same property as the debit to the other account. Therefore the accused could not be said to have obtained property belonging to another in relation to the bank transfers. Lord Goff also expressed doubts about whether a mortgage could constitute a service under s.3 Theft Act 1978.

Waites [1982] Crim LR 369. Court of Appeal
The appellant was convicted of obtaining a pecuniary advantage by deception: being allowed to borrow by way of overdraft contrary to subsection 16(2)(b) Theft Act 1968. She had used her cheque card to back cheques drawn on her account, thus obtaining an overdraft without authority. Her appeal was dismissed on the ground that although the bank had not agreed to the overdraft, she had been given the power to borrow by being issued with the cheque card.

Williams [1980] Crim LR 589. Court of Appeal
See Chapter 11 case notes.

Further Reading

For discussion on the nature of a deception see A. Smith. For consideration of issues raised with cheques and credit cards read Greenwood, J. Smith and Syrota (1980). The 1978 Theft Act is examined in J. Smith and Syrota (1979).

Greenwood, 'Causation and Credit Card Fraud' (1981) *Cambridge Law Journal* 209.
A. Smith, 'The Idea of a Criminal Deception' [1982] *Criminal Law Review* 721.
J. Smith, 'Comment on *Sibartie*' [1983] *Criminal Law Review* 470.
J. Smith, 'Obtaining Cheques by Deception} [1997] *Criminal Law Review* 396.
Syrota, 'The Theft Act 1978' (1979) *Modern Law Review* 301.
Syrota, 'Are Cheque Frauds Covered by s.3 of the Theft Act 1978?' [1980] *Criminal Law Review* 413.

14   Other Offences against Property

14.1   Criminal Damage

The Criminal Damage Act 1971, like the Theft Acts, protects property interests from harmful interference from others. It contains the offences relating to the destruction of, and damage to, property. Like the Theft Acts, this statute is written in language that was intended to be clear and non-technical, but has still caused difficulties in its interpretation. The most important criminal damage offences are found in s.1 of the Act which provides:

'(1) A person who without lawful excuse destroys or damages any property belonging to another intending to destroy or damage any such property or being reckless as to whether any such property would be destroyed or damaged shall be guilty of an offence.

(2) A person who without lawful excuse destroys or damages any property, whether belonging to himself or another –

  (a)   intending to destroy or damage any property or being reckless as to whether any property would be destroyed or damaged; and

  (b)   intending by the destruction or damage to endanger the life of another or being reckless as to whether the life of another would be thereby endangered; shall be guilty of an offence.

(3) An offence committed under this section by destroying or damaging property by fire shall be charged as arson.'

This section creates three offences: ordinary criminal damage in subsection (1); dangerous damage in subsection (2); and arson in subsection (3). Dangerous damage and arson are punishable with life imprisonment, while simple criminal damage is punishable with ten years' imprisonment. In addition to s.1, the Criminal Damage Act creates separate offences of threatening to destroy or damage property (s.2) and possession of anything (such as petrol, matches, stones, a knife or a crowbar) with the intention of destroying or damaging property (s.3), but these will not be discussed in detail here.

14.1.1   Ordinary Criminal Damage

The offence of criminal damage is found in s.1 Criminal Damage Act 1971 quoted above. The offence contains the following elements:

1.   Destruction or damage
The central element in the *actus reus* is the destruction of, or damage to, property. It is generally agreed that to destroy something is to damage it and so most of the cases concern what it means to damage property.

The word 'damage' should be given its ordinary meaning. What constitutes damage will depend on the nature and use of an item (*Roe* v. *Kingerlee*). Hence splattering mud on a parked car may not constitute damage, but it might be damage to put mud on a painting. Probably the most useful test to ascertain whether or not property has been damaged is to ask whether the defendant's act has impaired the value or usefulness of the item (*Morphitis* v. *Salmon**). The removal from a car of a wheel clamp by the owner of a clamped car might constitute criminal damage to the wheel clamp, as the wheel clamp is now of diminished usefulness (*Lloyd* v. *DPP*). Scratching a scaffolding pole neither impairs its usefulness nor reduces its value, and is therefore not to be regarded as damaging it (*Morphitis* v. *Salmon**).

The damage need not be permanent. In *Hardman*, graffiti that would eventually have been washed away by the rain was held to amount to damage, but if the damage can be easily removed then it is less likely to constitute damage. For example, in *R* v. *A* it was held that spitting on a policeman's coat did not damage it. In one case a defendant was arrested on the point of painting over a piece of National Front graffiti with white paint. This was found not to be criminal damage, partly on the ground that the wall was being returned closer to its intended (original) state (*Fancy*).

Damage is not restricted to breaking an item. It can be damage to attach something to a piece of property (for example, dumping rubbish onto a piece of land (*Henderson and Battley*)), to remove something (for example, taking away an essential part of a machine (*Tacey*)). Controversially it has been held that wrongfully wheel-clamping a car does not damage it (*Drake* v. *DPP*), because there has been no 'intrusion into the integrity of the object'. Although the wheel-clamping had affected the car's usefulness, it could (on payment) be quickly and easily removed without any long-term effects (unlike the land in *Henderson and Battley*). Perhaps the better charge in *Drake* would have been theft of the car, if dishonesty could be shown (see Chapter 11.6)

2. Property

'Property' is defined in s.10(1) Criminal Damage Act 1971 and is expressly restricted to tangible property. The term therefore includes land, but excludes patents, copyrights etc. Otherwise the definition is similar to that found in s.4 Theft Act 1968. In *Cox* v. *Riley*, the defendant erased a computer program from a printed circuit card. Convictions were upheld because the damage was to the card itself and not to the programs, which were intangible property and so not protected by the Act.

3. Belonging to another

You cannot be convicted of ordinary criminal damage of your own property. If you want you may rip up this book, if it is yours. (Although it will be noted that the offence of dangerous criminal damage can be committed against your own property.) A person who destroys his own property in the belief that it belongs to someone else could face the further annoyance of being convicted of attempted criminal damage of property belonging to another (see Chapter 18).

The phrase 'belonging to another' is defined in s.10(2) to include any person having custody, control, any proprietary right or interest, or a charge on the property. So you cannot destroy property which you own if someone else has a proprietary interest in it, for example. There are provisions relating to trust property and the property of a corporation which are counterparts to the provisions in s.5(2) and s.5(5) Theft Act 1968 (see Chapter 11.5).

4. Intention or recklessness

The *mens rea* for s.1(1) requires intention or recklessness as to causing damage to property belonging to another. It is enough if the defendant intended or was reckless as to the damage of some property belonging to another, even if it was not the property that was actually damaged. In other words, the doctrine of transferred *mens rea* can apply to these offences (see Chapter 4.6). The accused must intend or be reckless as to damaging property *and* intend or be reckless as to the property belonging to another (*Smith*).

The meaning of 'recklessness' is now governed by *Caldwell**, and is discussed in Chapter 4.4.2. In that case, as we have seen, Lord Diplock held that under s.1(1) Criminal Damage Act 1971 a person is reckless if:

'(1) he does an act which in fact creates an obvious risk that property would be destroyed or damaged and (2) when he does the act he either has not given any thought to the possibility of there being any such risk or has recognised that there was some risk involved and has none the less gone on to do it.'

5.   *Without lawful excuse*

The criminal damage offences do not contain that element of mens rea that is so typical of the Theft Acts: dishonesty. However, some of the elements of dishonesty are found in the requirement that the damage caused must be 'without lawful excuse'. The Criminal Damage Act 1971 contains in s.5 a partial definition of the phrase 'lawful excuse':

'(2) A person charged with an offence to which this section applies shall, whether or not he would be treated for the purposes of this Act as having a lawful excuse apart from this subsection, be treated for those purposes as having a lawful excuse –

  (a) if at the time of the act or acts alleged to constitute the offence he believed that the person or persons whom he believed to be entitled to consent to the destruction of or damage to the property in question had so consented, or would have consented to it if he or they had known of the destruction or damage and its circumstances; or

  (b) if he had destroyed or damaged . . . the property in question . . . in order to protect property belonging to himself or another or a right or interest in property which was or which he believed to himself or another or a right or interest in property which was or which he believed to be vested in himself or another, and at the time of the act or acts alleged to constitute the offence he believed –

    (i) that the property, right or interest was in immediate need of protection; and

    (ii) that the means of protection adopted or proposed to be adopted were or would be reasonable having regard to all the circumstances.

(3) For the purposes of this section it is immaterial whether a belief is justified or not if it is honestly held.

(4) For the purposes of subsection (2) above a right or interest in property includes any right or privilege in or over land, whether created by grant, licence or otherwise.

(5) This section shall not be construed as casting doubt on any defence of dishonesty recognised by law as a defence to criminal charges.'

This section is fairly straightforward. There are two key elements:

1. The defendant believes that the owner consented to the damage
The defence covers where the defendant believes that the owner consented to the damage, even if in fact the owner did not. The defence even applies if the defendant was aware that the owner's instructions were immoral (*Denton*). The belief that the owner consented or would have consented provides a defence even if it is an unreasonable belief (s.5(3)) and even if the mistaken belief is caused by the defendant's drunkenness (*Jaggard* v. *Dickenson*). A defendant who argued that he believed God owned the property (the Houses of Parliament) and that God authorized him to damage the property did not have a defence (*Blake* (1993)*). The court did not explain why this was so. The best explanation was that the defendant did not really believe that God owned (in the legal sense) the Houses of Parliament or that God had the legal authority to consent to the damage. It is not clear whether there is a defence if, unknown to the defendant, the owner has consented to the damage. In light of the *Dadson* principle (see Chapter 16.1) it is unlikely that this 'unknown justification' provides a defence.

2. The defendant was acting in order to protect his own or another's property
The defence in s.5 also covers damage done in order to protect other property. To be successful, the accused must believe both that the other property is in immediate need of protection and that the means of protection adopted are reasonable in the circumstances. In order to be able to rely on this defence, the courts have developed a rather complicated twofold test:

(a) Using a subjective test, did the defendant believe that the property was in immediate need of protection and that the means he used were reasonable (*Johnson* (1994))?
(b) Using an objective test, could the defendant's acts be said to be performed in order to protect the property (based on the facts as the defendant believed them to be)?

These may make more sense when applied to some cases. In *Ashford and Smith*, where the defendants were found outside a nuclear base armed with a pair of wire cutters, they tried to argue that they believed by cutting the wire and getting into the military base to protest they would lessen the chance of a nuclear war with its resulting damage to property. The defendants were prevented from using the s.5 defence as the court decided that, even taking the facts as the defendants believed them to be, it could not be said that *cutting the fence* would protect property. They believed that shutting down the base would protect property, but not cutting the fence. This suggests that it is necessary to show a clear causal link between the damage done and the anticipated protection of property. In *Hunt*, the defendant set fire to property in sheltered housing to demonstrate the lack of fire precautions and to persuade the owners to install better fire-prevention facilities. He was held not to have acted in order to protect property by that act (that is, the setting fire to the property). In both *Ashford and Smith* and *Hunt*, the defendants were acting in order to protect property, but they were not intending to protect other property directly by damage, but by actions that would follow from the damage.

In order to rely on s.5, the defendant must show that he believed that the property he was acting in order to protect was in need of immediate protection. This is judged subjectively on the defendant's state of mind. This is a further reasons why the defendants in *Blake*, *Ashford and Smith* and *Hunt* all faced difficulties. In *Ashford and Smith*, for example, it would be unlikely that the defendants believed a nuclear war was imminent.

The common law defences, which include self-defence, automatism and insanity (see Chapters 15 and 16), are also available to charges under the Criminal Damage Act 1971, as is made clear by s.5(5).

14.1.2 Dangerous Criminal Damage

In the case of dangerous criminal damage two elements are required:

1 There must be ordinary criminal damage, with two provisos. First, it is possible to commit dangerous criminal damage to your own property, the reasoning being that although you should be free to destroy or damage property that belongs to you, you should not do so in such a way as to endanger other people. This proviso also has consequences for the *mens rea* for this requirement. In the case of dangerous damage, only intention or recklessness as to damaging property is required. There is no need to have any *mens rea* as to the ownership of the property. Second, the lawful excuse defences explained in s.5 do not apply. The defendant may, however, still rely on the general defences, such as duress or lawful defence.

2 Dangerous damage also requires intention or recklessness (*Caldwell* recklessness) in relation to endangering the life of another person by the destruction or damage. The person whose life is endangered does not have to be the owner of the property (although it could be), but it cannot be the accused himself or herself. The mad scientist who blows up his garden shed and almost himself in an ill-fated experiment does not commit the offence, unless another person's life was thereby endan-

gered. It should be stressed that there is no need for there in fact to be an endangerment of someone's life. What must be shown is that there was intention or recklessness as to the endangerment. Thus, in *Sangha*, the defendant lit a fire in his room and left the house. The Court found he was guilty of dangerous criminal damage even though unknown to him the building was very well fireproofed and so in fact there was no danger to anyone living near by.

In *Steer**, the House of Lords held that there had to be a link between the damage to property and the endangering of life. It was not enough under s.1(2) to prove both recklessness as to the damage and recklessness as to endangering life; it had to be proved that there was at least recklessness as to endangering life by the damage to property. For example, where a defendant threw a brick through a car windscreen it was necessary to show that he was reckless that life was endangered by the damage to property (that is, the shattering of the windscreen – be it by obscuring the driver's vision or by the driver being hit by pieces of glass) and not by the driver being hit by the brick. That would not be endangering life through criminal damage, but an offence under s.47 or s.20 Offences Against the Person Act 1861 (*Webster and Warwick**).

Some commentators have complained that the offence is too widely drafted. *Merrick* demonstrates this concern. The defendant, acting with the consent of the homeowner, removed a television signal receiving box from the side of a house. While doing this, an electric cable was left exposed for six minutes. The defendant was convicted of dangerous damage. J. Smith has noted that the decision looks dubious because there is no offence to lay a dangerous cable. So why is there an offence to cut a cable (with the owner's consent) in a dangerous way?

14.1.3   Arson

The serious offence of arson requires no additional *mens rea* from that of simple criminal damage. What must be shown is that the destruction or damage was caused by fire. The charge may be brought under either s.1(1) or s.1(2), together with s.1(3). The lawful excuse defence in section 5 does apply, although the defendant may rely on the general defences, such as duress or lawful defence.

14.2   Blackmail

According to s.21(1) Theft Act 1968:

'A person is guilty of blackmail if, with a view to gain for himself or another or with intent to cause loss to another, he makes any unwarranted demand with menaces. . . .'

The section goes on to say that such a demand will be unwarranted unless:

'the person making it does so in the belief –
(a) that he has reasonable grounds for making the demand; and
(b) that the use of menaces is a proper means of reinforcing the demand.'

The maximum sentence for this offence is fourteen years' imprisonment. The offence is therefore made up of the following elements.

14.2.1   Making an Unwarranted Demand

The jury will have to use its common sense in determining whether the statement is a demand or not. The demand can be in writing or oral, and can be expressed or implied from the circumstances, tone of voice, physical gestures etc. There is obviously a fine line between an offer (which cannot form the basis of a blackmail charge) and a demand (which can). 'Give me £20 and I will make your life worthwhile', may be seen as an offer, but in some circumstances it may be a threat, by including the implied threat that unpleasant consequences will follow if you do not give me the money.

In a case of blackmail, a demand must be made. A victim of a crime would not commit blackmail if his assailant makes an unsolicited offer to hand over money in return for not reporting the crime (although the assailant may be guilty of incitement to commit an offence under s.5 Criminal Law Act 1967 (see Chapter 18.2)). Another consequence of the requirement that the demand needs to be made is that it seems to be irrelevant whether or not the victim actually hears or receives the demand (*Treacy*). If a letter containing a demand with menaces is lost in the post, the offence is still committed by the sender even though the intended victim did not receive the letter.

The demand may be that the victim or someone else acts or omits to act in a particular way. It need not be that specific money or property be handed over, but the demand must involve a financial gain or loss (s.34(2)(a)). Thus a demand that you be given a lucrative job would suffice, but not a demand to be appointed to an unpaid position in a voluntary organization.

14.2.2   Menaces

The second element of the *actus reus* is that the demand must be made with menaces. The term 'menace' is not defined in the Act, but it is to be given its 'normal meaning' involving the 'threats of any action detrimental to, or unpleasant to, the person addressed. It may also include a warning that in certain events such an action is intended' (*Lawrence and Pomroy* (1971)). Again, the menace can be express or implied from the circumstances. It does not matter whether the threat is that unpleasant consequences will befall the victim or someone else.

The menace must not be so trivial that it had no effect on the person threatened. Thus, the sale of a poster that exempted shops from 'rag activities' during a student fund-raising event was held not to constitute a menace (*Harry*). Normally it is enough for a judge to direct a jury that the threat involves menaces if that is how a reasonable person would interpret the words. However, there are two circumstances in which the judge will need to give further direction. The first is where the victim is not troubled by the menaces, even though a reasonable person would have been. This might be because the victim is unusually robust or because, unknown to the defendant, the facts are such that the threat is ineffective (for example, John threatens to persuade Sue's employers to sack her, even though, unknown to John, Sue had just handed in her notice). In these circumstances, the words are still threats with menaces despite the fact they have no effect on the victim (*Clear*).

The second situation where the judge will need to give a further direction is where the victim interprets the words as menaces even though a reasonable person would not have done so. Then, as long as the defendant was aware of the effect that his words would have on the victim, the threat can still be seen as menace (*Garwood*). Thus threatening to send the victim a bunch of flowers can amount to a menace if the defendant is aware that the victim is allergic to flowers. These decisions may sit a little uneasily with the rule that a threat does not need to be communicated to the victim, but the policy seems to be that if words are spoken by the defendant and she is aware of their potential effect, she cannot hide behind the victim's unlikely response.

14.2.3   Unwarranted

The definition of an unwarranted demand focuses on whether the defendant *believed* that there were reasonable grounds for his demand, not whether there *were* reasonable grounds. A demand will be unwarranted unless the defendant believes that '(a) he keeps reasonable grounds for making the claim' *and* (b) 'that the use of menaces is a proper way of enforcing the demand'. Consideration of (a) will focus on the legitimacy of the gain and of (b) will focus on the means used to obtain the loss or gain. These are expressed as *mens rea* to be proved by the prosecution, rather than defences for which the defence would need to introduce evidence. Let us consider these two elements separately.

First, when considering whether the defendant believes he has reasonable grounds for making the claim, she is to be judged on the facts as she believed them to be and by what she believes are the standards of the community (*Harvey*). So the question is whether on the facts as the defendant believed them to be, the defendant thought that ordinary people would say her demand was proper. The demand is 'proper' if the defendant believes that she is morally entitled to make the claim, even if there is not full legal entitlement. If Bob dies, leaving nothing to his son in his will, the son may believe he is morally entitled to some of Bob's estate, even though there is no legal entitlement. Therefore if the son demanded a part of the estate, the demand would not be improper.

Second, it must be shown that the defendant believed that the use of menaces is a proper way of enforcing the demand. This is usually a more difficult requirement for the defendant to satisfy. Although a defendant may readily persuade the jury that he believed that the victim owes him money, it will be more difficult to persuade a jury that he believed threats of violence were a proper way of enforcing the demand. The courts have decided that if a defendant is threatening to do an illegal act and the defendant is aware that it is an illegal act then he cannot claim that that was a proper way of enforcing the demand (*Harvey*).

An important consequence of the fact that the defendant must show both that he thought the demand and the method of enforcing the demand were reasonable, is that a blackmail charge can lie where the defendant is threatening to do something lawful. For example, if Mark catches Maria committing theft and says that he will report her to the police unless she gives him £100, this would amount to blackmail. Although Mark is entitled to report Maria to the police, the making of the demand is improper.

14.2.4   Intention to Make Unwarranted Demand with Menaces with a View to Gain for Oneself or Another, or Cause Loss to Another

The *mens rea* requirement of blackmail is an intention to make the unwarranted demand with menaces, with a view to gain for oneself or another, or cause loss to another. As stated earlier, the view to a gain must be one of property or money either for oneself or another. It is not necessary to show that the primary motivation is to receive money or property so long as it is a factor influencing the defendant in making the demand (*Bevans**).

Section 34(2) defines 'gain' as including 'a gain by keeping what one has as well as a gain by getting what one has not'; and a loss as including 'a loss by not getting what one might get, as well as a loss by parting with what one has'. A threat to tell the victim's husband about her adultery could not therefore form the basis of a blackmail charge as there was to be no gain or loss of monetary value. There is some dispute over whether 'a view to a gain' includes payment of a debt. An accountant might say that it is no gain to receive money legally owed to you, as it simply means that the money is recorded in the part of your accounts listing the money you actually have rather than in the part of your accounts detailing the money owed to you, but there is no judicial authority for this view. In reality, given the unreliability of creditors, most people would see it as a gain to receive payment, and there is some authority for this view (*Parkes*).

14.2.5 Why is Blackmail an Offence?

There has been much discussion over why blackmail is unlawful, especially when the defendant threatens to do what is lawful, or indeed to do what may be one's legal duty. Consider this example. Huw and Clare are co-workers. Clare catches Huw defrauding their employer. Clare says that she will report Huw to their boss unless Huw pays her £1000. Here Clare's threat (to report Huw) is lawful, indeed it may even be her legal duty, and simply asking for £1000 is lawful. So how can the two lawful acts combine to create a criminal offence? Perhaps the best explanation is that the core wrong in blackmail is not just the making of a threat, nor just the acquiring of another's property. It is the combination of the two: the threat of coercive force in order to obtain a financial gain. The offence is therefore similar to the crime of deception, where the victim's mind is manipulated in order to persuade him to hand over property. The difference is that in blackmail it is a threat (rather than deception) which is used to manipulate the victim's mind. An alternative understanding of the offence is to liken blackmail to an assault, putting the victim in fear of what the defendant is about to do.

14.3 Taking a Conveyance

It will be recalled that one of the elements of theft is that the defendant intended to permanently deprive the owner of the property. Therefore, it is normally no offence to borrow something, even without the owner's permission. Although there is some dispute over whether such borrowing should generally constitute theft, it is clear that borrowing cars (joy-riding, as it has become known) is a particular social problem. Hence it is a specific offence under s.12 Theft Act 1968:

> '. . . a person shall be guilty of an offence, if, without having the consent of the owner or other lawful authority, he takes any conveyance for his own or another's use or, knowing that any conveyance has been taken without such authority, drives it or allows himself to be carried in or on it.'

Notably there is no need to show an intention to permanently deprive the owner of the conveyance. The offence contains the following elements:

14.3.1   Conveyance

Conveyance here includes cars, motorbikes, boats and indeed 'any conveyance constructed or adapted for the carriage of a person or persons whether by land, water or air, except that it does not include a conveyance constructed or adapted for use only under the control of a person not carried in or on it'. This definition would include as well as the obvious, wheel-chairs and hang-gliders. It excludes supermarket trolleys (which are not designed to convey people and anyway do not 'carry' the driver) and horses (which are not 'constructions' (*Neal* v. *Gribble*)). There is a specific offence relating to bicycles in s.12(5).

14.3.2   'Taken'

The word 'taken' could be interpreted widely to include taking possession of a car, or narrowly to mean taking in the sense of causing the conveyance to move. The courts have accepted the narrow interpretation. The argument in favour of this interpretation is to contrast the word 'take' with 'use' later on in the section. If 'take' had been intended to have the wider meaning then the section could have been drafted 'to use the conveyance for his own or another's use'. So the present law is that starting the engine of a vehicle but not actually causing it to move does not amount to a taking, although it might constitute an offence of interfering with a motor vehicle with the intent that an offence under s.12(1) shall be committed (s.9 Criminal Attempts Act 1981; *Bogachi*). However there could be a taking even if the vehicle were only moved a few feet (*Marchant* v. *MacCallister*). There is no need for the conveyance to be moved on its own motion in order to be taken, it is sufficient if it is towed away, for example (*Pearce*). It is possible for a defendant to take a car which had already been taken by someone else and abandoned (*Spriggs*).

The offence can also be committed by someone who drives or allows herself to be carried in a conveyance that has been taken for the purposes of s.12, if she knows that the conveyance has been so taken. 'Carried' here requires a movement of the conveyance (*Miller* (1992)).

14.3.3 'For his Own or Another's Use'

This phrase has been interpreted to mean that it must be taken for use *as a conveyance* (*Bow**). Thus where a man pushed his ex-girlfriend's car around a corner so that she would think her car had been stolen as a 'practical joke', it was held that the car was not taken for use *as a conveyance* (*Stokes*). By way of contrast, where two people pushed a car around a corner, intending to return later in the day and drive it away, the offence was committed (*Marchant* v. *MacCallister*). Similarly, if a car's hand-brake was released and it travelled down a hill, but without carrying passengers, then again the taking would not be a taking as a conveyance; it was not being used to convey anyone. In *Bow*, the defendant moved a car 200 yards as he felt the vehicle was obstructing his way down a track. The court felt the question was one of fact, and on the facts of the case the car had been taken as a conveyance, although moving a car which was an obstacle for a couple of yards would not be. This decision seems dubious, as it is hard to see how he was using the car as a conveyance in this case. The defendant was not using the vehicle to convey himself or another anywhere. Indeed it took him out of his way, and he was using it so as to enable him to drive his own car down the track. It has also been argued that the court's interpretation of the section as requiring the car to be taken for use as a conveyance is an unduly restrictive reading of the offence. The loss to the victim is the same whether the car is taken as a form of transport, or towed away to form the basis of a bonfire or for a prank.

14.3.4 'Without Having the Consent of the Owner'

It is not enough to show that the owner would have consented if he had known of the circumstances; the owner has to consent at the time of the taking (*Ambler*). Although, as we shall see shortly, the defendant can raise a defence based on the fact that she believed that the owner would have consented to the taking. The prosecution will only need to prove the owner's lack of consent if the defence raises it as an issue at the trial (*McPherson*).

What if the owner had been deceived into giving his consent? The decided cases have not been very satisfactory, but the present position is as follows. If the defendant persuaded the owner to consent to lending the conveyance by a lie or deception, the offence is not committed and the owner is seen as consenting to the taking. This was stated in *Whittaker* v. *Campbell* where the court thought to decide otherwise would involve the court in having to distinguish between fundamental and non-fundamental mistakes, a complex question of civil law, and that if a 'common-sense' definition of consent is used there is consent even if it is induced by a deception. So, if the defendant obtains the consent of the owner to take the car by lying about his age, there is no offence under s.12. However, it is necessary to distinguish this from where the owner gives consent only for a specific use and the defendant uses the car outside the terms of permission, in which case he will be acting without the owner's consent. So the offence would not be committed if the accused asked the owner if he could take the car as he needed to go to Reigate for a wedding and the owner had said 'you can borrow the car', but the accused drove to Newcastle. However, the offence would have been committed if the owner had said 'you can borrow the car but only to go to Reigate and nowhere else'. In practice this distinction may be hard to draw.

Thus, if the owner gives a general consent for the defendant to take the car after the accused has lied about where he is going, this will not be seen as taking the vehicle without the owner's consent because the owner consented to the general taking at the moment when the defendant first drove off (*Peart*). However, if the owner agrees to the defendant taking the car on a specific journey and the defendant completes that journey but then departs on a new journey, the court has held that there is a second taking at the point when the driver departed from the agreed route. As this second taking is without the owner's consent, the defendant has committed the offence (*McGill*). That said, 'not every brief, unauthorised diversion from his proper route' is sufficient to constitute a new journey and a new taking (*McKnight* v. *Davies*). It is difficult, if not impossible, to find a sensible rationale behind these decisions.

14.3.5 Defence Based on Belief that the Owner would Consent

It should be noted that there is a specific defence to show that the defendant believed that the owner would consent to the taking or that he had lawful authority (s.12(6)). No doubt if a defendant took his friend's car to get his pregnant wife to hospital, the defendant would easily persuade the jury that he believed that his friend would have agreed to him taking the car. The test is subjective: it does not depend on whether the defendant's belief was reasonable but simply on whether there was such a belief. It may even be that a drunken and unreasonable belief will suffice (by analogy with *Jaggard* v. *Dickenson*).

14.3.6   An Intent to Cause Movement of the Conveyance

The *mens rea* for the offence is an intent to cause movement. Therefore if the defendant accidentally caused a vehicle to move there would be no offence (*Blayney* v. *Knight*). The crime is one of basic intent and so drunkenness is inadmissible as evidence of lack of intent (*McPherson*).

14.4   Aggravated Vehicle-Taking

The Aggravated Vehicle-Taking Act 1992 added a new s.12A to the Theft Act 1968, thereby creating a more serious form of the s.12 offence. This Act was introduced to combat behaviour which has been called 'joy riding', but which has lead to death, serious injury and damage. Section 12A provides:

'(1)   Subject to subsection (3) below, a person is guilty of aggravated taking of a vehicle if –

(a)   he commits an offence under section 12(1) above (in this section referred to as the 'basic offence') in relation to a mechanically propelled vehicle; and

(b)   it is proved that, at any time after the vehicle was unlawfully taken (whether by him or another) and before it was recovered, the vehicle was driven, or injury or damage was caused, in one or more of the circumstances set out in paragraphs (a) to (d) of subsection (2) below.

(2)   The circumstances referred to in subsection 1(b) above are –

(a)   that the vehicle was driven dangerously on a road or other public place;

(b)   that, owing to the driving of the vehicle, an accident occurred by which injury was caused to any person;

(c)   that, owing to the driving of the vehicle, an accident occurred by which damage was caused to any property, other than the vehicle;

(d)   that damage was caused to the vehicle.

(3)   A person is not guilty of an offence under this section if he proves that, as regards any such proven driving, injury or damage as is referred to in subsection (1)(b) above, either –

(a) the driving, accident or damage referred to in subsection (2) above occurred before he committed the basic offence; or
(b) he was neither in nor on nor in the immediate vicinity of the vehicle when that driving, accident or damage occurred.

In summary, aggravated vehicle-taking arises where, in addition to the straight-forward s.12 offence, one of the harms listed in s.12A(2) occurs. Probably the most common form of the offence would be where a defendant takes a vehicle contrary to s.12 and then drives the vehicle dangerously. Driving dangerously requires proof that 'it would be obvious to a competent and careful driver that driving in that way would be dangerous (s.2A(1)(b) Road Traffic Act 1988). Notably, these further harms do not require proof that the defendant intentionally or recklessly caused them. In *Marsh*, the defendant took a car without the owner's consent and then ran over the victim who ran out into the road in front of the defendant. His conviction under section 12A was upheld. The Court in *Marsh* explained that 'the policy of this statute is to impose heavier sanctions on those who take vehicles unlawfully and then cause an accident, whether or not the accident involves fault in the driving'. It is only necessary to show that the car's movement caused the accident that led to injury or damage. All those in the car are liable to conviction 'even though the passenger has protested at the driving which has caused damage to the vehicle' (*Davies*).

14.5 Computer Crime

It is, of course, possible to commit all kinds of crime using a computer. The most obvious is obtaining property by deception, but J. Smith and B. Hogan even suggest one could commit murder by computer if one hacked into an air-traffic controller's computer system and caused aircraft to crash, with the intent to kill the passengers. Here we will discuss crimes that specifically relate to computers. Not surprisingly, these are relatively recent creations of statute.

14.5.1 Computer Misuse Act 1990

There is no general crime of looking at other people's personal information, for example by looking inside their private diary. However, the Computer Misuse Act 1990 is designed to protect information kept on computers. The previous law was seen as inadequate following a House of Lords' decision where it was held that 'hacking' (gaining unauthorized access into a computer) was not *per se* a criminal offence. There are four particular reasons given by the Law Commission which suggest why it might be thought that information held on computers needs special protection by the criminal law. First, it is very hard to safeguard information stored on a computer, particularly as often the information is intended to be accessed by a number of authorized people. By contrast, information on paper can be kept in a safe or other secure place. Second, the ease of destroying or corrupting data on a computer means it deserves protection, particularly as it is not always possible for the owner of the computer to realize that the data has been looked at. Third, the highly confidential nature of the kind of information kept on computers (often concerning many members of the public) is such that it needs particular protection. Fourth, it may be sensible to deter people from searching for confidential information because of the temptation to use it for fraudulent purposes once they have found it.

The term 'computer' is not defined in the Act. No doubt any attempted definition would rapidly become out-of-date. In practice this is unlikely to create any problems as the term's meaning is generally understood. The courts appear to have taken a broad interpretation of the word 'computer' and it has been held to include machines which are not normally referred to as a computer, such as electronic personal organizers, boxes attached to televisions which control access to cable television channels (*Maxwell-King*) and cash registers (*Attorney-General's Reference (No. 1 of 1991)*).

14.5.2 Unauthorized Access to Computer Material

This offence is set out in s.1 of the Act and is designed to punish people who try to gain access to unauthorized data:

'1(1) A person is guilty of an offence if –
    (a) he causes a computer to perform any function with intent to secure access to any program or data held in any computer;
    (b) the access he intends to secure is unauthorised; and
    (c) he knows at the time when he causes the computer to perform the function that that is the case.
(2) The intent a person has to have to commit an offence under this section need not be directed at –
    (a) any particular program or data;
    (b) a program or data of any particular kind; or
    (c) a program or data held in any particular computer.

The *actus reus* and *mens rea* of this offence will be examined separately.

1. The actus reus *of the section 1 offence*

The *actus reus* of the offence is simply causing a computer to 'perform any function'. It seems that this could even include switching a computer on. It would not cover simply looking at a computer screen because this does not involve causing the computer to perform a function. There is no need to show that the defendant actually reached unauthorized material, only that he intended to do so.

2. The mens rea *of the section 1 offence*

The *mens rea* requirement can be broken down into three elements:

(a) An intention to secure access to any program or data on any computer. The phrase 'secure access' is narrower than may be at first assumed. Section 17(2) states:

> 'A person secures access to any program or data held in a computer if by causing a computer to perform any function he –
> (a)   alters or erases the program or data;
> (b)   copies or moves it to any storage medium other than that in which it is held or to a different location in the storage medium in which it is held;
> (c)   uses it; or
> (d)   has it output from the computer in which it is held (whether by having it displayed or in any other manner);
> and references to access to a program or data (and to an intent to secure such access) shall be read accordingly.'

This seems to mean that simply looking at unauthorized data on a computer does not infringe s.1. Once seeing the data, the defendant must do one of the four things with the data, using a computer. Writing down the data seen would not be regarded as copying it under (b), because the copying is not done by causing the computer to perform a function. 'Using' under (c) is restricted by the requirement that the computer must use the data. So finding confidential information on a database and then using it to blackmail someone would not be sufficient unless 'by causing a computer to perform any function he . . . uses it'.

It is made clear in s.1(2) Computer Misuse Act that there is no need to prove an intent to obtain access to any particular program or data. In other words, the offence is committed if a defendant is entering the computer just to see what she can find. Further, it does not matter whether the defendant is trying to reach data on the computer she is using, or attempting to reach data on another computer using her own computer *(Attorney-General's Reference (No. 1 of 1991))*.

Section 1 could be used to protect copyright in computer software, although it is not clear that the section was intended to do this. If someone received an unlicensed copy of some software and used it on her computer then this would seem to breach the terms of s.1 of the Act.

(b) The access to the data must be unauthorized. To be authorized to access data it must be shown that the defendant was either entitled to himself control access to that data, or he has been given authority to access the information by a person who is able to control access to it (s.17(5) Computer Misuse Act). It may be that a defendant is permitted access to some parts of a computer's database, but this would be no defence if she was attempting to reach parts of the database which she was not permitted to access. For example, in *R* v. *Bow Street Metropolitan Stipendiary Magistrate ex p Government of the USA** an employee of a credit-card company was allotted certain customers and access to data held about them on her company's computer. She accessed information about other customers. This would have constituted an offence under s.1 of the Act. It was no defence that she was authorized to access other customers' data; she was not authorized to access the data referred to in the charge.

Similarly, it may be that a defendant is authorized to access data for one purpose but not another. So, if a defendant is permitted access to data only for work purposes but accesses the data for her own reasons then this will be seen as unauthorized access (*R* v. *Bow Street Metropolitan Stipendiary Magistrate ex p Government of the USA**). Further, a person may be entitled to view certain data, but not to amend it. In such a case, amending the data could infringe s.1. It is also submitted that a person may be only authorized to access data in a particular way (for example, by using an office computer) and that accessing that data in an unauthorized manner (for example, by using a computer from home) could infringe s.1. However, the courts are yet to address this question.

In *DPP* v. *Ellis*, an employee of a university used computers which he was not entitled to use because they were restricted for use to certain staff. He simply used the computer to view web pages. It was held in the Divisional Court that he was not authorized to use the computer and that he was therefore not authorized to access the web-browser program on the computer. This was so, even though the web-browser program was widely available and the web pages did not contain secret information. The simple fact that he was unauthorized to use that computer meant he was not authorized to use the programs on the computer.

(c) The defendant knows that he or she is not authorized to access the program or data. It should be noted that this knowledge is based on a subjective test. There will therefore be borderline cases where a person is unsure whether he is authorized or not to access the data. If the defendant believes that access is unauthorized but in fact it is not, he will not have committed the offence although he may have committed an attempted offence. It must also be shown that the knowledge existed at the time when he caused the computer to perform a function. So if the defendant, believing he is authorized, enters a database and a message flashes on the screen that he is not authorized to use the data then he will not have committed an offence if he just watches the screen. He will however commit the offence if he then causes the computer to perform a function with the relevant intent.

14.5.3   Unauthorized Access with Intent

The offence in s.2 is a more serious one than that in s.1. It requires proof that a defendant committed an offence under s.1 and in addition that he intended to commit or facilitate the commission of a serious arrestable offence (see Chapter 2). The most common example of an arrestable offence in this context is likely to be a deception offence or theft. It is made clear in subsection 2(3) that there is no need for an intention that the serious arrestable offence is committed on the same occasion as the s.1 offence. Therefore a defendant who obtains data which he intends to use at some point in the future to commit an offence of obtaining property by deception will still be guilty of the s.2 offence. Further, according to subsection 2(4), it is not a defence that the arrestable offence he hopes to commit will in fact be impossible to commit. This is in line with the general law on 'impossible crimes' (see Chapter 18).

14.5.4   Unauthorized Modification of Computer Material

The *actus reus* of this offence, under s.3(1), is 'any act which causes an unauthorised modification of the contents of any computer'. The *mens rea* is:

> 'an intent to cause a modification to the contents of any computer and by so doing –
> (a)   to impair the operation of any computer;
> (b)   to prevent or hinder access to any program or data held in any computer; or
> (c)   to impair the operation of any such program or the reliability of any such data.'

It is also necessary to show that the defendant knew that the modification that was intended was unauthorized. Thus a defendant has a defence if he was authorized to modify a program to some extent but by mistake modified much more than he intended.

This section is clearly aimed at people who alter computer data with intent to corrupt a program or alter a database. The intent does not need to be directed towards any particular computer or data. Modification is defined as including removal of any program or data on a computer and includes adding to the contents or erasing them. It also includes temporary modification (s.3(5)). Section 3 would appear to cover sending someone a disk with a virus on it that was intended to damage the working of the computer.

14.5.5   Criminal Damage of Computers

Some cases have suggested that to damage computer software might be an offence under the Criminal Damage Act 1971. The information on software itself cannot be damaged under the Act as it is intangible property and so not covered by the Act. However, if the defendant is charged with damaging the computer or a disk then it seems that this might be an offence under the Act (*Cox* v. *Riley*). Under s.3(6) Computer Misuse Act criminal damage can only be charged in relation to computers if there has been a change in the physical condition of the computer. It is clearly intended that prosecutions involving corruption of data should be brought under the Computer Misuse Act. However, the wording of s.3(6) is rather vague, and the higher sentences and *mens rea* requirement of the Criminal Damage Act may persuade some prosecutors still to use the Criminal Damage Act in this area. Such a prosecution would involve expert witnesses arguing over whether changing information on a computer hard-drive, for example, involves a physical change in the computer.

14.6   Possession Offences

Several statutory offences have been created requiring possession, for example, of offensive weapons (Prevention of Crime Act 1953); drugs (Misuse of Drugs Act 1971); and articles for use in burglary, theft or deception (s.25 Theft Act 1968). The major difficulty with these offences has been to decide whether possession involves any *mens rea* element. In the leading case of *Warner* v. *Metropolitan Police Commissioner**, the defendant picked up two boxes which he thought contained perfume. In fact they contained drugs and he was charged with possession of drugs. The House of Lords held that if you possess a box or container then you possess the items in the container. The House of Lords has recently confirmed this ruling in *R* v. *Lambert**. Lord Clyde explained:

> 'Where the drug is in a container, it is sufficient for the prosecution to prove that the defendant had control of the container, that he knew of its existence and that there was something in it, and that the something was in fact the controlled drug which the prosecution alleges it to be. The prosecution does not require to prove that the accused knew that the thing was a controlled drug.'

There are two exceptions to this rule. The first is if the item has been placed in the defendant's pocket or handbag without her knowledge and she has not had an opportunity to discover that the item has been placed there. The second is if the accused believed that the box contained something completely different from what it actually held. However, in *Warner* v. *Metropolitan Police Commissioner* perfume was said not to be wholly different from drugs, which is a surprisingly narrow and rather harsh interpretation of the second exception. It seems that the burden of proof for proving either of these exceptions is on the defendant (*McNamara*). However these are evidential, rather than legal, burdens of proof (see Chapter 2 for explanations of these terms) and therefore do not infringe the Human Rights Act (*Lambert*; see Chapter 19).

Hot Topic: The GM Crop Protesters

In recent years the government has approved the planting of fields of genetically modified (GM) crops in certain places as part of a study into the benefits and disadvantages of such crops. These trials have proved highly controversial. Some activists went so far as to destroy the trial crops and this led to several trials with charges of criminal damage to the crops being brought against the protesters. Although none of these trials was reported in the official law reports, they provide an interesting example of how the law needs to balance the rights of protesters to protest and the rights of property owners to have their property protected.

Probably the best known trial involved Lord Melchett, the director of Greenpeace who along with 27 other Greenpeace activists were charged with criminal damage to a six acre trial GM crop field (*Melchett*). Their defence was that they believed by destroying the GM crops they were protecting non-GM crops in neighbouring fields from 'GM contamination'. The trial was abandoned after the jury was unable to reach a verdict on the criminal damage charge. On the retrial, the defendants were acquitted.

There could have been little doubt that the crops were damaged, that the crops were property (under s.10(1) Criminal Damage Act 1971), and that the defendants were *Caldwell* reckless. The key legal issue in the case is the defendants' belief that they were acting lawfully in order to protect other people's property. Could this belief provide a defence? After all, as the prosecutor in this case is reported as pointing out:

> 'In growing that crop [the farmers] were acting perfectly lawfully. All the authority had been given to do it; there was no legal reason why he should not have grown that crop.'

The key statutory provision was subsection 5(2)(b), the relevant part of which provides that a person has a lawful excuse for damaging property:

> 'if he had destroyed or damaged . . . the property in question . . . in order to protect property belonging to himself or another or a right or interest in property belonging to himself and another . . . , and at the time of the act or acts alleged to constitute the offence he believed –
> (i)   that the property, right or interest was in immediate need of protection; and
> (ii) that the means of protection adopted or proposed to be adopted were or would be reasonable having regard to all the circumstances.'

Section 5(3) adds: 'For the purposes of this section it is immaterial whether a belief is justified or not if it is honestly held'.

The provision clearly appears to provide the defendant with a defence. A few issues can be quickly disposed of. It was clear that the defendants believed that neighbouring crops would be damaged. They gave evidence that they believed that the neighbouring crops would be 'contaminated with GM and would therefore be less valuable, as they could not be marketed GM free'. As mentioned earlier in this chapter, an act which causes a reduction in value to a piece of property is likely to be regarded as an act which damages it. Subsection 5(2)(b) also makes it clear that the defence applies whether the defendant acts in order to protect his own or another's property. It therefore did not matter that the property 'at risk' did not belong to the defendants. Finally, s.5(3) makes it clear that it is irrelevant whether the defendant's belief is reasonable or not. It would therefore be of no use to the prosecution to demonstrate that in fact the GM crops did not pose a risk to the neighbour's crops.

The most difficult issue is whether the defendant's acts had been done in order to protect property. This was the requirement that had caused difficulties in similar cases in the past. As noted above in *Ashford and Smith*, the protesters at the nuclear base could not argue against the fact that the very act of cutting the fence damaged protected property. This simply enabled them to do other acts (enter the base and make a protest) which they thought might lead to the closing of the base, which would protect the property. As explained above, those defendants were denied a defence based on s.5 because the acts of damage were too remote from the protection. In the GM case, however, there is no such problem. The destruction of the crops meant that the threat they were posing to the neighbouring crops was brought to an end. It seems therefore that these protestors would certainly be able to rely on the defence of s.5.

This might lead some to call for a change in the law. If protesters are legally permitted to damage things they think are posing a risk to themselves, this could cause widespread disruption. People could destroy mobile phone masts, pylons, herds of cattle or incineration units without committing criminal damage if they honestly believed that these were posing a threat to people or property.

Perhaps surprisingly, an answer to this concern might be found in the law of theft since *Gomez*. By touching the crops, the protesters were committing an appropriation. Subsection 4(2)(b) Theft Act 1968 indicates that crops would be property for the purpose of the theft. If a crop is destroyed, this could constitute a permanent deprivation under s.6(1). The permanent deprivation requirement could cause problems if the property is damaged and not destroyed, as that may not be equivalent to an 'outright taking', although the interpretation of s.6 Theft Act 1968 in *DPP* v. *Lavender* (see Chapter 11.7) could be relied upon. This would leave the issue of dishonesty. Notably, the defendants in the GM crop case were acquitted of theft. We do not know why, but it is at least arguable that the defendants could legitimately claim that they believed most people supported the destruction of GM crops and would not regard the destruction as dishonest. This would be believable because of the apparent widespread opposition among the general public to GM crops. Defendants would be less likely to successfully persuade the jury that they were acting honestly in relation to less controversial issues.

Summary

14.1 Criminal damage is the offence of intentionally or recklessly destroying or damaging property belonging to another. Arson, where property is destroyed or damaged by fire, is a more serious form of criminal damage. There is also a separate offence of destroying or damaging property with intent to endanger life or being reckless as to whether life is endangered. Recklessness has been held to include the state of mind of the person who foresees an obvious risk that property would be destroyed or damaged, or life endangered. It also includes the state of mind of the person who fails to foresee that risk.

14.2 The essence of blackmail is the making of unwarranted demands, with menaces, with a view to gain something for oneself or someone else. Whether words or acts are demands with menaces is determined by considering all the circumstances, and the threat can be express or implied. The gain must be financial but need not be of directly gaining money.

14.3 It is an offence for the accused to take a conveyance for her own or another's use. 'Take' means that the conveyance must be taken in the sense of being moved. It must also involve taking the conveyance as a means of transporting someone and not for some other use. It is a defence if the owner consented to the taking.

14.4 Computers can be used to commit all kinds of crimes, although there are some specific crimes designed for computers set out in the Computer Misuse Act 1990. This Act prohibits gaining unauthorized access to computer material, and contains a more serious offence of doing this with the intent to commit another offence. There is also an offence of modifying computer material in an unauthorized way. It is possible to be guilty of criminal damage of computers if there has been a physical change to some component of the computer.

14.5 There are various offences relating to possession of particular items. There is dispute over the *mens rea* required for the notion of possession. The requirement has been decided to contain strict liability. One is held to possess without knowledge unless one thought the item was different in substance, or one lacked the opportunity to ascertain that one was in possession of an item.

Case Notes

Bevans [1988] Crim LR 236. Court of Appeal

The defendant, who suffered from osteoarthritis, took a gun to his doctor's surgery and threatened to kill a doctor unless he was given a pain-relieving drug. He was convicted, and appealed arguing that he had not made a demand for financial gain. The Court of Appeal upheld his conviction, holding that his demand was to be given the drug, which was property. The fact that his motive was to relieve his pain rather than make a financial gain was immaterial.

Blake [1993] Crim LR 586. Divisional Court

The accused wrote slogans opposing the Gulf War in felt-tip pen on a concrete pillar. He was charged with criminal damage, but attempted to argue that his conduct was justified by s.3 Criminal Law Act 1967. This argument failed because the writing did not constitute 'force'. He also argued that he believed that God owned the pillar and consented to the damage. The court rejected this argument, claiming that such questions were outside the provenance of the court.

Bow (1976) 64 Cr App R 54. Court of Appeal

The Crown alleged that the appellant and his brother were poaching when the gamekeepers approached them. The head gamekeeper parked his Land Rover so as to obstruct the only escape route for the appellant's car. The appellant got into the driver's seat of the Land Rover, released the handbrake and coasted 200 yards without switching on the engine. The appellant was convicted of taking a conveyance contrary to s.12 Theft Act 1968. He appealed and argued before the Court of Appeal that he had not taken the conveyance as a means of transport. The Court of Appeal decided that the motive of the appellant was irrelevant and he could be said to have taken the vehicle as a conveyance.

R v. *Bow Street Metropolitan Stipendiary Magistrate ex p Government of the USA* [2000] 2 AC 216.

Ojomo was an employee of the American Express credit-card company in the United States of America. Although she was able to access the accounts of any customer on her work computer, she was authorized to access only the accounts of certain customers assigned to her. She accessed the accounts of customers who had not been assigned to her. In proceedings to extradite her to the United States, the issue arose of whether she had committed an offence under UK law and in particular s.1(1) Computer Misuse Act 1990. She argued that s.1(1) dealt with hackers, 'outsiders' entering a database, not insiders who were entitled to enter part of the database. The House of Lords rejected such a distinction. As Ojomo was not entitled to have access to the part of the database which she accessed, she had committed the offence, even though she was authorized to access other parts of the database.

Caldwell [1982] AC 341. House of Lords

See Chapter 4 case notes.

R v. *Lambert* [2001] 3 WLR 206. House of Lords

See Chapter 19 case notes.

Morphitis v. *Salmon* [1990] Crim LR 48. Court of Appeal

The defendant removed a scaffolding clip from a barrier erected by a neighbour and was charged with causing criminal damage to the clip. He had scratched the clip but this was held not to be damage as scratch marks occurred as part of normal use of these clips. The court suggested that a conviction may have succeeded had he been charged with damage to the barrier as a whole.

Steer [1988] AC 111. House of Lords
The appellant was convicted of criminal damage, being reckless as to endangering the life of another person, contrary to subsection 1(2)(b) of the Criminal Damage Act 1971. He had fired a rifle at the door and bedroom window of a house. The trial judge held that under s.1(2), the danger to life need not come from the damage to property (in this case the damage to the door and window), but that it was sufficient if the danger came from the act of the accused which caused the damage (in this case the rifle shots). The Court of Appeal allowed the appeal and the House of Lords dismissed a further appeal by the prosecutor. It was held that under s.1(2) it was necessary that the accused should intend (or be reckless) as to endangering life by the destruction of, or damage to, the property itself.

Warner v. Metropolitan Police Commissioner [1969] 2 AC 256. House of Lords
See Chapter 6 case notes.

Webster and Warwick [1995] 2 All ER 168. Court of Appeal
The Court of Appeal heard two cases together. Webster and some others threw a stone from a railway bridge onto a passenger train. The stone crashed into the roof and showered the passengers with fibreglass. Warwick threw a brick at the rear window of a police car. In both cases the appeal concerned the correct direction on the *mens rea* of dangerous damage. The Court of Appeal stressed that it had to be shown that the recklessness as to endangerment of life had to be endangerment by criminal damage. In other words, it needed to be shown that Webster foresaw that passengers would be threatened by the splintering roof, not the stone itself, and that Warwick foresaw that the police officer would be endangered by the broken glass, not the brick itself. The Court of Appeal found that, in each case, although the trial judge had misdirected the juries, it was clear from the evidence and the juries' verdicts that the appellants were reckless as to whether the life of another would be endangered and so convictions on that basis under s.1(2) Criminal Damage Act would be substituted.

Further Reading

Blackmail is discussed by Aldridge and Lamond. Elliot considers criminal damage, Spencer the 1992 Aggravated Vehicle-Taking Act and Wasik computer crimes.

Aldridge, 'Attempted Murder of the Soul: Blackmail, Privacy and Secrets' (1993) *Oxford Journal of Legal Studies* 368.
Elliot, 'Endangering Life by Destroying or Damaging Property' [1997] *Criminal Law Review* 382.
Lamond, 'Coercion, Threats and the Puzzle of Blackmail', in Simester and Smith (eds), *Harm and Culpability* (1995, Oxford University Press).
Spencer, 'The Aggravated Vehicle-Taking Act 1992' [1992] *Criminal Law Review* 699.
Wasik, *Crime and the Computer* (1991, Oxford University Press).

PART IV
DEFENCES

15   Denial of Elements of Offences

> ### Key words
>
> - **Exemption** – an exclusion from the ambit of the criminal law because a person lacks the capacity to comply with the law.
> - **Self-defence** – the defendant uses a reasonable level of force in response against a person who is posing an unjust threat to him or her.
> - **Insanity** – the defendant suffers from a defect of reason caused by a disease of the mind which means they are not aware of what they are doing or not aware that what they are doing is wrong.

15.1   Defences

A defendant who faces a criminal charge and wishes to plead not guilty has essentially four courses open to her.

1. To claim an exemption from liability
Some defendants are excluded from the ambit of the criminal law altogether, however heinous their crime, for example those under the age of criminal responsibility and those who are insane. Such defendants are exempted liability because they lack a core requirement of criminal liability: they are people who lack the capacity to comply with the requirements of the criminal law. To punish infants or the insane would contravene profound principles that underlie the criminal law by punishing people who are not capable of being responsible for their actions. As J. Horder (1996) explains 'in a civilized legal system, only those who have the intellectual and moral capacity to understand the significance of their conduct will fall to be judged under its rules of criminal responsibility'.

2. To deny that the actus reus *has been proved*
A defendant can argue that the prosecution has not proved beyond reasonable doubt that the defendant's acts amounted to the *actus reus*. This may be a simple claim that the defendant was not present at the scene of the crime but somewhere else (an alibi); that she was at the scene of the crime but did not do the relevant act (for example, she did not pull the trigger, but someone else did); or that her act did not cause the injury. A less obvious

way of denying the *actus reus* is to admit that the defendant did the act which caused the injury, but argue that it was not an unlawful act, for example the defendant acted in self-defence. The courts have (rather oddly) seen unlawfulness as an aspect of the *actus reus* and so a claim of self-defence is in fact a claim that the defendant acted lawfully and thus a denial of the *actus reus*. Alternatively, the defendant may seek to argue that she did not really act but was an automaton at the time when the crime happened. This also is a denial of the *actus reus* – a denial that the defendant acted in the legal sense (see Chapter 3.6).

3.   To deny that the mens rea *has been proved*
The defendant may claim she did not have the required *mens rea*. This can be the straightforward claim that, for example, she did not intend the injury, or that she did not foresee that the injury might be caused, and so she was not reckless. Two particular ways of denying *mens rea* arise when the defendant claims that she lacked the necessary *mens rea* because she was intoxicated or had made a mistake.

4.   To rely on a defence
A defendant may admit that she performed the *actus reus* with the necessary *mens rea*, but seek to argue that she has a special defence, for example that she acted under duress or with the consent of the victim. If successful, these will result in an acquittal. When facing a charge of murder, the defendant can use a partial defence (for example, provocation) that, if successful, reduces the conviction from murder to manslaughter.

There are many different ways of classifying these defences. One way is to analyse them as we have done above (as exemptions, denial of *actus reus* or *mens rea*, or special defences). This method has the benefit of distinguishing those claims that argue that the wrong of the crime was not present (that is, there was no *actus reus* or no *mens rea*) and those claims which admit the wrongness of the act but argue that in all the circumstances the defendant should still not be blamed for it (that is, by relying on an exemption or defence). The classification of defences into '*actus reus* defences' and '*mens rea* defences' is also important because it has implications for the way that the defences develop and can be used. For example, if the offence is one of strict liability then only *actus reus* defences may be pleaded; lack of *mens rea* is irrelevant if there is no *mens rea* element to the offence. It also has the benefit of being the way that the judiciary most commonly discusses the defences.

However, to analyse defences in the above way has two drawbacks. First, there can be grave difficulties in deciding into which category a particular defence should fall. For example, the House of Lords has suggested that the consent of the victim (where it is relevant) should (in respect of offences against the person) be seen as a special defence (*Brown*). However, many (if not all) academic commentators believe that it is better to see consent as a denial of the *actus reus*, a denial that the act was harmful at all (see Chapter 7.7). Secondly, the analysis may hide the fact that the defences in different categories are closely linked. For example, there is a clear similarity between diminished responsibility and insanity, although in the above analysis they would be placed in different categories.

We have already noted that commentators have suggested some overarching theories that might explain all the defences (for example, the choice theory or the character theory; see Chapter 1.5). That would be another way of categorizing the defences. Another popular method would be to distinguish justifications and excuses, and we will discuss that distinction at the start of Chapter 16.

Before considering the defences in greater detail it is important to distinguish between a defence and mitigation. When the defendant is able successfully to raise a defence then he is found not guilty (except in the case of a partial defence where the defendant is convicted of a lesser offence than she would have been without the partial defence). By contrast, mitigation is a factor that becomes relevant at the sentencing stage. The mitigating factors can be so persuasive that only a nominal sentence is imposed (for example, an absolute discharge). But even where that occurs the defendant still has the censure of a criminal conviction, marking the law's disapproval of the accused's actions.

We will try and draw analogies between the defences where appropriate, but will divide the defences up on the basis mentioned earlier: that is, into those which are exemptions from the criminal law; those which deny the *actus reus*; those which deny the *mens rea*; and those which admit that the defendant has committed the *actus reus* with the necessary *mens rea*, but seek to use a special defence.

15.2   Exemptions from Liability

As explained above, an exemption applies to a person who lacks the moral capacity to be subject to liability under criminal law.

15.2.1   Infancy

Infancy is a clear example of an exemption from criminal liability. There is an age below which children are *doli incapax*, that is they are not responsible for their actions under the criminal law. If not responsible for their actions, children deserve not the censure of a criminal conviction but the assistance of social services. Different societies take different views on the appropriate age of criminal responsibility and in English law this has changed over the years. It is necessary to discuss three age groups:

1.   Under-ten-year-olds

At present, the age of criminal responsibility is set at ten-years-old by s.50 Children and Young Person Act 1933. If a nine-year-old commits the *actus reus* of a crime, be it the most premeditated, most heinous, most blame-worthy of crimes, she cannot be held criminally responsible for it. It is possible for care proceedings to be instigated under the Children Act 1989, which may result in a child being placed in secure local authority accommodation, but those are civil, not criminal, proceedings and are beyond the scope of this book.

If an under-ten-year-old's conduct would, in an adult, amount to the *actus reus* of an offence and it is proved that the child was manipulated by an adult, who had the necessary *mens rea* for that offence, then the adult can be convicted of the offence. The child is regarded as the 'innocent agent' of the adult if a causal link can be shown between the conduct of the adult and the *actus reus* of the offence (see Chapter 4.7).

2.   Ten to fourteen-year-olds

It used to be the law that between the age of ten and fourteen a child was presumed *doli incapax* and so could not be convicted of a crime, but that presumption could be rebutted if the prosecution proved that he had the capacity to differentiate between right and wrong. However, this presumption was abolished by s.34 Crime and Disorder Act 1998:

> 'The rebuttable presumption of criminal law that a child aged 10 or over is incapable of committing an offence is hereby abolished.'

Unfortunately this provision leaves great uncertainty as to the present law. There are two views.

(a)   Some commentators (such as Walker) argue that all s.34 does is to remove the presumption that those aged 10 to 14 are *doli incapax*. This means that it is still open to 10 to 14-year-olds to prove that they are *doli incapax* and do not know the difference between right and wrong. Few such children are likely to be able to do so and the defence is most likely to be relied upon by children suffering from learning difficulties.

(b) Other commentators take the view that the section abolishes the *doli incapax* rule for this age group all together. So a ten to fourteen-year-old can be convicted, even if she does not know the difference between right and wrong (provided she has the necessary *mens rea*).

It is suggested that the first view is the strongest, because it is the most straightforward interpretation of s.34. The long-established defence of *doli incapax* should only be abolished by the clearest statutory provision. Section 34 claims to abolish the presumption concerning capacity, not the actual defence itself. However, the Home Office circular on the Act (which is not binding on the courts) has taken the second view.

3. Over-fourteen-year-olds
A child over the age of fourteen is deemed as responsible as an adult, although the sentencing for children over fourteen and below eighteen is subject to a different regime.

15.2.2 Insanity

There are two ways in which a defendant's sanity may be relevant: if he is insane at the time of the actual trial itself or if he was insane at the time when he committed the offence. The two have quite different justifications. It is unfair to try someone who is insane at the time of the trial (unfit to plead), because if he is unable to understand the proceedings then he will be unable to participate and put forward his case. It is inappropriate to punish someone who is insane at the time he committed the offence because he was not responsible for his actions. Although such a person may be suitable for compulsory detention, the censure connected with a criminal conviction would not be appropriate. Given those different justifications, it is not surprising that the law regulating these two versions of the insanity defence are quite distinct.

1. Unfitness to plead
In relation to unfitness to plead, the law is now governed by the Criminal Procedure (Insanity and Unfitness to Plead) Act 1991. To be found unfit to plead it is necessary to show that the defendant is unable to give, receive or understand communications relating to the trial. So, if because of his disability, the defendant was unable to comprehend the evidence given or to instruct his counsel, he would not be fit to be tried. It seems that a defendant who is able to understand the proceedings but suffers from delusions (for example, that he is convinced he is guilty when he is not) will still be fit to stand trial.

If there is a question over whether the defendant is fit to plead, that question will be the first issue that the jury will have to decide, before hearing any evidence about the crime itself. If the defendant is found fit to plead then the trial will proceed as normal (although with a different jury). If it is decided that he is not fit then there will be a 'trial of the facts' using a different jury. Here the essential question for the jury is whether the defendant committed the *actus reus* of the crime with which he is charged. The jury do not need to consider whether the defendant had the *mens rea* (*Antoine*) or could rely on an excuse such as provocation (*Grant*). If it is decided that the defendant did not commit the *actus reus*, then obviously he can walk free. But if the defendant did commit the *actus reus* then the judge will have a wide range of orders available, ranging from a discharge, to a supervision order, to compulsory admission to hospital; although in the case of a murder charge, indefinite detention in a special hospital is mandatory. These different orders are available to a judge if the defendant committed the *actus reus*, even if it is not shown that he had the *mens rea* of the crime (*Attorney-General's Reference No. 3 of 1998*).

2.   Insanity at the time of the crime

The second way in which the issue of insanity could be raised is by introducing proof that the defendant was insane at the time that he committed the *actus reus*. This will only become relevant if the defendant is fit to stand trial. This area of the law was until recently overshadowed by the fact that if a defendant was found insane at the time of the crime then the judge would have no alternative but to send him to a hospital where he could be detained without a maximum sentence. This led many, who may otherwise have pleaded insanity, not to do so because they would rather be found guilty and receive a sentence which would at least have a maximum duration. Since the Criminal Procedure (Unfitness to Plead) Act 1991 the judge has a much wider discretion on sentencing and she can even order an absolute discharge, except in murder cases where indefinite detention in a special hospital is still mandatory. It was expected that this greater flexibility on sentencing would lead to a greater number of people attempting to use the defence, although in fact this has not occurred. Maybe the stigma of an insanity verdict is still a strong deterrent.

The legal definition of insanity dates back to the *M'Naghten** rules set out in 1873. It is important to realize that insanity here is a legal concept and the legal definition of the term is quite different from any medical or popular understanding of insanity. Some people who are insane under the law would certainly not be regarded as insane in medical terms. For example, courts have found epilepsy, sleepwalking and hypoglycaemia (caused by diabetes) to fall within the legal definition of insanity. Similarly someone who might be regarded as insane by doctors (although medical terminology tends to avoid the use of the term insanity) would not necessarily fall within the legal terminology. A person who heard voices telling him to kill traffic wardens and then did so might not fall within the legal definition of insanity.

Lawton LJ in *Quick** referred to insanity as 'this quagmire of law seldom entered nowadays save by those in desperate need of some kind of a defence'. In *Sullivan* (1984)*, Lord Diplock admitted that 'the nomenclature adopted by the medical profession may change from time to time . . . But the meaning of the expression "disease of the mind" as the cause of "a defect of reason" remains unchanged for the purposes of the application of the *M'Naghten* rules'.

The *M'Naghten** rules (as confirmed by the House of Lords in *Sullivan*) state that there are two requirements that need to be shown in order to establish insanity:

1 The defendant suffers from a defect of reason caused by a disease of the mind.
2 The defect of reason must mean that either: (a) the defendant is not aware of what he is doing or (b) he is not aware that what he is doing is wrong.

This definition contains the following elements:

- Disease of the mind
- Defect of reason
- The defendant did not know what he was doing or that what he was doing was wrong.

(a) Disease of the mind
'Mind' is used not to mean brain, but in the sense of 'the mental faculties of reason, memory and understanding' (Devlin J in *Kemp*, approved by Lord Diplock in *Sullivan* (1984)). So a condition which does not affect the brain as such but does affect the reasoning process could be classified as a disease of the mind. This widens the definition of insanity. This is especially so because a disease of the mind need not be permanent. In *Sullivan* (1984), Lord Diplock explained that if the disease impairs the faculties of reason, memory and understanding, 'it matters not . . . whether the impairment itself is permanent or is transient and intermittent, provided that it subsisted at the time of commission of the act'. Lord Diplock thereby cast doubt on *dicta* of Lord Denning in *Bratty* v. *AG for Northern Ireland**, twenty years earlier, who defined a disease of the mind in terms of a 'disorder which has manifested itself in violence and is prone to recur . . . At any rate it is the sort of disease for which a person should be detained in hospital rather than be given an unqualified acquittal'. This wide definition of

insanity means that epilepsy and conditions caused by diabetes can be classified as forms of insanity.

It is important to distinguish automatism from insanity. The crucial distinction depends on whether the impairment of mental facilities was caused by an 'external factor' or an 'internal factor'. In order to constitute insanity an internal factor must be involved. This distinction has already been discussed in Chapter 3.6.

(b) The defect of reason

The disease of the mind must cause a defect of reason. It was pointed out in *Clarke* (1972) that confusion or absentmindedness causing a failure to use the power of reasoning or failure of concentration, does not amount to a defect of reason. The accused must be deprived by the disease of the power of reasoning, even if temporarily.

(c) Did not know the nature and quality of his act or that the act was wrong

The defect of reason must be sufficiently severe that the accused either did not know the nature and quality of his act, or did not know that it was wrong. This is a difficult test to satisfy. The Report of the Butler Committee on Mentally Abnormal Offenders (1975, Cmnd 6244) commented:

'Just as a person must generally be very mad indeed not to know what he is doing (the nature and quality of his act) when he is killing a man or setting fire to a building, so he must be very mad not to know that these acts attract the unfavourable notice of the police (his knowledge of wrong).'

The 'nature and quality' of an act refers to its physical nature, and covers cases of severe delusions, where the accused believes he is doing something quite different from the act which is in fact done; for example, where the defendant thinks he is killing monsters from outer space when in fact he is killing a human being. It also covers cases where the accused has no control over his physical movements, as in an epileptic fit (*Sullivan*). Lord Diplock in *Sullivan* suggested that the phrase 'not knowing the nature and quality of his act' be explained to a jury as 'he did not know what he was doing'.

If the accused was aware of the nature of his act, he may still be found to be insane if it is proved that he did not know that it was wrong. 'Wrong' here means legally wrong rather than morally wrong. In *M'Naghten**, the judges said:

'We are of the opinion that, notwithstanding the party accused did the act complained of with a view, under the influence of insane delusion, of redressing or revenging some supposed grievance or injury, or of producing some public benefit, he is nevertheless punishable according to the nature of the crime committed, if he knew at the time of committing such crime that he was acting contrary to law; by which expression we understand your lordships to mean the law of the land.'

In *Windle*, the accused knew that in killing his wife, who had often talked of committing suicide, he was doing an act that the law forbade. It was accepted by Lord Goddard CJ in the Court of Appeal that 'he may have thought it was a kindly act to put her out of her sufferings or imagined sufferings', but that this was not the relevant question. He said, 'there is no doubt that the word 'wrong' in the *M'Naghten** rules means contrary to law and does not have some vague meaning which may vary according to the opinion of different persons whether a particular act might or might not be justified'. It should be stressed that the lack of knowledge of the legality of the defendant's acts must stem from her disease of the mind. Generally, ignorance of the law is no excuse.

It will be appreciated that the *M'Naghten** rules mean that a defendant who as a result of insane delusions believes that God has told him to kill people will not be regarded as insane. He will be aware of the nature of his acts and aware that what he is doing is contrary to the law. It would be different if he thought that God had told him that the people were in fact not humans but aliens from outer space whom he should destroy. In such a case the defendant would appear not to know that the quality of his acts is classified as insane. Whether it is proper to distinguish in this way between precisely the form of the delusion is open to debate.

The *M'Naghten** rules also do not cover a person who suffers from what is called an 'irresistible impulse' to act, if he knows what he is doing and knows that it is contrary to law. Lord Denning said in *Bratty* v. *AG for Northern Ireland*, 'when a man is charged with murder, and it appears that he knew what he was doing, but that he could not resist it, then his assertion "I couldn't help myself" is no defence in itself'. In the case of murder, however, irresistible impulse may be evidence of diminished responsibility (*Byrne*).

3. *Discussion of the law on insanity*

Although the *M'Naghten* rules are formulated in terms of insanity, Smith and Hogan argue that they are 'about responsibility rather than insanity'. As we have seen, the legal definition of insanity is not designed to take account of developments in medical opinion. Further, the courts have stressed that the law does not take into account the policy implications of the definition of insanity for example, by taking into account the possibility of dangers to the public. A point from a different perspective is that many defendants still prefer not to raise the insanity defence, but instead accept a straightforward criminal conviction. This means that such insane defendants are not receiving the treatment they need and instead are detained in prisons.

We have already noted that the Criminal Procedure (Unfitness to Plead) Act 1991 has given wide discretion to judges in deciding how to deal with a defendant found not guilty but insane. Another important change that the 1991 Act has made is that now the court must hear the evidence of two registered medical practitioners who have experience in diagnosis of mental disorder, before declaring a defendant not guilty by virtue of insanity. This may be required by article 5 of the European Convention on Human Rights which requires 'objective medical evidence before conviction'. However, there is no requirement that the court should follow the medical evidence, and some commentators have suggested that the law under the new Act may not be in full compliance with the Convention (see Chapter 19).

Four peculiarities of the procedural aspects of the insanity defence should be noted. First, the result of a successful insanity plea is not a straightforward acquittal: it is the 'special verdict' of 'not guilty by reason of insanity'. Second, there is a presumption of sanity, so that, as an exception to the general rule, an accused raising insanity has the burden of proving it on the balance of probabilities (on the burden of proof generally, see Chapter 2.4). This is controversial. Normally the prosecution has to rebut the defendant's claim that he had no *mens rea* beyond reasonable doubt. Where, however, the defendant's claim is that he is insane, the burden switches to the defendant. In Chapter 19 we will discuss the potential impact of the Human Rights Act on this area of the law. Third, the prosecution, as well as the defendant, may raise the issue of insanity. This may happen on a plea of diminished responsibility, another defence which puts in issue the accused's state of mind. The prosecution may counter with evidence of insanity in order to ensure detention in a hospital instead of a complete acquittal or a sentence of ordinary imprisonment. Alternatively, the trial judge may rule that a defence submission by the accused, such as a plea of automatism, amounts in law to a plea of insanity and direct the jury accordingly (*Bratty* v. *AG for Northern Ireland*). Such a situation may result in a change of plea to guilty by an accused who prefers a sentence of imprisonment to the stigma of the special verdict. Fourth, although the special verdict is formally an acquittal, it is possible for the accused to appeal against that verdict, under s.12 Criminal Appeal Act 1968. This is an exception to the rule that there is no appeal against an acquittal in the

Crown Court. The reason lies in the consequences of the special verdict for the defendant and the fact that insanity can be raised by the prosecution as well as the defence.

15.3   Denial of *Actus Reus*

As mentioned earlier, the defendant can seek to mount a defence on the basis that he did not satisfy the *actus reus* of the crime. This can be a straight-forward denial that he did the act alleged. In this section we will look at two special ways in which a defendant may allege that he did not commit the *actus reus*.

15.3.1   Self-defence and the Prevention of Crime

Here we will consider two closely aligned defences:

1 Section 3 Criminal Law Act 1967 provides a defence to a person who is using force to prevent a crime. It provides:

> '(1) A person may use such force as is reasonable in the circum-stances in the prevention of crime, or in effecting or assisting in the lawful arrest of offenders or suspected offenders or of persons unlaw-fully at large.
> (2) Subsection (1) above shall replace the rules of the common law on the question when force used for a purpose mentioned in the subsec-tion is justified by that purpose.'

This section would therefore apply where the defendant sees a friend being attacked and uses force to protect his friend.

2 The common law of self-defence can also be used. Subsection (2) makes it clear that where s.3(1) applies, the common law defence of use of force to prevent a crime or to effect or assist in a lawful arrest of offenders can be used. However, subsection (2) does not refer to the defence of self-defence. It is therefore generally assumed that the common law defence that a defendant can use force to protect himself or herself from an unjust threat, still exists.

In some cases both these defences will apply. If the defendant is attacked by someone and responds with violence, the defendant may be able to rely on either defence: to claim that his use of force was an attempt to prevent further attacks on him and therefore fell in s.3; or to rely on common law self-defence, arguing that the defendant was acting in order to defend himself. One or both of these defences apply to someone who is protecting themselves from an attack; to someone who is protecting someone else who is being attacked; to someone who is protecting her own property from attack; and to someone who is protecting someone else's property from attack.

Despite the similarities between the two defences there are two key differences:

1 Where the attacker is not acting unlawfully (for example, the attacker is a child or is insane) then s.3 does not apply (the defendant is not preventing a crime); but common law self-defence does apply.
2 The common law defence only applies if the defendant is acting in order to protect himself or herself. It does not apply where he or she is acting in order to prevent an attack on another, although s.3 does.

Fortunately, you do not need to get too worried about whether the correct defence to apply is s.3 or the common law defence because it is generally assumed that the legal rules applying to the two defences are the same. Unfortunately there is no case which explicitly states this, although that was assumed in *McInnes* and *Attorney-General for Northern Ireland's Reference (No. 1 of 1975)*.

The defences are readily justified. A society offers its citizens protection from violence from each other, usually by means of a police force. However, if someone is suddenly attacked, clearly the state cannot provide protection. Thus the law permits people to protect themselves, using force if necessary, to prevent an immediate attack or its continuation. In addition, the law allows a third party to intervene to protect someone from an attack. The law is sometimes justified by using the argument that the attacker forfeits her rights not to have personal violence used against her by attacking someone else. However, this can be a misleading explanation because the law does not permit any amount of force to be used against an attacker, only what is reasonable. Therefore an attacker does not lose all her rights. An alternative way of justifying the defence is to argue that there has been a net gain for society in repelling the attack. In other words, as a result of the defendant's intervention the situation is better than had the defendant not acted.

There are four main requirements that need to be proved if either defence is to be available:

• The defendant must respond to an unjustified threat to the defendant or her property or someone else
• The force used by the defendant was necessary to avoid the threat
• The force used by the defendant was proportionate

- The defendant acted in order to defend herself or someone else and not for some other reason.

We will consider these requirements separately.

1. The defendant must respond to an unjustified threat to the defendant or her property or someone else

The definition of the kind of attack that can give rise to self-defence has received relatively little attention in law, but it is important to find such a definition in order to distinguish self-defence from duress of circumstance (see Chapter 16.5). This is particularly true where the latter is not a defence to murder. S. Uniacke (1994) has suggested that at the heart of the notion of lawful defence is that the victim was posing an unjust threat to the defendant. The notion of an 'unjust threat' involves two elements:

(a) The victim must pose an unjust threat to the defendant or another. Lawful defence only applies where the threat comes from the victim, rather than from elsewhere. Consider Leonardo, who after a shipwreck is clinging onto a piece of wood when Kate tries to pull him off. Leonardo can use self-defence in repelling Kate's attack because she is posing a threat to his well-being. Because there is no reason why she, rather than he, should be entitled to the piece of wood, the threat is unjust. However, Kate is not being unjustly threatened by Leonardo and so she cannot claim to be acting in self-defence in using force against him in her attempt to get hold of the piece of wood. The threats to her welfare come from the inclement elements and the sea, not Leonardo.

(b) The threat must be an unjust one. It is important to appreciate that this does not require the victim to be blameworthy (*Re A (Conjoined Twins)*; see *Hot Topic* at the end of this chapter). Lawful defence applies, for example, where a sleepwalker or a child uses force against the defendant. Rather than showing that the threatener was blameworthy, it must be shown that the threat was unjust.

It follows that you may not be able to use self-defence if you are responsible for the attack against you. So for example, if Jack hits Arnold and Arnold responds by pushing Jack away, to which Jack responds by stabbing Arnold. Jack could not claim that he was using lawful defence in response to Arnold's push, because Arnold's push could not be regarded as unjust because it was an act of self-defence. This argument was extended further in one case where the defendant went round to see an enemy to discuss a matter with him. He took a weapon in case there was a fight. Any force used would not have been within the self-defence doctrine, as he would have sought out the incident that gave rise to the attack (*Malnik*). This rule must be read in the light of the decision in *Field* that the defendant is permitted to walk around in public, even though he knows that someone is looking for him and ready to attack him. Similarly a defendant can remain where he is, even though he knows that someone is on his way to attack him. The defence is only barred where the defendant deliberately encourages or seeks out the attack.

One issue which has troubled the courts is where the defendant thinks she is facing an unjust threat, but in fact she is not. For example, a woman is walking home at night and a man comes running towards her. She attacks him, believing that he is on the point of raping her. In fact he is just out for a jog. The leading case is *Williams (Gladstone)**. There the defendant thought that he was witnessing a person being mugged. He joined in the struggle and tried to help the victim of the mugging. In fact he had made a mistake and the 'mugger' was a plain-clothed police officer seeking to arrest the 'victim'. The court said that the defendant should be judged on the facts, as he believed them to be. As he perceived the facts to be, he was justified in using force and so the court held he had a defence. Later cases have followed this and it has now become a well-established principle (*Beckford**; *Oatridge*; *B* v. *DPP*). In *Williams (Gladstone)*, Lord Lane explained:

'The reasonableness or unreasonableness of the defendant's belief is material to the question of whether the belief was held by the defendant at all. If the belief was in fact held, its unreasonableness, so far as guilt or innocence is concerned, is neither here nor there. It is irrelevant. Were it otherwise, the defendant would be convicted because he was negligent . . . In other words the jury should be directed first of all that the prosecution have the duty of proving the unlawfulness of the defendant's actions; secondly, if the defendant may have been labouring under a mistake as to the facts, he must be judged according to his mistaken view of the facts; thirdly, that is so whether the mistake was, on an objective view, a reasonable mistake or not.'

In summary, what needs to be shown is that the defendant believed that he or she was responding to an unjust threat, whether or not in fact there was an unjust threat.

2.   *The force used is necessary to rebut the threat*
There are two aspects to this requirement.

(a) The defence is only available if the defendant uses force. This, it must be admitted, is unduly restrictive. Imagine Greg is sitting in a car when he sees Tim advancing towards him waving a hammer. It does not make sense to say that if Tim responds to the threat with force (for example, he drives into Greg) he can rely on lawful defence; but if he decides to escape from an attack by not using force (for example, driving away in excess of the speed limit) he cannot rely on the defence. It is true Tim can rely on duress of circumstances in such a case (see Chapter 16.3), but this defence is narrower in various ways than lawful defence (see Chapter 16.5). Fortunately the courts have been willing to interpret the term 'force' widely. For example, in *Renouf* the defendant driving one car compelled another car to leave the road and this was deemed to be force. One case, *Cousins*, went further and doubted that there need be use of force. On a charge of 'threat to kill', it was held that the defence of lawful defence was available as there was no need here to prove use of force. The court suggested that the only question was whether the defendant's actions were a reasonable way of preventing an attack. However, in *Blake**, the Divisional Court confirmed that to use the defence, a defendant must show he was using force. In that case the writing on property with a felt-tip pen did not constitute 'force'. The weight of authority therefore confirms the requirement of force.

(b) It must be shown that it was necessary for the defendant to use force in order to avoid the threat. If the defendant could easily have escaped from the attack but instead decides to use violence in return, the defence may not be available. Having said that, the courts are sympathetic to a defendant who is faced with unjustified threat but fails to see a means of escape. As long as the defendant believes that the use of force is the only effective way to repel the attack and there is no reasonable means for escape, he or she will be able to rely on the defence (*Bird*).

The law has even been willing to accept that it may be 'necessary' to use pre-emptive force before the aggressor has begun a threatened attack (*Cousins*). In one case, Lord Lane said that it may be considered necessary for the accused to have armed himself in advance of an expected attack, if 'his object was to protect himself or his family or his property against imminent apprehended attack and to do so by means which he believed were no more than reasonably necessary to meet the force used by the attackers' (*Attorney-General's Reference (No. 2 of 1983)**).

There is, therefore, no absolute rule in English law that in order to plead lawful defence the defendant must have first tried to retreat. However, the possibility of retreat will be taken into account by the jury in deciding whether or not force was necessary. In *Julien*, Widgery LJ said:

'It is not . . . law that a person threatened must take to his heels and run . . . but what is necessary is that he should demonstrate by his actions that he does not want to fight. He must demonstrate that he is prepared to

temporise and disengage and perhaps to make some physical withdrawal.'

In *Bird*, the Court of Appeal considered a direction to the jury based on
this passage and held that it was not necessary for the accused to have
demonstrated an unwillingness to fight. However, such a demonstration
would provide a convincing rebuttal of any suggestion that the accused was
the aggressor or that the force was used in retaliation or revenge, and not in
self-defence.

3.   The force must be reasonable

The force must be a proportionate (reasonable) response to the threat as the
defendant believed it to be. In deciding what is a proportional response, a
very important factor will be the seriousness of the threat and its object:
was it a threat of minor damage to property or a threat to someone's life?
In the case of a fight, the jury will consider what weapons were being used.
In *McInnes*, for example, Edmund Davies LJ said that in a fist-fight it was
'totally unreasonable' to pull out a knife and deliberately (in the words of
the accused) 'let him have it'. Even in the panic of a fist-fight, the defendant should show due regard to human life. If the defendant is aware that
his 'attackers' are police officers it is unlikely that the jury will accept that
the response was reasonable; although it still may be possible to persuade
the jury that the force used was reasonable if the defendant feared that the
police were to use more force than they are entitled to under the law
(*Burley*).

In deciding that the response was reasonable, the use of force must be
proportionate to the threat as it was perceived by the defendant. This does
not mean that it is up to the defendant to decide whether the response is
reasonable. The jury, not the defendant, must decide whether the defendant's response was reasonable on the facts as the defendant believed them
to be. As was explained in *Owino* by Collins J:

> 'The jury have to decide whether a defendant honestly believed that the
> circumstances were such as required him to use force to defend himself
> from an attack or a threatened attack. In this respect a defendant must be
> judged in accordance with his honest belief, even though that belief may
> have been mistaken. But the jury must then determine whether the force
> used was reasonable in the circumstances as he believed them to be.'

Thus if a defendant wakes up and finds a burglar in his room, he will not
be able to use the defence if he kills the burglar that he believes burglars
deserve to be shot or he thought that shooting the burglar was the only way

he could protect his property. In both cases the defendant would not be acting reasonably or proportionately on the facts as he believed them to be. By contrast, the defendant will be able to use the defence that he believed the burglar was about to kill him, however unreasonable that belief.

When deciding whether the response of the defendant was reasonable, the jury should not be unduly strict. Lord Morris in *Palmer** explained:

> 'If there has been an attack so that defence is reasonably necessary, it will be recognised that a person defending himself cannot weigh to a nicety the exact measure of his necessary defensive action. If a jury thought that in a moment of unexpected anguish a person attacked had only done what he honestly and instinctively thought was necessary that would be most potent evidence that only reasonable defensive action had been taken.'

In considering the reasonableness of the defendant's response, the jury can take into account the defendant's physical characteristics but not his psychological condition (*Martin*). So the defendant may be able to argue that his physical frailty meant that it was reasonable for him to use a weapon, rather than fight the attacker with his fists. However, his psychological condition cannot make a disproportionate response reasonable.

If the defendant's response is unreasonable then the defendant is guilty. There is no defence to murder if a defendant uses more force than is proportionate, even if he is a police officer acting in the course of duty (*Clegg**). The *Clegg* decision is controversial. If the defendant is attacked and is justified in using some force, but in the heat of the moment misjudges the appropriate level of force and kills, there is a strong case for saying he does not deserve the full censure of murder conviction. The Criminal Code proposes a change in the law here by suggesting a special defence of excessive force, reducing a murder charge to one of manslaughter (Clause 59).

Where a defendant claims that he was acting in order to protect property it will be rare for a jury to find that a defendant's very violent response was reasonable. However, a low level of violence may be thought to be appropriate. The issue is, of course, to be left for the jury and it may well be that individuals disagree on the appropriate levels of violence to protect property.

4.   The defendant acts in order to defend himself and not for some other reason

This is in line with the *Dadson* principle (Chapter 16.1). It needs to be shown that the defendant was not acting out of revenge or any other motive but acting in order to protect himself or another. This requirement also means that if the defendant helps someone, who unbeknown to him is in fact attacking someone else, he cannot rely on lawful defence as a defence.

It has been argued that the Human Rights Act will require a reconsideration of the law on lawful self-defence and the prevention of crime. This will be discussed in Chapter 19.

15.3.2   Damaging Property in order to Protect People or Other Property

Damage to property in order to protect property is governed by s.5 Criminal Damage Act 1971 (see Chapter 14.1). The defendant must believe both that the property is in immediate need of protection and that the means adopted are reasonable in the circumstances. Note that the means adopted do not actually have to be reasonable: it is enough if the accused believed that what was done was reasonable. In the case of damage to property in order to protect oneself or another person, the common law of lawful defence is also available (s.5(5)). That requires that only reasonable measures may be taken (for example, *Sears* v. *Broome**). The difference between the statutory and common law rules is an anomaly.

15.3.4   Automatism

This is another particular way of denying that the defendant performed the *actus reus*, by claiming that he did not act in the legal sense. Automatism has been already discussed in Chapter 4.6.

15.4   Denial of *Mens Rea*

As mentioned above, the defendant may simply deny that he intended or foresaw a consequence as required for the *mens rea* of the offence. Here we will deal with two more complex ways of denying a *mens rea*.

15.4.1   Mistake

One way of denying that the prosecution has made out its case is to say that the defendant is mistaken about a fact that is an aspect of the *actus reus*. Such a mistake will only succeed if the effect of the mistake is such that the defendant did not have the appropriate *mens rea*. This means that there is no defence of mistake as such. It is rather that some mistakes will lead to a finding that the defendant has no *mens rea*. So when will a mistake mean that the defendant lacks *mens rea*? This is answered by the following points:

1. *The mistake must relate to an aspect of the* actus reus

For example, if the defendant has sexual intercourse with Jane, a non-consenting woman, believing she is called Susan, this affords no defence. That is because the *mens rea* of rape does not require proof that the defendant was aware of the name of the victim. If, however, the defendant was mistaken about whether the victim was consenting, this would be a relevant mistake because the lack of consent of the victim is part of the *actus reus*. In *DPP* v. *B* and *R* v. *K* the House of Lords has confirmed that there is a presumption that a mistake as to any element of the *actus reus* provides a defence, unless there is a statutory provision making it clear that such a mistake does not provide a defence (see Chapter 6).

2. *The mistake does not need to be reasonable*

Lord Hailsham explained in Morgan*:

> 'I believe that *"mens rea"* means "guilty or criminal mind", and . . . to insist that a belief must be reasonable to excuse is to insist that either the accused is to be found guilty of intending to do that which in truth he did not intend to do, or that his state of mind, though innocent of evil intent, can convict him if it be honest but not rational.'

This approach was recently confirmed by the House of Lords in *B* v. *DPP** and *R* v. *K**. This is however, subject to an exception. If the offence is a statutory one which makes it clear that only a reasonable mistake affords a defence or indeed that no mistake will provide a defence then that provision governs the law. So if the offence is a strict liability one or a partial one (see Chapter 6), the mistake will provide no defence.

3. *The mistake must be one of fact, not law*

So far we have only considered mistakes of fact. Is it possible for a mistake as to the law to be a defence? There is a well-known maxim that ignorance of the law is no excuse: it will do the accused no good to argue that he did not know that having sexual intercourse with a woman without her consent was a crime; or that 'stolen goods' for the purpose of the offence of handling stolen goods includes goods obtained by deception.

So, a mistake as to the content of the criminal law does not affect liability. On the other hand, a mistake as to the civil law may do so. For example a mistake as to whether property belongs to oneself or another will be relevant to liability for theft (s.2(1)(a) Theft Act 1968 makes this clear), and this mistake may be based on an inaccurate view of the civil law of contract or sale of goods. As with mistakes of fact, the mistake must relate to an element of the *actus reus* which requires *mens rea*.

15.3.2   Intoxication

Strictly speaking, there is no defence of intoxication, however keen students seem to be to talk of it. Rather in some cases it is possible to introduce evidence of intoxication to support a defence of no *mens rea*. In such a case the defence is no *mens rea*, not intoxication. This is not surprising. It would be most peculiar if the law were to say: because you were drunk we will provide you with a defence.

In order to understand the law on intoxication it is necessary to distinguish cases where the defendant was voluntarily intoxicated and where he was involuntarily intoxicated.

Distinguishing voluntary and involuntary intoxication

To decide whether a defendant was voluntarily or involuntarily intoxicated, the key question is: did the defendant knowingly take alcohol or illegal drugs?

If the answer is 'yes', the defendant knowingly took alcohol or illegal drugs (for example heroin or cannabis) realizing what they were then the defendant will be voluntarily intoxicated. It is no defence for a defendant to claim that he was unaware of the strength of the alcohol in the drink (even if he believes that it is a low-alcohol drink: *Allen* (1988)). Likewise it is no defence for an accused to claim that he was unaware of the effect that alcohol or drugs would have on him.

If the answer is 'no', if the drink was non-alcoholic or the drugs were legal (for example, those prescribed by a doctor), or the defendant believed them to be, then the question will be whether the defendant was aware that the drugs might have the effect of causing him to lose control over his behaviour. If he did then he is voluntarily intoxicated; if he did not then he is involuntarily intoxicated. Common examples of involuntary intoxication arise where the defendant's non-alcoholic drink is (unknown to the defendant) spiked with alcohol. In *Hardie**, the defendant took Valium (an antidepressant drug), which had been prescribed by a doctor to a friend. The defendant went on to set fire to a room. It was found that the defendant believed that the Valium would have the effect of calming him down or sending him to sleep, but not of exciting him. He was therefore said to be involuntarily intoxicated. Had he been aware of the potential effect of the drug then he would have been voluntarily intoxicated.

Voluntary intoxication

In the leading House of Lords' case on voluntary intoxication, *Majewski**, a distinction was drawn between crimes of 'specific intent' and 'basic intent':

(a) *Crimes of specific intent.* In crimes of 'specific intent', the defendant can introduce evidence of intoxication to deny that he had the necessary *mens rea*. This is not to mean that in crimes of specific intent, just because the defendant is intoxicated he should be found not guilty. Rather, as the courts regularly confirm, 'a drunken intent is still an intent' (for example *Kingston*). Rather, the jury should consider all the evidence, including the defendant's intoxicated state, to decide whether or not he really had the *mens rea*.

(b) *Crimes of basic intent.* In crimes of 'basic intent', the defendant cannot introduce evidence of voluntary intoxication to rebut a claim that he had the necessary *mens rea*.

So how do we know which crimes are crimes of specific intent and which are crimes of basic intent? Although there is much dispute over the exact meaning of these phrases, the best interpretation is that 'basic intent' means recklessness (either *Cunningham* or *Caldwell* recklessness), while 'specific intent' means intention. It may help to remember that a specific intent crime requires proof that something specific was intended; a basic intent crime does not. Occasionally an offence may have some aspects which involve 'specific intent' and some which involve 'basic intent'. Rape is an example. There intoxication would be relevant in deciding whether the defendant intended to commit sexual intercourse (an issue of 'specific intent'), but not in deciding whether he believed the victim was consenting (an issue of 'basic intent').

So how might the law work in practice? First, consider a specific intent crime such as murder. The facts of *Moloney* provide a useful example. There the defendant and his step-father were both very drunk and decided to embark on a game involving guns. The defendant shot his step-father, but gave evidence that he did not mean to shoot him, but pulled the trigger to win the game. As murder is a specific intent offence, the evidence of his intoxication can be introduced. It was therefore up to the jury, considering all the evidence including the defendant's drunkenness, to decide whether he intended to kill or cause grievous bodily harm to his step-father. The fact of the drunkenness is crucial here because otherwise it would have been unbelievable that a sober man shooting a gun a few feet away from his step-father did not intend to seriously injure him. However, taking into account the drunkenness, the defendant's story becomes believable and it would be possible for a jury to decide that the defendant did not have the necessary intention. In *McKnight* Henry LJ suggested that the question in cases of specific intent was whether the defendant was *capable* of forming intent. This is inconsistent with all earlier cases which stress that the question is whether the defendant actually had the intent. Henry LJ's comments probably do not represent the present law.

Second, looking at a crime of basic intent, requiring proof of recklessness, we have already seen that a defendant who is voluntarily intoxicated cannot introduce evidence of his intoxication to rebut a claim that he was either *Caldwell* or *Cunningham* reckless (see Chapter 4). This will mean that if the risk was obvious, the jury is bound to assume that the defendant foresaw the risk and so he was reckless; unless in a case of *Cunningham* recklessness he can provide some other reason (apart from the intoxication) why he did not foresee the obvious risk (for example, he was blind).

Involuntary intoxication

If the defendant was involuntarily intoxicated, she can introduce evidence of her intoxication to rebut an allegation of recklessness (basic intent), and to argue that she did not foresee the consequences of her actions. As with voluntary intoxication, she can also introduce evidence of intoxication to show she did not intend a consequence (have specific intent). However, it must be stressed that if, after taking into account the involuntary intoxication and other evidence, the jury decides that the defendant did have the relevant *mens rea*, the defendant has no defence based on the involuntary intoxication. This was stressed in *Kingston** where the defendant, who had paedophilic desires, was lured into his enemy's flat. The enemy laced the defendant's cup of coffee with a drug. The defendant was taken to a room where there was a drugged naked boy. The defendant claimed that because of the drugs, his inhibitions were removed and although normally he would have been able to resist such a temptation, he committed an indecent assault on the boy. The House of Lords decided involuntary intoxication was only relevant in deciding whether the defendant had the necessary *mens rea*. Having decided that the defendant did intend to commit the assault, it was irrelevant that he only did so because drugs were administered against his will. This case stresses the point that there is no such thing as a defence of intoxication, it is simply that intoxication can be evidence supporting a defence of no *mens rea*. *Kingston* was a harsh decision, but the court seemed concerned that a defence of involuntary intoxication would be easy for a defendant to raise and difficult for the prosecution to disprove.

Intoxication and defences

What if a drunken defendant is seeking to raise a defence? Unfortunately the law has developed in a rather haphazard way and a general principle cannot be found. All we can do is discuss the individual defences separately.

(a) Mistake

What if the defendant, because of his drunken mistake, was not aware of an element of the offence? For example in a rape case because he was drunk he thought that the victim was consenting when in fact she was not. The correct view, it is submitted, is to follow the approach outlined above. For voluntary intoxication, the mistaken belief can be introduced as evidence of no *mens rea* in cases of specific intent, but otherwise will not provide a defence. So in a murder case, if the defendant was so drunk that he thought the victim was a deer and shot him, this could provide a defence: there was no intent to kill or seriously injure a person. This defendant would still be convicted of manslaughter. However in a rape case where the victim is drunk and so believes that the victim is consenting when she is not, the defendant will be guilty of rape because recklessness (basic intent) as to the victim's consent is required (*Fotheringham*). In cases of involuntary intoxication, the drunken mistake can provide a defence if that mistake negates *mens rea*. This approach is logical. If the law does not allow a voluntarily intoxicated defendant a defence to an offence of recklessness based on the fact that he did not foresee the consequences of his action because he was drunk, why should a drunken mistake as to the circumstances in which he acts provide a defence?

Unfortunately there are two cases which suggest that a drunken mistake as to a circumstance can provide a defence. In *Jaggard* v. *Dickenson*, the very drunk defendant damaged a house. She argued that she believed that the house was owned by her friend, who would have consented to the damage. In fact the house was not her friend's, but in her drunken state she had made a defence. Section 5(2) Criminal Damage Act provides a defence if the defendant believed that the owner would consent to the damage. Mustill J stated that the section provided a defence even if the belief was a drunken one. In *Richardson and Irvin*, the defendant believed that the victim was consenting to rough horseplay and therefore consented to the force. He therefore was not aware that his act was without the consent of the victim. This was held to be a defence to a charge of maliciously inflicting grievous bodily harm.

In the light of these two cases, therefore, the law cannot be stated with certainty. The better view is that *Jaggard* and *Richardson* are incorrectly decided and that a voluntarily intoxicated defendant cannot use evidence of intoxication to deny recklessness (basic intent) be that by denying foresight of consequences or awareness of circumstances. An alternative view is that an intoxicated belief as to the circumstances in which he acts can provide support for a no *mens rea* defence to any criminal charge; although a drunken mistake as to the consequences of a defendant's actions cannot provide support to a charge of basic intent.

(b)   Self-defence or prevention of crime

As explained above, in *Gladstone Williams* it was held that a defendant can use the defence of self-defence or the prevention of crime even though there was in fact no threat, as long as the defendant honestly believed that he was facing such a threat. However this is not true where the defendant, because he is intoxicated, incorrectly believes that he or another is being attacked. So if the defendant believes, because of his voluntary intoxication, that he is being attacked he cannot rely on a defence of self-defence. This was established in *O'Grady* and *O'Connor*. In cases of specific intent, the judge needs to direct the jury carefully here. The defendant can use his drunken beliefs as evidence that he had no intent to kill, but not as evidence that he was acting in self-defence.

(c)   Duress

If a defendant believes that there is a threat to life or of serious injury because he is intoxicated then this belief cannot form the basis of a duress claim, because the defendant must show that he has reasonable grounds for his beliefs that a threat has been made and will be carried out (see Chapter 16.2). Similarly, the defendant will not be able to argue that because he was intoxicated he gave in to the threat; he is required to show the level of firmness of a reasonable sober person.

(d)   Provocation

If a defendant mishears or misinterprets what is said or done because he is intoxicated and so believes that he is being insulted this, it seems can form the basis of defence of provocation (*Letenock*). It is very unlikely that the jury will decide that voluntary intoxication is a relevant factor when considering whether the defendant acted reasonably in response to the provocation (*Smith*).

(e)   Automatism

If the defendant commits a crime, having fallen over and banged his head while in an intoxicated condition, he may try to plead automatism. If he was in an automaton state, *Stripp* indicates that the key question is whether the defendant's state was caused predominantly by his intoxication or by his concussion. If it was the concussion then he would be able to plead automatism; if it was his voluntary intoxication then he would not (*Burns*; *Lipman*).

(f) Diminished responsibility
The relationship between diminished responsibility and intoxication is discussed in Chapter 10.9.2.

(g) Insanity
The leading case on insanity and intoxication is *Lipman*. There the defendant took LSD and (he claimed) as a result had an hallucination in which he was attacked by a many-headed monster. He killed the monster. On recovering, he discovered that in fact he had killed his girlfriend. He was not permitted to plead insanity because it was his voluntary intoxication, rather than any disease of the mind, which had caused him to be unaware of the nature of his acts. If however a person can show that although intoxicated it was his mental condition that primarily caused his lack of awareness then insanity may be available (*Burns*).

Discussion of the law on intoxication

There has been much dispute over the logic and policy which underlie the present law on intoxication. Understandably, the courts have been very unwilling to absolve completely from criminal responsibility those who incapacitate their mental processes with alcohol or drugs, and then go on to cause injury to other people or property. In *Majewski*, several of their Lordships accepted that their position owed more to policy than logic. Lord Salmon put it like this:

> 'A man who by voluntarily taking drink and drugs gets himself into an aggressive state in which he does not know what he is doing and then makes a vicious assault can hardly say with any plausibility that what he did was a pure accident which should render him immune from any criminal liability . . . In strict logic this view cannot be justified. But this is the view that has been adopted by the common law of England which is founded on common sense and experience rather than strict logic.'

This argument was expressed in differing ways by the judges in *Majewski*. Lord Simon of Glaisdale said:

> 'There is no juristic reason why mental incapacity (short of *M'Naghten*

insanity), brought about by self-induced intoxication, to realise what one is doing or its probable consequences should not be . . . a state of mind stigmatised as wrongful by the criminal law, and there is every practical reason why it should be.'

This view suggests that although intoxication may render a person incapable of forming a specific intention, such as an intent to kill, intoxication itself provides the *mens rea* necessary for a certain basic level of criminal culpability. Put this way, intoxication is seen as an alternative form of *mens rea*, rather than as an aspect of the rules on evidence which is how we have explained the law in this section. This would mean that even if the defendant could prove that had he been sober he would not have foreseen the risk (for example, because he was blind), he would not have a defence. This is how Lord Elwyn-Jones explained in *Majewski* why assault was a 'basic intent' crime:

'If a man of his own volition takes a substance which causes him to cast off the restraints of reason and conscience, no wrong is done to him by holding him answerable criminally for any injury he may do while in that condition. His course of conduct in reducing himself by drugs and drink to that condition in my view supplies the evidence of *mens rea*, of guilty mind, certainly sufficient for crimes of basic intent. It is a reckless course of conduct and recklessness is enough to constitute the necessary *mens rea* in assault cases.'

Mens rea is here regarded as a general requirement of culpability, rather than a precise state of mind such as intention or knowledge. This explanation for the law appears to be that if the accused takes illegal drugs or alcohol he is at that point reckless (*Cunningham* and *Caldwell* reckless). He must be aware that he may go on to commit a crime because, once intoxicated, no one can be sure how they will behave. The law presumes that everyone is aware of this potential effect of illegal drugs or alcohol. As was stated by Griffiths LJ in *Bailey*, 'it is common knowledge that those who take alcohol to excess or certain sorts of drugs may become aggressive or do dangerous or unpredictable things'. This explanation of the law has been criticized on two main grounds. First, it does not explain why those who drink a very small amount of alcohol or a low-alcohol drink should be seen as reckless. Secondly, the *mens rea* of foreseeing that one might go on to commit some kind of criminal act is not a sufficient *mens rea* for many crimes. For example, for a conviction under s.20 Offences Against the Person Act it has to be shown that the defendant foresaw that his act might cause some harm to the victim. Evidence that the defendant foresaw that he might commit some kind of crime would be insufficient. In any event, such a *mens rea* is not contemporary with the *actus reus*. One solution is to regard the whole sequence of events as one indivisible 'series of acts' under the doctrine of *Thabo Meli* (see Chapter 4.7). This was the approach of Lord Denning in *Gallagher**, a case where the link was clear because of evidence of a preconceived plan formulated before the accused got drunk, but this case involved an exceptional set of facts.

It may be that the law on intoxication represents a policy choice. Many crimes of violence are committed by those who are intoxicated. It is interesting to note that the Law Commission in its working paper suggested wholesale reform of the law in the light of the theoretical difficulties. However, as a result of the reaction to the working paper, and particularly the argument that the general public would not accept the acquittal of drunken defendants on the ground of lack of *mens rea*, the Commission decided in its final report to propose retaining the present law, albeit on a statutory footing.

Hot Topic: Mistakes and Self-Defence

One topic that has particularly troubled the law is where the defendant makes a mistake when acting in self-defence. It is useful to distinguish two kinds of mistakes that a defendant could make. The first is where she has made a mistake of perception: the defendant thinks she is being attacked but she is not. The second is where the defendant has made a mistaken judgement of value: the defendant correctly perceives the facts but decides to respond with an inappropriate level of violence. The test developed by the courts is that a defence is available if on the facts as the defendant believed them to be, the level of force used was reasonable. In other words, the law is sympathetic to a mistake of perception which will not lead to a denial of the defence; while the law is less sympathetic to a mistake of value which will cause the defendant to lose the defence. Why are these different kinds of mistakes treated differently?

In relation to mistakes of perception, the courts have relied on an analogy with the case of *Morgan*. *Morgan* was interpreted as arguing that it was necessary to show that the defendant had the necessary *mens rea* in respect of each part of the *actus reus*. So a defendant to a rape charge who believed (albeit unreasonably) that a victim was consenting was not guilty as he did not have the necessary recklessness as to the victim's consent, which was part of the *actus reus*. Likewise in *Williams (Gladstone)*, the court argued that if the defendant believed he was acting in legitimate self-defence then he did not have the necessary *mens rea* for the whole of the *actus reus*. That is because the court argued that it was an aspect of the *actus reus* of an assault that the act was unlawful. This reasoning is controversial. There are three particular difficulties.

First, there is doubt whether it is correct that unlawfulness is a part of the *actus reus*. It has been argued that unlawfulness cannot be part of the *actus reus* as such, because an act is not unlawful until both the *mens rea* and *actus reus* have been proved (Simester). In other words, to call unlawfulness an aspect of the *actus reus* is to put the cart before the horse.

Second, it was clear from their Lordships' speeches in *Morgan* that they did not intend to change the law on self-defence. Indeed their Lordships in *Morgan* appeared to assume that the mistake had to be reasonable if it was to be the basis of a self-defence.

Third, as moral issues it may be that mistakes in rape and self-defence can be distinguished. Simester argues it is important to appreciate in the case of a mistake over the consent of a victim of rape, that the defendant is not aware he is harming the victim. In the case of self-defence one can argue that the defendant is aware that he is harming the victim, but he is claiming that he had a good reason for doing so. The significance of this distinction is that the law could legitimately require a defendant who is aware that he is harming another to ensure he has reasonable grounds to believe that he has a good reason for injuring the victim; whereas if a person is unaware that he is harming the victim, the law cannot expect someone to ensure he has a good reason for performing the act. This argument might suggest that the law should be more sympathetic to the mistaken rapist than to the mistaken self-defence case. An alternative argument, made by J. Horder (1990), is to focus on the emotions that cause or explain the mistake. He suggests that fear of injury is a legitimate reason for making such a mistake (as in self-defence), but that sexual excitement is not a legitimate reason to make a mistake (as in *Morgan*). Seen this way, the law should be more sympathetic to the mistaken self-defence than to the mistaken rape case. Even though they have contradictory results, both arguments indicate that the two situations are not directly analogous.

Despite these concerns, the House of Lords in *DPP* v. *B* and *R* v. *K* has approved the *Morgan* approach as one of general application, including in relation to self-defence. So despite the above concerns, the courts appear persuaded by the analogy.

What about mistakes of value? As mentioned above, although the courts have been sympathetic about mistakes of perception, they have not to mistakes of value. In the *Tony Martin* case, a farmer argued that he believed he was justified in shooting a person he thought was a burglar because he believed that he was justified in doing so to protect his property. Had he thought (wrongly) that the burglar was about to kill him, he could have relied on the defence. Perhaps the best explanation of this position is that mistakes of perception are all too common. People mishear or misunderstand things all the time. There is no particular blame that attaches to such a mistake. Where someone believes he is about to be attacked there is no opportunity to double-check that this belief is justified. By contrast, a mistake of value is different. People who have values that are inconsistent with the law (for example, that it is permissible to shoot people dead to protect pieces of property) are not treated like those who mishear things. Adults are seen as responsible for their moral opinions. Such attitudes are themselves not criminal, but once they are put into action they can become so.

Before leaving mistakes and self-defence, we should consider the possible effect of intoxication. Suppose that the accused, because of self-induced intoxication, mistakenly believes that he is being threatened and that force is necessary to protect himself; he uses a degree of force which would be reasonable in the circumstances that he believes to exist. Although since *Williams (Gladstone)* self-defence has been based on the accused's own perception of the threat, in the face of an intoxicated mistake the policy demands that always surround intoxication have prevailed. In Chapter 10.3.2 above, we saw that the effect of intoxication on a mistake which amounted to a denial of *mens rea* depends on whether the offence is one of specific or basic intent. However, where the intoxicated mistake affects self-defence, the Court of Appeal has held that the accused has no defence even to specific intent crimes. In *O'Grady**, Lord Lane CJ held that no distinction should be drawn in this respect between offences of specific and basic intent. He drew support from the leading decision on intoxication, *Majewski**, and recognized 'two competing interests': on the one hand that of the accused, who had done what he believed necessary to defend himself; and 'on the other hand that of the public in general and the victim in particular who, probably through no fault of his own, has been injured or perhaps killed because of the defendant's drunken mistake. Reason recoils from the conclusion that in such circumstances a defendant is entitled to leave the court without a stain on his character'.

This means that if the defendant is so intoxicated that he believes that the victim is a large balloon, he will have a defence (as this is a mistake as to the *actus reus*). If, however, he is so intoxicated that he believes, unreasonably, that the victim is about to attack him, he will not have a defence. A difference is thus created between intoxicated mistaken beliefs that concern self-defence and those that concern other elements of the *actus reus* (such as consent: see Chapter 7.7) requiring specific intent or knowledge. The distinction which appeared to have been rejected in *Williams (Gladstone)* has reappeared in another guise, and it is interesting to note that Lord Lane CJ gave the judgement of the Court of Appeal in both cases.

Summary

15.1 A defendant who does not want to plead guilty to a criminal charge has a number of options available. She can simply claim that the prosecution has not proved its case – that the *mens rea* or *actus reus* has not been made out. Alternatively, she can seek to introduce evidence of a special defence, which involves admission of the *actus reus* and *mens rea* but seeks to claim that the defendant falls within one of the situations accepted by the law in which the defendant does not deserve the blame attaching to a conviction.

15.2 Some groups of people are exempt from criminal sanctions, as the criminal law cannot be addressed to them. Infancy and insanity are the two best-known examples. Infancy covers all those under the age of ten. Between ten and fourteen, a child is presumed to be incapable of committing an offence, but this presumption is rebuttable by evidence that the child was aware that her acts were wrong and not merely naughty. There is a presumption of sanity in all cases. However, insanity can be relevant in two ways. Firstly, if the defendant is insane at the time of the trial (she is unable to understand the trial or give her representative instructions), in which case if it is shown she committed the *actus reus* then the judge has a discretion as to what orders can be made in respect of the defendant. The defendant may also claim that she was insane at the time when she committed the offence. Insanity may be raised by the prosecution as well as the defence. The law on insanity is still governed by the *M'Naghten* rules, formulated in the last century and requiring a defect of reason caused by a disease of the mind.

15.3 Self-defence applies where it is necessary to use some force to defend oneself, another person or property, and the degree of force used is reasonable in the circumstances that the accused believed to exist. A person may also use a reasonable degree of force in the prevention of crime or in a lawful arrest, under s.3 Criminal Law Act 1967. Automatism is another way of denying that the accused has the required *mens rea*.

15.4 Two specific ways in which the defendant may argue that she lacks *mens rea* are by claiming she has made a mistake or that she was intoxicated when she committed the crime. A mistake of fact may amount to a denial of the *mens rea* of an offence, if it concerns a fact that forms part of the *actus reus*. But the mistake will not excuse if that part of the *actus reus* does not need a mental element. There is no general rule as to whether the mistake has to be reasonable; if the offence requires intention or knowledge there is no need for the mistake to be reasonable. If recklessness is sufficient, the position depends on the type of recklessness applied by the courts to that offence. If the offence is one of negligence then the mistake must be reasonable. Involuntary intoxication which results in the accused not possessing the necessary *mens rea* for the offence charged can form the basis of a defence. Voluntary intoxication will only be a defence to crimes which require intention as part of the *mens rea* (specific intent crimes); it is not a defence to crimes which can be committed recklessly (basic intent crimes). Involuntary intoxication is admissible as evidence of no *mens rea* for either specific or basic intent crimes.

Case Notes

***Attorney-General's Reference (No. 2 of 1983)* [1984] 2 WLR 465. Court of Appeal**
The accused was charged with having explosives in his possession without a lawful object, contrary to s.4 Explosive Substances Act 1883. His shop had been damaged during rioting and he was worried about another attack. He manufactured some petrol bombs 'as a last resort'. He was acquitted. The trial judge directed the jury that self-defence could be pleaded as a 'lawful object' for the purposes of s.4. The Court of Appeal held that this was correct. It was open to the jury to find that the making of the petrol bombs was a reasonable means of protection for the accused and his property in the face of an imminent apprehended attack.

***B v. DPP* [2000] Crim LR 403. House of Lords**
See Chapter 6 case notes.

***Beckford* (1987) 3 WLR 611. Privy Council**
The appellant was convicted of murder. He was a police officer who had been sent to arrest the victim who was reported to have been threatening another person with a gun. It was alleged by the prosecution that the appellant had shot the victim when he was unarmed and ready to give himself up. The defence case was that the victim had fired at the police and the appellant had shot and killed the victim in self-defence. The trial judge directed the jury that the killing would be in self-defence if the accused reasonably believed that he was in danger of death or serious injury, and used necessary and reasonable force to resist the attack. The Privy Council allowed the appeal on the ground that the accused would have been acting in self-defence if he had used such force as was reasonable in the circumstances as the accused honestly believed them to be, even if his belief was not reasonable.

***Blake* [1993] Crim LR 586. Divisional Court**
See Chapter 14 case notes.

***Bratty v. AG for Northern Ireland* [1963] AC 386. House of Lords**
See Chapter 3 case notes.

Caldwell [1982] AC 341. House of Lords
See Chapter 4 case notes.

Clegg [1995] 1 AC 482. House of Lords
Private Clegg was policing a checkpoint in Northern Ireland. He requested the driver of a car to stop but the car increased speed and drove through the checkpoint. He fired several shots at the car. The fourth shot, which killed a passenger, was fired after the car had passed through the checkpoint. The House of Lords upheld his conviction for murder, stating that killing by using excessive force in self-defence was murder. As the car had driven past the checkpoint and was driving away at speed, it could not be argued that the car or its occupants were threatening Clegg or his colleagues or posed an immediate threat to other people. Shooting at the car was an inappropriate amount of force to effect an arrest.

Collins [1973] QB 100. Court of Appeal
See Chapter 13 case notes.

Cunningham [1957] 2 All ER 412. Court of Criminal Appeal
See Chapter 4 case notes.

Gallagher [1963] AC 349. House of Lords
The accused was convicted of murder. He had killed his wife with a knife, having bought the knife together with a bottle of whisky. He pleaded insanity and intoxication. The Court of Criminal Appeal in Northern Ireland quashed the conviction on the ground that the trial judge had directed the jury to consider the state of the accused's mind before he started drinking the whisky. The House of Lords allowed the appeal by the prosecutor and restored the conviction. It was held that drunkenness which impaired the accused's powers of perception, moral sense or self-control was no defence. Intoxication would only be a defence to murder (though not manslaughter) if the accused was so drunk that he did not know what he was doing and could not form the necessary intention. If intoxication brings on a disease of the mind then the accused may be temporarily insane within the *M'Naghten* rules, and the insanity defence applies. This was not the case here. He formed the intention to kill while sober, and made preparations to do so. It was no defence that he then got drunk in order to give himself 'Dutch courage' to do the killing.

Hardie [1984] 3 All ER 848. Court of Appeal
The appellant was convicted of criminal damage. He was depressed after the breakdown of his relationship with the woman with whom he had been living. He took several Valium tablets, and then set light to the bedroom of the flat while the woman and her daughter were in another room. The trial judge directed the jury that since the drug was taken deliberately and not on prescription, it was no defence for the accused to argue that as a result of taking the Valium he had no *mens rea*. The Court of Appeal allowed the appeal. The jury should have been directed to consider whether the taking of the Valium itself was reckless, in light of its characteristics as a sedative drug 'wholly different in kind from drugs which are liable to cause unpredictability or aggressiveness'.

R v. K 25 JULY 2001; [2001] UKHL 41. House of Lords
See Chapter 6 case notes.

Kingston [1995] 2 AC 355. House of Lords
The defendant's coffee was spiked with a drug by a man who was seeking to blackmail him. The man then took the defendant to a room where there was a boy who was also drugged. The defendant assaulted the boy. The defendant admitted he had paedophilic inclinations but was normally able to resist any temptation to put them into

practice. However, he said that his inhibitions were removed by the spiked drink and he therefore committed the crime. The Court of Appeal suggested that an accused could have a defence where alcohol or drugs were administered against the accused's will by another. The Crown appealed and the House of Lords upheld the appeal. It accepted the principle that intoxication could only be relevant as evidence that the accused did not have the necessary *mens rea* for a crime. Here the accused admitted having the necessary recklessness and so the involuntary intoxication could only be relevant to mitigation.

Majewski [1977] AC 443. House of Lords

The appellant was convicted of assault occasioning actual bodily harm and assaulting a police officer in the execution of his duty. He had consumed a large quantity of drugs and alcohol before becoming involved in a fight in a pub. The trial judge directed the jury that the effect of the drugs and drink could not be a defence to the charges. The Court of Appeal and the House of Lords dismissed his appeal. It was held that although self-induced intoxication could be a defence to a crime such as murder that required a specific intent, it was no defence to a crime that could be committed recklessly. Self-induced intoxication is a reckless course of conduct which is itself an integral part of the crime (Lord Elwyn-Jones).

M'Naghten [1843–60] All ER Rep 229. House of Lords

The accused was charged with murder and the jury brought in a verdict of not guilty by reason of insanity. There was medical evidence that the accused suffered from delusions which affected his perceptions of right and wrong, and over which he had no control. The case was debated in the House of Lords and a number of questions were submitted to all the judges for their opinion. The judges said that every person is presumed to be sane and 'to possess a sufficient degree of reason to be responsible for his crimes' until the contrary is proved. A person suffering from partial insane delusions, concerning one or more subjects or persons, would nevertheless be criminally liable if he knew that his action was contrary to law. He should be judged as if the facts with respect to which the delusion exists were real. Lord Chief Justice Tindal stated the terms on which the jury should be directed as to the state of mind of such a person (see Chapter 15.2.2 above).

Morgan [1976] AC 182. House of Lords

See Chapter 8 case notes.

O'Grady [1987] 3 WLR 321. Court of Appeal

The appellant was charged with murder and convicted of manslaughter. He had been drinking with a friend and they both returned to his flat. During the night the two had a fight and the friend died of his injuries. The appellant claimed that he had woken up to find himself being attacked, and had been defending himself. The trial judge directed the jury that if the appellant had used an unreasonable degree of force to defend himself as a result of his intoxication, he could not rely on self-defence. The Court of Appeal dismissed the appeal, holding that a person cannot rely on self-defence where, as a result of voluntary intoxication, he mistakenly believes it is necessary to use a certain degree of force to defend himself. No distinction should be drawn between offences of specific and basic intent in relation to involuntary intoxication.

Palmer [1971] AC 814. Privy Council

The appellant was convicted of murder. The judge directed the jury on self-defence that in deciding whether it was reasonably necessary to have used as much force as was used, the jury should take into account all of the circumstances; if an unreasonable degree of force had been used, the jury should convict of murder. It was argued on appeal that in cases where the jury finds that it was necessary for the accused to use some force, but the defendant used an excessive, unreasonable amount of force, then it should be open to the jury to convict of manslaughter. The Privy Council dismissed the appeal. Self-defence either succeeds so as to result in an acquittal or it is disproved by the prosecution and therefore rejected. It cannot, unlike provocation, be a partial defence to murder. In deciding whether the force used was reasonable, the jury will recognize that a person defending himself cannot weigh precisely how much force is necessary to defend himself.

Quick [1973] QB 910. Court of Appeal
See Chapter 3 case notes.

Sears v. *Broome* [1986] Crim LR 461. Divisional Court
The appellant was convicted of criminal damage and acquitted of assault occasioning actual bodily harm. The victim had fallen through a shop window. The prosecution alleged that the appellant had pushed the victim through the window, and the appellant claimed that he had been acting in self-defence and had been trying to prevent the victim from attacking him. The Divisional Court allowed the appeal and quashed the conviction on the ground that as the appellant had been acquitted of assault on the basis of reasonable self-defence, he could not have been acting recklessly and without lawful excuse in relation to the damage to the window.

Sullivan [1984] 1 AC 156. House of Lords
See Chapter 3 case notes.

Williams (Gladstone) (1983) 78 Cr App Rep 276. Court of Appeal
The appellant was convicted of assault occasioning actual bodily harm. He had punched the victim, whom he thought was making an unlawful assault on a youth. In fact the victim had seen the youth rob a woman and had been lawfully attempting to prevent the youth from escaping. The Court of Appeal quashed the conviction on the ground that the jury had been misdirected as to the mistake of fact. The Court held that in cases where the accused makes a mistake of fact, he must be judged on the basis of the mistaken facts as he believed them to be. This is so not only in relation to a mistake as to consent (as in *Morgan**) but also where the mistake relates to the use of reasonable force in self-defence or the prevention of crime. If the mistake was genuinely held, its unreasonableness is irrelevant.

Further Reading

A discussion on the nature of defences is found in Horder (1996) and Sullivan. A discussion of insanity is found in Duff, Mackay and Kearns, and Mackay. Intoxication is considered in Ashworth, Gardner and Paton. Mistakes and defences are debated in Horder (1990) and Simester. Walker considers the criminal responsibility of children. Self-defence is analysed in Horder (1995) and Uniacke.

Ashworth, 'Intoxication and the General Defences' [1980] *Criminal Law Review* 556.
Duff, 'Fitness to Plead and Fair Trials' [1994] *Criminal Law Review* 419.
Gardner, 'The Importance of *Majewski*' (1994) *Oxford Journal of Legal Studies* 279.
Horder, 'Cognition, Emotion and Criminal Culpability' (1990) 106 *Law Quarterly Review* 469.
Horder, 'Drawing the Boundaries of Self-Defence' (1995) 58 *Modern Law Review* 431.

Horder, 'Criminal Law: Between Determinism, Liberalism and Criminal Justice' (1996) *Current Legal Problems* 159.

Mackay, *Mental Condition Defences in Criminal Law* (1995, Oxford University Press).

Mackay and Kearns, 'More fact(s) about the Insanity Defence' [1999] *Criminal Law Review* 714.

Mackay and Kearns, 'An Upturn in Unfitness to Plead? Disability in Relation to the Trial under the 1991 Act' [2000] *Criminal Law Review* 532.

Paton, 'Reformulating the Intoxication Rules: The Law Commission's Report' [1995] *Criminal Law Review* 382.

Simester, 'Mistakes in Defence' (1992) *Oxford Journal of Legal Studies* 295.

Sullivan, 'Making Excuses' in Simester and Smith (eds), *Harm and Culpability* (1995, Oxford University Press).

Uniacke, *Permissible Killing* (1994, Oxford University Press).

Walker, 'The End of an Old Song' (1999) 149 *New Law Journal* 64.

16   General Defences

16.1   Justifications and Excuses

When thinking about defences it can be useful to distinguish between justifications and excuses. A claim of justification is essentially an assertion that the act committed was permissible in all the circumstances. It need not necessarily be the most morally appropriate act, but it needs to be an act that is permitted by the law. For example, if the defendant is approached by a five-year-old child pointing a gun and at the point of pulling the trigger, shooting the child may be permitted (justified) by the law – even if morally the ideal thing to do would be to let the child shoot. A justification does not deny that the victim was wronged but explains that there were countervailing circumstances which made that conduct justifiable.

A claim of excuse, on the other hand, admits that the act was not justifiable but seeks to argue that in the circumstances the defendant does not deserve the blame attached to a criminal conviction. The claim is that the acts were understandable and excusable, given the defendant's mental state or the circumstances in which the defendant acted. Paul Robinson has neatly summarized the distinction between justifications and excuses: 'acts are justified, actors are excused'.

It is possible for excuses to be partial excuses. That is, the defendant is not fully to blame for the commission of the *actus reus*, but is nevertheless still somewhat to blame. For example, provocation is a defence to murder that reduces the sentence to manslaughter. A partial defence does not indicate that the defendant is blameless, otherwise there would be an acquittal, but implies that her blame is insufficient for a murder conviction and so can be seen as a partial excuse. Sometimes there is talk of 'partial justifications' but many commentators regard this to be an inaccurate phrase because an act is either justified or it is not.

Although this classification of defences into excuses and justifications is conceptually very useful, there are dangers in putting too much emphasis on it. In particular, the law's definition of defences was developed without the classifications of justification and excuse in mind. The law might have been clearer if it had been so.

One danger of placing too much weight on the excuse/justification distinction is that there is a temptation to believe that each defence should be classified as either a justification or an excuse. Within the legal definitions of a defence may fall factual situations, some of which are justifications and some of which are excuses. For example, as mentioned above, self-defence is a classic example of 'justification', but within the legal definition of self-defence falls the situation where the defendant makes a mistake and believes that he is being attacked when he is not. In such circumstances some commentators would argue that the defendant is not justified. Can it be said to be permissible for the defendant to use force against a victim who is in fact posing no threat to the defendant? No doubt the defendant would have an excuse. Although some defences cannot be neatly classified as either an excuse or a justification, some defences clearly fall into one category or the other: insanity, for example, is clearly an example of an excuse.

Another danger of putting too much emphasis on whether defences fall into the philosophical categories of justification or excuse is that practical considerations, policy factors and the need to make the law readily comprehensible to juries also influence the rules relating to defences. We should not, therefore, expect the justification/excuse distinction to be the sole influence on the development of the law relating to defences.

So far we have looked at the theoretical distinction between justifications and excuses. What are the practical implications that should follow? Several have been suggested, which will now be discussed, although, as we have just stated, there are many other influences on the law in this area.

1.   Accessories

If a third party assists someone who is acting in a justified way then she is not guilty of any crime. This is because she is assisting in the commission of an *actus reus* that is seen as desirable by society. However, an accessory to an excused principal will be guilty as she has assisted in the commission of an undesirable *actus reus* (unless the accessory has her own defence).

2.   Nature of the legal test

You might at first think that the test to determine the availability of a justification would be wholly objective because the law is considering whether the defendant's act was socially desirable. In contrast, you might expect the test for excuses would be essentially subjective because the law is considering the defendant's culpability. This is generally accurate but not wholly correct. First, in relation to justifications it is necessary to show that the defendant acted for a justified reason. For example if Mike sees his enemy George and shoots him, but unknown to Mike, George was about to detonate a bomb in a crowded marketplace and so Mike would have been justified in so acting, Mike cannot rely on that justification. The reason is that when considering whether an act is justified, one considers all the circumstances including the defendant's beliefs. A defendant is not acting as society would wish him to act if he is killing for an inappropriate motive. This is sometimes known as the *Dadson* principle.

Likewise an excuse sometimes does not rely on a wholly subjective test. Take provocation: if a defendant is insulted and is so angry that he loses his self-control, he is afforded a partial excuse. However, we may not want to make the defence available to a defendant whose response was totally unreasonable and caused by drunkenness or pride. So the defendant, in order to use provocation, must show that his response was reasonable and so worthy of an excuse. This could be explained in two ways: either an example of where a policy (the desire of the law to protect members of society from those who kill unreasonably following a provocation) affects the test which would be used if moral philosophy alone determined the test; or an argument that if the defendant was able to control his anger, but did not have a good reason for not controlling his anger, he is blameworthy and cannot claim an excuse.

3. Self-defence or prevention of crime
Another practical effect of the distinction between a justification and an excuse is that if a defendant is defending herself against force, she can defend herself against an excused attacker (for example, if the attacker is sleepwalking) but not against a justified attacker (see Chapter 15.3.1).

4. Strict liability offences
It also seems that excuses would be ineffective when facing a charge of a strict liability offence, but justifications are available to any crime.

5. Mistakes and defences
Some commentators argue that there should be a distinction between justifications and excuses where the defendant makes a mistake of perception. If the defendant misinterprets the facts and thinks they permit him to use justified force then he can have a defence even if the mistake is unreason-

able. However, if the defendant is relying on excuse, it must have been reasonable for him to make that mistake. The argument for this is that a person who is seeking to rely on an excuse is already admitting that his acts were unjustified, and if he is to deserve an excuse he should be blameless. If he has acted in an unjustified way and made an unreasonable mistake, an excuse should not be available.

There is one further general point that needs to be stressed before looking at the individual defences. With the exception of insanity and diminished responsibility, the accused does not need to prove her defence. This is not to say that the prosecution has to produce evidence to rebut every possible defence that could be proposed. The accused has the 'burden' (as it is known) of producing enough evidence to lay a foundation for her defence. Unless there is some evidence of the defence, raised on either the accused's or the prosecution's own evidence, the judge will not direct the jury to consider that defence and the accused cannot appeal against a conviction on the ground that the defence was not disproved by the prosecution. It is important to remember that the burden of proving all the elements of the offence is, with exceptions, on the prosecution (see Chapter 2.4). The burden on the accused is to produce some evidence of the particular defence that she seeks to raise.

We will now consider two defences in which the defendant admits he has the necessary *actus reus* and *mens rea*, but is seeking to rely on a defence.

16.2   Duress by Threats

The defence of duress may be pleaded where the accused admits that he committed the offence charged, with the necessary fault element, but claims that he only did so because he was threatened with death or serious injury if he did not comply with the demands of the threatener. The threat may be to harm the accused himself, or another person. Like self-defence, duress is a complete defence, resulting, if successful, in an acquittal. However, whereas self-defence is accepted as generally a justification for using force, it is not clear whether duress is also a justification or whether it is regarded primarily as an excuse.

A plea of duress based on justification would seek to argue that the wrong done in obeying the threatener (committing theft or a drug offence, for example) was less than the wrong that would have been done by the threatener (such as death or a serious assault). In other words, the offence committed under duress was the lesser of two evils. The problem with seeing duress as a justification is that the defendant is often ordered to injure an innocent bystander. For example, terrorist groups in Northern Ireland have in the past seized a taxi driver and threatened to kill him and his family unless he drove the terrorists and their weapons to a particular destination. Here the people who will be injured or killed in the explosion are blameless, and some commentators argue that therefore their injury or death cannot be justified. An important contrast is often drawn with self-defence where, like duress, the defendant is acting to prevent injury to himself or another, but, unlike duress, the person he injures (the attacker) is blameworthy, having attacked him and so legitimized the use of force against him. In other words, in self-defence the victim is posing a threat to the defendant, in duress he is not. Having emphasized this distinction, it should be remembered that you can use self-defence even where the victim is innocent, for example if there is no real attack but one believes that there is; or if the person who is attacking you is blameless, for example he is a child. This suggests that the distinction might not be as steadfast as might at first appear.

An alternative argument is to see duress as an excuse. Seen in this way, it could be claimed that the law cannot expect ordinary people to show extraordinary courage in resisting such fearsome threats, and that a person who succumbs to such a threat is not greatly culpable. Thus duress can be regarded as simply a concession to human frailty (Lord Hailsham in *Howe**) in that most people, when faced with a threat that they or their families would be killed, would commit the crime. A slightly different way of putting the argument is that in the inevitable panic that follows a threat of death or serious injury, the defendant is not able to think clearly and so would not be responsible for any decision made. It has sometimes been said that a defendant who acted under duress acted involuntarily. However, this claim must be treated with care. Acting under duress is not at all the same as being unable to control your actions, say because of a spasm. Indeed, in duress the defendant deliberately chose to commit the crime rather than suffer the harm. But the defendant chose to act as he did in circumstances such that the choice should not be seen as one for which the defendant is responsible. So perhaps the best way of expressing the effect of duress as an excuse is to state that the defendant did not have a fair opportunity to comply with the law; that she chose to act as she did, but that she had no morally acceptable alternative.

So is it best to see duress as a justification or an excuse? It may be the legal defence of duress in fact covers two types of situation: duress as an excuse or duress as a justification. If Harrison, a well-known terrorist, kidnaps Meg and threatens to kill all her family unless she steals a chocolate bar then surely she should steal the chocolate bar. That is what society would want her to do; she could be said to be justified. Indeed, an argument based on excuse – that she was so caught up in the dilemma of choosing between the two evils that she is not responsible for her choice – sounds inappropriate. However, in other cases where a defendant has to kill an innocent person or be killed, it may be that the killing would not be justifiable, but an argument based on the panic of the moment may lead us to excuse or partially excuse the defendant. If this view is correct then some of the difficulties that the law has faced with duress have resulted from the fact that it has failed to realize that in fact there are two different kinds of duress defences lurking under the single heading 'duress'.

It is, of course, possible to explain the existence of the defence without referring to the notions of justification or excuse. For example, it is possible to argue that when a person is faced with a threat of death or serious injury, the criminal law cannot hope to influence the behaviour of individuals. In other words, the law cannot have a deterrent effect and so there will be no gains to society in imposing criminal liability. Enough of the theory. What about the law on duress?

16.2.1   To What Crimes is Duress a Defence?

Duress is available as a defence to all crimes except murder (whether as a principal or an accessory; *Howe*), attempted murder (*Gotts*) and some forms of treason. No one really knows what kind of treason is referred to here as there are few cases to go on. It is clear that duress may be pleaded in at least some types of treason (such as propaganda for the enemy in wartime: *Purdy*).

The reason for excluding duress as a defence to murder is explained by Lord Hailsham in *Howe* who suggested it would not be:

'good morals, good policy or good law to suggest, as did the majority in Lynch . . . that the ordinary man of reasonable fortitude is not to be supposed to be capable of heroism if he is asked to take an innocent life rather than sacrifice his own. Doubtless in actual practice many will succumb to temptation . . . But many will not, and I do not believe that as a "concession to human frailty" the former should be exempt from liability to criminal sanctions if they do.'

The reasoning here sounds justificatory in tone. When faced with a threat, the law expects heroism and the defendant should lay down his own life rather than kill an innocent third party. Thus the law here seeks to uphold the sanctity-of-life principle and protect the innocent victim's life. One difficulty with this reasoning is that it does not cover the situation where the threat is to kill the defendant's family. It is one thing to expect someone to lay down his own life for another, it is another to expect him to lay down the lives of his family. The denial of the defence of duress to murder is particularly strange when it is recalled that the defence is only available if the defendant acted as a reasonable person would, and it would only be in the most unusual cases that the jury would decide that a defendant had acted reasonably if he had killed an innocent third party. Nevertheless, under no circumstances is duress a defence to murder.

The argument in favour of allowing duress as a defence to murder was eloquently made by Lord Morris in *Lynch*:

> 'If . . . someone is threatened with death or serious injury unless he does what he is told to do is the law to pay no heed to the miserable agonizing plight of such a person? For the law to understand not only how the timid but also the stalworthy may in a moment of crisis behave is not to make the law weak but to make it just. In the calm of the court room measures of fortitude or of heroic behaviour are surely not to be demanded when they could not in moments for decision reasonably have been expected even in the restrained and well disposed . . . .'

Duress is also not available as a defence to a charge of attempted murder (*Gotts*). The argument persuading the House of Lords was that it can be pure chance whether death results from the defendant's acts or not, and so the availability of duress in attempted murder should be the same as in murder. So the only defence for a defendant who was threatened and is facing a charge of murder or attempted murder is to try and plead a lack of intent. The argument would have to be that the defendant did not have the purpose to kill (but simply to avoid the threat) and, although he foresaw death as a virtually certain consequence to his actions, the jury should still hold back from saying that he had an intention (*Woollin**; see Chapter 4.3). However, although this argument can be made and has some caselaw support (*Bourne*; *Steane*) it was stressed in *Howe* that simply because one is acting under duress does not mean that one lacks intent.

Lord Griffiths in *Gotts* accepted that there is an anomaly in allowing duress as a defence to wounding with intent but denying it if the victim dies and a charge of murder is brought (the intention of the accused being the same). He thought that 'this flows from the special regard that the law has for human life, it may not be logical but it is real and has to be accepted'.

16.2.2 What Must be Shown if the Defence is to Succeed?

The requirements of the defence of duress were set out in *Graham** by the Court of Appeal and confirmed by the House of Lords in *Howe*. They are as follows:

1. The defendant was compelled to act in the way she did by threats of imminent death or serious physical injury

This is a subjective test. Did the defendant act in the way she did because of the threats? This will be fairly easily to show. It would only be in a most unusual case that the defendant did not commit the crime in response to the threat. If the defendant was ordered to kill his enemy whom he had been looking for an opportunity to kill for a long time, then maybe this requirement would not be made out.

It should be noted that the threat must be of death or serious injury of the defendant or any other person (*Conway*). It used to be thought that the threat had to be of injury to the defendant's family, but it now seems that the threat can be made towards a stranger (*Pommell**). However, the closeness of the relationship may be relevant when considering the reasonableness of the defendant's response (requirement **4** below). Any threats short of death or serious injury (such as loss of job or reputation or, perhaps most common, to inform the police of some other offence) will not excuse, and can only go towards mitigation of sentence (*Baker and Wilkins*). What about threats to cause serious psychological harm? In *Baker and Wilkins*, it was stated that the threat had to be of physical harm. However in *Ireland and Burstow*, the House of Lords stated that a clear distinction could not be drawn between physical injury and psychological injury. The House of Lords interpreted the term 'actual bodily harm' in the Offences Against the Person Act 1861 applied to psychological injuries (see Chapter 7). It is arguable that *Baker and Wilkins* will need to be reconsidered in the light of *Ireland and Burstow*. If other threats accompany the threat of death or serious injury, the accused may still rely on duress (*Valderrama-Vega*), as long as it was the threat of death or injury that caused him to commit the offence.

In *Hudson and Taylor*, one of the issues discussed was the need for the threat to be of immediate harm. The two accused were charged with perjury. They were young women who had been threatened that if they did not give false evidence, they would be injured. One of those who had made the threats was seen by the young women in court before they gave evidence. The Court of Appeal held that the crucial question was not whether the threat was capable of being carried out when it was made, but whether the threat was effective at the moment when the crime was committed. A threat of future violence may be too remote, but if the threat is 'sufficient to destroy his will' at the time when the accused has to decide whether or not to commit the offence, duress may be pleaded. In *Abdul-Hussain*, the Court of Appeal rejected an argument that the threat had to be immediate harm, as long as the threat was of imminent harm.

2. The defendant must have good grounds to believe that the threat had been made

This is an objective requirement. If a threat has not been made but the defendant unreasonably believes it has then he cannot rely on the defence. Unfortunately, in recent years there has been a division in judicial opinion on this issue. Brook LJ in *DPP* v. *Rogers* and recently the Court of Appeal in *Martin* have suggested that the defendant only has to actually believe that there has been a threat of death or serious injury; this belief does not have to be reasonable. However, the weight of authority, including the House of Lords in *Howe* and the Court of Appeal in *Abdul-Hussain* and *Cairns*, are in favour of a requirement that the defendant must have reasonable grounds to believe that the threat has been made. That said, in the light of *DPP* v. *B* and *R* v. *K*, with the House of Lords' resounding confirmation of *Gladstone Williams* and the emphasis that a mistake in self-defence or over a key element of the *mens rea* need only be honest and need not be reasonable in order to provide a defence, it may be that the House of Lords would prefer the *Martin* approach.

At present, therefore, the law appears to be that if the defendant had been kidnapped by a terrorist and the defendant unreasonably misheard the terrorist and believed that she was being threatened (but she was not), she will not be able to use the defence. This may seem harsh as one cannot expect defendants to show great powers of calmness and clarity of perception when placed in such a dilemma. On the other hand, when the jury is deciding whether the mishearing was unreasonable no doubt it will take into account the stressfulness of the accused's situation. The cases recognize that if there is in fact no threat but the defendant reasonably believes there is, she can rely on the defence (*Cairns*). Presumably also the defendant would only be expected to show those powers of perception of which she was capable. So a person with hearing difficulties would not be blamed for misunderstanding a threat. There is no caselaw expressly on this, but no doubt the court would take such disabilities into account.

3. The defendant must have good cause to believe that the threat will be carried out

Again, this is an objective test. If an American tourist was kidnapped by a terrorist who threatened to kill his family who were in the United States, it might be argued that there were no reasonable grounds to believe that the threat could be carried out and so he would not be able to rely on the defence of duress. In deciding whether there was good cause, the courts will bear in mind the unusual circumstances in which the defendant found herself. Again, presumably a defendant's disabilities can also be taken into account in deciding whether there was good cause to believe that the threat would be carried out.

4.   *The defendant must act as a reasonable person of reasonable firmness would have acted in those circumstances*

This is the part of the test that may be hardest for a defendant to fulfil. The test asks the jury to consider how an ordinary person, not an especially heroic one, would react to the threat. The defendant is expected to show 'the steadfastness reasonably to be expected of ordinary citizens in his situation' (*Graham*). One way of asking this question is to consider whether the defendant's response was proportionate to the threat that he or she was facing (*Abdul-Hussain*). Clearly, the more serious the offence, the greater the threat must be. As Lord Wilberforce explained in *Abbott*, 'the more dreadful the circumstances of the [crime], . . . the stronger and more irresistible the duress needed before it could be regarded as affording any defence'. S(D) went so far as to suggest that the evil done by the defendant must be less than the threatened evil.

As with provocation, the courts have had difficulty in deciding which of the defendant's characteristics to give to the reasonable person in deciding how she would react. The courts have allowed age, sex, pregnancy, recognized mental illness (for example, learned helplessness or post-traumatic stress disorder; *Emery*) and serious physical disability as characteristics that can affect the degree of firmness to be expected (*Bowen*). It is clear that neither voluntary intoxication (*Bowen*), nor other self-induced characteristics (*Flatt*), nor particular vulnerability to pressure (*Horne*), nor lack of firmness arising from sexual abuse (*Hirst*), nor emotional instability (*Horne*) nor low IQ (*Bowen*) can be taken into account as affecting the level of firmness required. The courts have not made it clear whether the defendant's characteristics can be taken into account in considering the gravity of the threat, as opposed to the level of firmness expected. Presumably the court would accept that to a concert pianist the threat to remove a finger might be graver than to someone else, but there is no caselaw on this. It should be noted that we have not yet had a case on duress since the House of Lords' decision on provocation in *Smith* (see Chapter 10.7). The Court of Appeal in *Graham* argued that provocation cases can be used as guidance for the development of the law on duress. It is not impossible that a new case on duress will follow the approach adopted in *Smith*.

The present law on duress has been criticized by Professor Smith (1996) who has commented:

'A jury may well have some difficulty with the question "Would a woman displaying the firmness reasonably to be expected of a women suffering from learned helplessness, have yielded to the threat?" Effectively, this seems to eliminate the objective test for this category of persons. The elimination of the objective test might in principle be a good thing but, if so, it should be done generally and not for limited categories'.

In fact the law here is trying to strike a delicate balance between the subjective and objective camps, attempting to mitigate the rigours of the objective test where it is not the defendant's fault that he is not a reasonable person. It is a shame that *Bowen* did not explain the basis of the distinction between those characteristics that were, and those that were not, relevant. The distinction drawn by the Court of Appeal in *Bowen* could be supported on the ground that there are two categories of characteristics that are not to be assigned to the reasonable person in ascertaining the level of firmness expected. Firstly excluded are those characteristics which cannot affect the level of firmness (for example, sexual orientation) simply because they are irrelevant. Secondly, also excluded are those characteristics for which the defendant is to be blamed (for example, drunkenness or cowardice etc.).

5.   *The defendant must not be responsible for the threats*
The defence of duress is not available where it is self-induced. That usually arises where the defendant is threatened by a gang which he has voluntary joined, in which case, if he was aware the gang was a violent one when he joined it, he cannot rely on the defence of duress (*Ali* (1995)). As Lord Lane explained in *Sharp*:

'Where a person has voluntarily, and with knowledge of its nature, joined a criminal organisation or gang which he knew might bring pressure on him to commit an offence and was an active member when he was put under such pressure, he cannot avail himself of the defence of duress.'

However, this only applies if the defendant voluntarily joined the gang and did so knowing that the gang was of a violent nature, and was likely to threaten him if he tried to leave (*Baker* (1999)). So it would seem to be no bar to duress if the defendant joined a shoplifting gang which later decided to perform armed robbery and threatened the defendant with violence when he tried to leave the organization. There also needs to be a close association between membership of the gang and the making of the threat. So where a defendant joined a gang and was later imprisoned, but while in prison he was threatened by a member of the gang, it was held that the threat was not closely related to his membership of the gang (*Lewis*).

Self-induced duress is not limited to membership of criminal gangs. A defendant may be thought to have put himself in a position where he would be liable to be threatened in other circumstances. In *Heath*, a defendant borrowed money from a drug dealer. When he did not pay the money back, the drug dealer threatened him with violence unless he played a role in transporting drugs. He was not able to rely on duress because he had put himself in a position where he was liable to be threatened by borrowing money from such a person.

A slightly different issue is where there is a gap in time between the making of the threat and the performance of the threat (see *Hudson and Taylor*). In *Abdul-Hussain*, the Court of Appeal stressed that it was not necessary to show that the defendant had reacted spontaneously in response to the threat, but the longer the gap in time between the point in time when the threat will be enacted and the performance of the crime, the less likely that it will be reasonable for the defendant to act in the way he or she did. The Court of Appeal explained that the threat of death or serious harm would have to be imminent, but not immediate. This is largely because the longer the gap in time, the more likely it is that the defendant will be able to find a way to escape from the threat, in particular by obtaining police protection or assistance. Although this will often be the reasonable course of action it is not always available, as in *Abdul-Hussain* where the victims were Shiite Muslims who had hijacked a plane to escape Saddam Hussein's Iraqi regime. By contrast, in *Heath* the defendant was told he would have to help with the transportation of drugs the next day or else face violence. The Court of Appeal felt this gave him enough time to seek police protection.

Reform of the law on duress

Clause 25 of the Draft Criminal Code, proposing reform of duress, states:

'(1) No act of a person constitutes an offence if the act is done under duress by threats.

(2) A person does an act under duress by threats if he does it because he knows or believes –

(a) that a threat has been made to cause death or serious injury to himself or another if the act is not done, and

(b) that the threat will be carried out immediately if he does not do the act or, if not immediately, before he or that other can obtain effective official protection, and

(c) that there is no other way of preventing the threat being carried out, and the threat is one which in all the circumstances (including any of his personal characteristics that affect its gravity) he cannot reasonably be expected to resist.'

If adopted, this proposal would make the defence notably more subjective than the present law, at least as regards mistaken beliefs, although the clause retains the reasonable firmness test. However, by simply asking whether the response was reasonable, the clause avoids the difficulties that the law has had with the reasonable person test.

16.3   Duress of Circumstances

This defence has only recently been recognized by the courts and has developed by analogy with duress by threats. The difference between the two defences is that whereas in duress by threats someone has threatened the defendant, in duress of circumstances there is no threat uttered by anyone else but the circumstances are such that unless the defendant commits a crime, someone will be killed or suffer serious injury. For example, in *Conway* the defendant was driving a car, with a passenger who had recently narrowly escaped death in a gun attack by two men. Two men approached the car and the defendant believed that his passenger was about to be attacked again. He drove off in a dangerous manner, exceeding the speed limit. The court found that he genuinely and reasonably believed that his friend was about to suffer death or serious injury (although in fact the two men were plain-clothed police officers) and could plead the defence of duress of circumstances to a charge of dangerous driving.

A case close to the borderline between the defences of duress by threats and duress by circumstances is *Cole*, where the defendant was told by creditors that unless he paid money that was due to them they would cause his family serious harm. The defendant committed a bank robbery. The court decided that this scenario was closer to duress of circumstances than duress by threats, as the defendant was not told that he must commit a particular crime and it was in reality his financial difficulties (a circumstance) that caused him to commit the crime.

The fact that it can be difficult to draw a sharp distinction between duress by threats and duress of circumstances does not need to be of concern, because the defences are identical in their extent and requirements. As with duress by threats, duress of circumstances is not available as defence to either murder or attempted murder. The test for duress of circumstances is identical to that for duress by threats (*Pommell*): was the defendant compelled to act as she did because of the circumstances as she reasonably believed them to be? Did she have good cause to believe that the circumstances threatened her life or presented the likelihood of serious injury, and would a reasonable person of reasonable firmness have reacted to the circumstances in the same way? One case suggested a slightly different formulation for the rules for duress of circumstances, requiring that the defendant acted not only in a reasonable way but also in a way that was necessary to avoid the harm (*Pittaway*). This *dictum* has not been picked up in later case and it is unlikely that it was intended to signal a change in the law. It seems harsh to punish a defendant who has acted reasonably when faced with a serious set of circumstances, even if the act was not strictly necessary. One point recently emphasized by the Court of Appeal is that it is not possible for duress of circumstances to be based solely on internal pressures. So a defendant cannot claim to be compelled to act in an illegal way by his own suicidal feelings (*Rodger*).

It is important for a defendant seeking to use duress of circumstances to show that he committed the crime only for as long as was necessary. For example if he is attempting to use the defence to a charge of drunk driving, he needs to show that he only drove for as long as was necessary to avoid the threat of death or serious injury (*Bell*). Once the threat has passed, the defendant should stop driving.

16.4   Coercion

Coercion is a particular form of duress and arises where a wife is threatened by her husband and so she commits a crime. It must be shown that the wife committed the crime because of her husband's threats (*Shortland*). It is not necessary for her to show that the threats were of death or serious injury; any threat will be sufficient as long as it compelled her to commit the crime. It must be shown that the pressures were such that she was 'forced unwillingly to participate'. The defence is only available to married couples and not to long-term unmarried partners, nor even to parties to a void marriage (*Ditta, Hussain and Kara*). This special rule for wives seems based on the clearly outdated notion that a wife is dominated by her husband (the defence is not available to a husband). Indeed the Law Commission has called for its abolition (Law Commission Report 83). Of course, there is nothing to stop a wife from relying on the defence of ordinary duress, although there seems no advantage in her doing so. Like duress, coercion is not available to a charge of murder or treason; although unlike duress it is available as a defence to attempted murder.

16.5   Self-defence and Duress of Circumstances

In this section we will briefly consider the interrelation of duress of circumstances and self-defence. We have noted that the distinction between duress by threats and duress of circumstances is not exact. This is not of particular concern as the scope of both defences and the rules governing them are effectively identical. More difficult is to distinguish between duress of circumstances and self-defence. This time the distinction needs to be clear, as duress of circumstances, unlike self-defence, is not available as defence to murder or attempted murder. Further, if a defendant thinks she is being attacked but is not, self-defence is available; whereas if the defendant thinks the circumstances are threatening her but they are not, duress of circumstances is only available if the mistake was reasonable. Although the law has failed to draw a clear distinction between the two defences, some work on this has been done by commentators. Consider the following hypothetical scenario of S. Uniacke's (as summarized by J. Horder):

'D and V are locked in a room with a diminishing supply of oxygen. D realises that only if he kills V will the oxygen supply be likely to last long enough for rescuers to save him. So he kills V. On Uniacke's view, this will not be killing in self-defence because V is not herself posing the threat; the threat stems from the lack of oxygen . . . It might be different, however, if instead of breathing normally, V began to hyperventilate . . . Now we may want to say that V has become part of the threat. V is, albeit involuntarily, assisting or enhancing the threat itself' [and so the defence of self-defence may be available].

This is a neat analysis but it might not be sufficient to justify why in one case the defendant can rely on self-defence and commits no crime but in the other is guilty of murder. The fineness of the distinction casts further doubt on the correctness of the ruling in *Howe*, that duress should not be available as a defence to murder.

16.6   Necessity

Unfortunately the term 'necessity' has been used by the courts and commentators to mean different things. Sometimes the courts have called duress of circumstances 'necessity'. However, in other cases and in other jurisdictions 'necessity' has been used to refer to a defence of pure justification: where the defendant was placed in a situation in which whatever he did would cause harm to someone and he performed an act that was the lesser of two evils. To avoid confusion in this book, 'necessity' will be used to refer to the notion of pure justification and not duress of circumstances. So when will necessity in this context provide a defence?

The present position has been summarized by the Court of Appeal in *Pommell*, where Kennedy LJ stated in *obiter dicta*:

'The strength of the argument that a person ought to be permitted to breach the letter of the criminal law in order to prevent a greater evil befalling himself or others has long been recognised (see for example Stephen's *Digest of Criminal Law*), but it has, in English law, not given rise to a recognised general defence of necessity . . .'

The leading case on necessity and murder is *Dudley and Stephens*. In that case, Lord Coleridge CJ held that necessity was no defence to murder, arguing from the authority of Hale (who wrote in the seventeenth century). The defendants had been shipwrecked and had killed and eaten a boy of seventeen after eight days without food and six days without water in an open boat. Lord Coleridge said:

'the temptation to the act which existed here was not what the law has ever called necessity. It is not needful to point out the awful danger of admitting the principle which has been contended for. Who is to be the judge of this sort of necessity? By what measure is the comparative value of lives to be measured? Is it to be strength, or intellect, or what? . . . We are often compelled to set up standards we cannot reach ourselves, and to lay down rules which we could not ourselves satisfy. But a man has no right to declare temptation to be an excuse, though he might himself have yielded to it.'

As A. W. B. Simpson pointed out in his book on this case (*Cannibalism and the Common Law*, 1986), the reasoning in the case reflects a view of the judicial function which is no longer widely accepted: that of laying down morally correct standards of behaviour. However, in more recent cases judges have been equally doubtful of the defence of necessity, on the ground that it would encourage all sorts of spurious claims.

So there is no general defence of necessity. However the courts have recognized four circumstances in which necessity provides a defence:

1 An action taken to preserve the life or wellbeing of another person who is unable to consent (Lord Goff *in Re F*). The most obvious example is where a doctor operates on a patient, who is unable to consent (because, for example, she is unconscious), if that treatment is immediately necessary for her wellbeing. Another example is where one person pulls another out of the way of a moving vehicle, when there is no time to obtain the consent of the other. It should be noted that if a person is

capable of consenting and wishes to die, treatment cannot lawfully be forced upon that person against his will (*S* v. *St George's*).

2 Where property is damaged in order to save other property then the defence may apply (Lord Goff, in *Re F*). An example of this might be where a house is pulled down to create a firebreak and prevent a fire engulfing a whole town.

3 Where property is damaged in order to avoid injury to a person, the defence may be available (Lord Goff, *in Re F*).

4 In the Court of Appeal decision of *Re A* (*Conjoined Twins*), Ward LJ suggested that necessity may be availiable on the special facts of that case (see Hot Topic, at the end of this chapter). It concerned the question of whether it was lawful to operate to separate conjoined twins in an operation that would end the life of one twin but would probably save the life of the other. Ward LJ was willing to permit the operation on the basis that it would not be unlawful, because the doctors could rely on the defence of necessity. However he provided a very narrow definition of when necessity could be available:

'Lest it be thought that this decision could become authority for wider propositions, such as that a doctor, once he has determined that a patient cannot survive, can kill the patient, it is important to restate the unique circumstances for which this case is authority. They are that it must be impossible to preserve the life of X without bringing about the death of Y, that Y by his or her very continued existence will inevitably bring about the death of X within a short period of time, and that X is capable of living an independent life but Y is incapable under any circumstances (including all forms of medical intervention) of viable independent existence.'

It is difficult to imagine circumstances, other than cases involving conjoined twins, when these requirements would be made out. Brook LJ also suggested that necessity was available. He gave a broader definition of necessity. Three circumstances had to be demonstrated:

'(a) the act is needed to avoid inevitable and irreparable evil;
(b) no more should be done than is reasonably necessary for the purpose to be achieved;
(c) the evil inflicted must not be disproportionate to the evil avoided.'

Controversially Brook LJ states that this kind of necessity provided a defence to murder. As neither of the other judges in the Court of Appeal accepted this definition, it is not binding on a later case. In any event there are difficulties with Brooke LJ's requirements. The core difficulty is that the Court of Appeal approved the decision in *Dudley and Stephenson*, even though the three requirements appeared to have been satisfied in that case. (See at the end of this chapter Hot Topic for further discussion.) It may be that it also has to be shown that the killing of this victim was the only way of avoiding the death of others. If the killing of another person would also have avoided the death (as was the case in *Dudley and Stephenson*, but not in *Re A (Conjoined Twins)*) then maybe the defence is not available. Notably, his wide definition of necessity was not adopted by their other Lordships in that case.

These are probably not a complete list of the circumstances in which necessity is available. It may be that if a case comes before the court and it feels that the defence should be available it will develop the defence. It should be noted that the second and third factors, as well as being forms of common law necessity, are also statutory defences under the Criminal Damage Act 1971. This reflects a wider point that in many circumstances where it might be thought that necessity should apply, there is in fact a statutory provision that provides a defence. Words such as 'reasonable' can in effect contain a defence where the defendant acts in performing the lesser of two evils. The point can work in reverse, however. In *Cichon* v. *DPP*, a defendant tried to use necessity as a defence to a charge under s.1(2)(d) Dangerous Dogs Act 1991 (which made it an offence not to muzzle some dogs under certain circumstances). The accused's argument was that the dog was ill and if the muzzle had been removed then there would be little danger to the public, but the dog's life might have been saved. However, the Divisional Court decided that the defence of necessity was not available, because if Parliament had thought the defence should be available in this scenario then it would have expressly provided for it, as it did in the Criminal Damage Act. This seems to suggest that necessity is not available as a defence to a statutory offence, unless the statute expressly states that it is. On other occasions the nature of the *mens rea* may include elements of necessity. But this, suggests *Backshall*, does not mean that the defence of necessity is necessarily unavailable.

There has been much discussion of an incident that occurred during the disaster of the *Herald of Free Enterprise*. It appears that as the boat began to sink, several passengers were attempting to escape by means of a ladder but one person was so terrified that he was unable to move. After many attempts to persuade him to move, someone pushed him off; he was never seen again. The others were able to use the ladder to escape. Had the other passengers been charged with murder, self-defence would not be available as defence because there was no threat posed by the victim, rather the threat was posed by the rising waters. Duress would not be available as it is not a defence to a charge of murder. Provocation cannot apply because there was nothing said or done which caused a loss of self-control. One possible defence would be a lack of intent. The hypothetical defendant could argue that it was not his purpose to kill the passenger (he would have been delighted if the passenger had managed to swim to safety). The case would therefore fall within the *Woollin* direction. Although the defendant was aware that it was virtually certain that death or serious harm would be caused by his actions, the jury may still be entitled not to find intention (see Chapter 4.4). More likely to succeed would be the defence of necessity as developed by Brooke LJ in *Re A (Conjoined Twins)*. The three requirements he set out would appear to have been satisfied in this case.

16.7   Superior Orders

It is no defence to state that you were ordered to commit a crime by a person in a senior position to you (*Yip Chi-Cheung*). The most likely circumstances in which this could arise is where a police officer or someone in the armed forces would try to argue that a more senior officer had ordered him to commit the crime. The reason behind the law's approach is the principle of the rule of law; that no one can escape the umbrella of the law. Even the most senior army officer is bound by the criminal law and cannot give an exemption to others. It is possible that if one was ordered to commit the crime then one could then deny having the necessary *mens rea* or seek to rely on duress.

Hot Topic: The Conjoined Twins

One of the most controversial cases before the courts in the last century was *Re A (Conjoined Twins)*, which concerned conjoined twins: Jodie and Mary. The issue before the courts was whether it would be lawful for doctors to separate the two twins. If the twins were separated, Mary would inevitably die but there was a promising prognosis for Jodie. However if they were not separated, both twins would die within three to six months. This was because Mary lacked effective organs to pump her blood around her body and was in effect relying on Jodie's organs to live. The problem was that Jodie's organs were not able to support two people for any length of time. The children's parents objected to the operation, largely based on their religious belief that no one should deliberately cause the death of someone else.

From the perspective of family law, the key question was what was in the best interests of the children (s.1, Children Act 1989). The difficulty is that the interests of Jodie and the interests of Mary pointed in different directions. It was said to be in Mary's interests not to perform the operation, but in Jodie's interests that the operation goes ahead. Faced with this dilemma the court suggested that it was permissible to weigh up the interests of the two children. Doing so the operation should go ahead as it was very much in the interests of Jodie; without it Jodie would die. Not performing the operation was less strongly in the interests of Mary because it would only mean that she could live for a few months longer. However the Court of Appeal held that despite this analysis under family law the court could only approve of the operation if it was lawful under the criminal law.

From the perspective of criminal law the case raised a host of issues:

1 Would the operation involve an act or an omission? Johnson J at first instance suggested that the operation could be seen as an omission in that from Mary's point of view the doctors were withdrawing the supply of blood that Jodie was providing. He drew an analogy with *Bland* where the House of Lords held that withdrawing feeding apparatus from a patient constituted an omission. The Court of Appeal, quite rightly, rejected this argument. In *Bland*, the doctors were removing the apparatus that they had originally connected to Tony Bland and thereby returning him to the position he was in when he arrived in the hospital. In that sense the overall effect of what the doctors had done could be regarded as nothing (that is, an omission). By contrast, the cutting into the twins was not returning them to the position they were in before. No sophistry could escape from the fact that the separation of the twins would involve an act.

2 Was Mary a separate person? The Court of Appeal was clear that Mary and Jodie should be regarded as two separate people. It rejected any argument that Mary was not an individual or that Mary and Jodie should be seen as one person. So the Court of Appeal was clear that if the operation went ahead it would involve an act that would cause the death of a person. This would be the *actus reus* of murder. But what of the *mens rea*?

3 If the doctors operated, could it be said that they would be intending to kill Mary? Here the Court of Appeal applied the decision of the House of Lords, case in *Woollin*. We have discussed this aspect of the case in Chapter 4. You may remember that the majority of the Court of Appeal controversially suggested that as the operation would be virtually certain to kill Mary and the doctors were aware of that, it therefore followed that the doctors intended to kill Mary. The majority rejected the more natural reading of *Woollin* which was that foresight of virtual certainty permitted, but did not require, the jury to find intention. Robert Walker LJ, in the minority, appeared to take this more natural reading and then argued that the court should not find intention in such a case because the doctors were acting for the best of motives (that is, saving Jodie's life). However, according to the majority of the Court of Appeal, if the operation went ahead both of the doctors would be intentionally ending the life of a person. The *actus reus* and the *mens rea* of murder would therefore be present. Could the doctors rely on any defence?

4 Could the doctors rely on defence of duress of circumstances? The short answer is 'no'. Following *Howe*, duress provides no defence to a charge of murder. In any event it could hardly be said that the doctors' will would be overborne if they were acting in pursuance of a court order authorizing the operation.

5 What about self-defence or prevention of crime? Could the doctors claim that they were operating to protect Jodie from Mary? Ward LJ, took the view that this could provide a defence for the doctors. The difficulty with this argument is that Mary could not be said to be attacking Jodie. Ward LJ, however, quite correctly stressed that self-defence is available even if there is no unjust aggressor. He gave an example of a six-year-old shooting other children in a playground. He

argued that the six-year-old could be killed to save the lives of other children, even though he is 'morally innocent'. Although the Court of Appeal did not discuss this issue in detail, it could be added that (using the analysis of Uniacke described in Chapter 15) although Mary was not attacking Jodie, she was posing a threat to her and this would be sufficient for the defence to be available

6 What about necessity? Brooke LJ, with the approval of Ward LJ, concluded that the doctors could rely on the defence of necessity in the circumstances of this case. As noted above, Ward LJ provided a narrow definition of necessity. Brooke LJ suggested that necessity could apply if three factors could be demonstrated:

1 that the act was required to avoid inevitable and irreparable evil;
2 that no more should be done than was reasonably necessary for the purpose to be achieved; and
3 that the evil inflicted was not to be disproportionate to the evil avoided.

These three factors were shown in this case. He distinguished *Dudley and Stephens* on the basis that the shipwrecked sailors had no reason to choose the cabin boy rather than any of the other sailors. By contrast, Mary was 'selected by nature'; killing her was the only way to save Jodie's life. There were no alternatives. It is not quite clear what he meant by 'selected by nature' except that Mary was the one whose existence posed the risk to Jodie's welfare. Brooke LJ preferred necessity because of the difficulty in private defence of finding an aggressive attack, which he saw as at the heart of private defence. Although Ward LJ preferred the self-defence route, he also appeared to accept that a defence based on necessity could apply:

'What are the doctors to do if the law imposes upon them a duty which they cannot perform without being in breach of Mary's right to life if at the same time the respecting of her right puts them in breach of the equally serious duty of respecting Jodie's right to life?... In those circumstances it seems to me that the law must allow an escape through choosing the lesser of two evils.'

7 Could the operation be justified on the basis that it was in the interests of Mary? Johnson J suggested that it would be in Mary's interests because if not separated, her life would be short and disagreeable. This argument was rejected by the Court of Appeal. Unless her life was regarded as utterly intolerable, the law does not accept that it is in a person's interests to die. Another argument suggested by Robert Walker LJ is that separating would be in the interests of both twins, as it would enable them to have their separate bodily integrity. The majority did not approve of this approach. Even if a person does have an interest in bodily integrity, it would be surprising if that were valued more highly than their interest in living. One argument not considered by the Court of Appeal or Johnson J is that it is in a person's interests to die well. It would be possible to see the case from Mary's point of view as involving a choice between two ways of dieing: either being killed in an operation that saved her sister's life or dieing with her sister. Could it be said that the former is a better death for Mary? In any event, as is made clear in Hot Topic at the end of Chapter 9, the law does not accept that it is in a person's interests to have his life shortened with the intention of killing him.

8 The court considered whether the Human Rights Act had any effect on the

outcome of the case. Again, different approaches were taken. Ward LJ took the view that Mary's right to life under article 2 was in conflict with Jodie's right to life. Faced with such a conflict, the courts were entitled to permit the operation to go ahead. Brooke LJ and Walker LJ preferred the view that article 2 only prevented the purposeful taking of a life. As the doctor's purpose was to save Jodie, not kill Mary, Mary's right to life was not infringed.

Summary

16.1 Certain defences can be seen as justifications for the conduct of the accused, whereas others are seen as total or partial excuses. English law has not developed with the distinction between justifications and excuses explicitly in mind, but they are useful theoretical tools.

16.2 Duress of threats is pleaded where the accused admits the commission of the act, with the required mental element, but claims that he acted under compulsion. The threat must be effective at the time of the crime, and only a threat of death or serious injury to the accused or another person will suffice. It must be a threat that an ordinary person of reasonable fortitude would have failed to resist. The possibility of avoiding the threat by seeking official protection will be taken into account, as will the immediacy of the threatened violence. A mistake as to the seriousness of the threat is only taken into account if it was reasonable. Duress is no defence to murder or attempted murder.

16.3 Duress of circumstances is available under similar conditions to duress by threats, except that in duress of circumstances the threat to life or serious injury is not made specifically by a particular person, but the circumstances are such that unless the defendant commits a crime there is risk of death or serious injury.

16.4 A wife who commits a crime following threats from her husband can plead a special defence of coercion if the threats compelled her to commit the offence.

16.5 It can be difficult to distinguish circumstances which give rise to duress of circumstances and those which give rise to self-defence. The key distinction is whether the threat is posed by the victim, by the surrounding circumstances or by third parties.

16.6 Necessity is available in a variety of situations. One is where the defendant is acting in order to promote the best interests of the victim whose life or wellbeing were in danger. Another is where the defendant is preventing a more serious harm and the only way of doing so is by committing an offence.

16.7 It is no defence to a criminal charge to claim that one was acting under orders.

Case Notes

Re A (Conjoined Twins) [2000] 4 All ER 961. Court of Appeal

The case concerned two conjoined twins: Jodie and Mary. If the twins were separated Mary would inevitably die, but there was a promising prognosis for Jodie. However if there was no separation, both twins would die within three to six months. This was because Mary lacked effective organs to pump her blood around her body and was in effect relying on Jodie's organs to live, but Jodie's organs were not able to support two people for any length of time. The children's parents objected to the operation. The Court of Appeal declared that the performance of the operation would not be unlawful. Although the doctors who performed the operation would be said to have intended to kill Mary, the operation would be lawful because the defence of necessity could apply.

Abdul-Hussain [1999] Crim LR 570 Court of Appeal

The appellants were Shiite Muslims fleeing from Saddam Hussein's regime in Iraq under which they claimed various forms of persecution. They had escaped to Sudan, but were on the point of being returned to Iraq where they feared they would be killed. They therefore hijacked an aircraft. At the trial, the judge withdrew the defence of duress because the threat was insufficiently immediate. The Court of Appeal held that the key issue was whether the threat was operating on the mind of the defendant. Whether the threat was immediate was a relevant factor in deciding whether the defendant's response was proportionate; duress was not restricted to where the defendant's criminal act was a spontaneous response to the threat. The Court of Appeal repeated calls for legislation to define duress with precision.

Cunningham [1957] 2 All ER 412. Court of Criminal Appeal

See Chapter 6 case notes.

Gomez [1993] AC 442. House of Lords

See Chapter 11 case notes.

Graham [1982] 1 All ER 801. Court of Appeal

The appellant was convicted of murder. He had assisted in the killing of his wife by another man with whom he had a homosexual relationship. The other man was violent and the appellant said that he had only acted out of fear. It was argued on appeal that the jury had been misdirected on the defence of duress. The Court of Appeal dismissed the appeal. It was held that the applicable test was twofold. First, was the accused taking part in the killing because of a well-grounded (reasonable) fear of death or serious physical injury as a result of his companion's words or conduct? Second, would a sober person of reasonable firmness, sharing the characteristics of the accused, have responded to those words or conduct by taking part in the killing? The effects of voluntary consumption of drink and drugs should be disregarded.

Howe [1987] 2 WLR 568. House of Lords

The appellant, with another man, was convicted of murder. They had pleaded duress as a defence, claiming that they believed that they would themselves be killed if they did not carry out the killing. The trial judge ruled that duress could only be raised as a defence in respect of the first count, in which they were charged as accessories to murder. Their appeals were dismissed by the Court of Appeal and the House of Lords. The House of Lords (departing from *Lynch*, an earlier House of Lords' decision) held that duress could not be a defence to murder, whether as principal or accessory. With respect to the test to be applied in cases of duress, the decision of the Court of Appeal in *Graham** (see above) was correct. It was also held that it was possible to convict an accessory of murder, as long as the accessory had the required intent, in cases where the principal was only guilty of manslaughter because of some special mitigating factor.

Pommell [1995] 2 Cr App Rep 607. Court of Appeal

The police found the accused in bed with a gun. He explained that he 'took it off a geezer who was going to do some people some damage with it'. He was convicted of unlawful possession of the gun. He was convicted after the trial judge had ruled that the defence of duress of circumstances was not available in the circumstances of the case. The Court of Appeal stated that, if true, the defendant's story could enable him to use the defence of duress of circumstances and quashed his conviction. The defence was available to the same crimes as duress by threats. The court stressed that the defendant might have an uphill task here showing that he took the earliest opportunity to hand the gun over to the police and so stop the commission of his crime.

Woollin [1999] AC 82. House of Lords
See Chapter 4 case notes.

Further Reading

The distinction between justifications and excuses is examined in Alldridge, Fletcher, J. Gardner, Hogan, J. Smith (1989), Smith and Wilson, and Williams. Duress is considered in Buchanan and Virgo, Elliott, Horder, J. Smith (1996) and K. Smith. Necessity is discussed in S. Gardner and Glazebrook.

Alldridge, 'The Coherence of Defences' [1983] *Criminal Law Review* 665.
Buchanan and Virgo, 'Duress and Mental Abnormality' [1999] *Criminal Law Review* 517.
Elliott, 'Necessity, Duress and Self-Defence' [1989] *Criminal Law Review* 611.
Fletcher, *Rethinking Criminal Law* (1978, Little Brown).
J. Gardner, 'Justifications and Reasons', in Simester and Smith (eds), *Harm and Culpability* (1995, Oxford University Press).
S. Gardner, 'Necessity's Newest Inventions' (1991) Oxford Journal of Legal Studies 125.
Glazebrook, 'The Necessity Plea in English Criminal Law' (1972) *Cambridge Law Journal* 87.
Hogan, 'The Dadson Principle' [1989] *Criminal Law Review* 679.
Horder, 'Autonomy, Provocation and Duress' [1992] *Criminal Law Review* 706.
Horder, 'Occupying the Moral High Ground: The Law Commission on Duress' [1994] *Criminal Law Review* 334.
Rogers, 'Necessity, Private Defence and the Killing of Mary' [2001] *Criminal Law Review* 515.
J. Smith, *Justification and Excuse in the Criminal Law* (1989, Sweet and Maxwell).
J. Smith, 'Commentry on *Bowen*' [1996] *Criminal Law Review* 22.
K. Smith, 'Duress and Steadfastness: In Pursuit of the Unintelligible' [1999] *Criminal Law Review* 363.
K. Smith and Wilson, 'Impaired Voluntariness and Criminal Responsibility' (1993) 13 *Oxford Journal of Legal Studies* 69.
Williams, 'The Theory of Excuses' [1982] *Criminal Law Review* 732.

PART V
PARTICIPATION IN CRIME

17 Accessories

> **Key words**
>
> - **Principal** – the person who satisfied the external elements of the offence.
> - **Accessory** – a person who assisted or encouraged the principal to commit the crime.
> - **Innocent agent** – a person whose conduct satisfied the external elements of the offence, but is blameless and was caused to act by another.

17.1   What is an Accessory?

Imagine a criminal gang which has three members who decide to commit a robbery, with each member performing a different role. One is the mastermind behind the gang who plans and co-ordinates the robbery; another obtains the gun that is used; and the third actually commits the robbery. It would be unsatisfactory if the criminal law were only able to convict the person who actually carried out the robbery. Indeed, sometimes the 'mastermind' behind such gangs is a greater threat to society than the individual who actually carries out the crime. The actual perpetrator may simply be a small cog in a huge machine. So it is not surprising that the law spreads the net of liability wider than just those who actually commit the crime, by enabling the conviction of those who assist or encourage others in the commission of the crime.

There are two main ways, at a theoretical level, in which the law could deal with accessories (or secondary parties, as they are sometimes known). This issue will be dealt with in greater detail as the Hot Topic at the end of this chapter, but a brief summary can be given now. The law could see accessories as guilty of a crime because they have partly caused the commission of the crime – without their assistance or encouragement the crime would not have taken place, at least not at the time or in the manner in which it took place. This view is sometimes known as 'derivative liability' (that is the accomplice's responsibility derives from that of the person who actually carries out the crime). Alternatively, one could punish accessories because the acts of assistance are in themselves harmful to society, independent of any causal link to the commission of the actual crime. Those who adopt this theory tend to draw an analogy between accessory liability and inchoate offences, such as incitement and attempts (see Chapter 18). The most significant difference between these derivative and inchoate theories would be where someone tries to help another commit a crime but the assistance is not used at all. In those circumstances the derivative theory would not attach accessorial liability as in no sense did the assistance contribute towards the commission of a crime, whereas the 'inchoate theory' would. At present the law largely adopts the 'derivative theory'. The Law Commission in its proposed Criminal Code has suggested a shift away from 'derivative liability' and towards inchoate liability. In fact these theories reflect a strain in the law between two competing concerns: on the one hand the law does not want criminal liability to be too extensive, while on the other it is understandable that the law should attempt to deter people who seek to aid criminal acts.

17.2   Principals and the Doctrine of Innocent Agency

It is necessary first of all to distinguish a principal from an accessory. There is no requirement for an indictment to state whether the defendant is charged as a principal or an accomplice. For example, a person will simply be charged with murder whether it is alleged that he was the principle or an accessory to murder. Although the charge will be the same, the indictment will specify how the accused is alleged to have participated in the offence. The accessory is liable to the same punishment, although whether the actual sentence differs from the principal will depend on the circumstances of the offence, the degree of involvement of the parties and the personal circumstances of the individual defendant. Although the charge will be the same for principals and accessories, the distinction is significant because the *actus reus* and *mens rea* requirements for principals and accessories sometimes differ.

Who is a principal? A principal is the person who fulfils the *actus reus* requirements for the crime. There is one exception to this and that is the doctrine of innocent agency, to be discussed shortly. Where the *actus reus* of the crime involves an act, such as damaging property or wounding, the principal will be the person who does that act. Where the *actus reus* of the crime involves bringing about a particular consequence, such as the death of another person, the principal will be the person who is the most direct cause of that consequence. It is, of course, possible to have two or more principals. For example, if two people together push a rock from the top of a cliff onto a victim below they will both be joint principals to the killing.

If two people were present at the scene of the crime but it is unclear who actually committed the crime, the law has developed a special set of rules. If one of them must have been the principal and the other either a joint principal *or* an accomplice, even if it is not clear who was which, then both can be convicted of the crime without it being established who actually was the principal. This is only possible as long as they both had the *mens rea* for being either a principal or an accomplice (*Gianetto*).

There is one circumstance in which the person who performs the *actus reus* is not the principal, and that is if she is an 'innocent agent'. If the person most intimately connected to the *actus reus* is an innocent agent then the person who caused the innocent agent to act in this way is to be regarded as the principal. Suppose a terrorist plants a bomb that is set to explode the moment someone touches it. A traffic warden touches the bomb, setting it off, and killing a passer-by. It would seem odd if the traffic warden was seen as the principal of the crime and the terrorist as an accessory (although in such a case the traffic warden would be not guilty because she had no *mens rea*). In such a case the traffic warden would be regarded as an innocent agent and the terrorist as the principal. A person may be an innocent agent in two ways:

1 She lacks the capacity to commit the crime, for example she is exempt from criminal liability because she is below the age of criminal responsibility (*Michael*) or she is insane (*Tyler*); or
2 she lacks the *mens rea* and is unaware of the criminal nature of her acts.

The traffic warden above would fall under heading **2**. Another example would be a secretary who types and posts a fraudulent letter dictated by her boss, unaware that it is fraudulent (*Stringer*). It appears that someone is not an innocent agent simply because she acts under duress or self-defence.

Although we have referred to the rule here rather grandly as the 'doctrine of innocent agency' in fact it is little more than an application of the rules of causation (see Chapter 5). The traffic warden's act would not be seen as breaking the chain of causation under the rules of causation, as she was not acting in a way which was 'free, voluntary and informed' and so was not a *novus actus interveniens* (see Chapter 5.4). Similarly when a person can be regarded as an innocent agent, his acts will not break the chain of causation so the primary cause of the chain of events could be regarded as the principal.

A particularly controversial example of the use of the doctrine of innocent agency is *Cogan and Leak*. Mr Leak persuaded his friend, Mr Cogan, to have intercourse with his wife, Mrs Leak. He told Mr Cogan untruthfully that Mrs Leak might appear to resist, but that she would act in this way in order to heighten her enjoyment of the occasion. In fact Mrs Leak did not consent to the sexual intercourse. Mr Cogan was acquitted on a charge of rape of Mrs Leak because he believed that the victim was consenting. However, the Court of Appeal suggested that Mr Leak could be seen as guilty of raping Mrs Leak through the innocent agency of Mr Cogan. This is seen as controversial for two reasons. The first is that Mr Leak at that time (before *R*; see Chapter 8.2.1) could not in law be guilty of raping his wife. It seems odd that he could be convicted of a crime for which he could not have been convicted had he committed the crime himself. Indeed the reasoning in the case would suggest that a woman could be convicted of raping another woman as a principal. Secondly, the case has been criticized as it is said that some crimes cannot 'linguistically' be committed through an innocent agent. Rape is such a 'physical' crime that it is inappropriate and unrealistic to refer to it as being committed through an innocent agent. Indeed another case has held that one cannot be said to 'drive' a vehicle through the innocent agency of another (*Millward*). A conviction for procuring rape would seem more realistic on the facts of *Cogan and Leak*, and was indeed said by the Court of Appeal to be available on the facts. However, despite these criticisms *Cogan and Leak* has not yet been over-ruled, although in a recent case on similar facts the prosecution relied on the charge of procuring rape rather than using the innocent agency rule (*K and B*). Indeed, whenever the innocent agency rule operates, a charge of procuring would be possible (*Wheelhouse*).

17.3   Aiding, Abetting, Counselling and Procuring

Having established who was the principal, it is then possible to decide whether anyone can be convicted as his or her accessory. Before outlining the ways in which the law recognizes how someone can be an accessory, it is important to emphasize two restrictions on accessorial liability. First, here we are dealing with those who assist or encourage the principal before or during the commission of the crime. Separate rules govern those who assist a principal after the crime is completed (see Chapter 17.13 below). Secondly, one can only be an accessory to a crime that has actually been committed. However much assistance or encouragement the accused offers the principal, unless the principal goes on to commit a crime the would-be accessory commits no offence, unless it constitutes incitement or conspiracy (see Chapter 18). Further, there is no charge of attempting to be an accessory, as is clear from s.1(4) Criminal Attempts Acts 1981.

Turning now to the definition of the ways of being an accessory. At one time the law distinguished between those who were present at the scene of a crime and those who were not (between aiding and abetting, and counselling and procuring; between principals in the second degree and accessories before the fact). This distinction is no longer of practical importance. Rightly so, whether an accomplice is present may be a matter of chance and of itself says nothing about the blameworthiness of his conduct. The accessory can be liable for acting in one or more of four ways set out in s.8 Accessories and Abettors Act 1861. The Magistrates Court Act 1980 is in similar terms for summary offences:

> 'Whosoever shall aid, abet, counsel, or procure the commission of any indictable offence, whether the same be an offence at common law or by virtue of any Act passed or to be passed, shall be liable to be tried, indicted and punished as a principal offender.'

The Court of Appeal has said that these four words (aiding, abetting, counselling and procuring) are to be given their ordinary meaning and that the words should be seen as indicating separate concepts *(Attorney-General's Reference (No. 1 of 1975))*. However, there is no need for the prosecution to specify which of the modes of accessory is alleged, although it is desirable to do so in order that the defendant may know the nature of the charge facing him. Surprisingly, the caselaw rarely discusses the differences between the different concepts, but the following definitions appear from the caselaw.

1. Aiding

This is the giving of assistance to a principal. It can range from supplying equipment (for example, *Bainbridge*), to acting as a look-out (for example, *Perman*). There is no need to show that the assistance was requested and indeed there may be no communication at all between the aide and the principal. For example, if an employee left a business premise with the door open, out of spite, and later a burglar wandered in and stole something, the employee could be seen as an aide to the burglary. However, it must be shown that the assistance was actually used in the performance of the crime *(Able)*. It seems sufficient for the act to be of only a small amount of assistance, although there is little authority on this. Certainly it is not necessary to show that 'but for' the act of assistance the crime would not have taken place.

2. Abetting

To be honest, no one knows the meaning of abetting. It appears to involve encouragement and support provided to a principal, but probably only if it is given during the performance of the crime. It seems that abetting has no separate role, the concept being covered by aiding or counselling.

3. Counselling

This involves giving encouragement, advice or information to the principal. There is no need to show that the counselling had any effect on the way that the principal acted, although it is necessary to show that the principal acted within the 'scope of the counselling'. So, if Clare suggests that Ellie kills Alex, and Ellie replies 'don't worry I was about to anyway' and goes on to kill Alex, Clare could still be convicted as an accessory. However, if Ellie went on to rob Alex, Clare could not be convicted as an accessory to robbery. An example discussed in *Calhaem** by Parker LJ also demonstrates this requirement. If the accused had counselled the principal to kill and

> 'if the principal offender happened to be involved in a football riot in the course of which he laid about him with a weapon of some sort and killed someone who, unknown to him, was the person whom he had been counselled to kill, he could not, in our view have been acting within the scope of his authority; he would have been acting outside it, albeit what he had done was what he had been counselled to do.'

This appears to mean that only exceptionally will the resulting act, if within the terms of the counselling, be considered too remote. The required link under the derivative theory between the assistance and the crime is stretched to its limits here.

4. Procuring

Procuring has been defined as 'to produce by endeavour. You procure a thing by setting out to see that it happens and taking appropriate steps to produce that happening' (*Attorney-General's Reference (No. 1 of 1975)*). This means that there must be a causal link between the act of procuring and the *actus reus*. A common example is where an accessory spikes a principal's drink (for example, by putting alcohol into someone's non-alcoholic drink), and the principal then goes on to drive. In such a case the accessory is seen to be guilty of procuring the drink driving offence.

Smith and Hogan have summarized the position as follows:

> '(1) procuring implies causation but not consensus
> (2) abetting and counselling imply consensus but not causation and
> (3) aiding requires actual assistance but neither consensus nor causation.'

This statement of the law was approved by Woolf J in *Able*.

17.4 The *Mens Rea* of Being an Accomplice

The *mens rea* for an accessory is far from clear and there is little direct caselaw on the issue and what there is, is difficult to interpret. Further, commentators are somewhat divided on this issue. Although it is difficult to be certain about the law, the following summary is proposed:

If *A* (the principal) performed crime *X*, and it is alleged that *B* was an accessory then it must be shown that at the time when *B* assisted or encouraged *A*, he or she foresaw:
(i)   *A* might go on to commit a crime similar to *X*; and
(ii) *A* would carry out the crime using *B*'s act of assistance or in accordance with his encouragement.

A very useful summary of the present law has been provided by the Court of Appeal in *Uddin**, which sets out the law in seven key principles, building on the decision of the House of Lords in *Powell and English**:

'(i) Where several persons join to attack a victim in circumstances which show that they intend to inflict serious harm and as a result of the attack the victim sustains fatal injury, they are jointly liable for murder; but if such injury inflicted with that intent is shown to have been caused solely by the actions of one participant of a type entirely different from actions which the others foresaw as part of the attack, only that participant is guilty of murder.
(ii) In deciding whether the actions are of such a different type the use by that party of a weapon is a significant factor. If the character of the weapon, e.g. its propensity to cause death, is different from any weapon used or contemplated by the others and if it is used with a specific intent to kill, the others are not responsible for the death unless it is proved that they knew or foresaw the likelihood of the use of such a weapon.
(iii) If some or all of the others are using weapons which could be regarded as equally likely to inflict fatal injury, the mere fact that a different weapon was used is immaterial.
(iv) If the jury conclude that the death of the victim was caused by the actions of one participant which can be said to be of a completely different type to those contemplated by the others, they are not to be regarded as parties to the death whether it amounts to murder or manslaughter. They may nevertheless be guilty of offences of wounding or inflicting grievous bodily harm with intent which they individually commit.
(v) If in the course of the concerted attack a weapon is produced by one of the participants and the others knowing that he has it in circumstances

where he may use it in the course of the attack participate or continue to participate in the attack, they will be guilty of murder if the weapon is used to inflict a fatal wound.

(vi) In a case in which after a concerted attack it is proved that the victim died as a result of a wound with a lethal weapon, e.g. a stab wound, but the evidence does not establish which of the participants used the weapon, then if its use was foreseen by the participants in the attack they will all be guilty of murder notwithstanding that the particular participant who administered the fatal blow cannot be identified: see *Reg.* v. *Powell*; *Reg.* v. *English* [1999] 1 A.C. 1. If, however, the circumstances do not show that the participants foresaw the use of a weapon of this type, none of them will be guilty of murder though they may individually have committed offences in the course of the attack.

(vii) The mere fact that by attacking the victim together each of them had the intention to inflict serious harm on the victim is insufficient to make them responsible for the death of the victim caused by the use of a lethal weapon used by one of the participants with the same or shared intention.'

This provides a reasonably clear summary of the law, but there are still several areas of difficulty.

1.   The importance of motive

Is it necessary to show that it was the defendant's purpose in acting that he wanted to aid the principal's crime? There are two key cases. In *National Coal Board* v. *Gamble**, the majority of the Divisional Court held that motive is irrelevant to the liability of an accessory, foresight alone is enough. This requirement caused problems in the House of Lords' case of *Gillick**, where the applicant challenged the legality of a government guidance which suggested that doctors could provide contraceptive advice to children under sixteen without their parents' consent. One of the issues that the case raised was whether the doctors would be guilty of aiding unlawful sexual intercourse with a girl under sixteen contrary to s.6 Sexual Offences Act 1956. The argument was that in some cases, had the doctor not provided the contraception the girl would not have engaged in the sexual intercourse. Lord Scarman appeared to decide that a doctor in such a case would not be committing a criminal act. This seemed to be because the doctor was acting in what she thought were the girl's best interests, in her clinical judgement. This appears to suggest that motive may be relevant, as it implies that if the doctor was not acting from what she thought was the girl's best interests, she might then be guilty of a criminal act. There is some indication that Lord Bridge thought that the provision of contraception was not aiding an illegal act, simply making it safer. This argument also appears to suggest that motive is crucial for determining liability for accessories.

If these two authorities, *Gamble* and *Gillick*, are in conflict then *Gillick*, although it is a House of Lords' decision, is probably the weaker authority as the case was mainly about medical and family law, and the criminal law aspects were only briefly touched upon by their Lordships. Some commentators have suggested that the case is really a recognition of a hidden defence of medical necessity. Indeed a recent case on accessories (*Powell**) stated that *Gillick* was of little relevance to the question of the *mens rea* for accessories in the criminal law. *Gamble*, by contrast, clearly focused on this question of the *mens rea* requirement of accessories and has been quoted with approval by the House of Lords in *Lynch* and *Maxwell**, and the Court of Appeal in *Able*. In *J. F. Alford*, the Court of Appeal confirmed that the motive of the accessory is irrelevant. It appears therefore that the present law requires that the accessory foresaw that the principal would commit the kind of crime he goes on to commit. It is not necessary to show that the accessory wanted the principal to commit that crime.

2. The degree of foresight required
The second issue of dispute is the level of foresight by an accessory that needs to be shown. It is clear that the accomplice must subjectively foresee at the time he commits his acts of assistance that the principal may go on to commit the crime, so the *mens rea* is *Cunningham* reckless rather than *Caldwell* recklessness (*Blakely**). The risk foreseen must not be minimal but it is unclear whether more than this is required. The simple answer given by the House of Lords in *Powell** is that the test is whether the accessory foresaw that the principal 'might' commit the crime. In other words, that the accessory thought it was a real, not negligible, possibility that the principal would commit the crime.

3. What must be foreseen?
The straightforward answer is that the accomplice must have foreseen that the principal may commit the crime. However, there are four points that need clarification.

First, it is clear that what must be foreseen is not just the act of the principal but the circumstances surrounding the act which make it a crime (*Johnson* v. *Youden*). In *Johnson* v. *Youden*, Lord Goddard CJ said that 'a person cannot be convicted of aiding and abetting the commission of an offence if he does not know of the essential matters which would constitute the offence'. So if Elizabeth assists Dennis in breaking a vase then it is necessary to show that Elizabeth foresaw that Dennis would break the vase and that the owner of the vase would not consent. However, it is not necessary to show foresight of circumstances that are irrelevant to the *actus reus* of the crime, for example the value of the vase.

Second, it is enough if the accomplice foresaw that the principal would commit the kind of crime that he committed. So if the accomplice gives assistance to a principal, foreseeing that he will commit a robbery, but using the assistance the principal commits a rape, the accomplice will not be liable under the criminal law. However, if the accomplice foresaw that the principal would burgle a bank and offers assistance, but the principal, using the assistance, burgles a different bank, the accomplice will be guilty (see, further, Chapter 17.7 below).

Third, in *Powell and English** the House of Lords made it clear that the accomplice needs to foresee that the principal will act with the necessary *mens rea*. In the context of murder this means that to be convicted as an accomplice of murder, the accomplice must foresee not only that the principal might kill, but that he or she will kill with the intention to kill or cause grievous bodily harm. So, if Emma gives Andrew a knife to assist in his plan to cause Joseph grievous bodily harm, but she knows that Andrew is liable to get carried away and accidentally kill Joseph, she will not be liable as an accomplice if Andrew in fact deliberately stabs Joseph to death. The explanation is that the deliberate killing is 'outside the scope of the joint enterprise'. What is unclear is what would happen if the accomplice foresaw that the principal would deliberately kill, but the principal accidentally killed.

Fourth, the House of Lords has developed a special rule in relation to weapons. If the accomplice is aware that the principal has a weapon, it is presumed that the accomplice foresees that the principal will use it. So, if the accomplice is assisting the principal in committing a burglary, but is aware that the principal has a knife and during the course of the burglary the principal stabs the house owner, it will be presumed that the accomplice foresaw the use of the knife. In *Powell and English**, Lord Hutton expanded this, explaining:

> 'if the weapon used by the primary party is different to, but as dangerous as, the weapon the secondary party contemplated he might use, the second party should not escape liability because of the difference in the weapon, for example, if he foresaw that the primary party might use a gun to kill and the latter used a knife to kill or vice versa.'

On the facts of *Powell and English**, the accused knew that the principal had a wooden post, but the principal pulled out a knife (which the accused knew nothing about) and stabbed the victim. These were held to be fundamentally different kinds of weapon and so the accused could not be held to be an accomplice to the stabbing. It was fundamentally different in that a knife is a 'deadly weapon' whereas a post is not. Had the accused pulled out an iron bar and hit the victim, a jury may well decide that the weapon was not of a different kind from that foreseen and so the accused would be guilty as an accomplice to the injuries caused by the bar. In *Greatrex*, the Court of Appeal stressed that the question of whether the weapon used by the principal is fundamentally different from that foreseen by the alleged accomplice is one for the jury to decide.

The decision of the Court of Appeal in *Roberts* suggests that this is a presumption of fact. For example the accessory would not have the necessary *mens rea* if it is shown that the accessory knew the principal had a gun, but thought that the gun was unloaded or that it was only to be used to frighten the victim (*Powell**), or did not foresee that the principal would encounter anyone while committing his crime (*Perman*).

4. Is the mens rea *for procuring different from that of other ways of being an accomplice?*

As stated earlier, the Court of Appeal has defined procuring as 'to produce by endeavour', which seems to indicate that an intention to produce a result is necessary (*Blakely*). However, later cases have not interpreted the *mens rea* for procuring to involve foresight rather than requiring intention (for example, *Roberts and George*). This seems sensible because it would seem to cause unnecessary confusion to have different *mens rea* for different forms of accomplice liability, especially as many forms of procuring could easily be classified as aiding or counselling.

5. Is the accessory liable for the unforeseen consequences of the principal's foreseen act?

What if the principal does an act which the accessory foresees, but the act has consequences which the accessory did not foresee; is the accessory still liable for those unforeseen consequences? The answer appears to be 'yes', if the principal's act causes those consequences in line with normal principles of causation (*Anderson and Morris**, *Gilmour* (a decision of the Northern Ireland Court of Appeal) and *Day*). So if *A* foresees that *B* might point a gun to frighten a victim but did not foresee that the victim would suffer a heart attack and die, *A* could still be liable as an accomplice to manslaughter.

6. *What if the accessory foresees the harm that the principal causes, but not the manner in which it is caused?*

What if the accessory foresees that the principal may cause a particular harm but the principal causes that harm in a way that the accessory did not foresee. Two recent cases appear to be in conflict on this issue. In one, *Mahmood*, two young men stole a car, drove it at speed and abandoned it without putting the hand-brake on. The car rolled onto a pavement and killed a baby. The court held that the passenger in the car must have foreseen that the driver might injure or kill someone by his speedy driving and would have been liable if the driver had. However, it found that the passenger would not have foreseen that the driver would abandon the vehicle in such a reckless way, and so he was not liable for the death of the baby. In contrast, in *Bamborough* the accomplice knew that the principal had a gun and foresaw that he might use the gun to pistol-whip the victim. In fact the principal shot the victim with the gun. It was held that as the accomplice foresaw that the principal would use the gun to cause serious injury, it did not matter that he did not foresee the precise way in which the injury would be caused. Of course, the same could have been said of *Mahmood* – the passenger foresaw that the driver would injure someone with the car but did not foresee exactly how. Of the two, *Bamborough* seems more in line with the ordinary principles of *mens rea*, which require foresight or intent of a result rather than of the means to obtain that result. It may be that *Mahmood* could be explained on the ground that by the time the principal left the hand-brake off, the joint enterprise (of 'joy-riding' the car) was at an end.

The question may be resolved in *Powell**, at least by implication. It will be recalled that their Lordships argued that if the accomplice believed that the principal had a weapon, but the principal used a different weapon, but one of a similar level of dangerousness, the accomplice could still be convicted. This implies that it is not necessary for the accomplice to foresee exactly the method by which the injury will be inflicted as long as it is similar to a method foreseen by the accomplice. This also seems to be implied by point (v) in the *Uddin* summary of the law.

7. *What if the principal does an act with less* mens rea *than that of the accessory?*

What should happen if the accessory intends that the principal will kill a victim, but the principal kills accidentally? The principal might be guilty of manslaughter, but could the accessory be guilty of murder? The problem is that the 'derivative principle' requires that the accomplice is only guilty if the defendant commits the crime, and this was thought to mean that an accomplice could not be guilty of a more serious offence than the principal. However, in *Howe** it was said that one could add the *mens rea* of the accomplice to the *actus reus* that the principal committed to create a more serious crime. Lord Mackay gives the following example:

> 'A hands a gun to D informing him that it is loaded with blank ammunition only and telling him to go and scare X by discharging it. The ammunition is in fact live (as A knows) and X is killed. D is convicted only of manslaughter. It would seem absurd that A should thereby escape conviction for murder.'

However, note this does not mean if *A* aids *B*, believing that *B* is going to kill *C*, but *B* only assaults *C*, that *A* can be guilty as an accomplice to murder or manslaughter. The accomplice cannot be convicted of assisting an offence with a more serious *actus reus* than that committed by the principal.

17.5 Criticisms of the Law on the Accessorial *Mens Rea* Requirement

This *mens rea* requirement may seem rather harsh, especially where the *mens rea* requirement for the principal is only intention. For example, for a principal to be guilty of murder he must have intended to cause death or serious injury; but for the accomplice to be liable for assisting the crime of murder he need only have foreseen that death or serious injury might occur (*Powell and English**). Lord Steyn in *Powell and English** sought to justify this position by three arguments. First, that the accessory who foresees that the principal may commit murder and nevertheless decides to join with him in a criminal enterprise can justly be convicted of murder. He noted that foresight is required both to the act which causes death and the *mens rea* of the accomplice. This means that the *mens rea* for an accessory to murder is not the same as that required for the principal in a manslaughter case where only foresight of death is required for recklessness manslaughter (see Chapter 9.3). Second, he argued:

> 'The criminal justice system exists to control crime. A prime function of that system must be to deal justly but effectively with those who join with others in criminal enterprises. Experience has shown that joint criminal enterprises only too readily escalate into the commission of greater offences. In order to deal with this important social problem the accessory principle is needed and cannot be abolished or relaxed.'

Thirdly, Lord Steyn in *Powell** relied on practical grounds: 'In the real world proof of an intention sufficient for murder would be well nigh impossible in the vast majority of joint enterprise cases', he argued. All these arguments carry force, but critics respond by arguing that convicting the accessory who foresees (but does not intend) that the principal will kill of manslaughter would better accord with principle and would perform the deterrence function to which Lord Steyn refers.

We will now examine three particular situations where the courts have applied these general principles on accomplices.

17.6   Presence of Accessory

One contentious topic has been whether a person's mere presence at the scene of a crime can amount to aiding, abetting, counselling and procuring. There are two circumstances in which the law recognizes that presence can amount to the *actus reus* for being an accessory:

1.   Presence as encouragement
Mere presence can itself amount to encouraging (counselling). It must be shown that the principal was actually encouraged by the accused's presence and the accused realized that his presence is encouraging the principal (*Coney*). It is not enough to show that the bystander was willing to intervene should his assistance become necessary, unless that willingness actually encourages the principal (*Sirat*). In *Clarkson*, the accused, a soldier, came across a fellow soldier raping a woman, and stayed and watched. He did nothing to stop the incident. However, he was acquitted on a charge of being an accomplice to rape as it was not shown that the rapist found any encouragement from his presence. Nor was it shown that he had the necessary *mens rea* of being aware that his presence might be an encouragement. By contrast, in *Collins* v. *Wilcox* the accused attended a performance by a saxophonist, an illegal immigrant, whom he had invited to play in England. His act of meeting the saxophonist on his arrival into England and his presence and clapping at the performance were encouragement to the illegal performance. The court suggested that had the accused attended the concert and shouted 'boo', and in other ways tried to disrupt the performance, he may not have been an accomplice. It is possible for a jury to infer assistance from mere presence at the scene of a crime, but the law is generally reluctant to do this without further evidence (*Coney*).

2.   Duty to prevent the crime
If the accused has a duty to intervene to stop the principal committing the

crime but fails to do so then this might establish him as an accessory. For example, in *Du Cros* v. *Lamborn* the owner of a car was convicted of speeding. In fact it was not clear whether he was the driving the car or was a passenger in the car when it exceeded the speed limit. Clearly, if he was the driver then he would be guilty of the offence. It was held, however, that if he was the passenger then he had a duty, as owner, to ensure that his car was not driven illegally. Therefore his presence in the car, together with a duty to stop the crime, could establish him as an accomplice. The Court of Appeal has recently confirmed that having a duty to intervene and failing to do so may constitute being an accessory to the crime, although it added that this would only be so where the defendant made a positive decision not to intervene (*J. F. Alford*).

17.7   Providing Equipment

In line with the basic principle on *mens rea* for accomplices, if the accused gives the principal a piece of equipment which is used in connection with a crime then the accessory will be liable if she foresaw that the principal would use the equipment during the crime. So if *A* lends *B* a screwdriver, believing that it will help *B* commit a burglary, which *B* duly commits, then *A* will be guilty as an accessory to the burglary. However, if *B* used the screwdriver to kill someone, *A* would not be guilty as an accessory to murder unless he foresaw that *B* might use it for that purpose. It is not necessary to show that *A* was aware of all of the details of the crime, for example it is not necessary to show that *A* knew precisely which house *B* would burgle, or exactly how *B* would effect entry, as long as *A* foresaw the type of crime that *B* would commit (*Bainbridge*). Indeed if *A* foresaw that *B* might commit a burglary, assault or a robbery with the screwdriver then *A* will be guilty as an accomplice if B does any of these things (*Maxwell*). This is sometimes called the 'shopping list' rule. It has even been suggested that *A* may write *B* a 'blank cheque' (Lowry CJ in *Maxwell*) by giving *B* the equipment and authorizing *B* to commit any crime that he wishes using the equipment. This *dicta* is notable as it describes the test for the *mens rea* of an accessory in terms of authorization, rather than foresight. It may be, therefore, that this is out of line with the other cases on accomplices (which had rejected a test based on authorization in favour of one based on foreseeability). That said, the law is unlikely to feel sympathetic towards an accomplice who hands over a gun and says 'you can commit any crime you like with this gun' and later complains 'but I didn't foresee he would do *that* with it'.

There are two particular difficulties that can arise in the provision-of-equipment cases. The first is how to deal with a defendant who is obliged in civil law to return a piece of property to the owner but who is aware that the owner is likely to use the equipment for criminal purposes; for example, where Tim asks Judith to return a gun that he had lent her, but Judith is aware that Tim plans to use the gun to kill someone. In *Gamble* Devlin J suggested that if one is obliged under civil law to return equipment to another then doing so should be classified as an omission and so not attract liability as an accomplice. The idea seems to be that if Tim is in law entitled to have possession of an item then by handing the item over Judith is not doing anything of legal significance. However, in *Garrett* v. *Churchill* the Court of Appeal refused to follow this reasoning and argued that civil law does not require the return of a piece which it is known is going to be used in a crime. It is certainly undesirable that the complexities of civil law should determine the issue. There is a need for an authoritative decision to decide how to balance the protection of property interests and the need to discourage crime.

The second difficulty is the so-called 'problem of the generous host'. If a host at a party provides alcohol for her guests, aware that some of those drinking are driving home after the party, is she aiding and abetting their drunk driving? Remember that the fact that it is not her purpose that they should drink drive seems to be irrelevant. It has been suggested (*in Attorney-General's Reference (No. 1 of 1975)*) that the host is not guilty as the decision to drink is entirely up to the driver; although this is not entirely convincing as it is always true that the principal has a choice of whether or not to commit the crime whenever there is a principal and an accessory. So it seems technically that the generous host is guilty, although unlikely to be prosecuted.

17.8   Joint Enterprise

A joint enterprise occurs where two or more people act together in order to pursue some unlawful enterprise. If there is a joint enterprise and the two carry out their plan, they will be jointly liable for each other's acts. In order for the doctrine to operate, two or more people must act in concert. So in one case where a man attacked a victim in a car park and a stranger came along and joined in the attack, it was held that there was no joint enterprise, although both were liable as principals for their own acts (*Petters and Parfitt*). This is not to say it is necessary for the members of the joint enterprise to agree expressly on a course of conduct, but they need to act together with a common purpose.

It had been suggested that joint-enterprise liability should be seen as distinct from accessorial liability. In *Stewart and Schofield* it was suggested:

> 'a person who is a mere aider or abettor etc. is truly a secondary party to the commission of whatever crime it is that the principal has committed although he may be charged as a principal . . . in contrast, where the allegation is that one defendant participated in the criminal act of another this is a different principle. It renders each of the parties to a joint enterprise liable for the acts done in the course of carrying out the joint enterprise.'

This was highly controversial and the House of Lords in *Powell** and the Court of Appeal in *Reardon* have now said that it is wrong. The doctrine of joint enterprise is simply an application of the general rules governing accessories. Being a party to a joint enterprise, then, is regarded as simply one way of being an aider, abettor, counsellor or procurer.

The doctrine of joint enterprise is relied upon where two people (*A* and *B*) act together to carry out crime *X*, in the course of which one (*B*) carries out crime *Y*. A typical example in the caselaw is where *A* and *B* agree to commit a burglary in the course of which *B* is disturbed by the owner and kills him. Clearly *A* is guilty of burglary as a joint principal, but is he also guilty of being an accomplice to murder?

Applying the normal rules for accomplices, the question (*Powell and English**) is: did *A* foresee that *B* might act in the way that he did? If *A* foresaw that *B* would kill with the *mens rea* for murder (that is, an intention to kill or cause grievous bodily harm) then *A* would be guilty as an accessory to murder. If *A* foresaw that *B* would kill without the *mens rea* for murder, *A* would be guilty as an accessory to manslaughter. If *A* did not foresee that *B* would kill, *A* is not liable as an accessory because *B*'s act is 'outside the joint enterprise'.

17.9 Acting Outside the Enterprise

We have already referred several times to the rule that the accomplice is not liable for the acts of a principal which were not foreseen by the accused. Such acts are described as outside the scope of the enterprise. A famous example of this is *Saunders and Archer*, where a husband and a friend agreed to poison the husband's wife with a poisoned apple. In the friend's absence, the husband gave the apple to his wife but she gave the apple to their child. The husband kept quiet while the child ate the apple, and died. It was held that the friend was not an accomplice to the child's murder as the husband chose not to intervene and stop the child eating the apple and this could not have been foreseen by the friend.

A classic statement by Lord Parker CJ of the law on this point is found in *Anderson and Morris*:

> 'where two persons embark on a joint enterprise, each is liable for the acts done in pursuance of that joint enterprise, and that includes liability for unusual consequences if they arise from the execution of the agreed joint enterprise but . . . if one of the adventurers goes beyond what has been tacitly agreed as part of the common enterprise, his co-adventurer is not liable for the consequences of that unauthorised act.'

In a much discussed South African case, three men agreed to kill the victim, who consented to the plan. The aim was to enable the victim's wife to claim on his life-insurance policy. Shortly before the three men were about to kill the victim, he changed his mind and told them not to kill him. However, one of the gang nevertheless went ahead and killed him. The question for the court concerned the liability of the other two members of the gang. The court held that not every departure from the plan could lead to an acquittal for the accomplices, but if it was a substantial variation then it would. Here the court decided that the killing without the consent of the victim was a substantial variation (*Robinson* (1968)). A deliberate variation by the principal was more likely to be outside the agreed plan than an unintended act (see also *Saunders and Archers*).

17.10   Withdrawal from Enterprise

The justification for enabling an accused to be able to withdraw from an enterprise is fairly obvious. There needs to be an incentive to persuade people to withdraw from criminal enterprises, and anyway one who has withdrawn is certainly less to blame than one who has been consistently involved. If any member of the gang effectively withdraws from the criminal enterprise, he may escape liability as an accomplice for any crimes committed after his withdrawal. He will remain liable for any crimes committed while he was a member of the enterprise.

The law is very strict about when an accomplice can withdraw from a planned criminal enterprise. It is not enough just to run away (*Becerra*); one must disassociate oneself from the crime in an unequivocal way (*Baker*). In *Fletcher*, the accused said to the principal 'don't do it' and 'don't be a fool'; these words were said to be equivocal and insufficient to end his association with the principal's actions. But the court stated that he could have withdrawn by attempting to prevent the principal from committing the crime. Simply not turning up on the day planned for the crime after being involved in its planning is also insufficient (*Rook*). However, announcing two weeks before the crime is due to take place that you are to have nothing more to do with the plan may be sufficient (*Whitefield*). The law is less strict when considering whether someone has withdrawn from a spontaneous joint enterprise. In such a case, simply no longer participating in the attack can constitute an effective withdrawal from the enterprise (*Mitchell*).

17.11   Interaction between Accomplice Liability and Principal Liability

If the principal is acquitted, can the accomplice still be found guilty? This depends on why the principal was acquitted. If the principal was acquitted because she had a special defence personal to her (for example, duress in *Bourne*, or infancy in *K* and *B*) or because she lacked *mens rea* (*Cogan and Leak*) then the accomplice can still be convicted. However, if the principal was acquitted because the *actus reus* had not taken place then the accomplice cannot be convicted (*Thornton* v. *Mitchell*). This can perhaps be made clearer by considering two recent driving offence cases. In *Millward**, the principal was a driver employed by a company which had inadequately maintained the vehicle; the vehicle crashed but the driver (the principal) was acquitted of reckless driving as he could not reasonably have been aware of the dangerous condition of the vehicle; but the company was convicted of procuring reckless driving as it should have realized that the vehicle was faulty. By contrast, in *Loukes* the appellant ran a business and was charged with procuring the offence of causing death by dangerous driving (an offence created by the Road Traffic Act 1991 which replaced the offence of causing death by reckless driving). One of the appellant's employees, who had driven a van that had been inadequately maintained by the firm, was involved in a car accident in which a death resulted. It was held that because the driver had been acquitted on the ground that he had not been driving dangerously, there was no *actus reus*. The case was distinguished from *Millward**, as there the *actus reus* was driving, and the principal was acquitted because he lacked *mens rea* (he was not reckless). By contrast, in *Loukes* the *actus reus* was dangerous driving (dangerousness does not involve a state of mind); there was no dangerous driving as the driver had taken all reasonable care, and so there was no *actus reus* and the defendant could not be said to have procured the offence.

17.12   Victims as Accomplices

If an offence is designed to protect a particular group of people then the victim cannot be said to aid and abet the offence against herself. So, in *Tyrell*, the court considered the offence of taking a girl away from her parents without her consent. A man did so and was convicted, but the girl was charged with aiding and abetting him, as it was said that she was willingly involved. The court held that as the offence was designed to protect young girls, it could not be used against them to charge them with aiding and abetting. Similarly a child who is the victim of incest by her father cannot be convicted of being an accomplice to his crime (as stated in *Whitehouse*).

17.13   Assistance after an Offence

According to s.4 Criminal Law Act 1967:

> 'Where a person has committed an arrestable offence, any other person who, knowing or believing him to be guilty of the offence or of some other arrestable offence, does without lawful authority or reasonable excuse any act with intent to impede his apprehension or prosecution shall be guilty of an offence'.

The offence typically involves misdirecting police, or providing a getaway car. It seems that the offence cannot be committed by omission because the statute refers specifically to 'an act'. The *mens rea* requires the defendant to know or believe that someone was guilty of an arrestable offence. There is no need to show that the defendant knew which arrestable offence had been committed, but simply that an arrestable offence had been committed. The other aspect of the *mens rea* is an intention to impede the apprehension of the offender. There is no need to show that the defendant was aware of the offender's identity (*Brindley*).

According to s.5(1) Criminal Law Act 1967:

> 'Where a person has committed an arrestable offence, any person who, knowing or believing that the offence or some other arrestable offence has been committed, and that he has information which might be of material assistance in securing the prosecution or conviction of an offender for it, accepts or agrees to accept for not disclosing that information any consideration, other than the making good of loss or injury caused by the offence, or the making of reasonable compensation for that

loss or injury, shall be liable on conviction on indictment to imprisonment for not more than two years.'

The *actus reus* of this offence requires that an arrestable offence be committed and that the defendant must accept consideration for not revealing the information. If the defendant requested the consideration then this would constitute the offence of blackmail and is a more serious offence (see Chapter 14.2). The *mens rea* is that the defendant knew or believed that the arrestable offence had been committed and intended to accept consideration (if it is more than reasonable consideration).

It is also a common law offence to refuse to go to the aid of a constable to assist in preserving the peace.

17.14   Reforms

The heart of the reforms found in the Law Commission Consultation Paper on accessories is a proposal to abandon the present derivative basis of liability and replace it with two basic crimes – assisting and encouraging crime. The explanation for this change is thus:

'An accused's legal fault is complete as soon as his act of assistance is done, and acts thereafter by the principal, in particular in committing or not committing the crime assisted, cannot therefore add to or detract from that fault.'

The offence of assisting would be any act that the defendant 'knows or believes assists or will assist the principal in consulting the offence'. It should be noted that the wording states that the offence 'will' assist, rather than 'may' assist. It also needs to be shown that the person assisted believed that the principal would go on to commit the crime with the necessary *mens rea*. It would also be an offence to solicit, command and encourage if the defendant intends the crime to be committed by the principal. The report rather strangely is seeking further advice on whether the notion of joint enterprise be retained, as there seems no obvious occasion when there could be a joint enterprise that would not also amount to an offence of assistance.

Hot Topic: Why do we have Liability for Accessories?

There is a range of ways in which a legal system could deal with those who help others to commit crimes. One of the difficulties with the English and Welsh law is that it has not clearly adopted an overarching approach to accessories which would provide the law with a clear conceptual basis. Here are some of the ways that a legal system could deal with accessories.

1. Derivative liability

This theory has been well explained by J. Dressler:

> 'A is held accountable for the conduct of P because, by intentionally assisting him, he voluntarily identifies himself with the primary party. His intentional conduct, therefore, is equivalent to manifesting consent to liability under the civil law.'

This is the theory that seems to best explain the present law. The principal is seen as the wrongdoer, the accessory is a person who by his or her action has associated himself or herself with that crime. In the same way that a person chooses to enter a contract and therefore to be bound by it, an accessory chooses to join in with the principal and is therefore liable for his or her crime. The criticisms of this approach can be seen in the following discussion on other approaches.

2. Inchoate theory

We could define being an accessory as an inchoate offence. It would be an offence to encourage or assist a crime. There would be no need to show that a crime took place or if it did the acts of the 'accessory' encouraged or assisted the principal. In other words, accessorial liability would look much more like the offence of incitement (see Chapter 18).

The argument in favour of this approach is a peculiarity of the present law. The argument is well made by J. Spencer (1987):

> 'If you commit the crime I knew you intended with my help to commit, I am likely to be an accessory, but if you do not, I may well commit no offence at all . . . This is very strange. In either case, I have done all that I have to do to incur criminal liability. It is no fault of mine – or to be accurate, it is not due to any lack of fault on my part – that the crime was never committed. If my behaviour was bad enough to punish where you actually made use of the help I gave you, it was surely bad enough to punish where I fully expected you to use it but you got caught before you had the chance.'

Adopting the inchoate model of accessorial liability would mean that whether the principal went on to commit the crime would be irrelevant to the liability of an accessory. The key wrong of the offence would be the offering of assistance to someone who is believed to be going to commit a crime.

Opponents of the inchoate offence model might argue that if someone offers assistance in the commission of a crime, but no crime takes place, there is insufficient harm to justify a conviction. Just as we do not punish a person for planning to commit an evil crime until he or she has gone beyond mere preparation and committed an attempt (see Chapter 18.3), even more so we should not punish a person who has offered help to someone who may be some time from committing an offence. In simple terms, there is not enough harm caused by an accessory if the principal does not commit a crime to justify a criminal conviction. This is a powerful objection to the inchoate model. However, supporters of the model would argue that the objection does not take sufficient account of the fact that the law is much stricter where people join together to commit crimes than where individuals act alone. Incitement and conspiracy are offences even where no objective harm results. In fact the line between incitement and where a person seeks to offer assistance is so fine that it is difficult to believe there is a fundamental difference between the two.

A second objection to the inchoate model is that it does not describe well the wrong committed. If Noel knew Myleene was planning to kill Kym and so Noel gave Myleene a machine gun which she then used to kill Kym, what would be a better description of what Noel did: that he contributed and to an extent was responsible for Kym's killing or that he gave Myleene a gun believing she would use it to kill? The general public might suggest that the former rather than the latter (as the inchoate model would have it) better describes what was done. This objection is another variation on the argument about whether we should only be responsible for our acts or whether we should also be responsible for the consequences of our acts (see Chapter 1.4.4).

3. A causation analysis

K. Smith (1991) has suggested that the law should ask whether the accessory caused, or was a cause of, the crime that the principal committed. In the example just discussed, Noel was a causal influence on the commission of the offence because his actions contributed to the way that Kym died. This would require a widening of the rules of causation and a removal of the rule that the free voluntary acts of a third party necessarily break the chain of causation. This may sound revolutionary but it should be recalled that in Chapter 5.4 we noted that in *Empress Car Co* v. *NRA* and *Kennedy* that the causation rules were not applied strictly.

Few commentators have been willing to follow K. Smith in this analysis, partly because if the *novus actus interveniens* doctrine is dispensed with, something needs to replace it if the potential net of criminal liability is not to be spread enormously wide. It is far from clear what rule could replace it which did not then exempt many accessories.

4. A specific statutory offence

It would be possible to create a specific statutory offence of involvement in a crime. There is an example of this in English and Welsh law. Under s.2(1) Suicide Act 1961:

> 'A person who aids, abets, counsels or procures the suicide of another, or an attempt by another to commit a suicide, shall be liable on conviction to imprisonment for a term not exceeding 14 years.'

Glazebrook (1996) suggests that a similar statutory offence could be created covering all forms of accessorial liability. If desired, the statute could set out clearly the meaning of the *actus reus* and the *mens rea* required. The benefit of this approach would be that there would be no need to have a special set of rules for 'accessorial liability'; there would be no need to distinguish principles and accessories; and accessorial liability would not need to (although it could) depend on the commission of a crime by someone else. However it may be that although it would mean helping the commission of a crime, it would simply be the *actus reus* of a crime and many of the real problems of accessorial liability would remain. This proposal in the end turns out to be really an issue about whether we wish to define accessorial liability in a statute (perhaps as part of a code) or whether we wish it to be defined by the common law. It does not provide an overarching solution to the complexities involved in accessorial liability.

Summary

17.1   The law not only punishes those who commit the *actus reus* but also those who assist them. Punishing accomplices could be based on seeing them as having partly caused the commission of the crime, their liability deriving from the crime that the principal commits. Alternatively one could see an act of assistance as in itself harmful and as appropriate for punishment, even if there is no actual crime committed.

17.2   The principal is the person who causes the *actus reus*. The one exception to this is where the *actus reus* is caused by a person who is an innocent agent. One can be an innocent agent if one lacks the capacity to commit the crime or has no *mens rea*. In such a case the person who causes the innocent agent to commit the *actus reus* will be regarded as the principal.

17.3   One can be an accomplice by aiding, abetting, counselling or procuring the principal. These words are to be given their ordinary meaning. If the person that the accused attempted to assist does not go on to commit a crime then the accused cannot be guilty as an accomplice.

17.4   The *mens rea* of being an accomplice is to do an act of aiding, abetting, counselling or procuring voluntarily and to foresee that the principal may go on to commit the crime with the assistance. There is no need to show that the accomplice wanted the principal to go on and commit the crime. It is sufficient to show that the accomplice foresaw that the principal would go on to commit the kind of crime that the principal went on to commit; there is no need to show foresight of the details of the crime.

17.5   The law on the *mens rea* for accessories is controversial. This is because an accessory can be liable with a lower *mens rea* than that required for a principal. This is justified in part by the policy of discouraging people joining together to commit crimes.

17.6   Merely being present at the scene of a crime is insufficient to constitute being an accomplice except in two situations. The first is where the presence of the accomplice is an encouragement to the principal and the accomplice is aware of this. The second is where the accomplice is under a duty to stop the principal committing the crime and deliberately fails to do so.

17.7   Providing equipment to a principal is the basis for a conviction as an accomplice if the accused foresaw that the principal might use that equipment for the kind of crime he goes on to commit with it.

17.8   If the accomplice and the principal act together in committing a crime then the accomplice can be liable as an accessory, under the principle of joint enterprise, for any other crime that he foresaw the principal might commit during their enterprise.

17.9   An accomplice is not liable for any act of the principal that is outside their enterprise; that is, any act that was not foreseen by the accomplice.

17.10   An accomplice may withdraw from a joint enterprise if she makes an unequivocal withdrawal. This may require some kind of action to positively try to stop the principal committing the crime.

17.11   If the principal is acquitted because she did not commit the *actus reus* then the accomplice cannot be convicted as an accomplice to that crime. However, if the principal is acquitted because of a lack of *mens rea* or because she has a special defence then the accomplice can still be convicted.

17.12 If the victim of the crime is of a class of people intended to be protected by the offence then she cannot be charged as an accessory to the crime committed against her.

17.13 It is an offence to impede the apprehension or prosecution of a person one believes to have committed an offence.

17.14 The Law Commission has suggested a complete reformation of the law on accomplices. The basis of liability is to be the act of assistance rather than any causal responsibility for the crime. There are to be two offences: assisting and encouraging crime; and it is to be no bar to a prosecution that the assistance or encouraging had no effect and a crime was not committed.

Case Notes

Anderson and Morris [1966] 2 All ER 644. Court of Criminal Appeal
The accused were both convicted of murder. They had been involved in a fist-fight with the victim, in the course of which Anderson pulled out a knife and killed the victim with it. Morris appealed on the ground that the trial judge had misdirected the jury on the liability of an accessory for acts committed by the principal. The court allowed the appeal, holding that where two persons embark on a joint enterprise and one of them goes beyond what has been tacitly agreed as part of the common enterprise, the other is not liable for the consequences of that unauthorized act.

Blakely [1991] Crim LR 763. Divisional Court
The accused were hoping to persuade a man to stay with them in a pub rather than return to his wife. They therefore spiked his non-alcoholic drink, intending to let him know before he drove off. He escaped when they were not looking and before they had an opportunity to tell him what they had done. He was later convicted of drink driving. The appellants were convicted of procuring the drink driving. The Divisional Court confirmed that the *mens rea* for being an accessory is foresight that the principal may go on to commit the crime. This is a subjective, not objective, test. As the trial judge had directed the jury in regard to an objective test, the Divisional Court allowed their appeals against conviction.

Calhaem [1985] 2 All ER 266. Court of Appeal
The appellant was convicted of murder. She had hired another person (who pleaded guilty to murder) to kill the victim. The killer claimed at the appellant's trial that he had only intended to pretend to attempt to kill the victim, but when the victim screamed he had killed her. The appellant argued on appeal that there must be a causal connection between the counselling and the killing. The court dismissed the appeal, holding that there was no need for such a causal connection, as long as the killing was within the authority or advice of the accessory. 'Counsel' should be given its ordinary meaning of 'advise' or 'solicit'.

Gillick [1986] AC 112. House of Lords
The plaintiff brought an action against her local area health authority and the Department of Health and Social Security (DHSS), seeking a declaration that a memorandum of guidance issued by the DHSS to area health authorities on giving contraceptive advice and treatment to children under sixteen was unlawful. The judge

at first instance held that the advice was not unlawful, but the Court of Appeal held that it was, on the ground that a doctor could not treat a girl under sixteen without the consent of her parents. The House of Lords allowed the appeal, holding that a girl under sixteen could validly consent to contraceptive advice and treatment, provided that she had sufficient understanding and intelligence to know what was involved. In exceptional cases, a doctor may be justified in prescribing contraception without the knowledge and consent of the girl's parents if: (i) he was satisfied that the girl, although under sixteen, understood his advice; (ii) she would not inform her parents; (iii) she was very likely to have sexual intercourse, whether or not contraception was prescribed; (iv) her physical or mental health would suffer if she were not given contraceptive advice or treatment; and (v) it was in her best interests to give her such advice or treatment without her parents' consent. It was also held that if the advice or treatment was given in a *bona fide* exercise of the doctor's clinical judgement then there would be no *mens rea* necessary for the offence of aiding and abetting unlawful sexual intercourse.

Howe [1987] 2 WLR 568. House of Lords
See Chapter 16 case notes.

Maxwell [1978] 3 All ER 1140. House of Lords
The appellant was convicted of planting a bomb at the Crosskeys Inn in Northern Ireland, contrary to s.3(a) Explosive Substances Act 1883. He was a member of the Ulster Volunteer Force, and had guided the bombers to the Inn in his car. He appealed against conviction on the ground that it was necessary to prove that he knew what offence was to be committed. His appeal was dismissed by the Court of Criminal Appeal in Northern Ireland and by the House of Lords. It was held that if the crime committed by the principal offender is one which was within the contemplation of the accessory, the accessory would be liable. In this case the appellant was a member of an organization which regularly committed acts of violence with explosives and firearms, and must have known that bombing was an obvious possibility which he was intentionally assisting.

Millward [1994] Crim LR 527. Court of Appeal
The appellant was convicted as an accomplice to the principal who was charged with causing death by reckless driving. The principal was a driver employed by the appellant to drive a tractor. The principal was said to be not guilty, as he was not reckless as to the dangerous state of the vehicle. However, the *actus reus* of the offence (causing death by driving) occurred and the accomplice had the *mens rea* (he should have been aware of the condition of the vehicle) and so the charge against the accomplice could be made out.

National Coal Board v. *Gamble* [1959] 1 QB 11. Divisional Court
The National Coal Board (NCB) was convicted of being an accessory to a contravention of the Motor Vehicles (Construction and Use) Regulations 1955. A weighbridge operator, an employee of the NCB, had allowed an overweight lorry to drive away, having issued the driver with the prescribed ticket. The NCB argued on appeal that knowledge of an illegal purpose was not sufficient for aiding and abetting; there must be a purpose of furthering the crime or encouraging the principal. The court held that there must be proof of an intent to aid. Supplying an article essential to the crime with knowledge of the use to which it is to be put is strong evidence of such an intention. However, there is no need to prove in addition a purpose or motive of encouraging the crime.

Powell and English [1997] 3 WLR 959. House of Lords
The House of Lords heard two appeals. In one, Powell (the accused) and two friends

called at the house of a drug dealer. A fight broke out and the drug dealer was shot dead. Powell stated that he had not killed the man and was unaware that either of the others had a gun. The prosecution argued that either he had fired the shot or he was an accomplice to the shooting. In the other appeal, English and Weedle had attacked a police officer with a wooden post. Weedle produced a knife and stabbed the police officer to death. English stated that he had not foreseen that Weedle would act in this way. Powell's conviction was upheld with the House of Lords holding that a party to a joint enterprise could be established if a party to a joint enterprise foresaw that the principal might have intent to kill or cause grievous bodily harm. English's appeal was allowed with the House of Lords holding that if in a joint enterprise one party acted in a way not foreseen by the other party then the other could be found not guilty as an accomplice to their crime. If a party to a joint enterprise was not aware that another was armed with a deadly weapon, the use of the weapon would be outside the scope of the joint enterprise and the party would not be liable as an accomplice to the principal's use of the weapon. However the party could be convicted if he or she was aware that the principal had a weapon of a similar level of dangerousness to the kind used by the principal. Applying this to the facts of the case, English knew that Weedle had a post but not a knife and so English could not be convicted as an accomplice to Weedle's act of murder.

Uddin [1999] Crim LR 987. Court of Appeal

After an altercation between the occupants of two cars, a group of six people attacked the victim. Three were hitting the victim with what appeared to one witness to be the bottom end of a snooker cue and three were kicking the victim to death. During the attack, one person pulled out a knife and stabbed the victim to death. The appellant argued that the use of the knife was outside the scope of any joint enterprise and so he should not have been convicted of murder. The Court of Appeal allowed the appeal, setting out the detailed guidelines quoted in the body of this chapter. Applying them to the facts of the case, it could not be shown that the defendant was aware that the principal had a knife. The jury should have been asked whether the stabbing was so different from hitting the victim with the sticks or shod feet that the stabbing was outside the common purpose of the attack.

Further Reading

K. Smith provides a detailed, if controversial, analysis of the whole subject. Alldridge considers innocent agency. The *actus reus* elements are discussed in Benyon and J. Smith (1978). The *mens rea* requirements are examined in Clarkson and J. Smith (1997). For reform proposals see Glazebrook, Spencer and Sullivan.

Alldridge, 'The Doctrine of Innocent Agency' (1990) 2 *Criminal Law Forum* 45.
Benyon, 'Causation, Omissions and Complicity' (1987) *Criminal Law Review* 539.
Clarkson, 'Complicity, *Powell* and Manslaughter' [1998] *Criminal Law Review* 556.
Duff, 'Can I Help You? Accessorial Liability and the Intention to Assist' (1990) 10 *Legal Studies* 165.
Glazebrook, 'Structuring the Criminal Code: Functional Approaches to Complicity, Incomplete Offences and General Offences', in Simester and Smith (eds), *Harm and Culpability* (1996, Oxford University Press).
J. Smith, 'Aid, Abet, Counsel or Procure', in Glazebrook (ed.), *Reshaping the Criminal Law* (1978, Stevens).

J. Smith, 'Criminal Liability of Accessories' (1997) *Law Quarterly Review* 453.

K. Smith, *A Modern Treatise on the Law of Criminal Complicity* (1991, Oxford University Press).

Spencer, 'Trying to Help Another Person Commit a Crime', in Smith (ed.), *Criminal Law: Essays in Honour of J.C. Smith* (1987, Butterworths).

Sullivan, 'The Law Commission Consultation Paper on Complicity: Fault Elements and Joint Enterprise' [1994] *Criminal Law Review* 252.

18 Inchoate Offences

Key words

- **Attempt** – where the defendant does an act which is more than merely preparatory to the commission of an offence, with intent to commit the offence.
- **Incitement** – where the defendant encourages another to commit an offence.
- **Conspiracy** – where two or more people agree to pursue a course of conduct which will necessarily involve the commission of a crime.

18.1 The Inchoate Offences

This chapter involves inchoate offences. But what are inchoate offences? The word 'inchoate' indicates that these offences are in a sense incomplete. They are not concerned with the direct causing of harm to a victim, but with either encouraging or planning with others to commit crimes, or trying to commit the crime itself. Several justifications for their existence have been offered. One is to see inchoate offences as preventative measures: liability is imposed for acts which fall short of a complete offence, such as murder or theft, but which come close enough to threaten public order and the Queen's peace. The criminal law intervenes to prevent the complete offence (usually termed the 'substantive offence') from being committed. This gives the state the justification for arresting and prosecuting an individual who is on the point of committing a crime. Another justification relies on the moral wrongfulness of the acts. It may be for example that someone's unsuccessful attempt to injure another only fails because of the quick response of the victim, in which case the attempt may be as morally blameworthy as a completed crime.

In each inchoate offence the mental element is crucial: it is the intention of the actor that the substantive offence be committed which makes her conduct potentially dangerous and justifies the intervention of the criminal law before any concrete harm has been done to another person or property. However, it is very important to remember that there is no liability for merely planning, alone, to commit an offence. There must be an *actus reus*, even for the inchoate offences, although, of course, this will differ from the *actus reus* of the substantive offence. In other words, merely having evil thoughts is not an offence.

If a plan to commit an offence is communicated to another person with a view to persuading the other to commit the substantive offence then this amounts to the inchoate offence of incitement. If the other person agrees to commit the offence, and a joint plan is formulated, this is a conspiracy. If the plan goes beyond the preparatory stage, and one of the conspirators embarks on committing the substantive offence, but is prevented from completing it, this will be an attempt. An attempt may be committed by one person acting alone and need not be preceded by a conspiracy.

The essence of the inchoate offence is that the substantive offence is not committed; if it is, then it will be appropriate to charge the accused with that substantive offence, although the mode of participation may vary. An inciter, who succeeds in getting the other person to commit an offence, becomes liable as an accessory (a counsellor and procurer). A conspirator may become either a principal offender or an accessory, depending on the part that he plays in the commission of the substantive offence. A person who succeeds in an attempt to commit an offence becomes a principal offender. That said, it is not a bar to a conviction for an inchoate offence that the substantive offence has been committed. In practice, conspiracy is sometimes charged even where the substantive offence has been committed, especially where there are a number of defendants and the prosecution may be unsure of the role played by each one. As conspiracy is easier to prove than many substantive offences and its boundaries more uncertain, this use of conspiracy is controversial.

18.2   Incitement

Incitement is an example of the way that the law recognizes the danger of people joining together to commit crimes. In incitement, the focus is on the menace of those who seek to persuade others to commit crimes. It can be argued that someone who is able to manipulate others to commit crimes on his behalf is particularly dangerous to society. The offence can thus be justified as a form of public protection. However, some see the offence as inappropriate because the act of incitement may be quite remote from the commission of the crime.

18.2.1   What Offences can be Incited?

The incitement can be tried either summarily or on indictment depending on the type of substantive offence incited (s.45 Magistrates Courts Act

1980). Punishment also varies according to the type of offence incited: if the incitement is tried summarily, the maximum punishment will be that available for the substantive offence on summary trial; if the incitement is tried on indictment, punishment is at the discretion of the court, except where specific provision is made (such as incitement to murder, punishable with a maximum of ten years under s.4 Offences Against the Person Act 1861). It is an offence to incite a person to commit any offence subject to the following exceptions:

1 Under s.5(7) Criminal Law Act 1977 it is not an offence to incite someone to conspire with another, as in effect this is an incitement to commit the offence and better labelled as such. However it is possible for a person to be convicted of inciting a person to incite someone else (*Sirat*).
2 It is probably true that there is no offence to incite a person to aid, abet, counsel or procure an offence (*Bodin and Bodin*)
3 It is not an offence to incite someone to do an act which if the inciter performed would not be an offence. So in *Pickford* a husband could not be found guilty of inciting his fourteen-year-old son to have sexual intercourse with his wife, because at that time a boy under fourteen was presumed incapable of sexual intercourse. However, the husband could be convicted of inciting his wife to commit incest with the son, as she was capable of committing the offence. Similarly, if the person incited would be able to rely on a defence, such as duress, if they committed the crime then there is no incitement.

18.2.2 The *Actus Reus* of Incitement

The essence of incitement is seeking to persuade another to commit a criminal offence. This may be by threat, pressure, encouragement or inducement (*Race Relations Board* v. *Applin*), but merely informing the other person of an opportunity to commit a crime is not incitement (*Hendrickson and Tickner*). The court will consider the words or actions in their context to decide whether or not they constitute an incitement (*Invicta Plastics* v. *Clare*). So the court may be willing to decide that certain words are an implied incitement, even if there is not an express encouragement to commit an offence. *Invicta Plastics* v. *Clare* also makes it clear that the incitement does not have to be directed at a particular individual: it may take the form of a newspaper advertisement addressed to the general public, for example. The encouragement, it seems, need not be particularly persuasive. In *Giannetto*, the Court of Appeal indicated that saying 'Oh goody' when someone announces they are about to commit a crime may be sufficient for incitement.

There are a wide variety of forms of incitement. The Court of Appeal in *Goldman* has recently approved the following comment of a South African judge on the meaning of incitement:

> 'An inciter . . . is one who reaches and seeks to influence the mind of another to the commission of a crime. The machinations of criminal ingenuity being legion, the approach to the other's mind may take many forms, such as a suggestion, proposal, request, exhortation, gesture, argument, persuasion, inducement, goading or the arousal of cupidity' (Holmes JA in *Nkosiyana*).

There is no need for the incitement to be effective, indeed an incitement may fail to influence the action of the other person in any way (*Marlow*). Therefore there will still be an incitement even if the person incited rejects the advice or because she had decided to commit the crime already (*Assistant Recorder of Kingston upon Hull ex p Morgan*). So even if Nicole suggests to Tom that they commit a robbery and Tom replies 'what a terrible idea', Nicole could still be convicted of incitement. An act of incitement which succeeds in persuading the other to commit the offence could lead to a charge of procuring or counselling that offence, or a charge of committing the offence as a principal acting through an innocent agent. In *Goldman*, it was an offence when the defendant replied to an advertisement and asked for indecent photographs of children. There was an incitement even though the incitee had invited people to incite them.

The *actus reus* of incitement occurs once the encouragement is communicated. An act of incitement which does not even reach its destination (for example, a letter sent encouraging another to commit a crime which is lost in the post: *Banks*) would be an attempted incitement.

18.2.3   The *Mens Rea* of Incitement

There are two elements of the *mens rea* for incitement:

1 It must be shown that the defendant intended the person incited to commit the offence which he was incited to commit. This includes knowledge of the circumstances which form part of the *actus reus*. So, if Carl incites Henry to have sexual intercourse with Barbara, this will only be an incitement to rape if Carl believes that Barbara would not consent to the intercourse.

2 The *mens rea* also includes an intent that the person incited would have

the *mens rea* for the substantive offence and have no defence. So in the above example, Carl would not be guilty of incitement to rape if he knew that Henry would believe Barbara was consenting. In such a case, Carl could be convicted of procuring the rape of Barbara.

Although this description of the *mens rea* for incitement is generally accepted, there are two cases that are inconsistent with it, although many commentators suggest that they are wrongly determined. In *Curr*, the court decided that there could be no incitement, as the women incited went on to commit the offences without the requisite *mens rea*. However, the court seemed to have overlooked the point that the offence is committed at the moment of incitement and the issue should have been whether the defendant believed at the time of the incitement that the women would commit the crimes with *mens rea*, not whether the women in fact did later act with the necessary *mens rea*. Indeed in the most recent case, *DPP* v. *Armstrong**, it was held that *Curr* should not be regarded as setting down a general rule. In *Armstrong*, the defendant telephoned an undercover police officer and asked for some child pornography. He was charged with incitement to distribute indecent photographs of children. The Divisional Court stated that he should be convicted, even though the police officer had no intent to distribute the photograph. This suggests that *Curr* will no longer be seen as setting down the law in this area.

In *Shaw*, the defendant was inciting a fellow employee to commit a fraud in order to reveal the weaknesses of their employer's security systems. The defendant himself therefore was not dishonest, although the person he incited was unaware of his purpose and so was dishonest. It was held that the defendant could not be guilty of incitement as he himself lacked the necessary *mens rea* for the offence he was inciting someone to commit. The case has been criticized on the ground that (as in *Curr*) the court failed to appreciate that the offence of incitement focuses on the act of encouragement and so the *mens rea* should relate to the defendant's state of mind at that point in time. The issue in *Shaw* should have been the defendant's beliefs about the incitee's state of mind, not whether he himself would have the *mens rea* for the crime. Indeed, as we have already stated, there is no need for the crime to be committed at all, and so to consider whether the defendant had the *mens rea* for the completed crime seems inappropriate. It is submitted that neither *Curr* nor *Shaw* should be followed.

The Law Commission Consultation Paper No. 131 suggests that incitement be replaced with an offence of encouraging crime, which would apply whether or not the person encouraged commits the crime.

18.2.4   Impossibility and Incitement

It the defendant incites someone to do an act which is in fact impossible, is this a defence? The following situations need to be distinguished:

1.   The defendant believes the conduct to be criminal, but in fact it is not
If the defendant believed that reading pornography was a criminal offence and incites someone to do that, there is no offence (by analogy with *Taafee*). Incitement only occurs when a person is encouraged to do an act which amounts to the *actus reus* of a crime.

2.   The means used are inadequate
If the defendant encourages someone to feed a child with peanut butter, saying that the child is allergic to peanut butter and it will kill her, this will be incitement to murder. This is true even if the child is not so allergic and the peanut butter will cause the child no harm. To establish the *mens rea* it is necessary to show that the inciter believed that the child might die as a result of eating the peanut butter. In *Armstrong*, where the defendant asked an under-cover police officer for some child pornography, the fact that the police officer would never hand over pornography and so the incitement was doomed to fail, did not prevent the defendant from being convicted.

3.   The offence could not be committed, whatever means were used
An example of this would be if the defendant encourages a person to kill someone who is already dead. This would not be an incitement. Similarly, inciting a person to steal a piece of property that did not exist would not be an offence. In *Fitzmaurice*, the appellant's father had incited the appellant and some men to rob a woman, whom the father said would be carrying wages at Bow on a Friday. In fact the woman was fictitious and the accused had been deceived into arranging the robbery by his father, who hoped to claim a reward by giving police information when the robbery was about to be carried out. The accused argued that he could not be guilty of inciting others to commit a robbery that could not have been carried out. However the court stated that 'the crucial question is to establish on the evidence the course of conduct which the alleged inciter was encouraging'. Here the incitement was to 'rob a woman at Bow'. This in itself was quite possible. The detail of the proposed robbery was only discussed by the parties after the incitement had taken place. However, if the incitement had been more specific (for example, to rob Ms *X* outside Bow Street station at 5 pm, when Ms *X* did not exist) then the offence could not have been established. It must be noted that this distinction is not always easy to make and there is

a strong argument for bringing incitement and common law conspiracy in line with attempts in this area so that impossibility is not a defence.

4. Incitement to do a crime which later becomes impossible
It is an offence to incite someone to commit a crime which is not possible at the time of incitement, but which will become possible later. For example it would be incitement to murder to encourage someone to kill a child who was as yet unborn (*Banks*).

18.3   Conspiracy

A conspiracy is essentially an agreement to commit a criminal offence. Conspiracy is an offence triable only on indictment. A charge of conspiracy to commit a summary offence requires the consent of the Director of Public Prosecutions (s.4(1) of the 1977 Criminal Law Act). The maximum term of imprisonment that may be imposed will depend on the maximum for the substantive offence involved (s.3 of the 1977 Act). The maximum term for conspiracy to defraud is ten years' imprisonment (s.12 Criminal Justice Act 1987). Conspiracy was a creation of the common law and still exists, to a limited extent, as a common law offence. However, a new offence of statutory conspiracy was created by ss.1–5 Criminal Law Act 1977, and the vast majority of conspiracies are now prosecuted under s.1 of this Act. The small compass of the common law was retained, with the intention that it should be replaced with statutory offences once the topic was considered by the Law Commission. However, the reform has not yet occurred and so the law is uncertain and complicated. In particular, the relationship between what is left of common law conspiracy and statutory conspiracy has proved difficult to apply in a rational and practical way.

18.3.1   Common Law Conspiracies

Only two categories of common law conspiracy survive:

1. Conspiracy to corrupt public morals
A conspiracy to engage in conduct which tends to corrupt public morals is a common law conspiracy, but only to the extent that such conduct would not amount to a criminal offence if committed by one person (s.5(3)). The offence is very narrow and is rarely prosecuted. One of the few successful prosecutions concerned a group of people who joined together to produce a magazine ('*Ladies Directory*') which contained advertisements encouraging readers to engage in 'fornication and . . . other disgusting and

immoral acts and exhibitions' (in the words of Lord Tucker, *Shaw* v. *DPP*). Corrupting public morals requires an agreement to perform acts that 'the jury might find to be destructive to the very fabric of society'. This type of common law conspiracy dates from two highly controversial decisions of the House of Lords, *Shaw* v. *DPP* and *Knuller* v. *DPP*, and has been retained pending statutory reform of sexual offences. The real significance of the two decisions lies not in their practical importance but in their implications for the role of the judiciary in the development and creation of criminal offences.

2. Conspiracy to defraud

The offence was defined by Viscount Dilhorne in *Scott* v. *Metropolitan Police Commissioner** as:

> 'an agreement by two or more by dishonesty to deprive a person of something which is his or to which he is or would be or might be entitled [or] an agreement by two or more by dishonesty to injure some proprietary right of his.'

It seems that there are two key requirements for a conspiracy to defraud:

(a) The conspiracy involves dishonesty (*Wai Yu-tsang*).
(b) The conspiracy if carried out will cause some prejudice to the victims' property rights (*Moses and Arsbo*).

It is not essential to demonstrate a deception, nor does it need to be shown that any victim has suffered a financial loss (*Moses and Arsbo*). It does not matter that the conspiracy to defraud is designed to persuade or encourage others to be dishonest rather than enable the conspirators themselves to carry out a dishonest scheme.

Conspiracy to defraud has been so widely defined that it covers agreements to commit many criminal offences, such as theft, robbery and obtaining property by deception, as well as agreements to do things which are not in themselves criminal (*Hollinshead**). Section 12 Criminal Justice Act 1987 makes it clear that even in cases involving an agreement to commit an offence, the prosecution has a discretion to charge conspiracy to defraud. This puts into statutory effect the decision in the case of *Cooke**, and prevents a defendant from seeking to claim that he should not have been convicted of a conspiracy to defraud as he planned to commit an offence. Undoubtedly, conspiracy to defraud still has an active part to play in criminal prosecutions and the Law Commission has proposed its retention (Law Commission Report No. 228).

18.3.2 Statutory Conspiracies

Any conspiracy to commit a criminal offence must now be charged under s.1 of the 1977 Act. Section 1 Criminal Law Act 1977, as amended by s.5(1) Criminal Attempts Act 1981, provides:

'(1) ... if a person agrees with any other person or persons that a course of conduct shall be pursued which, if the agreement is carried out in accordance with their intentions, either –
(a) will necessarily amount to or involve the commission of any offence or offences by one or more of the parties to the agreement, or
(b) would do so but for the existence of facts which render the commission of the offence or any of the offences impossible, he is guilty of conspiracy to commit the offence or offences in question.

(2) Where liability for any offence may be incurred without knowledge on the part of the person committing it of any particular fact or circumstance necessary for the commission of the offence, a person shall nevertheless not be guilty of conspiracy to commit that offence by virtue of subsection (1) above unless he and at least one other party to the agreement intend or know that that fact or circumstance shall or will exist at the time when the conduct constituting the offence is to take place.'

The effect of this section is that a conspiracy to commit any criminal offence is a statutory conspiracy. It used to be thought that a conspiracy to outrage public decency was a common law conspiracy but it has recently been stated that outraging public decency is an offence in its own right (*Gibson*) and so a conspiracy to outrage public decency should now be charged as a statutory conspiracy.

Having looked at the difference between common law and statutory conspiracies, the elements of a conspiracy will now be discussed.

18.3.3 The *Actus Reus* of Conspiracy

The *actus reus* of conspiracy is the agreement between two parties to engage on a course of conduct which necessarily involves an offence or one of the statutory conspiracies. This can be broken down into the following elements:

1. An agreement
The *actus reus* of conspiracy is then the agreement itself. There is no need

for the parties to have taken any steps to carry out their agreement (*Nock*). The agreement can be express or implied. It is sufficient if an agreement in general terms is reached, there is no need for all the elements of the plan to be settled upon. It is not even necessary for all the parties to the conspiracy to have met with each other, or even communicated with all the other members (*Ardalan*). So if *A*, *B* and *C* all agree with *D* to commit a crime, there can be a conspiracy even if *A*, *B* and *C* do not communicate with each other.

2.   *Two parties*

There must be at least two parties to a conspiracy (though there may be many more), and the statute provides in s.2(2) that if the only other party to the agreement falls within one of three exempt categories, there can be no conspiracy. The exempt categories are:

(a)   The victim of the conspiracy. This is not defined in the statute and the courts are yet to define the term.

(b)   The spouse of the alleged conspirator. This exemption does not apply where the spouses conspire with a third party (*Chrastny*). So, if there are only two parties to the conspiracy, husband and wife, no offence is committed. However if there are three parties to the conspiracy, husband, wife and a friend, then the offence is made out. The spousal exemption is controversial. It has been justified on the basis that husband and wife traditionally have been regarded as one for the purposes of the law, although there are few other examples in the law where this is reflected. It should be noted that this exemption does not apply to an unmarried cohabiting couple.

(c)   A person under the age of criminal responsibility (currently ten years old).

The need for at least two parties for there to be a conspiracy creates a problem where one party in a two-person conspiracy is acquitted (or all but one are acquitted in a larger conspiracy). Does this necessarily lead to the acquittal of the remaining party to the agreement? Not necessarily, because the answer will depend on the evidence in the particular case, and the reasons for the acquittal. The statute provides in s.5(8) that the acquittal of all the other parties to an agreement shall not be a ground for quashing the conviction of the remaining party 'unless under all the circumstances of the case his conviction is inconsistent with the acquittal of the other person or persons in question'. Such a conviction may be possible and consistent: for example, where one conspirator has confessed – his confession will only be admissible evidence against him, and the evidence against the alleged co-conspirators may be very weak; or a defendant may have a special defence.

The jury may be sure that the defendant is guilty of conspiracy, but unsure with whom he conspired: the alleged co-conspirators or persons unknown. It is for the judge to direct the jury whether all the accused must be convicted or acquitted together, or whether there is a material difference in the evidence against them so that a conviction of only one accused would be possible (*Longman and Cribben*).

3. The involvement of the parties in the agreement

In statutory conspiracy, the agreement must involve the commission of an offence 'by one or more of the parties to the agreement'. So an agreement which involves the commission of an offence by a third party is not covered. If Bryony and Steven reach an agreement that Sam will commit an offence, this will not amount to a conspiracy until Sam joins in the agreement. This is narrower than the common law, where the conspiracy can involve a plan which involves the commission of the offence by a third party.

4. The 'course of conduct' must be criminal

The Criminal Law Act states that the 'course of conduct' agreed upon must amount to a substantive offence; this must include all the elements of the offence, including the consequences and circumstances. So it is insufficient in establishing a conspiracy to murder just to show that the conspirators agreed to put poison in the victim's eggnog; it needs also to be shown that they agreed that the victim should die as a result. If the allegation is one of a conspiracy to rape, it must be shown that the parties intended or believed that the victim would not consent. If only one of the parties to the conspiracy is aware of the relevant circumstances or intends the consequences then the offence of conspiracy has not be committed.

5. The 'course of conduct' must necessarily involve an offence

The statutory definition uses the word 'necessarily', but this must be treated with care. It does not mean that the conspirators must agree to commit the offence in every conceivable circumstance. Every conspiracy will be conditional to some extent; an agreement to rob a bank may include an express or implied reservation relating to the presence of police on the premises. In *Jackson*, the Court of Appeal held that 'necessarily' does not mean inevitably; it can include planning for contingencies. In that case it was agreed that if W was convicted of burglary the others would shoot him in the leg in the hope that this would lead to a lower sentence. This was held to be a conspiracy. Indeed the court suggested that the parties to the conspiracy might believe that the plan is unlikely to succeed but can still be guilty of conspiracy. In a useful example, the court considered a scenario where two people agreed to drive from London to Edinburgh in a certain length of time. If it was possible to carry out that journey in the agreed time within the speed limits then there would be no conspiracy to break the speed limits, even if given the severity of the traffic it might be very unlikely that they could make the journey without breaking the speed limits. Whereas if they agreed to travel in a time only mathematically possible if the speed limits were exceeded, a conspiracy to break the speed limits could be shown. The clearest test (formulated by Donaldson LJ in *Reed*) is to ask whether the plan would have 'failed' if the offence had not been committed: there is a conspiracy if carrying out the agreement according to the parties' hopes involves the commission of an offence.

18.3.4   The *Mens Rea* of the Conspiracy

The wording of s.1(1) implies that all the conspirators must intend the full offence to be committed: the course of conduct must involve the commission of an offence 'if the agreement is carried out in accordance with their intentions'. However, in a surprising decision, Lord Bridge in the House of Lords has suggested that a person may be guilty of conspiracy even though she did not intend that an offence should be committed, as long as she intended to play some part in the agreed course of conduct and her co-conspirators intended to commit an offence (*Anderson**). So, for example, if a defendant intends to help in the preliminary stages, but then report her fellow conspirators to the police, the defendant would be convicted. As Smith suggests, it would be possible and more appropriate to charge such a person with being an accessory to the conspiracy, rather than a principal conspirator. This aspect of the decision in *Anderson** has been reconsidered by the Privy Council in *Yip Chiu-Cheung** which suggests that *Anderson** was wrong on this point and that it must be shown that each conspirator intended that the plan be carried out. Lord Griffiths explained:

'The crime of conspiracy requires an agreement between two or more persons to commit an unlawful act with the intention of carrying it out. It is the intention to carry out the crime that constitutes the necessary *mens rea* for the offence.'

In *Anderson*, Lord Bridge made a further point. He said:

'Beyond the mere fact of agreement, the necessary *mens rea* of the crime is, in my opinion, established if, and only if, it is shown that the accused, when he entered into the agreement, intended to play some part in the agreed course of conduct in furtherance of the criminal purpose which the agreed course of conduct was intended to achieve. Nothing less will suffice; nothing more is required.'

This seems to suggest that each conspirator must perform some kind of role in the plan. Professor Smith calls this a 'novel limitation' on the offence of conspiracy. Indeed a subsequent Court of Appeal decision, *Siracusa*, refused to apply Lord Bridge's *dicta* and instead held that if someone conspires with others to commit a crime but intends to play no role in actually carrying out the plan, she can still be convicted of conspiracy. There is much to be said for the approach in *Siracusa* because it enables the mastermind of a criminal gang who is the dominant force in the gang, but does not intend to play an active role in performing the crime, to be convicted.

18.3.5 Impossible Conspiracies

In looking at impossible conspiracies it is necessary to distinguish statutory and common law conspiracies.

1. Impossible common law conspiracies
As a result of the decision of the House of Lords in *DPP* v. *Nock*, an agreement to perform an act which is impossible may not amount to a statutory conspiracy. To decide whether impossibility is a defence to a statutory conspiracy you have to ask: why is it impossible? If it is impossible because what the conspirators were trying to do was impossible then there is a defence. If it is impossible because the means that the conspirators used were not adequate to do what they wanted to do then the impossibility does not provide a defence. The test for impossibility is to be judged at the time of the agreement. So, if the plan was possible at the time of the agreement then it may amount to a conspiracy.

2. Impossible statutory conspiracies
This is dealt with by s.1(1)(b) Criminal Law Act, quoted above. For statutory conspiracies, impossibility is not a defence. So it is an offence to conspire to kill someone who is already dead; or to conspire to handle goods believed to be stolen but which in fact are not.

18.3.6 Reform proposals

The draft Criminal Code suggests a redefinition of conspiracy (Clause 48):

'A person is guilty of conspiracy to commit an offence or offences if –
(a) he agrees with another or others that an act or acts shall be done

which, if done, will involve the commission of the offence or offences by one or more of the parties to the agreement; and

(b) he and at least one other party to the agreement intend that the offence or offences shall be committed.'

This, if enacted, would certainly clarify the present law.

18.4   Attempt

18.4.1   What are Attempted Crimes?

When criminal lawyers talk about attempted crimes they include within that phrase three different kinds of situation:

1.   A thwarted attempt
This is where the defendant plans to commit the crime but just before he is able do so, someone or something intervenes to prevent the defendant committing the crime. For example, the defendant is about to shoot the victim when a police officer knocks the gun out of the defendant's hands.

2.   A failed attempt
Here the defendant does everything he plans to do but his plan is ineffective. For example the defendant shoots at the victim but is so far away that the bullet misses; or the victim jumps out of the way at the last minute.

3.   An impossible attempt
Here what the defendant intends to do is in fact not possible. For example the defendant shoots at the victim, but the victim is in fact dead.

It should be noted that in attempted crimes, the intention of the defendant can play a crucial role. The same act could constitute attempted murder or be perfectly innocent, depending on the mental state of the defendant. Offering someone a cup of tea becomes attempted murder if you believe the tea to be poisoned and intend it to kill the recipient.

18.4.2   Why Punish Attempts?

Some of the most commonly cited reasons for punishing attempts are as follows:

1. Subjectivism

Subjectivists (see Chapter 1.4.4) focus on the moral wrong of the accused. The blameworthiness of an accused who attempts to commit an offence may be the same as that of someone who completes the crime. For example if Matthew shoots at Emma, but Emma at the last moment jumps out of the way, missing the bullet, some people would see Matthew as blameworthy as if he had succeeded in shooting her. It was no thanks to Matthew that his attempt did not succeed. Indeed a pure subjectivist would see no practical difference between an attempted crime and a complete one; in each, the defendant may have done all that she could to produce the desired result. What happened as a result of her actions was to some extent a matter of chance. Each should therefore receive the same sentence and be guilty of the same offence. Ashworth, while adopting a subjectivist stance, supports separate liability for attempts by referring to the popular understanding among the general public that there is a difference between an attempted crime and a successful crime. Ashworth (1987), argues that the labelling function of criminal law (see Chapter 1.5.1) requires that the law should reflect this commonly perceived difference, even if in moral terms there is no real distinction.

2. Objectivism

Objectivists (see Chapter 1.4) have tended to focus on the harm to the victim or the Queen's peace that has been caused by the attempt. This would justify criminal liability for an attempt where the victim is terrified by the efforts of the defendant or where passers-by are terrified at witnessing the attempted crime. However, some attempts under this approach would not appear to create such a harm. Where, for example, the defendant puts what he thinks is a poison into the victim's cup of tea, but in fact it was sugar. In such a case it would be difficult to locate a harm to the victim or the Queen's peace.

3. Duff

Some commentators try to take a middle approach between the purely objective and purely subjective approach. Duff (1997) has suggested that the law should consider attempts as attacks on interests protected by the law. This has the benefit of capturing both the subjective and objective elements of an attempt. It focuses on the intent of the accused as well as the threat to the victim's interests.

4. Incapacitation

Those who emphasize the importance of incapacitation in punishment (see Chapter 2.6) might argue that removing someone who has attempted to commit a crime from society protects law-abiding citizens from the danger by a person who has demonstrated that he is a danger to society. Such an approach typically places greater weight on protection of the public than 'minimalization' of the criminal law (see Chapter 1.3).

5. Police powers

Some argue that the justification for attempts lies in permitting and encouraging the police to arrest someone who is about to commit an offence, rather than waiting until the offence has been committed.

Much more could be written about the theoretical issues surrounding attempts (see Further Reading at the end of this chapter). The problem for the analysis of the law is that the courts have not clearly articulated the principles that underlie the law and so it is difficult to find a single approach that can explain the present law.

18.4.3   What Crimes is it an Offence to Attempt to Commit?

The law of attempts, like that of conspiracy, has been put into statutory form, and the Criminal Attempts Act 1981 abolishes the common law offence of attempt (s.6(1)). Attempting to commit a summary offence is not a crime; it is only an offence to attempt to commit an offence which is triable in England and Wales as an indictable offence (s.1(4)), although this includes offences which are triable either way. Some indictable offences cannot be attempted (s.1(4)): an attempt to conspire is not an offence. A criminal attempt is limited to an attempt to commit an offence as principal offender; an attempt to be an accessory is not an offence. This is one of the few remaining distinctions between the principal and the accessory. The exclusion of accessories extends to the separate offences of assisting offenders and withholding information about an arrestable offence, under s.4(1) and 5(1) Criminal Law Act 1967 (see Chapter 17.13). The thinking behind these limitations is that attempting to be an accomplice is too far removed from the commission of a substantive offence and the criminal law would become too broad if such acts were to be included within liability for attempts.

Section 1(1) of the Act (which is quoted below) requires the defendant to have performed an act and this, some commentators have suggested, indicates that there can be no attempts liability in relation to an omission. For example, if a husband seeing his wife dangerously ill leaves her and does not summon help hoping she will die, but fortunately a passer-by summons help and her life is saved, the husband could not be convicted of attempted murder. Other commentators argue that this is reading too much into the word 'act' in s.1(1) and a person, such as the husband in the above example, deserves a conviction, based on the law's general approach to liability for omissions (see Chapter 3.3).

A person charged with a substantive offence may be convicted of an attempt, for an allegation of attempt is impliedly included within the allegation of the substantive offence (s.6(3) and (4) of the Criminal Law Act 1967). Under the same provision, an accused who is charged with attempt and then proved to have committed the full offence, can still be convicted of attempt; alternatively, the judge may discharge the jury with a view to charging the full offence on a new indictment.

The punishment for an attempt is limited to the maximum punishment for the offence attempted, but in practice the sentence imposed will be lighter than the sentence that the court would have imposed had the full offence been committed. The reasons for this are essentially retributive: that is, based on the amount of harm actually caused by the offender.

18.4.4   The *Actus Reus* of an Attempt

What then needs to be proved in order to convict a person of a criminal attempt? The *actus reus* of an attempt marks the moment at which the non-criminal planning of an offence turns into a criminal attempt. It has proved elusive and difficult to define. Not only does the *actus reus* of every offence differ, but each offence can be committed in a variety of ways and circumstances (consider murder, for example).

The correct definition of the *actus reus* of attempts in theoretical terms depends upon what is regarded as the justification for punishing attempts. Those who focus on the moral blameworthiness of the defendant may just require an act that clearly indicates that the defendant intends to commit the crime. The *actus reus* is essentially playing an evidential role, revealing the defendant's *mens rea*. Those who focus on the harm caused in an attempt will require an act that produces that harm (harm to the victim or the Queen's Peace). Here the *actus reus* will play a crucial role in creating the justification for criminal liability.

As indicated above, the courts have refused to outline which justification for attempts liability explains the law and so the courts' discussion of the law on the *actus reus* for an attempt is difficult to explain in a principled way. Before 1981, the leading decision was one of the House of Lords: *Haughton* v. *Smith**. There, Lord Reid said that it must be left to common sense in each case to determine whether the accused has gone beyond mere preparation. The formulation chosen for the statutory offence, which represents the present law, is hardly more precise. Section 1(1) Criminal Attempts Act 1981 provides:

'If, with intent to commit an offence . . . [which is triable in England and Wales as an indictable offence], a person does an act which is more than merely preparatory to the commission of the offence, he is guilty of attempting to commit the offence.'

The basic distinction which was made at common law, and which the Criminal Attempts Act 1981 preserves, is between acts of mere preparation, which are not criminal, and acts of perpetration of the substantive offence (*Stonehouse*), which can amount to the *actus reus* of an attempted offence. Criminal liability arises at the point where the plan begins to turn into reality, and the accused embarks on the offence itself. The most useful test in the caselaw is that stated by the Court of Appeal in *Geddes**:

'has [the defendant] done an act which shows that he has actually tried to commit the offence in question, or . . . has [he] only got ready or put himself in a position or equipped himself to do so'?

Although the courts have been reluctant to go into greater detail, they have been willing to state what the 'more than merely preparatory' test does not mean. They have rejected a test suggesting that an attempt is committed when the accused has performed the first of a series of acts that will culminate in the commission of the *actus reus*. The courts have also rejected a test suggesting that an attempt only occurs when the defendant has done the act which is the last act to be performed before the *actus reus* occurs (*Gullefer*). So even if a number of acts have to be done before the *actus reus* occurs, the defendant can be convicted of an attempt. However if the defendant has performed the last act he needs to do before the *actus reus*, it is very likely that this will be regarded as more than mere preparation. The Court of Appeal in *Tosti* has recently stressed the importance of the requirement that it has to be shown that the defendants were acting in a way which was more than *merely* preparatory. The defendants, who were found with some cutting equipment examining the lock on a barn, could claim that they were preparing to commit the crime but could not claim they were *merely* preparing for the crime. Their conviction was therefore upheld.

It is useful to consider the facts of three of the leading cases, which give a flavour of how the courts have interpreted the 'more than merely preparatory stage'.

1 In *Jones* (1990), a man hid in bushes beside the victim's car. When the victim got into the car the defendant ran up, got into the car, and pointed a gun at him. This was held to be sufficient for an attempt to murder. The

court rejected the argument that the defendant could not be convicted of an attempt because he still had several acts to perform, namely the removing of the safety catch, putting his finger round the trigger and pulling it. The court added that while the defendant was waiting in the bushes he would be seen as acting in mere preparation; but by the time the accused was pointing the gun at the victim, the offence of attempt had been committed.

2 In *Kelly*, the defendant was charged with attempted rape. The defendant had dragged the victim behind a hedge and started to pull at her clothing. The Court of Appeal held this was more than mere preparation, even though a number of individual acts needed to take place before intercourse was to occur.

3 In *Campbell* (1991), a man wearing a balaclava and carrying a replica gun was seen outside a post office. He approached the post office door several times but did not enter it. He was held not to be guilty of an attempted robbery. The court suggested that the mere preparation would have ended and the attempt begun once the accused had entered the post office.

From these cases and similar ones, it seems the courts are more willing to find the defendant has embarked on the crime (and so is guilty of an attempt) once he is in the presence of the victim. Further, once it is clear that the defendant is not likely to change his mind and has clearly decided to carry out the crime then the court again is more likely to decide that the threshold has been crossed. Where there is a realistic possibility that the defendant will change his mind and decide not to complete the offence, the courts will be more reluctant to convict. This seems the best explanation for the decision in *Campbell*.

It is for the judge to decide whether the acts alleged are capable of being more than mere preparation. If they are not, the judge must withdraw the case from the jury. If they are, it is for the jury to decide whether it thinks the acts are more than mere preparation. The judge may give the jury guidance as to the law's understanding of what more than mere preparation means.

18.4.5 The *Mens Rea* of an Attempt

The *mens rea* of an attempt is an intention to commit the offence (s.1 Criminal Attempts Act 1981). For example, in order to be guilty of attempted murder it is necessary to show an intention to kill (*Mohan*). It would not be sufficient to show an intention to cause grievous bodily harm, even though such a state of mind would be sufficient for the crime of murder itself (*Fallon*). Intention here has the same meaning as that discussed in Chapter 4.3. That intention is key to the *mens rea* for an attempt is readily understandable: to attempt to commit a crime is to try to do it – to act with the purpose of committing the crime – which is what intention is. This observation has led some commentators to argue that intention here should be restricted to where the defendant has a purpose to commit the crime and should not cover defendants who did not have that purpose but knew that the forbidden result was virtually certain to result from their actions. However the Court of Appeal has stated that intention in the area of attempts is to have the same meaning as that generally applied in the common law, and so to include such an oblique intent (*Walker and Hayes*; *Pearman*).

This straightforward intent test can be difficult to use in crimes that require an act to be performed in certain circumstances. Unfortunately the position is confused and alternative tests have been proposed in the two leading cases before the Court of Appeal.

1. The 'Circumstances' test

The Court of Appeal in *Khan* suggested that it was necessary to distinguish the defendant's acts from the circumstances in which he acts. For those crimes in which only recklessness is required for a circumstance, the *mens rea* of an attempt to commit such a crime only requires recklessness as to the circumstances. In other words, the defendant must intend to do his act but can be reckless as to the circumstances in which he acts if recklessness as to the circumstances is sufficient for the actual crime itself. The facts of *Khan* involved an attempted rape where the defendant tried (without success) to have sexual intercourse with a woman without her consent. The Court of Appeal, looking at the *actus reus* of rape, explained that the lack of consent was a circumstance whereas the sexual intercourse was an act. The *mens rea* for an attempted rape was therefore that the defendant intended to perform sexual intercourse being reckless as to whether or not the victim was consenting.

The Court of Appeal purported to apply the *Khan* test in *Attorney-General's Reference (No. 3 of 1992)**), but in a controversial way. The case involved a charge of attempting to cause criminal damages thereby endangering the lives of others. It was held that it was sufficient if arson was intended, but that the defendant was reckless as to whether lives were endangered. The controversy surrounds whether it was correct to call the 'endangerment of lives' a circumstance. Is not the endangerment of lives better classified as a consequence of the defendant's actions, rather than a circumstance in which he acts? Some commentators have even suggested that following *Attorney-General's Reference (No. 3 of 1992)**, recklessness as to either the circumstances in which the defendant acts or the consequences of his actions is sufficient for the attempted offence, if it is enough for the substantial offence.

Controversy also surrounds the fact that *Caldwell* recklessness was sufficient for the criminal damage offence in *Attorney-General's Reference (No. 3 of 1992)** and so presumably the attempted offence. The problem is that *Caldwell* recklessness can include a case where the defendant gave no thought to the risk (see Chapter 4.4). Does it make sense to convict a defendant of attempting to cause criminal damage thereby endangering lives if it never crossed his mind that he might endanger lives?

2. The 'Missing Element' test

The Court of Appeal in *Attorney-General's Reference (No. 3 of 1992)** proposed an alternative test to the *Khan* test, which it thought may be easier for juries to understand. This was to decide what is the 'missing element' in the attempt. The missing element is the thing which prevents the offence from being a successful crime. It is then necessary to show that the defendant intended to supply that missing element. For those elements that are not missing, it is sufficient that the defendant had the *mens rea* required for the completed offence. An example may make this clearer. Imagine a defendant, like *Khan*, who tried but failed to have sexual intercourse with a woman who did not consent, aware that she was not consenting. Here the 'missing element' is the lack of sexual intercourse. If the sexual intercourse had occurred, the complete offence of rape would have been established. So, to be guilty of attempted rape the man must have intended to have sexual intercourse (*Kahn*). Note that it is not necessary to show that he intended that the woman would not consent, because the lack of consent is not 'missing' in this case. It is enough if he had the relevant *mens rea* in relation to the victim's consent that is necessary for rape. Another example is when some football fans jumped up and down on a fence. Although they did not break it, they were reckless as to whether it would be damaged. They would be not guilty of an attempt to commit criminal damage as the 'missing element' here was the damage to the property, and the defendants did not intend damage (*Millard and Vernon**).

Faced with these two conflicting tests, a subsequent court may prefer the 'missing element test' as it avoids the difficulty in distinguishing circumstances from other elements of the offence. That said, the 'missing element test' is not without difficulties of its own (see Further Reading at the end of this chapter).

Another issue over the *mens rea* which has caused fewer problems is 'conditional intent'. This is where the defendant has decided to perform a crime, but has not yet decided on all the details of the crime. For example, the defendant rummages in a woman's handbag to see if there is anything worth stealing, but is arrested by the police before he finds anything. What can it be said that the defendant has attempted to steal? The answer is to charge the defendant with attempting to steal from a handbag belonging to the victim, without specifying what is intended to steal. Similarly, if the defendant plants a bomb but has not decided who to kill by detonating it, a charge of simply attempting to kill persons unknown is likely to succeed. This issue was discussed in greater detail in Chapter 4.4.

18.4.6   Impossibility and Attempts

A persistent problem in attempts has arisen in cases where the substantive offence cannot possibly be completed. Does proof of attempt depend on proof that the attempt could have proceeded to the commission of the full offence? Is it possible to convict a person of attempting to steal from a wallet or pocket that is empty? Or of attempting to handle stolen goods, when it can be shown that the goods in question were not stolen at the relevant time? The common law in this area was notoriously difficult, and a number of not very convincing distinctions were made between allegedly different types of 'impossibility'. This led to the statutory reform that now governs attempts and statutory conspiracy. Section 1 Criminal Attempts Act 1981, after the basic definition of attempt in s.1(1) given above, provides:

'(2) A person may be guilty of attempting to commit an offence to which this section applies even though the facts are such that the commission of the offence is impossible.
(3)   In any case where –
    (a)   apart from this subsection a person's intention would not be regarded as having amounted to an intention to commit an offence; but
    (b)   if the facts of the case had been as he believed them to be, his intention would be so regarded, then, for the purposes of subsection (1) above, he shall be regarded as having had an intent to commit that offence.'

The meaning of the section was thrown into confusion by a decision of the House of Lords (*Anderton* v. *Ryan*), which suggested that the section had not reversed the case of *Haughton* v. *Smith**, which was the leading authority prior to the Criminal Attempts Act 1981. This was very surprising as the Act had clearly intended to change the law. This was recognized almost exactly a year later, in the case of *Shivpuri**, by the House of Lords itself. It is rare for the House of Lords to reverse one of its own decisions, and to do so within a year is extraordinary. However, Lord Bridge, who had given one of the judgements in *Anderton* v. *Ryan*, admitted that the earlier decision could not be justified. He said that he could not find 'a clear and coherent principle' in *Anderton* v. *Ryan* distinguishing cases of attempting the impossible which were criminal from those which were not. He argued that an attempt is an inchoate offence, and so by definition a substantive offence has not been committed. The reason for the failure of the attempt, whether inherent impossibility or an interruption by the police, should not affect the criminality of the attempt. The correct approach, giving effect to s.1(3) 1981 Act, was to concentrate on the intention of the accused. Lord Bridge said:

'What turns what would otherwise, from the point of view of the criminal law, be an innocent act into a crime is the intent of the actor to commit an offence.'

The present law therefore simply asks whether, on the facts as the accused believed them to be, he would have committed a crime if he acted in line with his intentions. If so, the *actus reus* of an attempt is made out. Thus, it is an attempted theft to try and steal property which does not exist if the defendant believes it does; and attempted murder to stab a pillow believing it to be person. No distinction is made between different types of factual mistake which render the commission of the intended offence impossible.

One final point needs to be made. In this section we have been examining cases where the accused intended to commit an offence (such as theft, handling stolen goods or murder) but failed to do so because of some mistake which made the commission of the offence impossible. He can now be convicted of attempted theft, or handling, or murder, as long as he had the necessary *mens rea*. If, however, the accused made a mistake, not of fact but as to the criminal law, so that he wrongly believed that what he intended to do was a crime, then he cannot be guilty of a criminal attempt (*Taafee*). For example, a person who commits adultery believing that it is a criminal offence has not committed an attempted crime. He cannot be guilty of attempting to commit the imaginary criminal offence of adultery. This principle is sometimes referred to as 'legal impossibility' because the mistake is one of criminal law, and a person cannot be convicted of attempting to commit a crime that is not known to the law.

The Draft Criminal Code proposes:

'A person may be guilty of incitement, conspiracy or attempt to commit an offence, although the commission of the offence is impossible, if it would be possible in the circumstances which he believes or hopes exist or will exist at the relevant time.'

This would bring a consistent approach to the entire law of impossibility and inchoate offences.

Hot Topic: Incitement and Free Speech

If you were to search the World Wide Web you could find pages telling you how to make a gun, how to grow cannabis plants and how to make poisons. Indeed the ignorant criminal seeking advice would be able to find help to commit almost any crime. But would the provision of such information involve an offence? When does telling someone how to commit a crime cross the line from giving information to amounting to incitement. Even this book, which has occasionally mentioned potential loopholes in the law, could be used by a rogue hoping to commit a dastardly deed without any punishment.

The case of *Marlow* is instructive. The case involved a defendant who wrote and published a book about a particular method of cultivation and production of cannabis. He advertised the book and about 500 copies were sold. On investigation by the police it was discovered that several people who had purchased copies of the book had followed its instructions and successfully grown cannabis. Marlow was charged with an incitement to cultivate cannabis contrary to s. 4(2) Misuse of Drugs Act 1971. Three main arguments were put forward by the defence. First, it was said that the book was in fact a 'genuine contribution to the debate about the legalisation of cannabis' and so should not be regarded as incitement to commit a crime. Secondly, it was said that the book provided information that was freely available elsewhere. Thirdly, it was suggested that the writing of the book was 'too remote' from the commission of any crime. The prosecution case was that the subject matter and nature of the book made it clear that the book was designed to encourage and enable readers to cultivate cannabis and so constituted an offence. The Court of Appeal accepted the prosecution's argument. The simple fact was, as the defendant knew, that people would read the book and be encouraged to grow cannabis. The fact that they were going to commit the crime anyway provided no defence to incitement (*Goldman*), nor would the fact that the information was provided elsewhere get away from these conclusions.

What the court did not consider is whether this is consistent with article 10 of the European Convention of Human Rights which protects 'the right to freedom of expression'. From one perspective it clearly is; after all, article 10(2) specifically states that restrictions on this right are permissible if they are 'prescribed by law and are necessary in a democratic society in the interests of . . . the prevention of disorder or crime, for the protection of health or morals . . .'. On the other hand, as mentioned above, there is a fine line to be drawn here. Imagine if *Marlow* had written an article discussing how cannabis is commonly cultivated, but then arguing that these were dangerous methods and that legalization of cannabis would enable safer methods to be developed. Such an argument might be seen as a useful contribution to the legal response to cannabis. It should be recalled that people writing or producing documentaries about criminal activities cannot seek protection by making a clear statement that the activity was unlawful, if the court interprets the overall effect of the publication is to encourage the readers or viewers to commit crimes.

Summary

18.1 There are three inchoate offences: incitement, conspiracy and attempt. They are committed before the substantive offence is completed, and should normally only be charged where the substantive offence is not completed.

18.2 Incitement consists of persuading or encouraging another person to commit an offence, intending that he should commit it. The incitement does not need to be effective; if it is, and an agreement to commit an offence is made, this will be a conspiracy.

18.3 There are a few areas where common law conspiracy is available, most notably conspiracy to defraud. However, most conspiracies are statutory conspiracies that involve an agreement between at least two persons to commit a criminal offence. A conspirator must know of any circumstance forming part of the *actus reus* of the substantive offence, and must intend the commission of the offence by one of the parties to the agreement.

18.4 It is a criminal offence to attempt to commit an offence which is triable on indictment. To be liable for an attempt, the accused must do an act which is more than merely preparatory to the commission of the substantive offence, and this means that she must have embarked on the *actus reus* of the substantive offence. She must intend to commit the 'missing elements' of the offence, including any consequences that form part of the actus reus. In cases of impossible attempts, a defendant can be convicted if on the facts as he believed them to be, he was performing an act which was more than merely preparatory to the commission of an offence.

Case Notes

Anderson [1986] AC 27. House of Lords

The appellant was convicted of conspiracy. He had agreed to supply diamond wire with a view to assisting the brother of a co-conspirator to escape from prison. He claimed that he had not intended to take any further part in the escape plan, and had not expected it to succeed. The Court of Appeal and the House of Lords dismissed his appeal. The House of Lords held that statutory conspiracy did not require the prosecution to prove an intention on the part of each conspirator that a criminal offence should be committed. Knowledge that the agreed course of conduct would necessarily involve the commission of an offence by one or more of the parties to the agreement, together with an intention to play some part in the agreed course of conduct, in furtherance of the criminal purpose, was enough.

Attorney-General's Reference (No. 3 of 1992) [1994] 1 WLR 409. Court of Appeal

The defendants were acquitted on a charge of attempted arson, being reckless as to whether life would thereby be endangered. The defendants threw petrol bombs at a car, missing the car. The Court of Appeal was asked whether on such a charge it was necessary for the prosecution to show that the defendants intended to endanger life. The Court of Appeal said that recklessness was sufficient as the missing element (the element that was lacking from the commission of the substantive offence) was the damage to the car; and the defendants intended that. For those elements that were not missing, it was sufficient for the defendants to have the *mens rea* required for the substantive offence.

Cooke [1986] AC 909. House of Lords

The appellant was convicted of conspiracy to defraud. He was a member of the buffet car crew on a British Rail train, who had taken their own food onto the train and sold it, keeping the proceeds. He argued on appeal that he should, following *Ayres*, have been charged with a statutory conspiracy under s.1(1) Criminal Law Act 1977, as the agreed course of conduct would involve the commission of an offence under s.25(1) Theft Act 1968 (going equipped to cheat). The Court of Appeal agreed with this submission and allowed the appeal, but the House of Lords restored the conviction. It was held that an agreed course of conduct might in part involve the commission of an offence, in which case s.1(1) could be used. However, it might also defraud the victim in such a way as not to involve the commission of an offence. In such a case, conspiracy to defraud could be charged in addition or in the alternative to the statutory conspiracy.

DPP v. *Armstrong* [2000] Crim LR 379. Divisional Court

The defendant telephoned an undercover police officer and asked to be sent some child pornography. He was acquitted on the basis that the incitement was impossible and because the person incited would not have the *mens rea* to distribute the material. On the prosecution's appeal to the Divisional Court it was held that this form of impossibility did not prevent the conviction of the defendant. The fact that the person incited did not intend to distribute the material was irrelevant if the defendant intends that if the person incited does what is asked he will commit an offence.

Geddes [1996] Crim LR 894. Court of Appeal

The appellant was found in a boys' lavatory block at a school, with a cider can, a knife, rope and masking tape. He had no right to be there. He was convicted of attempting to falsely imprison a boy. The Court of Appeal overturned his conviction, arguing that the evidence had not shown that he had moved beyond the realm of preparation into the commission of the offence. They noted that he had not actually approached a potential victim and his conduct did not clearly reveal his intentions. He had got himself in a position where he could commit the offence, but he had not embarked on the crime proper.

Haughton v. *Smith* [1975] AC 476. House of Lords

The appellant was convicted of attempting to handle stolen goods, contrary to s.22 Theft Act 1968. He had been involved in disposing of a van of corned beef that had been stolen a few days before. However, before the appellant met the van it had been stopped by the police and the stolen corned beef had been discovered. The policemen concealed themselves inside the van in order to trap the receivers. The conviction was quashed by the Court of Appeal and the House of Lords confirmed this decision, holding that it was not possible to convict a person of a criminal attempt in a case where a criminal offence would not have been committed even if the contemplated sequence of actions had been completed.

Hollinshead [1985] AC 975. House of Lords

The appellant was convicted of conspiracy to defraud. He had agreed to supply 'black boxes' to another man for sale to third parties. They would then be used to interfere with electricity meters and defraud electricity boards. The Court of Appeal allowed the appeal, but the House of Lords restored the conviction, holding that in the case of a conspiracy to defraud it was not essential for the act of defrauding to be carried out by a party to the agreement, as long as the parties to the agreement intended that dishonest use of the boxes (by a third party) should result from the sale.

Millard and Vernon [1987] Crim LR 393. Court of Appeal

The appellants were convicted of attempting to damage property belonging to another. They had pushed against the wooden wall of a football stand. They denied any intention to damage the wall, and the trial judge directed the jury that recklessness was sufficient. The appeal was allowed on the ground that, although the substantive offence could be committed recklessly, recklessness as to a consequence was not sufficient on a charge of attempt. The court expressly left open the question of whether recklessness with respect to a circumstance would be sufficient on a charge of attempting to commit a substantive offence, such as rape, where recklessness as to the circumstance was sufficient for the complete offence.

Scott v. *Metropolitan Police Commissioner* [1975] AC 819. House of Lords

The appellant was convicted of conspiracy to defraud. He had taken and made pirated copies of films in order to sell them on his own account. He argued on appeal that an element of deception or deceit was necessary in a conspiracy to defraud. His appeal was dismissed by the Court of Appeal and the House of Lords. It was held by Viscount Dilhorne in the House of Lords that although in very many fraud cases there will be deceit, this is not essential. The ordinary meaning of 'to defraud' is 'to deprive a person dishonestly of something which is his or of something to which he is or would or might but for the perpetration of the fraud be entitled'.

Shivpuri [1987] AC 1. House of Lords

The appellant was convicted of attempting to be knowingly concerned in dealing with a prohibited drug. He was arrested with a suitcase that he said he knew contained prohibited drugs. In fact the case contained a non-prohibited vegetable substance. His appeal was dismissed by the Court of Appeal and by the House of Lords. It was held by Lord Bridge that an attempt is committed if the accused does an act which is more than merely preparatory to the commission of the offence which he intends to commit, even if the commission of that offence is in fact impossible. Any distinction between the different types of factual impossibility could not be reconciled with the wording of s.1(1), (2) and (3) Criminal Attempts Act 1981.

Yip Chiu-Cheung [1995] 1 AC 111. Privy Council

The defendant was convicted of conspiracy to traffic in heroin. He was alleged to have conspired with Needham, an undercover drugs enforcement agent. The defendant argued before the Privy Council that he could not be convicted of a conspiracy as Needham did not have the necessary *mens rea* of a conspiracy and he could not form a conspiracy on his own. The Privy Council held that Needham (who was not charged) could have been convicted of a conspiracy as he intended the offence to be committed (in that he intended that the drugs be exported); he also intended that the defendant should be arrested after the trafficking. It was added that the *mens rea* for a conspiracy was an intention that the crime be carried out.

Further Reading

For a general discussion on inchoate crimes read Ashworth and Glazebrook. The leading work on liability for attempts is Duff. Other works on attempts include Buxton, Horder and K. Smith. Impossible attempts are considered in Hogan and Williams.

Ashworth, 'Defining Criminal Offences without Harm', in Smith (ed.), *Criminal Law: Essays in Honour of J.C. Smith* (1987, Butterworths).
Buxton, 'Circumstances, Consequences and Attempted Rape' [1984] *Criminal Law Review* 25.
Duff, *Criminal Attempts* (1997, Oxford University Press).

Glazebrook, 'Should we have a Law of Attempted Crime?' (1969) 85 *Law Quarterly Review* 27.

Hogan, 'The Criminal Attempts Act and Attempting the Impossible' [1984] *Criminal Law Review* 584.

Horder, 'Varieties of Intention, Criminal Attempts and Endangerment' (1994) *Legal Studies* 335.

J. Smith, 'Conspiracy to defraud: The Law Commission's Working Paper No. 104' [1995] *Criminal Law Review* 209.

K. Smith, 'Proximity at Attempt: Lord Lane's Midway Course' [1991] *Criminal Law Review* 576.

Williams, 'The Lords and Impossible Attempts, or *quis custodiet ipos custodes*' (1986) 45 *Cambridge Law Journal* 33.

19 The Human Rights Act and Criminal Law

19.1 The Human Rights Act 1998

The Human Rights Act 1998 is designed to ensure the protection of individuals' rights under the European Convention on Human Rights. It does this in two ways:

1. The interpretation of legislation
The Human Rights Act requires judges to interpret legislation in line with the European Convention on Human Rights. Section 3(1) states:

> 'So far as it is possible to do so, primary legislation and subordinate legislation must be read and given effect in a way which is compatible with the Convention rights.'

This makes it clear that if a statute is ambiguous and could be read in a way which is compatible with the Convention rights or could be read in a way which is not, then the statute should be read so as to be compatible. The key phrase is 'so far as it is possible'. What is unclear is how far this will be taken. Will the judges be willing to strain the natural meaning of words or even read words into statutes in order to ensure compatibility? Time will tell, and it may well be that some judges will be more willing to strive to ensure compatibility than others. If the judge decides that it is not possible to read a statute in line with the Convention rights then the court should issue a declaration of incompatibility which should (in brief) require Parliament to consider reform of the statute.

2. Duties on public authorities
Section 6 deals with the duties on a public authority. For our purposes it should be noted that both the courts (s.6(3)(a)) and the Crown Prosecution Service (CPS) are public authorities. Section 6 states:

> '(1) It is unlawful for a public authority to act in a way which is incompatible with a Convention Right.

(2)   Subsection (1) does not apply to an act if –
    (a)   as the result of one or more provisions of primary legislation, the authority could not have acted differently; or
    (b)   in the case of one or more provisions of, or made under, primary legislation which cannot be read or given effect in a way which is compatible with the Convention rights, the authority was acting so as to give effect to or enforce these provisions.'

This means that unless required to do so by statute, the court and the CPS (or any other public authority) should not infringe anyone's Convention Rights. The significance of these provisions on substantive criminal law is unclear. Here are three possible points of significance:

1   If the defendant is charged with a common law offence which infringes his Convention rights it is arguable that the court should interpret the common law to be in line with the Convention under s.6. It should be noted that s.3 only deals with the situation when a court is interpreting a statute which may or may not be incompatible with a Convention right; it does not apply when the court is considering the common law. However s.6 does. As there is no statute which compels a particular interpretation of the common law, s.6 may require the court to interpret the common law to be in line with the Convention rights.

    It should be added that this interpretation of the effect of s.6 is controversial. Did Parliament intend the courts to alter long and clearly established principles of common law if they conflict with the rights? Some (Buxton LJ, for example); argue that this cannot be so; others (Ashworth, for example) argue that that is what the Act says. The Court of Appeal in *R* v. *H* assumed that s.6 would lead to an alteration of an aspect of the common law which infringed the Convention, subject to an argument that an unforeseeable change in the law might infringe a defendant's rights under articles 6 and 7. In the context of that case it was held that it could not be said to be unforeseeable at the time of the offence that the common law would develop to adopt the stricter limits on what amounted to reasonable chastisement of children as required by the Convention.

2   If the CPS is considering whether or not to bring a prosecution, it is bound by s.6 because it is a public body. It should therefore not bring a prosecution if that would involve an infringement of the defendant's Convention rights. This would mean that if it was clear that a particular criminal law was incompatible with an individual's Convention rights then the CPS should not bring the case. Indeed it is arguable that if it

does bring a prosecution which infringes the defendant's Convention rights this could amount to an abuse of process, meaning that the court cannot hear the case.

3 It is also submitted that s.6 applies to the court at the sentencing stage. Imagine that the defendant has been convicted of a statutory offence which cannot be interpreted in line with the Convention and so a declaration of incompatibility has been issued by the court. In such a case, does s.6 mean that the Court must impose a nominal sentence (unless the offence is one of the rare ones for which there is a statutorily imposed minimum sentence)? To impose a substantial sentence would infringe the individual's Convention rights, which a court is not permitted to do under s.6 unless compelled to do so by a statute.

19.2 What Rights are Protected by the Act?

Before looking at these rights, it is important to appreciate that the rights protected by the Act can be relevant in the criminal law in two different ways:

1 A defendant may argue that to convict him of a particular offence infringes his rights.

2 A victim (or potential victim) may argue that the state has infringed his rights by not protecting him under the criminal law. For example, in *X and Y* v. *Netherlands* a girl with learning difficulties was sexually abused. Her abuser could not be prosecuted under Netherlands law because she could not sign the relevant paperwork. The fact that her abuser could not be punished led the European Court on Human Rights to hold that the Netherlands had infringed her rights under article 8 (see also *A* v. *UK**).

Now we will very briefly summarize the main rights in the Convention which are likely to be relevant in criminal cases. We will then consider some of the specific areas of the criminal law which might be under challenge following the Human Rights Act 1998.

Article 2
'1. Everyone's right to life shall be protected by law. No one shall be deprived of his life intentionally save in the execution of a sentence of a court following his conviction of a crime for which this penalty is provided by law.
2. Deprivation of life shall not be regarded as inflicted in contravention

of this article when it results from the use of force which is no more than absolutely necessary:

a. in defence of any person from unlawful violence;
b. in order to effect a lawful arrest or to prevent the escape of a person lawfully detained;
c. in action lawfully taken for the purpose of quelling a riot or insurrection.'

This right requires the protection of an individual's right to life. As we shall see, this will be relevant in discussions involving the defence of self-defence and protection of others; euthanasia; and the defence of necessity to a charge of murder.

Article 3

'No one shall be subjected to torture or inhuman or degrading treatment or punishment.'

Under this article, potential victims can claim protection from violence which constitutes torture or inhuman or degrading treatment.

Article 6

'1. In the determination of his civil rights and obligations and of any criminal charge against him, everyone is entitled to a fair and public hearing within a reasonable time by an independent and impartial tribunal established by law. Judgment shall be pronounced but the press and public may be excluded from all or part of the trial in the interests of morals, public order, or national security, where the interest of juveniles or the private life of the parties so require, or to the extent strictly necessary in the opinion of the court in special circumstances where publicity would prejudice the interests of justice.

2. Everyone charged with a criminal offence shall be presumed innocent until proved guilty according to the law.

3. Everyone charged with a criminal offence has the following minimum rights:

(a) to be informed promptly, in a language which he understands and in detail, of the nature and cause of the accusation against him;

(b) to have adequate time and facilities for the preparation of his defence;

(c) to defend himself in person or through legal assistance of his own choosing or, if he had not sufficient means to pay for legal assistance, to be given it free if the interests of justice so require;

(d) to examine or have examined witnesses against him and to obtain

the attendance and examination of witnesses on his behalf under the same conditions as witnesses against him;
(e) to have the free assistance of an interpreter if he cannot understand or speak the language used in the court.'

This article has important consequences for the law on criminal procedure and evidence, which cannot be discussed in detail in this book. However it also has significance for the law on burdens of proof and strict liability offences.

Article 7

'1. No one shall be held guilty of any criminal offence on account of any act or omission which did not constitute a criminal offence under national or international law at the time when it was committed. Nor shall a heavier penalty be imposed than the one that was applicable at the time the criminal offence was committed.
2. This article shall not prejudice the trial and punishment of any person for any act or omission, which, at the time when it was committed, was criminal according to the general principles of law recognized by civilized nations.'

This article prevents states passing retrospective criminal statutes. These are statutes that make conduct now criminal that was not at the time it was done. This was already a well-established common law principle. However the article, as we shall see, may be relevant if the courts wish to change well-established common law rules.

Article 8

'1. Everyone has the right to respect for his private and family life, his home and his correspondence.
2. There shall be no interference by a public authority with the exercise of this right except as is in accordance with the law and is necessary in a democratic society in the interests of national security, public safety or the economic well-being of the country, for the prevention of disorder or crime, for the protection of health or morals, or for the protection of the rights and freedoms of others.'

This article protects the right to respect for private and family life. It is clearly of significance in criminal law when discussing offences of a sexual nature.

Article 10

'1. Everyone has the right to freedom of expression. This right shall include freedom to hold opinions and to receive and impart information and ideas without interference by public authority and regardless of frontiers. This article shall not prevent States from requiring the licensing of broadcasting, television or cinema enterprises.

2. The exercise of these freedoms, since it carries with it duties and responsibilities may be subject to such formalities, conditions, restrictions or penalties as are prescribed by law and are necessary in a democratic society, in the interests of national security, territorial integrity or public safety, for the protection of the reputation or rights of others, for preventing the disclosure of information received in confidence, or for maintaining the authority and impartiality of the judiciary.'

This article protects the right to freedom of expression. It will be relevant in cases where the defendant's words are said to be the basis of a criminal charge.

Article 14

'The enjoyment of the rights and freedoms set forth in this Convention shall be secured without discrimination on any ground such as sex, race, colour, language, religion, political opinion, national or social origin, association with a national minority, property, birth, or other status.'

Significantly, this article calls into questions any offence which treats men and women differently. It should be noted that in *Da Silva Mouta* v. *Portugal* the European Court of Human Rights explained that discrimination on the basis of sexual orientation is also prohibited under article 14. It must be emphasized that the article only applies once it is shown that one of the applicant's other rights under the Convention has been infringed. It is not possible to rely on article 14 if you are only claiming that you have in general been discriminated against on the grounds of sex. It would be necessary to demonstrate, for example, that your right to respect for private life was infringed in a way that discriminated against you on the grounds of your sex.

19.3　Areas of the Law which may be Affected by the Human Rights Act

If what has been said so far has led the reader to expect that English and Welsh criminal law will be transformed by the Human Rights Act, you are likely to be disappointed. Some argue that there will be almost no change as a result of the Act, and even those who do see legitimate challenges list a relatively small number of changes. However, what may legitimately be expected is a change in language when discussing the interpretation of the criminal law. The Convention rights will appear as a way of justifying or supporting the criminal law, if not causing radical change to it.

So here are some of the main areas in which the Human Rights Act could have some relevance:

1. The standard of proof

The European Court of Human Rights has implied into article 6 a requirement that in a criminal trial, the charge must be proved against a defendant beyond all reasonable doubt (*Barbera, Messegue and Jabardo* v. *Spain*). However, the European Commission has held that this does not mean that the prosecution has the burden of disproving a defence that the defendant may wish to raise. It is legitimate to place the burden of establishing a defence on the defendant (*Lingens and Leitgens* v. *Austria*). It therefore appears that English and Welsh law is compliant with the Convention and so the Human Rights Act is unlikely to have any effect here (*R* v. *DPP ex p Kebilene**).

2. Burden of proof

Article 6.2 appears to state that the presumption of innocence is an absolute right. Of course, the English common law also purports to uphold the presumption of innocence (see Chapter 2.2), so it might be thought that this part of the law will be little affected by the Act. However there is an issue in relation to reverse onus clauses, where a statute places the burden on a defendant to establish his innocence. In *Attorney-General for Hong Kong* v. *Lee Kwong-Kut*, the Privy Council struck down as invalid a reverse onus offence on the basis of an article in the Hong Kong Bill of Rights which was worded in exactly the same way as article 6.2. Lord Woolf held that, in effect, the clause required the defendant to disprove the essential elements of the offence and this contravened the Hong Kong Bill of Rights. This may suggest that a reverse onus clause could be challenged under the Human Rights Act 1998.

However, in *Salabiaku* v. *France* the European Court of Human Rights considered presumptions of fact, where the burden lay on a defendant to rebut the presumption. It explained:

'Article 6(2) does not therefore regard presumptions of fact or of law provided for in the criminal law with indifference. It requires States to confine them within reasonable limits which take into account the importance of what is at stake and maintain the rights of the defence.'

The leading case now is *R* v. *DPP ex p Kebilene* which concerned s.16A Prevention of Terrorism (Temporary Provisions) Act 1989. The House of Lords stressed that it was important to distinguish between evidential burdens (where the defendant must raise a reasonable doubt by putting a point in issue before the prosecution must disprove the defence) and persuasive burdens (where the defendant must prove the existence of the defence on the balance of probabilities). The House of Lords suggested that an evidential burden will not infringe the Human Rights Act, while a persuasive burden might. Lord Hope suggested that in considering whether a persuasive burden infringed the Convention, the court should consider three questions:

'1. What does the prosecution have to prove in order to transfer the onus?
2. What is the burden on the accused – does it relate to something which is likely to be difficult for him to prove or does it relate to something which is readily in his knowledge or to which he readily has access?
3. What is the nature of the threat faced by society which the provision is designed to combat?'

After considering these three issues, the court can decide whether the presumption is within 'reasonable limits'. This indicates that these persuasive burdens could be found to infringe the Convention unless they can be justified on the grounds that they are necessary for the protection of the public and/or that they will be very easy for the defendant to meet.

The House of Lords in *Lambert* recognized that placing a legal burden of proof on the defendant is more likely to disproportionate than an evidential burden of proof (Chapter 2 explains the difference between these two terms). In *Lambert*, Lord Steyn explained that when considering whether a statute imposed a legal burden on the defendant:

'The principle of proportionality requires the House to consider whether there was a pressing necessity to impose a legal rather than evidential burden on the accused.'

So, the state must demonstrate that the pressing social need will not be met by placing an evidential burden and requires a legal burden.

3. Strict liability offences

In *Salabiaku* v. *France*, the applicant was convicted of illegally importing drugs. Under French law once the accused was shown to have been in possession of an article it was presumed that he or she was aware of the contents. This provision was held not to violate article 6. It was held by the European Court of Human Rights that

> 'Contracting states may, under certain conditions, penalise a simple or objective fact as such, irrespective of whether it results from criminal intent or from negligence.'

This suggests that strict liability offences will not infringe article 6. However the decision is subject to two important caveats. First, the Court stressed that such offences must be kept 'within reasonable limits' and 'take into account the importance of what is at stake and maintain the rights of the defence'. This may indicate that for serious offences, perhaps those involving potential prison sentences, a strict liability offence would not be appropriate (the Canadian courts have taken this approach).

The second is that the Court felt that the French law in the way it applied in this case was appropriate because the court was not prevented from having 'any genuine power of assessment'. In other words, although technically an offence of strict liability, in fact the court hearing did ensure that the defendant was culpable. This suggests that if a court interprets a strict liability offence so strictly that a defendant is convicted of an offence in circumstances where that appears unjust, it may be said that the court robbed itself of a 'genuine power of assessment' and therefore infringed article 6.

4. Uncertainty

It can be argued that if the definition of a criminal offence is too uncertain, this might infringe the Convention. First, there is article 7 which requires any offence to be a criminal offence at the time it was committed. Second is articles 8, 9 and 10 which protect various freedoms (for example, the right to respect for private life). These freedoms can be infringed under certain conditions, including where the infringement was prescribed by or is in accordance with the law. At first sight it is not apparent why these requirements require the criminal law to be certain, but they do so because, as the European Court of Human Rights in *Silver* v. *United Kingdom* explained:

> 'a norm cannot be regarded as "a law" unless it is formulated with sufficient precision to enable the citizen to regulate his conduct: he must be

able – if need be with appropriate advice – to foresee, to a degree that is reasonable in the circumstances, the consequences which a given action may entail.'

This suggests that to amount to 'a law' which complies with article 7, or to justify with the interference of the rights protected in articles 8, 9 and 10, the offence must be drafted with sufficient precision. In *Hashman* v. *United Kingdom**, the European Court held that the power under English law to bind the defendant to keep the peace on the basis that his conduct was *contra bonos mores* (contrary to the public good) was so imprecise that it did not amount to a law. It therefore could not justify the infringement of the defendant's right to freedom of expression under article 10.

However, it seems that the European Court of Human Rights will not be too strict in its requirements of precision. In *Steel* v. *United Kingdom*, the English offence of breach of the peace (defined as 'when an individual causes harm, or appears likely to cause harm, to persons or property or acts in a manner the natural consequence of which would be to provoke others to violence') was held to be sufficiently precise to amount to law and to justify an infringement of the applicant's rights of freedom of expression under article 10.2. The Court explained:

'given the importance of personal liberty, it is essential that the applicable national law meets the standard of "lawfulness" set by the Convention, which requires that all law, whether written or unwritten, be sufficiently precise to allow the citizen – if need be, with appropriate advice – to foresee, to a degree that is reasonable in the circumstances, the consequences which a given action may entail.'

So, only the most imprecise offences are likely to be successfully challenged under the Human Rights Act. Those offences which could possibly be challenged include: conspiracy to defraud, conspiracy to corrupt public morals and the definition of dishonesty. However, it would be a brave judge who would find these offences too vague to amount to law.

5. Retrospectivity

Article 7 specifically prevents retrospective criminal law. That means the state cannot punish a person for an offence which was not a crime at the time when the act was performed. Buxton LJ (writing extra-judicially) has argued that this principle is already accepted in the common law. The main difficulty in English law is where the criminal law is interpreted in a novel way as a result of which a defendant is convicted. Could this be said to be retrospective law? The issue arose in relation to the marital exemption in rape. In *R* v. *R*, the House of Lords confirmed that the marital exemption was now outdated and no longer existed. The defendant (who was married to the victim) could therefore be convicted of rape. The defendant applied to the European Court of Human Rights on the basis that at the time of the sexual intercourse the marital exemption was regarded as part of the law. Had he sought legal advice at the time he would have been told that he had a defence to a charge of rape. The decision of the House of Lords, removing the exemption and therefore enabling him to be convicted of rape, was in effect, he argued, retrospective criminal law-making. To the surprise of many commentators, the European Court of Human Rights in *SW* v. *United Kingdom** dismissed his application. Key to their reasoning was the following statement:

'Article 7 . . . cannot be read as outlawing the gradual clarification of the rules of criminal liability through judicial interpretation from case to case, provided that the resultant development is consistent with the essence of the offence and could be reasonably foreseen.'

This decision indicates that decisions by the courts, even ones that appear to change the law, are very unlikely to infringe article 7. Although, as *SW* v. *United Kingdom* indicates, if the court were to interpret an offence in an unforeseeable way this could infringe article 7.

6.   Protection from torture and inhuman and degrading treatment
Under English law, a parent has a defence of reasonable chastisement to a charge of violence against his or her child. In a very important decision, the European Court of Human Rights, in *A* v. *UK**, held that the English criminal law did not adequately uphold the child's rights under article 3 to protection from torture and inhuman or degrading treatment. The European Court held that chastisement could amount to torture or inhuman and degrading treatment. In deciding whether it did, it was necessary to consider the age of the child, the nature of the injury, the reason for the punishment and the degree of humiliation. In deciding whether chastisement was reasonable, a jury must now consider these factors (*R* v. *H*). This has led the UK government to announce a review of the law in this area.

   What is significant about this decision is the European Court's claim that the Convention *requires* a state to protect victims from torture and inhuman and degrading treatment by using the criminal law. Not only must the state not torture its citizens, it must make sure that one citizen is not tortured by another. This leads to the question of whether there are other offences in which a similar argument could be made. For example, could it be argued that the defence available to a defendant in a rape trial that he honestly (but unreasonably) believed that the victim consented, provides inadequate protection from rape, which no doubt is a form of inhuman and degrading treatment. Of course, there is a distinction between the rape case and reasonable chastisement in that the reasonable chastisement defence negates the *actus reus* – in effect, reasonable chastisement is a justification – whereas the defendant's belief in consent is a lack of *mens rea*. However it is difficult to see why these (what some would see as technical) distinctions are relevant as to the protection of the *victim's* rights. The victim of inhuman and degrading treatment lacks protection, whether the defendant's defence is a denial of *actus reus* or *mens rea*. Indeed, it is hardly believable that the decision of the European Court in *A* v. *UK* would have been different had the defence been based on an argument that the defendant believed he was using a lawful level of force and therefore lacked *mens rea*.

7.   Sex-specific offences

Any offence which distinguishes between people on the grounds of sex or sexual orientation is potentially liable to challenge under article 14. For example, ss.2 and 3 Sexual Offences Act which penalize the procurement of women (but not men) by threats or false pretences to have sexual intercourse could be challenged. If a man was procured to have sexual intercourse by threats, he may be able to argue that his article 8 rights were infringed in a way that was discriminatory. More significantly, the European Court of Human Rights in *Sutherland and Morris* v. *UK* found that having different ages at which men could consent to heterosexual and homosexual intercourse infringed gay men's rights under article 8. This led to the passing of s.1 Sexual Offences (Amendment) Act 2000, which equalized the age of consent for heterosexual and homosexual male sexual activity.

8.   Offending children

The leading case on the criminal acts committed by children is *T and V* v. *UK*, which concerned the notorious case involving the boys who killed Jamie Bulger. The European Court of Human Rights confirmed that having an age of ten for criminal responsibility did not infringe the European Convention. However the Court made some important points about the procedures to be adopted in trials of children. In particular, article 6 required the state to ensure that the accused were able to participate in the trial as effectively as possible.

9.   Sexual offences and privacy

Article 8 grants a right to respect for private and family life. This has significance for the criminalization of sexual acts performed between consenting adults in private. In *Laskey et al* v. *UK**, the European Court of Human Rights had to consider whether the decision of the House of Lords in *Brown* (see Chapter 7.7) was consistent with the Convention. To the dismay of civil rights activists, the Court held that *Brown* did not infringe the Convention because the acts involved violence and a 'significant degree of injury or wounding.' The decision was therefore justifiable under article 8.2. It is important to appreciate that the Court were only looking at the facts of *Brown* itself and not the general principle it set down. Technically, a person who gives another a consensual 'love bite', thereby causing a bruise, commits an assault occasioning actual bodily harm, but it is unlikely that a conviction would be seen as justifiable under article 8.2. In contrast to *Laskey* in *ADT* v. *UK**, the European Court found that the conviction of an applicant who engaged in homosexual non-violent group sexual acts infringed his right to respect for his private life.

10. Killing in the course of self-defence, lawful arrest or protection of others

Ashworth (2000) has argued that the rule in *Williams* and *Beckford* that the defendant can rely on an honest (even if unreasonable) mistake as the basis of self-defence or lawful defence (see Chapter 15.2) may infringe the victim's right to life in article 2 in a murder case. Article 2.2 permits killing in self-defence in cases of absolute necessity and this may be thought to justify the *Williams* rule. However, there have been several cases where the European Court has examined article 2.2 and restricted its meaning. In *McCann* v. *United Kingdom* and *Andronicou* v. *Cyprus*, it was confirmed that the belief of an accused trying to rely on article 2.2 to justify the killing must be based on 'good reason'. Ashworth argues that following these decisions, the *Williams* and *Beckford* approach is inconsistent with article 2.2.

Those who disagree with Ashworth tend to adopt one of two arguments. First, Buxton has argued that the Convention only applies to public officials. Indeed, the two leading cases (*McCann* v. *United Kingdom* and *Andronicou* v. *Cyprus*) have involved public officials. So although Ashworth's argument could be made where soldiers or police officers (for example) use force against citizens, the Convention has no application to where one citizen uses force against another. There is some support for this view in *NHS Trust A* v. *M; NHS Trust B* v. *H* where Butler Sloss P suggested that a doctor could not infringe article 2, because he or she was not acting as an official of the state. Those who oppose Buxton's approach argue that it takes insufficient regard of *A* v. *UK* which establishes that the obligation under article 3 is not limited to ensuring that the state does not infringe a citizen's rights under article 3, but extends to protecting one citizen's rights from being infringed by another citizen. The same is surely true of article 2.

Second, Buxton argues that the existence or otherwise of the defence is not likely to affect the response of the person who believes he is being attacked. In other words, the state's protection of the victim's rights under article 2 is of the same level whether the *Williams* defence is part of the law or not. He argues if a person believes he has to kill another to defend himself, he will kill whatever the law says. In other words, the *Williams* rule does not lessen the protection of citizens' rights to life. Ashworth argues that in *A* v. *UK* it would not have been a defence for the UK to argue that changing the law would not stop parents injuring their children in the name of corporal punishment. *A* v. *UK* makes it clear that states must ensure that their laws must protect the rights of individuals, regardless of the likely effectiveness of those laws.

11.   Victims of car and work killings

In Chapters 9 and 10 it was noted that killings involving cars and in the course of industrial activities are not normally charged as murder or manslaughter, but lesser offences, or indeed not prosecuted at all. Following the reasoning in *A* v. *UK* described above, it could be held that English and Welsh law therefore inadequately protects the right to life of victims under article 2.

12.   Insanity

The present law on insanity could be challenged in two ways under the Act. First, it could be claimed that the present law, with its placing on the defendant of the burden of proving that he is insane, contravenes article 6. This argument would follow the lines made above (point **2**) in relation to reverse onus clauses. The Court of Appeal in *R* v. *M*; *R* v. *Kerr*; *R* v. *H* held that article 6 had no application in cases of insanity, because the finding that a defendant is insane is not a criminal proceeding.

Secondly, article 5(1) allows the lawful detention of persons of unsound mind but only in accordance with a procedure prescribed by law. The European Court of Human Rights has held that unsoundness of mind must be established on objective medical evidence (*Winterwerp* v. *Netherlands*). The Criminal Procedure (Insanity and Unfitness to Plead) Act 1991 appears to comply with this requirement by insisting on two medical witnesses before a special insanity verdict can be given. However, these witnesses must use the legal definition of insanity and not the medical one. This would mean, as we have seen, that the medical evidence could be used to detain an epileptic (see Chapter 14.2). Could this mean that the detention is not established on 'objective *medical* evidence'? Indeed in the case of an epileptic the evidence would be that the person is not medically insane. Another issue raised by the Court of Appeal, but yet to be resolved, is whether the fact that a person found unfit for trial can be detained is compliant with article 5, given that the procedure does not involve a finding that the defendant's unfitness *requires* detention (*Grant*).

13. Euthanasia

We have already discussed the present law on euthanasia (see *Hot Topic*, Chapter 4). Can it be said that the present law infringes the Act? Interestingly, an argument can be made on both sides of the debate. Those who believe that the present law is too liberal could argue that it fails to adequately protect a patient's right to life under article 2 in two situations:

(a) The fact that a doctor can withdraw treatment from a patient in a case like *Bland* even though the patient will die without the treatment could be said to infringe a patient's right to life. However, article 2, by referring to deprivation of a life only protects the right not to be killed by an act, and does not cover omissions (*NHS Trust A* v. *M; NHS Trust B* v. *H*). Indeed, in *A National Health Service Trust* v. *D*, Cazalet J suggested that article 3 could require withdrawing treatment from a patient close to death who was suffering an intolerable level of pain.

(b) The fact that a doctor, it appears, can lawfully administer drugs for the purpose of relieving pain, but which will shorten a person's life, might also be said to infringe article 2. However in *Re A (Conjoined Twins)*, Brooke and Walker LLJ held that article 2 only protects a person from being purposively killed. The article may therefore not apply if the doctor is acting for the purpose of relieving pain.

Those who believe that the present law on euthanasia is too strict argue that not permitting doctors to kill a terminally ill patient who is living in agony infringes that person's rights under article 3 to be protected from torture or inhuman or degrading treatment. It may be that there is a conflict here between articles 2 and 3. Seen in this way, a court may decide that article 2 right is the stronger. In *A National Health Service Trust* v. *D*, Cazalet J accepted an argument that article 3 included a right to die with dignity. However he did not go so far as to state that article 3 could justify a positive act that caused someone's death. Indeed in *R* v. *Director of Public Prosecutions, ex parte Dianne Pretty & Secretary of State for the Home Department*, the House of Lords held that although articles 2 and 3 might *permit* a state to render assisted suicide lawful, they did not *require* a state to make it lawful. Nor did they require the state to allow a relative to kill a terminally ill person.

Summary

19.1 The Human Rights Act requires the courts to interpret statutes in a way which is compatible with individuals' rights under the European Convention on Human Rights if at all possible. The Act also requires public authorities (including courts and the CPS) to act in a way that is consistent with those rights, unless required to act otherwise by a statute.

19.2 The Human Rights Act protects a number of rights including the right to life, the right not to be tortured and the right to respect for one's private and family life.

19.3 The criminal law is largely compatible with the Act. Those areas which are most likely to come under challenge are those relating to the chastisement of children, offences which treat men and women differently and some 'reverse onus' clauses.

Case Notes

A v. *UK* (1999) 28 EHRR 603. European Court of Human Rights
The applicant was hit by his stepfather with a cane, causing severe bruising. The stepfather was acquitted of assaulting the applicant on the basis that he was using reasonable force in chastising him. The European Court of Human Rights found that the acquittal of the stepfather indicated that the applicant's rights under article 3 were not adequately protected by the state. It rejected the UK's argument that article 3 only applied where the state was torturing or imposing inhuman or degrading treatment on the citizen. It was explained that the state had a duty to protect a citizen's rights under article 3 from infringement by another.

ADT v. *UK* [2000] 2 FLR 697. European Court of Human Rights
The applicant was convicted under s.13 Sexual Offences Act 1956 of the offence of gross indecency. He and up to four other men engaged in sexual acts in the applicant's bathroom. The European Court found that the conviction infringed the applicant's rights under article 8 to respect for his family life. The infringement could not be justified under article 8.2 because (unlike *Laskey et al* v. *UK*) the acts did not threaten public health. The Court emphasized the importance of the fact that the acts took place in private.

R v. *DPP ex p Kebilene* [2000] 2 AC 326

The applicants were arrested for the offence of possession of items for the purposes of committing terrorism abroad, contrary to s.16A Prevention of Terrorism (Temporary Provisions) Act 1989. They sought to challenge the decision of the Director of Public Prosecutions to allow proceedings to be brought against them. Their argument was that the prosecution infringed their rights under the Human Rights Act as it breached their rights under article 6 of the European Convention. Their Lordships held that except in cases of bad faith or illegality, it would not be possible to challenge the decision of the DPP to prosecute. *Obiter*, Lord Hope acknowledged that 'persuasive burdens' could fall foul of article 6 unless required for the protection of the public.

R v. *H* [2001] 2 FLR 431. Court of Appeal
The defendant hit his son with a leather belt on a date before the Human Rights Act came into force. The prosecution appealed against the judge's proposed direction to the jury. The prosecution argued that the direction should be in line with the European Convention on Human Rights. The defence argued that the judge should direct the

jury in line with the common law at the time that he committed the offence, without regard to the Convention. The Court of Appeal was persuaded by the prosecution's arguments and stated that in considering whether chastisement was reasonable it was necessary to consider the nature and context of the defendant's behaviour, its duration, its physical and mental consequences in relation to the child, the age and personal characteristics of the child and the reasons why the punishment was administered.

Hashman v. *United Kingdom* [2000] Crim LR. European Court of Human Rights

The applicants were protesting against a hunt. They blew horns and shouted in an attempt to disturb the hounds. The Crown Court found that they had behaved *contra bonos mores* ('behaviour which was wrong rather than right in the judgment of the majority of contemporary fellow citizens') and should be bound over to be of good behaviour for a year. The European Court found that the applicants' freedom of expression under article 10 had been infringed. The *contra bonos mores* offence did not give the applicants sufficiently clear guidance as to how they should behave in future. Therefore it lacked the quality of law and so could not justify the infringement of the article 10 rights in article 10.2.

R v. *Lambert* [2001] 3 WLR 206 House of Lords

The appellant was charged with possession of a controlled drug with intent to supply contrary to s.5(3) Misuse of Drugs Act 1971. The appellant accepted that he was in possession of a bag which contained a controlled drug. However, at trial he relied on the defence under s.28 of the Act that he had neither known nor had reason to suspect the nature of the contents of the bag. He appealed against his conviction on the basis that having to establish his defence on the grounds of the balance of probability, rather than just being required to introduce evidence of his belief, contravened the presumption of innocence guaranteed by article 6(2) of the European Convention. The House of Lords held that the Human Rights Act could be used to quash a conviction made before the Act came into effect, which was the case here. Nevertheless their Lordships went on to hold that the correct interpretation (bearing in mind the Human Rights Act) of section 28 was that it only required the defendant to produce evidence of his belief, it did not require him to establish it beyond reasonable doubt. Still, his conviction was upheld on the basis that even if the jury had been correctly directed, it would inevitably have convicted him.

Laskey et al v. *UK* (1997) 24 EHRR 39. European Court of Human Rights

The applicants were convicted of assaults following sado-masochistic behaviour in private. They argued that the convictions infringed their rights under article 8 of the European Convention. The UK argued that the criminalization of such acts was necessary to protect public morals and the health of citizens and so justified under article 8.2. The European accepted this argument, arguing that the activities involved a risk of physical injury and undermined 'the respect which human beings should confer upon each other'.

SW v. *United Kingdom* (1996) 21 EHRR 363. European Court of Human Rights

The defendant was convicted of rape following a decision of the House of Lords that the marital exemption to rape was no longer part of the law. He argued before the European Court of Human Rights that in effect this was retrospective criminal law creation and therefore infringed article 7. The European Court rejected this argument on the basis that legal systems were permitted to gradual clarification of the definition of offences on a case-by-case basis.

Further Reading

The following are some of the writings to date on the potential impact of the Human Rights Act on criminal law.

Arden, 'Criminal Law at the Crossroads: The Impact on Human Rights from the Law Commission's Perspective and the Need for a Code' [1999] *Criminal Law Review* 439.

Ashworth, 'Article 6 and the Fairness of Trials' [1999] *Criminal Law Review* 261.

Ashworth, 'The Human Rights Act and the Substantive Criminal Law: A Non-Minimalist View' [2000] *Criminal Law Review* 564.

Ashworth, 'Criminal Proceedings After the Human Rights Act' [2001] *Criminal Law Review* 855.

Baker, 'Human Rights, *M'Naughten* and the 1991 Act' [1994] *Criminal Law Review* 84.

Buxton, 'The Human Rights Act and the Substantive Criminal Law' [2000] *Criminal Law Review* 311.

Centre for Public Law at the University of Cambridge, *The Human Rights Act and the Criminal Justice and Regulatory Process* (1999, Hart).

Lewis, 'The Human Rights Act 1998: Shifting the Burden' [2000] *Criminal Law Review* 667.

Sutherland and Gearty, 'Insanity and the European Court of Human Rights' [1992] *Criminal Law Review* 418.

Index